D1569206

THE TWO NEW YORKS

State-City Relations
in the Changing Federal System

THE TWO NEW YORKS

State-City Relations
in the Changing Federal System

❧

Gerald Benjamin
and
Charles Brecher

EDITORS

RUSSELL SAGE FOUNDATION · NEW YORK

The Russell Sage Foundation

The Russell Sage Foundation, one of the oldest of America's general purpose foundations, was established in 1907 by Mrs. Margaret Olivia Sage for "the improvement of social and living conditions in the United States." The Foundation seeks to fulfill this mandate by fostering the development and dissemination of knowledge about the political, social, and economic problems of America. It conducts research in the social sciences and public policy, and publishes books and pamphlets that derive from this research.

The Board of Trustees is responsible for oversight and the general policies of the Foundation, while administrative direction of the program and staff is vested in the President, assisted by the officers and staff. The President bears final responsibility for the decision to publish a manuscript as a Russell Sage Foundation book. In reaching a judgment on the competence, accuracy, and objectivity of each study, the President is advised by the staff and selected expert readers. The conclusions and interpretations in Russell Sage Foundation publications are those of the authors and not of the Foundation, its Trustees, or its staff. Publication by the Foundation, therefore, does not imply endorsement of the contents of the study.

Library of Congress Cataloging-in-Publication Data

The Two New Yorks: state-city relations in the changing federal
  system/edited by Gerald Benjamin and Charles Brecher.
    p.   cm.
  Bibliography: p.
  Includes index.
  ISBN 0-87154-107-6
  1. Intergovernmental fiscal relations—New York (State) 2. State-
local relations—New York (State)   I. Benjamin, Gerald.
II. Brecher, Charles.
HJ605.T86 1988
336.747—dc19   88-15778
                                                                        CIP

The paper used in this publication meets the minimum requirements of American National Standard for Information Sciences—Permanence of Paper for Printed Library Materials, ANSI Z39.48-1984.

10 9 8 7 6 5 4 3 2 1

Advisory Committee

Advisory Committee *(continued)*

C. Mark Lawton
  President, Commission of Independent Colleges and Universities
John Marchi
  Member, New York State Senate
John Mladinov
  New York State Department of Transportation
Jesse Nixon
  Director, Capitol District Psychiatric Center
David A. Pilliod
  Director, Office of Local Government Services, New York State
  Department of State
Edward V. Regan
  Comptroller, State of New York
James R. Tallon
  Member, New York State Assembly
Margie Van Meter
  Program Director, New York State Senate Committee on Child Care
Robert Wagner, Jr.
  President, New York City Board of Education
Arthur Y. Webb
  Commissioner, New York State Office of Mental Rehabilitation and
  Developmental Disabilities
Lois Wilson
  Administrator of School Finance, New York State School Boards
  Association

Contributors

RICHARD D. ALBA
  Professor, State University of New York at Albany
MARY JO BANE
  Associate Professor, Harvard University
GERALD BENJAMIN
  Professor, State University of New York at New Paltz
ROBERT BERNE
  Professor, New York University
SUSAN BLANK
  Program Associate, Foundation for Child Development
BARBARA B. BLUM
  President, Foundation for Child Development
CHARLES BRECHER
  Professor, New York University, and Director of Research, Citizens Budget
  Commission
MATTHEW P. DRENNAN
  Professor, New York University
BARBARA GORDON ESPEJO, ESQ.
  Webster & Sheffield
ESTER FUCHS
  Assistant Professor, Barnard College, Columbia University
CYNTHIA B. GREEN
  Senior Research Associate, Citizens Budget Commission
JAMES M. HARTMAN
  Former President, Citizens Budget Commission, and Vice President,
  Municipal Securities, Marine Midland Bank
RAYMOND D. HORTON
  Professor, Columbia University, and President, Citizens Budget Commission
SARAH F. LIEBSCHUTZ
  Professor, State University of New York at Brockport
DAVID LEWIN
  Professor, Columbia University
IRENE LURIE
  Associate Professor, State University of New York at Albany
PAUL D. MOORE
  Executive Director, New York State Legislative Commission on State-Local
  Relations
JAMES C. MUSSELWHITE, JR.
  Director of Planning, Fairfax Community Services Board
MARTIN SHEFTER
  Professor, Cornell University
KENNETH E. THORPE
  Assistant Professor, Harvard University
EMANUEL TOBIER
  Professor, New York University
KATHERINE TRENT
  Assistant Professor, State University of New York at Albany

Foreword

This book is the tangible outcome of an intellectual process that began with an intense, late-night conversation at the 1984 Setting Municipal Priorities conference. Mike Finnerty, then the budget director of New York State, Chuck Brecher, the co-director of the Setting Municipal Priorities project, and I were arguing about how the State treated the City fiscally. For every claim Chuck or I made about inadequate help, Mike had a counterclaim based on different data or a different perspective. We ended, literally at dawn's early light, by agreeing on a few propositions: first, that the State and the City were growing increasingly interdependent, largely though not entirely because of federal aid cuts; second, that only a handful of State and City officials know "the whole story" of state-city relations; third, that the relationship was too important to be understood by only a few specialists; and fourth, that the high level of suspicion between State and City officials was making it difficult for the "two New Yorks" to move in mutually advantageous ways. Finnerty closed the evening by recommending that the Setting Municipal Priorities project branch out to include a Setting State Priorities component. That seemed a mighty big undertaking to Chuck and me, but we began to think about a volume focusing on the New York State–New York City relationship.

Implementing even a first effort toward the goal of greater State-City understanding took several years. It was immediately evident that any effort to study the relationship could not be based only in New York City lest the effort be viewed as special pleading by denizens of Albany. The other problem was that the city's policy research community was relatively ignorant of State government. Consequently, a partnership was forged between an independent, nonpartisan organization in New York City, the Citizens Budget Commission, and the Nelson A. Rockefeller Institute of Government of the State University of New York in Albany. Warren Ilchman, director of the Rockefeller Institute applied his considerable skills to help organize and finance the project; equally important, he recruited Professor Gerald Benjamin from the New Paltz campus of the State University to work with Brecher as co-editor of the volume.

Brecher, Benjamin, Ilchman, and I worked to design a project that would contribute to a greater understanding in the media and among interested parties of the ways in which State and City actors influence each other's decisions. At the suggestion of several staff members of prospective foundation supporters, we also sought to make the analysis useful to a wider range of scholars and public officials in other states and cities with relationships analogous to those of the two New Yorks. These tasks required extensive expertise. Thus, our first challenge was to identify the critical subjects to be explored and to recruit a group of experts capable of making an objective and insightful contribution. The 22 contributors to this volume are drawn from multiple universities as well as governmental units and private, nonprofit organizations. They proved to be a unique collection of experts, and I, along with the editors, thank them for their substantial efforts and their patience with the editorial process.

The preparation of this volume benefited from reviews of outlines and drafts by a special Advisory Committee. The group consisted of 32 people, primarily State and City officials, who generously agreed to lend their expertise. Most attended group meetings with the authors and several spent time with authors individually.

In addition, a conference was held at Arden House in February 1987 at which the draft essays and the issues they raised were discussed. The conference provided the authors with another opportunity to obtain suggestions from the Advisory Committee as well as from the other participants.

The project required a reasonable level of financial support, and this was received from several foundations as well as in the form of in-kind contributions from both the Citizens Budget Commission and the Rockefeller Institute. We are grateful to the boards of both these organizations for their support. Special thanks are due to Frank P. Smeal, chairman of the Citizens Budget Commission, who made special efforts to help elicit support for the project, and to Jack Miller, chairman of the commission's research committee on State finances, who also took a special interest in this effort. The foundations that made essential, and much appreciated, contributions are the Ford Foundation, the Russell Sage Foundation, the New York Community Trust, the Morgan Guaranty Trust Company of New York, and the New York Times Foundation.

The Russell Sage Foundation also serves as publisher of this volume. The editors and authors are grateful to the Foundation, and particularly to Priscilla Lewis, the director of publications, for their interest in having the project produce a timely volume in a professional manner. In the organization of the project and its conference activities and in the production of the typescript and diskettes which led to this volume, two

Citizens Budget Commission staff members played critical roles: Barbara Weinstein, vice president for administration, kept all the balls in the air from crashing to the ground; Mary De La Fuente translated all the authors' disks and handwriting into the common language of Multimate, provided the editors hard copy with which they could work, and made it all into a presentable package with unfailing skill and patience. At the Rockefeller Institute the following staff members were especially helpful in managing this project in Albany and preparing for the Arden House conference: Barbara A. Plocharczyk, manager of administration and conferences; James K. Morrell, deputy director; and Susan C. Lenz, production manager. They were assisted by Diane Naughton, Maria Tudico, and Charlene Evans.

RAYMOND D. HORTON

President, Citizens Budget Commission

Contents

List of Tables

List of Figures

1
INTRODUCTION

❧

Gerald Benjamin
and
Charles Brecher

I N SEPTEMBER 1975 the two New Yorks—the State of New York and
the City of New York—were effectively merged. Fiscal mismanagement by municipal leaders led creditors to stop lending, and the
City faced bankruptcy. Eventually, the choice was between turning
over control of the City to a federal bankruptcy judge or to a new
State-authorized political body. State officials and reluctant municipal
leaders eventually chose the latter course. An Emergency Financial
Control Board was created, and, dominated by the governor and his
appointees, it assumed final authority over most major municipal policy
decisions.

It took more than a decade for elected municipal officials to regain
fully their autonomy from the renamed State Financial Control Board
(the "Emergency" was dropped after three years). The board "sunset" in
1986, as a consequence of continued efforts by Mayor Edward I. Koch,
elected in 1977, and of a revived local economy. The limited degree of
"home rule" granted the City in the State constitution was restored and
two separate, if interdependent, New Yorks were again functioning.

The forces leading to the demise of an independent City of New York
in 1975 and the subsequent rebuilding of relationships between the City
and the State are the subject of this volume. It is an interesting story
because the changing relations between the two New Yorks were
paralleled by changes in the role of the national government in the federal

system. After a period of increased federal activity to aid in the amelioration of multiple "urban problems," the national political mood shifted and brought to Washington leaders committed to reducing the federal role in domestic policy. The rebuilding of relationships between the City and the State took place in an environment of less federal intervention and a greater need to act autonomously.

Events in New York were perhaps more dramatic than those in other states with large cities, but the conditions in those areas have much in common with New York. Changing national policies and increased local fiscal stress forced many states and their urban centers to reassess the nature of their legal and fiscal relationships. Consequently, developments in relations between the two New Yorks, especially those associated with the recovery of New York City from its fiscal crisis, can be instructive for the rest of the nation.

This introductory essay serves two purposes. First, the historical evolution of relations among states, their large cities, and the national government is reviewed. This provides a broader context for the analysis of changing relations between the two New Yorks. Second, the next 15 essays are summarized to provide the reader with an overview of the volume's contents. These essays are a series of case studies of relations between the two New Yorks; viewed collectively they constitute a comprehensive analysis of the ways in which states and their large cities influence each other's performance.

HISTORICAL BACKGROUND

Unfortunately, enmity between big cities and their states is an enduring theme of American federalism. Traditionally, the states have been seen as the guardian of the Jeffersonian vision of America. The "state mind," Roscoe Martin wrote just 20 years ago, is characterized by "rural orientation, provincial outlook, commitment to a strict moral code, [and] a philosophy of individualism." Viewed from such a perspective, Martin continued, urban problems appeared to "spring from the unhealthy soil, even the misdeeds of the city."[1] With such attitudes ascendant, and with the states able to dominate the cities in law, it is little wonder that, as Norton Long noted, "rural legislatures often pillaged cities in their states and at best were frequently insensitive to urban interests and needs." And, in turn, "the history of state exploitation and neglect of cities has given rise to the cities' abiding suspicion of and hostility toward state governments."[2]

For much of American history, urban residents sought simply to be left alone by their states. If granted home rule, they believed, their resources would be sufficient to meet any demands placed upon them. But this view changed half a century ago, with the onset of the Depression. Faced with the overwhelming social and economic needs of the time, cities turned to the national government for help, and they did not want that help to pass through the hands of the states. Expressing a sentiment that has been echoed by big-city mayors ever since when issues of federalism are discussed, New York City Mayor Fiorello La Guardia, speaking for the U.S. Conference of Mayors, declared before a congressional committee: "I want to come to Washington to do business. I do not want to go to Albany to do business, and I do not think that my colleague, Mayor Kelly of Chicago, wants to go to Springfield."[3] Thus, the tensions between states and cities became exacerbated as they became rivals for direct national government assistance.

The case against the states was based not only on their lack of sympathy for cities, but upon fundamental questions about their capacity to govern effectively. Progressive era reforms in some states notwith-standing, Luther Gulick, one of the doyens of the emerging profession of public administration, declared in 1933: "The American states are finished. I do not predict that the states will go, but affirm that they have gone."[4] A decade and a half later, journalist Robert S. Allen made the case more colorfully: "State government is the tawdriest, most incompe-tent, and most stultifying unit of the nation's political structure. The whole system is moribund, corrosive and deadening. It is riddled with senescence, incompetence, mediocrity, ineffectiveness, corruption and tawdriness. It pollutes instead of purifying, destroys and obstructs instead of building and improving."[5] Even as late as 1972, political scientist Ira Sharkansky could declare, after reviewing the field, that "no prominent thinkers have defended the states in recent years."[6]

By the early 1970s things had already begun to change. Simultaneous with a new wave of reform and state constitutional revision, the federal Supreme Court had ordered reapportionment of state legislatures to conform to the one-man-one-vote principle. This fundamentally altered the composition of state legislatures by strengthening urban and suburban representation and weakening rural interests. There was new leadership, too, in the statehouses; as the title of one book on the governorship suggested, states were bidding "Goodbye to Goodtime Charlie" in those key offices.[7] In the intellectual community, new proponents of the politically reformed states, untinged by the racism that historically had marred the "states' rights" position, began to emerge. The Center for the Study of Federalism, a forum for the vigorous advocacy of the virtues of a decentralized system of governance, was established at Temple University in 1967. And Sharkansky's observations on the lack of advocacy for the states was prefatory to his spirited assertion that they were being "maligned," with regard to both their capacity to govern and their responsiveness to urban problems.

During the 1960s, debate continued as to whether the problems of the cities should be addressed in a direct relationship between them and the national government, or through the states. The focal point for the study of federal-state-local relationships in Washington, the Advisory Commission on Intergovernmental Relations (ACIR), consistently advocated the use of national funds as an incentive to draw state resources into the effort to address urban needs.[8] But mayors remained suspicious of the states; in the mid 1960s, one study described their attitudes as "at best ambivalent and at worst downright hostile."[9] Another extensive survey showed that most chief executives in large cities regarded state officials to be "only seldom or occasionally sympathetic or helpful."[10] This view was bolstered by prominent urbanologists such as Phillip M. Hauser, who in 1970 remarked that "for the first 69 years of this century [state governments] have demonstrated an utter disregard for urban problems."[11]

The domestic initiatives under President Lyndon B. Johnson established new direct relationships between the federal government and cities, but also linked the federal government directly to communities within cities. The result was considerable political turmoil as federal funds were sometimes used to help community leaders fight City Hall.[12]

President Richard M. Nixon sought to establish a "new federalism" that would place greater dependence on the states as middlemen in the federal effort to deal with urban problems. But not all of Nixon's plans were implemented, and some even reinforced the tendency of the national government to relate directly to cities and other local governments. The most notable of these were the federal revenue sharing program, which awarded funds directly to localities, and the new Comprehensive Employment and Training Act, which gave manpower training funds to cities. Consequently, despite Republican dominance of the national government during this time, the share of federal intergovernmental aid paid directly to localities more than doubled from 12 percent in 1970 to 27 percent in 1977 (see Table 1.1). During the presidency of Gerald Ford, federal loans to New York City in the 1975–1977 period, though reluctantly given, were perhaps the most dramatic example of a direct national–big-city relationship.

One observer, reviewing the intergovernmental system in the early 1970s, detected "conflicting values" in the "emerging approach." "It seeks new patterns between cities and the national government," Lawrence Herson wrote, "but exhibits considerable reluctance to break the traditional dependence of cities upon the States."[13] It was in this atmosphere that experts gathered at Arden House under the auspices of

TABLE 1.1

Federal Aid to States and to Local Governments
1955–1984 (in millions of dollars)

	Amount		Percentage	
	Aid to States	Aid to Localities	Aid to States	Aid to Localities
1955	$ 2,762	$ 368	88	12
1960	6,382	592	92	8
1965	9,874	1,155	90	10
1970	19,252	2,605	88	12
1975	36,148	10,906	77	23
1976	42,013	13,576	76	24
1977	45,938	16,637	73	27
1978	50,200	19,393	72	28
1979	54,548	20,616	73	27
1980	61,892	21,136	75	25
1981	67,868	22,427	75	25
1982	66,026	20,919	76	24
1983	68,962	21,021	77	23
1984	76,140	20,912	78	22

SOURCE: Advisory Commission on Intergovernmental Relations, *Significant Features of Fiscal Federalism*, 1985–1986 ed. (Washington, DC: ACIR, February 1986), table 43, p. 59.

Columbia University's American Assembly to consider the role of the states in addressing the urban crisis.

Dean Alan K. Campbell of Syracuse University's Maxwell School of Public Affairs, who edited the volume that emerged from this conference with his colleague Donna E. Shalala, identified four sets of barriers— constitutional, organizational, fiscal, and political—to state action in aid of cities. Campbell and Shalala found that "most of the ways in which states might help their urban areas are clearly within their legal competence. They could induce reorganization of local government. They could improve their aid system to reflect urban needs. They could assume direct responsibility for functions that are now performed locally. They could reallocate their resources." But, the authors noted, in most states, none of these actions had been taken. "It is this combination of legal ability and lack of action," they concluded, "which gives the political explanation [of inaction] its greatest force."[14] The same economic, political, and demographic trends that blocked the emergence of a national urban policy—suburbanization, the concentration of poor and minority populations in the big cities, the out-migration of business from those cities—also mitigated against state action. The cities' best hope for "genuine reconstruction," concluded journalist A. James

Reichley, a participant in the 1970 Arden House conference, was "some *total program* for the reconstruction of our entire society."[15]

Yet directing state efforts toward urban needs remained a tantalizing prospect, for, as Reichley wrote elsewhere, the states seemed "small enough to react sensibly to local needs and realities," while at the same time they were "large enough to coordinate programs for entire metropolitan regions."[16] Moreover, American constitutional realities made the boundaries of the states immutable, and metropolitanization was unlikely for a variety of compelling political reasons. This itself, wrote Leon Epstein in a survey of federalism published in 1978, was "a reason for turning to the states as instruments of decentralized authority."[17]

Then in the late 1970s, the national government began to retreat from its commitment to urban areas. In 1978, two years before Ronald Reagan's election to the presidency, growth of real federal aid to states and localities peaked. Confirming what that development implied, in 1980 President Carter's Commission for a National Agenda for the Eighties reported: "There are no 'national urban problems,' only an endless variety of local ones. Consequently, a centrally administered national urban policy that legitimizes activities inconsistent with a revitalization of the larger national economy may be ill advised."[18]

The Reagan Administration not only sought to accelerate the cuts in federal aid, but also wanted to "sort out" responsibilities for domestic functions between the national government and the states. An implicit aspect of Reagan's "new federalism" was severing direct links between the federal agencies and large-city government. One of the administration's most important legislative achievements, the Omnibus Budget and Reconciliation Act of 1981, consolidated several categorical government programs and in the process shifted federal funds from a direct pipeline to localities to distribution through the states. By 1983, federal intergovernmental aid paid directly to localities had been reduced to mid-1970s proportions. (See Table 1.1.)

During this time of declining federal interest in urban problems, state activity was enhanced significantly. This was documented in a study by the ACIR showing greater state aid to large cities in the late 1970s and in a study by the National Academy of Public Administration finding that many states had developed aggressive policies for urban development.[19] This and other evidence led Deil Wright, a leading student of American intergovernmental relations, to conclude that though "the states have been roundly and soundly chastised for their neglect of urban distress and decline, a balanced view, particularly taking into account developments in the 1970s, shows the states on record as taking numerous and varied urban-oriented policy initiatives."[20] Wright's analysis was confirmed in

1985 in a comprehensive examination, *The Question of State Government Capability*, by the ACIR. They found state governments "transformed in almost every facet of their operations" and "giving more attention to urban areas," especially through programs emphasizing economic development and growth management.[21]

Local governments, and especially big cities, were disquieted by the reductions in federal aid and the enhanced role of the states in distributing what remained. But studies that antedated the Reagan Administration demonstrated that state aid, especially in New York and the other large states, was better targeted on local need than was federal assistance. And after a period of uncertainty, it became clear that states generally were providing cities "greater-than-expected" help in replacing federal aid reductions of the early Reagan years, with some offsetting the entire loss, and preserving the real value of former federal aid.[22]

The state-local relationship has always been a crucial one, but it takes on added importance as a consequence of these recent developments. As befits their reputation as "federal laboratories," different states have developed different ways to aid their cities. One recent survey discerned two seemingly contradictory trends—both greater local autonomy and greater state involvement. "An expanded sphere of authority and state mandate cost reimbursement suggest greater power for local governments," Ann Bowman and Richard Kearney observed, "while increased state financial aid and greater involvement in urban areas pull in the opposite direction toward diminished local power."[23]

As these different patterns suggest, fruitful analysis of contemporary state-local relationships should go beyond general terms to the particulars of how those relationships actually work to effect day-to-day governance and service delivery. Each state government interacts in multifaceted ways with many local governments of different sizes and with different powers, some general and others special in purpose. Moreover, this network of governments is not an orderly system. Rather, it is an historic legacy, the cumulative result of generations of experience with public sector problem solving. Although it may appear a truism, it is worth noting that all local governments are not the same, and out of their differences arise different needs and expectations of state government. While officials in small towns may seek technical assistance to cope with the complexity they perceive in directives from the state capital, big-city managers may resent taking direction from state officials, people they believe to be less professionally accomplished than they and less familiar with the problems they face. Even within classes of similar local governments—big cities, for example—goals may differ. For example, New York City's objectives in Albany do not always coincide with those of its five sister big cities in the north and west of the state. Yet the state government struggles to accommodate this nonsystem of local government diversity in some systematic way, to achieve equity within and across classes of localities while at the same time more effectively reaching its policy goals.

OVERVIEW OF THE VOLUME

It is the premise of this volume that one set of special state-local relationships, those between states and their principal cities, has a major and distinctive impact on the performance of state and local governments. Big cities are repositories of much of a state's talent and wealth. Each helps give its state its very identity, shaping how the state is seen by outsiders. Their defining quality perhaps explains why these cities are rarely state capitals; the location of the seat of government in a smaller city helps to balance the big city's formidable presence in the state. Across the country—in New York, Pennsylvania, Illinois, Michigan, California, indeed, in any state in which there is a major city—the presence of that city both constrains and empowers state policymaking.

Case analyses of New York are an appropriate and fruitful point of departure for exploration of this subject because of the size of the city and the state, because of the leading roles they have traditionally played in subnational government in the United States, and because the historic relationship between New York City and New York State is undergoing change in ways that are similar to those occurring or likely to occur in other areas.

Despite a history of strong concern for home rule, New York State has always played a major role in the governance of New York City. New York, for example, is a state that relies heavily upon mandates; an ACIR study ranked it thirty-fifth among the states in discretionary authority given to local governments, and forty-fourth in such authority given to cities.[24] During the City's fiscal crisis of the mid 1970s, as noted earlier, the State created new oversight agencies and became directly involved in decisions in many areas of municipal policy. Since this period of strong State intervention, the City and the State have been reshaping their relationships. The following 15 essays in this volume thus constitute an extensive set of case studies in the methods—successful and unsuccessful—that states and their large cities can apply to attack jointly the nation's urban problems.

Comparative View

Any analysis involving New York inevitably raises a threshold question: Isn't New York different from the rest of the nation? The essay by James Musselwhite places the relationship between New York City and New York State in a comparative perspective. He identifies 20 American cities that both have more than 400,000 residents and are the largest in their state. This group includes not only the relatively well-known analogies to New York City and New York State, such as Chicago in Illinois and Boston in Massachusetts, but also "sunbelt" areas such as Phoenix in Arizona and Atlanta in Georgia.

Musselwhite finds that virtually all of these large cities have similar relationships to their states in several important respects. The large cities tend to have disproportionate concentrations of poor residents and social needs, yet they have less capacity to meet these needs than their states. For example, fully 18 of the 20 large cities have a greater share of their residents living in poverty than the rest of their states, with the average large city's share nearly one and a half times the statewide figure. New York falls near the middle of the group in most of these measures. The large cities also share certain political characteristics. Almost all of the cities (18 of the 20) vote more heavily Democratic than the rest of their states; again, New York City is close to the average for all of the large cities.

But Musselwhite also provides evidence that the relationship between the two New Yorks is unique. With approximately 7.2 million residents, New York City is in a class by itself; the nation's second largest city, Los Angeles, with a population of 3.1 million, has less than half as many inhabitants. New York City accounts for fully 40 percent of the statewide population; in contrast, Los Angeles represents only 12 percent of the California population. The only other cities that exceed one fifth of their state's populations are Phoenix (28 percent) and Chicago (26 percent).

In addition, the scale and scope of New York City's government distinguish it from virtually all other large American cities. Because local government in New York City performs functions often divided between cities and counties in other areas, and because it constitutes so large a part of the state, New York City is a relatively large public entity. Its employees represent 46 percent of all local government employees in the state; in contrast, the 20 large cities average only 10 percent of local government employees in their states. Indeed, the number of New York City employees actually exceeds the number of state government employees by a three-to-two margin; in all other large cities, the number of civil servants was about one fourth that of state government.

Economy and Demography

The next two essays place the economy and demography, respectively, of New York City in a national and statewide context. Matthew

Drennan's analysis, which documents the recent history of economic decline and resurgence, reveals three significant trends.

First, the two New Yorks are growing more slowly than the nation. In the 1976–1986 decade, the state and city populations fell slightly, while the nation's increased; state and city employment growth averaged 1.6 percent and 1.0 percent annually compared with a national rate of 2.4 percent; their respective growth rates for personal income were 8.5 and 8.2 percent versus 9.1 percent nationally.

Second, the city's economy is steadily becoming a smaller share of the state's economy. From 1969 to 1986, employment in New York City fell from almost 53 percent to just 41 percent of the statewide total; in the same period, the city's share of statewide personal income fell from nearly 46 percent to under 38 percent. Moreover, the consensus among analysts is that the city's share of statewide population, employment, and income will shrink even further by the end of the century.

Third, Drennan reports that New York City is becoming relatively poorer. Whereas the city historically had a higher average income than the rest of the state, that is no longer the case. In 1969, per capita personal income in New York City was about 5 percent above the statewide average; in 1986 it stood close to the statewide average; and in 1987 it is estimated to have slipped below the average.

The decline in the relative size and affluence of New York City is occurring despite the presence of vibrant economic sectors specializing in business services, such as finance, advertising, and the law. These activities continue to grow, but the suburbanization of the middle class and the concentration of the poor, particularly poor minorities, in central cities cause the city to decline relative to its surrounding areas.

These and other demographic factors are analyzed in the essay by Katherine Trent and Richard Alba. They find that the forces shaping the population of New York City differ significantly from those in the rest of the state. Their statistics support the traditional view of New York City as a magnet that attracts many disadvantaged and repels many of the middle class, particularly whites. The rest of the state also attracts new residents from a variety of income classes, but typically it does not lose as many middle-class residents to other locations. This helps explain how the city becomes relatively smaller and poorer.

New York City's strong attraction to new immigrants also causes it to be much more diverse ethnically than the rest of the state. A corollary is that the city is the center of the state's minority population. With only about 40 percent of the state's people, New York City is home to fully 74 percent of its blacks, 87 percent of its Puerto Ricans, and 70 percent of its foreign-born population.

Trent and Alba also identify distinctive ways New York City is affected by the national and statewide trends of an aging population and new family structures. Throughout the nation the elderly are becoming a larger share of the population, while children are relatively less numerous. This is evident in New York City, but with a unique twist. The relatively fewer children are increasingly from poor and minority group families. In 1980, nearly one third of the city's children were in families with incomes below the poverty level compared with 12 percent in the rest of the state; in the future this disparity is likely to become even greater. Similarly, New York City increasingly is the center for single individuals and female-headed households, while the rest of the state continues to be heavily dominated by families headed by married couples. Only 44 percent of New York City households contain a married couple compared with 64 percent in the rest of the state.

Political Dimensions

The next three essays explore political aspects of the relationship between the two New Yorks. Gerald Benjamin examines the legal and institutional structures that shape the relationship. He makes clear that in a strictly legal sense the State is able to dominate the City. New York's State Constitution and its highest court authorize State officials to exercise control over, including intervention in, matters of local government. The concept of home rule has little legal support. Moreover, special districts and State-chartered public benefit corporations, such as the Metropolitan Transportation Authority (MTA), are institutions accountable primarily to the governor and the State legislature; previously, the services they provided were municipal functions.

Benjamin recognizes that legal analysis should be supplemented with understanding of political institutions. And within political structures that govern the State of New York, City officials exercise considerable and growing influence. Benjamin traces this influence to two sources: the City's lobbying and changes in the composition of the legislature to abide more closely to one-man-one-vote. The City's annual lobbying effort, typically launched by a mayoral visit to Albany, generally targets a wide range of issues from direct fiscal aid and new taxing authority to nonmonetary items, such as revision of the City's administrative code. On many issues, such as State funding of Medicaid, the City has formed alliances with other localities.

The City's effectiveness in influencing the legislature also has been strengthened by reapportionment. The Supreme Court ruling in 1964 requiring state legislatures to apply the one-man-one-vote rule upset a system in place since 1894, one that strongly favored upstate Republicans. Since 1964, the State legislature has been fully reapportioned four times. The first two times, in 1965 and 1966, were direct responses to the federal and subsequent New York State court requirements. The revisions of 1971 and 1981 followed population changes revealed in the decennial federal censuses. In addition, partial redistricting was required in 1974 and 1981 to conform to the federal Voting Rights Act protection of minority groups, whose members now constitute over one quarter of the Assembly delegation from New York City.

Because reapportionment took place over a period when New York City's share of the statewide population was declining, it did not increase the size of the city's delegation in either house. In fact, the number of New York City seats in the 150-member Assembly fell from 65 in 1964 to 60 in 1987; in both 1964 and 1987, the City had 25 Senate districts, but the body was enlarged from 58 to 61 seats. The more significant change has been the shift to Democratic party control of the Assembly; Democrats grew from a 62-member minority in 1965 to a 93-member majority in 1987. Over 60 percent of these Democrats, including the Speaker, are from New York City. In addition, Republicans from New York City account for 6 members of the 35-member Republican majority in the Senate; without them, the Republicans would be a minority in the Senate as well. The important roles of New York City Democrats in the Assembly and Republicans in the Senate give the City great influence in the State legislature.

Martin Shefter's essay examines the results of New York's elections over recent history and the impact upon them of election law, leadership strategies, and national political trends. His analysis of gubernatorial elections finds a resurgence of Democratic strength even greater than that which Benjamin notes in the legislature. In 1962, a Republican was elected governor by a margin of more than 500,000 votes; 20 years later, a Democrat was elected by a margin of more than 1.4 million votes. Comparing the 1962 and 1982 elections, Shefter shows that in 1982 New York City Democrats actually accounted for about 200,000 *fewer* votes for the winner. The unsuccessful Democratic candidate in 1962 received over one half of his votes from New York City and barely one quarter from suburban areas; in 1982, the successful Democratic candidate received only 40 percent of his votes from New York City and nearly an equal share from suburban areas. Thus, the growing Democratic strength has resulted from shifts in both upstate and New York City area suburbs from Republican to Democratic candidates. Shefter shows that the Democrats no longer are a party overwhelmingly identified with New York City.

Another political dimension to the relationship between the two New Yorks is their interactions with the third partner in the American federal system, the national government. The essay by Sarah Liebschutz indicates that the stakes are enormous. The federal government spends about $57 billion in New York State annually, or about $3,200 per capita—with a large share of the money going directly to citizens in the form of Social Security, Medicare, and other entitlement payments. Federal grants provided about $8.7 billion to New York State in fiscal year 1986, accounting for nearly 23 percent of the State's budget. Similarly, federal aid provided about $3 billion to the City of New York, or about 19 percent of its operating budget.

Liebschutz analyzes the degree of agreement between the City and the State and the relative priority each assigns to specific issues as they seek to influence federal policy. She finds that there are few cases where the City and the State actually disagree over major federal policy issues, but the mayor and the governor often assign them different priorities. Therefore, the two New Yorks pursue somewhat different agendas. The battle led by Governor Cuomo to retain deductibility of state and local taxes in the federal personal income tax illustrates how effective New Yorkers can be in Washington when the State and the City work together and in alliance with others. In contrast, the recent difficulty in locating a naval base on Staten Island demonstrates that ideological differences still may divide them, as in the past.

Fiscal and Human Resources

In order to function, both the City and the State require resources in the form of money and personnel. The next three essays examine the ways in which these resources are secured and managed by the two New Yorks. Cynthia Green and Paul Moore analyze the system of public finance for localities in New York State, James Hartman reviews the distribution of public capital investments within the state, and Raymond Horton and David Lewin compare the manner in which human resources are managed by the City and the State.

Green and Moore's essay highlights two broad points. First, the ways in which New York City raises its money differ significantly from those of other localities in the state. It relies less on property taxes than other municipalities or counties and has a far more diverse set of revenue sources. In 1985, the City of New York obtained only about one sixth of its (nonschool) revenues from the property tax compared with one third for all other local governments in the state. However, the City levies personal income and business taxes not used in many other areas and a sales tax that is higher than that of virtually all other localities. This distinctive situation has evolved historically because the City's desire for more revenues has been accommodated with the State's desire to limit its aid to the City. How? By having the State legislature grant the City special taxing authority. This option of granting broad taxing authority to their cities, instead of new local aid, increasingly is being considered by states across the nation in the face of federal cutbacks.

Second, Green and Moore indicate that the fiscal balance of "getting and giving" between the two New Yorks has steadily been shifting in the City's favor. That is, the City has been contributing relatively less to the State's fisc, but has been receiving a growing share of the State's funds. Between fiscal years 1976 and 1983 (the most recent year for which data are available), the share of the State's revenues originating in New York City fell from 39.8 percent to 36.6 percent; available evidence suggests that the trend predates this recent period, though the earlier data are less reliable. However, the City's share of State assistance to localities has grown slightly over the same period, largely because of growth in the share of education aid allocated to the City. Moreover, the State has taken other fiscal actions of special benefit to the City not reflected in data on aid to localities. These include State assumption of City University senior college costs, certain court costs, and costs for the supplementary payments under the Supplementary Security Income (SSI) program.

James Hartman's essay on capital resources highlights the enormous scale of public infrastructure within the state. The State has a five-year capital plan calling for $17.6 billion in spending; the City has a ten-year plan totaling $31.4 billion; the separate capital needs of the Metropolitan Transportation Authority require $19.5 billion in the next ten years. After allowing for the financial transfers among these units, their ambitious plans suggest total average capital spending of about $8 billion yearly.

In most instances the division of responsibility for capital needs between the two New Yorks follows functional lines. The State has major financing responsibility for highways and bridges, higher education, mental health, environmental conservation, and its prisons. Together, these five functions account for nearly 90 percent of the State's capital plan, with transportation alone representing just over 50 percent. For most of these functions, the State also carries out the construction plans, but for highways and sewage treatment much of the money is transferred to the City to support its capital plan. The City, in turn, devotes about one sixth of its capital resources to highways, about one eighth to waste disposal, and divides much of the rest among numerous primarily locally financed projects in education, hospitals, water mains, and police, fire, and sanitation facilities and equipment. In some instances, notably water and waste treatment, these local investments are required by increasingly stringent State regulations.

The major exception to the seemingly well established and mutually accepted division of responsibility is mass transit, the service which makes the largest demand on capital resources. Additional—and as yet unidentified—resources are needed to realize the MTA's capital plans, but there is no consensus over the best source. Consequently, conflicts between the two New Yorks emerge. Upstate and suburban legislators oppose taxing their constituents to finance New York City subway facilities; City officials emphasize the regional character of the MTA's mission and its status as a State-chartered body.

Raymond Horton and David Lewin shift our attention from fiscal to human resources. Their essay assesses the quality of human resources management by the two New Yorks in terms of four elements: (1) staffing, or the adequacy of the number of workers employed; (2) compensation, or the adequacy of the pay levels for employees; (3) personnel administration, or the effectiveness of the mechanisms for recruiting and promoting workers; and (4) productivity, or the development of programs to increase the efficiency of the workforce. In each case, they reach provocative conclusions.

Using a method that adjusts for both the size of the population served and the range of functions performed, Horton and Lewin compare the size of the two New Yorks' workforce to that of a group of similar states and cities. They show that New York State employs about one fifth more people than the average for other large states and that New York City employs about one fourth more workers than the norm for other large cities. A similar comparative analysis of compensation levels reveals that the two New Yorks pay their workers at rates roughly comparable to the average for other large states and cities. The combination of relatively high staffing levels with pay levels that match those of other areas leads Horton and Lewin to question the appropriateness of current policies.

In assessing personnel administration and productivity, Horton and Lewin contrast the two New Yorks. They find that the municipal agency for personnel administration, the City's Department of Personnel, has been permitted by successive mayors from Robert Wagner to Edward Koch to deteriorate to its current level of barely minimal performance. The exigencies of budgeting and collective bargaining have displaced serious concern for maintaining an independent civil service system. Similar pressures are at work at the state level, but the New York State Department of Civil Service has fared better, perhaps because of a more pervasive civil service ethos combined with a younger system of collective bargaining in State government. With respect to productivity initiatives, Horton and Lewin find an area where the State could learn from the City. The leaders of the City of New York began developing programs to improve productivity even before the 1975 fiscal crisis, and these efforts accelerated in the late 1970s. In contrast, the State has done less, and proceeded more slowly, in developing explicit productivity initiatives that are integrated into the budgetary process.

Service Provision

The remaining six essays are devoted to major public service areas in which the State and the City play a role. In all cases the authors consider how the nature of the service differs in New York City and how each of the two New Yorks has attempted to accommodate the other's special interests and needs.

Education. In New York, as in almost every other state, elementary and secondary education is provided by a network of school districts which rely on both local tax sources and State aid. Robert Berne's essay focuses on the nature of the fiscal relationship between New York State and the local units it relies upon to deliver public education.

Berne finds the relationship to be both distinctive and dynamic. Public schools in New York City receive and spend less per pupil than large city school districts in other states, except for San Antonio, Baltimore, and Jacksonville. The nation's 21 other largest cities had per pupil expenditures above their statewide average. In most cities, the greater needs of poorer and more disadvantaged students lead to higher-than-average spending for large urban school systems. In New York City, when adjustments are made for higher prices and greater needs, per pupil resources are approximately 20 percent below the rest of the state. Moreover, the disparity is due entirely to the level of State aid rather than local tax effort for education. The City's share of education aid is below its share of statewide pupil enrollment, which higher-than-average levels of local tax support do not offset.

The lower level of available resources is one of several factors that lead New York City's public schools to perform poorly relative to the rest of the state. For example, more than one third of the City's public elementary school students read below minimum levels established by the State Education Department compared with less than one tenth elsewhere in the state. Similar disparities exist for mathematics skills.

The dynamic aspect of the relationship that Berne identifies is the improved position of the City in recent years. Since the mid 1970s, increments to the annual statewide appropriation for State education aid have been distributed more favorably to the City. As a result, there has been steady progress in bringing the City's share of aid and enrollment closer together, although a sizable disparity remains. At the same time, modest progress in the performance of New York City public schools has occurred. While the data are far from conclusive, they suggest that an increasing share of elementary school students are performing at or above national norms.

In considering the forces behind the improved fiscal treatment of education in New York City, Berne is drawn to a political explanation. Legislative decisions on the share of education aid allocated to the City are not "automatic" in the sense that they flow from predetermined formulas; rather, the legislative leaders decide explicitly on the City's share and adjust the formulas to achieve the desired result. The factors identified by Benjamin and Shefter—growing Democratic strength in the legislature with leadership based in New York City—appear to be linked to the dynamic quality of the education aid relationship.

Health Care. The distinguishing features of New York City's health care delivery system are identified in Kenneth Thorpe's essay. The city has an abundant supply of physicians and hospital beds; but perhaps more important, its health care providers are concentrated in large academic medical centers. More than two thirds of the city's hospitals have graduate medical education programs compared with less than one tenth nationally. These institutions tend to be unusually large. The city's hospitals have an average size of over 400 beds, more than twice the national average and 100 beds larger than the statewide average. Finally, the city has an unusually large municipal hospital system in absolute and relative terms. The New York City Health and Hospitals Corporation operates 11 acute care hospitals and four long-term care facilities that account for about one fifth of the citywide number of hospital beds and more than two fifths of all outpatient and emergency room visits.

Until the 1960s, local circumstances did not require extensive State policy adjustments because the State had only limited involvement in financing personal health care. However, passage of the federal Medicaid program changed the relationship by giving the State a major role in financing health care for the indigent. As Medicaid spending soared and fiscal pressures tightened in the 1970s, the State began to aggressively regulate the entire hospital industry. By the early 1980s, the State had become a major actor in health care policy; and under a federal waiver of Medicare policy it exercised control over virtually all hospital revenues. This expanded role generated conflict throughout the state between private hospitals and public regulators.

However, the State's more aggressive role in health care has not generated extensive conflicts with the City. The City, in its dual role as partial financer of the Medicaid program and operator of its own public hospital system, has shared objectives of lowering Medicaid costs; moreover, the City has benefited from the State's regulatory system in that the municipal hospitals are recognized as a "special" category of provider. While the City continues—with some success—to seek reductions in its State-mandated share of Medicaid financing and has fought vigorously for fair treatment of HHC facilities in the State's reimbursement system, Thorpe finds that the State's role in health care has adjusted appropriately to the special concerns of the City.

Mental Health and Mental Retardation. Care for the mentally ill and retarded historically has been provided by State-operated institutions. Barbara Blum and Susan Blank's essay concentrates on how these systems adjusted to the policy of deinstitutionalization first inaugurated for mental health services in the late 1950s, when the development of psychotropic drugs made it possible, and later applied to mental retardation services as a result of court actions in 1972. They find the responses to be far more satisfactory for mental retardation than for mental health.

What explains the contrast between the successful shift from residential centers to community-based services for the retarded and the unsatisfactory, unplanned discharge of State mental hospital patients to locally sponsored outpatient facilities? To Blum and Blank, the answer is politics and money. One objective of the deinstitutionalization policy for the mentally ill was to reduce costs per patient by shifting to a new form of care, but the State was unable to shift resources from the direct operation of public hospitals to grants to localities for community-based services. In contrast, the emptying of Willowbrook and other facilities for the retarded was accompanied by increased appropriations virtually from the start, which meant that the funds did not have to be shifted to local aid because the State retained primary responsibility for community-based care to the retarded. Such additional funding also was easier to provide because of the smaller scale of mental retardation services; the number of patients in mental hospitals was cut from over 93,000 in 1955 to less than 21,000 in 1985 compared with a reduction in residents of developmental centers from about 20,000 in 1975 to just under 10,000 in 1985.

Political forces were also important. Parents of the retarded were an active and powerful force in initiating and monitoring deinstitutionalization of their children. The families of the mentally ill, when present, did not play so strong a role, and there were no other groups to serve as political advocates on behalf of them. Moreover, Governor Hugh Carey evidenced special concern for the retarded, bringing additional political support to their cause. Contraction of the mental hospital system was made especially difficult by union pressure to retain jobs in often-isolated communities where institutions are located and by the need to upgrade standards of care to maintain accreditation. At the same time, localities were not adequately funded or well enough organized to take on the new responsibilities; thus, they were politically resistant from the beginning.

Social Services. The essay by Irene Lurie and Mary Jo Bane considers the structure of social service programs in New York State and examines child welfare services as a case study in the dynamics of the city-state relationship. They begin by noting that social welfare services under New York's constitution are a responsibility of the State and that extensive programs, often drawing upon federal assistance, have been established by the legislature. However, the State generally has chosen not to administer these programs directly; instead it relies on counties and the City of New York to perform line functions. The system, unlike that in most other states, is State-supervised rather than State-administered.

Within the state, social service needs and expenditures are concentrated in New York City. As noted earlier, about 40 percent of all New Yorkers live in New York City; however, the city accounts for fully two thirds of the state's welfare recipients and receives an equivalent share, about $2.8 billion annually, of the State's social service spending.

Although the legal arrangements place the City in a subordinate position to the State in the making of social welfare policy, State supervision rather than administration, plus the concentration of expenditures in New York City, lets its officials bargain with their ostensible superiors in Albany. Although they might eventually lose in court challenges, the City's immediate administrative control over the system permits it to disobey (and thereby embarrass) the State, while mustering constituency and public support to further its interests. The Lurie-Bane reconstruction of the formulation and implementation of the Child Welfare Reform Act of 1979 illustrates this bargaining pattern; for example, the record-keeping and utilization review requirements established initially by the State were modified in response to resistance by City officials. As long as the City bears day-to-day responsibility for delivering services to a majority of the state's social service clients, the State will have to adjust to the City's needs.

Child welfare illustrates another important feature of the relationship between the two New Yorks in social services; a variety of State and City agencies and legislative committees are involved in making policy. Because most programs receive federal support, federal officials also must review or approve most State decisions; and they assert new and different interests. Similarly, because localities—and especially New York City— rely on voluntary agencies to help deliver services, these agencies become actively involved in policymaking in order to protect their interests. Thus, the real picture of decision making is not a State-City hierarchy, but a

multi-party set of negotiations involving federal officials and the
voluntary providers.

Housing. Three features combine to distinguish the New York City
housing market from that of virtually every other major urban area in the
state and even the nation. First, a large proportion of residents rent rather
than own their homes. Fully 77 percent of all housing units in New York
City are rented compared with 58 percent in the other "big five" cities,
28 percent in the rest of the state, and 36 percent nationwide. Second,
vacancy rates in the city's rental market have remained low for an
extended time period creating potential for exploitative rent levels. While
the national vacancy rate is estimated at about 5 percent, the New York
City figure is just 3 percent (a level never exceeded since the end of World
War II). Finally, the city has a large number and proportion of poor
residents who, without sizable subsidies, cannot afford rents sufficient to
enable landlords to maintain their buildings.

Under these circumstances, strong political pressures for government
intervention in the housing market have arisen, both to provide subsidies
and to regulate rents. Emanuel Tobier and Barbara Gordon Espejo's
essay provides a largely historical review of the ways in which the two
New Yorks have responded to these pressures. Their analysis includes six
major types of housing programs—rent control, the Mitchell-Lama
limited-profit programs, the Urban Development Corporation (UDC)
initiatives, federal subsidies made available through public housing
authorities and the Section 8 program, shelter allowances under public
assistance programs, and local subsidies through property tax exemptions.

Tobier and Espejo find no clear and consistent division of responsibilities between the City and the State and no uniform pattern of
interaction. Programs begun at different times lack an integrated quality.
In some cases, notably rent control, responsibility for the program has
shifted back and forth between State and City agencies. In other
cases—for example, the UDC—the State assumed extraordinary powers
and acted directly without involving local agencies. Finally, in instances
such as public housing and Mitchell-Lama projects, the State supported
direct action by locally controlled agencies.

These diverse forms of intervention have resulted from widely varying
patterns of interaction. Programs such as Mitchell-Lama involved joint
State-City action that generated little direct conflict between the two New
Yorks. In other instances—for example, legislative changes in local tax
exemption programs—the State sought to thwart City initiatives.
Finally, the City sometimes resisted State actions, such as Governor

Nelson A. Rockefeller's vacancy decontrol program and some of UDC's planned projects.

The most persistent theme in the Tobier-Espejo history of New York housing programs is the important role of federal funding. Many State and City actions have been responses to opportunities to tap federal funds. Changes in federal programs at the beginning of Richard M. Nixon's second presidential term helped bring the UDC to its knees. The retreat of the federal government from this policy arena under President Reagan led to a withering of some State and local activities. The current attention to the homeless and the recent spate of gubernatorial, mayoral, and private sector proposals for housing initiatives indicates a new willingness to allocate substantial nonfederal resources, but these are emerging within an ill-defined framework of State and City responsibility.

Criminal Justice. Crime, like many other social pathologies, is disproportionately concentrated in New York City. With 40 percent of the statewide population, the city is the site of 61 percent of all violent crimes; its rate of 8,397 crimes per 100,000 population is more than 50 percent above the statewide average. Because criminals in New York City are more likely than their counterparts elsewhere to be sentenced to prison, 70 percent of the cells in State prisons are filled by people sent from New York City.

Ester Fuchs's essay on the public agencies responsible for administering criminal justice in the two New Yorks reveals a complex network of relationships. Not only are responsibilities divided between State and City, but there also are divisions among highly autonomous units at each of these levels. The State, largely under the direction of the governor, operates prisons, but a separate judicial branch oversees criminal court activities. Similarly, the City, under mayoral leadership, maintains a police force and operates its Correction and Probation departments, but other independent local actors also play major roles. These include five separately elected district attorneys, autonomous local criminal court judges, and a private Legal Aid Society.

Fuchs argues that this fragmentation of authority and lack of central coordination lead to poor, even disastrous, performance by the criminal justice system as a whole. To support her argument, she points to the jail overcrowding crisis of 1983 and the subsequent failure to develop any viable, long-run response. In November 1983 a federal judge found the city's jails to be intolerably, in fact unconstitutionally, overcrowded and ordered the mayor to reduce the jail population. In the next two weeks 613 inmates were released on parole, much to the dismay of the mayor and a large segment of the public. This temporarily relieved the problem, but overcrowding again became an issue in 1986 as accelerated narcotics enforcement by City police led to renewed problems of overcrowding in city jails.

Both the emergence of and the ineffective responses to the crisis are attributed by Fuchs to the fragmented nature of the system. As legislative initiatives, local police policies, and independent judicial actions vastly increased the number of sentenced criminals over the past two decades, the City looked to the State to house them. The State, however, did not expand its prison capacity in an adequate and timely fashion. The City unsuccessfully sued the State over responsibility for sentenced inmates, while the City itself was simultaneously being sued on behalf of prisoners to remedy their poor treatment. Conflicts and finger pointing between judges and the mayor over responsibility for speedier processing of defendants were frequent. This atmosphere of contentious intergovernmental (and intragovernmental) relations hampers the development of viable solutions; in Fuchs' view, consolidation of authority is essential to progress.

The foregoing brief summaries hardly do justice to the authors' efforts; each essay provides greater detail and fuller elaboration. While some important areas such as higher education and transportation are absent because of limited resources and available expertise, the contributions together constitute a relatively comprehensive analysis of relationships between the two New Yorks. Moreover, because the essays also often contain comparative analyses, and because the two New Yorks often resemble other large cities and their states, the volume can provide insights for those concerned with state and local government throughout the nation. The broader themes emerging from the individual essays are discussed in the conclusion.

NOTES

1. Roscoe Martin, *The Cities and the Federal System* (New York: Atherton, 1965), p. 77.
2. Norton Long, "The Three Communities," in Marilyn Gittell, ed., *State Politics and the New Federalism* (New York: Longman, 1986), p. 139.
3. Quoted in Martin, *Cities*, p. 98.
4. Quoted in U.S. Advisory Commission on Intergovernmental Relations, *The Question of State Government Capacity* (Washington, DC: ACIR, 1985), p. 1.
5. Quoted in Donald F. Lufton, *Many Sovereign States* (New York: McKay, 1975), p. 30.

6. Ira Sharkansky, *The Maligned States* (New York: McGraw-Hill, 1972), p. 2.
7. Larry Sabato, *Goodbye to Goodtime Charlie: The American Governorship Transformed* (Washington, DC: Congressional Quarterly Press, 1983).
8. See Arthur W. McMahon, *Administering Federalism and Democracy* (New York: Oxford University Press, 1972).
9. James L. Sundquist and David W. Davis, *Making Federalism Work* (Washington, DC: Brookings Institution, 1968), p. 215.
10. B. Douglas Horman, "The Block Grant: Readings from a First Experiment," *Public Administration Review* 30 (1970):141–142.
11. Quoted in Sharkansky, *Maligned States*, p. 132.
12. See Daniel P. Moynihan, *Maximum Feasible Misunderstanding* (New York: Basic Books, 1969).
13. Lawrence Herson, "Pilgrims' Progress: Reflections on the Road to Urban Reform," in *Political Science and State and Local Government* (Washington, DC: American Political Science Association, 1973), p. 14.
14. Alan K. Campbell and Donna E. Shalala, "Problems Unsolved, Solutions Unfound: The Urban Crisis," in Alan Campbell, ed., *The States and the Urban Crisis* (New York: Prentice-Hall, 1970), p. 26.
15. A. James Reichley, "The Political Containment of the Cities," in Campbell, *States and the Urban Crisis*, p. 195.
16. A. James Reichley, "The States Hold the Keys to the Cities," *Fortune* (June 1969): p. 154.
17. Leon D. Epstein, "The Old States in a New System," in Anthony King, ed., *The New American Political System* (Washington, DC: American Enterprise Institute, 1978).
18. Quoted in Nicholas Henry, *Governing at the Grassroots* (Englewood Cliffs, NJ: Prentice-Hall, 1984), p. 250.
19. U.S. Advisory Commission on Intergovernmental Relations, *State Community Assistance Initiatives: Innovations of the Late 1970s* (Washington, DC: U.S. Government Printing Office, 1979); and Charles R. Warren, *The States and Urban Strategies: A Comparative Analysis* (Washington, DC: U.S. Government Printing Office, National Academy of Public Administration, and Department of Housing and Urban Development, 1981).
20. Deil S. Wright, *Understanding Intergovernmental Relations* (Monterey, CA: Brooks-Cole, 1982), p. 384.
21. U.S. Advisory Commission on Intergovernmental Relations, *Question of State Government Capability*, p. 2.
22. See Thomas Dye and Thomas L. Hurley, "The Responsiveness of Federal and State Government to Urban Problems," *Journal of Politics* 40 (February 1978): 196–207; Peter D. Ward, "The Measurement of Federalism and State Responsiveness to Urban Problems," *Journal of Politics* 43 (February 1981): 83–99; Robert M. Stein, "The Targeting of State Aid: A Comparison of Grant Delivery Systems," *Urban Interest* 3 (1981): 47–59; Fred Teitelbaum, David D. Arnold, and Dorrett Lyttle, "State Assistance to Distressed Cities," *Urban Interest* 3 (1981): 47–59; John P. Pelissero, "State Aid and City Needs: An Examination of Residual State Aid to Large Cities," *Journal of Politics* 46 (August 1984):

916–935; quotation from George E. Peterson, "Urban Policy and the Cyclical Behavior of Cities," in George E. Peterson and Carol W. Lewis, eds., *Reagan and the Cities* (Washington, DC: Urban Institute, 1986), p. 34.

23. Ann Bowman and Richard Kearney, *The Resurgence of the States* (Englewood Cliffs, NJ: Prentice-Hall, 1986), p. 184.

24. Joseph F. Zimmerman, *State-Local Relations: A Partnership Approach* (New York: Praeger, 1983), pp. 39–40.

2

A COMPARATIVE VIEW

James C. Musselwhite, Jr.

A S THE DOMESTIC role of the federal government has shrunk in the 1980s, large cities are focusing more attention on their state capitals and less on Washington. Moreover, the federal government has chosen to redirect many of its remaining domestic programs toward the states and away from cities. Given the pronounced withdrawal of the federal government from urban affairs, states and large cities are redefining their relationships in ways that make each more important to the other. Relationships between big cities and their states are likely to become the crucial intergovernmental link for future urban policy.

To better understand these relationships, this book focuses on New York City and New York State. Yet a comparative analysis provides a useful perspective in which to consider that experience. To develop a broader perspective for the New York case, this essay compares the relationship between New York City and New York State with the relationships of other large cities and their states. The first section summarizes the historical and legal background of city and state relations in America and outlines the major contemporary issues; the second section identifies the specific cities and states to be examined in the chapter and explains how they were chosen; the third section examines how socioeconomic conditions in big cities compare with those in their states; the fourth section examines the political and institutional linkages between states and big cities; and the final section considers big-city and state fiscal relations.

BACKGROUND

Contemporary city-state relations can be understood best in the context of their evolution. This requires an appreciation of the major factors responsible for the environment in which big cities operate today.

General History

In the country's early years, cities played minor roles in the body politic and were too small to expect or need much from state governments. Indeed, urban areas of all sizes did not constitute even 10 percent of the population until nearly the middle of the nineteenth century.[1] State governments also played small roles during this period, and their activities were rarely concerned with urban affairs. The American city became a crucial force in the nation's economic and political life only after the industrial revolution in the mid-1800s. Cities such as New York, Pittsburgh, and Baltimore became the engines of economic growth for their states as the manufacture and shipping of goods increased. Cities grew in employment and population to become the center not only of many states' economies, but also of their social, educational, and cultural life. This was reflected by the rapid population growth of cities, which represented one third of the nation's population in 1900 and one half by 1920. Cities of this time were largely self-contained business and residential units. City governments were almost solely responsible for financing and providing governmental services in urban areas. Public services were largely infrastructure and utility oriented and were generally concerned with encouraging business expansion within the city. These services included water, streets, bridges, and transportation.

States in the nineteenth century were not generally boosters of cities. At best, most states ignored their cities. At worst, many states placed considerable constraints on cities because of a widespread notion that urban life corrupted its citizens and made them less fit to govern themselves than rural citizens. Rooted in America's rural founding and echoed by Thomas Jefferson and others, this anti-urban bias has played a major role throughout America's history. Large-scale foreign immigration to the cities beginning in the mid-1980s further reinforced the notion that the cities differed from the rest of the country in undesirable ways. Dennis Judd characterized city-state relations this way:

Politics in the states had operated on this perception of cities as "enemy country" throughout the nineteenth century. State legislatures had placed stringent limits on the powers of municipal officials and had frequently assumed control of police departments, utilities boards, and other city functions. In the twentieth century, the distrust of cities became amplified into several national movements, all intent on keeping the "dangerous elements" within the cities in their place.[2]

The role of state governments did not change greatly as the twentieth century began. In only a few of the more progressive areas, such as New York and Minnesota, did states offer assistance to distressed urban populations. In general, however, states had neither the interest nor the capacity to deal with these problems. As a result, city officials began to demand publicly federal assistance when they were no longer able to deal with the human misery occasioned by the Depression. At this point, the cities looked increasingly to the federal government for help, a trend which was substantially reinforced and continued until the late 1970s.

Big-city relationships with the rest of the country began to change fundamentally after World War II. Social and economic changes during this period were as fundamental as those which had brought big cities to the forefront of American life a hundred years earlier. Large numbers of people and businesses left the cities for the suburbs, and many moved from cities in the older part of the country to new cities in the South and West. Urban life was no longer a phenomenon to be experienced only in the big city, but spread out in different forms to Westchester County, Shaker Heights, and other suburban locations. Moreover, the nation's big cities were no longer only those found along the Atlantic seaboard and in the Midwest industrial heartland. Los Angeles became the nation's second largest city; Texas came to have three of the country's ten most populous cities.

During this period many big cities declined in terms of population and economic base. This was particularly true of the older cities concentrated in the Northeast and Midwest. But even in the South and West where many big cities were expanding rapidly, the growth of most cities was slower than the growth in the balance of their states by the 1980s. And some like New Orleans and Atlanta experienced declines that paralleled the frostbelt cities.

As a result of these major changes, the dynamics of urban life no longer conformed to big city jurisdictional boundaries, but spread unevenly across large metropolitan areas and a myriad of local governments. Consequently, big cities often found themselves facing a disproportionately large share of the nation's metropolitan problems with a disproportionately small share of local resources to deal with them. Big cities increasingly confronted metropolitan problems concentrated within their borders because of the special needs of their large poor, minority, and elderly populations. In addition, many of the older cities were experiencing severe deterioration of their infrastructure. Yet the tax base and political power to deal with many of these problems was now found outside the big cities in nearby suburban towns and counties, as well as in state capitals.

The decline of large cities was a cause of national concern during the 1960s and 1970s. Urban policy, coupled with civil rights and anti-poverty initiatives, lead to many new federal programs. The expanded federal role was accompanied by a perception that states were either reluctant to aid cities or, in the worst case, that states were actually contributing to urban problems. Federal aid to cities took many forms and went through a number of evolutions in both Democratic and Republican administrations. Some have argued that big cities became unhealthily dependent on the federal government, while others argued that not enough was done. What is important, however, is that federal funding became a major source of city revenues during this period.[3] In 1978, for example, direct federal funding to cities equaled $10.2 billion, or about 16 percent of city revenues. By the late 1970s, however, these federal programs were being reduced as the Carter Administration began a retreat from the Great Society programs that the Reagan Administration has accelerated. In 1984, direct federal aid to cities had declined to $7 billion in inflation-adjusted terms, or 10 percent of city revenues.[4]

Legal Background

Law plays a powerful role in all walks of American life, including city-state relationships. There is extensive variation in this experience among states, but two legal decisions are crucial to a general understanding of contemporary city-state relations in all states. First, in *Dartmouth College* v. *Woodward*, the Supreme Court ruled that cities are legal creations of the state and derive their legal authority from the state.[5] Second, in *Baker* v. *Carr*, the Court applied the one-man-one-vote principle to state and local legislatures.[6]

The *Dartmouth College* case affirmed the states' authority to decide city rights and responsibilities. This dominant role of the states has lead to greatly differing roles for big cities across the country that have been shaped by particular state traditions. For example, St. Louis can no longer annex adjoining lands and therefore finds population growth impossible. Houston, by contrast, can annex territory and grow virtually at will. This legal superiority of states also has served as a vehicle by which rural and later suburban interests could use state government to limit or shape the role of big-city government.

Given the crucial role of state government in defining city prerogatives, adequate representation in the state legislature is vital to urban residents. Yet for much of the nation's history, big cities were not represented in state capitals in proportion to the size of their population. The Supreme Court changed this in *Baker* v. *Carr*. The initial impact of this decision was to strengthen big-city political representation in state legislatures, which enabled them to more ably represent big-city interests. Given the continuing shift of people and jobs out of the big cities, however, the major impact of the decision for the rest of the century will be a strengthening of the political power of suburban areas at the expense of the big cities.

Current Issues

Today, the most pressing priority of most large cities is improved fiscal health. The continuing movement of business and population to the suburbs and reductions in federal aid to cities promise little fiscal relief for most of the nation's large cities in the foreseeable future. Large cities will be increasingly on their own fiscally, unless they can convince their states to play a more supportive role in city affairs or work out more cooperative agreements with nearby local governments.

In their quest for fiscal health, big cities can pursue several strategies. Perhaps the most emphasized strategy is the promotion of economic growth to enhance city revenues. Economic development programs, including reduced taxes and other inducements to business expansion, are the principal means by which cities have pursued this strategy.[7] Another popular strategy is "load shedding," or the transfer of fiscal responsibility for services or capital outlays to other governments. Until recently, the federal government was the primary target of this off-loading.[8] Now, however, cities are turning more often to their states, and in some cases to neighboring local governments, to share their fiscal burdens. A third strategy is simply reduction of city services. At various times cities such as Detroit, New York, and Cleveland have reduced their appropriations for fire, police, garbage, or other services. A fourth strategy is more efficient delivery of services, either through improved performance of city personnel or contracting out to private providers.[9] And for those cities allowed by state law, a fifth strategy is expansion of the city limits to increase the tax base.

Apart from fiscal issues, cities may face other problems depending upon their circumstances. These include the social and economic challenges of the underclass, deteriorating infrastructure in older cities,

the need to expand infrastructure in newer cities, and matching revenue
responsibilities to services in broader metropolitan areas. The latter issue
includes coordination of program responsibilities with other local
governments whose residents benefit from a city's services or facilities but
live outside it. In many cases this requires creating an appropriate
regional institution or creating special relationships between existing
institutions.

SELECTING BIG CITIES AND THEIR STATES

There is no standard definition of a "big" city to use in selecting a set
of cities for comparative purposes. For this analysis, 20 city-state pairs
were chosen based on two criteria. First, the city had to have a large
population, specifically a population of 400,000 or more in 1984. There
were 32 cities of this size. Second, the city had to be the largest in its state.
This criteria eliminated 11 large cities. Washington, DC was also omitted
from the analysis because it is not part of a state. The remaining cities and
states selected for analysis are listed in Table 2.1.

To provide a baseline against which to measure changes over time, the
same criteria were used to select large cities in 1970. (See Appendix Table
A.1.) That process identified 17 of the 20 cities in Table 2.1, but excluded
Columbus, Kansas City, and Oklahoma City. Those three cities were
replaced by Cleveland, St. Louis, and Minneapolis.

Variations in City Size

Even among "big" cities there is wide variation in population size.
New York, the largest city in the analysis, is about 17 times larger than
the smallest "big" city. Although the mean size of these cities is 1.3
million, only 6 of the 20 cities exceed 1 million in population. Moreover,
only 3 of the cities—New York, Phoenix, and Chicago—constitute as
much as a quarter of their state's total population. This suggests that few
large cities have substantial political influence in their states solely
because of their size. Rather, if they are important actors at the state
level, it is because of their strong individual efforts or because they
successfully ally themselves with other local jurisdictions.

These data reveal that New York City is unique in two respects. First,
New York is more than twice as populous as any other city. Indeed, it is
more populous than all but nine states.[10] Second, no other city
constitutes nearly as high a percentage of total state population. Only
Phoenix and Chicago are even close in this respect. This situation is not
new. In 1970, New York City stood out as even larger in absolute size
and as an even greater share of total state population. (See Appendix

TABLE 2.1
Large Cities, 1984

City	Population (in thousands)	Population as a Percentage of State Population
New York	7,165	40%
Los Angeles	3,097	12
Chicago	2,992	26
Houston	1,706	11
Philadelphia	1,647	14
Detroit	1,089	15
Phoenix	853	28
Baltimore	764	18
Indianapolis	710	13
Memphis	648	14
Milwaukee	621	13
Jacksonville	578	5
Boston	571	10
Columbus	566	5
New Orleans	559	13
Denver	505	16
Seattle	488	11
Kansas City	443	9
Oklahoma City	443	13
Atlanta	426	7
Unweighted Mean	1,294	15

SOURCE: U.S. Bureau of the Census, *Statistical Abstract of the United States: 1986* (Washington, DC: U.S. Government Printing Office, 1985).

Table A.1.) Because of its huge size, New York City may have developed its local government institutions on a scale not seen elsewhere, and New York State may have recognized the city's importance in ways not common to other cities. These issues are explored below.

SOCIOECONOMIC CHARACTERISTICS

New York City is unique among large cities because of its size. Does this uniqueness carry over to its socioeconomic characteristics? This is a complex question, but for comparative purposes it may be examined in terms of resources and needs.

Resources

Income and wealth are the two principal economic resources. These resources can be measured as income per capita and assessed property value per capita. For comparative purposes, these indicators are expressed as the ratio of city to state per capita personal income and as the ratio of city to state per capita property assessment.[11] Where the indicators have a value of one, city and statewide per capita incomes and wealth are equal. When an indicator is greater than one, large city per capita income and wealth are greater than the statewide figure. (See Table 2.2.)

Income. On average, big cities' per capita income is below that of their states. However, this is a misleading average figure because of the very low city incomes in such older declining cities as Baltimore, Detroit, and Philadelphia. Eleven of the 20 cities actually have per capita incomes higher than those of their states. All but a few of these are newer cities in the West and South. These data suggest a significant regional trend

TABLE 2.2
Income and Wealth, Big Cities and Their States

City	Ratio of City to State per Capita Income, 1979	Ratio of City to State Assessed Property Value per Capita, 1982
Houston	1.220	NA
Oklahoma City	1.165	1.073
Seattle	1.150	NA
Kansas City	1.081	NA
Phoenix	1.072	.860
Denver	1.070	.929
Indianapolis	1.063	.580
Memphis	1.041	1.189
Atlanta	1.021	1.091
Los Angeles	1.014	.883
New Orleans	1.001	.907
New York	.970	1.078
Milwaukee	.970	.781
Columbus	.931	NA
Jacksonville	.931	.750
Boston	.879	.234
Chicago	.860	.659
Philadelphia	.855	1.350
Detroit	.808	.445
Baltimore	.709	.509
Unweighted Mean	.991	.832

SOURCES: U.S. Bureau of the Census, *County and City Data Book: 1983*; and *Taxable Property Values and Assessment Sales Price Ratios, 1982 Census of Governments* (Washington, DC: U.S. Government Printing Office, 1983).

NOTE: NA = not available.

corresponding to the familiar frostbelt-sunbelt dichotomy. In this context, New York is in the frostbelt category, but at the better-off end of it. New York City has a slightly lower per capita income than the entire state, but New York City's ratio is higher than that of almost any other frostbelt city. In fact, New York City's absolute per capita income of $7,271 was slightly higher than the overall average in 1979, but New York State's even higher per capita income drove down the city's ratio.[12]

There have been interesting changes in city-state per capita income relations since 1969. (See Appendix Table A.2.) In that year, big cities' per capita incomes were greater than their states' on average, and the dichotomy between frostbelt and sunbelt cities was less evident. New York City still ranked twelfth among the 20 cities, but its per capita income was slightly higher than that of New York State. New York City and other frostbelt areas experienced significant declines in per capita income relative to their states between 1969 and 1979.

Wealth. Big cities generally have less wealth than other parts of their state. The average big city has only about 83 percent as much wealth per capita as the state as a whole. Only 5 of the 20 cities have greater per capita wealth than their states as a whole. This is clear evidence of the extent to which the nation's large cities have lost businesses and middle-class residents to the suburbs and smaller cities.

Unlike most large cities, New York has greater wealth per capita than the state as a whole. New York City is still home to many of the nation's largest businesses and is the nation's major commercial and financial center. As a result, the city has highly valuable commercial property, particularly in Manhattan, one of the world's prime real estate locations. In this respect, New York City has a larger relative property tax base than all but three of its counterparts.

Similar data for 1967 show a serious decline in big-city wealth relative to state wealth over the 15-year period. (See Appendix Table A.2.) In 1967, 12 of the 20 cities had greater wealth per capita than did their states. New York City ranked sixth, suggesting that it may have been somewhat more successful in preserving its relative share of wealth than other cities. It is clear, however, that big cities including New York lost a far greater share of their relative wealth than of their income during this period.

Human and Physical Needs

Urban needs have both a human and a physical dimension. While each is difficult to measure, suitable proxies for these dimensions are people living in poverty and infrastructure needs. The poverty dimension can be measured as the portion of the population with incomes below the federal poverty threshold. Infrastructure is best examined along two different lines. First, the need to repair or replace deteriorating infrastructure is gauged by the share of housing constructed before 1939.[13] Second, the need to build new infrastructure is measured by increases in the population over the past decade. Each of the three indicators is expressed as a ratio of the city indicator to the state indicator in Table 2.3.

Human Needs. Human needs are significantly greater in big cities than in the rest of their states. While this is not surprising, the magnitude of difference is worth noting. As a share of the population, the poverty population in big cities, on average, is half again as large as it is

TABLE 2.3

Poverty and Infrastructure Needs Among Large Cities and Their States

City	Ratio of City to State Share of Population in Poverty, 1979	Ratio of City to State Share of Pre-1939 Housing, 1980	Ratio of City to State Rate of Population Growth 1970–1980
Baltimore	2.337	2.246	*
Detroit	2.106	1.652	*
Boston	2.104	1.332	*
Philadelphia	1.962	1.304	*
Chicago	1.845	1.493	*
Atlanta	1.657	1.429	*
Columbus	1.602	0.744	3.538
Milwaukee	1.586	1.139	*
New York	1.493	1.141	*
Los Angeles	1.439	1.544	.297
New Orleans	1.419	2.358	*
Denver	1.356	1.633	*
Memphis	1.321	0.814	.213
Indianapolis	1.186	0.807	*
Jacksonville	1.185	1.746	.168
Houston	1.156	0.689	1.081
Seattle	1.143	1.892	*
Kansas City	1.082	1.241	*
Oklahoma City	0.896	0.792	.522
Phoenix	0.841	0.857	.663
Unweighted Mean	1.471	1.343	.926

SOURCE: U.S. Bureau of the Census, *County and City Data Book: 1983* (Washington, DC: U.S. Government Printing Office, 1984).

*City population declined; therefore ratio is not shown.

statewide. In Baltimore, Detroit, Boston, and Philadelphia the poverty population share is double or more the state figure! This pattern of high concentrations of the poor in large cities is the most uniform big-city characteristic explored in this chapter. Only two of the big cities have a smaller share of the poor than do their states—Oklahoma City and Phoenix.

Like most of its counterparts, New York City has a considerably greater share of its population in poverty than does New York State. Yet the concentration of poverty in New York City relative to New York State is close to the average for all large cities—1.493 versus 1.471.

The concentration of poverty in large cities is increasing. The average ratio of city to state poverty increased from 1.277 in 1969 to 1.471 in 1979. New York City's ratio of poverty increased as well during this period, but not as rapidly as in big cities as a whole. New York City's ranking among the 20 cities examined, however, was ninth during both periods. (See Appendix Table A.3.)

Infrastructure Needs. A primary concern of most big cities is replacing or repairing deteriorating infrastructure. Relative to their states, big cities have a 34 percent greater share of older infrastructure. This concentration of older infrastructure is not noticeably higher in any particular region, but appears to be endemic to big cities. Only five of the big cities have less older infrastructure than their states; this group includes Columbus and Indianapolis, as well as the sunbelt cities of Houston, Memphis, and Oklahoma City.

A major concern of newer cities in the West and South has been the construction of infrastructure to meet the needs of their growing populations. However, from 1970 to 1980, only 7 of the 20 big cities experienced population growth. Two of these were in the Midwest. Although all may have legitimate needs for expanding their infrastructure, it is important to note that only two of these cities grew faster than their states—Columbus and Houston. Relative to their states, growing large cities have limited needs for new infrastructure.

Although New York City has greater infrastructure needs than the state as a whole, it compares favorably with other large cities on this dimension. New York City's ratio of infrastructure needs relative to the state is lower than that of 12 other cities. This means that New York City infrastructure needs are more like those statewide than those in most other big cities.

As big cities' human needs are increasing relative to their states, so are their physical needs. From 1970 to 1980, the proxy of pre-1939 housing shows a 7 percent increase in city needs relative to statewide needs for repairing deteriorating infrastructure. (See Appendix Table A.3.) New

York City, however, did not experience an increase in physical needs on this measure, but remained below average in both periods.

POLITICAL AND INSTITUTIONAL RELATIONS

Political and institutional relations between big cities and their states define the structure within which many urban issues are decided and subsequent policies carried out. These relations are so complex and rich in their variation that they can be explored only at their most general level here. This exploration, however, should provide a basic understanding of city-state norms and whether New York City and New York State conform to these norms.

Political Relations

A basic issue is whether big-city voters have a political orientation fundamentally different from voters in the rest of the state. This question can be analyzed in terms of voting behavior. The most simple and direct way to examine the issue is with presidential election returns. The 1984 presidential race is instructive because it is the most recent, and because it clearly differentiated the two major philosophical streams of modern American politics.

Since the New Deal, big-city voters have favored more liberal and Democratic candidates. Growing minority and disadvantaged support for social welfare programs in the cities have reinforced these tendencies in the last two decades. Therefore, it is no surprise that in only two of the big cities did the Democratic share of the 1984 presidential vote fall below that of their states. (See Table 2.4.) Detroit was twice as Democratic as Michigan; and Atlanta, Baltimore, Chicago, and New Orleans were one and half times or more as Democratic as their respective states.

New York City is slightly below average in its Democratic bias. This is partly a function of the City vote being so large that it affects state averages more than in other states. Nonetheless, New York City is not as different politically from the balance of the state as are Baltimore, Atlanta, and Detroit. What is unique about New York City's Democratic vote, however, is its sheer size. In the 1984 presidential election, the New York City Democratic vote amounted to 1,343,875. Its nearest competitor, Chicago, had only a little more than half this total.[14]

The big-city vote is of declining importance. It averaged only about 14 percent of the statewide total in 1984, and in Atlanta, Boston, Kansas City, and Jacksonville was less than a tenth of votes cast. In 1968 the

TABLE 2.4
Big-City Voting Compared with Statewide Voting, 1984

City	Ratio of City to State Democratic Share of Vote for President	City Share of Total State Vote for President
Detroit	2.00	11%
Atlanta	1.79	8
Baltimore	1.52	17
Chicago	1.50	25
New Orleans	1.50	12
Kansas City	1.46	8
Denver	1.44	17
Philadelphia	1.41	16
Milwaukee	1.41	13
Seattle	1.39	14
New York	1.33	32
Memphis	1.32	16
Boston	1.31	8
Houston	1.27	11
Los Angeles	1.21	10
Indianapolis	1.09	14
Jacksonville	1.08	5
Columbus	1.04	5
Oklahoma City	0.99	11
Phoenix	0.96	25
Unweighted Mean	1.35	14

SOURCES: Richard M. Scammon and Alice V. McGillivray, *America Votes 16: A Handbook of Contemporary American Election Statistics* (Washington, DC: Congressional Quarterly, 1985); and unpublished information supplied by Alice V. McGillivray at the Elections Research Center in Washington, DC, and by the Franklin County, Ohio, Board of Elections.

big-city vote averaged 17 percent of the statewide vote for president. (See Appendix Table A.4.) Perhaps more important, that election marked the first presidential contest in which the suburban vote exceeded the central city vote.[15] In this sense, the era of the big city clearly has passed. Yet there are three big cities whose vote is still crucial to statewide voting—New York, Chicago, and Phoenix, and New York City leads this group.

Institutional Relations

Two important dimensions of institutional relations between big cities and their states are the degree to which government is decentralized and the size of city governments relative to other governments. The greater the decentralization, the more latitude big city governments may have to develop and carry out their own programs. The size of city government provides an indication of its importance as an institution in the state.

Decentralization. The notion that particular traditions and organizational modes encourage or discourage certain kinds of behavior has proved to be an important insight for understanding American federalism. Foremost in this school of thought has been Daniel Elazar.[16] Based on a fairly elaborate theory, Elazar classified the American states as having either centralized or decentralized traditions. Interestingly, only 6 of the 20 states of concern here fall into Elazar's decentralized classification, and one of these is New York. (Elazar categorized 19 of the 48 continental states as decentralized.)

A more recent examination of structural relationships between states and their local governments confirms and elaborates on many of Elazar's conclusions. The index reported in Table 2.5 is a composite of three measures concerned with personnel, service delivery, and financial responsibility. These measures reflect the relative distribution of personnel between state and local governments, which level of government delivers services, and which funds the services. Higher numbers represent greater centralization at the state level, and lower numbers less centralization.[17]

New York State has the lowest level of centralization of those states with a big city. Only Nebraska among all 50 states had a lower level of centralization. New York State's institutional arrangements seem to give New York City greater autonomy than is true of any other big-city state. Massachusetts and Maryland, by contrast, limit the autonomy of Boston and Baltimore.

Centralization in big-city states is increasing, suggesting that big cities may be losing some of their autonomy. From 1969 to 1982, the average centralization score increased 9 percent. Throughout this period New York State was the least centralized state, but its level of centralization rose more rapidly than the average. In this context, New York City may have seen its autonomy limited by state action more than most other large cities. Nonetheless, its absolute autonomy probably remains greater than that of any other big city.

Size of Big-City Government. While measures of centralization characterize the institutional environment in which cities operate, they do not necessarily reveal how important big city institutions are relative to others. If California is relatively decentralized, for example, this may mean it delegates responsibilities to counties rather than cities. And if

TABLE 2.5
Index of State Centralization, 1982 and 1969

State	1982	1969
Louisiana (New Orleans)	60.2	58.2
Oklahoma (Oklahoma City)	59.3	*
Massachusetts (Boston)	57.7	47.3
Maryland (Baltimore)	57.3	43.9
Pennsylvania (Philadelphia)	55.6	53.2
Ohio (Columbus)	53.9	39.9
Michigan (Detroit)	52.5	45.5
Indiana (Indianapolis)	52.4	43.2
Illinois (Chicago)	51.7	44.6
Missouri (Kansas City)	51.2	54.8
California (Los Angeles)	49.3	39.1
Washington (Seattle)	49.3	53.3
Wisconsin (Milwaukee)	49.3	42.8
Arizona (Phoenix)	47.5	48.9
Georgia (Atlanta)	46.9	49.7
Texas (Houston)	46.2	47.5
Tennessee (Memphis)	45.4	50.7
Colorado (Denver)	44.9	46.2
Florida (Jacksonville)	43.9	45.6
Minnesota (Minneapolis)	*	41.6
New York (New York)	42.8	36.1
Unweighted Mean	50.9	46.6

SOURCE: G. Ross Stephens, "State Centralization Over The Last Quarter Century," a paper prepared for a conference on the Reagan domestic program, Woodrow Wilson School, Princeton University, 1984.

*Not a state with one of the large cities.

both New York City and Columbus operate in decentralized environments, there is surely a tremendous difference in the size and sophistication of institutions in the two cities. One way to examine this dimension of big cities' institutions is to compare their sizes in terms of the number of employees relative to other governments. (See Table 2.6.)

How do big-city governments compare with state governments in terms of size? Big-city governments generally are large enough to be major partners in statewide policy deliberations and service provision. Indeed, the average big-city government has a fourth as many employees as does its state government.

New York City government is unique because of its size. Largely because New York City government performs many services not provided by cities in other states, it has 42 percent more employees than does the state! No other big city comes close to this ratio of city to state employees.

TABLE 2.6

Relative Size of Big-City Governments, 1982

City	Big-City Employees as a Percentage of State Government Employees	City Employees as a Percentage of All Local Government Employees
New York	142%	46%
Baltimore	41	24
Chicago	38	12
Memphis	34	15
Denver	27	11
Philadelphia	27	10
Boston	25	10
Phoenix	23	8
Detroit	18	7
Indianapolis	17	6
Los Angeles	16	5
Milwaukee	15	5
Seattle	13	7
New Orleans	12	7
Houston	11	3
Kansas City	10	4
Atlanta	9	3
Oklahoma City	7	4
Jacksonville	7	2
Columbus	6	2
Unweighted Mean	25	10

SOURCES: U.S. Bureau of the Census, *Employment of Major Local Governments, 1982 Census of Governments;* and *Compendium of Public Employment, 1982 Census of Governments* (Washington, DC: U.S. Government Printing Office, 1984).

NOTE: All figures are full-time equivalent employees. The big-city totals and all local government totals include elementary, secondary, and higher education employees when these school systems are legally dependent upon municipal governments for their operation. They generally do not include special authorities unless those authorities are also legally dependent upon the municipality for their operations.

Another way to assess the importance of big-city governments is to examine their size relative to other local governments in the state. As Table 2.6 shows, big-city governments account for only one employee in ten of all local government employees in their state. This suggests that in most states big cities are just one of many local governments with which the state deals. Once again, however, New York City is unique, constituting nearly half of all local government employees in the state. This suggests that in New York State, local government concerns are heavily weighted by New York City.

The relative importance of large-city governments has declined. (See Appendix Table A.5.) Between 1967 and 1982 the average ratio of large-city to state employees fell from 37 to 25 percent and the large-city share of all local government employees dropped from 12 to 10 percent. This trend was evident in New York where the ratio of city to state employees went from nearly 2-to-1 in 1967 to 42 percent above the state figure in 1982.

FISCAL RELATIONS

One of the most important aspects of city-state relations is fiscal relations, particularly the extent to which the state provides funds for city-administered activities. These state funds consist of state own-source revenues and federal funds initially paid to the state, and then "passed through" to localities. The state often may allocate among communities federal funds it receives on a discretionary basis, and the state has even greater control over the distribution of its own-source revenues. The state also may choose to provide services directly in a community, contract out to for-profit or nonprofit agencies, or provide funds to county, regional, or special district governments rather than city government.

Big cities depend on state-administered funds for about 15 percent of their revenues. (See Table 2.7.) Although this is a substantial amount, it suggests that big cities should not be characterized as "wards of state government."[18] However, this average figure masks tremendous differences among cities. In Oklahoma City, Los Angeles, and Atlanta, state-administered funds are almost inconsequential to the running of city government. However, in Baltimore, New York, Boston, and Milwaukee state-administered funds constitute between 32 and 48 percent of total revenues and are crucial to the city's operations.

When state-administered revenues are considered on a per capita basis, New York City emerges as receiving more such revenue than any other large city. Only Baltimore approaches New York in this respect. High levels of state funding for New York City are partly explained by the fact that New York City government has a broader role than any large city in America; it carries out services often provided by counties, other local governments, and even state governments in many communities. As a result, state funding that is usually dispersed among county governments, state agencies, and special districts in most other communities is concentrated in one New York City government total. The extraordinarily broad scope of government in New York City is crucial to understanding the city's fiscal relations and will be explored in more detail below.

Big-city reliance on state funds decreased slightly in the 1970s. (See Appendix Table A.6.) In 1967, 17 percent of big cities' revenues came

TABLE 2.7
State Financial Support of Large Cities, 1982

City	State-Administered Revenues as a Percentage of City Budget	Per Capita State Support of City Budget
Baltimore	48%	$871
New York	32	901
Boston	32	587
Milwaukee	32	261
Indianapolis	24	162
Phoenix	19	130
Detroit	15	215
Denver	14	185
Memphis	12	215
Seattle	12	144
Chicago	12	90
Philadelphia	11	155
New Orleans	10	91
Columbus	8	49
Jacksonville	7	97
Los Angeles	4	45
Atlanta	4	45
Kansas City	4	36
Houston	1	6
Oklahoma City	1	6
Unweighted Mean	15	215

SOURCE: U.S. Bureau of the Census, *Finances of Municipal and Township Governments: 1982 Census of Governments* (Washington, DC: U.S. Government Printing Office, 1984).

from their states compared with 15 percent in 1982. New York City reliance on state funds during the same period dropped from 35 to 32 percent.

State funding of big-city governments is just one type of state transfer to local government. State governments also provide funding to other cities, towns, counties, school districts, and other units of local government. States have different traditions in this respect. Some states choose to have local governments provide many state-funded services, while other states choose to provide these services directly. The range on this dimension is great, as Table 2.8 shows. At one extreme, Tennessee allocates only about a quarter of state funds to local governments. At the other extreme, California allocates almost half of its state expenditures to local governments. However, California's high support for local government does not yield significant funding for Los Angeles (refer to Table 2.7) because it is primarily directed toward county governments.

TABLE 2.8
State Financial Support of Local Governments, 1967 and 1982

	Percentage of State Expenditures Allocated to Local Government	
State	1982	1967
California (Los Angeles)	47%	41%
New York (New York)	46	54
Wisconsin (Milwaukee)	43	46
Arizona (Phoenix)	42	31
Indiana (Indianapolis)	40	37
Florida (Jacksonville)	40	32
Colorado (Denver)	38	34
Ohio (Columbus)	34	33
Washington (Seattle)	33	33
Pennsylvania (Philadelphia)	33	29
Texas (Houston)	32	30
Oklahoma (Oklahoma City)	31	*
Maryland (Baltimore)	31	43
Illinois (Chicago)	31	34
Georgia (Atlanta)	30	37
Missouri (Kansas City)	29	26
Louisiana (New Orleans)	28	30
Michigan (Detroit)	28	39
Massachusetts (Boston)	27	46
Tennessee (Memphis)	26	33
Minnesota (Minneapolis)	*	31
Unweighted Mean	34	37

SOURCES: U.S. Bureau of the Census, *State Payments to Local Governments: 1982 Census of Governments* (Washington, DC: U.S. Government Printing Office, 1984); and *State Payments to Local Governments: 1967 Census of Governments* (Washington, DC: U.S. Government Printing Office, 1968).

*Not a state with one of the large cities.

New York State allocates an unusually large share of its expenditures to local governments. In this respect, the environment in New York is particularly amenable to state funding of its large city. The same environment characterizes Milwaukee, one of the three other cities receiving state support comparable to New York City's. Baltimore and Boston are different, however. Both cities receive substantial support from their states, yet neither Maryland nor Massachusetts allocates unusually large shares of its state budget to local governments.

The share of state expenditures allocated to local governments declined modestly. From 1967 to 1982, the average share of state spending going to local government fell from 37 percent to 34 percent in the 20 big-city states. The portion of state spending going to local governments in New York, however, fell substantially more, dropping from 54 to 47 percent. Nonetheless, New York State continued to allocate an unusually large share of its spending to local governments.

Big-city governments do not play the same roles in their communities across the country for two reasons. First, as already noted, states may choose to provide some services directly in communities or finance city and other local governments to differing degrees. Second, big cities play differing roles in their communities depending upon their relationships with other local governments in the area.

A big city's role in its regional complex of local governments can be quantified as big-city revenues as a share of total local government revenues in the area. This is calculated in two ways in Table 2.9: first, in terms of all local governments in the county where the big city is located; second, in terms of all local governments in the Standard Metropolitan Statistical Area (SMSA) in which the big city is located. By either measure, big cities are not the dominant actor among local governments. They account for about one half of and one third of all local revenues, respectively.

As discussed earlier, New York City's role relative to other large cities is extensive. The City performs functions normally carried out by other local governments and state government in other communities. For example, there are only three local government or public school units located in New York City. Yet in less populous Cook County there are 516 such units and in Los Angeles County 276 such units.[19] New York City also operates a university system that is larger than a number of state systems and has the largest local public hospital system in the country. The City provides large matching payments for Medicaid and Aid to Families with Dependent Children (AFDC), a role normally played by states.[20] New York City also has financial responsibilities for bridges and roads, the largest mass transit system in the country, and the largest public housing program in the country.

New York City's dominance of regional local government is sharply delineated in Table 2.9. Because there are no county units within the city, municipal government represents 100 percent of local government activity within the county. Within its SMSA New York City accounts for fully 83 percent of all local government activity. New York's dominance is unique. Interestingly, neither Chicago, Los Angeles, nor Phoenix controls as much as a third of local government revenues. Clearly, county and other local governments play roles in these areas that are carried out by the city in New York.[21]

In short, New York City is unique among big cities in the enormous scope of its activities. The City is responsible for the full range of activities carried out by a combination of local governments in most

TABLE 2.9

Big-City Government Role in Regional Government, 1982

| City | Big-City Revenues as a Percentage of All Local Government Revenues in | |
	County	Metropolitan Area
New York	100%	83%
Memphis	79	73
Jacksonville	69	60
Philadelphia	67	35
New Orleans	66	35
Denver	61	26
Boston	56	19
Kansas City	44	22
Indianapolis	42	31
Detroit	39	25
Oklahoma City	34	24
Columbus	32	27
Atlanta	32	15
Houston	30	26
Milwaukee	29	22
Seattle	29	23
Chicago	26	21
Los Angeles	22	22
Phoenix[a]	20	20
Baltimore[b]	—	49
Unweighted Mean	46	33

SOURCES: U.S. Bureau of the Census, *Compendium of Government Finances: 1982;* and *Local Government in Metropolitan Areas: 1982* (Washington, DC: U.S. Government Printing Office, 1984).

[a]County and metropolitan area are the same.

[b]Baltimore is not part of a county.

communities and also carries out and finances activities that are normally the responsibility of state government elsewhere. For this reason, New York City government is qualitatively different from big-city government nationally.

CONCLUSION

The relationship between New York City and New York State is in many ways unique. No other city is in the same class with New York in absolute size or relative importance to its state. This, in part, explains why New York State has shown special concern for New York City in financing its services and generally in supporting its administration of a vast local government. These factors and a history of strong local governments in New York State have helped to make New York City the largest and most comprehensive city government in America by far. As a result, New York City dominates local government in its area in a way not seen elsewhere and even carries out activities normally performed by states in some other areas of the country.

If New York City is unique with respect to New York State in its enormity and scope of government, it is fairly typical of other big cities and their relationships with their states with respect to resources, needs, and political orientation. Big cities across the country generally have less income, more poor residents, more deteriorating infrastructure, and more liberal political orientations than do their states as a whole. New York City also has these characteristics.

NOTES

1. Population data in this paragraph from Dennis R. Judd, *The Politics of American Cities: Private Power and Public Policy*, 2nd ed. (Boston: Little, Brown, 1984), p. 16.
2. Judd, *Politics of American Cities*, p. 119.
3. For an analysis of the federal role in big-city finances, see James W. Fossett, *Federal Aid to Big Cities: The Politics of Dependence* (Washington, DC: Brookings Institution, 1983).
4. Numbers were derived from data in various issues of *City Government Finances* (Washington, DC: U.S. Bureau of the Census).
5. 4 Wheat 518 (1819). This relationship was further elaborated in *City of Clinton* v. *Cedar Rapids and Missouri Railroad Co.*, 24 Iowa 455, 475 (1818), which came to be referred to as Dillon's rule.
6. 369 U.S. 186, 82 S.Ct. 691 (1962). This case was further elaborated upon by the Supreme Court in *Reynolds* v. *Sims*, 377 U.S. 533, 84 S.Ct. 1362 (1964).
7. See R. Scott Fosler and Renee A. Berger, eds., *Public-Private Partnership in American Cities: Seven Case Studies* (Lexington: Lexington Press, 1982), for case studies of these strategies.
8. For an analysis of fiscal responsibility for social welfare services by level of government in 12 cities, see James C. Musselwhite, Jr., "The Impacts of New Federalism on Public/Private Partnerships," *Publius: The Journal of Federalism* 16, no. 1 (Winter 1986): 113–131.
9. For a discussion of social welfare privatization, see James C. Musselwhite, Jr., and Lester M. Salamon, "Social Welfare Policy and Privatization: Theory and Reality in Policymaking," in Mark S. Rosentraub, ed., *Urban Policy Problems: Federal Policy and Institutional Change* (New York: Praeger, 1986).
10. If these comparisons are made on the basis of entire metropolitan areas, New York's dominance is not as stark, though it remains the largest such

area in the country. Comparisons of metropolitan areas, however, are problematic because of how they are defined. The Census Bureau changes the composition of metropolitan areas periodically, and these areas do not necessarily correspond to local perceptions of metropolitan areas.

11. There is necessarily some imprecision in comparisons of property tax assessments, because assessments within a single state can be carried out by different units of government that may value property differently. However, this indicator still appears to be the best single proxy for estimating relative wealth within a state.

12. U.S. Bureau of the Census, *Statistical Abstract of the United States: 1986* (Washington, DC: U.S. Government Printing Office, 1985), calculated from data on p. 454.

13. This indicator is used to measure the same type of need in formulas used to allocate federal funds under the Community Development Block Grant program.

14. Data are from Richard M. Scammon and Alice V. McGillivray, *America Votes 16: A Handbook of Contemporary American Election Statistics* (Washington, DC: Congressional Quarterly, 1985); and unpublished information supplied by Alice V. McGillivray at the Elections Research Center in Washington, DC, and by the Franklin County, Ohio, Board of Elections.

15. *The 1968 Elections* (Washington, DC: Research Division of the Republican National Committee, 1969).

16. Daniel J. Elazar, *American Federalism: A View from the States* (New York: Crowell, 1966).

17. For a full description of the methodology, see G. Ross Stephens, "State Centralization Over the Last Quarter-Century," a paper prepared for a conference on the Reagan domestic program, Woodrow Wilson School, Princeton University, 1984; and G. Ross Stephens, "State Centralization and the Erosion of Local Autonomy," *Journal of Politics* 36, no. 1 (February 1974): 51–66.

18. This does not mean that big cities generate 85 percent of their budget from own-source revenues. As noted earlier, cities also receive more than 10 percent of their revenues directly from the federal government.

19. U.S. Bureau of the Census, *Governmental Organization: 1982 Census of Governments* (Washington, DC: U.S. Government Printing Office, 1983).

20. For an analysis of New York City's financial role in social welfare services, see Alan J. Abramson and Lester M. Salamon, *Government Spending and the Nonprofit Sector in New York City* (Washington, DC: Urban Institute Press, 1987).

21. For a discussion of local government financial roles for social welfare in the Chicago and Phoenix areas, see Kirsten Gronbjerg, James C. Musselwhite, Jr., and Lester M. Salamon, *Government Spending and the Nonprofit Sector in Cook County* (Washington, DC: Urban Institute Press, 1984); and John S. Hall, James C. Musselwhite, Jr., Lori E. Marczak, and David Altheide, *Government Spending and the Nonprofit Sector in Two Arizona Communities: Phoenix/Maricopa County and Pinal County* (Washington, DC: Urban Institute Press, 1985).

APPENDIX TABLE A.1
Large Cities, 1970

City	Population (in thousands)	Population as a Percentage of State Population
New York	7,896	43%
Chicago	3,369	30
Los Angeles	2,812	14
Philadelphia	1,949	17
Detroit	1,514	17
Houston	1,234	11
Baltimore	905	23
Cleveland	751	7
Indianapolis	737	14
Milwaukee	717	16
Boston	641	11
Memphis	624	16
St. Louis	622	13
New Orleans	593	16
Phoenix	584	33
Seattle	531	16
Denver	515	23
Jacksonville	504	7
Atlanta	495	11
Minneapolis	434	11
Unweighted Mean	1,371	17

SOURCE: U.S. Bureau of the Census, *Statistical Abstract of the United States: 1986* (Washington, DC: U.S. Government Printing Office, 1985).

APPENDIX TABLE A.2
Income and Wealth, Big Cities and Their States

City	Ratio of City to State per Capita Income, 1969	Ratio of City to State Assessed per Capita, 1967 Property Value
Houston	1.212	0.873
Seattle	1.207	1.224
Atlanta	1.195	1.404
New Orleans	1.161	1.469
Minneapolis	1.146	1.458
Denver	1.138	1.223
Memphis	1.134	1.582
Indianapolis	1.130	1.200
Phoenix	1.108	0.857
Los Angeles	1.093	1.092
Milwaukee	1.050	0.930
New York	1.025	1.443
Philadelphia	0.984	1.487
Chicago	0.973	0.938
Detroit	0.953	1.260
Jacksonville	0.933	0.467
St. Louis	0.923	1.447
Boston	0.908	0.915
Cleveland	0.881	0.763
Baltimore	0.819	0.763
Unweighted Mean	1.049	1.135

SOURCES: U.S. Bureau of the Census, *County and City Data Book: 1973* (Washington, DC: U.S. Government Printing Office, 1973); and *Taxable Property Values and Assessment Sales Price Ratios: 1967 Census of Governments* (Washington, DC: U.S. Government Printing Office, 1968).

APPENDIX TABLE A.3
Poverty and Infrastructure Needs Among Large Cities and Their States

City	Ratio of City to State Share of Population in Poverty, 1969	Ratio of City to State Share of Pre-1939 Housing, 1970	Ratio of City to State Rate of Population Growth, 1960–1970
Boston	1.888	1.266	*
Baltimore	1.847	1.835	*
Cleveland	1.753	1.550	*
Detroit	1.587	1.478	*
Seattle	1.515	1.352	*
Chicago	1.459	1.316	*
St. Louis	1.414	1.577	*
Philadelphia	1.411	1.182	*
New York	1.364	1.117	0.172
Los Angeles	1.215	1.359	.493
Milwaukee	1.181	1.044	*
Jacksonville	1.172	1.387	4.396
Denver	1.145	1.224	.163
Minneapolis	1.139	1.379	*
New Orleans	1.052	1.750	*
Indianapolis	1.021	0.771	4.974
Atlanta	0.976	1.059	.122
Memphis	0.958	0.735	2.530
Phoenix	0.773	0.806	.900
Houston	0.764	0.724	1.858
Unweighted Mean	1.277	1.246	1.734

SOURCE: U.S. Bureau of the Census, County and City Data Book: 1972 (Washington, DC: U.S. Government Printing Office, 1973).

*City population declined; therefore ratio is not shown.

APPENDIX TABLE A.4
Big-City Voting Compared with Statewide Voting, 1968

City	Ratio of City to State Democratic Share of Vote for President	City Share of Total State Vote for President
Atlanta	1.97	5%
Cleveland	1.57	7
Detroit	1.48	18
St. Louis	1.48	12
New Orleans	1.44	9
Baltimore	1.41	23
Chicago	1.38	31
Memphis	1.37	15
Philadelphia	1.30	18
Indianapolis	1.26	10
Milwaukee	1.25	15
Los Angeles	1.25	14
Denver	1.23	26
New York	1.22	38
Boston	1.20	10
Seattle	1.09	19
Minneapolis	1.09	12
Jacksonville	1.06	8
Houston	1.04	10
Phoenix	0.97	36
Unweighted Mean	1.30	17

SOURCES: Richard M. Scammon, *America Votes 8: A Handbook of Contemporary American Election Statistics, 1968* (Washington, DC: Congressional Quarterly, 1970); *The 1968 Elections* (Washington, DC: Research Division of the Republican National Committee, 1969); and unpublished information supplied by various county boards of elections.

APPENDIX TABLE A.5

Relative Size of Large-City Governments, 1967

City	Large-City Employees as a Percentage of State Government Employees	City Employees as a Percentage of All Local Government Employees
New York	199%	48%
Baltimore	91	33
Memphis	52	19
Boston	50	16
Chicago	43	14
Detroit	32	11
Philadelphia	31	13
Denver	29	12
St. Louis	29	11
Phoenix	25	10
Milwaukee	24	8
Seattle	22	9
Los Angeles	21	6
Cleveland	21	5
New Orleans	19	10
Atlanta	16	5
Minneapolis	13	5
Houston	10	3
Jacksonville	8	2
Indianapolis	8	3
Unweighted Mean	37	12

SOURCES: U.S. Bureau of the Census, *Employment of Major Local Governments: 1967 Census of Governments;* and *Compendium of Public Employment: 1967 Census of Governments* (Washington, DC: U.S. Government Printing Office, 1969).

NOTE: All figures are full-time equivalent employees. The large-city totals and all local government totals include elementary, secondary, and higher education employees when these school systems are legally dependent upon municipal governments for their operation. They generally do not include special authorities unless those authorities are also legally dependent upon the municipality for their operations.

APPENDIX TABLE A.6
State Financial Support of Large Cities, 1967

City	State-Administered Revenues as a Percentage of City Budget	Per Capita State Support of City Budget
Baltimore	41%	$169
Milwaukee	36	64
New York	35	208
Boston	33	159
Memphis	29	60
Denver	27	54
Phoenix	18	18
Indianapolis	16	11
Detroit	15	30
Seattle	14	21
New Orleans	14	20
Cleveland	13	18
Los Angeles	11	15
Chicago	10	14
Minneapolis	10	14
Philadelphia	8	16
St. Louis	7	12
Atlanta	5	6
Houston	0	0
Jacksonville	0	0
Unweighted Mean	17	45

SOURCE: U.S. Bureau of the Census, *Finances of Municipal and Township Governments: 1967 Census of Governments* (Washington, DC: U.S. Government Printing Office, 1969).

3

THE ECONOMY

ᘒᔋᘒ

Matthew P. Drennan

I N THE SECOND half of the 1970s, there was a popular view that New York State and New York City, along with other old industrial states and cities of the Northeast, were in a condition of permanent decline or at least economic stagnation. The pervasive judgment was that economic growth had shifted, perhaps forever, to the sunbelt. Economic growth can be defined in an operational, bloodless manner by economists, but the notion (and the reality) carries with it a bundle of related and subjective visions: vigor, youth, optimism, and the excitement of newness and change. Economic decline carries the opposite subjective visions. The subjective visions themselves, when widely shared, probably influence the reality. Sometime in that decade, Cities Service moved its headquarters from 27 Wall Street to Tulsa and then had its vacant office tower torn down for lack of a buyer. That vast gaping vacant lot on Wall Street was a powerful negative symbol.

That land is now occupied by a new skyscraper, and no doubt the appreciation in its value since Cities Service moved to Tulsa would have made it a far better investment than Cities Service stock. In the second half of the 1980s the popular perception is of a selectively tarnished sunbelt (Houston, Tulsa, and other energy and agriculture states and cities) and a selectively booming Northeast—Boston, New York, and Baltimore.

55

But those popular perceptions, both the former one of a permanently stagnant northeastern economy and the present one of a rebound, are flawed. They lack a theoretical structure, a paradigm of growth and decline. An urban economic analysis which classifies cities and states by their existing mix of industrial activities and then superimposes on that taxonomy the broad sweep of changes in technology and shifts in the composition of demand leads to a clearer understanding of why some places decline or grow, or why decline might shift to growth. Thomas Stanback and Thierry Noyelle have developed and refined such a taxonomy,[1] which makes comprehensible the stagnation of some sunbelt cities (New Orleans, Birmingham) while others boomed, and the boom in some snowbelt cities (Columbus, New York) while others languished.

This essay analyzes and compares the economies of New York State and New York City. The first part describes the secular decline and recovery of those economies. The second part analyzes the sources of decline and recovery by explaining the transformation of the export bases of the state and city. In the third part, the relative decline in the role of New York City in the state's economy is related to national forces affecting all large central cities. The fourth part focuses on patterns of economic growth among the diverse parts of the state economy outside New York City. The fifth part presents the economic outlook for the state and the city.

TRENDS IN THE STATE AND CITY ECONOMIES

Economists are often tempted to make the analogy that the economies of states and cities are like ships in the harbor of the national economy, rising and falling inexorably with the national economic tides. While national forces undoubtedly influence local economic fortunes, the connection is less obvious or inevitable than the analogy suggests. The problem with this nationally oriented view is well illustrated by the fortunes of New York State and New York City, especially in the period since 1969.

The year 1969 was the end of an incredibly strong national growth era. There were no recessions from 1962 until 1969, the longest unbroken period of economic expansion on record. In 1969, the national unemployment rate was 3.5 percent, and only slightly higher in New York State (4.3 percent) and New York City (4.6 percent). These rates seem unbelievably low in the present era when dips below 7 percent are considered a splendid economic performance.

From 1969 to 1976, population and employment fell in the state and the city, particularly in the city. In the nation, however, both population and employment expanded (see Table 3.1). Personal income increased in the state and the city, but at rates considerably below the national growth in personal income of 9.4 percent per year. A better measure of the average standard of living is real per capita personal income, which adjusts for the effects of both inflation and population changes. That measure reveals unambiguously the poor performance of the state's and city's economies relative to the United States. Compared with national growth of 2.0 percent annually from 1969 to 1976, real per capita personal income in the state expanded at a feeble 0.6 percent per year, while the city had no increase in those seven years.

That long period of sluggish or no growth in real per capita income resulted in a marked change in the affluence of the state and the city relative to the nation. In 1969 real per capita personal income in the state was 16 percent above the national average, and in the city it was almost 22 percent above the national level. By 1976 the state was only 5 percent, and the city only 6 percent, above the national average.

In 1976, the U.S. unemployment rate was 7.7 percent, or more than double its 1969 level of only 3.5 percent. But the deterioration in the state and the city was far worse: The state unemployment rate rose from 4.3 percent in 1969 to 10.3 percent in 1976, and the city unemployment rate rose from 4.6 to 11.2 percent. Thus, the unfavorable unemployment rate spread between the nation and the state rose from 0.8 percentage points in 1969 to 2.6 percentage points in 1976. And the city's unfavorable spread rose from 1.1 percentage points in 1969 to 3.5 percentage points in 1976.

After 1976, recovery began in the state's economy. Employment recovery in the city did not resume until 1978 because of layoffs of municipal government workers in 1977 tied to the fiscal crisis. State employment expanded 1.6 percent annually from 1976 to 1986, and employment growth in the city over that period was 1.0 percent annually. Although those rates were not as strong as the national employment growth, they represented a marked turnaround from the previous declines.

Personal income growth in the state and city from 1976 to 1986 was much stronger than in the prior period: 8.5 percent annually in the state and 8.2 percent annually in the city. This was almost as high as the national growth in personal income of 9.1 percent annually. But most important, real per capita personal income in the state and the city expanded at average annual rates above 2 percent for the ten years ended in 1986. That was above the U.S. annual growth rate of 1.7 percent. Consequently, some of the decline in relative affluence from 1969 to 1976 was recovered by 1986. In 1986, real per capita personal income in both the state and the city were 10 percent above the national level.

TABLE 3.1
Levels of Economic Activity, United States and New York State, New York City, and Rest of State, 1969, 1976, and 1986

	1969	1976	1986	Average Annual Percentage Change	
				1969–1976	1976—1986
United States					
Population (millions)	202.7	218.0	241.5	1.0%	1.0%
Personal Income (billions)	$772.9	$1,451.4	$3,487.0	9.4	9.2
Employment (millions)	70.38	79.38	100.17	1.7	2.4
Unemployment Rate	3.5%	7.7%	7.0%		
Real per Capita Personal Income (1982 dollars)	$9,287	$10,631	$12,610	2.0	1.7
New York State					
Population (millions)	18.11	17.98	17.81	-0.1%	-0.1%
Personal Income (billions)	$79.8	$125.7	$284.6	6.7	8.5
Employment (millions)	7.18	6.79	7.93	-0.8	1.6
Unemployment Rate	4.3%	10.3%	6.9%		
Real per Capita Personal Income (1982 dollars)	$10,731	$11,163	$13,894	0.6	2.2

TABLE 3.1 *(continued)*

	1969	1976	1986	Average Annual Percentage Change 1969–1976	Average Annual Percentage Change 1976–1986
New York City					
Population (millions)	7.86	7.42	7.24	−0.8%	−0.2%
Personal Income (billions)	$36.4	$52.5	$115.9	5.4	8.2
Employment (millions)	3.80	3.20	3.55	−2.4	1.0
Unemployment Rate	4.6%	11.2%	7.9%		
Real per Capita Personal Income (1982 dollars)	$11,291	$11,305	$13,919	0.0	2.1
Rest of State					
Population (millions)	10.25	10.56	10.57	0.4%	8.7%
Personal Income (billions)	$43.4	$73.2	$168.7	7.8	2.0
Employment (millions)	3.38	3.59	4.38	0.9	
Real per Capita Personal Income (1982 dollars)	$10,302	$11,063	$13,877	1.0	2.3

SOURCES: U.S. data from Council of Economic Advisors, *Economic Report of the President* (Washington, DC: U.S. Government Printing Office, January 1987); and New York population and income data from U.S. Bureau of Economic Analysis, *Survey of Current Business*, various issues.

NOTE: State and city data for 1986 are partly estimated based on data for first three quarters of 1986.

Because the city accounts for almost half of all jobs in the state, it is useful to analyze the state's economy in two separate parts: New York City and the balance of New York State. The balance of New York State did not suffer a long decline in its economy from 1969 to 1976. So the decline in state population and employment over that period can all be attributed to the depressed condition of the New York City economy.

From 1969 to 1976, personal income in the balance of the state expanded 7.8 percent annually, on average. That was well above the growth of personal income for New York City in that period of 5.4 percent. Indeed, the city growth was less than the rate of inflation (over 6 percent per year) from 1969 to 1976. The growth of employment in the balance of the state proceeded at 0.9 percent annually over that period. Although below the national employment growth rate of 1.7 percent annually, it was nonetheless closer to the national pattern than the massive employment losses experienced by New York City. In 1969, the city had 3.8 million jobs, or 400,000 more than the balance of the state. By 1976, the city had lost 600,000 jobs, falling to 3.2 million, while the balance of the state gained 200,000 jobs, rising to 3.6 million. Thus, by 1976 the situation had reversed and the balance of the state had 400,000 more jobs than New York City.

In the ten years from 1976 to 1986, labeled as the recovery period for the city, the balance of the state continued to perform better than New York City on broad economic measures. Personal income growth was 8.7 percent annually compared with 8.2 percent for the city. Employment growth in the balance of the state, at 2.0 percent per year, was double the rate of employment expansion (1.0 percent) of the city. Also, real per capita income for the balance of the state grew faster than in the city.

The result of those long trends of poorer performance by the New York City economy relative to the balance of the state has been to reduce the importance of the city's economy within the state (see Table 3.2). In

TABLE 3.2
Relative Importance of New York City in the State's Economy, 1969–1986

| Year | New York City as a Percentage of New York State | | | |
	Population	Employment	Personal Income	Per Capita Income
1969	43.4%	52.9%	45.7%	105.2%
1976	41.3	47.1	41.8	101.3
1986	40.7	44.8	40.7	100.2

SOURCES: See Table 3.1.

1969 over 43 percent of the New York State population was in New York City; by 1986 the city share of state population had fallen below 41 percent. The drop in the city's share of jobs and income was more severe. In 1969 the city had 52.9 percent of all jobs in the state; by 1986 the city share was down to 44.8 percent. In 1969 New York City's share of state personal income was 45.7 percent; by 1986 it was down to 40.7 percent. In terms of relative affluence, in 1969 the city's per capita income was 5 percent above the state average; by 1986, city per capita income was the same as the state's.

SIGNIFICANCE OF EXPORT ACTIVITIES

If national trends do not explain the changing economic performance of New York State and New York City, what does? The answer rests, at least in part, with what urban economists refer to as an area's "export base." States and cities, like nations, are engaged in a competitive struggle for markets beyond their borders. States and cities have industries which specialize in "export" sales as well as serving local markets. Obvious examples are aerospace and defense in California, tourism in Florida, and automobiles in Detroit. The long-term health of a state or city's economy is critically linked to the fortunes of its export industries. Changes in technology and tastes and changes in demand throughout the nation and the world can spur or depress the export industries of an area.

Because there are no direct measures of trade into and out of states and cities, it is not easy to identify export industries for those areas. However, a method of estimating export activity has been devised and can be applied to New York State and New York City.[2] This method reveals that of 52 detailed industries for which data are available, 19 are export industries of the state and 21 are export industries of the city.

The 19 export industries of New York State are grouped into three functional categories in Table 3.3—goods production and distribution, producer services, and consumer services. Goods production and distribution includes export industries in manufacturing, transportation, and wholesale trade. Producer services include export industries which provide services to business firms, government, and nonprofit organizations not only within the state but also throughout the nation and internationally. Of course, some also provide services to consumers (banking, for example), but they are not identified as export industries if their primary orientation is to serving local consumers and businesses. Banking and legal services, for example, are export industries not because of an unusually large number of neighborhood branch banks and law

TABLE 3.3

Employment in Export Industries of New York State,
1976 and 1986 (in thousands)

Industry	1976	1986	Average Annual Percentage Change
Goods Production and Distribution	1,059.1	1,017.9	−0.4%
Apparel	186.0	128.4	−3.6
Printing and Publishing	145.9	159.7	+0.9
Petroleum and Coal Products	8.1	5.4	−4.0
Leather Goods	30.1	16.8	−5.7
Instruments and Related Products	122.5	125.2	+0.2
Miscellaneous Manufacturing	67.4	46.2	−3.7
Water Transportation	67.4	51.1	−0.9
Wholesale Trade	431.7	485.1	+1.2
Producer Services	1,297.5	1,712.5	+2.8
Communication	128.7	120.4	−0.7
Banking	192.8	245.2	+2.4
Other Finance, Insurance, and Real Estate	382.5	462.4	+2.4
Business Services	285.1	484.7	+5.5
Amusement Services	58.7	75.6	+2.6
Legal Services	53.6	93.4	+5.7
Membership Organizations	118.2	115.0	−0.3
Miscellaneous Services	77.9	115.8	+4.0
Consumer Services	636.7	923.9	+3.8
Health Services	395.5	548.2	+3.3
Educational Services	143.3	198.5	+3.3
Social Services	97.9	177.2	+7.7
Total Export Industry Employment	2,993.3	3,654.3	+2.0
Total Private Employment	5,515.9	6,541.7	+1.7
Total Employment	6,789.5	7,924.7	+1.6

SOURCE: New York State Department of Labor, unpublished data.

offices in the state, but because the large banks and large law firms provide services to corporations, governments, and nonprofit organizations around the nation and the world.

Consumer services include two large export industries: private health and private education. New York has an unusually large number of prestigious academic health centers which train about 10 percent of the medical students in the nation. In addition, they draw hundreds of millions of dollars of health-related research support into the state and many thousands of out-of-state patients come to New York hospitals for specialized treatment.[3]

Employment in the goods production and distribution part of New York's export base suffered a precipitous decline in the 1969–1976 period of contraction, falling 2.8 percent annually. As noted above, total state employment fell less rapidly (0.8 percent annually) over that period. In the 1976–1986 recovery phase, the goods production and distribution part of the export base continued to decline, albeit at a slower rate (0.4 percent annually). Thus, the strong recovery of the state's economy since 1976 has not been driven by the goods production and distribution component of the export base.

In 1976, the low point for employment in New York State, the producer services component of the export base already was larger than the goods production and distribution component. In the expansion phase of the state's economy, producer services added 415,000 jobs, an average annual growth of 2.8 percent. Consumer services' employment expanded by about 287,000 jobs, or 3.8 percent annually. Thus, the recovery and expansion in the New York economy since 1976 has been driven by the producer services and consumer services components of the export base.

The strong expansion of producer and consumer services lead to their increased dominance of the export base in 1986. These industries account for 72 percent of export sector employment, while production and distribution of goods accounts for only 28 percent. That shift is an important reason New York was less hard hit than the nation by the severe 1981–1982 recession. Producer and consumer services are less cyclically sensitive than goods production and distribution.

Employment in the 21 export industries of New York City is shown in Table 3.4. The goods production and distribution component of the city's export base fared worse than it did in the state, dropping 1.6 percent annually since 1976. Again, producer services is the largest component and grew 2.6 percent annually since 1976. The consumer services export component in the city grew faster (3.1 percent annually), but not as fast as it did statewide. By 1986 producer services accounted for over half the export base of the city.

Considering the state's and city's export bases in a national context helps explain the precipitous decline and subsequent recovery in the local economy. In 1969 New York State was a major force in the national production of goods, accounting for 9 percent of all such jobs in the nation, while its share of total U.S. jobs was 10 percent. The production of goods in New York State was a large-scale activity with 2.1 million jobs. From 1969 to the present the national economy gained over 27 million jobs, but only 0.7 million in goods production. The national stagnation in goods production employment hit New York very hard. In the zero-sum national goods production employment picture since 1969,

TABLE 3.4

Employment in Export Industries of New York City,
1976 and 1986 (in thousands)

Industry	1976	1986	Average Annual Percentage Change
Production and Distribution of Goods	581.6	495.6	−1.6%
Apparel	153.2	107.1	−3.5
Printing and Publishing	90.0	90.2	+0.2
Leather Goods	15.4	7.3	−7.2
Miscellaneous Manufacturing	46.3	29.1	−4.5
Water Transportation	24.3	14.7	−4.9
Wholesale Trade	252.4	247.2	−0.2
Producer Services	840.2	1,084.4	+2.6
Air Transportation	49.6	48.1	−0.3
Transportation Services	23.6	25.6	+0.8
Communication	78.9	71.0	−1.0
Banking	134.4	170.9	+2.4
Security Brokers	69.8	133.2	+6.7
Insurance Carriers	79.2	68.4	−1.5
Insurance Agents	23.2	26.7	+1.4
Real Estate and Miscellaneous Financial	87.5	92.8	+0.6
Business Services	187.6	293.5	+4.6
Motion Pictures	19.6	27.0	+3.3
Legal Services	36.8	63.6	+5.6
Miscellaneous Services	50.0	63.6	+2.4
Consumer Services	358.9	485.5	+3.1
Health Services	184.6	231.3	+2.3
Educational Services	64.6	87.2	+3.0
Social Services	109.7	167.0	+4.3
Total Export Industry Employment	1,780.7	2,065.5	+1.5
Total Private Employment	2,687.4	2,978.5	+1.0
Total Employment	3,209.7	3,551.7	+1.0

SOURCE: New York State Department of Labor, unpublished data.

gains in the sunbelt, in the suburbs, or in former pastures where now two interstate highways cross came at the expense of older areas like New York.

Also important were the national recession in 1970 and the more severe 1973–1975 recession, coupled with soaring energy prices in an energy-importing state. Population loss diminished local demand, and the fiscal crisis directly lowered government employment and indirectly had depressing economic effects. But the mix of employment in the state in 1969 was well suited for the coming national boom in services and particularly in finance, insurance, and real estate (F.I.R.E.) jobs. Those sectors include New York's major export industries. From 1969 to 1986, national employment in services grew 4.3 percent annually and in F.I.R.E. 3.3 percent annually, well above the national growth in total jobs of 2.1 percent annually. That boom has driven the recovery of the state and the city.

In the Stanback-Noyelle taxonomy referred to earlier, areas which specialize in producer and consumer services are classified as "nodal." Places which specialize in goods production are classified as "manufacturing." In the transformation of the U.S. economy since 1969, metropolitan areas which have fared well tend to be nodal places while those which have suffered most tend to be manufacturing places. The northeastern and north central states had the major manufacturing centers in 1969 while the sunbelt had more nodal centers than manufacturing centers. Similarly, New York City and its environs have had a growing economy since 1977, as have Boston, Columbus, and Baltimore, because they are nodal places. But Buffalo, Cleveland, Detroit, St. Louis, and Birmingham, for example, have not experienced similar growth because their economies are heavily dependent on goods production.

ADDITIONAL FACTORS IN THE RELATIVE DECLINE OF NEW YORK CITY

The preceding sections documented trends in the city and state economies and related them to the transformation of their export bases. But two central questions which the trend data pose remain to be answered. Despite a rebound in New York City's economy and its strong export base; (1) why is New York City becoming a smaller part of its state's economy, and (2) why is New York City becoming poorer relative to the rest of the state?

As mentioned earlier, in 1969 the city had 43 percent of the state's population, almost 53 percent of its jobs, and 46 percent of its personal income. By 1976 all those shares were lower. And by 1986 they were even lower: 41 percent of the population, 45 percent of the jobs, and 41 percent of the personal income. In terms of relative affluence, the city also has declined and that trend is expected to continue. In 1969, per capita personal income in the city was 5.2 percent higher than the state average. By 1986, per capita personal income in the city was the same as the state.

The answers to these questions lie in the diminished importance of large central cities in the national economy as economic activity has become more dispersed, and in the increasing concentration of poor, minority populations in these large central cities. A corollary to the diminished economic importance of the large central city is that the political divisions "state" and "city" are no longer useful economic units of analysis, particularly "city." New York State is a heterogeneous grouping of metropolitan areas, where the bulk of its jobs are concentrated, and nonmetropolitan counties. The metropolitan areas are quite dissimilar in their economic makeup and trends. Thus, an improved dimension for analyzing the economy of New York State is in terms of its metropolitan areas, which we will present after considering the diminished importance of large, central cities.

The 1970 census was the last one in which large cities (here defined as cities with more than 500,000 residents) collectively showed a gain in population. There were 26 such cities in 1970, up from 21 in 1960, and their aggregate population was 31.8 million, a rise of 3.2 million over 1960. In 1970 those 26 cities accounted for about half the population of their metropolitan areas. By 1980 there were only 22 such cities with an aggregate population of 28.4 million, down 3.4 million from 1970, (see Table 3.5). And in 1984 there were 23 such cities, but their aggregate population was down 4.3 million to 24.1 million. Their share of their metropolitan areas' population had diminished to 38 percent by 1984, from 49 percent in 1970. Thus, suburbanites outnumbered city dwellers in the metropolitan areas containing the nation's largest cities.

That was true in all metropolitan areas collectively in 1980, not only the metropolitan areas with large cities. Although the vast majority of the U.S. population was metropolitan in 1980 (172 million out of 226 million, or 76 percent), most people (99.8 million) lived in suburbs, not central cities (see Table 3.6). The central cities of all metropolitan areas

TABLE 3.5

Population of Central Cities with 500,000 or More People and Their Metropolitan Areas, 1960–1984

Year	Number of Cities	Population (in millions)	Central Cities as a Percentage of Their Metropolitan Area Population
1960	21	28.6	*
1970	26	31.8	49.1%
1980	22	28.4	47.5
1984	23	24.1	37.9

SOURCE: U.S. Bureau of the Census, *Statistical Abstract of the United States: 1986* (Washington, DC: U.S. Government Printing Office, December 1985).
*Not available.

TABLE 3.6

U.S. Population by Race and Residence, 1980 (in thousands)

	Total	Nonblack[a]	Black	Spanish Origin[b]
United States	226,546	200,040	26,506	14,612
Metropolitan	172,297	150,569	21,727	12,871
Central Cities	72,546	56,731	15,815	7,755
Suburbs	99,751	93,839	5,912	5,116
Nonmetropolitan	54,249	49,470	4,779	1,741
22 Largest Central Cities				
Number	28,400	20,090	8,310	4,173
Percentage of				
U.S. Total	12.5%	10.0%	31.4%	28.6%

SOURCE: U.S. Bureau of the Census, *Statistical Abstract of the United States: 1986* (Washington, DC: U.S. Government Printing Office, December 1985).

[a]Primarily whites, including whites of Spanish origin, but also orientals and other racial groups.
[b]Includes both white and black Spanish origin.

had 72.5 million residents in 1980, or 32 percent of the national population. Among the nonblack population, the share living in central cities was even smaller, just 28 percent. Almost half (47 percent) the nation's nonblack population lived in suburban parts of metropolitan areas.

For blacks, the picture is strikingly different. About 60 percent of all blacks live in central cities compared with only 28 percent of all whites and other nonblacks. Similarly, more than half (53 percent) the population of Spanish origin lived in central cities. Thus, the racial and ethnic mix in central cities is more weighted with minorities than the nation as a whole. That is particularly true for the 22 largest central cities. Blacks are less than 12 percent of the U.S. population, but they constitute 22 percent of central city population and 29 percent of the population in the 22 largest cities.

Looked at another way, the 22 largest central cities had only 12 percent of the U.S. population in 1980, and an even smaller share of the white and other population (10 percent). But those same cities had 31 percent of the nation's black population and almost 29 percent of the Spanish-origin population.

Blacks were not always concentrated in central cities. In 1920, one half the black population lived on farms compared with one quarter of the white population. As recently as 1950, 21 percent of the black population lived on farms compared with 14 percent of the white population. By 1983, less than 1 percent of the nation's black population lived on farms while 3.4 percent of the white population still lived on farms.[4]

The black share of the large central city population is continuing to increase. For the same set of 20 large cities identified by James Musselwhite in another essay in this volume, Table 3.7 presents the black share and Spanish-origin share of the cities' population. From 1970 to 1980 all of the large cities showed an increase in the percentage of black population, except Los Angeles and Phoenix.

Having shown that large central cities are declining and are a shrinking part of their metropolitan areas (New York City is not unique in shrinking relative to New York State), it is now appropriate to consider why they are becoming relatively poorer (like New York). The level of income is linked to residential patterns within the metropolitan area. Families in metropolitan areas have higher median incomes than nonmetropolitan families (see Table 3.8), which accords with the popular

TABLE 3.7

*Black and Spanish-Origin Population
as a Percentage of Central City Population, 1970 and 1980*

City	Percentage Black		Percentage Spanish Origin, 1980
	1970	1980	
New York	21.1%	25.2%	19.9%
Los Angeles	17.9	17.0	27.5
Chicago	32.7	39.8	14.0
Houston	25.7	27.6	17.6
Philadelphia	33.6	37.8	3.8
Detroit	43.7	63.1	2.4
Phoenix	4.8	4.8	14.8
Baltimore	46.4	54.8	1.0
Indianapolis	18.0	21.8	0.9
Memphis	38.9	47.6	0.8
Milwaukee	14.7	23.1	4.1
Jacksonville	22.3	25.4	1.8
Boston	16.3	22.4	6.4
Columbus	18.5	22.1	0.8
New Orleans	45.0	55.3	3.4
Denver	9.1	12.0	18.8
Seattle	7.1	9.5	2.6
Kansas City	22.1	27.4	3.3
Oklahoma	13.7	14.6	2.8
Atlanta	51.3	66.6	1.4

SOURCES: U.S. Bureau of the Census, *1970 Census of Population, U.S. Summary,* Table 82; *1980 Census of Population, U.S. Summary,* Tables 87 and 135.

TABLE 3.8

Median Family Income by Race and Residence, 1983, and Poverty Rates, 1984 (in thousands of dollars)

	All Races	White	Black	Spanish Origin
United States	$24.6	$25.8	$14.5	$17.5
Metropolitan	26.4	27.9	15.3	17.1
Central Cities	22.3	24.7	13.9	15.6
Suburbs	29.2	29.9	18.9	20.3
Nonmetropolitan	21.0	21.8	12.0	15.7
Percentage of Families Below Poverty Level	11.6%	9.1%	30.9%	25.2%

SOURCE: U.S. Bureau of the Census, *Statistical Abstract of the United States: 1986* (Washington, DC: U.S. Government Printing Office, December 1985).

and long-held perception of greater affluence in urbanized areas. But within metropolitan areas there is a sharp divergence, with central city median family income $5,000 lower than suburban median family income. That huge difference prevails for the three major racial groups: white, black, and Spanish origin. Clearly, central city families are not nearly so affluent as suburban families. The poverty data show wide differences by race. There is a markedly lower poverty rate for white families than for black and Spanish-origin families.

Given that the median family income of blacks is lower than that for whites, the poverty rate among black families is three times greater than that for white families, and the black population's concentration in cities is great and growing, it is not surprising that *all* large cities, not just New York, are becoming poorer relative to their states. As shown in Table 3.9, every one of the 20 large cities identified by Musselwhite had a decline in median family income relative to their respective states from 1969 to 1979. In 1969, 11 of the 20 cities had median family incomes higher than their respective states. New York City, at 91.5 percent of the state's median family income in 1969, was not one of them. For the most part, the ones higher than their states in 1969 were newer sunbelt cities with much developable land within city limits. By 1979, all 20 were in a lower relative position than they had been in 1969, and only 8 were still higher than their respective states. The most marked drop was for Atlanta; from 102 percent of the state median family income in 1969 to 78 percent in 1979. New York City dropped from 92 percent of the New York State median family income to 83 percent.

The worsening relative income position of those large cities is mirrored in their changing poverty position. (See Table 3.10.) In 1969,

TABLE 3.9
Large-City Median Family Income as a Percentage of State Median Family Income, 1969 and 1979

City	1969	1979
New York	91.5%	83.2%
Los Angeles	98.1	90.7
Chicago	92.7	82.8
Houston	116.5	111.7
Philadelphia	97.9	82.0
Detroit	90.9	76.9
Phoenix	108.7	107.4
Baltimore	79.3	68.0
Indianapolis	108.0	101.0
Memphis	116.2	101.8
Milwaukee	102.0	94.7
Jacksonville	104.8	101.7
Boston	84.3	75.9
Columbus	94.2	89.0
New Orleans	98.7	82.9
Denver	101.0	91.5
Seattle	105.8	101.8
Kansas City	111.2	106.4
Oklahoma City	118.2	110.7
Atlanta	102.4	78.2

SOURCES: U.S. Bureau of the Census, *1970 Census of Population, Social and Economic Characteristics, U.S. Summary,* Table 41; *1980 Census of Population, Social and Economic Characteristics, U.S. Summary,* Table 43.

12 of those 20 cities had poverty rates higher than their states. New York City was among them, with 11.5 percent of its families below the poverty level compared with 8.5 percent of all New York State families. By 1979, 16 of the 20 cities had poverty rates higher than their respective states. Over those ten years the cities and states moved in opposite directions. Fully 16 of the 20 cities had increases in the incidence of poverty while 15 of the 20 states had decreases in the incidence of poverty. In New York City, for example, the poverty rate rose from 11.5 percent in 1969 to 17.2 percent in 1979. Over the same period, the New York State poverty rate fell from 8.5 to 7.6 percent.

If the suburbs are becoming larger and more affluent than their central cities, what accounts for their prosperity and growth? The specific suburban employment data are not available to identify export industries and their growth trends in the suburbs. However, it is widely recognized

TABLE 3.10
Poverty Level, Large Central Cities and Their States, 1969 and 1979

| City | Percentage of Families Below Poverty Level | | | |
| | 1969 | | 1979 | |
City	City	State	City	State
New York	11.5%	8.5%	17.2%	7.6%
Los Angeles	9.9	8.4	13.0	8.7
Chicago	10.6	7.7	16.8	8.4
Houston	10.7	14.6	10.0	11.1
Philadelphia	11.2	7.9	16.6	7.8
Detroit	11.3	7.3	18.9	8.3
Phoenix	8.8	11.5	8.1	9.5
Baltimore	14.0	7.7	18.9	7.5
Indianapolis	7.1	7.4	8.8	7.3
Memphis	15.7	18.2	17.1	13.1
Milwaukee	8.1	7.4	11.2	6.3
Jacksonville	14.1	12.7	12.9	9.9
Boston	11.7	6.2	16.7	7.6
Columbus	9.8	7.6	12.1	8.0
New Orleans	21.6	21.5	21.8	15.1
Denver	9.4	9.1	10.3	7.4
Seattle	6.0	7.6	6.6	7.2
Kansas City	8.9	11.5	9.4	9.1
Oklahoma City	10.6	15.0	9.3	10.3
Atlanta	15.9	16.7	23.7	13.2

SOURCE: U.S. Bureau of the Census, *Statistical Abstract of the United States, 1986* (Washington, DC: U.S. Government Printing Office, December 1985).

that economic activity has been expanding faster in the suburbs than in the large, built up central cities. Moreover, it is possible to identify one very important export activity for most suburban areas—namely, the export of highly skilled labor to the central city. The earnings of commuters produce a substantial inflow of income to suburban areas. For example, the net inflow of commuter earnings in the Nassau-Suffolk metropolitan area amounted to $9 billion in 1983, or one-third of the earnings of all residents of Nassau-Suffolk.[5] No export industry of Nassau-Suffolk, including defense, comes close to the importance of commuters' earnings for the local economy. In contrast, large cities such as New York suffer an outflow of income due to the substantial numbers of commuters from the suburbs. In 1983, earnings of all people who work in New York City were about $77 billion. Of that amount, about $20 billion, or 26 percent was a net outflow to individuals who work in the city but reside elsewhere.[6]

A CLOSER LOOK AT THE REST OF THE STATE

The division of New York State into New York City and the remainder of the state is a useful analytic tool for exploring the diminishing role of New York City, but it has limitations for exploring trends in the rest of the state. The "rest-of-the-state" is not an instructive unit of analysis because its parts are so heterogeneous. It includes booming Nassau-Suffolk, troubled Buffalo, and depopulated Adirondack counties, to name some of its disparate parts.

Table 3.11 presents total employment for the metropolitan areas of New York State, grouped into downstate and upstate sectors. The three contiguous downstate metropolitan areas are New York, Nassau-Suffolk, and Poughkeepsie. The New York (which includes New York City, Westchester, Rockland, and Putnam counties) and Nassau-Suffolk metropolitan areas are the largest two of the ten metropolitan areas in the state in terms of population and employment.

The three downstate metropolitan areas had almost 5.2 million jobs in 1985, or 67 percent of all jobs in New York State. The seven upstate metropolitan areas had 1.8 million jobs in 1985, or 23 percent of the statewide total. The remaining 10 percent of state employment was outside those ten metropolitan areas.

In the 1977–1985 period employment grew in the downstate areas almost three times faster than in the upstate areas: 1.7 percent annually compared with 0.6 percent annually. However, three of the seven upstate areas had employment growth higher than that of the New York metropolitan area (1.3 percent per year): Rochester (1.7 percent), Albany-Schenectady-Troy (2.2 percent), and Syracuse (2.0 percent). The other four upstate areas showed either employment declines or sluggish growth.

Buffalo, the fourth largest metropolitan area, is in the upstate group and showed the worst employment change—down 2.3 percent. It is interesting to note that if Buffalo were excluded from the upstate group, their employment growth would almost match downstate growth: 1.6 percent versus 1.7 percent annually. But to make the comparison more meaningful, New York City should be excluded from the downstate group because it, too, is shrinking either absolutely or relatively as a center of economic activity. Excluding New York City, the downstate

TABLE 3.11
Employment, Metropolitan Areas of New York State, 1977 and 1985
(in thousands)

	1977 Employment	1985 Employment	Average Annual Percentage Change 1977–1985
Downstate Metropolitan Areas	4,505.7	5,173.9	1.7%
New York[a]	3,590.9	3,987.2	1.3
New York City	3,187.3	3,486.1	1.1
Three Suburban Counties	403.6	501.1	2.7
Nassau-Suffolk	827.5	1,071.9	3.3
Poughkeepsie	87.3	114.8	3.5
Upstate Metropolitan Areas	1,720.5	1,806.5	0.61%
Buffalo	497.8	414.2	−2.3
Albany-Schenectady-Troy	321.7	382.1	2.2
Rochester	395.0	451.5	1.7
Syracuse	246.5	288.1	2.0
Binghamton	111.7	118.3	0.7
Utica-Rome	111.3	117.4	0.7
Elmira	36.5	34.9	−0.6
Nonmetropolitan Counties	631.4	774.3	2.6%
New York State	6,857.6	7,754.7	1.55%

SOURCES: U.S. Bureau of Labor Statistics, *Supplement to Employment and Earnings for States and Areas, 1977–81* (Washington, DC: U.S. Government Printing Office, 1983); and *Employment and Earnings*, May 1986.

[a]Includes New York City plus Westchester, Rockland, and Putnam counties.

area had employment growth of 3.1 percent annually versus 1.6 percent annually for the upstate area excluding Buffalo.

The downstate area is not only larger and experiencing more rapid employment growth, but it is also more affluent than the upstate area. In 1984 per capita personal income in the downstate area was $15,636, or 9 percent higher than the state average of $14,341. For the seven upstate metropolitan areas combined, per capita personal income was $12,727, or 11.3 percent below the state average and almost $3,000, or 18.6 percent, below the downstate metropolitan area average. None of the seven upstate metropolitan areas had a per capita income as high as any of the three downstate areas, or indeed not even as high as the state average. The nonmetropolitan counties are the least affluent, with an average per capita income of only $10,711, or 25 percent below the state average.[7]

What accounts for the slower growth and lesser affluence of the upstate metropolitan areas compared with the downstate areas? A good part of the answer emerges from applying the Stanback-Noyelle paradigm of nodal and goods producing places. Given the shift in national demand toward relatively more producer services and relatively less goods production and distribution, those places (like New York City) with an export base primarily in producer services are well situated to gain. Similarly, those places with an export base oriented to the production, transport, and marketing of goods are generally badly situated. The available employment data for the state's metropolitan areas is too aggregated to permit a full empirical test of this paradigm. Ideally, one would add employment in manufacturing and mining (excluding central office jobs), water, rail, and truck transportation, and wholesale trade and compute that "goods production and distribution" sector's share of total employment. Metropolitan areas with large shares of their jobs in that sector would be expected to have done less well over the past decade than areas with small shares. Lacking that data, a cruder analysis, based on the share of all jobs in manufacturing in the metropolitan areas, is presented in Table 3.12.

TABLE 3.12
Manufacturing Employment
in Metropolitan Areas of New York State, 1985

Metropolitan Area	Manufacturing Employment	
	Thousands of Jobs	Percentage of Total Jobs
New York	494	12.4%
Nassau-Suffolk	181	16.9
Poughkeepsie	35	30.2
Total Downstate	709	13.7
Buffalo	79	19.0
Albany-Schenectady-Troy	52	13.6
Rochester	148	32.8
Syracuse	58	20.1
Binghamton	40	33.8
Utica-Rome	26	22.1
Elmira	7	20.6
Total Upstate	410	22.7
Nonmetropolitan Counties	176	22.8
New York State	1,295	16.7

SOURCE: U.S. Bureau of Labor Statistics, *Employment and Earnings*, May 1986.
NOTE: Parts may not add to totals because of rounding.

Only 14 percent of the 5.2 million jobs in the downstate metropolitan areas are in manufacturing. In the seven upstate metropolitan areas the share is markedly larger, 23 percent. Thus, the structure of the downstate metropolitan economy is more favorable to gaining from the secular trends in the national economy. But there are exceptions, because upstate is not homogeneous. Rochester, with 33 percent of its jobs in manufacturing, showed strong growth from 1977 to 1985, as did Syracuse with 20 percent of its jobs in manufacturing. The mix of manufacturing in those places is oriented to high technology and defense industries (like San Jose, California, with 40 percent of its jobs in manufacturing), and so they have gained from national trends over the past decade. Albany-Schenectady-Troy stands out as the only upstate metropolitan area with a relatively small share of manufacturing jobs (14 percent). Stanback and Noyelle would classify it as a "government-education" place; it is neither nodal nor goods-producing in its orientation.

THE ECONOMIC OUTLOOK

Recently, the U.S. Bureau of Economic Analysis published national and individual state economic forecasts for the year 2000.[8] The national forecast points to a continuation of recent trends with projected growth in real personal income of 2.6 percent annually compared with 2.5 percent annually over the 1973–1983 period. Similarly, employment growth is projected to the year 2000 at 1.5 percent annually compared with 1.4 percent annually from 1973 to 1983. The break with past trends, however, is the projected acceleration in the growth of real earnings. Real earnings growth is projected to accelerate to 2.9 percent per year from 1983 to 2000, twice as fast as the recent historical rate. As noted above, employment growth is projected to rise at about the same rate as in the past ten years. Consequently, real earnings per employee (the main source for improvements in living standards) are projected to increase 1.4 percent per year. In the past decade, there was no growth in real earnings per employee—neither in the nation nor in the state.

Historically, real earnings per employee grow when demand for labor is strong relative to supply and when capital investment per worker accelerates, raising the value added per employee. These two factors are not independent. In a tight or tightening labor market, with moderate to low inflation, employers cannot easily pass on wage increases in higher prices. So to protect profit margins, they tend to invest in labor-saving capital equipment. The fears of modern-day Luddites aside, no period of sustained massive capital investment has ever lead to massive unemployment, but rather to rising real wages and employment. Of course, final demand must be adequate as a precondition leading to a tightening labor market.

If the growth in final demand, as measured by, say, the growth in personal income, is projected to be no stronger through the year 2000 than over the past decade, why should labor markets tighten? The answer is in the supply of labor. The national figures summarize a remarkable shift over the remainder of the century from the past 15 years.[9] From 1970 to 1985, national employment expanded by 28.5 million, or 1.9 million per year on average. But the prime working age population expanded more: 31.4 million, or 2.1 million per year. On average, job expansion was 200,000 less per year than the expansion in the working age population. Not surprisingly, in such a long-run labor supply-demand situation, real wages did not rise, capital spending per worker was sluggish, and the unemployment rate went from 3.5 percent in 1969 to 7.2 percent in 1985.

The employment and working age population situation will reverse in the remainder of the century. Projected employment growth is 22.9 million, or 1.5 million per year, much lower than the 1970–1985 expansion in employment. The working age population, however, will expand even less: 18.9 million, or 1.3 million per year. Thus, employment growth will exceed working age population growth by 200,000 per year on average. Hence a blessed phenomenon that has not been visited upon the United States since the late 1960s is around the corner: labor shortage.

The caveat in this analysis is the employment projection, but it is not a serious downside risk. In the past 25 years, employment growth averaged 2.0 percent per year. The projected gain of 22.9 million jobs by the year 2000 assumes average employment growth of only 1.3 percent per year.

The working age population projection is more firm than most economic forecasts because all of the people who will be in that age group from now until the year 2000 have already been born. The projection also takes immigration into account.

The broad economic outlook for New York State and New York City is presented in Table 3.13. Real earnings per employee and real per capita income are expected to grow 1.1 percent and 1.4 percent per year, respectively, in the state. Employment growth of 1.0 percent per year is double the expected rate of population growth in the state. The city is also expected to have healthy growth in real per capita income (1.3 percent per year), no population growth, and moderate employment growth of 0.4 percent per year. The projected growth rates are compared with the 1976–1986 experience as follows:

	New York State		New York City	
	1976–1986	1985–2000	1976–1986	1985–2000
Real Personal Income	2.1%	1.9%	1.9%	1.3%
Population	−0.1	0.5	−0.2	0.0
Real per Capita Personal Income	2.2	1.4	2.1	1.3
Employment	1.6	1.0	1.0	0.4

On every measure except population, the 1976–1986 actual experience is slightly better than the projected growth. However, it must be remembered that the state and city were rising out of a very deep hole in the 1976–1986 period. When adding to a relatively small base, growth rates are larger than when added to an expanded base.

Considering the city in relation to the state, the projected pattern is similar to the past. As noted earlier, in 1969 the city had 43 percent of the state's population, almost 53 percent of the jobs, and 46 percent of the personal income; by 1986 all those city shares were lower. And by the year 2000 they are expected to be still lower: 38 percent of the population, 41 percent of the jobs, and 38 percent of the personal income. In terms of relative affluence, the city has been edging lower and that trend is also expected to continue. In 1969 per capita personal income in the city was 5.2 percent higher than the state average; by 1986 per capita personal income in the city was the same as the state. And by 2000 it is expected to be somewhat lower than the state average.

None of this means that the city is "going to hell in a hand basket." It has been documented here that as a nation or region grows, its older, developed, densely settled cities grow less fast while its newer, less developed, less densely settled areas grow faster. California has been growing faster than Massachusetts for at least 150 years, long before anyone ever heard of the sunbelt. Slower employment growth in the city relative to the balance of the state occurs as economic functions get "passed down" from a major center to lesser centers, as the smaller places reach critical market sizes, and as cost pressures at the center push out less specialized functions that get outbid for space in the central business district. The much-heralded and bemoaned departures of corporate headquarters from Manhattan in the 1970s (they had been leaving since the 1950s) have not led to a long-term depressed office market. The space they vacated, plus millions of square feet of new space, has been occupied by firms from among the major export industries of the city, the producer services.

In many respects the decline in the relative size of New York City's population and economy is less important than the projected rise in real

TABLE 3.13

Economic Outlook, New York State and New York City, 1986, 1990, and 2000

	1986	Forecast 1990	Forecast 2000	Average Annual Percentage Change 1986–2000
New York State				
Real Personal Income (billions of 1982 dollars)	$247.5	$274.1	$320.4	1.9%
Population (millions)	17.81	18.26	18.97	0.5
Real Per Capita Personal Income (1982 dollars)	$13,894	$15,009	$16,890	1.4
Employment (thousands)	7,925	8,410	9,109	1.0
Real Earnings (billions of 1982 dollars)	$172.7	$194.6	$232.8	2.2
Real Earnings per Employee (1982 dollars)	$21,797	$23,135	$25,555	1.1
New York City				
Real Personal Income (billions of 1982 dollars)	$100.8	$107.5	$121.0	1.3
Population (millions)	7.24	7.18	7.26	—
Real Per Capita Personal Income (1982 dollars)	$13,919	$14,979	$16,670	1.3
Employment (thousands)	3,552	3,640	3,750	0.4

SOURCES: New York State forecast data from U.S. Bureau of Economic Analysis, *Survey of Current Business*, May 1985; New York City forecast data prepared by the author using GOTHAM, the Drennan Economic Data Base and Forecasts for New York City.

per capita income. This improves the welfare of all. In addition, unemployment in the city is projected to become lower than it is now. The prospects for these positive possibilities are much stronger now than they have been for 15 years.

NOTES

1. Thomas Stanback, Jr., and Thierry Noyelle, *The Economic Transformation of American Cities* (Montclair, NJ: Rowman & Allanheld, 1984).
2. The method for identifying export industries is based on the concept of location quotients. If the value of output produced by a given industry in the city represents a larger percentage share of total city output than that same industry's national output represents of total U.S. output, then that

industry would have a location quotient (ratio of the industry's percentage share of city output to its percentage share of national output) greater than one. If the location quotient is greater than one for all recent years, then the industry is classified as a export industry of the city. For a full explanation, see Matthew P. Drennan, *Modeling Metropolitan Economies for Forecasting and Policy Analysis* (New York: New York University Press, 1985), pp. 16–22.

3. In 1984, health research grants, out-of-state patients, and medical school students are estimated to have drawn in over $1 billion in income. See Eli Ginzberg and Matthew Drennan, *The Health Sector—Its Significance for the Economy of New York City* (New York: Commonwealth Fund, 1985).

4. U.S. Department of Agriculture, Economic Research Service, *Farm Population Estimates 1910–1970* (Washington, DC: U.S. Government Printing Office, 1973); and U.S. Bureau of the Census, *Current Population Reports*, Series P-27, no. 59, April 1985.

5. U.S. Bureau of Economic Analysis, "Local Area Personal Income, 1979–1984," *Survey of Current Business*, August 1986; and unpublished data provided by the Bureau of Economic Analysis.

6. U.S. Bureau of Economic Analysis, "Local Area Personal Income."

7. U.S. Bureau of Economic Analysis, "Local Area Personal Income."

8. U.S. Bureau of Economic Analysis, *Survey of Current Business*, May 1985.

9. Population projections and historical data from the U.S. Bureau of the Census, *Statistical Abstract of the United States: 1986* (Washington, DC: U.S. Government Printing Office, December 1985); and employment projections from the U.S. Bureau of Economic Analysis, *Survey of Current Business*, May 1985.

4

POPULATION

❦

Katherine Trent
and
Richard D. Alba

DEMOGRAPHIC examination of New York City in relation to its state illustrates the profound influences of a principal city on the population history and fortunes of a larger geographic area. New York City lies at the vortex of the most powerful population currents affecting New York State, and demographic changes in the City exert a potent influence on the rest of the state.

The forces altering the composition of the city and state population include foreign immigration, movement between the city and its suburbs, out-migration to the sunbelt, aging of the population, growing ethnic and racial diversity, and changing household and family structure. These forces have made New York City different from the rest of the state and are likely to widen the differences in the future. This essay examines the major forces affecting the populations of New York City and New York State. Two important questions guide the discourse: Have the demographic forces currently affecting the city and the state always been in play? Are these agents of change likely to remain influential in the future? The essay is organized into five sections, each covering an important aspect of population dynamics—migration, immigrant characteristics, racial and ethnic diversity, age structure, and family and household structure.

POPULATION GROWTH AND MIGRATION

During the 1970s, New York City's population fell 10 percent to just over 7 million people. (See Table 4.1.) The state's population also declined, but the city's loss explains the state's loss; other areas of the state added about 140,000 people. This 1970–1980 decline was not a continuation of a long-term, downward trend. Both the city and the state

TABLE 4.1
Population of New York City and New York State, 1790–2000

Year	Population[a] New York City	New York State	New York City as a Percentage of State
1790	33,100	340,100	9.7%
1800	60,500	589,100	10.3
1810	96,400	959,000	10.1
1820	123,700	1,372,800	9.0
1830	202,600	1,918,600	10.6
1840	312,700	2,428,900	12.9
1850	515,500	3,097,400	16.6
1860	813,700	3,880,700	21.0
1870	942,300	4,382,800	21.5
1880	1,206,300	5,082,900	23.7
1890	2,515,300	5,997,900	41.9
1900	3,437,200	7,268,900	47.3
1910	4,766,900	9,113,600	52.3
1920	5,620,000	10,385,200	54.1
1930	6,930,400	12,588,100	55.1
1940	7,455,000	13,479,100	55.3
1950	7,892,000	14,830,200	53.2
1960	7,782,000	16,782,300	46.4
1970	7,895,600	18,241,400	43.3
1980	7,071,600	17,558,100	40.3
1985[b]	7,254,200	17,782,800	40.8
1990[c]	7,180,400	18,023,100	39.8
2000[c]	7,260,700	18,548,300	39.1

SOURCES: Ira Rosenwaike, *Population History of New York City* (Syracuse: Syracuse University Press, 1972), tables 2 and 19; *1984–1985 New York State Statistical Yearbook* (Albany: Nelson A. Rockefeller Institute of Government, 1985), table A-3; *Statistical Abstract of the U.S.: 1904* (New York: Johnson Reprint, 1970), table 2; *Abstract of the 13th Census of the U.S.: 1910* (Washington, DC: U.S. Bureau of the Census, 1910), table 28; New York State Department of Commerce, State Data Center.

NOTE: Numbers rounded to nearest hundred.

[a]Population counts refer to geographic boundaries in effect for given census years.

[b]Population estimates.

[c]Population projections.

had grown steadily since the first national census of 1790 with the sole exception of a slight decline in New York City between the 1950 and 1960 censuses.

Since 1980, the city and the state have again experienced population growth. Between 1980 and 1985, the city's population grew an estimated 183,000, or 2.6 percent. This percentage gain is larger than the state's gain in the same period (1.3 percent), but well below the national rate of increase—5.4 percent.

The decline in the city's population during the 1970s implies a shift in the balance between the city and the rest of the state. In fact, this shift has an earlier origin. The city's population grew more slowly than the state's during the 1960s, 1950s, and even 1940s. Since 1910 and until 1950, residents of New York City accounted for at least half of all New York State residents; but by 1980, their share had slipped to 40 percent. So far, the recovery of the 1980s has not changed this proportion substantially.

The decline since the 1940s in New York City's relative position represents more a gain for its suburbs than a change in the balance between upstate and downstate regions. For example, Long Island's share of the state's population grew from 4.5 percent in 1940 to 11.7 percent in 1960, and to 14.8 percent in 1980; the suburban counties north of New York City—Putnam, Rockland, and Westchester—also gained relative to the total state population.[1]

The prospects are for continued slow growth in the city's and state's populations. The State's official projections anticipate New York City's population in the year 2000 to be 7,260,000 people, only 190,000 more, or 2.7 percent higher, than in 1980. The projected figure is still more than 600,000 below the city's 1970 population. The same projections indicate that the state's population will increase 5.6 percent between 1980 and 2000. By contrast, the U.S. Census Bureau projects a national population increase of 18 percent. Thus, the nation's population is expected to grow much faster than the state's or the city's.[2]

It should be noted that New York City's population is growing faster than the official projections anticipated. The city's growth in the 1980–1985 period accounted for 80 percent of the total state increase. Nonetheless, these figures indicate continued slow growth for both New York City and New York State relative to the nation as a whole.

Migration patterns are the principal explanation for the population losses experienced by New York City and New York State during the 1970s. The negative effect of migration dates back to earlier periods. Between 1940 and 1950, net migration loss occurred for the first time in New York City's modern history.[3] Although more persons left than entered the city, a substantial excess of births over deaths (that is, natural increase) resulted in population growth for the 1940–1950 period.

During the next decade, however, natural increase and in-migration were
not great enough to offset out-migration—thus, the slight population
decline in the 1950s. Although an exodus of persons from the city
continued in the 1960s, a large number of entrants and natural increase
during the period resulted in slight population growth between 1960 and
1970. But population growth did not occur in the following decade,
largely because of a substantial increase in net out-migration. This
out-migration slackened in the early 1980s, but the migration balance is
likely to remain precarious. Neither New York City nor New York State
is likely to gain significantly from migration in the foreseeable future.

Three currents predominate in the migration flows into and out of the
city—suburbanization, interregional movement, and foreign immigration. Suburbanization is directed to adjacent areas within and across state
boundaries and has been continuing for decades. During the first half of
the century, residents left Manhattan for less congested areas in the other
boroughs. This outward movement slowed during the Great Depression
and World War II. In the post World War II period, suburbanization
increased and was evident in each decade including the 1970s.[4] For
example, in the 1975–1980 period about 190,000 city residents moved
to Long Island (while just 55,000 moved in the opposite direction). But
a substantial number also crossed state boundaries to suburbs in New
Jersey and Connecticut, thereby creating a migration deficit for the state
as well as the city. New Jersey is one of the most popular destinations for
migrating New York State residents, and the great majority of New
Yorkers who relocate there are moving from one of the five boroughs.[5]

During the 1970s, interregional movement caused an enormous
population loss. Over 484,000 New York City residents and approximately 1.1 million New York State residents moved to the sunbelt
between 1975 and 1980; few moved in the opposite direction. This
migration consisted not only of retirees, but also of young adults, many
of them college educated, who appear to have left the stagnant New York
economy of the 1970s for job opportunities in Florida, California, and
Texas. The improvement of the city and state economies in the early
1980s appears to have brought some relief, and the period of massive
migration loss to the sunbelt may be ending (in part because the baby
boom generation is maturing out of the age range most prone to
migration). But even in a period of relatively robust economic growth,
the losses have not ceased. Internal Revenue Service data indicate that
New York State has had significant net losses through migration to the
sunbelt states, and especially Florida, in each of the years following
1980.[6]

Population shifts from New York City and New York State to
southern regions of the nation are a new phenomenon. Historically,

regional migration patterns did not favor the South at the expense of the North. The recent population growth in the South contrasts sharply with net migration losses the South experienced in every decade between 1900 and 1960.[7] This regional turnaround is fed by many factors, including a growing retirement population, lifestyle changes, changing racial attitudes, a more progressive political climate in the South and, perhaps most important, broad economic shifts affecting regional employment opportunities.[8]

The changing pattern of black migration also has influenced the regional population redistribution. The migration northward of blacks from the South dates from before the beginning of the twentieth century. During the "Great Migration" of 1916–1918, over 500,000 blacks left the South. This movement was related to the outbreak of war, which depressed immigration from abroad and increased the demand for labor in northern industrial centers. The recruitment of blacks to northern industrial cities slowed during the Great Depression and then resumed heavily during the 1940s, 1950s, and 1960s.[9] An important counter-stream of blacks moving or returning south in recent decades, however, has coincided with the overall south-to-north migration turnaround. Between 1965 and 1970, there were half as many blacks moving to the South as to the North.[10] In the 1975–1980 period, 112,000 blacks left New York State for southern destinations, while only 33,000 migrated in the opposite direction.[11] Thus, black migration has contributed to and followed the overall turnaround in interregional migration.

The stream of blacks moving south has not been great enough to reverse the steady growth of the black population in New York City and New York State. (See Table 4.2.) Between 1900 and 1940, the black population in New York City grew from about 61,000 to over 458,000. Between 1940 and 1980, the black population in the city grew 1.3 million, reaching nearly 1.8 million. By 1980, blacks in New York City accounted for 25 percent of the total city population, and nearly 75 percent of the state's total black population.

The flow of Puerto Ricans into New York City and New York State is another important source of population growth. (See Table 4.3.) Puerto Rican movement to the United States dates from the end of the Spanish-American War when the island was ceded to the United States by Spain and is similar to black migration in that the flow of Puerto Ricans grew larger with the onset of World War I and the restrictive immigration laws of the 1920s.[12] In 1920 there were 7,000 Puerto Ricans living in the city. By 1930 this number had grown to 45,000 and by 1940 to 61,000. Between 1950 and 1980, persons of Puerto Rican birth or parentage grew from 246,000 to 861,000. In the 1975–1980 period alone, over 53,000 persons migrated from Puerto Rico to New York State; 86

TABLE 4.2

Black Population of New York City and New York State, 1900–1980

	New York City[a]		New York State[b]		New York City Blacks as a Percentage of State Blacks
Year	Number	Percentage[c]	Number	Percentage[c]	
1900	60,700	1.8%	99,000	1.4%	61.3%
1910	91,700	1.9	134,000	1.5	68.4
1920	152,500	2.7	198,000	1.9	77.0
1930	327,700	4.7	413,000	3.3	79.3
1940	458,400	6.1	571,000	4.2	80.3
1950	747,600	9.5	918,000	6.2	81.4
1960	1,087,900	14.0	1,418,000	8.4	76.7
1970	1,668,100	21.1	2,169,000	11.9	76.9
1980	1,784,300	25.2	2,402,000	13.7	74.3

SOURCES: Ira Rosenwaike, *Population History of New York City* (Syracuse: Syracuse University Press, 1972), table 69; U.S. Bureau of the Census, *1980 Census of Population, General Population Characteristics, New York*, table 15; *Historical Statistics of the U.S.: Colonial Times to 1970* (Washington, DC: U.S. Government Printing Office, 1975), tables A195–209.

[a]Numbers rounded to nearest hundred.

[b]Numbers rounded to nearest thousand.

[c]Percentage of total population in given census year.

percent of these migrants moved to New York City. In 1980, Puerto Ricans living in the city accounted for 87 percent of all Puerto Ricans residing in the state.

The third major current is immigration from abroad. While changes in U.S. immigration policy during the twentieth century affected the volume and composition of these flows, New York City has a long-standing and continuing role as a mecca for new immigrants to the United States.

The immigrant population in New York City was 1.3 million in 1900 and grew steadily to 2.3 million in 1930. (See Table 4.4.) The foreign-born population declined during the 1930s, 1940s, and 1950s because of the Great Depression, World War II, restrictive immigration laws, and the migration to the suburbs of earlier-arriving groups. In 1965, immigration law reforms ushered in a new era of immigration. Between 1960 and 1980, the city's immigrant population again grew; over 1.6 million immigrants were living in New York City in 1980.

During the 1970s, New York State received annually about 90,000 immigrants, approximately one in every six immigrants to the United States. New York State is the second most frequent destination for immigrants, after California. But immigration into the state usually means immigration into the city, the latter taking in about three quarters of the foreign immigrants entering New York State.[13]

TABLE 4.3
Puerto Rican Population of New York City and New York State,
1900–1980

Year	New York City Number	New York City Percentage[a]	New York State Number	New York State Percentage[a]	New York City Puerto Ricans as a Percentage of State Puerto Ricans
1900	300[b]	0.0%	NA	NA	NA
1910	554[b]	0.0	641[b]	0.0%	86.4%
1920	7,364[b]	0.1	7,719[b]	0.1	95.4
1930	44,908[b]	0.6	45,973[b]	0.4	97.7
1940	61,463[b]	0.8	63,281[b]	0.5	97.1
1950	246,306	3.1	301,375	2.0	81.7
1960	612,574	7.9	642,622	3.8	95.3
1970	811,843	10.3	916,608	5.0	88.6
1980	860,552	12.2	986,389	5.6	87.2

SOURCES: Ira Rosenwaike, *Population History of New York City* (Syracuse: Syracuse University Press, 1972), tables 43, 57, and 68; and unpublished information provided by the U.S. Census Bureau.
NOTE: NA = Not available.
[a]Percentage of total population in given census year.
[b]Born in Puerto Rico only.

New York City's foreign-born population is fed not only by formal immigration. Temporary movements across international borders, such as those by tourists, businessmen, and students, and illegal immigration also play significant roles. And not all of the traffic is incoming: Emigration, frequently by the foreign born but also by the U.S.-born, is an important influence, but one for which a precise numerical estimate is lacking. Indeed, it is nearly impossible to make precise statements about the contributions of these various forces to the city's population because of limits inherent in available records. But undoubtedly immigration is numerically the most important contributor. For example, the alien registrations in New York State for January 1980 indicate that of the 801,000 aliens counted, some 690,000 (86 percent) were immigrants, that is, permanent resident aliens.[14]

Estimates of the number of illegal aliens are subject to all sorts of challenges, but there is little question that illegal aliens represent another important segment of New York City's population. One attempt to estimate their number compared the 1980 census with an estimate developed from Immigration and Naturalization Service records.[15] This comparison indicated that the 1980 census counted at least 234,000 undocumented aliens in New York State; given the distribution of immigrants in New York, more than four fifths of these illegals would

TABLE 4.4

Foreign-Born Population of New York City and New York State, 1900–1980

Year	New York City Number	New York City Percentage[a]	New York State Number	New York State Percentage[a]	New York City as a Percentage of State
1900	1,270,100	37.0%	1,900,400	26.1%	66.8%
1910	1,944,400	40.8	2,748,000	30.2	70.8
1920	2,028,200	36.1	2,825,400	27.2	71.8
1930	2,295,200[b]	33.1	3,193,900[b]	25.4	71.9[b]
1940	2,080,000[b]	27.9	2,853,500[b]	21.2	72.9[b]
1950	1,860,900	23.6	2,577,100	17.4	72.2
1960	1,558,700	20.0	2,289,300	13.6	68.1
1970	1,437,100	18.2	2,109,800	11.6	68.1
1980	1,670,200	23.6	2,388,900	13.6	69.9

SOURCES: Ira Rosenwaike, *Population History of New York City* (Syracuse: Syracuse University Press 1972), table 69; Ellen P. Kraly, "U.S. Immigration Policy and the Immigrant Populations of New York," in Nancy Foner, ed., *New Immigrants in New York* (forthcoming), table 2; U.S. Bureau of the Census 1900 Census of Population, table 2; 1910 Census of Population, table 1; 1920 Census of Population table 7; 1940 Census of Population, table B; 1950 Census of Population, *New York*, table 14; 197(Census of Population, *General Social and Economic Characteristics, New York*, table 45; and 198(Census of Population, *General Social and Economic Characteristics, New York*, tables 61 and 116.

NOTE: Numbers rounded to nearest hundred.

[a]Percentage of total population in given census year.

[b]Foreign-born whites only.

have been residing in New York City. How many went uncounted by the census is unknown.

Clearly, immigration plays a major role in shaping the city and state population. Immigration adds to population growth and the continued flow of immigrants changes the composition of the city and state populations in significant ways.

CHARACTERISTICS OF FOREIGN IMMIGRATION

The impact of foreign immigration extends beyond its important role in population growth. Federal reforms to immigration law in 1965 ended the discriminatory system of admissions based on national origin quotas and began a system of preferences based on family relationships and occupation. Moreover, these reforms ended the exclusion of Asian immigrants. The result has been an upsurge in the number of immigrants and a shift in their origins away from the countries of Europe, which dominated the mass immigration before 1930, to those of Asia, Latin America, and the Caribbean.

In recent years, between 15 and 25 percent of immigrants admitted to the United States have identified New York State as their intended place of residence. Immigrants coming to the state do not settle evenly throughout it; as noted above, the great majority settle in New York City. As a result, the city and state contain substantial proportions of the nation's recent immigrants. In 1980 nearly 1.2 million state residents were foreign born and had come to the United States since 1965; the state held 16 percent of all such persons in the nation. New York City alone held nearly 940,000 of the post-1964 arrivals, more than one eighth of the nation's total.[16]

These immigrants differ in important ways from U.S.-born residents of New York City and New York State. Young adults constitute a majority of the immigrants. Of all post-1964 immigrants residing in New York City in 1980, 56 percent were between ages 20 and 44; in contrast only 34 percent of the rest of the city's population was in this age category. Thus, immigration contributes to an age stratum that has felt the heaviest impact of migration loss in recent years. Accordingly, recent immigrants constitute a substantial proportion of young adults in the city; in 1980, they represented one in every five city residents between ages 20 and 44.[17]

Preferences in immigration law have encouraged the entry of women and family groups. Consequently, recent immigrants are more likely than other city residents to live in family settings as opposed to single-person or other nonfamily households. In addition, immigration is contributing to the city's population of children. Immigrants are concentrated in the childbearing ages, and the impact is substantial. In 1980, nearly one child in every four city children under age 10 lived in an immigrant household; for New York State as a whole, this proportion was one in eight. For both New York City and New York State, the great majority of recent immigrants' children—about 80 percent—have been born in the United States.[18]

One of the great strengths of New York City's recent immigration is its ethnic diversity. This diversity is revealed in the 1980 census portrait of immigrants arriving since 1965. (See Table 4.5.) Fully 30 percent have come from the Caribbean; this group is composed mainly of Dominicans (9.1 percent), Jamaicans (7.5 percent), Haitians (4.1 percent), Trinidadians (3.1 percent), and Cubans (2.3 percent). About 12 percent were born in South America, with Colombians (3.3 percent), Ecuadorians (3.0 percent), and Guyanese (2.6 percent) the largest groups. About 20 percent are from Asia; significant in numbers among Asian immigrants are the natives of China and Hong Kong (5.3 percent), India (2.7

TABLE 4.5
Foreign-Born Population by Place of Birth and Year of Immigration, 1980

| | Total Foreign-Born Persons | | | | | Year of Immigration to New York State | | | |
| | New York City | | New York City as a Percentage of State | New York State | | 1965 to 1980 | | Before 1965 | |
	Number	Percentage Distribution		Number	Percentage Distribution	Number	Percentage	Number	Percentage
Total	1,670,199	100.0%	69.9%	2,388,938	100.0%	1,181,183	100.0%	1,207,755	100.0%
Europe	666,447	39.9	59.8	1,115,249	46.7	271,693	23.0	843,556	69.8
Austria	26,263	1.6	67.7	38,779	1.6	1,697	0.1	37,082	3.1
Germany	60,749	3.6	45.0	134,991	5.7	12,273	1.0	122,718	10.2
Greece	42,080	2.5	76.9	54,738	2.3	31,521	2.7	23,217	1.9
Hungary	21,457	1.3	67.6	31,732	1.3	4,374	0.4	27,358	2.3
Ireland	41,354	2.5	62.1	66,639	2.8	6,819	0.6	59,820	5.0
Italy	156,413	9.4	55.1	283,990	11.9	68,738	5.8	215,252	17.8
Poland	78,135	4.7	69.0	113,262	4.7	15,417	1.3	97,845	8.1
United Kingdom	33,542	2.0	40.1	83,736	3.5	25,127	2.1	58,609	4.9
USSR	88,415	5.3	78.4	112,725	4.7	38,620	3.3	74,105	6.1
Yugoslavia	21,419	1.3	73.3	29,225	1.2	16,072	1.4	13,153	1.1
Other Europe	96,620	5.8	58.4	165,432	6.9	51,035	4.3	114,397	9.5
Asia	214,663	12.9	73.9	290,456	12.2	231,519	19.6	58,937	4.9
China	60,824	3.6	88.4	68,839	2.9	46,498	3.9	22,341	1.8
India	21,880	1.3	65.4	33,434	1.4	31,375	2.7	2,059	0.2
Korea	18,358	1.1	67.7	27,104	1.1	25,392	2.1	1,712	0.1
Philippines	20,212	1.2	73.5	27,493	1.2	24,381	2.1	3,112	0.3
Other Asia	93,389	5.6	69.9	133,586	5.6	103,873	8.8	29,713	2.5

TABLE 4.5 (continued)

| | Total Foreign-Born Persons | | | | | Year of Immigration to New York State | | | |
| | New York City | | New York City as a Percentage of State | New York State | | 1965 to 1980 | | Before 1965 | |
	Number	Percentage Distribution		Number	Percentage Distribution	Number	Percentage	Number	Percentage
North and Central America	80,570	4.8	53.2	151,474	6.3	72,076	6.1	79,398	6.6
Canada	15,874	1.0	21.7	73,142	3.1	16,249	1.4	56,893	4.7
Other North and Central America	64,696	3.9	82.6	78,332	3.3	55,827	4.7	22,505	1.9
West Indies	414,032	24.8	89.3	463,759	19.4	356,791	30.2	106,968	8.9
Cuba	46,880	2.8	82.4	56,895	2.4	26,713	2.3	30,182	2.5
Dominican Republic	124,088	7.4	94.5	131,313	5.5	108,050	9.1	23,263	1.9
Jamaica	90,756	5.4	84.7	107,130	4.5	88,004	7.5	19,126	1.6
Other West Indies	152,308	9.1	90.4	168,421	7.1	134,024	11.3	34,397	2.8
South America	153,714	9.2	84.1	182,818	7.7	146,711	12.4	36,107	3.0
Africa	23,578	1.4	72.3	32,621	1.4	23,651	2.0	8,970	0.7
North Africa	10,918	0.7	74.0	14,757	0.6	9,127	0.8	5,630	0.5
Other	12,660	0.8	70.9	17,864	0.7	14,524	1.2	3,340	0.3
All Other Countries	2,190	0.1	52.1	4,200	0.2	2,619	0.2	1,581	0.1
Country Not Reported	115,005	6.9	77.5	148,361	6.2	76,123	6.4	72,238	6.0

SOURCES: U.S. Bureau of the Census, 1980 Census, Population, *General Social and Economic Characteristics, New York*, table 116; *Detailed Population Characteristics, New York*, table 195.

percent), Korea (2.1 percent), and the Philippines (2.1 percent). European countries have also made their presence felt; 23 percent of the post-1964 arrivals are from European countries, with the largest groups coming from Italy (5.8 percent), the USSR (3.3 percent), and Greece (2.7 percent). Of the major sources of immigration into the United States, only Mexican and Vietnamese immigrants are not represented in large numbers in New York. The origins of recent immigrants contrast sharply with those of immigrants who arrived prior to 1965; fully 70 percent of these earlier immigrants were of European origin.

The diversity of recent inflows is one sign that immigration is likely to exert a powerful influence on the city and state populations for the foreseeable future. Although one can only guess at future levels of immigration to the nation and at the numbers of immigrants who will settle in New York, the importance of New York City is bolstered by the number of its burgeoning ethnic communities, since these are natural destinations for newly arriving immigrants. It is also enhanced by the nature of U.S. immigration policy; currently, the great majority of foreign nationals granted immigrant status are relatives of U.S. citizens or of permanent resident aliens. These two factors make it likely that, in the near future at least, new immigrants will follow the pathways established by recent immigrants. And these lead to New York City.

RACIAL AND ETHNIC DIVERSITY

Both interregional and foreign migration have helped make New York State one of the most ethnically and racially diverse states in the nation. The locus of this diversity is New York City. (See Table 4.6.) In 1980, New York City contained 85 percent of the state's Hispanic population (87 percent of the state's Puerto Ricans) and 74 percent of its non-Hispanic blacks and Asians.[19] The city was home to just 28 percent of non-Hispanic white New Yorkers. In other words, three out of every four minority New Yorkers resided in New York City.

Minorities are likely to make up a majority of New York City's population in the future, although they constitute a small percentage of the rest of the state's population. The 1980 census showed New York City to be 48 percent Hispanic and nonwhite; minorities made up only 9 percent of the population elsewhere in the state. The city's minority population is likely to grow even larger because of further in-migration of minority groups, generally higher fertility among minorities, and an age structure favoring minority population growth.

Hispanics and nonwhites are substantially younger on average than whites. In New York City 64 percent of children (ages 0 to 19) were

TABLE 4.6
Racial and Ethnic Groups in New York City and New York State, 1980

Racial/Ethnic Groups	New York City		New York State		New York City as a Percentage of State
	Number	Percentage Distribution	Number	Percentage Distribution	
Non-Hispanic Whites	3,703,203	52.4%	13,211,516	75.2%	28.0%
Non-Hispanic Blacks	1,694,505	24.0	2,298,672	13.1	73.7
Hispanics	1,406,389	19.9	1,660,901	9.5	84.7
(Puerto Ricans)	(860,552)	(12.2)	(986,389)	(5.6)	(87.2)
Asians	239,338	3.4	322,751	1.8	74.2
American Indians	9,907	0.1	39,434	0.2	25.1
Other	18,297	0.3	24,798	0.1	73.8
Total	7,071,639	100.0%	17,558,072	100.0%	40.3%

SOURCES: Richard D. Alba and Katherine Trent, *The People of New York: Population Dynamics of a Changing State* (Albany: Nelson A. Rockefeller Institute of Government, State University of New York, 1986), tables 4.1 and 4.4; and U.S. Bureau of the Census, 1980 Census of Population, *General Population Characteristics, New York,* tables 23 and 31.

Hispanic or nonwhite in 1980; in contrast, majority whites (non-Hispanic whites) were disproportionately represented among New York City's elderly, constituting 82 percent of those aged 75 and over and 75 percent of those aged 65–74.

The substantial age differences between minority and majority New York City residents imply a shifting racial and ethnic composition through natural increase alone. Majority whites are concentrated in the older age groups where mortality rates are higher; on the other hand, fertility disproportionately increases minority groups who have higher fertility rates than majority whites and who are more concentrated in the young adult ages of highest fertility. These factors, in combination with the continued immigration of Hispanics and nonwhites, strongly suggest higher growth rates among minority populations in the city.

The racial and ethnic contrast between New York City and the rest of the state reflects profound cleavages which separate Hispanics and nonwhites from the majority white population. (See Table 4.7.) Education is one example of these disparities. Among adult New York City residents 35 percent of non-Hispanic whites had completed at least one year of college, and 22 percent had completed four or more years of college. In contrast, among adult blacks only 24 percent had completed one year of college and only 9 percent had completed four years. Just 16 percent of Hispanics had completed one year of college, and only 6 percent had completed four years. Puerto Ricans in the city fared the worst—only 12 percent had completed one year of college and under 4 percent had completed four years.

TABLE 4.7

*Selected Social and Economic Characteristics of Racial
and Ethnic Groups, New York City and New York State, 1980*

	New York City	Balance of State	New York State
Adults with Four Years of College[a]			
Non-Hispanic Whites	22.1%	18.4%	19.6%
Non-Hispanic Blacks	8.9	9.3	9.0
Hispanics	5.8	10.8	6.5
Puerto Ricans	3.9	6.3	4.2
Asians	34.6	53.1	38.8
Adult Males Employed[b]			
Non-Hispanic Whites	77.2%	77.6%	77.5%
Non-Hispanic Blacks	60.0	56.9	59.2
Hispanics	66.7	71.8	67.6
Puerto Ricans	62.0	65.7	62.5
Asians	78.8	79.2	78.9
Persons Below Poverty Level			
Non-Hispanic Whites	10.1%	7.7%	8.4%
Non-Hispanic Blacks	29.1	24.5	27.9
Hispanics	34.9	20.0	32.6
Puerto Ricans	41.9	26.6	40.0
Asians	15.5	7.2	13.6
Children Below Poverty Level			
Non-Hispanic Whites	14.3%	9.3%	10.3%
Non-Hispanic Blacks	39.6	31.4	37.3
Hispanics	47.8	29.0	44.7
Puerto Ricans	54.2	35.4	51.6
Asians	16.8	7.5	14.3

SOURCE: U.S. Bureau of the Census, 1980 Census of Population, 1 percent B sample of the Public Use Microdata Samples.

[a]Persons aged 25 and over.

[b]Persons aged 16–64.

Such educational disparities translate into labor-market inequalities. In 1980, among men between ages 16 and 64, 77 percent of non-Hispanic whites in the city and the rest of the state were employed. However, 60 percent of black men in the same age range living in the city were employed, and only 57 percent of blacks in the remainder of the state were employed. Among Hispanics 67 percent of adult males were employed in the city, but nearly 72 percent were employed in the rest of the state.

Moreover, employed majority and minority group members do not typically work at the same kinds of jobs. Majority whites are more likely to have jobs with high prestige and pay. In 1979, the year for which income data were collected in the 1980 census, the average annual earnings of employed majority white men living in New York City were $17,014. Black men averaged $11,242 and Hispanic men $10,317. While minorities fared better outside the city, the substantial differences between groups remained.

Given these striking labor market difficulties, there are substantial inequalities in the income available to support households and families. In 1979, the average New York City household headed by a non-Hispanic white received $20,294; the average household headed by a black received $13,513, and the average household headed by a Hispanic received $12,342.

The substantial social and economic disparities among racial and ethnic groups are also reflected in poverty rates. Poverty among non-Hispanic blacks and Hispanics is dramatically higher than among whites. Nearly 30 percent of blacks living in New York City, and 25 percent living in the rest of the state were poor in 1980. Poverty among Hispanics was even more pervasive—35 percent of Hispanics in New York City, and 20 percent elsewhere in the State were poor.

Because, as shown earlier, an increasing proportion of children in New York State are minorities, the extent and distribution of poverty among these groups is of special concern. Indeed, the chances that children are being raised in poverty vary in dramatic ways by ethnicity and race; and New York City children are at a much greater risk of being poor than children in the rest of the state. In 1980, nearly one third of New York City's children were living in households with incomes below the poverty line compared with 12 percent of children in the remainder of the state. Only 14 percent of white children in New York City were living in poverty, but nearly 40 percent of black children, 48 percent of Hispanic children, and 54 percent of Puerto Rican children in New York City were poor. Put starkly, two in every five black children and one in every two Hispanic children in New York City were living in poverty.

POPULATION AGING

One of the most important demographic trends in New York State and New York City, as well as the nation, is the aging of the population. This trend is in part a function of increased longevity, which adds to the supply of older persons, and decreased fertility, which reduces the supply of younger ones. The aging of the massive baby boom generation (those born between the late 1940s and the mid-1960s) also plays an important role.

The aging of the baby boom generation has been likened to a snake digesting a large animal, an image intended to convey the baby boom's bulge in the age distribution and its changes over time. Between 1950 and 1970, children in New York City increased from 27 to 31 percent of the total population; children grew from 29 percent of the New York State population in 1950 to 36 percent in 1970. (See Table 4.8.) In the 1970s, the baby boom generation began reaching adulthood. Between 1970 and 1980, persons between ages 20 and 34 grew from 22 to 26 percent of the city's population; similar changes occurred for New York State as a whole.

In New York State and New York City, the aging of the population has been augmented by the out-migration of young adults and families during the 1970s. This helped make the state's population the fifth oldest

TABLE 4.8

Population of New York City and Balance of New York State by Age,
1940–2000

Age Group	New York City		Balance of State	
	Number	Percentage Distribution	Number	Percentage Distribution
1940				
0–19	2,072,500	27.8%	1,829,100	30.4%
20–34	2,037,300	27.3	1,436,500	23.8
35–64	2,930,700	39.3	2,250,600	37.4
65+	414,400	5.6	508,000	8.4
1950				
0–19	2,111,600	26.8	2,144,400	30.9
20–34	1,902,200	24.1	1,562,800	22.5
35–64	3,272,900	41.5	2,577,900	37.2
65+	605,200	7.7	653,300	9.4
1960				
0–19	2,344,700	30.1	3,381,100	37.6
20–34	1,538,900	19.8	1,582,400	17.6
35–64	3,084,500	39.6	3,192,800	35.5
65+	813,800	10.5	845,400	9.4
1970				
0–19	2,474,100	31.3	3,991,100	38.6
20–34	1,725,200	21.9	1,882,400	18.2
35–64	2,747,700	34.8	3,449,500	33.4
65+	947,900	12.0	1,018,900	9.9

TABLE 4.8 *(continued)*

| Age Group | New York City | | Balance of State | |
	Number	Percentage Distribution	Number	Percentage Distribution
1980				
0–19	1,987,800	28.1	3,337,600	31.8
20–34	1,807,100	25.6	2,493,100	23.8
35–64	2,325,100	32.9	3,446,600	32.9
65+	951,700	13.5	1,209,100	11.5
1990				
0–19	1,836,200	25.6	2,992,800	27.0
20–34	1,767,300	24.6	2,637,000	24.3
35–64	2,555,000	35.6	3,805,400	35.1
65+	1,021,900	14.2	1,477,500	13.6
2000				
0–19	1,838,800	25.3	2,975,700	26.4
20–34	1,521,100	20.9	2,128,000	18.9
35–64	2,844,200	39.2	4,539,700	40.2
65+	1,056,600	14.6	1,644,100	14.6

SOURCES: U.S. Bureau of the Census, 1950 Census of Population, *Characteristics of the Population, New York,* table 15; 1970 Census of Population, *Characteristics of the Population, New York,* table 138; 1980 Census of Population, *General Population Characteristics, New York,* table 19; "Official Population Projections" of the New York State Data Center; and Ira Rosenwaike, *Population History of New York City* (Syracuse: Syracuse University Press, 1972), table B-1.

NOTE: Numbers rounded to nearest hundred.

(in terms of median age) in the nation.[20] While both the state and city populations will age considerably for the foreseeable future, the impending changes are likely to bring about greater convergence in their age structures. In 1980, for instance, the proportion of elderly in New York City's population (14 percent) was notably higher than elsewhere in the state (12 percent). But the disparity is expected to be much less in the year 2000. The proportion of elderly in New York City's population is projected as 15 percent, exactly the same as in the rest of the state.

The aging of the population is not just a matter of changes among the elderly, but reflects shifts throughout the age distribution. Not only are the elderly increasing in number; so, too, are middle-age persons. But this change, which is expected for both the New York City and New York State populations, may be less rapid in the city for several reasons. New York City's elderly appear to be more likely than those from elsewhere in the state to move to the sunbelt, and it experiences a significant loss of adults on the brink of middle age as a result of movement to the suburbs.

At the same time, New York City receives a steady inflow of young adults as a result of immigration, and it attracts native-born persons in their 20s because of its educational, professional, and social opportunities. Finally, its child population is likely to be buoyed by the concentration of minority groups, with higher than average fertility, in the city.

Nevertheless, the number of children in New York City is expected to decline during the last two decades of the century. Persons under age 20 will drop from just under 2 million in 1980 to 1.84 million in 2000. This represents an approximately 8 percent decline over the period compared with a nearly 10 percent decline projected for the state as a whole. Young adults are also projected to decline in number, but at about the same rate in both the city and the state. Between 1980 and 2000, persons aged 20 to 34 in New York City are expected to decrease by nearly 290,000, or almost 16 percent, compared with a decline of about 15 percent for the state as a whole. Young adults made up nearly 26 percent of the New York City population in 1980; they are expected to constitute only about 21 percent in 2000. This age group is projected to decline from 25 to 20 percent of the New York State population.[21]

While children and young adults are expected to decline as part of the New York City and New York State populations, the opposite is true for middle-aged persons. The largest growth is expected in the middle-age range (designated here as ages 35–64), because of the aging of the baby boom generation. Between 1980 and 2000, the middle-aged group in New York City is expected to swell by more than half a million persons, or 22 percent. This group's share of the total population will also increase dramatically: the middle-aged were 33 percent of the New York City population in 1980; they are projected to account for 39 percent in 2000. Despite this substantial growth, the middle-aged group in New York City is expected to increase at a slower pace than elsewhere in the state: outside of New York City, this group is projected to expand by 32 percent between 1980 and 2000. Nonetheless, the middle-aged share of the population will be similar in the city and state at the end of the century.

Although the elderly are expected to make up nearly 15 percent of the population in both the city and the state by the year 2000, the rate of growth is expected to be dramatically slower in the city. Over the 20-year period, 1980 to 2000, the projected rate of growth for the city's elderly population is 11 percent, while in the rest of the state the elderly are expected to increase 36 percent. Growth among the elderly is expected to be concentrated among persons aged 75 and over. The "young old," persons between ages 65 and 74, are expected to decline 8 percent in the city in this period. The number of persons aged 75 to 84 is expected to rise 18 percent, and those aged 85 and over are expected to more than double in number between 1980 and 2000.

The aging of the population raises a host of important issues, stemming from the shifting composition of the workforce, alterations in household and family structure, and impacts on such age-related institutions as schools and nursing homes. One obvious repercussion is the increased demand for health care, a result of the growing elderly population and especially the rapid growth in the number of the "very old" (those aged 85 and over). The "very old" are at a greater risk of suffering from chronic diseases and have higher rates of institutionalization. Moreover, persons in this age group often find it difficult physically or financially to maintain their own homes.

The aging of the population will have pronounced effects on New York City households and on the demand for housing in particular. The changing age structure has been a major force behind the decline in average household size over the last two decades, and that decline is likely to continue, although probably not at as steep a rate as in the recent past. One reason for the continuation of the decline is the expected increase in the elderly population. The elderly typically reside in one- or two-person households, below average in size. The aging of the baby boom generation is also linked to family and household changes. Currently a large part of the city population are at ages when family formation and also disruption are most likely. The formation of families puts additional strain on the city's housing and fuels continuing movement to the suburbs. The disruption of families, by separation and divorce, also strains housing resources, by creating two or more households out of one. The anticipated growth in the number of single-parent families and divorced persons is another factor driving average household size downward.

Another consequence of population aging, and in particular of the arrival to middle age of the large baby boom generation, is that the labor force will grow steadily older by the end of the century. Many social scientists expect this will lay a foundation for economic stability, if not prosperity, because higher productivity should accompany the greater experience of New York workers. But the aging of the workforce could also produce strains, a result of intensified competition for promotion among the growing number of workers at the ages where career mobility traditionally has been expected. Even though its middle-aged group is not expected to grow as rapidly as in other parts of the state, New York City might feel these strains strongly because a significant part of its workforce commutes to work from neighboring suburbs expected to experience rapid growth in their middle-aged population. On Long Island, for example, the middle-aged group is projected to expand 31 percent between 1980 and 2000, and in the suburban counties north of the city, this group is expected to grow 27 percent.

Perhaps the most portentous changes may be those among younger age groups. The shrinking pool of young adults holds potent implications for the labor force. On the one hand, it may ease the strain on the economy to create new jobs and thereby pave the way for fuller, if not full, employment. On the other hand, it may mean a scarcity of entry-level workers, not only making young workers expensive for employers but also leading to a mismatch between the characteristics of the youthful part of the workforce and those sought by employers. This is a potentially serious issue in New York City, because so much of its future entry-level workforce will be minority-group members; the current high high school dropout rates among New York City minorities suggest how serious the mismatch might be. Alternatively, if minority-group members are adequately prepared for the future economy, the shrinking overall size of the young adult group might cause significant amelioration of ethnic and racial inequalities, as currently underutilized groups experience higher rates of labor force participation and social mobility.

Another serious implication of an aging population is the cleavage between New York City and the rest of the state regarding the status of children. In the near future, children are likely to be fewer in number and a smaller proportion of the population than they are today or than they were in the past. Fewer adults will have a personal, direct stake in the welfare of children, and pressures for the maintenance and enhancement of the institutions and resources devoted to children may weaken. At the same time, pressures on the public purse may grow from the other end of the age spectrum, since the number of elderly, and particularly the number of the very old, will be larger than ever before.

The severity of these tensions differs between New York City and the rest of the state. New York City more strongly feels these threats to children's welfare because it has large populations of single-parent families and of people living in poverty. New York City is home to a majority of the state's minorities and houses over half of its single-parent households. Moreover, many births in New York City occur to nonmarried women. In 1983, 38 percent of the city's births occurred to nonmarried women compared with 26 percent for all births in the state.[22] All these factors cause a greater threat to the welfare of New York City's children.

FAMILIES AND HOUSEHOLD STRUCTURE

The living arrangements of New Yorkers have changed since the 1960s. These changes reflect national trends, including higher divorce rates, lower fertility, postponement of marriage, the arrival of the baby boom generation to adulthood, and increased longevity. Together, these trends have led to a sharp decline in the proportion of households containing families, especially married-couple families. At the same time, the proportion of households headed by single parents has risen (particularly those maintained by women). Households composed of individuals living alone or with unrelated persons have also grown. A significant accompaniment of these trends has been the declining average size of households. As a consequence, the rate of growth of households is higher than the rate of population growth.

Between 1970 and 1980, the number of households in New York State grew about 7 percent, even though the population declined 4 percent. The proportion of households containing families declined from 82 percent in 1960 to 70 percent in 1980. Married-couple families declined both in number and as a proportion of all households. Between 1960 and 1980, married-couple families declined 6 percent—dropping from 71 to 55 percent of all households. In contrast, single-parent families grew from 16 percent of all the state's families with children in 1970 to 25 percent in 1980. Nonfamily households more than doubled between 1960 and 1980, growing from 18 to 30 percent of all households. Increases in nonfamily households were due largely to an increase in households maintained by persons living alone, which by 1980 constituted 26 percent of all households in New York State. In concert with these changes, the average size of households has dropped from 3.1 persons in 1960 to 2.7 persons in 1980.[23]

Although both New York City and New York State have experienced these changes in family and household structure, the contrast between the city and state is striking. New York City more dramatically illustrates the patterns resulting from the decline of married-couple households, the growing number of single-parent families, and the rapid increase of nonfamily households. The total number of households in New York City declined about 2 percent between 1970 and 1980, but family households declined 14 percent. Fewer than two in every three of New York City households contained a family unit in 1980; in contrast, more than three in four households in the rest of the state contained a family. (See Table 4.9.) Between 1970 and 1980, married-couple households in the city declined 25 percent. Only a minority of New York City households—just 44 percent—contained married couples in 1980, while 64 percent of households in other parts of the State contained married couples. New York City also had a disproportionate number of households with nonmarried-couple families in 1980; these households grew 26 percent between 1970 and 1980. Such family units, the majority of which are single-parent families, made up nearly 20 percent of the city's households in 1980; and particularly numerous were families

TABLE 4.9

Household Characteristics of New York City and New York State, 1980
(in thousands)

Type of Household	New York City		Balance of State		New York State	
	Number	Percentage	Number	Percentage	Number	Percentage
Total Households	2,793	100.0%	3,553	100.0%	6,346	100.0%
Family Households	1,771	63.4	2,697	75.9	4,468	70.4
Married-Couple Family	1,234	44.2	2,263	63.7	3,497	55.1
Other Family, Male Householder	89	3.2	83	2.3	172	2.7
Other Family, Female Householder	449	16.1	350	9.9	799	12.6
Nonfamily Households	1,022	36.6	856	24.1	1,878	29.6
Person Living Alone	908	32.5	737	20.7	1,645	25.9
Other	113	4.0	120	3.4	233	3.7
Persons per Household	2.49		2.86		2.70	

SOURCES: U.S. Bureau of the Census, 1980 Census of Population, *Detailed Population Characteristics, New York,* table 206; 1980 Census of Population, 1 percent B sample of the Public Use Microdata Samples.

headed by women with no husband present, which constituted 16 percent of all households in New York City. Indeed, more than half of New York State's female-headed families were located in New York City.

The large number of nonfamily households also distinguishes New York City from the rest of the state. While about a quarter of the households in other areas of New York State did not contain a family in 1980, this was true of 37 percent of households in New York City. The great majority of these nonfamily households are persons living alone; in New York City in 1980, one household in every three contained just one person. About one household in every five in the rest of the state contained one person. The large proportions of single-parent families and persons living alone in New York City results in the city having a smaller number of persons per household (2.49) than the balance of the state (2.86).

The concentration of single-person households and the small proportion of married-couple families in New York City is related to its age structure, life-cycle factors, and migration. The migration into and out of New York City has had a noticeable impact on the mix of family and household types. The exodus of families out of New York City to neighboring suburbs has contributed to the decline of married-couple households. The in-migration of many young, single adults also contributed to the decline of married-couple families and the rise of single-person households. Moreover, the migration of New Yorkers to sunbelt states includes many married couples and especially elderly couples. By contrast, the widowed are a disproportionate part of the much smaller migration of elderly returning to the city from the sunbelt.

Whites, blacks, and Hispanics all have experienced the changing patterns in living arrangements discussed above. Nevertheless, there are substantial racial and ethnic differences in household and family composition, especially in the prevalence of female-headed, single-parent families. Blacks and Hispanics have higher percentages of single-parent households than do whites, and blacks are more likely to be found in nonfamily households than members of other racial and ethnic groups.

The transformation in living arrangements of the last two decades is expected to slow during the remainder of the century. The slowing is due in part to the aging of the baby boom generation, which will be moving beyond the ages of strongest impact on household formation. This is expected to end the decline of the married-couple family and slow the growth of persons living alone. However, single-parent families are expected to continue to be one of the fastest growing household types.[24]

CONCLUSION

New York City has a continuing, strong effect on the population of New York State. Although the city's population is currently 40 percent of the state's, its demographic impact is not dictated by size alone.

Foreign immigration is an important example of how New York City population dynamics affect the state's overall population. The city serves as the gateway and home for newly arriving groups and has been the point of dissemination for immigrants to other parts of the state. The growth of the state depends on immigrant flows to the city, and immigration makes an important contribution to this growth. Moreover, immigration may prove an important source of young adults as the proportion of persons in this age group shrinks toward the end of the century.

It should be noted, however, that New York State's share of national immigration has been declining. In 1970, New York State received about 26 percent of all immigrants entering the United States; by 1980 the state's share had dropped to 17 percent.[25] The future role of immigration in New York City and New York State will depend on immigration policy, housing availability, and the continued attractiveness of the city.

New York City and New York State, already racially and ethnically diverse, will become even more diverse in the future. Because of the impending age structure changes in the population, racial and ethnic

concentrations will be more pronounced among the younger age groups.
As of 1980, 35 percent of New York State residents under age 5 were
Hispanic or nonwhite.[26] This suggests that children and young adults,
who will be fewer in number than they are today, will also be more likely
to come from minority groups.

These trends, along with the existing serious racial and ethnic
inequities described in this chapter, pose a major challenge to the future
health of New York State's economic and political life. Affirmative steps
to substantially ameliorate, if not end, racial and ethnic inequalities are
needed, not only as a matter of social justice, but to protect New York
State's competitive position and to guarantee that its labor force can meet
the demand of the future.

NOTES

1. *1984–1985 New York State Statistical Yearbook* (Albany: Nelson A.
   Rockefeller Institute of Government, State University of New York,
   1985).
2. Michael Batutis and Robert Scardamalia, "The Official Population
   Projections for New York State Counties: 1980 to 2010" (Albany: New
   York State Department of Commerce, State Data Center, 1985); and
   "Projections of the Population of the United States by Age, Sex, and Race,
   1983–2080." *Current Population Reports*, series P-25, no. 952, May
   1984, table 6 (middle series).
3. Ira Rosenwaike, *Population History of New York City* (Syracuse:
   Syracuse University Press, 1972). See page 131.
4. Rosenwaike, *Population History*, pp. 131–132.
5. Richard D. Alba and Michael Batutis, Jr., *The Impact of Migration on
   New York State: A Report* (Albany: Center for Social and Demographic
   Analysis, Public Policy Institute, and New York State Job Training
   Council, 1984).
6. Alba and Batutis, *Impact of Migration*; Richard D. Alba and Katherine
   Trent, *The People of New York: Population Dynamics of a Changing
   State*, (Albany: Nelson A. Rockefeller Institute of Government, State
   University of New York, 1986); Richard D. Alba and Katherine Trent,
   "Population Loss and Change in the North: An Examination of New
   York's Migration to the Sunbelt," *Social Science Quarterly*
   67(1986):690–706.
7. John D. Kasarda, "The Implications of Contemporary Redistribution
   Trends for National Urban Policy," *Social Science Quarterly*
   61(1980):373–400.
8. Kasarda, "Implications;" Alba and Trent, "Population Loss." Migration
   patterns are not the sole demographic forces affecting regional shifts in
   population growth. While the shifts in net migration are the most
   important factors in population redistribution between the North and
   South, a continuing drop in birth rates also feeds these population shifts.
   The lower birth rates in the Northeast exacerbate the differences in

population growth between New York and southern states. See Peter A. Morrison, "New York State's Transition to Stability: The Demographic Outlook," in Benjamin Chinitz, ed., *The Declining Northeast: Demographic and Economic Analyses* (New York: Praeger, 1978).

9. Rex R. Campbell, D. M. Johnson, and G. Stangler, "Return Migration of Black People to the South," *Rural Sociology* 39(1974):514–528.

10. Rex R. Campbell et al, "Counterstream Migration of Black People to the South: Data from the 1970 Public Use Sample," *Public Data Use* 3(1975):13–21.

11. Alba and Trent, "Population Loss."

12. Rosenwaike, *Population History*.

13. *1978 Statistical Yearbook of the Immigration and Naturalization Service*, table 12; *1983 Statistical Yearbook of the Immigration and Naturalization Service*, table IMM 5.2.

14. Alba and Trent, "Population Loss." These registrations, recorded by the Immigration and Naturalization Service, do not include post-1964 immigrants who have become citizens through naturalization and thus understate the impact of recent immigration.

15. Jeffrey Passel and Karen Woodrow, "Geographic Distribution of Undocumented Immigrants: Estimates of Undocumented Aliens Counted in the 1980 Census by State," *International Migration Review* 18 (Fall 1984): 642–671. Illegal aliens, it is worth noting, are not simply people who enter the United States by clandestine means, such as crossing the border. Many illegal aliens enter the United States legally and overstay the limits of their visas.

16. Alba and Trent, *People of New York*.

17. Alba and Trent, *People of New York*.

18. Alba and Trent, *People of New York*.

19. It should be noted that the racial/ethnic categories used are based on combined racial and Hispanic-origin data and are defined to be mutually exclusive. The Hispanic category contains anyone who is identified as Hispanic on either the Hispanic origin question or the race question in the census. The remaining categories, which are racial in character, are understood to contain persons of the appropriate races, with Hispanics excluded. (An exception is the Puerto Rican category which is classified as a subset of the Hispanic category.)

20. U.S. Bureau of the Census, *County and City Data Book, 1983*, table A.

21. All projections of age groups are derived from Batutis and Scardamalia, "Official Population Projections."

22. New York State Department of Health, "Vital Statistics of New York State, 1983," tables 21 and 25.

23. Alba and Trent, *People of New York*; and New York State Council on Children and Families, "A Profile of Families," *Trends* 2 (January 1985).

24. New York State Council on Children and Families, "Provisional Projections of New York State Households 1980–2000," unpublished paper, October 1984.

25. Alba and Trent, *People of New York*, table 3.1. The decline in the state's share of immigrants admitted to the United States is partly due to the diminished flow of Europeans in recent years.

26. Alba and Trent, *People of New York*.

5

THE POLITICAL RELATIONSHIP

❧

Gerald Benjamin

"THE POWER has shifted to Albany."[1] This was the reason Ed Koch gave for his gubernatorial candidacy in 1982, an effort undertaken only three months after he had been reelected Mayor of New York City, and despite his pledge to serve out a full second term. Mario Cuomo, Koch's successful rival for the Democratic nomination, agreed. "The state saved the city," Cuomo noted in his diary on April 21, 1982, "and controls its destiny even now."[2]

If there was an error in Koch's observation, it was its contemporaneity. He attributed the power shift to the "New Federalism" of the 1980s, the desire of President Ronald Reagan to deal with New York City and other cities through their state governments. But actually, the degree to which the State ought to control the City has been one of the two core city-state issues for all of New York history. The other concerns the degree to which City priorities and politicians are able to dominate State policymaking.

In the modern history of the city-state relationship in New York, the State, as sovereign, has had the upper hand. Its historic strength grew as a consequence of State efforts during the 1960s and 1970s to deal with pressing urban problems and of responses to the 1975 New York City fiscal crisis. But in a seeming paradox, New York City has simultaneously gained influence in State policymaking, because of alterations imposed by

the courts in New York's electoral system and other long-term political
changes. Thus, though the power is indeed in Albany, it is more and more
the case that New York City politicians wield that power and will do so
in the future.

In the five sections that follow, an historical overview of the complex
and ambiguous city-state political relationship is followed by a review of
the most visible manifestation of that relationship, the interactions
between these governments' two chief executives. The third section
explains how the State has come to assume a legally dominant position
in the state-city political relationship with emphasis on the failure of the
"home rule" movement and the emergence of State authorities with
substantial activities within the city. With the State's role so important,
the City's lobbying efforts in Albany are critical; these activities are
analyzed in the fourth section. Finally, a case study of reapportionment
politics demonstrates the reasons for the decline of the size of the city's
presence in state government, the altered nature of its legislative
delegation, and the concomitant rise in its influence.

AN HISTORIC AMBIGUITY

At the 1821 constitutional convention, Chancellor James Kent argued
for a property qualification for voting that would keep power in the
hands of New York's "moderate and moral farmers," and out of those of
"the mostly motley assemblage of paupers, emigrants, journeymen
manufacturers, and those indefinable classes of inhabitants" attracted to
the state and the city. Noting that New York City had increased in size
fivefold between 1773 and 1821, from 21,000 to 123,000 inhabitants,
Kent prophesied that with universal manhood suffrage "in less than a
century the *city will govern* the state. And can gentlemen seriously and
honestly say," he continued, "that no danger is apprehended from those
combustible materials that such a city must enclose?"[3]

Over a century and a half later, upstaters were still expressing similar
concerns about New York City. In a Gannett news poll taken in the early
spring of 1982, three out of four of them agreed that a "serious conflict"
existed between upstate and the city. New Yorkers living outside New
York City were particularly suspicious that the City was poorly managed
and wasteful, and getting too large a share of federal aid.[4]

But upstate attitudes are not entirely negative. A leading historian of
New York sees in them a "love-hate relationship, a mixture of pride and
envy, of alternative fascination and revulsion."[5] Another observer,
political scientist Lynton Caldwell, captured this ambiguous feeling as
well in his description of upstate "Yorkers'" attitudes toward New York

City as similar to those of the "French provincial, alternately fascinated and repelled by the city of Paris. The city is an object of interest and even of pride, yet also a symbol of the social changes that threaten his status and values. He dislikes the big city not so much for what it is, but for what it represents."[6]

In part, too, the upstater's attitude toward New York City may stem from the insight that to those outside the state, all of New York is seen as an extension of the city. Certainly, this is the case abroad. It is also the case in Washington. Recently, New York's U.S. Senator, Daniel Patrick Moynihan, observed that "New York State means New York City" in the nation's capital, and corruption in the city was endangering programs important to all of the state. He and the late Senator Jacob Javits did not fight for aid to the city during the 1970s fiscal crisis, Moynihan commented, to have the money gained "turned into loot."[7]

From the city perspective, the fear was of control of local governance by a nonresponsive, rural-dominated Albany establishment. Consider these pained observations made by city partisans at half century intervals over the last 150 years:

> Our city occupies the position of a conquered province, entirely dependent on the will of a distant indifferent and alien government. Fernando Wood, New York City mayor in 1861
>
> Every time we danced together, the New York chickens have been stepped on by the upstate donkey. Alfred E. Smith, New York City assemblyman in 1915
>
> Governor Tom Dewey has turned City Hall into Uncle Tom's cabin. Rudolph Halley, City Council president in 1953[8]

City dwellers, too, have their ambivalences. They rush to upstate forests and lakes for summer vacations and crowd the mountain slopes on winter weekends. But many share the sentiments of their mayor, whose disdain for gingham dresses and Sears, Roebuck suits, expressed in a *Playboy* interview in early 1982, may have cost him the governorship.[9]

Part descriptive and part metaphoric, differences in upstate and city perspectives nevertheless lead to a clear conclusion. The concentricity of real social, economic, and political differences between it and the rest of the state makes New York City a defining element in state politics. Over three centuries of history, New York in the city became first very Catholic and then very Jewish; New York outside the city was and long remained largely Protestant. New York in the city quickly was ethnic and then later black and brown; New York outside the city was native for far longer, and overwhelmingly white. New York in the city was very Democratic; New York outside the city, even in other cities, was far more Republican. No wonder that New York City, a great mercantile, commercial, and industrial center, the entrepot for a polyglot of peoples of every ethnic and racial description, developed a politics and political culture different from upstate's more homogeneous, mostly agricultural heartland. No wonder that there was from the first a "discontinuity between city and state government [that] has been the cause of electoral antagonisms between city and upstate, which, once established, have furthered the conflicts."[10]

The dominant issues in the city-state relationship reflected these concentric economic, social, and political differences. Some of these—anti-Catholic and temperance measures, for example—passed with time or were resolved in the policy process, only to be replaced by new social questions—for example, "welfare" and "gay rights." Other issues, mostly those of structure and process, were more persistent. City officials wanted the authority to organize local governance, freely manage the public resources of the City, and respond directly to the demands of its citizens. Their goals were home rule, control of City finance in all its aspects, and greater support to the City from the State. In contrast, upstate officials wanted structures that would limit the City's taxing and spending; systems that would break the power of the city's numbers; institutions that would be responsive to those elements of the state that, though less numerous, were perceived as more virtuous.

City-state relations reflect not only differences that create real conflict, but also public position-taking designed to create issues that will rally political support in home constituencies. Upstate leaders attack the city as a substitute for seeking substantive, and perhaps expensive, solutions to hard problems. New York City officials blame the State with similar intent and effect.

Often, a policy debate reflects both these elements. For example, political ethics legislation emerged as an upstate-downstate issue in the 1986 legislative session. Burgeoning scandals in New York City created a point of vulnerability for all Democrats, since their party was dominant in the city. In response to the scandals, Governor Mario Cuomo proposed legislation, supported by the City, that included tightened financial disclosure requirements for all elected officials and that barred them from practicing law before State agencies. Senate Republican Majority Leader Warren Anderson, in a letter to the *New York Times*, called the governor's plan an "overreaction" designed to divert attention from the "Democratic scandals in New York City." As an alternative, Anderson suggested legislation that increased disclosure requirements and limited campaign contributions to Board of Estimate candidates in the city alone.[11] Later, during the special legislative session of December 1986, debate continued between Cuomo and Anderson over whether a proposed new commission to investigate unethical conduct by public officials should operate statewide or be limited to New York City.

The tensions and ambiguities in the New York City-New York State relationship are most evident in the public interactions between the city's mayor and the state's governor. Though clashing personalities or partisan differences may exacerbate the tension between them, even in the best circumstances differences of constituency and role create conflict.

THE GOVERNOR AND THE MAYOR

Governor Franklin D. Roosevelt faced a dilemma during the summer of 1932. After long investigations of Tammany Hall, Judge Samuel Seabury had placed 15 specific charges of criminality by New York City's mayor, Jimmy Walker, before the governor in early June. Two months later, the mayor's response was in Roosevelt's hands. The presidency hung in the balance. If the governor removed the mayor, Roosevelt would appear opportunistic and alienate many regular Democrats in key northeastern states. If he did not, he would appear insensitive to corruption, losing the backing of western and midwestern liberals inclined to his cause.[12]

Ultimately Walker resigned, sparing Roosevelt the necessity to choose. But this dramatic incident illustrated the governor's ultimate power over mayors and other city officials, the power to hold them accountable and, if justified, to remove them.

An array of provisions in State law gives not only the governor but also the courts, the legislature, and various State agencies the power to conduct inquiries and investigations into the operations of the City. Sometimes spurred by election-year politics or by partisan differences between upstate and downstate, the list of these investigations is long.[13]

Most recently, in the wake of the 1986 Parking Violation Bureau scandals in New York City, Governor Cuomo, a potential president as FDR was, appointed the State-City Commission on Integrity in Government, chaired by Columbia University president Michael I. Sovern, to study the structure and operation of City government. Later the competition among an array of prosecutors—federal, State, and local— to reveal further corruption in City government led Republicans to demand that the governor take a more vigorous role, perhaps by appointing a special prosecutor. By the end of 1986, after a reelection victory of unprecedented size, and facing media pressure that included a rare front page editorial in the *Daily News*, Cuomo appointed a special Moreland Act Commission to investigate unethical conduct by public officials throughout the state.

Ordinarily, however, state-city relations are not conducted in the shadow of impending indictments. Rather, the political interactions between City and State leaders are based upon the meshing of their institutional roles and personal chemistries. And recently, these relationships are between city politicians in City government and city politicians in State government.

In 1982, all the contenders for governor, Democratic and Republican, were from New York City. In fact, almost all New York governors in the last half century have emerged from the city. To obtain the visibility for a credible gubernatorial run, and the necessary financial backing, a base in the world's media and financial capital has proved almost indispensable. This is even more true as the geography of electoral politics becomes defined by media markets rather than by counties.

In New York State, Democrats recruited for governor and other top offices in their area of strength, New York City, and sought to build on that strength to win. But Republicans recruited in the city as well, seeking a Hughes or Dewey who was known through the downstate media, could cut into Democratic majorities there, and could therefore win with strong upstate support. Nelson Rockefeller dramatized the Republican approach. An archetypical east-side New Yorker in style and substance, Rockefeller maintained the fiction of Westchester County political origins for Republican consumption outside the city.

Governors are from the city, but not of the city. Mayors, on the other hand, are living symbols of the city. Perhaps this is why they have failed to advance politically. Citing one of Wallace Sayre's famous laws, "New York City Mayors come from nowhere and go nowhere," Theodore Lowi observed that no mayor has been elected to higher office, and few have been nominated, since the creation of the greater city at the end of the nineteenth century.[14] Ed Koch's defeat in the 1982 gubernatorial primary, well after Lowi wrote, shows this law is still ironclad.

The relationship between the current governor and mayor was affected by their confrontation in this contest and by their previous run against each other in the 1977 mayoral primary. Observers commented that there was "a reservoir of personal animus" between Mario Cuomo and Ed Koch. Koch held Cuomo responsible for innuendos that Koch was a homosexual that emerged during these campaigns. Cuomo believed that Koch was behind rumors that Cuomo was anti-Semitic. One associate quoted the governor as having later said: "Despite being elected governor, and despite giving the keynote speech at the 1984 Democratic national convention, nothing can ever be as satisfying as beating Ed Koch."[15]

But "even if Governor Cuomo and Mayor Koch weren't long time rivals," the New York Times noted in an editorial, "even if they were brothers married to loving sisters, their political offices would drive them apart."[16] A decade and a half earlier, Governor Nelson Rockefeller expressed a similar sentiment in greater detail:

Frankly, it is always difficult for the Mayor of the City of New York and the Governor of New York State. There is a built in conflict there because the Mayor has got a lot of problems and he's got a constant desire to get more support from Albany. When he can't solve a problem here, because he doesn't have enough money or whatever the problem is, Albany is always there to either call upon or to involve in some way in the reason why the problem wasn't solved.[17]

Rockefeller's difficulties with John Lindsay were legendary, as were Tom Dewey's with Fiorello La Guardia; party ties did not necessarily mitigate personal enmities or the clash of ambitions. Governor Carey's objections to his co-partisan as mayor, Abe Beame, was less personal than professional. Carey failed to back Beame for reelection in 1977 because he felt the mayor's handling of the fiscal crisis to be inadequate.

Carey worked better with Ed Koch, whom he endorsed after Mario Cuomo lost the mayoral primary in 1977. But there were tensions. As an incoming mayor wanting to establish his own powers, Koch was restive under the authority of the State Emergency Financial Control Board (EFCB). Later, he strained his relationship with the governor by characterizing him as weak-willed and enigmatic during the 1978 transit strike. "One simply doesn't understand what he says," Koch remarked of Carey, whose endorsement for reelection he later withheld.[18]

Intraparty rivalries did not always produce gubernatorial-mayoral tensions. Mayor Robert Wagner got along well with Governor Averell Harriman. Harriman endorsed Wagner for the U.S. Senate and strongly backed the city before a hostile Republican legislature in Albany, despite the risks for his own reelection of too close an identification with the metropolis.

Nor did partisan differences necessarily reinforce conflict between the offices. Governor Herbert Lehman was "amicable" with Mayor La Guardia. Dewey had "informal understandings" with Mayor Impellitteri.[19] Similarly, though publicly at odds, Wagner and Governor Rockefeller got along well behind the scenes. "I did much better with Rockefeller than with Harriman," Wagner recalled, "since Averell had much more serious problems with the legislature." In fact, according to Ken Auletta, a too close relationship between Rockefeller and Wagner led to the adoption of practices in 1964 and 1965 that contributed significantly to the fiscal crisis a decade later.[20]

Governor Carey's involvement in the 1977 mayoral primary and Koch's reluctance to later endorse Carey were not unusual. Gubernatorial involvement in city politics, and the potential effect of mayoral words and deeds on gubernatorial prospects, is a regular theme of New York politics. Nelson Rockefeller recruited John Lindsay as the Republican candidate for mayor in 1965 and provided $500,000 for his campaign, only to find that Lindsay's actions in the 1968 city sanitation strike compromised the governor's presidential ambitions. Later, in 1973, Rockefeller sought to recruit Robert F. Wagner, the former Democratic mayor, as the Republican candidate for that office! Given this pattern, and Ed Koch's overwhelming prospects for victory, Governor Cuomo's reticence in 1985 was notable. The best he offered was an off-handed endorsement of the mayor's third-term bid at a bill-signing ceremony at Battery Park City in Manhattan. They had "extraordinary success" in working together over the past three years, Cuomo said.[21]

Partisan differences or intraparty rivalries might be overcome, or might enhance mayoral-gubernatorial conflict. Personalities or ambitions might mesh or clash. But the tension between the two offices is institutional, and therefore omnipresent. As Wallace Sayre has noted, "As the two leading elected officials in a populous and nationally influential state, the governor and the mayor cannot avoid friction or even overt collision."[22]

SOURCES OF STATE DOMINANCE

Home Rule: Issue, Practice, Consequences

It was the 1986 legislative session in Albany. As usual, the City wanted legislation—for new taxes, to close its budget gap; to renew old taxes, to avoid a new gap; for authority to build a dormitory at Brooklyn College; for still another plan to finance moderate-income housing; even for the food vending arrangements on Liberty Weekend. As usual, the City opposed legislation—to enrich pension benefits for its workers; to allow upstate pistol permit holders to carry their weapons into the city. And, as usual, the City was affected—by increased local and school aid; by exemptions to residence laws for its uniformed employees; by changes in rent control legislation, and by requirements that subway car overhauls be done partly within the state.

Big issues and small, home rule notwithstanding, in 1986 as in previous years they all seemed to come to Albany. Although mid-year ceremonies in New York City marked the end of some of the emergency State fiscal powers imposed during the crisis ten years before, even a casual reading of the daily press revealed that the nation's greatest metropolis was in large measure governed from a much smaller city 150 miles to its north.

The Legal Capture of the City. This was not always the case. When New York City was first chartered, the feudal concept of the corporation prevailed in British law. "Commerce was the organizing principle of the municipality's government, and its offices, suffrage requirements, ordinances and pageantry all reflected the economic practicalities underlying its existence."[23] The distinction between public and private corporations, later enshrined in American law by the Dartmouth College case, was not recognized and did not exist. Thus, as a municipal corporation, New York City was distinct in law from other unincorporated forms of local government, created by the State for its convenience. And the city's charter was inviolable, protecting it even from State intrusion.

The concept of the city as an autonomous legal entity survived well beyond the turn of the nineteenth century. In the 1780s, the State Council of Revision spoke of New York City as an "independent republic." Between 1800 and 1830 New York courts continued to accept British law on this matter, and "charter inviolability provisions in the New York State Constitution kept New York City's charter rights immune from state intrusions." In fact, an 1815 State Supreme Court decision concerning the City's powers referred to "the almost invariable course of proceeding of the legislature not to interfere in the internal concerns of a corporation, without its consent."[24]

By this time, however, things were changing. No longer able to do all it had to with corporate resources alone, the City by the early nineteenth century was seeking additional positive authority from the State, thus at once inviting Albany into its affairs and implicitly acknowledging its legitimate role. Furthermore, the transformation of the city from a "commercial" to a "residential" community in the eighteenth century led to pressures to democratize its governance in post-revolutionary America.[25] The moment of decisive change came in 1804, when the State altered the City's ward boundaries and extended the franchise within it. With this action, hotly contested, the municipal charter as a bastion against State action was decisively breached. Although, as noted, it took the courts some time to recognize the new political realities, by the 1820s "the singularity and autonomy of the city as a local government had been obliterated."[26]

In the decades that followed, the consequences of "state ascendence" were most evident at times of highly publicized corruption in the city, or of stark political differences between upstate and the city. Following the election of Mayor Fernando Wood in 1857, for example, "a coalition of wealthy New York City Democrats and Republicans joined upstate

Republicans in the state legislature to deprive the city's mayor and council of power over most municipal functions, including most police, fire and public health activities." Often city officials resisted. In one instance, police responsive to the mayor battled those of the State-controlled Metropolitan force in the streets. In the post-Civil War period newspapers characterized the treatment of the Democratic city by upstate Republicans as analogous to national Republican treatment of the defeated South.[27]

One legal device used by the State to subsume City government was the creation of a number of special districts for single purposes, the jurisdiction of which extended beyond the geographic limits of the city. These districts were governed by commissioners appointed by the governor, but their bills were paid from City coffers. The mayor sued, asserting that the creation of such agencies violated "home rule" provisions included in the 1846 State constitution that guaranteed the local election or appointment of local officials. But the Court of Appeals took the side of the State, setting early upon the course it would follow thereafter. The agencies were not coterminous with the City's boundaries, the Justices said; thus the constitution did not bar their creation. Only the legislature could determine if there was sufficient cause for such action, and once it did, this action was valid.[28]

The Home Rule Movement. In the competitive political environment of the final third of the nineteenth century, City-State differences were exacerbated. New York City remained a Democratic stronghold. Republicans, when they won in Albany, sought, often in the guise of reform, to use that base to control the City's patronage and resources. Of one plan to create a State police constabulary for large cities, for example, the Republican "easy boss," Thomas C. Platt, wrote to an associate, "we will pass it through, home rule or no home rule."[29] Upstaters were facilitated in their goals by the entrenchment in law during this period of Dillon's Rule, which regarded cities as "mere creatures of the state" and without inherent rights.[30]

In response, downstate reformers of both parties attempted to enshrine protections for the City and limitations upon the State in home rule laws, and more important, in home rule provisions of the State constitution beyond the reach of ordinary legislative action. As Sayre pointed out, this was not done without ambiguous feelings. For reformers knew that victory for home rule would place power in the hands of the Tammany machine and the "ignorant proletariat" it led.[31]

In Albany, Democratic governors championed home rule. The system of State intervention in the city, Samuel Tilden wrote in his 1875 annual message, "insures bad government of the city, and tends to corrupt the legislative bodies of the state." The history of "withdrawing from the city of New York the powers of local government which it held under its charter, and supplying their place with acts of the State Legislature," Tilden's upstate successor Lucius Robinson agreed, was "one long record of confusion, robbery and wrong."[32]

Gradually, beginning in the nineteenth century and stretching into the twentieth century, home rule had its successes. In 1874 the State constitution foreclosed local bills and required general laws in some areas of concern to cities. In 1894, the same year in which apportionment rules greatly disadvantageous to cities were adopted, so was a landmark constitutional provision that gave mayors a suspensive veto over local laws passed in Albany that affected their jurisdictions and otherwise required the legislature to act by general law "in relation to the property, affairs or government" of any city. A generation later, during a rare moment of Democratic control of State government, the Home Rule Act was passed. It gave every city the "power to regulate and control its property and local affairs," including authority to perform a broad range of specific functions "subject to the Constitution and general laws of the state." A decade later, another Home Rule Amendment was adopted that made the passage of laws local in "terms or effect" in Albany without local consent even more difficult and allowed cities to roll back by their own actions some special legislation already passed. Moreover, this 1923 amendment enshrined in the constitution cities' affirmative powers to act with regard to their own property, affairs, or government. Finally, in 1938 an additional amendment was passed, requiring a local request in writing by the mayor and council, or two thirds of the council alone, before special legislation applying to one city could be passed.[33]

All these efforts to limit the State and carve out a sphere of autonomy for cities, however, were rendered moot by that old friend of State sovereignty, New York's high court, the Court of Appeals. "As viewed by the courts," one former New York City corporation counsel once wrote, "home rule was merely a pleasant myth."[34] Constitutional limits on special legislation could be overcome, the court ruled, by legislation general in form that placed New York City, the state's only city with a population greater than 1,000,000, in a class by itself. The constitutional sphere of autonomous City action, that of its property, affairs, and government, was narrowly construed, given a "Court of Appeals definition, not that of Webster's dictionary."[35] And in the case of *Adler v. Deegan*, the "state concern" doctrine was established. While sustaining a State multiple dwelling law that adopted needed housing codes applicable to New York City alone, but opposed by City leaders, Justice Benjamin Cardozo wrote, "if the subject be in substantial degree a matter of state concern, the legislature may act, though intermingled with it are concerns of the locality."[36]

Home rule struggles continued, but to little effect. The constitutional language that permitted regular State intervention in New York City's governance was debated but not changed at the 1938 Constitutional Convention. Nor was it substantially altered in 1963 and 1964, when home rule was extended by constitutional amendment and enabling legislation to local governments other than cities in New York State. The 1960s constitutional language did include a directive that home rule be liberally construed, but this was largely ignored by the courts. Half serious suggestions that the City become the "Fifty-first state," raised in the Mailer-Breslin mayoral campaign in 1969, and Mayor John Lindsay's contemporaneous proposal for a semi-autonomous, federal city that would have direct links to the national government, bypassing the state, were in part expressions of frustration with this situation. These, too, were not new. Before the adoption of the 1923 Home Rule amendment, an annual "State of Manhattan Bill" was a regular feature of the legislative session in Albany.[37]

At the 1967 Constitutional Convention, the struggle was renewed. Judge Francis Bergen of the Court of Appeals argued for a new formulation of home rule that would reverse Dillon's Rule, allowing cities to exercise any powers not denied by constitution or statute. Frank C. Moore, a former Lieutenant Governor and the Republican eminence on local government questions, defended the new 1963 amendment, including its retention of the "property, affairs, and government" language so narrowly construed by the Court of Appeals. Interestingly, City officials were chary of any expansive redefinition of its constitutional power. "The city did not wish to risk a new approach, even though it would provide more power to local government. Fearful of the state exercising its prohibitive alternative, the corporation counsel decided it was safer to live with the known."[38]

Besides, by this time partisans of the City were coming to regard the struggle for home rule as a sideshow. In modern government, they argued, functions of the nation, the state, and the city were inextricably intermixed. "Home rule" assumed that a separate sphere could be defined for the City and the State, but this was no longer the case. Even if borrowing, taxing, and spending limits were lifted—another City goal at the convention—the resources would not be there to meet burgeoning urban needs. The answer then was full State assumption of urban functions, for example, for community development and what was then called "welfare."

The 1967 Constitutional Convention marked the last serious discussion of the alteration of home rule as a legal concept in New York State.

With the failure of the product of that convention at the polls, the complexities of home rule remain integral to city-state relations. Indeed, whether or not a home rule message is needed for State action affecting the City sometimes becomes a matter for negotiation, giving considerable power to the home rule counsels in both houses of the legislature. In 1986, for example, the final removal of the requirement for a home rule request, after a period of on-again, off-again negotiations, accelerated the passage of the Harbor Festival legislation.

Ambiguities in home rule law often set up the possibility for a sort of governmental Alphonse and Gaston routine. City inaction in dealing with a problem may be blamed on the absence of local authority. State inaction, in turn, may be blamed on the absence of a home rule message. For example, journalist Ken Auletta described the politics of a City tax increase in mid 1966 in this way: "Not wanting to accept responsibility, the City Council joined [Mayor] Lindsay in demanding that the state legislature mandate these taxes upon the city. The state insisted that the city request permissive legislation and then mandate the taxes itself. The feud was not about whether to tax but about who would get blamed."[39]

The New Public Authorities in the City. On the reform agenda that emerged in the 1960s, direct State involvement in meeting New York City's needs, formerly viewed with distrust and even hostility, came to be regarded as positive and necessary. And the State wanted to be involved, for the city of the 1960s was where the governmental action was. To Governor Nelson Rockefeller, "state government [was] the logical leader of intergovernmental cooperation in the solution of urban problems."[40]

Public authorities were a principal vehicle for this involvement. These are agencies created by the legislature to function as "public benefit corporations," outside the regular structure of State government. Their flexibility arose from their independence of the hiring, budgetary, and procedural rules that constrained ordinary executive agencies, and most important, from their ability to borrow on their own, based upon projected revenues from their projects. This allowed the State, through the use of authorities, to bypass New York's constitutional referendum requirement for "full faith and credit" state borrowing.[41]

Some authorities, already established, such as the Port Authority, were adapted to new purposes during the Rockefeller years. Others, such as the Metropolitan Transportation Authority (MTA), the Urban Development Corporation (UDC), and the Housing Finance Agency (HFA), were created in the 1960s to meet urban needs. Thus, in transportation, housing, economic development and other areas, largely autonomous agencies, with boards appointed in Albany, functioned in the city. Although established with an independent, though often inadequate, revenue base, these agencies were reminiscent of the mid-nineteenth-century State commissions in that they delivered vital city services but served areas broader than the city and were not controlled by its elected officials.

It is virtually impossible to isolate, for all State public authorities active in New York City, a precise aggregate level of spending or investment in the city. The activities of some—the Battery Park City Authority, for example—are confined entirely to the city. Others, such as the Power Authority of the State of New York are focused largely upstate, but have significant projects in New York City. But at least 15 State public authorities spend billions of dollars a year within the boundaries of the five boroughs and have tens of billions invested there. And the boards of these agencies are controlled by the governor, through the ex officio service on them of his budget director and selected commissioners and through additional appointments of board members and chairmen, usually with the advice and consent of the State Senate.

The mayor of New York City has some say in the governance of only three State public authorities active in the city: the MTA, the United Nations Development Corporation (UNDC), and the Municipal Assistance Corporation (MAC). The City's chief executive makes direct appointments and has a hand in the selection of the chairman of only one of these agencies, the UNDC. For both the MAC and the MTA boards, the mayor is confined to recommending four members for gubernatorial appointment. (MAC has 9 voting board members and the MTA has 14.) Clearly, even where the mayor's role with regard to public authorities active in the city is formally acknowledged, it is purposively minimized.

The mayor and other local elected officials are thus left with relatively little say in a number of major policy arenas in which the city's future will be substantially shaped. The periodic wrangling in Albany over subsidies for the MTA provides a regular and visible example of this. Regularly during the Christmas season, most recently in 1986, New Yorkers witness the drama of last-minute negotiations in the state capital for aid, taxing authority, or borrowing authority for that beleaguered public authority, money needed to meet the enormous capital and operating needs of the city's subways and commuter railways. When the subway fare was 35 cents, it was the mayor to whom city residents turned to save it. Now the fare is a dollar, and it is the governor to whom they turn. During the 1978 city transit strike, for example, Mayor Koch recalled, it was clear to him that the MTA chairman, Richard Ravitch, "would do what the governor wants, because he was appointed by the governor." "My role with regard to the MTA board," Koch wrote, "was that of a minority stockholder."[42]

The State government influences the activities of most public authorities that work in New York City not only through the governor's appointment power, but also through the Public Authorities Control Board (PACB). This board, created during the fiscal crisis, must give its approval before many of these agencies may finance any project. In addition, it is required to approve certain procurement contracts negotiated by the MTA for the New York City Transit Authority and must authorize any "moral obligation debt," except that of MAC, before it may be incurred. Such debt, though not backed by New York's full faith and credit, involves an implied State obligation to stand behind it.

The PACB is chaired by the governor's budget director. The other voting members, the chairmen of the Senate Finance Committee and the Assembly Ways and Means Committee, are designated by the Senate majority leader and the Assembly speaker. The control by the major State political institutions of this board is total.

Hunter's Point and Times Square. Two early disputes between the Koch and Cuomo administrations, both concerning public authority development plans, illustrate the governance issues embedded in the deep involvement of these agencies in the city. The first was a $125 million Port Authority project for a 70-acre tract in the Hunter's Point area of Queens, part of a billion dollar effort for the bi-state port area. The City was originally opposed because of the lack of specificity of the New York portion of the plan compared with the New Jersey portion and, through Republican Senate Finance Committee Chairman John Marchi of Staten Island, blocked the package in Albany. After the matter was ironed out in a personal meeting, Governor Cuomo emerged with his arm around Mayor Koch and announced to the press, "This resolves the differences between us." To this Koch responded, "That's right. But there'll be others."[43] And there were.

The Times Square Redevelopment Project was being handled by a subsidiary public authority to the Urban Development Corporation (UDC) established for this purpose. The governor appointed three of this corporation's board members, including UDC chairman, William Stern, and the mayor appointed two. Following a dispute over who would be the principal developer for a major portion of the project, the governor's directors selected Paul Milstein. The mayor's appointees, who backed Trammell Crow of Houston, abstained in the vote and then walked out. For Mayor Koch, the City's autonomy was at stake. "The City of New York is not a vassal city," he announced. "What you always have with these independent authorities," Koch continued, "is they want to do it their own way. But it's always going to be 50–50, never 60–40. Unless it's 60–40 for us."[44]

Again, despite the ostensible independence of the authority, the governor got personally involved. On a Sunday in August 1983, he met with the mayor at the World Trade Center, their second meeting since Cuomo entered office. Each man's memory of this encounter is subtly different, reflecting their different roles. Cuomo reported telling Koch that "the city must be respected and the state must be respected." Koch recalls Cuomo saying, "We are never going to impose ourselves on the city."[45] In any event, the tone was conciliatory, and again a compromise was arranged.

The MAC Surpluses. MAC, created as a consequence of the fiscal crisis, is a source of city-state issues similar to those arising out of the operation of other public authorities in the city. During the crisis in the mid 1970s, the State became directly involved fiscally through the assumption of certain costs and through increased aid to the City. In addition, MAC was established to stretch out New York City's short-term debt, control and limit its borrowing, review and audit budgets and accounts, and advise on fiscal and management practices. Later, finding "a state of emergency" and "overriding state concern" the legislature created an office of Special Deputy Comptroller for New York City and an Emergency Financial Control Board (EFCB) "designed specifically to engage the State of New York in the creation, monitoring and possible enforcement of a retrenchment plan for New York City."[46]

Ten years later, with the City's financial health restored, the powers of the EFCB were diminished. But MAC was still going strong, and, in fact, was producing surpluses from interest on reserves; refinancing debt at lower interest rates; and making reductions in required reserves as the City reentered the bond market. MAC debt, as a consequence, declined. In 1983, differences of opinion among the mayor, the governor, and MAC chairman Felix Rohatyn about the spending of an anticipated $1 billion five-year surplus produced what Rohatyn called a "massive political struggle." The revenue stream behind MAC's borrowing was composed of dedicated City sales taxes, and City officials insisted that therefore they should have the "ultimate decision" concerning the allocation of these funds.[47]

The problem for the City was, as Deputy Mayor Kenneth Lipper put it, that "it's our money, but it's in their cash register." Finally, the matter was resolved in a compromise among Mayor Koch, Governor Cuomo, and Rohatyn. The sum of $160 million was allocated for the City's operating expenses, $550 million for its capital budget, and the rest to meet economic development goals (the governor's priority) to be specified in later City-State negotiations.

The same issue arose again in 1985, with Rohatyn projecting an additional MAC surplus over ten years of $1.6 billion. After consultations with the governor, Rohatyn suggested using $1 billion of this for mass transit. Although he professed to having an "open mind" on the matter, Mayor Koch again reminded Rohatyn and the governor that "MAC does not have any money that does not belong to the city."[48] The mayor especially objected to linkage of this commitment of funds to the MTA with a proposal to create a panel to oversee transit spending, a sort of control board for one function. Finally, in April 1986, an agreement allocated $925 million over nine years to mass transit and $700 million to City debt reduction and operating expenses.

Observing from the sidelines, State Comptroller Ned Regan was disappointed with this outcome. He favored use of the MAC surplus for a more rapid retirement of outstanding agency debt. But Regan did put his finger on the power shift that the allocation of this money represented. "MAC debt is city debt," Regan wrote to the *New York Times*. "The distribution of the MAC surplus should be determined by the City's elected representatives and taxpayers. Instead, Governor Cuomo and Felix G. Rohatyn, MAC Chairman, are making the decision in this area, with Mayor Koch presumably having a secondary role and little alternative but to agree."[49]

One analyst of the fiscal crisis, Robert W. Bailey, termed it the occasion for the greatest incursion by the State into City affairs since the adoption of the 1923 Home Rule Amendment, greater even than similar State actions during the Depression of the 1930s.[50] Certainly, crisis provided an opportunity for an extraordinary increase in the State role. With the governor himself on the Control Board, and with a majority of it appointed by him, it may be only a slight exaggeration to say that at the height of the crisis he was simultaneously the chief executive of both the City and the State. This, at least, was Governor Carey's claim.[51]

But the fiscal crisis accelerated tendencies evident in other public authorities, created far earlier than MAC or the control board. State power grew in the city, not only out of crisis, but out of an attempt by the State to take a creative and positive role in addressing seemingly intractable urban problems, with resources beyond those available to the City alone.

THE CITY IN ALBANY

The influence of the State and its agencies on New York City's governance makes it essential that the City government maintain an effective presence in Albany. This involves not only direct contact among

political leaders, but a major institutional effort by the City as well. Every
year the mayor and his top aides develop a set of fiscal and programmatic
goals through a coordination committee that reports to the first deputy
mayor. After a review of unmet objectives of previous years and an
evaluation of new proposals made by City departments and agencies,
priorities are set by the beginning of the legislative session in January.
About ten major items are identified each year. They are then pursued by
the City's legislative lobbying office, staffed with a director, five full-time
assistants, and four others on temporary assignment from nonmayoral
agencies. This office has been operating for about 30 years; earlier, its
functions were handled by the corporation counsel.

In the lobbying process the mayor is a resource that is carefully used,
both through largely symbolic annual visits to Albany and through direct
contact with the governor and legislators when issues are joined. Because
the governor is the State official with the biggest and most obvious stake
in the city, he is the prime target of City lobbying in Albany. In the
legislature, as on the executive side, personal relationships are important
and partisanship is consequential.

> If the mayor's party is the majority party in one or both houses, he may expect
> at least pro forma support, particularly if the governor is of the opposite
> party; if, on the contrary, the mayor's party is in the minority, he will get less
> help. Democratic mayors may find state legislatures of their own party
> determined to press again for claims they or their allies have earlier lost at city
> hall, or to secure compensatory concessions on new matters from the mayor as
> the price of their help at Albany. Fusion mayors encounter upstate Republican
> legislators who doubt the mayor's party loyalty and New York City
> Democratic legislators who regard him as a city hall interloper.[52]

Mayor Wagner found the Republican legislature of the 1950s and
1960s cordial but nonresponsive. John Lindsay could get little out of the
Senate in 1969, the year that its Finance Committee chairman, John
Marchi, ran against him for mayor. Mayor Koch has been especially
careful not to alienate Republicans, even in the Assembly where they
have been in the minority since he has been mayor. During the early
stages of the Republican contest for the gubernatorial nomination in
1982, Koch reported having told Lew Lehrman, who was ultimately
nominated: "I'll talk to you, but also tell [Warren] Anderson and [Jim]
Emery. I can't afford to have any enemies. I need them in the state
legislature."[53] Mayor Koch has even gone so far as to endorse
Republican senators for reelection, both because of their support for the
city in the State Senate and because of his own desire for the GOP line in
the city.

THE POLITICAL RELATIONSHIP

His support of Republicans, of course, did not endear Koch to upstate Democratic senators, or to the Senate minority leader, Manfred Ohrenstein. And mayoral comments and actions can make one year's friends the next year's adversaries. It did not help Koch's budget balancing program during the 1986 session, for example, when he attacked Republican legislators from the city for opposing it and threatened to campaign against their reelection, though later this fence was mended, and the backing of these key senators helped pass the needed taxes.

One of New York City's strategies for pursuing its legislative goals is to work as much as possible in concert with or through others, so as to broaden its base of support. Coalitions are built on every issue, and shift from issue to issue. John Lindsay coalesced the mayors of the "Big Six" cities for a collective effort in Albany, and achieved considerable success in increasing state aid in 1970, a gubernatorial election year. More recently, the City has worked actively not only with other cities, but also through the New York State Association of Counties, in which it is a member by virtue of being composed of five counties.

But when its self-interest does not correspond with that of others, the City goes it alone. In 1986, for example, conflict between Democratic Assemblyman Dennis Gorski and Republican Executive Ed Rutkowski of Erie County (Gorski ultimately unseated Rutkowski), and between Democrats and Republicans in Nassau County, blocked a bill that included new taxing authority for New York City. New York, not wishing to be held hostage to political differences elsewhere in the state, sought and obtained separate action on its taxing authority, after providing a home rule message to satisfy Assembly Speaker Stanley Fink that City Council support for the new taxes was on the record.[54]

Both legislators in Albany and council members in the city are in a complex of political and personal relationships that all may be consequential for the pursuit of the City's ends in the capital. Often holders of citywide office—Comptroller Harrison Golden and Council President Andrew Stein are two current examples—began their political careers in the State legislature and retain strong personal and political connections there. In a reversal of usual patterns, some council members even have served in the State legislature before returning to the city. Aspiring to advance in the city political system, state legislators often make their committee and subcommittee chairmanships in Albany the base for investigative or other activity downstate. In addition, senators and Assembly members may be in the same or rival party factions as counterparts in the City Council or on the Board of Estimate. And, as deputy majority leader of the Assembly Alan Hevesi noted in his book on the State legislature, legislators from the city often see themselves as representing not only their districts but also county party organizations.[55]

In 1986, under its new president, Peter Vallone, and as a gesture of a desire for greater legislative independence from the mayor, the City Council announced the beginning of an independent lobbying effort in Albany on behalf of the City. Although this move has not yet produced tangible results, it may improve, at least marginally, the passive image of the council, which has traditionally labored in the shadow of the Board of Estimate.

State Aid and Budgetary Authority

The City's legislative goals fall in two general categories: those bills that involve money and those that do not. Although the latter may be extremely important—for example, the 3,088-page version of the City administrative code passed after full revision in 1985—the former get most of the attention.

The fiscal issues, in turn, may also be divided into two categories: those that are resolved in the early spring, in connection with passage of the State budget, and those that are resolved in the later spring, in connection with the City's balancing of its budget. The first phase focuses on State aid and increased State expenditures in programs with heavy impact on the city; the second focuses on new or reauthorized taxing authority and the avoidance of additional mandated costs. Alan Hevesi found it "natural and inevitable" that the mayor claim the City to be shortchanged during this process and that the governor emphasize either the City's hidden resources or, in hard times, its wastefulness.[56] On those rare occasions that the governor is inclined to be generous, he exposes himself to criticism from other quarters. This was the case, for example, in 1983, when Governor Cuomo's budget won praise from Mayor Koch but condemnation from Senator Majority Leader Anderson. It was, Anderson said, too generous to New York City during a time in which State workers outside the city were being disproportionately affected by layoffs.[57]

Throughout, of course, there is lively debate about the City's projected revenues and expenses, and consequent fiscal needs, with the claims made by the mayor, the City comptroller, and their aides closely scrutinized by the executive chamber and both legislative houses. Often, the question of whose numbers are right—with regard to what is needed, or what is being offered, or even what has been passed—becomes a matter of controversy. In 1984, after the State budget was passed, Mayor Koch complained that the City had been "treated unfairly," for it had gotten only $140 million in new aid of the $240 million he originally said he needed. "We are not vassals," Koch asserted, "content with crumbs from the table."[58]

Governor Cuomo found "nothing new" about the mayor's position. Earlier he had jokingly suggested that the City, with a projected surplus of $500 million, might give the State some money for a change. By State Budget Director Mike Finnerty's account, the City received $550 million in new money that April. The City objected and suggested that though the total was accurate, some forms of State aid actually cost it money, by driving up matching fund requirements. When the mayor denounced Finnerty's figure as a "ruse" and "contrived," Assembly Majority Leader Fink supported the governor. "While it might not necessarily be there for the [financial plan] gap closing," Fink said, "there is a lot of money that gets poured down to New York City."[59]

With regard to City taxing authority, there are two categories of issues: reauthorization of taxes that have expired and new authority. Many fiscal crisis era taxes, worth over $1.5 billion in revenues, expire annually. The failure of their reauthorization would be a massive blow to the City. Thus, they create a major vulnerability, especially in the Republican Senate which claims, not entirely accurately, that the City has never relinquished a temporary tax.

New taxing authority is even more controversial. It was an issue in 1986, when the mayor sought $100 million of it to close that year's budget gap. Koch was supported in the Democratic Assembly, but his real estate transaction tax proposals, including a transfer tax on cooperative apartments, was blocked in the Senate. Senators preferred an added levy on hotel rooms, which would export a good deal of the burden to non-New Yorkers.

Cost Avoidance

Budget balancing also involves the avoidance of the imposition of additional costs upon the city. "What we are concerned about," Deputy Mayor Lipper said during one recent budget cycle, "is the increase in the number of programs mandated on the city."[60] Although New York City's lobbying effort is generally evaluated on its affirmative achievements—bills passed, new money obtained—the City's "kill list" is as important as the "positive list." After all, expenses avoided are as great a benefit as dollars obtained to meet expenses.

One perennial City concern is legislation that enriches pension or other fringe benefits for current or former City employees. Every year, a vigil is kept by City representatives to guard against "midnight pension bills" offered during the hectic final days of the legislative session. The governor is urged to deny messages of special necessity required to bring such measures to the floor in the eleventh hour. If this fails, he is lobbied hard to veto these bills.

Public employee unions are very politically active in New York State and support majority party incumbents in both legislative houses, Republicans and Democrats alike. Moreover, these unions have long followed the practice of seeking through legislation what they may have failed to get at the bargaining table. As the *New York Times* noted in a 1984 editorial, this made the State legislature "remarkably receptive" to unions, especially if it was "conferring benefits to be paid with taxes imposed by someone else," that is, the City.[61]

The governor was thus the final bastion, but public employee unions were an important part of his constituency. Often Mario Cuomo held firm, but not in 1985. Suggesting that the need of long-term retirees, many without Social Security, was real, and that the City was having a "banner year" financially, Cuomo signed a pension enhancement bill that he estimated would cost the City $39 million annually after two years.[62] Predictably, Mayor Koch put the cost higher and denounced the governor's action as signaling a revival of the "union raids" against the City treasury that had been common before the fiscal crisis.

The 1986 legislative year was a good one for the City. It exceeded its fiscal goals, making important education aid gains; helped block major new pension bills; and saw over 75 measures it backed pass into law. Clearly however, the City does not always win, on fiscal or on other issues. Its attempts, with other local governments in New York State, to repeal the Wicks Law governing contracting for public construction failed, as did another of the mayor's perennial attempts to capture firm control of the City Board of Education.

Despite Mayor Koch's expectation that Mario Cuomo would seek to "torture" him, and therefore the City, when Cuomo assumed the governorship, and though the two men have been characterized as living a "no first strike existence, like two nervous superpowers," they do seem, on the whole, to have worked together effectively on legislative matters concerning New York City.[63] But perhaps this is as much because of changes in the configuration of legislative power in Albany as it is a consequence of these chief executives' ability to overcome their differences.

REAPPORTIONMENT AND CITY INFLUENCE

Legislative districting in New York State historically has involved factors other than population, in part to avoid dominance of the State legislature by New York City. But the scheme that assured that the State would be "constitutionally Republican," as Al Smith later described it at the 1915 Constitutional Convention, was put in place in 1894. Although approximately reflective of the geographic balance of population in the state then, several provisions disadvantaged the city as time passed. For the Assembly, each county was assured at least one member, with counties having more than one and a half but less than two "population ratios" given a second seat before the remainder of the 150 were distributed on a population basis. In the Senate, no county could have more than one third the membership, and no "two counties adjoining or separated only by public waters" (Manhattan and Kings, or Brooklyn) more than half. Large counties, those with four or more senators, could add another only when they achieved "a complete ratio" of population, and then, unlike in the Assembly, new seats were added, not taken from other areas of the state by reapportionment. Finally, a provision that apportionment be on the basis of citizenship, not total population, worked to the city's disadvantage. In 1894, 18 percent of the city's people were noncitizens, compared with 5 percent of those living outside the city.[64]

Republican reapportionment plans drawn under the provisions of the 1894 constitution were regularly challenged by New York's Democrats in the courts. In fact, new districts created by the legislature in 1906 and 1916 were declared unconstitutional by the Court of Appeals. Moreover, legislation enacted in 1907 was allowed to stand not on its merits, but because it was challenged too late, after four legislative elections had been held using the districts created by it. Thus, in the first 50 years under the 1894 constitution, only one reapportionment plan, that of 1917, went into effect unchallenged.[65]

The unfairness of the State constitution's provisions on reapportionment, and the need to enhance New York City's representation in Albany by making the allocation of legislative seats more closely proportional to population, was a perennial electoral issue for downstate Democrats during the first third of the twentieth century. But when, under extraordinary political circumstances—during the depression in 1935, for example—Democrats were able to win control of the governorship and both houses of the legislature for brief periods, they were still unable to reapportion because of intraparty differences. Even if they did act, however, the Democrats' action would be constrained by overarching State constitutional provisions that limited city gains. After 1894, real gains required constitutional change. But when conventions were held, they also were Republican dominated.

The election of Republican Tom Dewey to the governorship in 1942 ended a generation of Democratic domination of that office. With both the executive and legislative branches again firmly in GOP hands,

TABLE 5.1

New York City Representation in the New York State Assembly and Senate, 1895–Present

	1895–1917	1917–1943	1945–1953	1955–1965
Assembly Seats				
New York City	64	63	67	65
Total	150	150	150	150
Percentage				
New York City	42.7	42.0	44.7	43.3
Senate Seats				
New York City	22	23	25	25
Total	50	51	56	58
Percentage				
New York City	44.0	45.1	44.6	43.1

SOURCE: Compiled by the author from *New York Legislative Manual* (Albany: New York State Legislature, various years).

reapportionment resumed. Based on the federal census for the first time, in accord with a constitutional amendment ratified in 1931, legislative districts were altered in 1943, and again in 1953. New York City remained disadvantaged, however, because the 1894 constitutional provisions continued to define the parameters of change. In 1944, for example, five new Senate seats were added. (See Table 5.1.) Two of these were in the city, but it made no proportional gain. Under the old apportionment, New York City, with 55 percent of the population, had

TABLE 5.2

Congruence Between Geography and Party, New York State Assembly, 1943–Present

	1943	1945	1953	1955	1961	1963	1965	1966	1967
Democrats									
New York City	55	50	48	56	54	55	57	64	57
Rest of State	5	5	4	4	11	10	5	26	23
Total	60	55	52	60	65	65	62	90	80
Percentage									
New York City	91.7	90.1	92.3	93.3	83.1	84.6	91.9	71.1	71.2
Republicans									
New York City	8	17	19	9	11	10	8	11	11
Rest of State	82	77	79	81	73	75	80	64	59
Total	96	94	98	90	84	85	88	75	70
Percentage									
New York City	8.3	18.1	19.4	10.0	13.1	11.8	9.1	14.7	15.7

SOURCE: Compiled by the author from *New York Legislative Manual* (Albany: New York State Legislature, various years).

TABLE 5.1 *(continued)*

	1966	1967–1971	1973–1981	1983–Present
Assembly Seats				
New York City	75	68	65	60
Total	165	150	150	150
Percentage				
New York City	45.4	45.3	43.3	40.0
Senate Seats				
New York City	30	26	25	25
Total	65	57	60	61
Percentage				
New York City	46.1	45.6	41.7	41.0

23 of 51 senators, or 45.1 percent. Under the new system it had 25 of 56, or 44.6 percent. In the Assembly, the allocation of four additional seats to the city did increase its proportional representation, from 42 to 44.7 percent, but the new percentage still did not approach the city's proportion of the state population.

The congruence between geography and partisanship, and consequently between geography and reapportionment, cannot be overemphasized. In 1953, admittedly an exceptional year, all but one Democratic senator and 48 of the 52 Democrats in the Assembly (92 percent) came from New York City. In the 1961 legislature, 23 of 25 Democratic senators (92 percent) and 54 of 65 Assembly members (83 percent) were from the city (see Tables 5.2 and 5.3).

TABLE 5.2 *(continued)*

	1969	1971	1973	1975	1977	1979	1981	1983	1985	1987
Democrats										
New York City	56	57	53	56	57	58	58	59	57	58
Rest of State	16	14	14	32	33	28	28	38	37	36
Total	72	71	67	88	90	86	86	97	94	94
Percentage										
New York City	77.8	80.3	79.1	63.6	63.3	67.4	67.4	60.8	60.6	61.7
Republicans										
New York City	12	11	12	9	8	7	7	1	3	2
Rest of State	66	68	71	53	52	57	57	51	52	54
Total	78	79	83	72	60	64	64	52	55	56
Percentage										
New York City	15.4	13.9	14.4	12.5	13.3	10.9	10.9	1.9	5.4	3.6

TABLE 5.3
Congruence Between Geography and Party, New York State Senate, 1943–Present

	1943	1945	1953	1955	1961	1963	1965	1966	1967
Democrats									
New York City	18	17	18	23	23	23	22	25	22
Rest of State	2	4	1	1	2	2	10	3	4
Total	20	21	19	24	25	25	32	28	26
Percentage									
New York City	90.0	80.1	94.7	95.8	92.0	92.0	68.7	89.3	84.6
Republicans									
New York City	5	8	7	2	3	3	2	5	4
Rest of State	26	27	30	32	30	30	23	32	27
Total	31	35	37	34	33	33	25	37	31
Percentage									
New York City	16.1	22.8	18.9	5.9	9.1	9.1	8.0	13.5	12.9

SOURCE: Compiled by the author from *New York Legislative Manual* (Albany: New York State Legislature, various years).

But even in the 1950s and 1960s Republicans depended substantially upon New York City seats. Members elected there provided breathing space for the Republican Assembly majority in 1953 (19 percent of the party conference), and the margin of control ten years later (12 percent of the conference). In the Senate, by the early 1960s, Democratic gains outside the city were being offset by Republican districts carved out within New York City's boundaries.

Reapportionment in New York

Reapportionment came to New York, as it did elsewhere, in 1964. In the case of *WMCA* v. *Lomenzo* (decided with *Reynolds* v. *Sims*) the U.S. Supreme Court established the "one man, one vote" principle for apportionment of both houses of the New York State legislature and directed that a special election be held in districts reapportioned on the basis of that principle in 1965.[66] The decision was hailed by New York City's Democratic mayor, Robert F. Wagner, as "a new Magna-Charta for the Democratic party." In response, the Republican governor, Nelson Rockefeller, in consultation with GOP legislative leaders, appointed a Citizen's Committee on Reapportionment headed by Dean William H. Mulligan of Fordham University. According to the closest student of these events, Professor Richard Lehne, the Mulligan Committee proceeded to employ techniques for a new apportionment that would "permit a reversal of the apparent intent of the original decisions."[67] These included increasing the size of the legislature, maintaining county

TABLE 5.3 *(continued)*

	1969	1971	1973	1975	1977	1979	1981	1983	1985	1987
Democrats										
New York City	21	21	19	19	20	19	19	20	19	19
Rest of State	3	3	4	7	5	6	5	6	7	7
Total	24	24	23	26	25	25	24	26	26	26
Percentage										
New York City	87.5	87.5	82.6	73.1	80.0	76.0	79.2	76.9	73.1	73.1
Republicans										
New York City	5	5	6	6	5	6	6	5	6	6
Rest of State	28	28	31	28	30	29	29	30	29	29
Total	33	33	37	34	35	35	35	35	35	35
Percentage										
New York City	15.1	15.1	16.2	17.6	14.2	17.1	17.1	14.2	17.1	17.1

boundaries, giving some members a fraction of a vote, and changing the basis of representation from citizens to voters (not population).

Matters were further complicated when the Democrats unexpectedly gained control of both houses of the legislature in November 1964. In December Governor Rockefeller convened a special, lame duck session of the Republican legislature elected in 1962, which Democratic State Chairman William H. McKeon, enraged, urged his copartisans to boycott. Undeterred by the uproar, the Republicans passed four separate apportionment plans, ranked from most to least favored, with a provision that if one was invalidated by the federal courts the next would come into force.

In these plans, the legislature reapportioned both houses, a departure from previous practice and from the procedure set out in the State constitution. Formerly, Senate districts were designed in Albany with Assembly boundaries within them, when required, defined by local legislative bodies (in New York City, the City Council). Thus, one little-noticed casualty of federal court reapportionment action in New York State was the local role in redistricting.

The federal court accepted the Republicans' least-favored plan, which increased the size of the Assembly and Senate and based apportionment on the 1960 census of citizens. But then the New York courts precipitated a crisis in federalism by their 1965 decision in *In Re Jerome Orans*, rejecting the alternative accepted by the federal judiciary because it violated the State constitutional limit on the size of the Assembly. Facing the imminence of the 1965 elections, the federal court then directed that these go forward anyway on the basis of the plan it had approved, with a new reapportionment following in 1966 that would meet State court objections. When the New York Court of Appeals again attempted to intervene to block action on the basis of its primacy in State constitutional law, it was overruled by the federal district court and the election was held.[68]

The Democratic controlled legislature of 1965 could not agree on a reapportionment plan before the special election of that year. Bitter internal Democratic party disputes blocked the organization of the two legislative houses. Reform, minority, and upstate Democrats did not trust regulars and their county leaders, who traditionally controlled apportionment in the city when Republicans held the majority. This was a process of great importance to the county leaders, for New York City's internal party politics were based upon Assembly district lines. Furthermore, the Republican plan for 1966 created a number of new city seats, and thus new opportunities for minorities. These would be lost with a return to the 150 seat limit ordered by the State courts. Finally, the 165 seat plan also followed traditional political and neighborhood boundaries and found favor among some Democrats for that reason.

The 1965 special election produced a Democratic Assembly; the margin was 90 to 75. But control of the Senate returned to the Republicans, 37 to 28. (See Table 5.4.) In the short-lived 165-member Assembly of 1966, New York City had 75 seats, 45 percent of the total and about its share of the state population. In the 1966 Senate the city had 30 seats, a gain of 5, but only a small proportional advance because of the increase in size of that body. Interestingly, the city's representation as a percentage of each house was not substantially higher than in the

TABLE 5.4

Seats in the New York State Senate by Party, New York City and Statewide, 1943–Present

	1943	1945	1953	1955	1965	1966	1967
Statewide							
Democratic	20	21	19	24	32	28	26
Republican	31	35	37	34	25	37	31
Total	51	56	56	58	58*	65	57
Percentage							
Republican	60.7	62.5	66.1	58.6	43.1	56.9	54.3
New York City							
Democratic	18	17	18	23	22	25	22
Republican	5	8	7	2	2	5	4
Total	23	25	25	25	25*	30	26
Percentage							
Republican	21.7	32.0	28.0	8.0	8.0	16.7	15.4

SOURCE: Compiled by the author from *New York Legislative Manual* (Albany: New York State Legislature, various years).

malapportioned body of a decade and a half earlier. Just as the rules changed to remove its political disadvantage, New York City's share of the state's population declined.

The partisan consequences of the 1965 reapportionment in the city reflected its Republican origins. In the Senate there was an increase of Republican New York City strength over 1961 from three to five. In addition, Republican Assembly seats in the city were protected. Although there was a small proportional decline because of the increased size of New York City's delegation, the number of Republican Assembly members from the five boroughs actually increased by one.

Despite a court-imposed deadline, the 1966 Senate and Assembly also failed to produce a reapportionment plan. The Republicans in the Senate offered a proposal designed by their expert on reapportionment, New York City lawyer Donald Zimmerman. Democrats in the Assembly appointed a "Professors' Commission." Seeking to recognize "communities of interest," this commission concentrated Democratic strength upstate and dispersed Republican strength in the city, creating the hypothetical possibility of between 92 and 94 Democratic Assembly seats. But also, by ignoring traditional lines, this plan worked to the disadvantage of minority groups and put at risk almost half the incumbent members of the legislature, including the Senate Minority Leader.[69]

A solution was finally imposed by a five-member, bipartisan court-appointed panel. By first identifying and codifying areas of Republican and Democratic agreement in the two plans, which were mostly in rural areas, and then by giving weight to traditional arrangements, the results produced by this panel tended to favor Republicans and, in the city,

TABLE 5.4 *(continued)*

	1969	1971	1973	1975	1977	1979	1981	1983	1985	1987
Statewide										
Democratic	24	24	23	26	25	25	24	26	26	26
Republican	33	33	37	34	35	35	35	35	35	35
Total	57	57	60	60	60	60	60*	61	61	61
Percentage										
Republican	57.9	57.9	61.7	56.7	58.3	58.3	58.3	57.4	57.4	57.4
New York City										
Democratic	21	21	19	19	20	19	19	20	19	19
Republican	5	5	6	6	5	6	6	5	6	6
Total	26	26	26	25	25	25	25	25	25	25
Percentage										
Republican	19.2	19.2	23.1	24.0	25.0	24.0	24.0	25.0	24.0	24.0

*Column does not add because of a vacancy at the time the data were gathered and reported.

regular Democrats. After all, it was they who had created the "traditions" in apportionment. Thus, for example, the "tradition" of having one Republican senator and three Republican assemblymen from Manhattan was followed in the compromise plan. In sum, "the court-imposed plan worked to the advantage of the regular party leadership and of incumbent legislators of all factions and to the disadvantage of insurgents, upstate Democrats, Puerto Ricans and Blacks."[70]

New York City emerged in 1967 with 68 Assembly seats and 26 Senate seats, about 45.5 percent of each house. (See Table 5.1.) Four city Republican senators provided their party with the margin of control in that body. The 15-member reduction in size of the Assembly cost Democrats seven seats in the city and three upstate. (See Table 5.5.) Assembly Republicans held their own in the city, but lost five seats elsewhere. The overall partisan division was thus narrowed from 90–75 to 80–70 in the Democrats' favor. Calculations by political scientist Howard Scarrow demonstrated that controlling the reapportionment, when separated from other factors, was worth ten seats to the Assembly Democrats, as it had been to Republicans in the past. It was thus decisive in 1966. By making further inroads in suburban areas in 1968, however, Republicans recaptured the Assembly with a margin of control dependent upon a core of strength in New York City.[71]

TABLE 5.5
Seats in the New York State Assembly by Party, New York City and Statewide, 1943–Present

	1943	1945	1953	1955	1965	1966	1967	1969
Statewide								
Democratic	60	55	52	60	62	90	80	72
Republican	90	94	98	90	88	75	70	78
Total	150	149*	150	150	150	165	150	150
Percentage Republican	60.0	62.7	65.3	60.0	58.7	45.4	46.6	52.0
New York City								
Democratic	55	50	48	56	57	64	57	56
Republican	8	17	19	9	8	11	11	12
Total	63	67	67	65	65	75	68	68
Percentage Republican	12.7	25.4	28.4	13.8	12.3	16.2	16.2	17.6

SOURCE: Compiled by the author from *New York Legislative Manual* (Albany: New York State Legislature, various years).

The GOP's Last Hurrah

The 1971 reapportionment was thus once again carried out at a special session, with Republicans in control of both houses of the legislature and the governorship. Because of continued decline in New York City's proportion of the state population, its representation in both the Senate and the Assembly again dropped. The number of city Assembly members returned to 65, the pre-1964 level; it would, however, have been 13 seats less had reapportionment not occurred. The number of senators from the city remained the same, again because of a decision to enlarge that body.

With the issue of the proportionality of the city's representation resolved by federal court intervention, the 1971 reapportionment was focused upon the nature of district boundaries. For city Democrats, these were "life or death" decisions, made "behind locked doors and in the dead of night."[72] In the minority, Democrats sought to protect themselves and the party organization in the city, rather than developing strength elsewhere in the state. With that accomplished, 7 Senate Democrats and 22 Assembly Democrats voted with the Republicans on reapportionment over the protests of the minority leadership, giving the Republican plan a veneer of bipartisanship. One former Democratic state senator described the process in this way: "The Republicans get through protecting their guys upstate and in places like Queens. Then they let the county leaders handle things in the city. It's a madhouse—each legislator goes to his county leader with his own dream district, hoping for the best. You put in your order, like groceries."[73]

TABLE 5.5 (continued)

	1971	1973	1975	1977	1979	1981	1983	1985	1987
Statewide									
Democratic	71	67	88	90	86	86	97	94	94
Republican	79	83	62	60	64	64	52	55	56
Total	150	150	150	150	150	150	149*	149*	150
Percentage									
Republican	52.7	55.3	41.3	40.0	42.7	42.7	34.7	36.7	37.3
New York City									
Democratic	57	53	56	57	58	58	59	57	58
Republican	11	12	9	8	7	7	1	3	2
Total	68	65	65	65	65	65	60	60	60
Percentage									
Republican	16.2	18.5	13.8	12.3	10.8	10.8	1.7	5.0	3.4

*In 1945 there was one American Labor party member in the Assembly. In 1983 and 1985 there was a vacancy when the data were compiled. All percentages are based on 150, the number of seats in the Assembly, except for 1966, when the number of seats was increased to 165.

Republicans worked to secure the growing suburbs, guard their New York City Assembly seats, and carve out increased Senate strength in the city. This sometimes resulted in primary battles between Democratic incumbents outside the city. It also resulted in some odd-shaped districts. One was the thirty-fourth in the Bronx, in which two areas of Republican strength were connected by one lane of a drawbridge.[74] The results in 1973 showed the effectiveness of Republican efforts. Twelve Republican Assembly members and seven Republican senators were returned to Albany from New York City; the losses from reapportionment downstate were again absorbed by the Democrats.

Largely because of the shape of some city Senate districts, disappointed Democrats planned to challenge the 1971 State legislative apportionment on constitutional grounds before a sympathetic State Supreme Court judge in New York City. They would act, they thought, as soon as the bill was signed by the governor. But when their suit was filed, on Monday, January 17, 1972, these Democrats found that a group of Republicans had preemptively filed a similar suit in Albany County the previous Friday, only minutes after Governor Rockefeller had acted. The Republicans knew that, under the rules of procedure, the case would be heard where the first suit was filed; and it was—before Judge Edward Conway, a former Albany County Republican leader.

The litigants in *Schneider* v. *Rockefeller* claimed that the 1971 apportionment violated the "compact" and "contiguous" requirements for districts in the State constitution. But the State Supreme Court, and later the Court of Appeals, agreed with the State government's view that New York's constitutional requirements might have to be relaxed so as to meet the federal standard of population equality. In addition, in a very generous interpretation of the constitution's language, the Court of Appeals found that compactness and contiguity for State constitutional purposes meant "touching, adjoining and connecting, as distinguished from territory separated from other territory."[75] In home rule decisions, the court used narrow construction to protect the State's interest; on reapportionment, broad construction accomplished the same end.

Enter the Voting Rights Act. The matter of legislative apportionment now appeared settled for the next decade. But the federal courts again intervened, though this time not on constitutional but on statutory grounds. The federal Voting Rights Act was originally passed in 1965 to deal with discrimination against blacks in southern states. Amendments to the act in 1970, however, allowed the Justice Department to review electoral practices in any state or local jurisdiction in which less than half the voting-age population had registered or voted in 1968. This opened three New York City boroughs—Manhattan, the Bronx, and

Brooklyn—to possible scrutiny. As a result of a lawsuit brought by the NAACP Legal Defense Fund on behalf of three black political leaders in the city, this scrutiny was ordered by the federal courts early in 1974.

There had been continuous minority presence in the State Assembly since World War II, and a black member was first elected to the Senate in 1953. But black and later Hispanic representation in the legislature, though it grew slowly, remained far smaller than the proportional presence of those groups in New York's population. Reapportionments in the 1950s and 1960s had only limited impact on the legislative strength of these groups, and it appeared that the story for the 1970s was likely to be the same. (See Tables 5.6 and 5.7.)

But as a consequence of the NAACP Legal Defense Fund suit, in April 1974 the federal Department of Justice ordered the redrawing of Republican constructed State Senate and Assembly district lines in Manhattan and Brooklyn. The "effect" of the 1971 lines, Assistant Attorney General J. Stanley Pottinger announced, was to concentrate or dilute minority voting power so as to "abridge the right to vote because of race or color."[76] Five Senate and ten Assembly districts were directly at issue, but others would be affected as a consequence of changes made in these.

Again, a special legislative session was called to deal with reapportionment. Again, the fate of individual political careers, and the distribution of power in the Democratic party, was in Republican hands.

The early expectation of NAACP attorneys was for four additional minority Senate seats and five Assembly seats. These goals became more modest, however, when the courts failed to include the Bronx in the redistricting. Actually, minority State legislators were not initially united behind this lawsuit. Nine of 15 members of the Black and Puerto Rican Caucus, those tied to the regular Democratic organization in New York City, had voted for the 1971 reapportionment bill. Once the lawsuit was successful, however, none openly opposed its goals.

The issue of reapportionment within the city tended to set minority members against their allies on many other issues—white reform Democrats. The dominant Republicans could be expected to protect their own city seats, and even seek to take the opportunity to add to their strength. They also could be expected to adhere to their long-term alliances on reapportionment with organization Democrats in the city. Clearly, the price for minority progress would have to be paid by junior and reform Democrats. And it was. Those who lost their seats or were forced into primaries included reformers Carol Bellamy, Chester Straub, Peter Mirto, and Franz Leichter.

Minority group leaders were not satisfied with the lines that emerged from the special session in 1974, though the new districts were again

TABLE 5.6
Black and Puerto Rican Members
of the New York State Legislature, 1943–1985

	1943	1945	1953	1955	1963	1965	1966	1967	1969
Assembly									
Black									
Number	3	3	3	4	3	6	9	7	8
Percentage	2.0	2.0	2.0	2.7	2.0	4.0	5.4*	4.7	5.3
Puerto Rican									
Number	0	0	0	1	3	3	3	3	1
Percentage	0.0	0.0	0.0	0.7	2.0	2.0	1.8*	2.0	0.7
Senate									
Black									
Number	0	0	1	1	2	3	3	3	3
Percentage	0.0	0.0	1.8	1.7	3.4	5.2	4.6	5.3	5.3
Puerto Rican									
Number	0	0	0	0	0	0	0	1	1
Percentage	0.0	0.0	0.0	0.0	0.0	0.0	0.0	1.7	1.7

SOURCE: Compiled by the author from *New York Red Book* (Albany: Williams Press, various years).

TABLE 5.7
Black and Puerto Rican Proportion of the
Democratic Membership and the New York City Delegation,
New York State Assembly, 1943–1987

	1943	1945	1953	1955	1963	1965	1966	1967	1969
Democrats	60	55	52	60	65	62	90	80	72
Black									
Number	3	3	3	4	3	6	9	7	8
Percentage	5.0	5.4	5.8	6.7	4.6	9.7	10.0	8.7	11.1
Puerto Rican									
Number	0	0	0	1	3	3	3	3	1
Percentage	0.0	0.0	0.0	1.7	4.6	4.8	3.3	3.7	1.4
Minority									
Percentage	5.0	5.4	5.8	8.4	9.2	14.5	13.3	12.4	12.5
City Members	63	67	67	65	65	65	75	68	68
Black									
Number	3	3	3	4	3	5	8	6	7
Percentage	4.8	4.5	4.5	6.1	4.6	7.7	10.6	8.8	10.3
Puerto Rican									
Number	0	0	0	1	3	3	3	3	1
Percentage	0.0	0.0	0.0	1.5	4.6	4.6	4.0	4.4	1.5
Minority									
Percentage	4.8	4.5	4.5	7.6	9.2	12.3	14.6	13.2	11.8

SOURCE: Compiled by the author from *New York Red Book* (Albany: Williams Press, various years).

TABLE 5.6 (continued)

	1971	1973	1975	1977	1979	1981	1983	1985	1987
Assembly									
Black									
Number	7	9	9	9	10	12	15	16	16
Percentage	4.7	6.0	6.0	6.0	6.7	8.0	10.0	10.7	10.7
Puerto Rican									
Number	3	3	4	4	5	5	4	4	4
Percentage	2.0	2.0	2.7	2.7	3.3	3.3	2.7	2.7	2.7
Senate									
Black									
Number	3	3	4	4	4	4	4	4	4
Percentage	5.3	5.0	6.7	6.7	6.7	6.7	6.6	6.6	6.6
Puerto Rican									
Number	1	1	2	2	2	2	2	2	2
Percentage	1.7	1.7	3.3	3.3	3.3	3.3	3.3	3.3	3.3

*Membership of the Assembly was fixed at 150, except for the 1965 special election.

TABLE 5.7 (continued)

	1971	1973	1975	1977	1979	1981	1983	1985	1987
Democrats	71	67	88	90	86	86	97	94	94
Black									
Number	7	9	9	9	10	12	15	16	16
Percentage	9.9	13.4	10.2	10.0	11.6	13.9	15.5	17.0	17.0
Puerto Rican									
Number	3	3	4	4	5	5	4	4	4
Percentage	4.2	4.5	4.5	4.4	5.8	5.8	4.1	4.2	4.2
Minority									
Percentage	14.1	17.9	14.7	14.4	17.4	19.7	19.6	21.2	21.2
City Members	68	65	65	65	65	65	60	60	60
Black									
Number	6	8	8	8	9	11	12	13	13
Percentage	8.8	12.3	12.3	12.3	13.8	16.9	20.0	21.7	21.7
Puerto Rican									
Number	3	3	4	4	5	5	4	4	4
Percentage	4.4	4.6	6.1	6.1	7.7	7.7	6.7	6.7	6.7
Minority									
Percentage	13.2	16.9	18.4	18.4	21.5	24.6	26.7	28.3	28.3

supported by large bipartisan majorities in the Senate and the Assembly. Puerto Rican leaders were angered by the sacrifice of Hispanic to black interests in Brooklyn. Black politicians, such as Manhattan Borough President Percy Sutton and City Councilman Samuel Wright, argued that the 65 percent minority population target, used by the Republicans with the informal approval of the Department of Justice, neither substantially increased the number of black and Puerto Rican districts nor assured victories for minority candidates, because of differential registration and turnout rates between white and nonwhite voters. To assure black and Hispanic winners, Wright insisted, 80 percent minority districts were necessary. Later research confirmed this view. "A 65 percent minority population does not assure that a minority candidate will have a chance to gain an electoral majority," Roman Hedges and Jeffrey Getis wrote after a thorough analysis in 1983. "Rather the standard must be in the neighborhood of 80–90 percent."[77]

Events also bore out this view. In four of five newly designed districts with white incumbents, whites were able to win reelection in 1974. The number of black and Hispanic members in the Assembly increased by one, and in the Senate by two. But the long-term effect was much greater. By 1981, the last year in which elections were conducted in the districts redefined as a result of the 1974 litigation, the number of blacks in the Assembly had risen to 12, and the number of Hispanics to 5. In 1981 minority representation was up 42 percent to 17 members from 12 members in 1973, the year before the lawsuit was filed.

Nevertheless, there was a serious question of how far redistricting could be pushed to solve what was really a problem of low registration and turnout, especially when political leaders were not committed to solving this problem. As elections analyst Arthur Klebanoff observed, organization political leaders of all races in the city favored "small, controllable constituencies." They "want to be able to beat insurgents," he said, "and if they let the rolls increase with all these strange voters they'll lose control of the process."[78]

Black and Puerto Rican leaders were not the only ones upset by the 1974 state legislative district reapportionment in New York City. The Hassidic Jewish community of Williamsburg in Brooklyn found that its neighborhoods, formerly concentrated in one Senate and one Assembly district, were now divided in order to meet the informal 65 percent minority/35 percent white Justice Department guidelines. Hassidic leaders, asserting their status as a minority, sought redress under the fourteenth and fifteenth amendments. Their action was to no avail. The Supreme Court denied that Hassidic Jews had minority status for the purposes of the law and affirmed the necessity for the Attorney General to employ strict racial criteria for the enforcement of the Voting Rights Act.[79]

Democratic Gains, City Gains

For the post-1980 reapportionment, both the governorship and the Assembly speakership were held by Democrats from Brooklyn, Hugh Carey and Stanley Fink. Carey, in his second term, was the first person of his party to become governor in a decade and a half. Fink, speaker since 1979, presided over a majority initially elected in 1974, the post-Watergate year. The State Senate, led by Warren Anderson, was the sole Republican bastion. Assembly Democrats hoped to make the most of this historic opportunity. Another Brooklyn politician, Mel Miller, then co-chairman of the Legislative Task Force on Reapportionment, declared to the press: "For 88 years, the Republicans drew the district lines, cutting up cities. This is the first time in almost a century that the Democrats have a real role."[80]

They gained that role because the careful Republican gerrymandering of the early 1970s misfired. Its efforts were completely overcome, and even reversed, by the combined effects of the movement of city Democrats to the suburbs and the anti-Republican reaction to the Watergate crisis that swept the nation in 1974. Scarrow's analysis revealed that "after 1972 the Republican gerrymandering was no longer effective; changing voting patterns completely undid careful work of Republican cartographers. By 1974 the Assembly districting scheme had become virtually unbiased; and beginning in 1976 it turned against the party which designed it."[81] In the Senate, because of larger districts, the advantages of gerrymandering wore off more slowly and Republican incumbents were able to hold on through 1980, even though district boundaries no longer favored them.

The one-man-one-vote principle required that New York City's Assembly delegation shrink in the 1980s to reflect the city's relative decline in population; it did, from 65 to 60 seats. In the Republican Senate, not constitutionally limited to a fixed membership, contraction of the city delegation was again avoided by increasing the size of the body, this time by one member. (See Table 5.1.) There the goal of the Republican majority became to increase the number of seats outside the city, so as to diminish its dependence upon city districts that might be lost if incumbents retired or died.

The "nonretrogression rule" for minority representation, set out by the Supreme Court in *Beer* v. *New Orleans*,[82] required no decline in the number of minority-dominated districts. This protected black and Hispanic members, and thus guaranteed their proportional increase in strength in the city delegation in Albany as its total size shrank. Previously, Republican domination of the Assembly allowed them to exploit divisions among city Democrats; now other constituencies were protected. The remaining seven city Republicans became the prime targets.

Some effort was made by Senate Republicans to protect their colleagues in the other house. Majority Leader Anderson broke off negotiations in the 1981 special session. Senate Republicans charged Democrats in the Assembly with trying to lock up 104 of the 150 seats (they then held 86), including 59 of 60 in New York City. This, said Jay P. Rolison, the lead senator on reapportionment, would "destroy any vestige of the Republican party in the Assembly." "I go into this with the idea of extracting fair representation for minorities," Donald Zimmerman added, "and in New York City one of those minorities is Republicans."[83]

Democrats denied these assertions. At least four city seats in the Assembly, they said, would be winnable by Republicans. As for the 104 seat target, Assemblyman Miller responded: "I'll go before a grand jury and testify under oath we don't have 104 seats."[84]

Seeking delay until the 1982 election, with a remote hope for a reversal of control in the Assembly, Republicans repaired to the State constitution, as insurgent Democrats had in the past. They said that, in violation of its provisions, Democratic reapportionment proposals too frequently failed to honor county and town lines. They also argued that, unlike congressional district lines, which had to be adjusted for the 1982 election, State legislative district boundaries need not be changed until mid-decade. But, after almost two decades of federal reapportionment decisions and voting rights legislation, it was unclear which State constitutional provisions still had force and effect, and these arguments failed.

Again, a lawsuit, this one brought by the Black and Puerto Rican Caucus under the Voting Rights Act and joined by the speaker, brought a federal court-imposed deadline, which the legislature again failed to meet. The court then appointed a special master, and the threat of his drawing a reapportionment plan that ignored incumbency produced movement. The reapportionment bill, which was said to assure 36 or 37 Republican seats in the Senate, passed on a straight party vote there. But, having protected themselves, the Senate majority could do little for their Assembly copartisans. In the Assembly vote, eight Republicans from Nassau County provided the margin of comfort for Democratic leaders, an insurance policy against the votes of disaffected Democratic members put at risk by district changes. These were delivered by the Nassau County Republican leader, who, like Democratic organization leaders in New York City in earlier years, was consulted on the lines in his county.

The symmetry in the switch in circumstances and roles from 1971 was complete.

Black leaders who were dissatisfied with state legislative and congressional district lines filed another lawsuit. The Department of Justice found several districts in Brooklyn, the Bronx, and Manhattan biased, either because of excessive concentration or dilution of minority strength. In response, Governor Carey promptly signed legislation delaying the State's primary elections and allowing the legislature time to react.

The black and Puerto Rican coalition was again strained by the divergence of ethnic interests, especially in Brooklyn, where the final reapportionment plan eliminated an Hispanic congressional seat. The leader of the legislature's Black and Puerto Rican Caucus continued to press for more 80 percent minority districts to assure the election of minority representatives. The federal deputy attorney general rejected this view, as he did Puerto Rican claims for special, separate consideration of their interests. Both, he said, were outside the intent of the Voting Rights Act.[85]

The final redistricting plan passed the legislature on July 3, 1981. There was a gain of two black members in the Assembly the next year, both outside New York City. Hispanic representation in that body actually declined. Nevertheless, there was an increase in the black and Puerto Rican proportion of the city delegation to 28 percent as a consequence of the overall loss of five seats. White Democratic incumbents again prevailed, as predicted by black leaders, in three quarters of the 65 percent minority districts.

It was now Republicans who were an endangered species in the New York City Assembly delegation; in 1982 one was elected; in 1984 three, and in 1986 two. In contrast, six Republican senators were returned from the city in those years. Senate minority representation remained the same, with a seat lost in Brooklyn balanced by one gained in Queens.

More important were the overall results. In the Senate, there was no change; the Republicans held on to a majority with a continued dependence on city seats. The real change was in the Assembly. The Democratic majority that was gained in the post-Watergate year and held relatively narrowly until 1980 was institutionalized. Although this majority depended upon seats from outside the city (one third of them), it produced leadership from the city in the powerful speaker's chair and in the chairs of two thirds of the Assembly committees. In contrast, during 1974, the last year in which the Republicans controlled the Assembly, the speakership and 19 of 22 committee chairs were held by members from outside New York City. In New York State's highly disciplined legislative system, this was a change of major consequence.

CONCLUSION

The political tensions between the two New Yorks are historic, continuing, and inevitable. They are based on real differences in the people, the economies, and the political cultures of New York inside and New York outside "the city." These contrasts lead to differences in constituency and interest to which political leaders respond. And they are based, too, upon the clash of ambitions that lead political leaders to emphasize upstate and downstate differences, and in doing so, to exacerbate them. No matter how personally friendly they may be, no matter how united under one partisan banner, the governor of the State and the mayor of the City will clash.

Law, both constitutional and statutory, has been one instrument employed by the State first to capture and then to perpetuate control of the City. This is evident in the history of both home rule and legislative apportionment. Although the City gained home rule in form over its many years of struggle for it, it never gained home rule in fact. The 1894 legislative apportionment provisions are the best example of the use of law to subordinate New York City in the State. In both home rule and reapportionment policies, the role of the State's high court, the Court of Appeals, as a guardian of State sovereignty against City incursions cannot be overstated. Strict interpretation or broad, the court read New York's constitution so as to assure State dominance.

The reapportionment revolution swept the nation too late to give New York City numerical dominance of the State legislature; by the early 1960s the city's proportion of the state population was already in decline. But the movement of city people to the suburbs and upstate ultimately made elections there more competitive, and in 1974, the post-Watergate year, Democrats were able to capture the governorship for the first time in almost a generation and to gain lasting control of the Assembly. Thus, the city, though it contained fewer voters and fewer legislative seats, actually gained in political influence. It remained the keystone of any Democratic strategy for continued control of the State, the recruiting ground for Democratic gubernatorial candidates, and the home town of Democratic Assembly speakers. The city was smaller, but it remained a Democratic monolith in an increasingly Democratic state.

Although reapportionment failed to increase the size of the city's Albany delegation, the Voting Rights Act substantially altered the composition of that delegation. Change was slow, but by the mid-1980s minority members constituted more than a quarter of New York City's State legislators and more than a fifth of the Democrats in the Assembly. Federal intervention altered the rules of the game in district making in Albany and further opened opportunities for advancement for black and

Hispanic New York City politicians. In addition, minority members, most of them from the city, are now numerous enough to block action in the Assembly Democratic Conference; there they have an opportunity for the exercise of statewide power.

The State dominates the City. This is evident in the influence of public authorities in a range of crucial policy areas as well as in the demise of home rule. These agencies operate outside the control of elected City officials and are responsive to the priorities of the governor who appoints their boards. The new institutions that grew from the fiscal crisis, the MAC and the EFCB, dramatized the State's dominance, and perhaps incrementally advanced it, but the trend was already evident. The commitment of State resources to address the urban ills of the 1960s was inexorably followed by the greater assertion of State power.

But more and more, New York City politicians dominate the State. Two of the three most important State leaders—the governor and the Assembly speaker—are now from the city, and this has been the case for almost a decade and a half. Moreover, in the State Senate, the margin of Republican control is provided by members from New York City. As a consequence, the city's fate will be determined largely by leaders it has produced; but, ironically, those leaders will be at work in the State capitol, not in City Hall. Ed Koch was right; the power has shifted to Albany.

NOTES

1. Edward I. Koch, *Mayor: An Autobiography* (New York: Simon & Schuster, 1984), p. 333.
2. Mario M. Cuomo, *Diaries of Mario M. Cuomo: The Campaign for Governor* (New York: Random House, 1984), p. 195.
3. W. Bernard Richland, "Constitutional City Home Rule in New York," *Columbia Law Review* 54 (March 1954): 311–337.
4. Paul A. Smith, "New York," in Alan Rosenthal and Maureen Moakley, eds., *The Political Life of the American States* (New York: Praeger, 1984), p. 249.
5. David M. Ellis, *New York: State and City* (Ithaca: Cornell University Press, 1979), p. 181.
6. Lynton K. Caldwell, *The Government and Administration of New York* (New York: Crowell, 1954), pp. 10–11.
7. Quoted in Andy Logan, "Lawyers, Guns and Money," *New Yorker*, April 28, 1986, p. 100.
8. Ellis, *New York*, pp. 192 and 197.
9. Arthur Browne, Don Collins, and Michael Goodwin, *I, Koch* (New York: Dodd, Mead, 1985), p. 254.
10. Theodore Lowi, "Why Mayors Go Nowhere," *Washington Monthly*, January 1972, p. 59.

11. *New York Times*, May 19, 1986, p. A20.
12. Kenneth S. Davis, *FDR: The New York Years, 1928–1933* (New York: Random House, 1985), pp. 353–355.
13. Wallace Sayre and Herbert Kaufman, *Governing New York City* (New York: Russell Sage Foundation, 1960), pp. 579–581.
14. Lowi, "Why Mayors Go Nowhere," p. 55.
15. Browne et al., *I, Koch*, p. 263; and Cuomo, *Diaries*, p. 216.
16. *New York Times*, September 5, 1983, p. 18.
17. Quoted in Robert Connery and Gerald Benjamin, *Rockefeller of New York* (Ithaca: Cornell University Press, 1979), p. 256.
18. Koch, *Mayor*, p. 110.
19. Sayre and Kaufman, *Governing New York City*, pp. 586–587.
20. Wagner quotation from Alan G. Hevesi, *Legislative Politics in New York State* (New York: Praeger, 1975), p. 197; and Ken Auletta, *The Streets Were Paved with Gold* (New York: Random House, 1979), p. 56. On the Rockefeller-Wagner relationship, see also Martin Shefter, *Political Crisis/ Fiscal Crisis* (New York: Basic Books, 1985), pp. 75–76.
21. *New York Times*, August 1, 1985, p. B3.
22. Wallace Sayre, "The Mayor," in Lyle Fitch and Annmarie Hauck Walsh, eds., *Agenda for a City: Issues Confronting New York* (Beverly Hills: Sage, 1970), p. 586.
23. Jon C. Teaford, *The Municipal Revolution in America* (Chicago: University of Chicago Press, 1975), p. 4.
24. See Henrick Hartog, "Because All the World Was Not New York City: Governance, Property Rights and the State in the Changing Definition of a Corporation, 1730–1860," *Buffalo Law Review* 28 (Winter 1979): 91–109; and Joan C. Williams, "The Invention of the Municipal Corporation: A Case Study in Legal Change," *American University Law Review* 34 (Winter 1985): 369–438. Quotation is cited in Williams on p. 395.
25. Teaford, *Municipal Revolution*, pp. 47–48.
26. Hartog, "Because All the World," p. 108.
27. David C. Hammack, *Power and Society: Greater New York at the Turn of the Century* (New York: Russell Sage Foundation, 1982), p. 130; James C. Mohr, *The Radical Republicans and Reform in New York During Reconstruction* (Ithaca: Cornell University Press, 1973), p. 43.
28. James F. Richardson, *The New York Police* (New York: Oxford University Press, 1970), pp. 107–108.
29. Richard L. McCormack, *From Realignment to Reform: Political Change in New York State, 1893–1910* (Ithaca: Cornell University Press, 1981), p. 171.
30. See the formulation in *Trenton v. New Jersey*, 262 U.S. 182, at 187 (1923).
31. Wallace Sayre, "New York City and the State," in Sigmund Diamond, ed., *Modernizing State Government* (New York: Academy of Political Science, 1967), pp. 314–321.
32. Tilden is cited in Richland, "Constitutional City Home Rule," p. 319, fn. 27; Lucius Robinson, "Veto Message of May 18, 1877," in Charles Z. Lincoln, ed., *Messages from the Governors*, vol. 7 (Albany: J. B. Lyon, 1909), p. 101.
33. For a summary through the late 1950s, see Sayre and Kaufman, *Governing New York City*, p. 585.

34. Richland, "Constitutional City Home Rule," p. 326.
35. Judge Crane, cited in Richland, "Constitutional City Home Rule," p. 333.
36. *Adler v. Deegan,* 251 N.Y.S. 467 (1929); and J. D. Hyman, "Home Rule in New York, 1941–1965: Retrospect and Prospect," *Buffalo Law Review* 15 (1965): 335–369, at p. 343.
37. Belle Zeller, *Pressure Politics in New York* (Englewood Cliffs, NJ: Prentice-Hall, 1937), p. 6, fn. 15.
38. Donna Shalala, *The City and the Constitution* (New York: National Municipal League, 1972), p. 47.
39. Auletta, *Streets Were Paved with Gold,* p. 64.
40. Connery and Benjamin, *Rockefeller,* p. 245.
41. For a good overview of authorities and their functioning, see Annmarie Hauck Walsh, *The Public's Business* (Cambridge: MIT Press, 1978). The brief definition used here is drawn from Walsh's essay with James Leigland, "The Only Planning Game in Town," *Empire State Report,* May 1983, pp. 6–12.
42. Koch, *Mayor,* pp. 169 and 175.
43. *New York Times,* November 19, 1983, p. 29. The Port Authority Project is discussed in Norman Fainstein and Susan Fainstein, "Economic Restructuring and the Politics of Land Use Planning in New York City" (unpublished paper, April, 1986).
44. *New York Times,* March 9, 1984, p. B4.
45. *New York Times,* March 10, 1984, p. 25. For a detailed treatment of issues surrounding the redevelopment of the 42nd Street area, see Susan Fainstein, ed., "The Redevelopment of 42nd Street," a special issue of the *City Almanac* 8, no. 4 (Summer 1985).
46. See Robert W. Bailey, *The Crisis Regime* (Albany: SUNY Press, 1984), pp. 29, 36, and 39.
47. *New York Times,* December 3, 1983, p. 25; November 24, 1983, p. 1. See also Felix G. Rohatyn, "New York City's Economy and the Municipal Assistance Corporation," in *Gallatin Review* 5, no. 1 (Winter, 1985–1986): 13–19.
48. *New York Times,* December 15, 1985, p. 1.
49. *New York Times,* February 20, 1986, p. A22.
50. Bailey, pp. 16–17.
51. Hugh Carey, "The Governor," in Gerald Benjamin and T. Norman Hurd, eds., *Making Experience Count* (Albany: Rockefeller Institute, 1985), pp. 1–26.
52. Sayre, "The Mayor," pp. 586–587.
53. Koch, *Mayor,* p. 328.
54. Interview with Jim Brenner, director of New York City's Legislative Office, July 9, 1986.
55. Hevesi, *Legislative Politics,* p. 169. See Fred H. Goldner, "The Daily Apple: Medicine and the Media," in Vernon Boggs, Gerald Handel, and Sylvia F. Fava, eds., *The Apple Sliced* (South Hadley, MA: Bergin and Garvey, 1984), pp. 214–233, for an example of a State legislative position being used to pursue political goals in the city.
56. Hevesi, *Legislative Politics,* p. 196.
57. *New York Times,* February 1, 1983, p. B4.
58. *New York Times,* April 3, 1984, p. B1.
59. *New York Times,* April 3, 1984, p. B1.

60. *New York Times*, January 31, 1986, p. B2.
61. *New York Times*, August 2, 1984, p. 22.
62. *New York Times*, August 1, 1986, p. B2.
63. Koch, *Mayor*, p. 331; Browne et al., *I, Koch*, p. 264.
64. New York State Constitutional Convention Committee, *New York City Government Functions and Problems*, vol. 5 (Albany: J. B. Lyon, 1938), pp. 47–49; Richard Lehne, *Legislating Reapportionment in New York* (New York: National Municipal League, 1971), p. 3; and Leonard Ruchelman, *Political Careers: Recruitment Through The Legislature* (Rutherford, NJ: Fairleigh Dickinson University Press, 1970), pp. 35–38.
65. See *Matter of Sherrill* v. *O'Brien*, 188 N.Y. 185 (1906); *Matter of Dowling*, 219 N.Y. 44 (1916); and *Matter of Reynolds*, 202 N.Y. 430 (1911).
66. 377 U.S. 633 (1964). For the story of this case, see Calvin B. T. Lee, *One Man, One Vote: WMCA and the Struggle for Equal Representation* (New York: Scribner, 1967).
67. Lehne, *Legislating Reapportionment*, p. 12.
68. See the chronology in David Schultz and Richard Lehne, "New York," in Leroy Hardy, Alan Heslop, and Stuart Anderson, eds., *Reapportionment Politics* (Beverly Hills: Sage, 1981), pp. 234–235.
69. Lehne, *Legislating Reapportionment*, p. 12.
70. Lehne, *Legislating Reapportionment*, pp. 15–17; Hevesi, *Legislative Politics*, p. 151. For the perspective of a member of this commission, see Harvey L. Mansfield, "Modernizing the State Legislature," in Sigmund Diamond, ed., *Modernizing State Government* (New York: Academy of Political Science, 1967), pp. 42ff.
71. Howard Scarrow, *Parties, Elections and Representation in the State of New York* (New York: New York University Press, 1983), p. 101.
72. Hevesi, *Legislative Politics*, p. 146.
73. *New York Times*, April 7, 1974, sect. 4, p. 6.
74. David Wells, "The Reapportionment Game," in *Empire State Report*, February 1979, p. 8.
75. See Schultz and Lehne, "New York," p. 238.
76. *New York Times*, April 2, 1974, p. 1.
77. Roman Hedges and Jeffrey L. Getis, *A Standard for Constructing Minority Legislative Districts: The Issue of Effective Voting Equality*, Working Paper no. 6 (Albany: Rockefeller Institute, 1983), pp. 16–17.
78. *New York Times*, January 13, 1974, sect. 4, p. 4.
79. 430 U.S. 144 (1977); Calvin B. Almquist, "United Jewish Organizations v. Carey," *Southwest Law Journal* 31 (Winter 1977): 1143–1149.
80. *New York Times*, May 9, 1982, p. B3.
81. Scarrow, *Parties*, p. 108.
82. 425 U.S. 130 (1976).
83. *New York Times*, February 10, 1982, p. B2.
84. *New York Times*, December 13, 1981, p. 46.
85. *New York Times*, June 25, 1982, pp. 1 and D3.

6

THE ELECTORAL FRAMEWORK

❧

Martin Shefter

A STORY, which might be titled "A Tale of Two States," is commonly told, and it runs like this: Although legally New York is a single state, socially and politically there are two New Yorks. New York City is heavily ethnic, increasingly nonwhite, and quintessentially urban; upstate New York has a population and a way of life that is less cosmopolitan. Since the colonial period, residents of the two New Yorks have viewed one another with considerable hostility, and the state's major political parties have reflected these antipathies. For over a century the Democrats have been the dominant party in New York City, and the Republicans have prevailed upstate because they have represented the interests of that region in the electoral arena.[1]

Like many good stories, this one embodies much truth but simplifies for dramatic force. It fails to note that patterns of partisan dominance within the state are shaped not only by regional loyalties and antipathies, but also by national political developments, the strategies of party leaders, and the laws that structure electoral competition. In addition, downstate and upstate New York are not as politically homogeneous as this tale implies, and each party seeks votes in the territory of the opposition as well as in its own bastion. Finally, this story does not explain changing electoral patterns in New York—in particular, the Democratic resurgence since the mid 1970s.

This essay analyzes the electoral framework of city-state relations in New York with these qualifications in mind. The first section describes electoral patterns in the state in recent decades. The next four sections analyze how national political tides, intraregional cleavages, the strategies of political elites, and election laws have shaped electoral outcomes during the three decades following World War II. The sixth section analyzes the character and sources of the Democratic resurgence in state politics in the 1970s, and the concluding section considers the prospects that the recent decline in partisan cleavages between the city and the rest of the state will endure.

PATTERNS OF PARTY COMPETITION IN NEW YORK

Political scientists generally date the modern era of American party politics from Franklin Roosevelt's election to the presidency in 1932. Since then, the Democratic and Republican parties have been fairly evenly balanced in New York State, and statewide elections have generally been quite competitive. As Table 6.1. indicates, elections for different offices have had sharply different outcomes.

Presidential elections are closely contested in New York State. Dwight Eisenhower in 1956 and Lyndon Johnson in 1964 were the only candidates in the modern era to carry the state with more than 60 percent of the vote. With the exception of the four successive victories of Franklin Roosevelt, alternation between the parties has been frequent.

Elections for governor are also closely contested. Mario Cuomo's 1986 victory was the only 60 percent landslide in the modern era. Nonetheless, the Republicans dominated the Executive Mansion between 1942 and 1974, winning seven of the eight gubernatorial elections in that period. The Democrats have won all four elections for governor since 1974.

Historically, the Republican (GOP) grip on the State legislature has been firmer than on the governorship. Between 1932 and 1974 the Republicans controlled the State Assembly for all but five years (1935 and 1965–1968), and it controlled the State Senate for all but seven years (1933–1938 and 1965). In 1974 the GOP lost its majority in the Assembly, but it has continued in control of the Senate.

During the decades following World War II, the GOP's dominance of State offices in New York was as strong or stronger than its position in any of the other urbanized states. On an index of state party competition based upon the percentages of the gubernatorial vote and of seats in the state legislature won by the major parties, New York ranked among the most Republican of the two-party states in the postwar era. Compared

TABLE 6.1

*Party Winning Elections in New York
for Major National, State, and Local Offices, 1932–1986*

	President	Governor	State Senate	State Assembly	New York City Mayor
1932	Dem	Dem	Dem	Rep	Dem
1933				Rep	Rep/Fus
1934		Dem	Dem	Dem	
1936	Dem	Dem	Dem	Rep	
1937				Rep	Rep/ALP
1938		Dem	Rep	Rep	
1940	Dem		Rep	Rep	
1941					Rep/ALP
1942		Rep	Rep	Rep	
1944	Dem		Rep	Rep	
1945					Dem
1946		Rep	Rep	Rep	
1948	Rep		Rep	Rep	
1949					Dem
1950		Rep	Rep	Rep	Dem
1952	Rep		Rep	Rep	
1953					Dem
1954		Dem	Rep	Rep	
1956	Rep		Rep	Rep	
1957					Dem
1958		Rep	Rep	Rep	
1960	Dem		Rep	Rep	
1961					Dem
1962		Rep	Rep	Rep	
1964	Dem		Dem	Dem	
1965			Rep	Dem	Rep/Lib
1966		Rep	Rep	Dem	
1968	Dem		Rep	Rep	
1969					Lib
1970		Rep	Rep	Rep	
1972	Rep		Rep	Rep	
1973					Dem
1974		Dem	Rep	Dem	
1976	Dem		Rep	Dem	
1977					Dem
1978		Dem	Rep	Dem	
1980	Rep		Rep	Dem	
1981					Dem
1982		Dem	Rep	Dem	
1984	Rep		Rep	Dem	
1985					Dem
1986		Dem	Rep	Dem	

SOURCE: Compiled by the author from *New York Legislative Manual* (Albany: New York State Legislature, various years).

NOTE: Dem = Democratic party; Fus = fusion coalition; ALP = American Labor party; Rep = Republican party; Lib = Liberal party.

with the states with large cities identified in James Musselwhite's essay in this volume, New York was more Republican than any state but Wisconsin during the years 1946–1963.[2]

In New York City, by contrast, the Democrats have long been the dominant party. Democrats controlled the Board of Estimate, the City's highest governing body, for 42 of the 54 years between 1932 and 1986 and occupied the mayoralty for 36 of these years. Interestingly, the only victories by Republican mayoral candidates during this period—in 1933, 1937, 1941, and 1965—occurred during interludes in which the GOP's monopoly on State government was broken.

These patterns of party dominance and competition are consistent with the image of an electorate divided along regional lines into two mutually antagonistic camps. The GOP's greater strength in state than federal elections during long stretches of recent history might be taken to indicate that some New Yorkers who were prepared to vote for the Democrats in Washington were wary of turning the government in Albany over to a party so strongly identified with New York City. The tendency to vote Republican in gubernatorial and State legislative elections might have been greater in New York than in other urbanized states because New York City accounts for a larger proportion of its state's population than any other major city in the nation and hence poses a greater threat of dominating its state.

Although tensions between New York City and the remainder of the state contributed to these patterns of party competition and dominance, other factors were important. National political tides, intraregional cleavages, the strategies of political elites, and the laws that structure electoral competition have also shaped electoral outcomes in New York State.

PARTY ENROLLMENTS
AND NATIONAL POLITICAL TIDES

The best predictor of an individual's voting behavior is his or her party identification: not surprisingly, persons who identify with the Democrats are most likely to vote for that party's candidates; those who regard themselves as Republicans more often than not support GOP candidates; and independents fall in between. Survey data on the party identification of New York voters over time are not available, however, so the closest one can come to this measure is data on party enrollments. Table 6.2 reports the Republican share of major party enrollments in New York

TABLE 6.2

Republican Share of Major Party Enrollments, 1930–1982

	New York City	Outside New York City	New York State
1930	26.6%	70.2%	50.1%
1934	17.7	61.1	40.3
1938	19.2	66.7	44.1
1942	22.1	69.3	47.0
1946	31.5	72.7	52.0
1950	23.7	69.1	46.8
1954	23.2	69.3	48.6
1958	24.7	67.6	49.5
1962	25.9	64.4	46.8
1966	22.2	60.7	43.4
1970	22.6	61.1	45.3
1974	20.7	59.0	43.7
1978	17.1	56.1	41.6
1982	16.5	56.3	42.3

SOURCE: Compiled by the author from *New York Legislative Manual* (Albany: New York State Legislature, various years).

City, outside New York City, and in the state as a whole between 1930 and 1982.

The Democrats have enjoyed overwhelming dominance in New York City throughout the past half-century, and the GOP has been the stronger of the two major parties elsewhere in the state. Since the New Deal, the GOP has generally enrolled fewer voters than the Democrats statewide. Consequently, Republican candidates have had to win considerable support from independent, Democratic, or minor party voters to prevail in statewide elections. Although GOP candidates have been able to accomplish this feat, the smaller the deficit they have had to overcome, the easier has been their task. The period of Republican hegemony in gubernatorial elections—1942 to 1970—coincided with the years in which the GOP share of statewide two-party enrollments exceeded 45 percent.

The strength of the major parties in New York State has been heavily influenced, in turn, by developments in the national political arena. The sharp decline in the Republican share of enrollments between 1930 and 1934 is explained by the advent of the New Deal and the associated realignment of the national party system. The resurgence of the GOP in New York in the late 1930s and early 1940s was part of a general trend in northern states that coincided with the coming to power within the national party of such liberal Republican leaders as Wendell Willkie, Earl Warren, and New York's Thomas Dewey.[3]

National political developments also played a role in the subsequent decline of the GOP. GOP enrollments began declining in 1958 in Republican strongholds upstate, as in traditionally Republican areas elsewhere in the nation; after 1964, when Barry Goldwater's nomination signaled that power within the national GOP was shifting toward the South and West, GOP enrollments began to fall in New York City as well. The Republican vote in congressional elections in the state also fell after 1964, which further suggests voter alienation from the national party.[4]

In the mid 1950s, the State began reporting the number of voters who chose not to enroll in any party. Table 6.3 shows for the state as a whole the percentage of registered voters enrolling as Republicans and Democrats, and the percentage filing blank enrollment forms between 1958 and 1984. The failure of the Democrats to gain enrollees as the GOP declined suggests that voters were being repelled by the Republicans, rather than being attracted to the Democrats. Only the nonparty category has experienced gains in recent years.

TABLE 6.3
Republican, Democratic, and Nonparty Enrollments, New York State, 1958–1984
(percentage distribution)

	Republican	Democratic	Nonparty
1958	45.0%	46.0%	7.8%
1960	43.7	47.2	7.7
1962	42.5	48.3	7.9
1964	42.2	48.5	7.9
1966	38.9	50.9	8.5
1968	40.0	49.2	8.6
1970	39.8	47.9	9.4
1972	38.1	48.2	10.3
1974	37.5	48.3	10.8
1976	37.5	49.0	10.3
1978	34.8	48.8	13.7
1980	35.3	47.9	14.2
1982	33.9	46.3	17.2
1984	32.8	47.3	17.4

SOURCE: Compiled by the author from *New York Legislative Manual* (Albany: New York State Legislature, various years).

NOTE: Rows do not sum to 100 percent because minor party enrollments are omitted.

INTRAREGIONAL CLEAVAGES

Although the Democrats have long been dominant in New York City and the Republicans stronger elsewhere in the state, "downstate" and "upstate" New York are not homogeneous politically; moreover, voters in each region have often been willing to sit out elections or to defect to the opposition. Such divisions and defections played a major role in enabling the Republicans to dominate the governorship under Dewey and Rockefeller and to gain control of Gracie Mansion under La Guardia and Lindsay.

The data in Table 6.4 provide some indication of the extent of these divisions and defections. In this table, upstate New York is partitioned into urban, suburban, and rural areas, and downstate is partitioned into urban and suburban areas (that is, New York City and its suburbs).[5] The table shows three measures of party strength in these regions at the midpoint of the era of GOP dominance in state elections—the Republican percentage of party enrollments in 1962, of the presidential vote in 1960, and of the gubernatorial vote in 1962.

On every measure of party strength, the GOP clearly was weaker— and, correlatively, the Democrats were stronger—in New York City than in any other region of the state. However, in upstate cities the Democrats did almost as well in the 1960 presidential election and 1962 gubernatorial election as in New York City, and they won a considerably larger share of the vote in these cities than in the remaining regions of the state. Even in the state's three most heavily Republican areas—the downstate suburbs, upstate suburbs, and rural counties—there was a measure of political heterogeneity. Measured by party enrollments, the

TABLE 6.4
Republican Strength in Five Regions of
New York State, 1960–1962
(Republican Percentage of Total)

	Party Enrollment 1962	Presidential Vote 1960	Gubernatorial Vote 1962
New York City	23.7%	37.2%	45.7%
Upstate Cities	48.4	40.8	47.8
Downstate Suburbs	58.2	56.9	66.5
Upstate Suburbs	64.4	58.1	61.9
Rural Counties	61.1	61.1	65.3

SOURCE: Compiled by the author from *New York Legislative Manual* (Albany: New York State Legislature, various years).

GOP was strongest in the upstate suburbs; in presidential elections the Republicans were strongest in the rural counties; and in gubernatorial voting the party was strongest in the downstate suburbs. Finally, it is noteworthy that in every region of the state the Republicans won a larger share of the vote in the gubernatorial than presidential elections, but their gains were particularly great in New York City, the upstate cities, and the downstate suburbs.

The Republicans were able to dominate gubernatorial elections from the early 1940s through the early 1970s because they were more successful than the Democrats in holding on to their core supporters and winning votes in the other party's strongholds. The success of the GOP in this regard was a consequence, in part, of the candidates it nominated: the victorious Republican candidates during this period, Thomas Dewey and Nelson Rockefeller, were identified with downstate and had a strong appeal to voters in New York City and its suburbs. Each candidate also profited in his first successful campaign from deep cleavages within the opposition camp between New Deal liberals and organization Democrats.[6]

Finally, as Table 6.5 indicates, the decline of electoral turnout between presidential and gubernatorial elections cost the Democrats considerably more votes in their urban strongholds—especially New York City—than it did the Republicans in their areas of greatest strength. The Democrats amassed only two thirds as many votes statewide in the gubernatorial election of 1962 as in the presidential election two years earlier. These losses can be explained largely, as Gerald Benjamin has noted, by the social composition of the party's electoral base.[7] In off-year elections, even more than in presidential races, turnout rates are considerably lower among working-class than middle-income voters. The dependence of the Democrats upon blue collar, urban voters thus made them vulnerable to this decline in participation.

The Republicans, on the other hand, held on to a much larger proportion of their vote in off-year elections—and nowhere more so than in New York City. Consequently, in the areas of greatest Democratic strength, the Democrat's margin of victory over the GOP declined sharply between the presidential election of 1960 and the gubernatorial election of 1962. By contrast, in the areas of greatest GOP strength, the Republican victory margins were as large or even larger than they had been two years earlier. Taken together, these shifts turned a GOP deficit of 383,666 votes in the 1960 presidential election to a surplus of 529,169 in the gubernatorial election of 1962.

Table 6.6 shows that GOP support in New York City was crucial to its success in gubernatorial elections during the postwar period. The first column of this table reports the GOP vote in each region as a percentage

TABLE 6.5

Vote for President and Governor in Five Regions of New York State, 1960 and 1962
(in thousands)

	President, 1960			Governor, 1962		
	Democratic Liberal	Republican	Republican Margin	Democratic Liberal	Republican	Republican Margin
New York City	1,936	1,145	−791	1,280	1,078	−202
Upstate Cities	522	360	−161	352	321	− 31
Downstate Suburbs	529	699	170	333	660	327
Upstate Suburbs	438	605	167	315	511	195
Rural Counties	405	636	231	272	512	230
Total State	3,830	3,446	−387	2,552	3,082	529

SOURCE: Compiled by the author from *New York Legislative Manual* (Albany: New York State Legislature, various years).

TABLE 6.6

Republican Vote as a Percentage of Statewide Republican
and Total Vote by Region, 1962

	Percentage of Statewide GOP Vote	Percentage of Statewide Total Vote	Cumulative Percentage of Total Vote
Rural Counties	16.6%	9.1%	9.1%
Upstate Suburbs	16.6	9.1	18.2
Downstate Suburbs	21.4	11.7	29.9
Upstate Cities	10.4	5.7	35.6
New York City	35.0	19.1	54.7

SOURCE: Compiled by the author from *New York Legislative Manual* (Albany: New York State Legislature, 1964).

of the party's statewide vote. The second column reports the Republican vote in each region as a percentage of the total (Democratic, Republican, Liberal, and Conservative) vote in the state, and the third column cumulates these last percentages. The data in the first column show that the GOP received a considerably larger percentage of its statewide vote in New York City than in any other region. The data in the third column indicate that this New York City vote was vital to the party: The support the Republicans received outside New York City amounted to only 35.6 percent of the total vote in the state; without the votes it won in New York City the GOP could not have gained control of the governorship.

Divisions, defections, and abstentions within the opposition camp historically have been even more crucial to the GOP's prospects for victory in New York City municipal elections. Because the Democrats long have been the dominant party in the city, the Republicans can win citywide elections only by joining with minor parties, reformers, and dissident Democrats in a "fusion" coalition. Divisions between Tammany and New Deal Democrats enabled a coalition of Republicans and reformers to elect Fiorello La Guardia mayor in 1933. La Guardia was able to win reelection in 1937 and 1941 by forging a coalition between the GOP and the American Labor Party.

A quarter-century later, in 1965, John Lindsay was elected mayor by securing the nominations of the Republican and Liberal parties. Lindsay's bid for the mayoralty was greatly assisted by divisions between reform and regular Democrats both during and after that party's primary and by William F. Buckley's candidacy for mayor on the Conservative party line in the general election. In the presence of these divisions, Lindsay was able to win election with less than 43 percent of the total vote. In his 1969 quest for renomination, Lindsay was defeated in the

Republican primary by John Marchi, but he was able to win reelection on the Liberal line because he again faced a divided opposition. In the general election, Marchi, running as the candidate of both the Republican and Conservative parties, won 23 percent of the vote; Mario Procaccino, the Democratic candidate, won 35 percent; and Lindsay carried the election with 42 percent of the total vote.

ELITE POLITICAL STRATEGIES

The emergence of both cleavages within and alliances across New York's regions and parties is influenced by the strategies political leaders pursue. The strategic choices of political leaders in New York City are shaped, in turn, by the balance of power at other levels of government. Such choices help explain why the Republicans historically played their largest role in New York City politics when the party was weakest at other levels of government, and they often contributed to the maintenance of a partisan cleavage between Albany and New York City.

Because the Democrats are the dominant party in New York City, Republican politicians in the city have had to rely chiefly upon the resources of the State and federal governments to fuel their local organizations. When the Democrats are in power in Albany or Washington, however, such resources are not available to the city's Republicans, and then GOP leaders historically have been most willing to ally with reformers, third parties, and dissident Democrats in a fusion coalition.

This consideration accounts for the formation of the fusion coalition that elected Fiorello La Guardia mayor in 1933. The Seabury investigations of the early 1930s uncovered evidence of pervasive corruption in the city and drove Mayor Jimmy Walker to resign in September 1932. The election to fill the balance of the mayor's term coincided with the presidential and gubernatorial elections of November 1932. Because Republican leaders did not want to blur party lines and discourage voters from supporting the full GOP ticket, they had no interest in joining a fusion coalition that year and no effort was made to organize one.[8]

When the Democrats won control of both the White House and New York's governorship in the 1932 elections, however, the GOP faced the prospect of being frozen out of power at the federal, State, and local levels, and therefore Republican leaders were willing to make the concessions that fusion entails. In the 1933 municipal elections, they joined with reformers and nominated Fiorello La Guardia for mayor, despite their concerns about his record of party irregularity.[9] Continued Democratic dominance in Washington and Albany helps explain why they renominated La Guardia in 1937 and 1941, even though this meant collaborating with a party, the American Labor Party, in which radical political forces played a significant role. But after Thomas Dewey's election as governor in 1942 gave the Republicans control of the State government, GOP leaders in the city refused to nominate La Guardia for a fourth term, and the Democrats under William O'Dwyer recaptured City Hall.

Once the Democrats returned to power in New York City, Democratic mayors cooperated with Republican governors in ways that helped maintain the partisan cleavage between the State and City governments. For example, in 1946 Mayor O'Dwyer rejected advice of the City comptroller and Democratic State legislators that he seek to secure the revenues the City needed to close its budget gap by publicly pressuring the governor and State legislative leaders to turn over to the City a portion of the $570 million surplus Albany had accumulated during the war. Instead, he chose to ask for increases in municipal taxes—a request that Republican leaders in Albany were happy to grant. This enabled O'Dwyer to obtain revenues to finance the construction program that was to be the centerpiece of his reelection campaign, and it enabled Dewey to skirt an issue that could cost him votes either upstate or downstate. Similar deals were struck by Mayor Vincent Impellitteri and Governor Dewey and Mayor Robert Wagner and Governor Rockefeller, and these enabled the Democrats to cement their control over New York City and the Republicans to buttress their position in Albany.[10]

The strategic choices made by party leaders in response to political changes outside the city also played a role in the election of New York City's most recent Republican mayor, John Lindsay. In 1964, the leader of the conservative wing of the national GOP, Barry Goldwater, defeated Nelson Rockefeller, leader of the party's liberal wing, in a bitter struggle for the Republican presidential nomination. In the general election, however, Goldwater was trounced by Lyndon Johnson. In the wake of this disaster, Rockefeller and other GOP liberals sought to demonstrate that their political formula was still effective—and thereby reassert themselves in the national party—by securing the election of a liberal Republican as mayor of overwhelmingly Democratic New York City. Towards this end, they induced GOP Congressman John Lindsay, whom the Liberal party was prepared to endorse, to run for mayor, and raised millions of dollars to finance his campaign from liberal Republicans throughout the nation.[11]

THE LEGAL ENVIRONMENT

The electoral framework of city-state relations in New York has been shaped not only by the alliances political leaders have forged across party lines, but also by the efforts of those leaders to alter the laws governing the conduct of elections in ways that would work to the advantage of their party. Some of these efforts achieved their purpose and had the intended political effects; others, however, had unintended political consequences.

Legislative apportionment is the most obvious of these techniques for influencing the balance of power between the city-based Democrats and upstate Republicans. As Gerald Benjamin notes in the preceding essay, the State constitutional provisions that governed legislative apportionment between 1895 and 1965 were intended to enhance the power of upstate areas relative to the city, and these provisions worked as intended. Although each U.S. Census between 1910 and 1950 indicated that a majority of the state's population lived in New York City, the city's representation in the Assembly and Senate during these decades fluctuated between 43 and 45 percent. At the same time, because of the congruence of geography and partisanship in New York State, legislative malapportionment advantaged the Republicans relative to the Democrats. Between 1952 and 1962, for example, Republican representation in the Assembly and Senate was from 6.9 to 11.5 percent greater than the popular vote received by GOP candidates.[12]

The political influence of New York City was also diluted for a long time by State laws governing voter registration. In 1866 the State legislature enacted a law requiring voters in New York City and Brooklyn to assume the burden of registering in person each year as a condition of retaining their eligibility to vote. At the turn of the century, this requirement was extended to all cities and to villages with a population exceeding 5,000, but it was not imposed on smaller villages or unincorporated areas. Differential registration requirements almost certainly served to depress voter turnout in New York City and other cities relative to more rural areas in the state.[13] In the mid 1950s, New York City was authorized to adopt a system of permanent personal registration, which permitted voters to retain their eligibility so long as they voted at least once every two years, and in the mid 1970s voters were permitted to register by mail. This easing of registration requirements, however, coincided with other developments that tended to depress electoral turnout—in particular, the decline of voter attachments to the party system—and hence it did not lead to increased voter participation rates.[14]

The separation of State and federal elections has also diminished the influence of predominantly Democratic voters in New York City, as the discussion of Table 6.5 indicated. This consequence, however, was unintended by the political leaders most responsible for the 1937 amendment to the State constitution providing for the election of governors in nonpresidential years. Prior to that time governors had been elected for two-year terms in even-numbered years. The Democrats dominated the governorship, but not the State legislature, in the 1930s and advocated that governors be elected for four-year terms in nonpresidential years so as to strengthen that office and eliminate the opportunity for the Republicans to capture it in years when the GOP nominated the more popular presidential candidate. They failed to foresee, however, that urban party organizations would grow weaker, reducing the turnout of Democratic voters in off-year elections.

Over the years the laws structuring elections in New York City also have been altered in efforts to influence the strength of various parties and the outcome of elections within the city itself. Indeed, one reason that Republicans in the State legislature were willing to authorize the consolidation of Greater New York in 1898 was they calculated that by adding suburban areas in the outer boroughs to Manhattan, the GOP would have a better shot at capturing the municipal government of New York City. This calculation proved faulty.

Forty years later, the La Guardia administration secured the enactment of proportional representation (PR) for New York City Council elections to enable the Republican and American Labor parties to obtain greater representation on the council. Proportional representation, however, also enabled Communists to win seats on the council, and in 1947 the major parties, arguing that this was intolerable, secured the abolition of PR and a return to district representation in City Council elections.[15]

Finally, in 1970 the State legislature enacted a law requiring a run-off primary for citywide offices in New York City, when no candidate wins more than 40 percent of the vote in the first round. This law was enacted because the 1969 Democratic primary was won with less than 33 percent of the vote by a candidate, Mario Procaccino, whom blacks and white liberals believed appealed to "racial backlash" sentiment. Nonwhite politicians now argue, however, that a two-stage primary is biased against blacks and Hispanics. They calculate that a black or Hispanic could win the Democratic mayoral primary with the support of the city's racial minorities if white voters divided their support among several candidates. A run-off round, by enabling white voters to unite behind a single candidate, makes it more difficult for a black or Hispanic mayoral contender to profit from such divisions.

THE DEMOCRATIC RESURGENCE

The mid-1970s witnessed major changes in the electoral framework of State-City relations in New York. On the state level, the Democrats won control of the governorship and Assembly (but not the Senate) in 1974 and have been able to maintain control of these institutions in each subsequent election. In New York City, the Republican party has become all but moribund: in mayoral elections since the mid 1970s the GOP has not managed to win even 10 percent of the vote. Consequently, the partisan cleavage between the State and City governments that had prevailed during all but a few of the preceding 40 years has essentially disappeared. Many of the above-mentioned forces shaping electoral outcomes have contributed to these changes in state and city politics.

Party Enrollments and National Political Tides

As Table 6.7 indicates, between 1962 and 1982 the Republican share of party enrollments declined in all regions of the state, and this decline

TABLE 6.7

Party Enrollments in Five Regions, 1962 and 1982
(percentage distribution)

	1962	1982	Percentage Point Change
New York City			
Republican	23.7%	13.9%	− 9.8
Democratic	68.0	70.3	+ 2.3
Blank	6.3	13.4	+ 7.1
Upstate Cities			
Republican	48.4	29.4	−19.0
Democratic	44.0	52.2	+ 9.2
Blank	7.0	15.9	+ 8.9
Downstate Suburbs			
Republican	58.2	43.1	−15.1
Democratic	29.8	32.4	+ 2.6
Blank	11.3	21.3	+10.0
Upstate Suburbs			
Republican	64.4	51.6	−12.8
Democratic	25.9	26.0	+ 0.1
Blank	9.2	20.0	+10.8
Rural Counties			
Republican	61.1	44.3	−16.8
Democratic	29.9	35.3	+ 5.4
Blank	8.4	16.3	+ 7.9

SOURCE: Compiled by the author from *New York Legislative Manual* (Albany: New York State Legislature, various years).

NOTE: This table omits minor party enrollments, and therefore the percentages in the first two columns do not sum to 100.0.

was even greater outside than in New York City. The GOP's losses, however, were not matched by Democratic gains. With the exception of upstate cities, the independent category enjoyed the greatest percentage increases.

The drop in Republican enrollments was steepest in the mid 1960s and the mid 1970s. The first of these declines, as mentioned above, probably reflected disaffection among some former Republican adherents in New York as the influence of the party's northeastern wing came under attack in the mid 1960s, and the national GOP became increasingly associated with the interests and cultural values of the South and Southwest. The second stage of this decline can be attributed at least in part to the introduction in 1976 of mail registration forms which explicitly indicated that voters need not enroll in any party, thereby facilitating this choice. In addition, however, there are reasons to believe that the attachment of many voters to the national parties continued to weaken in the 1970s and 1980s. An indication of this is the extraordinary volatility of the Republican presidential vote in the party's former upstate strongholds. In the upstate suburbs, where this volatility is most spectacular, the vote for the Republican presidential candidate more than doubled between the Goldwater debacle of 1964 and the Nixon landslide of 1972, fell by 25 percent between 1972 and 1980, and then increased by 38 percent between 1980 and 1984.[16]

Intraregional Political Cleavages

The decline of the Republican party worked to the advantage of the Democratic candidates for State office. Its effect upon patterns of competition in gubernatorial elections varied among the state's regions, however. The trajectories of the Republican and Democratic vote for governor in the different regions suggest some sources of the political changes New York experienced in the 1970s.

In upstate rural and suburban areas, the vote for Republican gubernatorial candidates exhibited no clear trend between 1958 and 1982. (See Figures 6.1 and 6.2.) The Democratic gubernatorial vote displayed only a slight upward trend in rural counties, but in suburban areas it increased markedly, making these areas more competitive in elections for governor. What is most notable in both regions, however, is increasing electoral volatility, which suggests that party ties became weaker and the characteristics of particular candidates and the issues of the day more important. This made it possible for the Democrats in 1974 to carry the upstate suburbs and to come close to carrying the rural counties as well.

FIGURE 6.1

Rural Counties: Vote for Governor, 1958–1982

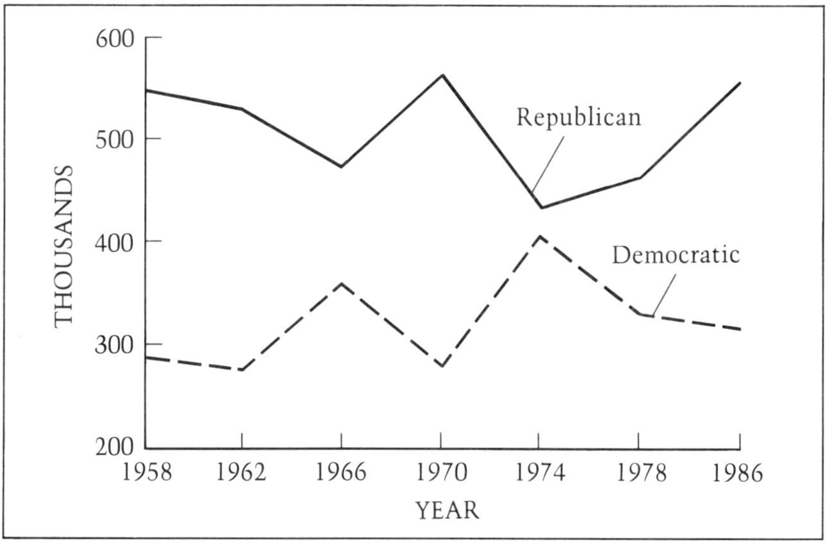

SOURCE: Compiled by the author from *New York Legislative Manual* (Albany: New York
State Legislature, various years).

In upstate cities, as Figure 6.3 indicates, the gubernatorial vote has
been less volatile. Rather, there has been a reasonably steady, though
slow, erosion of the vote for Democratic candidates and a more rapid
decline in the Republican vote. As a result of these trends, upstate cities,
which formerly were the site of close competition in gubernatorial
elections, have been reliably Democratic since the mid 1970s.

It is likely that migration played a role in this development: As the
(raw) Democratic vote declined in upstate cities, it increased in the
upstate suburbs. However, the decline of the Democratic vote in these
cities has not been as large as the party's gains in the surrounding
suburbs, and the drop in the upstate Republican urban vote has not been
matched by GOP gains in those suburbs. This suggests that there has
been a net movement of voters from the Republican to Democratic camps
in upstate cities. Because this secular trend toward the Democrats
coincided with the secular decline of industry in upstate cities, one can
speculate that it is related to the change in the national party system
mentioned above—the increasing identification of the national Democratic party with the problems of the industrial Northeast and of the
national GOP with the sunbelt.

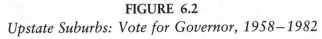

FIGURE 6.2
Upstate Suburbs: Vote for Governor, 1958–1982

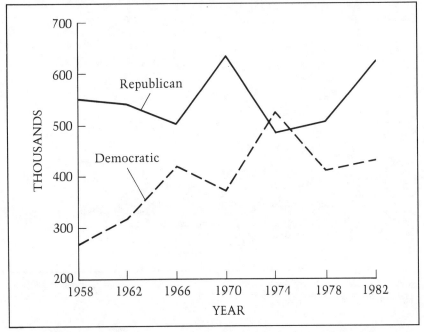

SOURCE: Compiled by the author from *New York Legislative Manual* (Albany: New York State Legislature, various years).

The 1974 election was more of a turning point downstate than it was in any region upstate. In New York City the Democratic gubernatorial vote declined only modestly during the 24-year period depicted in Figure 6.4, but the Republican vote plunged by roughly half between the elections of 1970 and 1974. This transformed the Republicans from narrow losers to the position of a hopeless minority. In the downstate suburbs, as Figure 6.5 indicates, the Republicans won almost twice as many votes as the Democrats in the four gubernatorial elections between 1958 and 1970, but the GOP vote dropped by roughly 25 percent in 1974 and gubernatorial elections subsequently became highly competitive in these counties.

In New York City and its suburbs 1974 was a turning point in state but not national elections, and hence one must look to developments on the state level to explain its significance. The most obvious of these, of course, is that Nelson Rockefeller was the Republican gubernatorial candidate in the elections of 1958 through 1970, whereas he left Albany prior to the election of 1974. But what was it about the four-term

FIGURE 6.3

Upstate Cities: Vote for Governor, 1958–1982

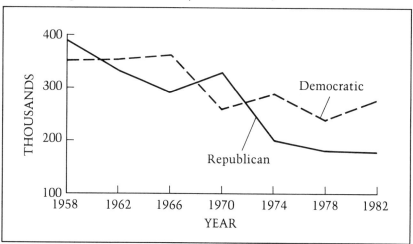

SOURCE: Compiled by the author from *New York Legislative Manual* (Albany: New York State Legislature, various years).

governor that explained his success in the downstate counties? The most common explanation is the enormous sums Rockefeller was able to spend on his campaigns, but his extraordinary appeal to normally Democratic Jewish and Catholic voters was of equal significance. When Rockefeller no longer led the Republican ticket, Hugh Carey and Mario Cuomo were able to attract many of these voters in New York City and its suburbs back to the Democratic ticket.[17]

Together these developments undermined the Republican advantage in gubernatorial elections. As Table 6.8 indicates, the Democrats owe their recent successes less to an increase in their vote than to a decline in support for the GOP: between 1962 and 1982, the statewide vote for the Democrats rose by only 123,000, while the Republican vote declined by 603,000. Most of the GOP decline was in New York City and the upstate cities, but the party also suffered losses in the downstate suburbs. At the same time, there were smaller declines in the Democratic gubernatorial vote in New York City and the upstate cities and a very large increase in the party's vote in the downstate suburbs. The net result of these trends was to increase the Democratic margin by 379,000 in New York City and by 74,000 in the upstate cities and to cut the party's deficit by 284,000 votes in the downstate suburbs. By contrast, in the upstate suburbs and rural counties the increases in the vote for the gubernatorial candidates of the two major parties between 1962 and 1982 essentially

FIGURE 6.4

New York City: Vote for Governor, 1958–1982

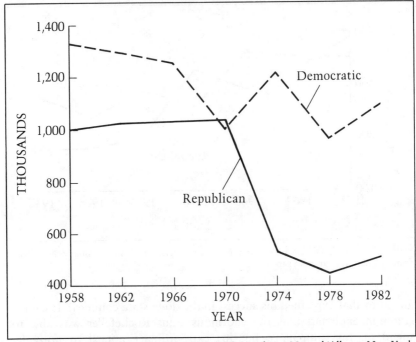

SOURCE: Compiled by the author from *New York Legislative Manual* (Albany: New York State Legislature, various years).

counter-balanced one another. (The strong vote for Lewis Lehrman in the upstate suburbs and rural counties explains why the Democrats did not achieve a net gain between 1962 and 1982 despite the underlying trend of increasing support for the party's gubernatorial candidates in these regions.)

For the purposes of this essay, the most noteworthy characteristic of the coalition the Democrats have constructed in gubernatorial elections over the past dozen years is that it cuts across divisions between downstate and upstate New York and between urban and suburban areas. This has enabled the Democrats to win control of the Executive Mansion even though New York City's weight in statewide elections has been declining. Between 1962 and 1982 New York City's share of the total statewide gubernatorial vote declined from 41.9 to 30.6 percent. As Table 6.9 indicates, the proportion of the Democratic gubernatorial vote cast in New York City fell from 50.1 percent in 1962 to 40.4 percent in 1982. The downstate suburbs increased their share of the statewide

FIGURE 6.5

Downstate Suburbs: Vote for Governor, 1958–1982

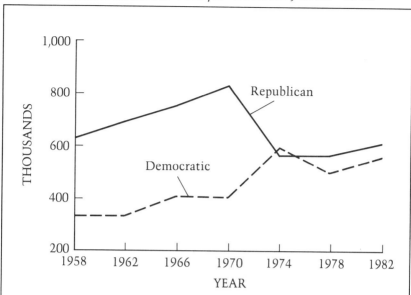

SOURCE: Compiled by the author from *New York Legislative Manual* (Albany: New York State Legislature, various years).

TABLE 6.8

Change in Vote for Gubernatorial Candidate, 1962–1982 (in thousands)

	Democratic Margin 1962	Change Democratic Vote 1962–1982	Change Republican Vote 1962–1982	Change Democratic Margin 1962–1982
New York City	+201	−200	−579	+379
Upstate Cities	+ 31	− 69	−143	+ 74
Downstate Suburbs	−327	+234	− 50	+284
Upstate Suburbs	−195	+117	+124	− 7
Rural Counties	−230	+ 41	+ 45	− 4
Total State	−520	+123	−603	+726

SOURCE: Compiled by the author from *New York Legislative Manual* (Albany: New York State Legislature, various years).

NOTE: The Liberal party vote is included in the Democratic totals in 1962 and 1982. The Conservative vote is included in the Republican total in 1982, when the two parties nominated the same candidates, but not in 1962, when they did not.

TABLE 6.9

Statewide Democratic-Liberal Votes for Governor by Region,
1962 and 1982 (percentage distribution)

	1962	1982
New York City	50.1%	40.4%
Upstate Cities	13.8	10.6
Downstate Suburbs	13.0	21.2
Upstate Suburbs	12.4	16.2
Rural Counties	10.7	11.7
Total State	100.0	100.0*

SOURCE: Compiled by the author from New York Legislative Manual (Albany: New York State Legislature, various years).

*Figures do not add to 100.0 because of rounding.

Democratic vote from 13.0 to 21.2 percent, and the upstate suburbs from 12.4 to 16.2 percent. As a result of these changes, the Democrats have become a party that is not so overwhelmingly identified with New York City.

Elections for the Assembly display a similar pattern. The Democrats gained control of the Assembly in 1974 by winning 20 new seats in districts that previously had been held by Republicans and losing only one of their seats to the GOP. Of the 20 new Democratic members, only one was from a predominantly rural county (Chautauqua). Two were from New York City. Seven were from counties near the city that were heavily suburban (Nassau and Suffolk) or increasingly becoming so (Orange and Ulster). The remaining ten were from upstate metropolitan counties: one from a city (Niagara Falls), one from a district (in Erie county) that was entirely suburban, and eight from districts (in Erie, Monroe, Onondaga, and Broome counties) that were partly urban and partly suburban. This increased the number of Democratic members of the Assembly from outside New York City from only 15 of 69 in 1973–1974 to a weightier 32 of 88 in 1975–1976. On the other hand, elections for the Senate were not marked by such dramatic changes in the mid 1970s, for reasons that are discussed in the section below.

Finally, regarding municipal elections in New York City, the Republican party essentially collapsed as a significant participant in local politics in the mid 1970s. As recently as the 1960s, the GOP had played a meaningful role in the city's politics. In 1965, Republican John Lindsay, running as a fusion candidate, won the mayoralty with 44 percent of the vote. In 1969, John Marchi's victory over Lindsay in the GOP primary gravely threatened the mayor's political career, and in the general election Marchi won 23 percent of the vote. Then the GOP's position declined precipitously. It won 16 percent of the vote in the 1973 mayoral election and a mere 4 percent in 1977. In 1981, the GOP threw in the towel and endorsed Mayor Koch, and in 1985 it won only 9 percent of the vote when it nominated a political unknown in a nominal challenge to Koch's bid for a third term.

Elite Political Strategies

The strategies pursued by political elites have contributed to the new patterns of party dominance that have prevailed on the state and municipal levels since the mid 1970s. In an effort to keep his prospects for national office alive, Nelson Rockefeller resigned from the governorship in 1973. He had little to gain by enduring yet another reelection campaign in 1974, and turning over the Executive Mansion to Lieutenant Governor Malcolm Wilson, he calculated, could give his designated successor the advantage of incumbency in that election. By chairing a commission on national goals, Rockefeller hoped to tap new sources of publicity as the nation's bicentennial approached. His resignation, however, deprived the Republicans of a candidate with a strong appeal among downstate Jewish and Catholic voters, thereby contributing to the victory of the Democrats in the gubernatorial and Assembly elections of 1974.

Control of these institutions enabled the Democrats to exploit the advantages of incumbency from which the Republicans had benefited for so many years. As indicated in Table 6.10, which reports the vote received by the candidates running for major offices in the 1986 elections, those advantages are formidable. In that election, incumbent Democratic Governor Mario Cuomo and Attorney General Robert Abrams defeated

TABLE 6.10
Vote for State Officials, 1986

	Democratic	Republican	Democratic Margin
Governor	2,681,629	1,342,125	+1,339,504
U.S. Senator	1,674,927	2,366,789	− 691,862
Attorney General	2,436,018	1,299,448	+1,136,570
Comptroller	1,546,558	2,219,452	− 672,862
State Senator	1,493,000	1,641,000	− 148,000
Assemblyman	1,826,000	1,436,000	+ 390,000

SOURCE: *New York Times,* November 6, 1986, p. B14.

NOTE: Based upon election-day tallies. Included in the Democratic and Republican columns are votes cast on minor party lines for candidates of the major parties.

their Republican challengers by margins of 1,339,504 and 1,136,570 votes, respectively. At the same time, the Democratic candidates for comptroller and U.S. senator, running against incumbents, received only 58 and 62 percent as many votes as Cuomo and were defeated by margins of almost 700,000 votes. Evidently the incumbents successfully established themselves as local institutions—much as their predecessors had done 20 years earlier.

Table 6.10 also suggests that many Republican State senators have successfully entrenched themselves. GOP candidates for the Senate won a majority of the statewide vote in 1986, while the party's gubernatorial candidate was being defeated by a landslide margin. Because State senatorial districts in New York approach the size of congressional districts, incumbents are able to establish some visibility and insulate themselves from adverse trends. (Notable examples are the five Republican State senators from New York City, who have managed to secure repeated reelection despite the near-collapse of the GOP in municipal politics.) This helps explain how the GOP retained control of the State Senate in 1974, in the face of that year's Democratic gubernatorial landslide, and have held on to a majority of seats ever since.

It is more than visibility, however, that explains the success of incumbents holding both statewide and legislative offices. Democratic and Republican officeholders have generally done little in their official capacities to undermine one another. The usually cordial relations between Governors Carey and Cuomo, on the one hand, and Comptroller Regan, on the other, is a case in point. Democrats Carey and Cuomo also cooperated frequently with the Republican majority in the State Senate, under GOP leader Warren Anderson, to the point that Democratic Senate leader Manfred Ohrenstein bitterly complained in 1986 that his party's governor was doing nothing to help the Democrats gain control of that house. Within the legislature itself, collusion across party lines by incumbents is manifested in the willingness of each chamber to approve the "member items" the other adds to the budget.

Incumbents also make strategic use of their powers within the electoral arena itself. The ability of incumbents to outspend their challengers by as much as eight-to-one in 1986 reflects the advantages they enjoy in raising campaign contributions. The party holding the governorship also has been able to avoid bitter primary fights and prevent the minor parties from intervening in its nominating processes. The Republicans under Rockefeller avoided primaries altogether and refused to deal with the Conservatives. The Democrats under Carey and Cuomo conducted a serious primary only in 1982, when Carey did not stand for reelection; in 1986, Cuomo was even able to derail a primary challenge to his candidate for lieutenant governor. And Democratic governors have used their patronage powers to establish virtual control over the Liberal party. The out-party, on the other hand, has suffered from disorganization and disunity, been subject to minor party intervention in its nominating processes, and faced the attendant problem of presenting itself as competent to govern. The Democrats labored under all of these burdens when Nelson Rockefeller was governor. After his departure, the strength of the Republican organization proved to be illusory (or at least transitory); the party leadership was unable, in 1982, to prevent a candidate possessing great personal wealth and Conservative backing from winning the GOP gubernatorial nomination; and, in 1986, the party found itself incapable of conducting a credible campaign against Governor Cuomo.

Elite political strategies have also played a role in the decline of the Republican party in New York City. After being elected mayor, Ed Koch established an entente with leading Republican politicians. In 1980 he all but endorsed Ronald Reagan for president and helped secure the Democratic nomination for a number of the city's incumbent Republican State senators. In return for this support, as well as for some mayoral patronage and assistance in raising contributions, four of the city's five Republican organizations supported Koch's nomination in the 1981 GOP mayoral primary. In 1985 the GOP nominally opposed Koch's bid for a third term, but the mayor traded endorsements with the most powerful Republican public official from the city—John Marchi, chairman of the State Senate's finance committee—and also maintained close relations with State Senator Roy Goodman, the chairman of the Republican organization in Manhattan. The party gave little more than its nomination to Diane McGrath, the political novice who ran on the Republican line against Koch, and her campaign ended in disarray with the GOP candidate for City Council president endorsing Koch for mayor.

The Legal Environment

Finally, changes in the legal environment contributed to the political changes New York has experienced in recent years. On the state level, legislative reapportionment in the 1960s and 1970s increased the Assembly representation of a number of the downstate and upstate suburban areas in which the Democrats were growing stronger. The reapportionment plan enacted after the 1980 census was strongly biased in favor of the Democrats in the Assembly and the Republicans in the Senate, and solidified the pattern of party control that had emerged during the previous decade.

In New York City, changes in the laws governing relations between the state and municipal governments in the mid 1970s indirectly contributed to the weakening of the Republican party in the metropolis. Historically, fiscal crises such as the City experienced in 1975 served as preludes to fusion campaigns: political forces that wanted the municipal government to reorder its fiscal priorities would join with the Republicans and various reform groups in an effort to defeat the administration responsible for the City's financial problems.[18] The creation of the Municipal Assistance Corporation and the Emergency Financial Control Board during the 1975 fiscal crisis, however, substituted for fusion by enabling the advocates of retrenchment directly to compel the municipal government to alter its budgetary policies. The creation of these monitoring agencies also discredited the Beame administration, and the policies they insisted the mayor pursue further weakened him politically. This enabled Beame's opponents (most notably, Governor Carey) to intervene in the 1977 Democratic mayoral primary and secure his defeat. The winner of the primary, Ed Koch, subsequently established close relations with many of the traditional supporters of the GOP—bankers, businessmen, and homeowners—further weakening the Republicans as an independent force in the city's politics.[19]

PROSPECTS

Whether the changes in New York politics over the past dozen years will endure beyond the immediate future remains an open question. The triumph of individual Democratic *candidates* does not imply, or automatically translate into, commensurate gains for the Democratic *party*. Governors and State legislators have done much in recent years to buttress their own chances for reelection, but little to strengthen their party as an institution.

Consequently, short-term forces may at any time lead the party controlling the State government to lose an election, thereby tranferring the benefits of incumbency to the opposition. In the mid 1970s, Governor Rockefeller's departure from Albany at a time of national political crisis and local economic distress enabled the Democrats to come to power. A less momentous series of events could enable the Republicans to regain power in New York State at any point in the future.

In New York City, the scandals that erupted in 1986 weakened Mayor Koch politically and could lead to his departure from office at the end of his third term. To date, however, there are no indications that Republicans in the city have benefited from revelations of corruption on the part of Democratic politicians. Moreover, black and Hispanic voters—a growing proportion of the city's electorate—are overwhelmingly attached to the national Democratic party, and the Liberal party's capacity to serve as a vehicle for fusion is waning as it fails to replenish its aging membership. Consequently, it is probable that the Democrats will continue to monopolize public office in New York City in the foreseeable future. It is not unlikely, then, that in the years ahead the Republicans could win control in Albany while the Democrats retain power in New York City—reinstituting the partisan cleavage between State and City that had prevailed prior to the mid 1970s.

NOTES

The research reported in this chapter was supported by the Jonathan Meigs Ford Foundation and Project Ezra of Cornell University. Bruce Frohnen provided invaluable research assistance.

1. See, for example, David Maldwyn Ellis, *New York: State and City* (Ithaca, NY: Cornell University Press, 1979), chap. 8.
2. Austin Ranney, "Parties in State Politics," in Herbert Jacob and Kenneth Vines, eds., *Politics in the American States* (Boston: Little, Brown, 1969), p. 65.
3. James Sundquist, *Dynamics of the Party System* (Washington, DC: Brookings Institution, 1983), chap. 11.
4. Howard Scarrow, *Parties, Elections, and Representation in the State of New York* (New York: New York University Press, 1983), pp. 14, 18.
5. The "upstate cities" are Albany, Binghamton, Buffalo, Niagara Falls, Rochester, Rome, Schenectady, Syracuse, Troy, Utica, and Yonkers. The "upstate suburbs" are the counties of the 1970 upstate SMSAs, excluding these cities: Albany, Rensselaer, Saratoga, Schenectady, Herkimer, Oneida, Madison, Onondaga, Oswego, Broome, Tioga, Wayne, Monroe, Livingston, Orleans, Niagara, and Erie. The "downstate suburbs" are the counties of the 1970 New York City SMSA, excluding New York City and Yonkers. The "rural counties" are the remaining counties in the state.
6. In 1942 divisions between FDR's supporters and the regulars headed by James Farley were so deep that the ALP refused to endorse the regular Democratic candidate for governor. In 1958 the Democrats were deeply divided between a reform wing, headed by Eleanor Roosevelt and Herbert Lehman, and a regular wing, headed by Carmine De Sapio.
7. Gerald Benjamin, "Patterns in New York State Politics," in Robert Connery and Gerald Benjamin, eds., *Governing New York State: The Rockefeller Years* (New York: Academy of Political Science, 1974).
8. Martin Shefter, "Economic Crises, Social Coalitions, and Political Institutions: New York City's Little New Deal," paper delivered at the annual meeting of the American Political Science Association, New York City, September 1, 1981.
9. Arthur Mann, *La Guardia Comes to Power, 1933* (Philadelphia: Lippincott, 1965).
10. Robert Caro, *The Power Broker* (New York, Knopf, 1974), chap. 34.
11. *New York Times*, October 14, 1965, p. 42.

178 THE TWO NEW YORKS

12. Scarrow, *Parties, Elections, and Representation*, p. 110.
13. Stanley Kelley et al., "Registration and Voting: Putting First Things First," *American Political Science Review* 61 (June 1967):359–379.
14. Scarrow, *Parties, Elections, and Representation*, p. 88.
15. Martin Shefter, "Political Incorporation and the Extrusion of the Left: Party Politics and Social Forces in New York City," *Studies in American Political Development* 1 (1986):50–90.
16. *New York Legislative Manual* (Albany: New York State Legislature, various years).
17. Rockefeller's appeal to Jewish and Catholic voters is analyzed in Mark Levy and Michael Kramer, *The Ethnic Factor* (New York: Simon & Schuster, 1972). Carey's recapture of these voters is noted in *New York Times*, November 6, 1974, p. 30; November 7, 1974, p. 1. For data on the relationship between ethnicity and party identification on the eve of the 1982 gubernatorial election, see John K. White and Dwight Morris, "The Electoral Riddle," in Peter Colby, ed., *New York State Today*, (Albany: SUNY Press, 1985), p. 73.
18. Martin Shefter, *Political Crisis/Fiscal Crisis: The Collapse and Revival of New York City* (New York: Basic Books, 1987), chap. 2.
19. Shefter, *Political Crisis/Fiscal Crisis*, pp. xiii—xiv, 174–183.

7

THE CITY AND THE STATE
IN WASHINGTON

℃∿℃

Sarah F. Liebschutz

NEW YORK'S place in the federal system always has been distinctive; its early characterization as a "reluctant pillar" still holds. New York's adoption of the federal constitution in 1788—it was the eleventh state to ratify the Constitution, when nine was the minimum number necessary—came after careful assessment of the substance and the timing of ratification. The final action was pragmatic, best captured in the words of a delegate who voted for ratification "not from a conviction that the Constitution was a good one or that the Liberties of men were secured. No—I voted for it as a Choice of evils in our own present Situation."[1] This pragmatism, this calculation of net benefits, remains the attitude and modus operandi of contemporary New York officials in Washington.

The other side of the relationship—federal officials' view of New York—was captured in the 1975 *Daily News* headline "Ford to City: Drop Dead," at a time when the President's assistance was sought to prevent the impending bankruptcy of the City of New York. Washington's disdain reflected the alienation of many Americans from the fast-talking, fast-thinking, fast-spending New Yorkers whose City and State, in the public mind, were undifferentiated.

Both of these characterizations—New York State's seeming aloofness from the federal government and Washington's indifference to the problems of New York State and New York City—are, of course, overdrawn. Yet the characterizations have some basis in reality, in the ways that New York State and New York City attempt to influence federal policy and in the ways that decision makers at the national level respond to them.

The purpose of this essay is to examine the relationship among New York City, New York State, and the federal government. The first section sketches the dimensions of the relationship, which encompass federal spending and regulatory policies. The next section describes the multiple structures used to advance state and city interests and focuses on the composition and cohesion of the state and city congressional delegations. How effective are New York City and New York State in advancing their policy interests? The last sections of the essay present two case studies which illustrate collaboration and competition between the two governments in Washington.

NEW YORK'S STAKES IN FEDERAL POLICIES

"The idea of the federal union as a partnership is a key aspect of federalism."[2] For New York State and New York City, the federal partnership involves recognition by Washington of state and city interests, and, in return, their acknowledgment and support of national interests. The range of federal decisions affecting New York is enormous, encompassing virtually every facet and instrument of public policy—from domestic to foreign issues and including direct federal expenditures in the state, intergovernmental grants-in-aid, and regulations. This section concentrates on two of the most significant dimensions—expenditures and regulations. The stakes for the state and the city in both policy areas are high.

Federal Expenditures

The importance of federal expenditures to states and localities can be viewed from a variety of perspectives: the level and composition of expenditures, the level of federal grants to state and local governments, and their dependence on these grants as a source of funding.

Per capita federal expenditures in New York State in 1985 were $3,192, less than 2 percent below the national average. But as shown in Table 7.1, the distribution of expenditures among activities in New York was considerably different from the distribution in the nation as a whole. Fewer federal civilian and military employees are located in New York, and federal wages and salaries are three fifths of the national average.

TABLE 7.1
Per Capita Federal Expenditures, Fiscal Year 1985

	United States	New York State	New York City
Total	$3,252	$3,192	NA
Salaries and Wages	476	282	NA
Procurement Contract Awards	800	645	291
Direct Payments to Individuals	1,439	1,559	NA
Medicare	286	345	NA
Social Security	759	863	NA
Other	100	81	NA
Grants to State and Local Governments	435	623	752
Department of Agriculture	14	13	NA
Department of Education	17	10	NA
Environmental Protection Agency	11	24	NA
Department of Health and Human Services	139	297	NA
Medicaid	93	224	NA
Social Services	11	11	NA
AFDC	35	62	NA
Department of Housing and Urban Development	42	73	NA
Community Development	15	25	NA
Housing Assistance	27	48	NA
Department of Labor	11	10	NA
Department of Transportation	62	58	NA
Highway Trust Fund	49	32	NA
Urban Mass Transportation Administration	13	26	NA
Department of the Treasury	18	26	38
Other	114	108	NA

SOURCES: U.S. Bureau of the Census, *Federal Expenditures by State for Fiscal Year 1985* (Washington, DC: U.S. Government Printing Office, March 1986); and *Consolidated Federal Funds Report,* vol. 2: *Subcounty Areas, Fiscal Year 1985* (Washington, DC: U.S. Government Printing Office, March 1986).
NOTE: NA = not available.

Fewer procurement contracts, defense and other, are awarded to New York firms.

In contrast, direct payments to individual New Yorkers and grants to New York's state and local governments are greater than the national average. Both Medicare and Social Security payments exceed national norms by significant amounts. Federal grants for Medicaid were 140 percent above the per capita national average. Federal spending in New York State for other income transfer programs (public assistance and housing assistance) and for community development and mass transit is also higher than the national average.

Federal spending in New York City contrasts in important ways with that in the state as a whole. The limited available data (see Table 7.1) reveal that the local governments in the city (including the Metropolitan Transportation Authority) received nearly 20 percent more federal aid per capita than did such governments statewide. As elaborated below, such aid reflects both the City's heavy service obligations and the large number of its residents dependent on public assistance.

The opposite situation holds regarding federal procurement awards. These were less than one half, on a per capita basis, in New York City than statewide. Thus, the disparities between federal spending in New York State and in the nation are explained in large part by the City's experience: Federal grants-in-aid to the State exceed the national average because New York City's unique governmental and demographic characteristics attract more grants; federal expenditures for military and other goods and services in the state are below the national mean because of the low level of procurement awards in New York City.

Federal Aid to the State Government

From the mid 1970s to the mid 1980s, federal aid has constituted about one fourth of the State's revenues. This proportion has remained fairly constant, dipping in 1985 as State revenue growth outpaced that of federal receipts. Federal aid projected for 1987 at $9.4 billion represents an increase of 40 percent over such aid received in 1982, despite the Reagan Administration's initiatives to decrease federal aid to state and local governments.

The explanation for this seeming paradox is that the State of New York benefits from the cost-sharing provisions of many federal entitlement programs, particularly public assistance and Medicaid. When the State increases its spending in those areas, either because of State decisions to increase benefits or because economic conditions contribute to higher caseloads, federal aid grows proportionately. Since 1981, the State has increased its public assistance benefits at least three times and the federal government shared in financing these improvements. The single largest source of federal aid to the State government (see Table 7.2) is Medicaid, where economic conditions and inflation have rapidly increased State and federal expenditures in recent years. However, federal aid to New York State under entitlement programs would have been even higher in the absence of the Reagan Administration initiatives.[3]

Federal aid for operating and capital programs has actually decreased since 1981—dramatically, in some cases. Aid for job training

TABLE 7.2

Federal Funds to New York State, Fiscal Years 1981–1984
(in millions of dollars)

	1981	1982	1983	1984
Entitlement Funds				
AFDC[a]	$1,053.3	$1,062.5	$1,016.3	$ 965.8
Medicaid	2,637.0	3,000.0	3,227.0	3,400.0
Food Stamps	929.3	878.4	986.7	982.0
Operating Funds				
Low-Income Energy Assistance Block Grant	223.1	237.8	250.6[b]	263.2[c]
Health Block Grants				
Alcohol, Drug Abuse, Mental Health	55.4	36.4	28.5[b]	28.5
Preventive Health	6.5	5.8	6.1	6.1
Maternal and Child Welfare	28.8	23.8	31.1[b]	75.0
Education Block Grant	54.6	31.2	31.6	31.6
Compensatory Education	261.4	273.7	313.6	349.8
Social Services	236.0	184.9	202.0[b]	209.0
Community Services Block Grant	46.7	30.4	30.2[b]	28.6
CETA/JTPA	489.0	252.0	230.3	194.9[d]
Capital Programs				
Highways	515.9	404.2	596.3	749.4
Mass Transit				
Operating	199.4	171.6	138.9	138.9
Capital	520.7	353.7	640.1	568.0
Housing				
Public Housing	165.4[e]	144.2[e]	243.8[f]	NA
Section 8	63.9	25.9	38.0	NA
Wastewater Treatment	268.1	252.7	271.4	271.4

SOURCES: New York State, *Executive Budget*, *1982–1983*, *Executive Budget, 1983–1984*, *Executive Budget, 1984–1985*, and *Executive Budget 1985–1986*. These data were supplemented with interviews with staff from the New York State Departments of Education, Health, Labor, Social Services, State, and Transportation, and the U.S. Department of Housing and Urban Development, Buffalo Area Office.

[a]Calendar year figures for this program.

[b]Includes emergency jobs bill supplement.

[c]Includes mid 1984 supplement of $25.4 million.

[d]October 1–June 30 transition year.

[e]Comprehensive Improvement Assistance Program (CIAP) funds only.

[f]CIAP and Operating Subsidy funds.

TABLE 7.3

New York City Revenues, Fiscal Years 1981–1987
(in millions of dollars)

Source	1981	1986	1987	Percentage Change 1981–1987
Local Revenues	$8,688	$12,975	$14,272	64.2%
State Aid	2,942	4,609	5,065	72.1
Federal Aid	2,469	3,001	2,366	− 4.2
Unrestricted Aid	287	257	130	−54.7
Categorical Aid	2,182	2,744	2,106	*
CETA/JTPA	329	88	79	−75.9
Community Development	267	274	195	−26.9
Welfare	1,109	1,563	1,382	24.6
Education	319	479	422	32.2
Other	158	340	158	*
Total Revenues	14,098	20,585	21,703	53.9

SOURCES: Data for 1981 are from City of New York, *Executive Budget Fiscal Year 1983, Message of the Mayor,* May 10, 1982, p. 239; data for 1986 and 1987 are from City of New York, *Executive Budget Fiscal Year 1987, Message of the Mayor,* May 5, 1986, pp. 50 and 261.

*Change less than 1 percent.

and housing assistance has been sharply cut. These trends are expected to continue.

Federal Aid to New York City

New York City, because of its size and because it administers and finances a broad range of services, is more dependent on federal grants than other city governments. In both absolute and relative terms, federal aid to New York City is impressive. It received $3 billion in federal grants in 1986—an amount that dwarfed aid received by any other city. Federal aid to all American cities in 1983 was 15 percent of all local revenues; for New York City, such aid represented 25 percent of own-source revenue.[4]

Federal funds reach the City directly and through the State government. Most categorical grants listed in Table 7.3 are channeled by the State to local governments using formulas that are determined in whole or in part at the federal level. Because these formulas take into account such population characteristics as unemployment and low income, the City receives a large share of federal job training, education, and social service funds distributed by the State to its localities.[5]

Federal aid varies in importance by program area. Most federal funds to the City are for public assistance, Medicaid, foster care, and other social services. Accordingly, program impacts are important in relatively few of the more than 100 municipal agencies. Of the large City agencies, the Human Resources Administration and Department of Housing Preservation and Development received federal assistance in 1981 amounting, respectively, to 94 percent and 82 percent of their total revenues. [On the other hand] the Department of Social Services and Board of Education received 38 percent and 14 percent respectively [of their operating revenues from the federal government].[6]

Since the advent of the Reagan Administration, the City's reliance on federal aid for operating programs has decreased. Between fiscal years 1981 and 1986, the annual level of federal aid increased from $2.5 billion to $3 billion (see Table 7.3). But this increase represented a relative decline in the contribution of federal revenues to the City—from 17.9 to 14.6 percent.[7] The decreases were most severe for job training, community development, and housing assistance programs.

For 1987, the City projected a decrease of nearly $400 million in federal aid—mostly because of the expected termination of the federal general revenue sharing program. The resulting aid will represent an even smaller share of local revenues—11.9 percent.

Federal Regulatory Policy

Federal regulations have great potential to affect the lives and fortunes of New Yorkers. For example, deregulation of natural gas impacts the costs of heating the nearly 40 percent of homes in New York State heated by natural gas. Federal regulation of air traffic affects two of the nation's busiest airports, Kennedy and La Guardia, as well as other airports in the state. The interpretation and application of remedies against textile imports influence the health of the New York City apparel manufacturing industry. The designation of routes for transportation of hazardous waste by the U.S. Department of Transportation could alter the environmental conditions for the millions who work and live in New York City.

Recent research indicates that regulation by the federal government of states and by the federal and state governments of local governments "has become a significant political institutional and intergovernmental issue in the United States."[8] The State and City are not unique in the increasing penetration of their policy preferences by the federal government. As they rely so heavily on federal revenues for health, welfare, and transportation programs, however, federal regulatory policies in these areas are particularly salient for both governments.

Both the State and City monitor the rule writing and rule interpretation aspects of the regulatory process through their Washington offices.

When a state and/or local match is required as a condition of federal aid, the surveillance is especially keen, as the magnitude of the required state and local spending is directly affected. Thus, New York State, which maintains one of the most generous and comprehensive Medicaid programs in the nation, was very active as Medicaid regulations were developed following enactment of the Omnibus Budget Reconciliation Act (OBRA) of 1981. OBRA contained an important experiment with State financial incentives for Medicaid cost containment; the "incentives" were in the form of penalties that reduced the federal matching payment to states which failed to limit their expenditures. Staff from the State's Division of the Budget and its Washington Office worked closely to influence subsequent regulations to ensure that New York would qualify for rebates under the incentive program.[9]

Federal regulatory policies have provoked clashes with the City and the State where State and local prerogatives, not the financial match, were at issue. The Surface Transportation Assistance Act of 1982 provided increased federal highway and mass transit aid to states within a framework of new national standards regarding truck dimensions and interstate highway routes. The thorny issue for the State was the stipulation by the Federal Highway Administration that tandem trailers be permitted to use highways on Long Island and in New York City which previously excluded them. Both the State's general power to control safety on its highways and the City's specific power, under special State legislation, to set its own standards for vehicle weights and dimensions on local highways were challenged.

The State "was faced with the dilemma of whether to maintain its position of clear nonconformity with the national standards or to risk the loss of between $750 million for one year and up to $4 billion for the next five years. Pragmatism triumphed over state prerogative"[10] in the end, as the State legislature complied with federal policy, enacting the required legislation that undermined the City's authority.

Large potential losses can occur when federal regulations impose conditions of aid that are unacceptable to a recipient government. New York City's 1986 federal highway aid of $17 million was jeopardized because of a conflict between the City's anti-apartheid law and federal competitive-bidding regulations. Local Law 19 of 1985 requires bidders on business with the City to state that they do not have dealings with the South African government or with firms whose goods originate in South Africa. The federal Department of Transportation, asserting that "apartheid is not the issue, maintains that the local law violates a federal prohibition against municipalities limiting competitive bidding on federally funded contracts to certain classes of bidders."[11] At the urging of Mayor Koch, a supplemental appropriations bill allowing an exemption to the regulation for New York City for fiscal 1986 was enacted by the Congress. However, as of this writing, more than $700 million in federal highway aid to the City for the next five years still remains in jeopardy because of the conflict between Local Law 19 and federal regulations on competitive bidding.

In sum, the stakes for New York State and New York City in federal policies are high. Billions of federal aid dollars as well as City-State policy preferences are involved. Consequently, both governments are well organized to exert influence in Washington on these matters.

STRUCTURES FOR INFLUENCE

The City and the State seek to influence federal policies through multiple channels. They are institutional and ad hoc, formal and informal. The Congress is the constitutionally sanctioned institution for formal participation by New York State's two senators and its 34 members of the House of Representatives in the legislative process. Both general governments are represented through permanent Washington offices. Informal communication channels exist between program specialists in State, City, and federal agencies. Finally, coalitions involving one or more of these groups frequently emerge around specific issues on an ad hoc basis. This discussion focuses on the formal, institutional channels which New York State and New York City use to exert influence in Washington.

State and City Washington Offices

Lobbying in Washington by states dates to 1908 and the initiation of an annual Governors' Conference (later National Governors' Conference, or NGC) by President Theodore Roosevelt. However, as Donald Haider has observed, the conference's early, dominant tone of

> restricting business to state issues precluded a national focus during [its] first fifty years. [Then, in the 1960s] as issues involving intergovernmental relations and support for federal revenue sharing assumed greater import, a movement emerged among governors across party lines for overhauling the Conference and strengthening its then diminutive role as a government interest group. [In 1967 the NGC established a permanent Washington office] whose mission consisted of gathering and disseminating information on matters related to issues of federal-state relations.[12]

Lobbying by cities in Washington dates to the 1930s and the close relationship between President Franklin D. Roosevelt and the nation's large-city mayors:

The key political group linking the President to his urban constituency, supportive of greater federal-urban ties, long on votes and long on programs at the time, was the United States Conference of Mayors. The Conference, initially comprising mayors from the 100 largest cities, developed goals [which] remain largely intact today: to expand direct federal-city programs, increase federal fiscal support for these programs, gain federal assumption of specific programs like public assistance, establish federal instrumentalities and safeguards for maintaining urban fiscal solvency and enhance the autonomy of cities as general-purpose units of government.[13]

Since the mid 1960s, lobbying in Washington by states and cities has surged in response to the "rapid increase in the size and complexity of federal domestic programs."[14] Such lobbying occurs, in part, under the auspices and orchestration of organizations such as the Governors' Conference. For most cities, the Conference of Mayors and the National Center for Municipal Development provide a Washington presence. All cities and states, individually and on an ad hoc basis, engage Washington law firms to advance their interests on specialized matters. In 1985, 35 states, including New York State, and most of the nation's largest cities, including New York City, Los Angeles, Chicago, and Philadelphia, maintained permanent Washington offices to advance their interests.

It was his disappointment, in part, with the inability of the National Governors' Conference to surmount partisanship that led Governor Nelson A. Rockefeller in 1971 to establish a New York State office in Washington. The initial purpose of the office was to press for enactment of a federal revenue sharing program. Persuaded that members of the state's large, but uncohesive congressional delegation had the potential to influence a favorable outcome for such legislation, he "set up a new state office in Washington to work more closely with the delegation and assigned one of his key aides, Jim Cannon, to work full-time for revenue sharing."[15]

The mayors of New York City have played an active role in the Conference of Mayors from its earliest days. Mayors La Guardia, Wagner, and Lindsay all assumed leadership roles in the effort to "build public and congressional support for urban legislation."[16] It was not dissatisfaction with the Conference that led Mayor John V. Lindsay to establish a New York City office in Washington in 1966. Rather, he sought to develop more direct links to the federal bureaucracy and procure more federal funds for the City. Haider indicates that in his 1969 campaign for reelection, Lindsay "credited [the Washington] office with helping to raise federal aid to the City to more than $1 billion annually."[17]

Today, New York State and New York City have separate, strong institutional presences in Washington. The New York State Office of

Federal Affairs, the governor's lobby, is located near the Capitol. Its professional staff consists of six program specialists and a director. The New York City Washington Office, the mayor's lobby, is also a short walk from the Capitol on New Jersey Avenue. Its director oversees seven legislative representatives, a grants coordinator, and the representative of the City Board of Education. Additionally, the State Assembly and Senate and the State Department of Education are each represented by one- or two-person Washington offices; New York City's Board of Education and its Health and Hospitals Corporation (both housed within the City Washington Office), the Port Authority, and the Metropolitan Transportation Authority complete the roster of New York agencies with formal representation in the nation's capitol.

The State Office of Federal Affairs and the City Washington Office pursue a wide range of monitoring and coordinating activities. The span of issues in which these offices is involved is enormous, extending from agricultural subsidies to sewage treatment plant regulations to reimbursement of police costs to the City for protecting foreign diplomats to immigration policy to tax incentives for developers. No particular issue occupies an enduring primacy within this panoply. Rather, as one official remarked, "We fight each battle as it comes along, and sometimes we fight two or three battles simultaneously."

"Fighting the battles" for New York in Washington sometimes takes the form of a team effort between the two offices. When the governor and mayor share positions on issues, as, for example, on retention of state and local tax deductibility and extension of general revenue sharing—both elaborated later—the directors coordinate efforts. On other issues, where City and State positions and/or priorities differ, the view of the governor or the mayor is advanced separately—as in the Medicaid and anti-apartheid examples already discussed. Whether the City and the State join forces or "go it alone," however, communication is ongoing and open between the two offices. This is because they share two common challenges in dealing with the Congress. One is "dealing with dissension within the New York delegation. The other is working to convince the rest of Congress that New York is not the enemy of all good."[18] This historically unruly New York delegation warrants separate consideration.

The New York Delegation

The New York State delegation, second largest in the Congress, was characterized in the past as "openly hostile"[19] and "schizophrenic."[20] In more recent years, the delegation—although its ideological cleavages remain sharp—has developed greater internal civility and somewhat more cohesion.

An analysis in the late 1960s of seven state party delegations to the House of Representatives found that New York members ranked lowest in terms of interaction, ideological homogeneity, and joint action.[21] The following quotation illustrates the cleavages that then characterized the delegation:

> [New York] is like two states. The city congressmen, Republicans as well as Democrats, don't know where upstate is. The upstaters don't like this. They know where the city is but they can forget it. This makes cooperation difficult. They just don't use their potential power. New York didn't get reimbursed on the Thomas E. Dewey Thruway and [U.S. Senator from New York James] Buckley was chairman of Public Works at the time. He couldn't care less.[22]

The ideological rifts which typified the state delegation in the 1960s still persist. Table 7.4 presents ratings by liberal (Americans for Democratic Action) and conservative (Americans for Constitutional Action) groups of the delegation members for selected years. The ratings are based on votes by representatives on policy issues of importance to the rating organizations. Irrespective of the year when the ratings were obtained, Democratic members are more liberal than their Republican colleagues; New York City members are more liberal than noncity representatives. The state delegation remains as ideologically heterogeneous in the 1980s as it did in the 1960s.

Since the 1970 census, the size of the New York delegation in the House of Representatives has decreased from 41 to 34 seats; the loss of 5 seats after the 1980 census was the greatest for any single state. Redistricting and subsequent elections to the House of "politicians with pragmatic, rather than Rooseveltian approaches to issues"[23] appear to have contributed to a less rancorous delegation in the 1980s.

Of equal importance, however, for understanding behavioral change within the delegation is the altered environment in which the City and the State now operate. New York is no longer the largest or the richest state; its adjustment during the 1970s from high taxing and high spending policies to those designed to regain the state's competitive economic advantage was—and is—difficult. Similarly, the fiscal crisis of New York City, necessitating loan guarantees from the federal government, revealed the City's vulnerabilities. "The issues are harder now," said one staffer who served two New York congressmen. "It's not a question of arguing dollars upstate versus downstate anymore, it's a question of keeping dollars altogether, and that's simply harder to do."[24]

TABLE 7.4

*Ratings of New York Members of the House of Representatives,
Selected Years*

	1972	
	Americans for Democratic Action	Americans for Constitutional Action
Democrats (*n* = 25)	70.0%	15.5%
Republicans (*n* = 16)	20.0	60.0
New York City Members (*n* = 19)	75.4	12.1
Rest of State (*n* = 22)	31.0	50.9
Total (*n* = 41)	50.3	32.9
	1982	
	Americans for Democratic Action	Americans for Constitutional Action Research Institute
Democrats (*n* = 22)	86.3%	10.6%
Republicans (*n* = 17)	26.2	67.6
New York City Members (*n* = 17)	77.2	15.3
Rest of State (*n* = 22)	46.9	51.3
Total (*n* = 39)	60.1	35.4
	1984	
	Americans for Democratic Action	Americans for Constitutional Action Research Institute
Democrats (*n* = 20)	84.3%	13.9%
Republicans (*n* = 14)	28.6	65.9
New York City Members (*n* = 14)	82.1	15.1
Rest of State (*n* = 20)	47.3	49.3
Total (*n* = 34)	61.3	35.2

SOURCES: *Congressional Quarterly Weekly Report*, December 9, 1972; May 7, 1983; April 20, 1985.

The New York City fiscal crisis is frequently cited by members and their aides as the turning point in sensitizing the delegation to the need to develop greater cohesion. During the 1960s through the mid 1970s, Democrats and Republicans met only two or three times a year as separate groups within the delegation "mostly for organizational purposes or to pick its candidate for an important committee position; the reason for the low level of interaction was age and ideological splits."[25] Meetings of the delegation as a whole were even more rare and were characterized by stridency.[26]

Since the New York City fiscal crisis, the state delegation meets monthly under bipartisan leadership to discuss and take action on issues whose implications transcend the boundaries of individual districts. In recent years, these meetings have resulted in strong majorities for renewal of general revenue sharing, retention of tax incentives for industrial investment, location of additional army divisions at Fort Drum, building of jet trainer aircraft on Long Island, and retention of the deduction for state and local taxes from federal personal income taxes. Despite the wide differences in philosophy that still exist within the delegation, a shared interest in attracting federal funds in the form of grants or procurement contracts to create jobs more frequently overrides individual differences than was the case in the past.

All is not sweetness and light, however, within the New York delegation. While internal stridency in the state delegation has diminished, the New York City delegation has not attained a comparable sense of identity. City members do not meet separately with their own leadership and do not relate as a group to the mayor and the governor. Reapportionments, high turnover, and the resulting paucity of committee or party leadership positions have worked against the city delegation being a key reference group for its members. Haider wrote in 1973: "When confronted by their collective impotence, individual members of the city delegation assert constituency prerogative, campaign pledges or dictates of conscience."[27] Such behavior is still evident.

The Staten Island Homeport Vote

A recent, well-publicized example of city members' independent behavior involved a June 1986 vote in the House of Representatives on the navy's plan to build new bases for its expanding fleet. The plan included a "homeport" on Staten Island for the USS Iowa and its escort ships. An appropriation to fund construction of homeports on Staten Island and Everett, Washington, was defeated by a 241–190 vote. Twenty-five New York representatives supported the appropriation. All eight New York votes against it came from New York City members, who committed the unusual action of voting against a military construction project for their own region.[28] Even more extraordinary is that all but one of the eight had been supporters of the project three years earlier. Intervening events reveal the influences of constituents and ideology on these members.

The basing of the battleship Iowa on Staten Island was part of a buildup to a 600-ship navy advocated by President Reagan during his first term. Once spending for the enlarged fleet was approved by the Congress, the Secretary of the Navy tried to "lock up long-term political patronage for [the concept] by giving many members of Congress a tangible stake in the expanded Navy."[29] His strategy was to disperse the fleet to ports on the east, west, and Gulf coasts rather than concentrating the ships at San Diego and Norfolk, the navy's existing large homeports. The advocates of dispersal claimed that the new bases would bring forces closer to potential trouble spots and that enemy forces would have to attack more targets to immobilize the fleet.

Following the Secretary's announcement of the dispersal strategy in 1983, Mayor Koch, the New York City Council, and Representative Guy V. Molinari, whose district includes Staten Island, began to seek support for a Staten Island homeport. The Mayor wrote editorials in various newspapers and letters to the Secretary. The City Council passed resolutions of support in 1983 and 1985.

Representative Molinari and Mayor Koch achieved some important early successes. All of the members of the state delegation, with the exception of Representative Theodore S. Weiss from Manhattan, who has consistently opposed the project because of the specter of a nuclear accident, signed a letter on March 16, 1983, urging a homeport in New York (Staten Island) Harbor. Several months later, the navy Secretary selected Staten Island over other east coast sites as the homeport for the Iowa.

But the near unanimity among the House members from New York City was short-lived. Supporters of the nuclear freeze movement mounted a campaign against the plan to equip the battleships with nuclear weapons. Opponents gathered more than 100,000 signatures on a petition in 1984 to force a New York City referendum on the homeport. Although the courts later barred the vote, the lobbying continued, including a demonstration when the Iowa sailed into New York Harbor in 1984. On August 9, 1984, 11 New York representatives—8 of them from the city—wrote the Secretary urging him to "reconsider the [Navy's] policy of neither confirming nor denying the presence of nuclear weapons or components on board any ship. The citizens of New York, our constituents, [they asserted] deserve to know whether they are inviting a conventionally-armed or nuclear-armed Surface Action Group to take up residence in their harbor."

The nuclear issue soon became joined with the budgetary implications of building the new ports. Proponents of the homeport expansion strategy argued that "building new ports would cost $799 million—only about $200 million more than expanding the existing homeports."[30] Opponents, who labeled the appropriations measure "homeporking not homeporting," argued that "personnel costs, transportation costs, costs of building infrastructure, hospitals, training schools" would drive the costs up to $1.5–$2 billion.[31]

The cost factors turned out to be the justification given by seven of the eight city representatives who voted against the homeports. Four of the eight signed a letter to the Secretary three weeks before the vote which cited the budgetary arguments. "The question at hand [they wrote] is not simply whether New York should have a homeport, but whether a national homeporting plan is appropriate for the nation at this time of severe budgetary restraints."[32]

The vote of the eight city members against the Staten Island Homeport appropriation was a source of considerable dismay to other members of the state delegation. Representative Stratton, delegation chair, commented that "saving the plan would take some miracle. I think it tells a good deal about the New York delegation. If New York is going to have any clout, we've got to work together."[33]

Is the Staten Island homeport vote typical or atypical behavior for the New York State congressional delegation in the 1980s? There is considerable evidence to indicate that it is atypical. A year before that vote, in 1985, all members of the delegation, except for two upstate representatives, had supported the retention of deductibility of state and local taxes from the federal income tax. A month after the homeport vote, 30 of 34 delegation members present voted to spend $151 million in funds to construct trainer aircraft on Long Island. Yet the popular perception of a New York delegation in disarray, with New York City members "aloof and arrogant," persists.

THE CITY AND THE STATE: COMPETITORS OR COLLABORATORS VIS-A-VIS WASHINGTON?

Both New York City and New York State are well organized to respond to federal policy initiatives. Do their positions and priorities on issues diverge or are they similar? Are they collaborators or competitors in Washington?

A simple typology of modes of collaboration and competition can be created based on policy preferences and priorities. (See Figure 7.1.) Four outcomes are possible. When both parties hold similar positions and assign high priority to an issue, collaboration in lobbying efforts is expected. When their positions are similar, but only one party places a high priority on the issue outcome, the party for whom the issue is a low priority can be expected to acquiesce, that is, follow the lobbying leadership of the other. Where issue positions and priorities diverge the party for whom the matter is of high priority can be expected to advocate

FIGURE 7.1

Typology of Two-Party Competition and Collaboration

	Issue Priorities	
	SIMILAR	DIVERGENT
Issue Positions — SIMILAR	collaboration	acquiescence
Issue Positions — DIVERGENT	competition	minimal or no competition

actively its position while opposition activities of the other party, if any, will be minimal. Only when the two parties diverge on issues of high mutual priority will they actively compete.

Most of the time, the City and the State find themselves broadly in agreement on federal issues, but with different priorities. Accordingly, acquiescence and minimal competition are the most common patterns of behavior.

In general, the City and the State emphasize different issues for federal action. Recent reports of the New York State Office of Federal Affairs and the New York City Washington Office reveal considerable overlap in topics for legislative action, but differing emphases within each area.[34] For example, while the City's thrust was to retain full community block grant funding for entitlement cities, the State emphasized continued eligibility of the State Division of Housing and Community Renewal for technical assistance grants under the Small Cities part of the program.[35] With respect to the federal housing development program, the City advocated capping low-income rents at 30 percent of individual income, while the State supported expanding the number of large cities eligible for new construction and substantial rehabilitation grants.

These examples illustrate that City and State perspectives yield different, but not necessarily incompatible, positions within the same policy arena. As the legislative director for an upstate representative put it, "New York City presses for social programs and mass transit, while the State stresses interstate highway funding. But we don't see these as conflicts."

More frequently, the situation involves similar issue positions taken by the City and the State, but with different intensities of importance. As one congressional staffer suggested, "Koch and Cuomo both support federal housing and homeless and highway aid programs. But it is a matter of the priority assigned to each." The efforts of Governor Cuomo in 1985 and 1986 to retain state and local tax deductibility and those of Mayor Koch in 1986 to continue the general revenue sharing program illustrate high priority issues for the State, in the former instance, and for the City, in the latter, where the other government was highly supportive.

For New York City, the loss of general revenue sharing funds—about $270 million for City fiscal year 1987—"is equivalent to 5,400 police officers or 5,490 teachers."[36] Mayor Koch convened a meeting at Gracie Mansion of other large-city mayors and other local officials and also testified before congressional committees in cooperation with the U.S. Conference of Mayors to publicize the adverse effects on all local governments of the termination of general revenue sharing. For the mayor's Washington Office, the continuation of general revenue sharing was a legislative priority for 1986.

As state governments did not receive general revenue sharing funds, the issue did not command as high a profile for the State. Nonetheless, the effects of termination of general revenue sharing on the State government were worrisome, as New York City and other local governments who were to lose general revenue sharing probably would look to the State for replacement revenues. Thus, the State's lobbyists and its upstate representatives supported the efforts of Mayor Koch to renew the program.

Issues where the City and the State are in direct competition with each other in Washington are rare. They tend to involve matters where the City's demands for federal action are perceived by the State as undermining its own prerogatives. The City-State dispute over federal AFDC two-party check regulations, elaborated below, is the only recent example of direct competition discovered by this writer.

Least frequent of all are instances where the City and the State share precisely issue positions and priorities. Given the different perspectives and responsibilities of each government, that is understandable. Rather, as indicated, the typical issue is one where the City and the State "go along" with each other in the federal arena; that is, each acquiesces to the higher priority of the other because the outcome will be good for both.

CITY-STATE COMPETITION:
THE TWO-PARTY RENT CHECK CASE

The provision of suitable and affordable housing for welfare clients is a concern of both New York City and New York State governments.

First, the City and the State share equally the nonfederal costs of the Aid to Families with Dependent Children (AFDC) program. Second, although the City's AFDC program is administered by the municipal Human Resources Administration (HRA), the State has long played an active part in exercising its own policy prerogatives. The two-party rent check, made payable to both the client and the landlord and cashable only when signed by both, has been advocated by the City as one way to alleviate the welfare housing problem. The State, concerned about the restraints on freedom of welfare clients to manage money implied by this device, resists its unbridled use. Different perspectives on this issue created a competitive situation for the City and the State vis-a-vis the federal government.

The Problem

The availability of housing for welfare recipients in New York City is extremely limited. In 1986, the city vacancy rate for all rental housing units, at 2 percent, was very low; for low-income rentals, it was even lower—1.6 percent. The number of homeless families, in contrast, is high and growing rapidly. By 1986, there were over 4,000 homeless families. Because the cost of providing temporary housing for homeless families is much higher than the rents for more permanent shelter, the fiscal impact of growing homelessness is considerable.

The causes of the low vacancy rate and the growing problem of the homeless are complex. One reason for the scarcity of low-income rental housing is a long-standing reluctance of landlords to rent to public assistance recipients "because they fear that the rent will not be paid. Often they are right. As a result, many tenants are evicted; many landlords abandon their buildings because they cannot afford to maintain them."[37]

Such behavior by welfare clients sometimes is understandable. "It is tempting for the welfare client to use the money granted for rent for other items—more food or clothing or other purchases. Indeed, welfare clients to an increasing extent [have been, in the past 15 years] doing just that, sometimes catching up on the rent late in the month but frequently not paying rent at all for several months and then moving if they were evicted first."[38]

Homelessness does not result only from evictions. Other causes include cutbacks since 1981 in eligibility for federal AFDC and food stamp programs and denials of SSI benefits; and the release of psychiatric patients from State mental institutions without sufficient community support. From the New York City perspective, however, the failure of welfare clients to pay rent is more amenable to local remedy than are attempts to change other federal or State policies.

The Two-Party Check

Two tools are available to local AFDC administrators to assure rent payment in the case of nonpayment because of mismanagement of the welfare grant by the client. One is the two-party check made out to both the client and the landlord and the other is the direct vendor check, that is, a check made out solely to the landlord.

Federal policy toward the use of restricted rent checks has changed in two important respects over the past decade. The first change concerns limitations on the use of this device. When first allowed under federal law, restricted checks were limited to 5 percent of a state's AFDC caseload. Later, the statutory limitation was increased to 10 percent. In 1977, Congress raised the ceiling to 20 percent. In 1981, the Omnibus Budget Reconciliation Act (OBRA) deleted the limitation entirely.

The second change concerns the process and criteria for determining mismanagement by the client—the necessary precondition for issuing the restricted check. Prior to OBRA, nonpayment of bills could be used as an indication of mismanagement, but determination of mismanagement could not be made solely on that basis. Hearings were mandated, after failure by the welfare client to pay rent, to determine the reason for such nonpayment. Only then, and only if mismanagement was ascertained, could the two-party or the direct vendor rent check be used.

Following enactment of OBRA, the federal Health and Human Services Department (HHS) developed regulations concerning procedures and criteria for imposition of the restricted payment check. The process was begun under HHS Secretary Richard Schweiker. Proposed regulations were issued in November 1984 by his successor, Margaret Heckler; final rules were promulgated in March 1986 by her successor, Otis Bowen. During that period of nearly five years, New York City and New York State advocated and advanced different points of view.

The City's Position

HRA has long favored the two-party check as a method to deal with nonpayment of rent by welfare clients and has pressed the federal government to liberalize regulations concerning its use. Blanche Bernstein, former HRA administrator, wrote, "In 1975, as many as 26 percent of clients receiving AFDC were on two-party checks."[39] Under her leadership, HRA made "special efforts to reduce the proportion below 10 percent. [Fortunately for the city and the state, Congress, in the

1977 amendments,] forgave past sins so that no penalties were imposed on New York State"[40] for exceeding the 10 percent limit. Shortly after the 1977 action, however, the proportion of New York City's AFDC clients on two-party rent checks began to rise again—nearly reaching the new 20 percent limit within a year.

During the late 1970s, Mayor Koch and his Washington Office staff aggressively advocated greater flexibility for the City in the use of two-party checks for welfare clients. Their efforts paid off, as Congress deleted the ceiling in OBRA.

Besides statutory change, the City also requested waivers from current law and regulations. In 1978–1979, HRA sought permission from New York State and the federal government to mount a demonstration project in two South Bronx community planning districts. The project proposed expanded use of the two-party check in exchange for landlords' agreements to maintain and improve their properties. In this case, the City failed to secure the necessary State and federal approvals. Blanche Bernstein, writing from the perspective of HRA, asserts:

> State and federal officials have their responsibilities. Certainly, these officials must ensure that a proposal, such as the Bronx demonstration project, is feasible and provides adequate protection to welfare clients. We adopted many of their suggestions, which served to strengthen the proposal substantially, but one cannot escape the conclusion that the decision to reject was a political decision, not reflective of the objective situation but only of political pressures from one bloc of special interest groups [that] regarded the principle of money management as untouchable forever.[41]

The issue of adequate protection for welfare clients and the principle of unencumbered money management did not die with the Bronx demonstration project. On the contrary, City and State differences over OBRA regulations revolved around these very points.

Although OBRA deleted the 20 percent ceiling, it did not directly address the other major concern of City officials—the delays involved in determination of mismanagement before the restricted rent check can be imposed. As Senator D'Amato asserted in a May 1985 letter to Secretary Heckler, "During this time the family may be evicted and join the growing ranks of homeless. Many landlords are unwilling to risk such a delay; therefore, there is a growing shortage of rental housing made available to AFDC recipients."

The principal concerns of New York City, as the OBRA regulations were being developed, were practical: HRA wanted greater flexibility in determining mismanagement and in placing welfare clients on restricted checks. Specifically, the City wanted (l) presumption of mismanagement after two months of nonpayment of rent and (2) ability to place welfare recipients on restricted checks immediately thereafter, that is, prior to the opportunity for a hearing. The City also wanted HHS to establish these procedures and not leave flexibility with the states.

These concerns were actively and aggressively advocated. Mayor Koch, Senators D'Amato and Moynihan, and New York City Deputy Mayor Brezenoff wrote letters to President Reagan, Chief of Staff Donald Regan, OMB Director David Stockman, and HHS Secretaries Schweiker, Heckler, and Bowen. Mayor Koch personally advanced the City's position in Washington meetings at the White House, OMB, and HHS.

The proposed rules issued under the direction of Secretary Heckler in November 1984 incorporated the City's positions exactly. Mayor Koch, in a January 1985 "Dear Margaret" letter to the Secretary, urged her to issue the final rules quickly.

The State's Position

New York State reacted quickly and negatively to the November 1984 proposed rules. The State Department of Social Services (DSS) saw them as undermining its own authority to set policy. Further, DSS contended that the proposed remedies failed to distinguish between two groups of welfare clients: those who deliberately withhold rent because the landlord fails to provide essential services and those who mismanage the AFDC check. For the former group, DSS argued, "allowing hearings only after the imposition of a restriction might actually contribute to the deterioration and loss of housing stock, since it would severely limit a tenant's opportunity to withhold rent to challenge housing code violations."[42] For those welfare clients suspected of mismanagement, DSS proposed to expedite fair hearings to forestall evictions, an approach that it asserted would be "less injurious to the independence and dignity of recipients of public assistance" than imposing the restricted checks prior to hearings.[43]

New York State's position put it directly at odds with the City. The State wished to maintain its traditional prerogatives and to safeguard, as far as possible, the ability of the welfare client to manage his or her own welfare check. The City's practical objective to increase the supply of low-income housing units was dismissed tersely by DSS in its comments to HHS on the 1984 regulations: "We think that failure of recipients to pay rent is but one very minor aspect of the homeless problem."

Resolution of the Dispute

When the final regulations were issued on March 18, 1986, New York State turned out to be the winner. The specific criteria for determining mismanagement contained in the November 1984 proposed rules were removed. Instead, states were given "maximum flexibility to establish criteria for such a determination [which could be nonpayment of rent]." Such flexibility extended to the timing of the imposition of restricted payments; at the option of the state, they could (or could not) be imposed prior to a hearing.

The fact that Otis Bowen, not Margaret Heckler, was Secretary of HHS when the final regulations were signed was critical to this outcome. A former governor of Indiana, Bowen's strong predisposition toward strengthening the role of states vis-a-vis both federal and local governments was well known. In a letter to him one month before the final regulations were issued, Mayor Koch acknowledged the Secretary's bent ("As a former Governor, you would want this authority to reside in the State Government"), but argued that "the New York case is different because localities pay a significant part of the cost."[44]

Despite the Mayor's plea, the final regulations revealed the key factor of Secretary Bowen's partiality for state over local options. Consequently, the locus for decision making for New York City's welfare housing problem shifted from Washington to Albany where the City now faced the challenge of influencing New York State regulations on two-party rent checks.

CITY-STATE COLLABORATION:
THE DEDUCTIBILITY CASE

Proposals to revise the federal income tax system, first advanced by the Treasury Department in 1984 and then endorsed by President Reagan in 1985, put the State and the City on a collision course with Washington. The key issue was the deductibility of state and local taxes from the federal income tax, the elimination of which the President favored and the retention of which Governor Cuomo, Mayor Koch, Senators D'Amato and Moynihan, and a nearly unanimous House delegation advocated. The governor played a highly visible role in the campaign against elimination of deductibility. The campaign was aimed at activating support for retention both inside New York and elsewhere. This case study demonstrates not only City and State collaboration, but also a deliberate strategy to defuse state and local tax deductibility as an exclusively New York issue.

Historical Background

State and local taxes, along with federal taxes, were the only deductions specified in the Revenue Act of 1862, the country's first income tax, enacted to finance the Union effort in the Civil War. The original rationale was to ensure that the federal government and the state governments each possess adequate powers to raise revenues and to protect individuals from double taxation.[45]

Deductibility of state and local taxes was included in the first modern income tax law of 1913 and in subsequent tax laws. In January 1984, when President Reagan proposed in his State of the Union address "an historic reform for fairness, simplicity and incentives for growth" deductions for major state and local taxes were a long-standing tradition.

Treasury I and Treasury II

The Treasury Department, responding to the President's State of the Union directive to prepare a tax reform proposal, presented its report in November 1984. Among its many recommendations was repeal of deductions for state and local taxes. The report, known as Treasury I, supported repeal by contending that (1) state and local expenditures provide benefits primarily for residents of the taxing jurisdiction, not all federal taxpayers; (2) there is no more reason for a federal subsidy for spending by state and local governments than for private spending; (3) the deduction is not equitable because the benefits of the subsidy accrue primarily to high-income individuals and high-income communities.[46]

The drafters of Treasury I also recognized that repeal of deductibility would raise more revenue than any other single provision in the President's tax reform package. Given the revenue decreases anticipated from proposed cuts in tax rates, elimination of state and local tax deductions was crucial to accomplishing "revenue neutral" tax reform.

From the time of its issuance, Treasury I was viewed as a first effort, not necessarily the final plan to be espoused by the President. Treasury II, issued in May 1985, modified several provisions in Treasury I, but retained repeal of state and local tax deductibility. The reasons for repeal remained the inefficiencies and inequities cited in Treasury I, but this time the arguments singled out "high-tax" states where the "current deduction for state and local taxes disproportionately benefits high-income taxpayers."[47] In that context, the targeting of New York as a high-income, high-tax state whose residents gain most from deductibility was evident.

Effects on New York

Eliminating deductibility would have had adverse effects on individual taxpayers and public services in New York, and the state's economic competitiveness. Individual taxpayers gain from the deductibility of state and local taxes only if they specifically claim this deduction by itemizing. The amount of gain increases with the amount of state and local taxes they pay and with their marginal tax rate. Tax savings are largest in states with high state and local taxes and high-income taxpayers, who face high marginal rates and are most likely to itemize.

Compared with residents of all other states, New Yorkers stood to lose the most from elimination of state and local tax deductibility. In 1982, savings per itemizing return ranged from $1,292 in New York to $257 in Wyoming, while savings on a per capita basis ranged even more widely, from $233 in New York to $20 in South Dakota.[48] Total savings for New York taxpayers in 1982 was $4 billion, or 17 percent of the national total.

Deductibility also has implications for state and local services. The potential effects of ending deductibility were two-fold: the costs to the itemizing taxpayer of government services were raised in the absence of deductibility; consequently, the amount of government services provided would be lowered as the taxpayer reacts to increased tax prices. Public education would be particularly hard hit because school taxes are so visible and politically vulnerable. The annual public school budget is determined by direct referendum in most districts.[49]

Elimination of deductibility could also undermine the efforts of New York State to retain businesses and attract new investment. One of the most impassioned arguments for deductibility is its role in reducing interstate competition. Deductibility reduces the differences in after-tax incomes between residents of high- and low-tax states. States and localities thus have less incentive to compete for taxpayers by cutting tax rates.

Governor Cuomo, Senators Moynihan and D'Amato, and State Comptroller Edward Regan publicly contended in December 1984 that elimination of deductibility would be "devastating" to New Yorkers. "It would interfere," they stated in a press conference, "with the ability of State and local governments in New York to provide essential services, endanger the State's middle-class families, and erode the State's economic base by driving businesses out of New York."

The Governor's Leadership and Strategy

At the outset, New York's strong position against repeal was unique among state governments. Governor Cuomo articulated New York's case and, in so doing, quickly attained national recognition "for picking a fight that few Democratic leaders [were] willing to join, at least publicly."[50] Political observers noted that the Governor's posture on deductibility was risky for his own political future as well as for the

Democratic party, which had been "struggling to position itself closer to the political values and issues that have yielded Republican gains in recent elections."[51]

Nonetheless, the Governor persisted, speaking before congressional committees and in other national forums and taking on opponents from Governor Richard Thornburgh of Pennsylvania to White House Communications Director Patrick Buchanan. Cuomo's arguments focused on his views of federalism:

> The President's plan has been caught in an embarrassing contradiction. He invented the New Federalism. He said he wanted to encourage state and local governments to deliver more of the services that the Federal Government had previously delivered. But by disallowing the deduction of state and local taxes, the plan would impede their ability to do so. In effect, the President is suggesting that he would excuse his failure to supply us bread and his interference with our ability to produce our own by requiring us to starve altogether.[52]

Cuomo was unyielding in his opposition to compromise on deductibility of state and local taxes throughout the two-year course of tax reform. The Governor's calls for vigilance in the face of "tax restructuring proposals that would work, unfairly, to the serious detriment of New Yorkers,"[53] were part of an "inside" strategy to stimulate bipartisan unity among officials in Albany, New York City, and other local governments and in the state's congressional delegation.

Governor Cuomo's early and unequivocal position was communicated to each member of the state's congressional delegation. It was followed by a request that House members cosponsor a resolution crafted by Representative Raymond J. McGrath, Republican from Long Island and a member of the Ways and Means Committee. McGrath's resolution declared deductibility "essential to the well-being of moderate-income Americans, state and local governments and the housing industry."[54] Thirty-two of the 34 New York members signed as cosponsors.

The three New York members on the Ways and Means Committee—Republican McGrath and Democrats Thomas J. Downey and Charles B. Rangel—stood firmly for retention. For McGrath and Downey, whose districts on Long Island contain high proportions of tax itemizers, this position was consistent with their constituents' interests. Between May and December 1985, during Ways and Means Committee deliberations, McGrath and Downey made it clear that deductibility was the *sine qua non* for their support of any committee tax reform bill.

Congressman Rangel's posture against repeal was based on concern for the indirect cuts in government services that would adversely affect his low-income New York City constituents. He also was concerned with securing several "poverty package" elements that would benefit his district more directly; these included increases in the zero bracket and personal deduction amounts. Once he was assured that these elements were protected, he stood firmly on retention of full deductibility with his two colleagues.

New York's Senators D'Amato and Moynihan actively advocated full retention of deductibility from the time Treasury I was presented. Both spoke at numerous functions within the state and elsewhere. They lobbied fellow senators using material detailing the negative effects repeal would have on public education and on revenues for state and local services in all regions of the nation. As a condition for facilitating their access to campaign funds in New York City, Senator D'Amato secured pledges of support for deductibility from Republican senators running for re-election.

Shortly after Treasury II was issued, Senator D'Amato called a meeting of about 200 business leaders in New York City to alert them to the negative implications for New York of the President's proposal. This meeting led to the formation of An Ad Hoc Committee on Deductibility of State and Local Taxes. Renamed the Tax Bill Working Group in June 1985, it was co-chaired by Lewis Rudin, a New York City real estate developer, and Amory Houghton, chairman of the board of Corning Glass Works. Its purpose was to coordinate the efforts of the business community and labor unions in New York City and upstate in support of continued deductibility. In support of the strategy to nationalize the deductibility issue, described below, the Tax Bill Working Group was instrumental in the formation of the National Coalition Against Double Taxation.

Senator Moynihan, member of the Senate Finance Committee and its core group of six senators who developed the committee bill that ultimately was considered by the full Senate in June 1986, was in a pivotal position to promote retention of deductibility. He was not fully successful. The Senate Finance Committee bill, which was unanimously reported out of Committee in May 1986, continued full deductibility for income and property taxes, but not for sales taxes. Senator Moynihan supported that bill, he wrote in a June 1986 special report to his constituents, "for the simple reason that whatever our state or regional interests, we all knew something radical had to be done and there would never be a better time to do it." But he also pledged to press the deductibility issue in the Conference Committee.

Governor Cuomo and his allies felt it was important to downplay deductibility as a "New York" issue that pitted high-tax states against low-tax ones, high-income itemizers against lower-income persons.

"Nationalizing" deductibility was approached in two ways: stressing the concept of federalism as partnership and emphasizing the widespread negative effects on government services that might result from ending deductibility.

Such negative effects were projected to occur disproportionately in the Northeast and Midwest and in the field of public education. The Northeast-Midwest Congressional Coalition in the House of Representatives, representing 18 states, took a position against repeal of deductibility, contending that "repeal would place an unfair and disproportionate burden on taxpayers" in those two regions.[55] Those states rely most heavily on revenues from personal income, sales, and property taxes; states least hard hit by repeal rely on energy severance taxes "that would be considered business taxes and remain deductible."[56]

While many government services could be affected if deductibility were repealed, the national strategy emphasized that education was the prime target for cuts. About 36 percent of all state and local expenditures are earmarked for education; the effects of repeal would be especially harsh for public education. The Washington offices of the New York State Department of Education and the New York City Board of Education were instrumental in alerting major lobby groups, including the American Federation of Teachers, the National Education Association, and the National School Boards Association, to these potential consequences. Under the aegis of the broader National Coalition Against Double Taxation, these educational groups collected data on each state's reliance on sales, property, and income tax revenues for funding education. Their research led them to predict that 32 states would lose between 15 and 18 percent of their spending per pupil if deductibility were repealed.[57] Through these arguments and other activities involving the National Coalition Against Double Taxation, Cuomo and other opponents demonstrated that the repeal of deductibility affected every region of the country—not just New York State.

Conclusion: The Congress Disposes

The Tax Reform Act passed by the House in December 1985 retained full deductibility of state and local taxes. The Senate version adopted in June 1986 retained full deductibility for income and property taxes but not for the sales tax. The House-Senate Conference Committee subsequently adopted the Senate's position. (Senator Moynihan's optimism that the sales tax deduction would be put back by the Conference Committee was not borne out. The foregone revenues that the deduction would represent could not be compensated for.)

In September 1986, both the House and the Senate approved the Conference Agreement by wide margins. The Tax Reform Act of 1986 signed into law by the President in October 1986 retained the itemized deductions for state and local income taxes, real estate taxes, and real property taxes and repealed the itemized deduction for state and local sales taxes.

This outcome did not reflect total success for New York's lobbying efforts. Nonetheless, it was an impressive achievement. Deductibility for income and property taxes, which represent 77 percent of New York's deductible revenues, was retained. The high risk "all or nothing" strategy led to an outcome that, while not completely successful, would have been far more damaging for New York in its absence.

CONCLUSION

This essay shows that New York City and New York State—independently and in collaboration—are active participants in the federal system. For each government, the stakes are high; as a result, each is well organized and poised to respond to federal initiatives and to influence federal policies.

On the whole, the City and the State are inclined to work together, or at least to avoid being visibly at odds. Tensions between them are inevitable, but they are now more frequently overcome within the New York congressional delegation than was the case in past years.

Closer City-State collaboration reflects recognition of the difficult national environment within which New York operates. Population shifts since 1960 and subsequent reapportionments have resulted in decreases in congressional representation and electoral college strength for New York. These trends are expected to continue; Texas and Florida are projected to overtake New York by 1990, dropping New York State from the second to the fourth largest delegation.

Successful outcomes for New York cannot be taken for granted in the federal arena. Two lessons are worth repeating. First, ongoing collaboration between New York City and New York State is important for favorable distributions of federal resources. As Representative Stratton said after the divided House vote on the Staten Island homeport, "If New York is going to have any clout, we've got to work together."

Second, the City and the State can neutralize their sometimes negative image in Washington and achieve their goals by demonstrating, as in the deductibility case, that their position is not unique, but, rather, is shared by taxpayers and governments all around the nation. In the future, as New York's numerical presence in the Congress continues to shrink, the need to stress the congruity between the goals of New York City and New York State and those of other states and cities will become even more imperative.

NOTES

1. John P. Kaminski, "New York: The Reluctant Pillar," in Stephen L. Schechter, ed., *The Reluctant Pillar: New York and the Adoption of the Federal Constitution* (Troy, NY: Russell Sage College, 1985), pp. 116–117.
2. Daniel J. Elazar, *American Federalism: A View from the States* (New York: Harper & Row, 1984), p. 2.
3. For an analysis of the effects on the New York State government of the Reagan domestic program, see Sarah F. Liebschutz and Irene Lurie, "New York," in Richard P. Nathan and Fred Doolittle, eds., *Reagan and the States* (Princeton, NJ: Princeton University Press, 1987).
4. The percentage for all cities is from the U.S. Advisory Commission on Intergovernmental Relations, *Significant Features of Fiscal Federalism* (Washington, DC: ACIR, 1985), p. 65. For the New York City percentage, see City of New York, *Executive Budget Fiscal Year 1987, Message of the Mayor*, May 5, 1986, p. 50.
5. See Richard H. Silkman, "Old Federalism and New Federalism in New York State," in Morton Schoolman and Alvin Magid, eds., *Reindustrializing New York State* (Albany: SUNY Press, 1986), pp. 331–355.
6. Fred C. Doolittle, "Federal Aid," in Charles Brecher and Raymond D. Horton, eds., *Setting Municipal Priorities 1986* (New York: New York University Press, 1985), p. 129. This chapter contains an analysis of the fiscal impacts on the City of recent federal cutbacks.
7. See City of New York, *Executive Budget Fiscal Year 1987*, p. 50.
8. Catherine Lovell and Charles Tobin, "The Mandate Issue," *Public Administration Review* 41 (May–June 1981):318.
9. For an analysis of the effects on New York State of 1981 federal Medicaid policy changes, see Liebschutz and Lurie, "New York."
10. Sarah F. Liebschutz, "New Federalism Modified: Jobs and Highways in New York," *Publius* 14 (Summer 1984):96.
11. "City, U.S. in Dispute on Antiapartheid Law," *Newsday*, May 1, 1986, p. 18.
12. Donald Haider, *When Governments Come to Washington* (New York: Free Press, 1974), pp. 21–30.
13. Haider, *When Governments Come to Washington*, pp. 1–3.
14. David L. Cingranelli, "State Government Lobbies in the National Political Process," *State Government* 56 (1983):122.
15. Robert H. Connery and Gerald Benjamin, *Rockefeller of New York* (Ithaca: Cornell University Press, 1979), pp. 400, 402.
16. Donald Haider, "The New York City Congressional Delegation," *City Almanac*, 7, no. 6 (April 1973):4.
17. Haider, "New York City Congressional Delegation," p. 4.
18. Michael Oreskes, "For New York Lobbyists, It Was Westway Week," *New York Times*, September 22, 1985, sec. 1, p. 60.

19. James Barron, "The New York Delegation," in Peter W. Colby, ed., *New York State Today* (Albany: SUNY Press, 1985), p. 205.
20. Barbara Sinclair Deckard, "State Party Delegations in the House of Representatives," doctoral thesis, University of Rochester, 1969, p. 139.
21. Deckard, "State Party Delegations."
22. Deckard, "State Party Delegations," p. 139.
23. Barron, "New York Delegation," p. 204.
24. Barron, "New York Delegation," p. 207.
25. Deckard, "State Party Delegations," pp. 72–73.
26. Deckard, "State Party Delegations," p. 208.
27. Haider, "New York City Congressional Delegation," p. 12.
28. One of the fourteen New York City seats was vacant because of the death of Congressman Joseph Addabo.
29. "House Balks at Navy's Homeporting Plan," *Congressional Quarterly Weekly Report*, June 28, 1986, p. 1484.
30. *Congressional Quarterly Weekly Report*, June 28, 1986, p. 1493.
31. U.S. Congress, House, *Congressional Record*, June 25, 1986, p. 4199.
32. Michael Oreskes, "House Vote on Navy Port for Staten Island," *New York Times*, June 28, 1986, sec. 1, p. 31.
33. Oreskes, "House Vote on Navy Port."
34. New York State, Office of Federal Affairs, *Report on the Second Session of the 98th Congress*, October 24, 1984, and New York City, Washington Office, *Federal Program, 99th Congress Second Session*, February 1986.
35. Because New York is one of only three states that has not elected to administer the small cities block grant program, this was a special issue for the State. For background on New York and the small cities program, see Liebschutz and Lurie, "New York."
36. City of New York, Washington Office, *Federal Program*, p. 1.
37. Letter from Edward I. Koch to Otis Bowen, February 18, 1986.
38. Blanche Bernstein, *The Politics of Welfare* (Cambridge, MA: Abt, 1982), p. 166.
39. Bernstein, *Politics of Welfare*, pp. 166–167.
40. Bernstein, *Politics of Welfare*, pp. 166–167.
41. Bernstein, *Politics of Welfare*, p. 200.
42. Letter from Caesar Perales to Margaret A. McSteen, January 14, 1985.
43. Letter from Perales to McSteen.
44. Letter from Koch to Bowen.
45. See Sarah F. Liebschutz and Irene Lurie, "State and Local Tax Deductibility," *Publius* 16 (1986):51–70.
46. U.S. Department of the Treasury, *Tax Reform for Fairness, Simplicity and Economic Growth*, vol. 1, *Overview* (Washington, DC: U.S. Government Printing Office, November 1984), pp. 78–80.
47. U.S. Department of the Treasury, *The President's Tax Proposals to the Congress for Fairness, Growth and Simplicity* (Washington, DC: U.S. Government Printing Office, May 1985), p. 62.
48. U.S. Advisory Commission on Intergovernmental Relations, "Federal Income Tax Deductibility of State and Local Taxes," Discussion Draft, June 1985, table 5, p. 22; and U.S. Department of the Treasury, *The President's Tax Proposals to the Congress*, pp. 68–69.
49. For further discussion of these points, see Liebschutz and Lurie, "State and Local Tax Deductibility."

50. Phil Gailey, "Risky Stand on Tax Plan," *New York Times*, June 21, 1985, sec. 1, p. 30.
51. Gailey, "Risky Stand," p. 30.
52. Gailey, "Risky Stand," p. 30.
53. Mario M. Cuomo, *State of New York Annual Budget Message 1985– 1986*, January 22, 1985, p. m9.
54. House Resolution 105.
55. Northeast-Midwest Congressional Coalition, "Fact Sheet, State and Local Tax Deductibility," September 12, 1985.
56. Northeast-Midwest Congressional Coalition, "Fact Sheet."
57. Donald Phares, "Adverse Consequences of the Proposed Elimination of State-Local Tax Deductibility," an Issue Paper for the SALT-D Action Group, June 1985.

8

PUBLIC FINANCE

❧

Cynthia B. Green
and
Paul D. Moore

THE CITY of New York is the largest single component in a complex public service delivery system in New York State that includes over 9,800 separate counties, cities, towns, villages, fire districts, school districts, and special districts. This essay analyzes New York City's financial relationships with the State and compares them with those of New York's other local governments. A key question is whether the City's relationships are "special" within New York State, and, if so, in what ways. The first section summarizes the history of the state-local fiscal partnership, focusing on the changing balance between control and flexibility. The second section compares New York City's revenue, expenditure, and debt characteristics with those of the State's other local governments. The third section focuses on the balance between the contribution of New York City taxpayers to State revenues and the benefits to City residents of State spending for services in New York City. The essay concludes with a discussion of the forces shaping the current City-State fiscal relationship, highlighting those which are expected to continue and identifying new forces which are likely to emerge.

HISTORICAL BACKGROUND[1]

Before the 1890s, New York City included only Manhattan and the southern portion of the Bronx. The remainder of the Bronx, Brooklyn, Queens, and Staten Island were under several separate local governments. At that time, there was little sharing of functional or financial responsibility between the State and its local governments. The only major interaction was a result of the State's requirement that localities annually submit a taxing and spending plan for legislative approval. However, the legislative review was not rigorous or systematic. As a result, the nature of state-local fiscal relationships changed irregularly and the treatment of localities differed widely.

Beginning in the 1820s, high debt burdens and bond defaults among local governments became a serious problem. Eager to attract industry and population, local governments issued bonds to buy stock of railroad companies that agreed to construct routes through their territory. Interest on the bonds was to be paid through local taxes, while the principal was to be paid from stock dividends. Problems arose because the stock dividends were often insufficient to cover bond liabilities. Also, in 1871, the "Tweed Ring" and its associated corruptness in New York City was exposed.

State concern over local fiscal mismanagement and corruption led to amendments to the State Constitution in 1884 that established tighter State control over local finances. These amendments replaced the ad hoc, annual legislative reviews of local financial plans with constitutional limits on local taxing and borrowing. Under these provisions, the large cities in the state, including the City of New York, were granted permission to levy only one tax, the real property tax. This tax was limited to 2 percent of the assessed value of taxable real estate.

In 1898, New York City and its surrounding counties of Brooklyn, Staten Island, Queens, and the Bronx consolidated into the "Greater City of New York," becoming the first and largest metropolitan government in the state.[2] As power was transferred to the new City's legislative and executive branches, the old county governments' role was limited. However, the newly consolidated City was still held to the earlier 2 percent constitutional limit on real property taxation.

Unforeseen was the degree to which the City of New York would experience urbanization, industrialization, and population growth. Like most cities facing these changes, New York experienced strong and growing demand for public services. To meet these needs, higher revenues were necessary. However, under the State constitution, the City's ability to generate these revenues was restricted.

Increased Interdependence

As budgetary problems began to occur, the City turned to the State for assistance. Often this took the form of requests for State aid or a transfer of responsibility for funding of particular functions from the local to the state level. After 1900, the State involved itself fiscally in areas that had previously been local responsibilities, notably education and roads.

Beginning in 1916 and continuing into the 1930s, the State began to share with localities revenues from State taxes on business corporations, personal income, occupational licenses, financial institutions, motor vehicle fees, and alcoholic beverages. However, these efforts were hampered by perceived inequities in the distribution of funds among the localities and by the unpredictability of the annual amounts localities would receive. In addition, income from the single local revenue source, the property tax, often proved unreliable, particularly during periods of economic downturns.

In these circumstances, the City sought greater revenue generating capacity. Generally, the State was reluctant to grant such requests, not wishing to relinquish control over its localities' finances. The State was concerned about local financial mismanagement, the erosion of its own revenue base, and the economically harmful consequences that might result from higher levels of taxation. However, at the same time, the State did not wish to restrict severely local discretion, particularly for New York City. It had become the largest and most economically important locality in the state.

To maintain control, yet provide additional revenues to the City, the State had four options: provide more direct State assistance; assume additional local costs; grant greater latitude in City taxing authority; or establish higher constitutional property tax limits. Most often, the third choice was selected and the City was permitted to further "tax itself." In the 1930–1949 period, the State allowed the City to enact taxes on retail sales, gross receipts, and consumption items. Further, the constitutional tax limit was amended in 1938 to be 2 percent of a five-year moving "average" of assessed value.

Yet the City quickly exhausted the additional revenue from these measures and continued to experience budget problems. In 1955, the State responded with constitutional amendments permitting the substitution of full value for assessed value in calculating the property tax limit and raised the City's limit from 2 to 2.5 percent of the five-year average.

However, the City's fiscal responsibilities and demands continued to grow. After much debate and consideration, in 1966 the State granted the City the right to impose a tax on the personal income of its residents and on the earnings of persons employed in the city but residing elsewhere.

Clearly, the State had relaxed its control over the City's revenue generating capacity. As a result, the City-State fiscal relationship differed from that of other localities. Of all localities in the state, the City of New York had the broadest revenue base.

State relaxation of fiscal control over the City was accompanied by other changes in State policy that further intertwined fiscal relationships. Under the governorship of Nelson A. Rockefeller, which spanned 15 years beginning in 1959, the State expanded its activities. Rockefeller's policies reflected the national mood. President John F. Kennedy's "New Frontier" and President Lyndon B. Johnson's "Great Society" fostered the notion that "no problem was beyond solution if enough money, time, energy, talent and knowledge could be brought to bear in an organized, systematic way."[3]

Rockefeller dramatically increased State taxes and spending. For localities, two important broad initiatives were taken. First, State aid to localities expanded rapidly. Second, the State expanded its use of public benefit corporations, or authorities, to finance regional capital needs.

Rockefeller expanded local assistance for education and transportation and began assistance to localities for health, housing, and community development. In addition, large increases were made in general purpose aid. During the 1960s the share of the City's budget derived from State funds increased from 18.5 to 32.4 percent.[4]

Simultaneously, the State improved its capital plant. Initially, Rockefeller's efforts were stymied when in referenda voters failed to approve new debt for capital construction. In response, the governor created public authorities that could issue debt without voter approval, but which lacked direct State financial guarantees. To help ensure that the obligations of these agencies would be accepted by investors, Rockefeller introduced the concept of "moral obligation," an implied promise of the State to guarantee debt service payments. Such creative mechanisms permitted the State to embark upon the largest capital program in history, including the building of facilities for localities. Today there are 17 major State authorities.[5] While all are State entities, several concentrate their activities on the capital needs of New York City.

Although the City and other localities benefit from this infusion of State resources, it has reduced local autonomy and increased State involvement in local financial affairs. To illustrate the nature of this increased interdependence, three of these major capital financing mechanisms are described briefly below.

The Urban Development Corporation, created in 1968, is now concerned with economic development. It is mandated to generate industrial, commercial, and civic development in distressed urban areas and to create jobs through the construction of low- and moderate-income housing and the renovation or expansion of industrial and commercial facilities. In 1986, its investments totaled $4.0 billion, of which 80 percent are within the City of New York.[6]

The Metropolitan Transportation Authority (MTA) was created in 1967 and is responsible for mass transportation in the New York metropolitan area. It operates seven train and bus systems located in the City of New York and the counties of Nassau, Suffolk, Orange, Dutchess, Putnam, Rockland, and Westchester. Under the MTA's 1982 to 1986 capital plan, three quarters of a total investment of $8.5 billion was for projects in New York City.[7]

The Housing Finance Agency was created in 1960 to finance the construction of facilities for the State University of New York; the Department of Mental Hygiene; and public and private housing, hospitals, nursing homes, community mental health facilities, and youth and senior citizen centers. Most of the agency's recent projects involve housing activities. In 1986, of this agency's total $6.7 billion commitment, 40 percent was for projects within the city.[8] Other State authorities—notably the New York State Battery Park City Authority, the Housing Development Corporation, and the Dormitory Authority—finance capital projects exclusively in New York City.

The Fiscal Crisis and Renewed Controls

By the middle of the 1970s, the State's and City's fiscal affairs were bound together; few City services were not supported financially by both the City and the State. Despite this substantial assistance, the City experienced little direct fiscal interference from the State. However, fundamental changes began in 1975. The State, in response to a fiscal crisis and loss of confidence in the City's financial management, imposed strong fiscal controls.

Despite the additional State aid and increased revenue generating capacity, the City still experienced budgetary problems in the early 1970s. The use of short-term debt and capital budget expenditures to finance operating expenses grew as a way of circumventing the State's constitutional tax limits. As a result of "overspending, overtaxing, overborrowing, chaotic accounting and deceptive financial reporting,"[9] the City of New York lost access to the public credit markets in the spring of 1975. State efforts to advance funds to the City, provide new programs of assistance, and assume a greater portion of the funding of many City-financed services strained the State's fiscal resources. There was serious concern that the City's difficulties would force it into bankruptcy and this, in turn, would jeopardize the market access of State authorities and even the State itself.

The State responded with actions to avert municipal bankruptcy. In September 1975, the State passed the Financial Emergency Act.[10] A "Control Period" was established during which the City was required to take specific actions under State supervision. The City had to prepare and maintain a budget balanced in accordance with Generally Accepted Accounting Principles (GAAP) and to submit its financial statements to an independent audit. The City also was required to revise its accounting practices. In order to provide more timely and accurate information, between 1977 and 1980 the City implemented the Integrated Financial Management System. It provides financial information for the City in a single, integrated system that aids in preventing expenditure overruns.

New State agencies and procedures were established in order to provide ongoing oversight of the City's finances. The Financial Emergency Act created the New York State Emergency Financial Control Board, later renamed the Financial Control Board (FCB). This agency, composed of seven members including the governor, state comptroller, and mayor, had direct oversight responsibility. The City was required to submit annually a four-year financial plan encompassing its revenues, expenditures, cash flow, and capital projections to the FCB. The FCB's responsibilities included reviewing, and then approving, modifying, redesigning, or rejecting the City's financial plan; reviewing the City's operations and determining its compliance with the financial plan; approving or disallowing long- or short-term City borrowing and certain contracts, including collecting bargaining agreements; and reexamining the approved financial plan quarterly to determine its conformance to statutory standards. These powers were intended to ensure that the City's fiscal practices were sound and its financial plans and labor contracts were affordable.

To assist the FCB in exercising its responsibilities, the State created the Office of Special Deputy Comptroller for New York City. The Special Deputy Comptroller, appointed by the New York State Comptroller, is directed to conduct analyses of the City's revenues, expenditures, and indebtedness as well as to perform special studies.

Also in 1975, the State established the Municipal Assistance Corporation for the City of New York (MAC), an authority empowered to issue bonds to finance the City's accumulated deficits.[11] MAC alleviated the City's cash flow problems by refinancing its short-term debt with long-term bonds. MAC also oversees and reviews the City's finances.

The establishment of these oversight bodies placed the City in a more regulated and dependent position than had been the case for some time and than was the case for any other local government in the State (except Yonkers). Clearly, after 1975 the ability of the City to make independent financial and operating decisions was limited and the nature of public financing of City operations fundamentally altered.

The City's fiscal crisis also triggered shifts in other State policies. The State's historical approach of granting the City taxing power to finance needed services rather than providing direct State financing for these functions was modified. In January 1976, for example, the City's Temporary Commission on City Finance concluded that "the State must assume all operating costs of higher education, courts, correction services and probation (in New York City)."[12] Parallel recommendations concerning the welfare system, made decades earlier, were renewed. The trauma of the fiscal crisis resulted in implementation of a number of these recommendations.

Until 1986, the policies of strong State control over the City's finances and increased State involvement in previously financed local services continued. However, improvements in the city's economy and its financial management system led to the end of the control period in June 1986. Each of the three required conditions had been met. First, the City had balanced its budget under GAAP for three consecutive years. Second, the City had regained access to private credit markets. Third, the City had retired all of its federally guaranteed long-term debt. Although the Financial Control Board will continue to exist until 2008, its formal power to reject or approve the City's budget and financial plans, long- and short-term borrowing, and contractual agreements is in abeyance.

Full power will be restored to State control agencies if the City experiences an operating deficit of over $100 million, fails to meet its debt service payments, or loses significant market access. This seems unlikely, however, because under State law the City still is required to maintain GAAP balanced budgets and continue its sophisticated financial management system; and MAC remains empowered to manage and refund the City's outstanding debt. In addition, City fiscal authorities have become sensitive to avoiding the mistakes of the past.

The 1975–1985 period is especially significant because it witnessed the shift in State policy from primarily broadening the City's revenue raising capacity to enforcing strict monitoring and control of its finances. Since these reforms were institutional in nature, they will continue to determine the future direction of the City-State fiscal relationship. Therefore, the remainder of this essay focuses on that period and the major components of the new relationship.

How Different Is New York City?

To determine how New York City's pattern of public finance differs from that of localities in the rest of the state, it is useful to compare selected measures for the City with comparable figures for all jurisdictions outside New York City.[13] The latter figures combine the activity of the State's 57 counties, 61 cities, 932 towns, 556 villages, and 837 fire districts. (To facilitate meaningful comparisons, data relating to public education, which is sometimes financed by independent school districts spanning other local boundaries, have been excluded for New York City and all comparison units.) Additional comparisons are made with the aggregate activity of all local governments, except school districts, in the counties of Erie, Monroe, Onondaga, and Westchester. These counties' combined total population is in excess of 3 million. They also contain the State's next four largest cities—Buffalo, Rochester, Syracuse, and Yonkers. The most important reason for using this framework of analysis is the unique nature of New York City as a comprehensive provider of services that in other parts of the State are provided by some combination of county, city, town, and village governments as well as fire districts and other special districts. The combined activities of these units constitute an entity comparable to New York City. The relevant comparative data for expenditures are presented in Table 8.1, for revenues in Table 8.2, and for debt and full value of real property in Table 8.3.

The Preeminent Size of New York City

By almost any measure, the magnitude of public finance in New York City eclipses all other units of local government in the state. With only 40 percent of the state's population, New York City accounted for over 55 percent of all (nonschool) local government expenditures and revenues in the state and for 58 percent of all local government outstanding debt. As these figures suggest, per capita spending by New York City was nearly 90 percent higher than the average for other localities in the state, and its per capita outstanding debt was more than double the average for all other local units. A similar relationship exists between New York City and the four other large urban counties in the state. Per capita total spending, total revenues and outstanding debt in New York City vastly exceeded the comparable figure for all four areas.

An elaboration of the factors behind the greater spending and borrowing in New York City is beyond the scope of this essay, but an important observation can be derived from Table 8.1. The disparities appear to be roughly proportional for the three types of spending examined—current operations, debt principal, and debt interest. That is, the City has relatively high per capita figures for each category.

It is important to note that the substantial gap between the scale of public finance in New York City and other localities is narrowing. Between 1975 and 1985 total spending by the City increased about 53 percent, well below the other localities' rate of 69 percent and below the figures for each of the four other large areas. Similarly, outstanding debt for New York City rose less than 25 percent over the decade compared with an average of 54 percent for all other local governments. As this suggests, New York City in recent years has issued less debt annually than localities in the rest of the state. In 1985, the City issued not quite $3.0 billion of new debt, while the combined total issued in the rest of the state exceeded $3.1 billion.

A significant aspect of public finance for which the general pattern described above does not apply is the value of real property. Contrary to commonly held perceptions, New York City does not have a greater real property tax base than the rest of the state. New York City's 1985 full value of taxable property was almost $98.6 billion, in itself a staggering sum. Yet the aggregate full value tax base for localities in the rest of the state was over four times greater at $432.5 billion. On a per capita basis, the property tax base in the rest of the state ($41,248) was nearly three times that of New York City ($13,941). Moreover, that disparity has been increasing. The City's growth in full value between 1975 and 1985 was 39 percent, while the property tax base for the rest of the state rose 89 percent.

New York City's Unique Revenue System

In addition to scale, New York City differs significantly from other localities in its heavy reliance on nonproperty taxes other than sales taxes. (See Table 8.4.) In 1985 the City derived 28 percent of its revenues from taxes on personal, corporate, and bank income and similar sources. For all other localities in the state the equivalent share is 3 percent. Among the four other large urban areas, only Yonkers derives more than 5 percent of its total revenues from such sources.

Currently, every county and city in New York State levies a tax on real property. In four of the state's 57 counties the property tax is the sole source of local tax revenues.[14] The 53 other counties utilize additional revenue sources, although their reliance on them is much less than that of New York City.

The nonproperty tax revenue on which many local units primarily rely is the sales and use tax. All but four of the state's counties, and just under half of its 62 cities, impose such a tax. New York City and three other cities (Mount Vernon, Yonkers, and Glen Cove) together with two counties (Nassau and Suffolk) have received State permission to increase their sales tax rates to 4 percent. All other counties and cities are restricted to a combined sales tax rate that may not exceed 3 percent.[15]

TABLE 8.1
Expenditures in Selected Urban Areas of New York State, Local Fiscal Years 1975 and 1985

Government Unit(s)	1985 Amounts		Percentage Change 1975 to 1985
	Total (in millions)	Per Capita	
TOTAL EXPENDITURES			
New York State Total	$28,942.3	$1,648	59.9%
New York City Total	16,243.3	2,297	53.3
NYS Total (excluding NYC)	12,699.0	1,211	69.1
Erie (all units)	1,262.0	1,243	64.2
Monroe (all units)	960.1	1,367	88.1
Onondaga (all units)	652.2	1,406	90.3
Westchester (all units)	1,377.0	1,589	95.8
CURRENT OPERATIONS EXPENDITURES			
New York State Total	22,712.9	1,294	73.9
New York City Total	12,660.3	1,790	66.8
NYS Total (excluding NYC)	10,052.5	959	83.7
Erie (all units)	1,010.5	995	69.6
Monroe (all units)	697.2	993	84.6
Onondaga (all units)	460.1	992	90.2
Westchester (all units)	1,206.0	1,392	108.9
EQUIPMENT AND CAPITAL EXPENDITURES			
New York State Total	3,088.8	176	27.2
New York City Total	1,587.4	224	9.9
NYS Total (excluding NYC)	1,501.4	143	52.6
Erie (all units)	143.9	142	38.1
Monroe (all units)	157.1	224	139.3
Onondaga (all units)	64.0	138	(4.9)
Westchester (all units)	96.1	111	23.7
DEBT SERVICE PRINCIPAL EXPENDITURES			
New York State Total	1,781.6	101	(2.8)
New York City Total*	1,121.8	159	11.7
NYS Total (excluding NYC)	659.9	63	(20.3)
Erie (all units)	52.6	52	14.0
Monroe (all units)	71.0	101	61.2
Onondaga (all units)	96.2	207	393.4
Westchester (all units)	41.0	47	16.0

TABLE 8.1 *(continued)*

Government Unit(s)	1985 Amounts Total (in millions)	Per Capita	Percentage Change 1975 to 1985
DEBT SERVICE INTEREST EXPENDITURES			
New York State Total	$1,359.1	$77	74.3%
New York City Total*	873.9	124	57.5
NYS Total (excluding NYC)	485.2	46	115.7
Erie (all units)	54.9	54	143.6
Monroe (all units)	34.8	50	51.1
Onondaga (all units)	31.9	69	127.8
Westchester (all units)	33.8	39	161.7

SOURCES: Office of the New York State Comptroller, *Special Report on Municipal Affairs*, for local fiscal year ended in 1975; Office of the New York State Comptroller, *Special Report on Municipal Affairs*, for local fiscal year ended in 1985; Office of the New York City Comptroller, *Report of the Comptroller of the City of New York for the Fiscal Year 1974–1975*; and Office of the New York Comptroller, *Comprehensive Annual Financial Report of the Comptroller for the Fiscal Year Ended June 30, 1985*.

*These figures are taken from or combined with data from the *Comprehensive Annual Financial Report* and are not directly comparable to the other figures presented in the table, which are from the *Special Report on Municipal Affairs*, since they were compiled under different accounting principles; the most important of these principles is the treatment of financing activities of the Municipal Assistance Corporation (MAC), which are included in these figures.

Between 1966 and 1984, the City of New York was the only local government in the state to levy a personal income tax. In 1984, the City of Yonkers also received State permission to enact such a tax. The Cities of New York and Yonkers also share another revenue instrument not permitted elsewhere in the state; both have a tax on real estate transfers, New York since 1980 and Yonkers since 1984. The City of New York also taxes commercial activity, through mechanisms such as a general corporation tax levied on the income of corporations conducting business in the city, a financial corporation tax imposed on the income of banking corporations conducting business in the city, an unincorporated business tax, and a commercial rent tax.

The distinctive features of New York City's revenue system have become even more pronounced in the period since the fiscal crisis. Between 1975 and 1985 the share of City revenues from its nonsales and nonproperty taxes jumped from 15 to 28 percent; in contrast all other

TABLE 8.2
Revenues in Selected Urban Areas of New York State, Local Fiscal Years 1975 and 1985

Government Unit(s)	1985 Amounts		Percentage Change 1975 to 1985
	Total (in millions)	Per Capita	
TOTAL REVENUES			
New York State Total	$27,049.1	$1,541	81.0%
New York City Total	14,835.1	2,098	70.1
NYS Total (excluding NYC)	12,214.0	1,165	96.5
Erie (all units)	1,219.2	1,201	84.5
Monroe (all units)	894.7	1,274	94.3
Onondaga (all units)	554.7	1,196	92.4
Westchester (all units)	1,335.6	1,541	101.3
REAL PROPERTY TAXES			
New York State Total	6,590.2	375	91.8
New York City Total	2,553.7	361	89.5
NYS Total (excluding NYC)	4,036.5	385	93.3
Erie (all units)	335.7	331	64.2
Monroe (all units)	242.3	345	85.2
Onondaga (all units)	162.9	351	123.6
Westchester (all units)	522.5	603	104.7
SALES TAXES			
New York State Total	3,553.6	202	151.1
New York City Total	1,827.8	258	131.0
NYS Total (excluding NYC)	1,725.8	165	176.6
Erie (all units)	175.5	173	176.4
Monroe (all units)	79.0	113	95.5
Onondaga (all units)	77.8	168	130.5
Westchester (all units)	166.6	192	241.9
OTHER NONPROPERTY TAXES			
New York State Total	4,493.3	256	213.9
New York City Total	4,106.3	581	204.9
NYS Total (excluding NYC)	387.0	37	356.9
Erie (all units)	13.8	14	357.6
Monroe (all units)	56.3	80	185.0
Onondaga (all units)	21.2	46	97.1
Westchester (all units)	39.0	45	455.2

TABLE 8.2 *(continued)*

	1985 Amounts		
Government Unit(s)	Total (in millions)	Per Capita	Percentage Change 1975 to 1985
STATE AID			
New York State Total*	$4,306.3	$245	46.0%
New York City Total*	2,521.7	357	30.2
NYS Total (excluding NYC)	1,784.6	170	76.3
Erie (all units)	232.5	229	99.8
Monroe (all units)	136.3	194	108.2
Onondaga (all units)	96.2	207	78.6
Westchester (all units)	178.4	206	49.6
FEDERAL AID			
New York State Total	3,942.6	225	2.7
New York City Total	2,439.2	345	(3.0)
NYS Total (excluding NYC)	1,503.3	143	13.6
Erie (all units)	185.7	183	106.0
Monroe (all units)	155.3	221	44.2
Onondaga (all units)	60.6	131	(11.6)
Westchester (all units)	97.5	113	(21.0)
ALL OTHER REVENUES			
New York State Total	4,163.1	237	122.7
New York City Total	1,386.4	196	76.6
NYS Total (excluding NYC)	2,776.7	265	156.1
Erie (all units)	276.2	272	161.6
Monroe (all units)	225.4	321	134.3
Onondaga (all units)	135.9	293	180.5
Westchester (all units)	331.6	383	202.0

SOURCES: Office of the New York State Comptroller, *Special Report on Municipal Affairs*, for local fiscal year ended in 1975; Office of the New York State Comptroller, *Special Report on Municipal Affairs*, for local fiscal year ended in 1985; Office of the New York City Comptroller, *Report of the Comptroller of the City of New York for the Fiscal Year 1974–1975*; and Office of the New York City Comptroller, *Comprehensive Annual Financial Report of the Comptroller for the Fiscal Year Ended June 30, 1985*.

*The increases since 1975 have been adjusted to reflect a State advance of $785 million to the City.

TABLE 8.3

Full Value and Debt in Selected Urban Areas
of New York State, Local Fiscal Years 1975 and 1985

| | 1985 Amounts | | |
Government Unit(s)	Total (in millions)	Per Capita	Percent Change 1975 to 1985
FULL VALUE			
New York State Total	$531,131.4	$30,250	77.0%
New York City Total	98,583.1	13,941	38.9
NYS Total (excluding NYC)	432,548.3	41,248	88.8
Erie (all units)	30,345.6	29,883	76.5
Monroe (all units)	25,243.6	35,947	77.3
Onondaga (all units)	14,904.3	32,127	94.9
Westchester (all units)	55,281.6	63,791	197.5
TOTAL DEBT ISSUED			
New York State Total	6,098.5	347	203.9
New York City Total*	2,997.7	421	206.7
NYS Total (excluding NYC)	3,120.8	298	201.4
Erie (all units)	459.1	452	67.5
Monroe (all units)	198.7	283	132.5
Onondaga (all units)	140.7	303	30.8
Westchester (all units)	342.1	395	110.7
TOTAL DEBT OUTSTANDING			
New York State Total	20,265.9	1,154	35.6
New York City Total*	11,716.7	1,657	24.7
NYS Total (excluding NYC)	8,549.2	815	54.0
Erie (all units)	856.1	843	49.9
Monroe (all units)	597.7	851	30.4
Onondaga (all units)	455.0	981	51.9
Westchester (all units)	664.9	767	62.4

SOURCES: Office of the New York State Comptroller, *Special Report on Municipal Affairs*, for local fiscal year ended in 1975; Office of the New York State Comptroller, *Special Report on Municipal Affairs*, for local fiscal year ended in 1985; Office of the New York City Comptroller, *Report of the Comptroller of the City of New York for the Fiscal Year 1974–1975*; and Office of the New York Comptroller, *Comprehensive Annual Financial Report of the Comptroller for the Fiscal Year Ended June 30, 1985.*

*These figures are taken from or combined with data from the *Comprehensive Annual Financial Report* and are not directly comparable to the other figures presented in the table, which are from the *Special Report on Municipal Affairs*, since they were compiled under different accounting principles; the most important of these principles is the treatment of financing activities of the Municipal Assistance Corporation (MAC), which are included in these figures.

localities in the state continued to place small reliance on those sources and their share grew only from 1 to 3 percent.

The City's receipt of intergovernmental transfers also has not followed the pattern of all other government units in the state. According to the published data, State aid to New York City decreased by over $201 million between 1975 and 1985, while every other government unit received increased aid. However, this figure is misleading, because the 1975 data include a $785 million advance of State aid that was part of the State's response to the City's fiscal crisis.[16] If the 1975 data are adjusted to represent a more typical aid flow, then State aid to New York City would have increased by about $584 million, or 30 percent. Nonetheless, this rate of increase is still well below that for all other localities—76 percent (see Table 8.2).

Federal aid to New York City actually decreased by about $77 million, or 3 percent, between 1975 and 1985. Such aid to all other localities in the state increased by almost 14 percent. Yet like New York City, the local governments in Onondaga and Westchester counties received less federal aid. In Westchester, the decline was an especially severe 21 percent.

New York City's Unique Debt Structure

As with property taxes, the State Constitution limits a local government's debt incurring power to a fixed percentage of its real property tax base. New York City's limit is 10 percent of the average full value of property over the past five years (including school purposes), while it is 9 percent for the four other large cities (also including school purposes) and 7 percent for all other cities, towns, and villages (excluding school purposes). However, overlapping limits for county purposes (7 percent) and school purposes (5 percent) make the combined limits for other localities more generous than those on New York City.

Despite its more restrictive limits, the City of New York has substantially more debt outstanding than other localities. As shown in Table 8.3, the City's outstanding debt in 1985 was over $11.7 billion, or $1,657 per capita, compared with equivalent figures for all other localities of $8.5 billion and $815 per capita. As these figures suggest, New York City has been able to issue substantial debt outside its constitutional limit.

New York City's heavy reliance on short-term borrowing—borrowing not subject to the constitutional tax limit—was a major reason for its fiscal crisis. Since 1975, and with help from the State-created Municipal Assistance Corporation (MAC), the City's debt

TABLE 8.4
Composition of Municipal (Nonschool) Revenues, 1975 and 1985

Government Unit(s)	Local Fiscal Years Ending in		Percentage Point Increase (Decrease) Between 1975* and 1985
	1975*	1985	
REAL PROPERTY TAXES AS PERCENTAGE OF TOTAL			
New York State Total	23.0%	24.4%	1.4
New York City Total	15.4	17.2	1.8
NYS Total (excluding NYC)	33.6	33.1	(0.5)
Erie (all units)	30.9	27.5	(3.4)
Monroe (all units)	28.4	27.1	(1.3)
Onondaga (all units)	25.3	29.4	4.1
Westchester (all units)	38.5	39.1	0.6
SALES TAX AS PERCENTAGE OF TOTAL			
New York State Total	9.5	13.1	3.6
New York City Total	9.1	12.3	3.2
NYS Total (excluding NYC)	10.0	14.1	4.1
Erie (all units)	9.6	14.4	4.8
Monroe (all units)	8.8	8.8	0.0
Onondaga (all units)	11.7	14.0	2.3
Westchester (all units)	7.3	12.5	5.2
OTHER NONPROPERTY TAXES AS PERCENTAGE OF TOTAL			
New York State Total	9.5	16.6	7.1
New York City Total	15.4	27.7	12.3
NYS Total (excluding NYC)	1.4	3.2	1.8
Erie (all units)	0.5	1.1	0.6
Monroe (all units)	4.3	6.3	2.0
Onondaga (all units)	3.7	3.8	0.1
Westchester (all units)	1.1	2.9	1.8
STATE AID AS PERCENTAGE OF TOTAL			
New York State Total	19.7	15.9	(3.8)
New York City Total	22.2	17.0	(5.2)
NYS Total (excluding NYC)	16.3	14.6	(1.7)
Erie (all units)	17.6	19.1	1.5
Monroe (all units)	14.2	15.2	1.0
Onondaga (all units)	18.7	17.4	(1.3)
Westchester (all units)	18.0	13.4	(4.6)

TABLE 8.4 *(continued)*

Government Unit(s)	Local Fiscal Years Ending in		Percentage Point Increase (Decrease) Between 1975* and 1985
	1975*	1985	
FEDERAL AID AS PERCENTAGE OF TOTAL			
New York State Total	25.7	14.6	(11.1)
New York City Total	28.8	16.4	(12.4)
NYS Total (excluding NYC)	21.3	12.3	(9.0)
Erie (all units)	25.4	15.2	(10.2)
Monroe (all units)	23.4	17.4	(6.0)
Onondaga (all units)	23.8	10.9	(12.9)
Westchester (all units)	18.6	7.3	(11.3)
ALL OTHER AS PERCENTAGE OF TOTAL			
New York State Total	12.5	15.4	2.9
New York City Total	9.0	9.4	0.4
NYS Total (excluding NYC)	17.4	22.7	5.3
Erie (all units)	16.0	22.7	6.7
Monroe (all units)	20.9	25.2	4.3
Onondaga (all units)	16.8	24.5	7.7
Westchester (all units)	16.5	24.8	8.3

SOURCES: Office of the New York State Comptroller, *Special Report on Municipal Affairs*, for local fiscal year ended in 1975; and Office of the New York State Comptroller, *Special Report on Municipal Affairs*, for local fiscal year ended in 1985.

*Published 1975 data for State aid to New York City have been reduced by $785 million, to eliminate distortion caused by an "advance" of aid made by the State to help alleviate the City's cash flow problem.

has been refinanced. MAC's success in restructuring the City's financial position is summarized in the corporation's 1985 annual report.[17]

> The numbers alone are formidable. During the ten years since 1975, the corporation has completed transactions cumulating more than $15 billion. From those financings, it has provided the City with nearly $5.0 billion to pay off its accumulated budget deficit, almost $2 billion of relief from its short-term debt burden, and about $2.5 billion toward re-starting its critical capital construction program, plus substantial debt service savings from favorable restructuring of previous financings.

The importance of MAC's role is evident in the changing composition of City debt. In 1975, the City reported total outstanding debt of $11.3

billion, all of which had been issued by the City. Table 8.5 shows that by
1985, however, total debt had grown to $12.5 billion with only 42
percent issued by the City. The majority, 53 percent, had been issued by
MAC.

GIVING AND GETTING

Historically, the State of New York has been charged with fiscal
discrimination against the City. This charge rests upon the notion that
the City does not receive a fair share of the State's spending on behalf of
its localities. As early as 1861, Mayor Fernando Wood claimed that the
State's fiscal treatment of New York City was inequitable and suggested
that serious action was needed: secession from the State. Although such
action was obviously not taken, in the early 1920s William Randolph

TABLE 8.5
*Impact of Municipal Assistance Corporation (MAC)
on New York City's Borrowing, Debt, and Debt Service, 1985*

	Amount (in millions)	Percentage of Total
Total Debt Issued	$ 3,922	100.0%
New York City	1,832	46.7
Component City Units	13	0.3
MAC	2,077	53.0
Total Net Debt Outstanding	12,508	100.0
New York City	5,219	41.7
Component City Units	652	5.2
MAC	6,637	53.1
Total Debt Service Principal	1,969	100.0
New York City	1,543	78.4
Component City Units	21	1.1
MAC	566	28.7
Adjustments and Eliminators	(161)	(8.2)
Total Debt Service Interest	1,212	100.0
New York City	612	50.5
Component City Units	70	5.8
MAC	709	58.5
Adjustments and Eliminators	(179)	(14.8)

SOURCE: Office of the New York City Comptroller, *Comprehensive Annual Financial
Report of the Comptroller for the Fiscal Year Ended June 30, 1985*, pp. xxi, 19, and 47.

NOTES: Data for New York City include both school and higher education purposes, in
addition to general City purposes. Component City Units include the New York City
Educational Construction Fund and the City University Construction Fund.

Hearst, Sr., the publisher of the *New York Journal American*, made the same claim and called for the same remedy.[18]

Shortly after World War II, this argument surfaced once more, and Mayor William O'Dwyer threatened to seek independent statehood if the State did not improve its treatment of the City. To document the inequities of the State's financial assistance to the City, O'Dwyer established a study committee to identify the percentage of State tax collections generated within the City and compare it with the City's share of State aid. They found that in 1952 some 60 percent of the State's revenues were derived from city sources, but the City received less than half of the State's local assistance. Despite these findings, the committee concluded that the City was not a victim of State fiscal discrimination and the controversy diminished, at least for a time.[19]

In 1969, the Citizens Budget Commission analyzed the "balance of trade" between the City and the State. They concluded that since the 1950s, the City's fiscal relationship with the State had become increasingly favorable. Over time, the City contributed proportionally less revenue to the State, while receiving proportionally more State aid. The share of State revenues attributable to New York City sources declined from 60 percent in 1951 to under 50 percent in 1961 and to 46 percent in 1968. Despite the City's declining contribution to State revenues, the City's share of the State's local assistance budget grew from under 39 percent in 1959 to 47 percent in 1969. During this period, State aid became an increasingly important component of the City's budget, accounting for 27 percent in 1969 compared with only 18 percent ten years earlier.

There has been little talk of independent statehood for New York City in recent years. However, there are annual struggles between the City and the State over whether the City receives its fair share of the State's resources. How does the balance of trade equation look today, and has it changed since it was last studied?

New York City's Contribution to State Taxes

The State of New York funds its programs through four major types of revenues—taxes, federal aid, transfers from other funds, and miscellaneous activities including investments, fees, and sales of abandoned properties (see Table 8.6). Taxes represent the largest category of State revenues, accounting for almost 94 percent of the total in fiscal year 1987. Four types of taxes are imposed in New York State. The most significant is the personal income tax, accounting for over half of the State's total tax revenue. User taxes and fees, which are imposed on such activities as sales transactions, the consumption of motor fuel, cigarettes,

TABLE 8.6

New York State Receipts for the General Fund, Fiscal Year 1987 As Adopted (dollars in millions)

	Total Amount	Percentage of Total
Total Receipts	$24,789	100.0%
Total Taxes	23,200	93.6
Personal Income Tax	12,630	51.0
User Taxes and Fees	6,357	25.6
Business Taxes	3,119	12.6
Other Taxes	1,094	4.4
Miscellaneous Receipts	1,340	5.4
Federal Grants	90	0.4
Transfers from Other Funds	159	0.6

SOURCE: New York State, *Official Statement, 1986 Tax and Revenue Notes*, April 11, 1986.

and alcohol, and licenses to sell alcoholic beverages, furnished over 25 percent of the State's tax revenues in fiscal year 1987. Business taxes, imposed on the gross receipts of corporations, utilities, and banks, supply about 13 percent of the total. Other taxes—such as those imposed on estate and gifts, pari-mutuels, lotteries, and real estate transfers—generate the remaining 4 percent of all State taxes.

New York City is a large contributor to State revenues. The greatest controversy arises over the largest single source of State revenue: the personal income tax. Determining New York City's contribution to State personal income tax revenue requires specifying the relevant taxpayers and estimating the taxes these individuals pay. Is the relevant taxpayer group the residents of the city, regardless of whether their income is earned within or outside the city, or is the relevant group those who are employed in the city, regardless of where they reside? Legitimate arguments can be made on both sides, and the estimate of revenues contributed will differ depending on the approach selected.

Unfortunately, data availability limits the alternative estimates that can be analyzed. The State's personal income tax records identify place of residence, but not place of employment. Therefore, the State Department of Taxation and Finance estimates a locality's share with the residence approach. By drawing on survey data and City tax records, the New York City Office of Management and Budget (OMB) estimated the City's share of State personal income taxes in fiscal years 1983 and 1984 defining New York City taxpayers as nonresident employees and all residents, regardless of place of employment. Under the resident approach, used by the State, the city accounted for 35 percent of the

State's personal income tax in 1984. (See Table 8.7.) When all residents and employees are included, that figure rises to 45 percent.[20] Clearly, the City's contribution is higher when nonresident employees are counted as well as residents. However, since New York City residents employed outside the City have not been removed, this approach overstates the City's contribution. In addition, it is not possible to analyze trends under this approach since these data are not available for earlier years. Therefore, recognizing its possible limitations, the following analysis draws on the State's figures which base the City's contribution on income taxes paid by city residents.

Similarly, the only trend data available on each of the State's other major revenue sources is the series prepared by the State Department of Taxation and Finance. It is possible that these figures understate the City's contribution; however, since this analysis is particularly concerned with trends in the City's proportional "giving" to the State, it is necessary to rely on the State's figures. However, identifying a locality's precise contribution to State revenues is not a straightforward task. The State's revenues are not derived from local governments, but rather from residents, employees, and firms located within a locality's boundaries. As a result, unavoidable definitional and estimating problems arise.

In State fiscal year 1984, almost 37 percent of the State's own source revenue was collected from New York City (see Table 8.7). In each of the major categories of State taxes, the City contributed more than one third of the revenue: 36 percent of total user taxes and fees, 35 percent of the personal income tax, 45 percent of various business taxes, and 47 percent of "other" taxes. Among the specific levies that constitute each of these four major categories in 1984, the City's contribution was substantial, ranging from 23 percent (motor fuel tax and motor vehicle fees) to 85 percent (real property gains tax).

Historically, the City's role in the generation of State tax revenues has declined. In State fiscal year 1976, New York City contributed just under 40 percent of the State's taxes. (See Table 8.7.) In the most recent year for which data are available, fiscal year 1984, that figure was 37 percent. The reduction in the City's relative contribution to State tax revenue over the past decade is the result of small but steady annual declines primarily between fiscal years 1976 and 1980. In fiscal year 1981, the City's share increased, but that was followed by two years of a return to small annual declines. In 1984 the City's contribution increased from 36.6 to 37.4 percent. That year's increase is the result of a sizable (85 percent) City contribution to a newly enacted State revenue source, the real property gains tax.

The overall downward trend since 1976 is evidenced specifically by declines in the City's share of all but four of the 18 specific taxes levied

TABLE 8.7

Estimated Share of New York State Tax Revenue Provided by New York City (in millions)

	State Fiscal Year 1976			State Fiscal Year 1980			State Fiscal Year 1984		
	Paid from NYC	State Total	NYC as Percentage of Total	Paid from NYC	State Total	NYC as Percentage of Total	Paid from NYC	State Total	NYC as Percentage of Total
Total Tax Revenue	$3,780	$9,490	39.8%	$4,530	$12,380	36.6%	$6,900	$18,427	37.4%
Personal Income Tax	1,470	4,013	36.6	2,034	5,962	34.1	3,300	9,417	35.0
User Taxes and Fees	1,266	3,416	37.1	1,436	4,114	34.9	1,892	5,261	36.0
Sales and Use Tax	816	2,149	37.8	1,030	2,845	36.9	1,414	3,744	37.8
Motor Fuel Tax	143	480	29.9	116	475	24.3	96	422	22.8
Cigarette Taxes	139	337	41.1	135	332	40.7	178	440	40.6
Motor Vehicle Fees	79	263	30.0	68	278	24.3	96	420	22.8
Alcoholic Beverage Tax	73	154	47.5	71	150	47.5	79	172	46.0
Alcoholic Beverage Control Licenses	16	33	47.5	16	34	47.5	29	63	46.0
Business Taxes	839	1,696	49.5	886	1,974	44.9	1,245	2,763	45.1
Corporation Tax*	46	111	41.1	69	171	40.7	202	499	40.6
Corporation FranchiseTax	426	877	48.6	456	1,014	45.0	615	1,199	51.3
Corporation and Utilities Tax	108	279	38.8	128	365	35.0	228	680	33.6
Insurance Taxes	71	173	41.0	82	202	40.6	86	213	40.6
Bank Taxes	156	191	82.0	130	182	71.7	114	172	66.3
Unincorporated Business Tax	32	65	49.9	21	40	53.2	NA	NA	NA

TABLE 8.7 (continued)

	State Fiscal Year 1976			State Fiscal Year 1980			State Fiscal Year 1984		
	Paid from NYC	State Total	NYC as Percentage of Total	Paid from NYC	State Total	NYC as Percentage of Total	Paid from NYC	State Total	NYC as Percentage of Total
Other Taxes	204	363	56.2	173	332	52.1	463	986	47.0
Estate and Gift Taxes	67	147	45.6	58	125	46.4	120	259	46.2
Real Estate									
Transfer Tax	2	7	23.8	4	13	31.1	21	58	36.8
Pari-Mutuel Taxes	122	182	67.0	76	117	65.0	69	121	57.1
Lottery	13	27	46.1	35	77	46.1	119	390	30.6
Real Property Gains Tax	NA	NA	NA	NA	NA	NA	134	158	85.0

SOURCE: New York State, Department of Taxation and Finance, Office of Tax Policy Analysis, Bureau of Tax Statistics.

NOTES: Rounding of revenue figures may affect the figures on City's share of total State revenues. NA = tax not in place at that time.

*Excludes Sections 180 and 186-A.

and in each of the four major categories of tax revenue. The decline for the personal income tax was from 36.6 to 35.0 percent. Although this relative decline appears small (1.6 percentage points), its effect on total revenue is substantial, because the personal income tax is the largest single source of State revenue. In fact, one third of the overall decline is attributed to the City's reduced contribution from this source.

Although this analysis focuses on the period between 1976 and 1984, evidence suggests that the downward trend in the City's relative contribution to State tax revenues long predates 1976. Recall that earlier analyses identified that at the beginning of the 1950s New York City accounted for about 60 percent of State taxes. Ten years later that figure had dropped to just under 50 percent. At the end of the 1960s, the City's share was even lower: 46 percent.[21] Clearly, New York City's share of State revenues has been declining steadily and significantly for some time.

What explains the City's declining proportional "giving," especially via the important personal income tax? As documented in Matthew Drennan's essay in this volume, since 1969 the city's economy has not fared as well as that of the state as a whole or the areas outside the city. An important consequence of this was that personal income growth in the city was slower than that statewide: 5.4 percent versus 6.7 percent. Additional evidence suggests that this trend began at least a decade earlier. In 1959, the city accounted for 52 percent of the state's personal income. That share declined annually during the 1960s, dropping to under 50 percent in 1963 and to 47 percent in 1967.[22]

The city's revenue-generating capacity under the personal income tax has slowed, while the State's reliance on this source has increased. During the first half of the 1970s, the personal income tax accounted for about 42 percent of total State taxes.[23] Since that time, the relative importance of the personal income tax has grown steadily and dramatically. By fiscal year 1980, over 48 percent of all State tax collections were from this source. Two years later, it generated more than half (53.6 percent) of the State's taxes.[24] As shown earlier, the figure is currently over 54 percent.

The structure of the State's finances has shifted in favor of the personal income tax, and areas outside of New York City have become better able economically to provide the State revenues in this form. As the city's personal income base has weakened relative to other areas in the State, its contribution to the largest single State tax and the overall State tax system has declined.

State Spending in Support of New York City

State spending in support of its localities takes two basic forms. First, the State devotes about 60 percent of its operating budget to local

assistance programs that directly transfer State funds to local governments. Second, State expenditures finance direct State operations providing services to local residents such as corrections, courts, parks, health,
and mental health. The residents of New York City receive benefits from
the State in both these forms.

Direct State Aid. The State provides local aid through 127 programs
in seven major categories. Some 111 programs provide specific categorical aid for one of six major services; the other 16 provide general
purpose grants. The largest major category is education, which accounted for over 56 percent of all direct State aid during fiscal year 1986.

As Table 8.8 shows, New York City's percentage of total State aid has
risen slightly since 1976. The City accounted for 46.5 percent of all State
aid disbursements in 1976 compared with 47.7 percent in 1985.

The City's share varies widely by program. In State fiscal year 1985,
the City's share of categorical programs ranged from 29 percent for
highway and transportation aid to 66 percent for social services. For
unrestricted aid, the City received 48 percent of the total.

The amount of aid going to New York City increased for all major
program areas between 1975 and 1984, except health and environment
and the "all other" category. This pattern is consistent with total aid
distributions to all communities.

However, the City's percentage of State aid fell between 1976 and
1985 in all of the aid areas except education. The declines were above 10
percentage points in unrestricted (10.6), highway and transportation
(12.6), mental hygiene (19.2) and health and environment (23.8), and
"all other" (20.5). Yet, the dollar increase in education aid was so large
that it pulled the City's percentage of total State aid 1.2 percentage points
above its 1976 share. This relatively large increase in education aid also
had the effect of making more money available to the City for
unrestricted purposes. Since New York City is one of only five places in
the state with a fiscally dependent school district, increased education aid
effectively frees up locally generated revenues for other purposes.

Indirect State Aid to New York City. In addition to categorical and
unrestricted aid programs, the State assists the City through indirect
measures. Spending for these measures is not included in the City's
budget and does not appear under the State's local assistance budget.
Nevertheless, these efforts provide substantial fiscal relief to the City.

This indirect assistance takes two forms. First, the State has assumed
a larger, and sometimes the complete, responsibility for financing
functions previously supported predominantly or entirely by localities.
Once assumed by the State, these expenditures are often not considered

TABLE 8.8

State Aid Disbursements to New York City by Program Area, State Fiscal Years 1976–1985

State Fiscal Year	Total	Education	Social Service	Health and Environment	Mental Hygiene	Highway and Transportation	Unrestricted	All Other
Amount Paid to New York City (in millions)								
1985	$5,019	$1,907	$2,336	$ 40	$108	$57	$484	$ 87
1984	4,654	1,712	2,151	59	102	48	484	98
1983	4,154	1,733	1,632	41	98	65	484	102
1982	3,933	1,581	1,523	90	84	57	484	115
1981	3,547	1,439	1,327	76	67	56	484	97
1980	2,621	1,235	606*	72	71	53	482	103
1979	2,719	1,137	794*	68	89	54	484	93
1978	2,753	1,075	989*	69	58	51	434	77
1977	2,842	1,044	1,032	103	57	51	434	119
1976	2,769	1,000	995	103	56	50	405	160
New York City as Percentage of State Total								
1985	47.7%	36.2%	66.4%	37.1%	45.7%	29.2%	48.1%	46.4%
1984	47.4	34.6	67.4	39.6	50.4	30.5	55.5	33.5
1983	45.7	35.0	66.9	35.9	47.9	28.9	55.0	36.3
1982	46.1	34.4	67.7	51.1	39.3	34.2	55.0	43.6
1981	46.5	34.1	70.0	48.4	43.1	38.0	60.0	40.6
1980	40.6	32.1	54.6	46.6	46.2	42.6	58.1	42.9
1979	43.2	31.7	60.9	52.6	56.4	43.1	60.4	51.3
1978	44.8	31.0	68.8	51.7	54.0	42.4	60.4	45.5
1977	45.5	30.6	69.5	61.9	53.3	42.7	60.4	49.1
1976	46.5	30.7	71.4	60.9	64.9	41.8	58.7	66.9

SOURCE: State of New York, *Annual Report of the Comptroller*, 1976 to 1985 editions.

*During these years State aid for some categories of Medicaid are not included in the figures shown. This distorts the trend for these years. The distortion is due to phased implementation of a State system to make Medicaid vendor payments directly by the State rather than reimbursing localities for the payments.

as local assistance because they are accounted for under direct State operations. Second, the State provides direct services that assist the residents of the State's localities.

Specific areas in which the State assumed greater financial responsibility are described below. However, it is important to recognize that estimates of the resulting savings to the City are necessarily inexact. It is possible to identify State funds allocated for these purposes, but this is not necessarily the level of City budgetary relief. To assume that the current State cost of a program corresponds to savings to the City, it must also be assumed that the size, nature, and associated costs of the program remain the same over time. However, this has not been the case. With greater State financial participation, the size, nature, costs, and, at times, goals of programs have changed. Nonetheless it is useful to consider the general dimension of the City's savings, and the current State cost of these programs provides such an estimate.

One of these "takeover" efforts benefited the City only, while others assisted local governments statewide. The action specific to New York City was an assumption by the State of about half of the costs of the City University of New York (CUNY). Prior to 1978, the City and the State shared evenly the operating costs of the senior colleges of the CUNY, while the City financed the debt service on senior college bonds. Between 1978 and 1982, the State assumed total responsibility for these operating and capital costs. Current State financing of the City University includes nine senior colleges, one technical college, a graduate center, a law school and an affiliated school of medicine. In State fiscal year 1987, the State cost of the share previously borne by the City amounted to $400 million.[25]

New York City also shared in statewide savings for localities in costs of courts, Medicaid, and certain Supplemental Security Income (SSI) payments. Between 1978 and 1982, the State phased in a takeover of the noncapital costs of local court systems. In 1987, this constitutes an estimated $320 million in additional State assistance to New York City.[26]

In 1984, State legislation decreased over a three-year period the local share of funding for Medicaid long-term care services from 25 to 10 percent. Long-term care services include nursing home care, personal care, home health, and nursing services. In addition, localities were relieved of financial responsibility for medical services to mentally disabled persons. In State fiscal year 1987, the final year of the phased-in takeover, the fiscal relief for the City from these initiatives exceeded $300 million.[27]

The State of New York augments federal payments to the elderly and disabled under the nationwide Supplemental Security Income program. Prior to 1979, the State required localities to finance 50 percent of these augmented payments. In 1979, the State assumed the local portion of these payments. In 1987, this represented a saving to the City of about $85 million.[28]

The State also provides significant direct services to city residents. In 1987, with the exception of the State University of New York, corrections and mental health are the most costly of the direct services. These two programs account for over 20 percent of the State's direct operating budget.[29] The bulk of State prisoners are from New York City. Between 1980 and 1986, no fewer than 66 percent and as many as 70 percent of all State inmates were New York City residents.[30] Similarly, State mental health facilities are anticipated to serve over 460,000 patients in 1987, with about 60 percent from New York City.[31] City residents are overrepresented in these programs, since during the same period the City's share of total state population was only 40 percent.

New York's Localities Support Services Elsewhere Financed at State Level

It is important to consider New York State's large and growing aid programs in a national context, because New York is unique in an important respect. New York State requires local governments to finance a larger share of combined state and local government spending than any other state. For all states in 1984, 56 percent of state and local expenditures (excluding federal assistance) were financed by the state; New York financed only 43 percent of these expenditures. In contrast, Hawaii, Alaska, North Dakota, and New Mexico were responsible for at least 75 percent.[32]

The arrangements for financing three major services explain New York's unique position. In public welfare and highways, New York State's contribution to combined expenditures is the lowest in the country. The State finances 50 percent of public welfare spending compared with a nationwide average of 82 percent. The average state finances 63 percent of highway expenditures, yet New York contributes only 35 percent. In education, New York's 43 percent share is closer to—but still below—the national average of 52 percent.

New York's financial arrangements for public welfare differ most dramatically from those of other states. The State requires its localities to finance 50 percent of the nonfederal portion of Aid to Families with Dependent Children (AFDC); 50 percent of the cost of the State's Home Relief and emergency assistance to adults programs, and at least 10 percent of Medicaid costs. In no other state is the local share of these programs so high.[33] In fact, in half of the states, the local share of public welfare is less than 10 percent, including six states which finance the total cost of these programs.[34]

MORE OF THE SAME?

A clear finding of the foregoing analysis is that New York City's 1975 fiscal crisis had a profound effect on the State-City fiscal relationship. As a result of the crisis, the State ended its period of relatively relaxed control over the City. State required improvements in the City's financial management system have been put into place and New York City now has one of the most sophisticated systems in the country. The State's Financial Control Board will continue to oversee City financial management practices until at least the year 2008. Although its powers are now diminished, its continued presence reduces the likelihood of future crisis. The City also has been totally or partly relieved by the State of responsibility for funding certain costly services including courts, the CUNY, Medicaid, and SSI grants.

More generally, for at least the past three decades the City has received improved fiscal treatment from the State. The City's proportional "giving" is down and its proportional "getting" is up. Are these trends likely to continue in the future?

The City's proportional contribution to State taxes declined primarily because the City's share of the State's largest revenue base, personal income, decreased. According to Matthew Drennan, the future economic outlook for New York City includes growth in real per capita income, no population growth, and moderate employment growth. The State as-a-whole is anticipated to experience sizable growth in real personal income, small population growth, and significant increases in employment. These projections result in a continuation of the patterns established between 1980 and 1985; the city will account for a declining share of the state's jobs and personal income. As a result, the share of State revenues attributable to New York City is likely to continue to drop.

Will the City continue to account for a growing share of State spending? Since 1975, the State's willingness to provide high levels of assistance was related directly to the City's poor financial condition. New efforts will be hard to justify on these grounds, since the City's financial condition is substantially stronger and no longer perceived as warranting special State support. In addition, a number of other localities in the state are facing serious economic difficulties, and their claims to special State aid may be stronger than those of New York City. Thus, future State actions probably will not be specifically targeted at New York City.

Two recent State policies limit the prospects for significantly higher levels of assistance for New York City and other localities. First, the governor and legislature have a commitment not to increase any of the three broad based taxes (personal income, corporate income, and sales tax), which are the State's major revenue generators. Second, the State has embarked upon a multiple-year program to reduce its accumulated deficit. This requires annual devotion of cash resources of approximately $150 million that cannot be used for other purposes. With revenue growth constrained by pledges to avoid higher taxes and new monies committed to deficit reduction, there are few possibilities for major new local aid programs.

However, the distribution of even limited new funds among various State aid programs will have an important impact on the City's future share of total direct State aid. In recent years, the State has directed much of its new aid funds to education and social service programs. Since 1977, the City has received a growing share of education aid (from under 31 percent in State fiscal year 1977 to over 36 percent in 1985). Also, the City receives a significant portion of all social services aid (over 66 percent). Should a sizable share of any new State resources be devoted to these areas, the established trend of increased proportional "getting" for the City will continue.

In the area of indirect State aid, again, specific actions aimed at assisting only New York City are unlikely. However, statewide actions to assist localities that do not involve direct financial assistance to the City may be initiated. Such indirect measures could take the form of State assumption of the cost of certain local services and increased use of State-authorized public benefit corporations to provide capital for infrastructure projects. New York City would gain from these types of initiatives.

NOTES

1. The discussion of City-State fiscal relations from the 1800s through the 1950s was developed from the following sources: New York State—New York City Fiscal Relations Committee, *A Report to the Governor of the State of New York and the Mayor of the City of New York,* November 1956; New York State Legislative Commission on State-Local Relations, *New York's Limits on Local Taxing and Borrowing Powers,* December 1983; and New York State Legislative Commission on State-Local Relations, *New York's Revenue Sharing Program—At the Crossroads,* March 1985.
2. For a discussion of the events leading to the creation of the Greater City of New York, see David C. Hammack, *Power and Society* (New York: Russell Sage Foundation, 1982), chap. 7.
3. New York State Division of the Budget, *The Executive Budget in New York State: A Half Century Perspective,* 1981, p. 110.
4. New York City Temporary Commission on City Finances, *The Role of Intergovernmental Fiscal Relations in New York City,* Fourteenth Interim Report to the Mayor, May 1977, p. 13.
5. As of September 1985, there were 17 authorities with outstanding debt of at least $100 million. See New York State, *Official Statement, 1986 Tax and Revenue Anticipation Notes,* April 11, 1986, p. 34.
6. Figures were provided by the Urban Development Corporation.
7. Metropolitan Transportation Authority, "Amendment to the Capital Program of the MTA," February 19, 1986.

8. New York State Housing Finance Agency, *Annual Report, Fiscal Year 1985–1986*, October 31, 1985.
9. New York City, Comptroller's Report, "A Short History of City Fiscal Crisis," vol. 12, no. 2, August 1986, p. 3.
10. Financial Emergency Act for the City of New York, New York State Unconsolidated Laws, Chapter 22. The City of Yonkers is the only other local government in New York ever to be placed under State monitoring agencies. A State Financial Control Board for Yonkers was established in November 1975 and continued through December 1978. In 1984, Yonkers experienced another fiscal crisis and the State Financial Control Board was reestablished.
11. MAC is a public benefit corporation the obligations of which are backed by sales taxes, stock transfer taxes, and per capita aid. The State designated a "fiscal agent" to ensure that specified monies of the City would be impounded and made available to meet the necessary debt service on existing City obligations. The State includes a covenant in all City long-term and certain short-term debt which requires the establishment of a separate fund for the purposes of servicing the debt. This fund is administered and maintained by an officer or agency of the State, not the City. Usually the New York State comptroller has performed this function.
12. New York City, Temporary Commission on City Finances, *Role of Intergovernment Fiscal Relations*, p. 8.
13. The data presented in this section are compiled by the New York State Department of Audit and Control and published annually in the *Comptroller's Special Report on Municipal Affairs*. Although these data are "official," since they are compilations of audited data, they may differ sometimes significantly from figures published by the U.S. Bureau of the Census and the New York City Comptroller's Office. Also, revisions to the data occur subsequent to publication, and consequently the data shown here may not coincide with published figures. Further, definitional changes occurred in some measures between 1975 and 1979. Finally, New York City is the only unit of local government that does not use the State Comptroller's standard annual reporting form. These difficulties required the authors to adjust certain data items to facilitate comparability. These adjustments were made in consultation with staff from the State Department of Audit and Control.
14. Office of the New York State Comptroller, *Special Report on Municipal Affairs*, for local fiscal year ended in 1984, Legislative Document no. 91, February 28, 1985.
15. Office of the New York State Comptroller, *Special Report*. Erie County received permission to temporarily raise its rate to 4 percent until January 1, 1988.
16. Office of the New York City Comptroller, *Comprehensive Annual Financial Report of the Comptroller for Fiscal Year 1976*, p. 25.
17. Municipal Assistance Corporation for the City of New York, *Tenth Annual Report*, September 1985, p. 1.
18. Information in this paragraph is reported in Donna E. Shalala, *New York City—Statehood: An Idea Whose Time Has Passed*, a Report to the Executive Secretary of Citizens Union, July 1971.
19. This remaining discussion on the history of the "balance of trade" disputes between the City and the State is from Citizens Budget

Commission, *Does New York State Shortchange New York City? A New Look at an Old Problem,* December 1969.

20. New York City, Office of Management and Budget, Memo from Diane Brosen to Anthony Shorris, Re: New York City's Contribution to New York State Tax Revenues, March 17, 1987.

21. See Citizens Budget Commission, *Does New York State Shortchange New York City?,* table 1.

22. Shalala, *New York City—Statehood,* p. 5.

23. Data for 1970 from Citizens Budget Commission, *Does New York State Shortchange New York City?;* and data for 1975 from David Grossman, "Intergovernmental Aid," in Charles Brecher and Raymond D. Horton, eds., *Setting Municipal Priorities 1984* (New York: New York University Press, 1983).

24. Data for 1980 and 1982 from Grossman, "Intergovernmental Aid."

25. Figure provided by the New York State Division of the Budget, Fiscal Planning Unit.

26. Figure provided by the New York State Unified Court System, Office of Court Administration.

27. New York State, *1986–87 Executive Budget Briefing Book,* no date, p. III-23.

28. Figure provided by the New York State Division of the Budget, Fiscal Planning Unit.

29. Cynthia B. Green, "The State Budget: What Are Governor Cuomo's Priorities?" *Citizens Budget Commission Quarterly* 6, no. 2 (Spring 1986), table 4, p. 5.

30. Data provided by the New York State Department of Correctional Services.

31. Data provided by the New York State Office of Mental Health.

32. Figures in this paragraph are from U.S. Advisory Commission on Intergovernmental Relations, *Significant Features of Fiscal Federalism,* 1985–1986 ed., p. 31, table 20.

33. New York City, *Executive Budget Fiscal Year 1986, Message of the Mayor,* May 3, 1985, pp. 34–35.

34. U.S. Advisory Commission on Intergovernmental Relations, *Significant Features.*

9

CAPITAL PROJECTS

❧

James M. Hartman

C APITAL development is big business for both New York State government and New York City government. The State's capital plan for 1986–1991 projects appropriations of $17.6 billion for the activities of its executive departments. The City's capital plan for 1987–1996 anticipates commitment of $31.4 billion for municipal agencies. Moreover, the independent Metropolitan Transportation Authority has estimated its capital needs at $19.5 billion over the next decade.[1] The projects encompassed in these ambitious plans are fundamental to the delivery of public services by the State and City governments.

The capital development efforts of the State and the City are intertwined in certain key areas. In other functions, however, the State and the City manage their capital affairs with significant independence from the other's influence. To understand the overall pattern of decision making for capital projects requires answering several questions: Where does State government make its own investments in New York City? Where does the State assist the City with municipal projects? How do administrative and regulatory actions of the State affect the City's capital priorities? In which areas does the City operate with relative autonomy? How do needs in New York City influence statewide capital policies?

This essay contains four sections which address these crucial questions. The first section describes the State's five-year capital plan; the second section describes the City's ten-year capital program, with an emphasis on the areas of City financial autonomy. The next section examines six functional areas for which the State has heavy financial involvement in New York City: higher education, environmental conservation, highways and bridges, corrections, mental hygiene, and mass transit. The final section discusses three areas in which the State asserts nonfinancial controls with a major impact on City capital spending: water supply, waste disposal, and hospitals.

THE STATE CAPITAL PROGRAM

In 1983 the State Legislature passed a bill requiring the governor to prepare annually a rolling five-year plan for the capital expenditures of State government.[2] The plan must include estimates from the executive branch for appropriations, the authorizations to undertake capital work, and for disbursements, the actual spending likely to occur. The plan is intended primarily as a strategic policy document; implementation still requires annual appropriation decisions by the legislature. Nonetheless, the plan is the best source to discern the overall direction of capital development by State government.

In January 1986 Governor Cuomo submitted the third annual version of the capital plan. It covers fiscal years 1987 through 1991.[3] The plan includes $17.6 billion in suggested appropriations for the major agencies of State government and $10.2 billion in expected disbursements.[4] These amounts do not include the various capital activities of the State's independent public authorities—except where an entity, like the Dormitory Authority, is used as a financing vehicle. Large authorities such as the Housing Finance Agency and the Urban Development Corporation engage in extensive capital programs. But their major projects are not generally regarded as part of the public infrastructure, and they are discussed in other essays in this volume.

The major categories of spending and sources of funding for the State's five-year plan are shown in Table 9.1. Five functional areas constitute nearly 90 percent of the State's capital program. The Department of Transportation, whose program is largely for highways and bridges, receives $9.3 billion, or 53 percent of the total. Capital development in higher education, at the State and City universities, is the second largest item with $2.7 billion, or 15 percent of the total. Third in magnitude of planned appropriations is the $1.7 billion for mental hygiene facilities. The departments of Environmental Conservation and Correctional Services receive $1.2 billion and $.8 billion, respectively. All of the other agencies of State government share the remaining $1.9

TABLE 9.1

New York State Five-Year Capital Plan, Fiscal Years 1986–1987 Through 1990–1991
(in millions of dollars)

Function	Total Appropriations		Funding Sources				
	Amount	Percentage	Federal Aid	General Obligation Bonds	Current Revenues	Agency Financing	Other
Transportation[a]	$9,256.3	52.7%	$5,714.2	$1,286.6	$2,017.4	$95.3	$142.8
Higher Education[b]	2,686.6	15.3	3.4	—	591.9	2,040.6	50.7
Mental Hygiene[c]	1,719.9	9.8	0.4	—	1,719.5	—	—
Environmental Conservation	1,177.3	6.7	120.9	815.2	82.6	—	158.6
Corrections	811.1	4.6	—	—	529.2	281.9	—
Other	1,870.6	10.6	99.3	73.1	1,657.8	—	40.3
Total[d]	17,521.8	100.0	5,938.1	2,174.9	6,598.4	2,417.8	392.5

SOURCE: New York State, *Five-Year Capital Plan, Fiscal Years 1986–87 through 1990–91*, no date. Summary of funding sources developed with assistance from Division of Budget staff. Figures may not add up to totals due to rounding.

[a]Department of Transportation.

[b]State and City universities.

[c]Office of Mental Health and Office of Mental Retardation and Developmental Disabilities.

[d]Includes all appropriations in the capital plan, with the exception of the "bond proceeds" appropriations, which represent a double-counting with general obligation bonds.

billion, or 11 percent of the planned total. The concentration of capital activities in these five major functions reflects the State's extensive service delivery responsibilities in these areas.

Four major sources of funding support the $17.6 billion in appropriations: general obligation debt, independent agency debt, current revenues, and federal aid. Interestingly, general obligation bonds, a $2.2 billion amount, constitute the smallest funding share, 12 percent. This situation stems from the State constitutional requirement for voter approval of any general obligation debt backed with the full faith and credit of the State. Placing a bond issue before the public and winning its approval can be a long and difficult process. One major recent success in such an effort was the 1983 "Rebuild New York" bond issue. Most of the $1.3 billion in general obligation debt for transportation was approved in the 1983 vote. The only other major State general obligation bonding in the five-year plan is the $815 million for environmental conservation. This amount represents funds that remain from the 1965 Pure Waters Bond Act and the 1972 Environmental Quality Bond Act.

Because voter approval is difficult, the State often turns to its independent agencies to issue debt in support of the capital program. The most widespread technique for agency financing is the so-called lease purchase debt. The independent agencies issue bonds and construct facilities. The State then becomes the tenant under an agreement in which it pays the debt service and eventually takes title to the property. The State long has used this method to have the Dormitory Authority and Housing Finance Agency pay for higher education facilities. Over $2 billion of the five-year-plan funds for the State and City universities are derived from this source. The other major use of agency financing is for prison construction. In 1981 the voters turned down a general obligation bond issue for this purpose. Subsequently, in a controversial action, the State authorized the Urban Development Corporation to borrow $513 million to construct new prison space. Of that amount, $281 million remains to be utilized. In total, agency financing equals $2.5 billion, or 14 percent of the overall plan.

Because of the restraints on borrowing, the largest funding source for the State's capital program is current tax revenues. The total in the plan is $6.6 billion, or 37.6 percent. Current revenues support the entire mental hygiene program and constitute dominant or significant shares of corrections, higher education, and transportation. The capital program competes directly with the operating budget for use of the State's current revenues. When combined with the borrowing restrictions, this situation seriously limits the resources available for capital projects. Limited resources is an overriding fact of life in the State's capital planning.

The State's only source of external capital aid is federal assistance for highway and bridge repair. The approximately $6 billion of projected federal monies in the five-year plan is nearly all for the Department of Transportation. The federal government supports State and local highway work through numerous aid programs, funded principally with the Highway Trust Fund. In return for this support, however, the federal government, as discussed later, exercises powerful control over highway capital priorities.

THE CITY CAPITAL PROGRAM

Like State government, the City in recent years has undertaken a process of long-range capital planning. The City's effort results in a ten-year plan which is revised every two years. The first of these plans covered City fiscal years 1983 through 1992. It was designed to provide strategic guidance to the formulation of the annual capital budget— which requires the approval of the Board of Estimate and City Council. The concept of a ten-year capital plan gradually took hold throughout City government and has been updated twice.

The current plan encompasses fiscal years 1987 through 1996.[5] As shown in Table 9.2, it anticipates total commitments of $31.4 billion. The plan addresses the basic infrastructure and facility needs of City government. Among the major City functions, allocations range from $5.6 billion for highways and bridges to $505 million for City jails. The planned projects include "catch-up" from the neglect of the fiscal crisis period, attention to ongoing replacement and repair needs, and the initiation of certain new capital ventures.

Table 9.2 shows the heavy extent to which the City relies upon its own capital resources. Over $24 billion, or 77 percent of the total plan, is to come from municipal funds. City borrowing does not require voter approval, and about $17 billion will be raised in municipal general obligation bonds and $7 billion in revenue bonds backed by water and sewer fees. The City uses no current revenues in its capital budget. The level of City borrowing may need to grow even higher if, as expected, federal tax reform undermines the strategy of having private companies finance and build waste disposal plants. The City had hoped to generate $3.8 billion in private capital for this purpose.

The situation of the City "on its own" in capital development is typical of all counties and municipalities in New York State. Local governments traditionally have carried the principal burden for their own capital inventory. Accordingly, as Table 9.2 indicates, the City is entirely responsible for infrastructure such as sewers, water mains, and water

TABLE 9.2

New York City Ten-Year Capital Plan, Fiscal Years 1987 Through 1996 (in millions of dollars)

Function	Total Commitments		Funding Sources			
	Amount	Percentage	City	State	Federal	Private
Highways and Bridges[a]	$5,621.4	17.9%	$4,056.4	$269.4	$1,295.3	—
Waste Disposal	4,338.0	13.8	538.0	—	—	3,800.0
Water Mains	2,431.9	7.6	2,431.9	2.3	—	—
Education	2,122.5	6.8	2,120.2	—	—	—
Sewers	2,033.8	6.4	2,033.8	—	—	—
Water Supply	1,939.2	6.2	1,939.2	—	—	—
Hospitals	1,872.5	6.0	1,419.9	—	2.7	449.6
Sewage Treatment	1,844.6	5.9	892.1	247.2	705.3	—
Police, Fire, Sanitation[b]	1,562.0	5.0	1,562.0	—	—	—
Parks	1,308.0	4.2	1,234.6	25.7	47.0	0.6
Public Buildings	824.8	2.6	824.8	—	—	—
Equipment	704.0	2.2	704.0	—	—	—
Economic Development	616.4	2.0	613.7	—	2.6	—
Corrections	504.6	1.6	504.6	—	—	—
Other	3,631.7	11.6	3,295.8	178.8	134.0	17.8
Total	31,355.4	100.0	24,171.0	723.4	2,193.0	4,268.0

SOURCE: New York City, Office of Management and Budget, *Ten-Year Capital Plan, Fiscal Years 1987–1996*, May 1986.

[a]Excluding funds for the Transit Authority as shown in the City's ten-year document.

[b]The Sanitation total excludes waste disposal, shown separately.

supply, and for facility needs in police, fire, sanitation, corrections, education, and public hospitals.

Only two major areas, highways and sewage treatment, receive substantial federal and State assistance. In both cases the initiative lies with the federal government, which established programs that require State financial participation. Consequently, the State is expected to provide $269 million to the City for local highway work and $247 million for sewage treatment projects over the ten-year period. The $179 million in "other" State aid is composed largely of support for social services, juvenile justice, and museum facilities.

In fairness to the State, the data in Table 9.2 do not include the local service for which the State has primary responsibility: buses and subways. The organization of the Metropolitan Transportation Authority as a State agency in 1968 relieved the City of the main financial burden for mass transit. Significantly, the MTA is projecting bus and subway capital needs of $16.2 billion over the next decade.[6] As discussed later, finding those resources is now largely a State problem.

AREAS OF STATE FINANCIAL INVOLVEMENT IN NEW YORK CITY

The State is involved financially in New York City capital development both as a direct service provider and as an aid source for the City government. Higher education, corrections, and mental hygiene are three functions for which the State provides directly most services to City residents. Environmental protection, highways, and mass transit involve a mix of direct State service provision and State financial aid to local units providing services. In all six areas, however, the special needs and circumstances of New York City impact on statewide capital policies.

Higher Education

One major structural change produced by the City's fiscal crisis was the State's 1979 takeover of the City University (CUNY). This action put CUNY's graduate and four-year colleges on a fiscal basis equivalent to that of State University (SUNY) institutions. The two-year community colleges in the CUNY system continue to be a joint responsibility of the State and the City. This arrangement resembles the upstate pattern in which county governments fund a share of their community colleges.

The State takeover of CUNY came at a time when its physical facilities were in dire condition. Growth in the number of students during the open enrollment period of the early 1970s created serious overcrowding.

Many buildings were old and neglected. The City's effort to construct new facilities had been thwarted by the fiscal crisis. By contrast, SUNY enjoyed the benefits of a 20-year construction program initiated during the administration of Governor Rockefeller. The cost of that program was nearly $3 billion, and it left SUNY with a network of largely new campuses.

Much of the State's efforts on behalf of CUNY in recent years have been to address the imbalance of physical facilities between CUNY and SUNY. This continuing effort is reflected in the comparison of the five-year plans for the two systems, shown in Table 9.3. Projected spending for CUNY is higher on both an absolute and a relative basis. The senior colleges of CUNY, with 89,000 students, are slated for $1.3 billion compared with the $1.1 billion for SUNY, with its 150,000 students.

The composition of planned spending for the two systems is also different. Nearly 88 percent of the CUNY total is for new, expanded, and renovated facilities. The objective is to relieve all ten senior campuses in the system of reliance on outdated, overcrowded, or rented facilities. By contrast, only 58 percent of the SUNY program is for new construction or renovation. The goal here is to complete facilities that have been established pieces of campus master plans for many years. Few entirely new projects are planned. Moreover, 31 percent of the SUNY total is for general maintenance and improvements to well-established facilities.

This general pattern of capital priorities is similar for the community colleges. The two-year CUNY institutions, where the City shares the cost,

TABLE 9.3

New York State Five-Year Capital Plan for Higher Education
(in millions of dollars)

	State University		City University	
	Graduate and 4-Year Colleges	Community Colleges	Graduate and 4-Year Colleges	Community Colleges
General Maintenance and Improvements	$349.1 (31.4%)	$23.6 (31.4%)	$140.8 (10.8%)	$41.0 (21.2%)
New, Expanded, and Renovated Facilities	649.3 (58.4%)	47.0 (62.6%)	1,150.3 (87.7%)	150.0 (77.7%)
Other	114.2 (10.2%)	4.6 (6.1%)	19.6 (1.5%)	2.2 (1.1%)
Total	1,112.6 (100.0%)	75.0 (100.0%)	1,310.7 (100.0%)	193.3 (100.0%)

SOURCE: See Table 9.1.

receive $193 million in the plan. Two thirds of that amount is for new construction or renovation. By comparison, the total program for upstate community colleges is $75 million. A larger share of those funds than at CUNY are earmarked for maintenance and repair.

In sum, the State is seeking to provide modern facilities for the previously neglected CUNY. That is a costly effort. The capital needs at SUNY, by comparison, reflect the situation of a physically mature campus system in need of refinement and attention to the first signs of age.

Corrections

Criminal justice policies in New York have imposed an increasing demand in recent years upon the State's prison system. Expansion in the number of cell spaces is a major capital goal. Legislation passed in 1983 and 1985 authorized $513 million in Urban Development Corporation bonds to finance prison construction. This effort is intended to provide for 39,700 beds by 1989.

Table 9.4 charts the growth in prison space since 1980—when the system had 21,799 regular beds. That number had increased to 35,430 by September 1986. Throughout this period, however, new construction was unable to keep pace with the rise in the inmate population. The system was forced to house 38,050 prisoners in 1986. This demand compelled the use of 3,659 beds in makeshift facilities such as dormitories, recreational space, and infirmaries. The Department of Correctional Services hopes to minimize the reliance on such temporary beds when it reaches the goal of 39,700 cell spaces in 1988.

TABLE 9.4

New York State Prison Capacity and Population, 1980–1988

	Capacity			Population	
Year	Regular	Special Facilities	Total	Number	Percentage from New York City
1980	21,799	1,196	22,995	21,848	66.4%
1982	25,236	4,017	29,253	28,466	68.0
1984	31,868	3,167	35,035	33,829	70.0
1986*	35,430	3,659	39,089	38,050	69.9
1988 (projected)	39,700	700	40,400	—	—

SOURCE: Data provided by the New York State Department of Correctional Services.

*September; all others are end of calendar year.

The cost of reaching the 1988 goal totals $811 million. (See Table 9.5.) Approximately, one half of that amount is earmarked for the expansion program. The other half is needed for repair and modernization of the older facilities in the system. The average age of the 13 maximum-security prisons is 67 years. It is 36 years for the 30 medium- and minimum-security facilities.[7]

The New York State prison system represents something of a paradox. The inmates come from New York City, but the prisons are located upstate. Nearly 70 percent of the September 1986 prison population of 38,050 were legal New York City residents. As shown in Table 9.4, that percentage had increased from 66 percent in 1980. However, there are only 2,440 State prison beds located in New York City. There are 1,250 beds in the medium-security Arthur Kill and Queensborough facilities and 1,190 beds in the minimum-security Edgecombe, Fulton, Lincoln, and Bayview facilities. None of the recent or planned expansion is located in New York City.

Why are there so few State prisons in the city? Two reasons seem most apparent: political opposition and cost. First, most New York City neighborhoods do not want prisons. The families of inmates, who often must travel long distances for visitation, do not have the political strength to overcome that opposition. By contrast, many upstate communities welcome the jobs that accompany State prisons. Second, the higher cost of land and labor make site acquisition and construction in New York City expensive. In 1983 the State examined the feasibility of building a 1,000-bed, maximum-security prison on North Brother's island. The cost per bed was estimated at $200,000, more than double the statewide average.[8]

The paramount question facing the prison system is: Will the expansion to 39,700 beds be sufficient? Many criminal justice analysts predict continued growth in the inmate population. One report for the

TABLE 9.5
New York State Capital Plan for Corrections
(in millions of dollars)

	Amount	Percentage
Maintenance and Improvement to Existing Facilities	$394.6	48.7%
Expansion of Existing Facilities	117.9	14.5
New Facility Construction	281.9	34.8
Other	16.0	2.0
Total	810.4	100.0

SOURCE: See Table 9.1.

State's Project 2000 forecast over 50,000 inmates by the turn of the century.[9] That forecast was based upon assumptions about demography, arrests, sentencing, and length of time served. As a result, in his 1987 State of the State address, Governor Cuomo suggested the need for even more new prison construction. Significantly, however, he urged consideration of community-based alternatives to incarceration. One interesting implication of such alternatives would be to keep more New York City criminal offenders in the city during their correctional time.

Mental Hygiene

State mental hygiene services fall into two main categories—mental illness and mental retardation. The Office of Mental Health provides services to patients with mental illness. Its five-year capital allocation is $1.2 billion. The Office of Mental Retardation and Developmental Disabilities serves persons disabled by mental retardation or other developmental or neurological disorders. Its five-year capital plan amount is $548 million. Because of their larger scale, it is appropriate to focus on mental health facilities.

In 1955 New York State's mental hospitals had residential space for over 90,000 patients. The equivalent number in 1986 is just 20,335. This marked reduction stems from the controversial policy of "deinstitutionalization," which is examined in a separate essay in this volume. Significantly, the State plans to reduce its inpatient population further over the next five years by expanding the capacity of community-based facilities. This goal has important implications both for capital planning and for service to New York City residents.

Table 9.6 provides an overview of the current and planned system of mental health services. The 20,335 beds in State-run hospitals were expected to serve 40,614 patients during the course of the 1986–1987 year. The 5,270 beds in local hospital psychiatric wards throughout the state were expected to serve a yearly total of 55,616 patients. Community-based residential facilities—many run under contract with nonprofit agencies—have 6,054 beds expected to house 7,578 patients. Outpatient clinics run by the State, local governments, and nonprofit agencies expected to treat a total of 356,250 patients.

Is New York City adequately served by this system? As Table 9.6 shows, there are 4,252 State hospital beds located in the city. They are expected to accommodate 12,495 of the 19,617 city residents needing State hospitalization during the 1987 fiscal year. The remaining New York City residents must be treated at upstate institutions. The community-based residences in the city have 1,742 beds, which were expected to serve 2,136 of the 3,353 New York City residents to be

TABLE 9.6
New York State Mental Health Facilities, Capacity and Patients Served

| | Projected for Fiscal 1986–1987 | | | | | Planned for Fiscal 1990–1991 | |
| | Statewide | | New York City | | | | |
	Beds	Individuals Served	Beds	Patients from New York City	Number Served in New York City	Statewide Beds	New York City Beds
Residential							
State-Run Hospitals	20,335	40,614	4,252	19,617	12,495	15,251	4,252
Local Inpatient	5,270	55,616	2,593	27,365	27,365	5,770	2,933
Community-Based Residential	6,054	7,578	1,742	3,353	2,136	13,250	4,568
Total	31,659	103,808	8,587	50,335	41,996	34,271	11,753
Nonresidential	—	356,250	—	222,560	181,688	409,688[a]	208,940[b]

SOURCE: Data provided by the New York State Office of Mental Health.

[a]Individuals to be served statewide.

[b]Individuals to be served in New York City.

treated in such facilities. Similarly, only 181,688 of the 222,560 out-patients from New York City will be served in city-located clinics. In short, many New York City residents must receive their mental health care elsewhere in the state.

The State's plan to develop more community-based treatment capacity will improve services to New York City residents in the sense that fewer will have to be treated at upstate locations. Although the State plans to shrink its total institutional bed capacity to 15,251, the number of beds located in New York City would remain at its current level of 4,252. The plan calls for expanding the contingent of community-based beds in the city from the current 1,742 to 4,568. Moreover, the capacity of outpatient clinics in New York City would increase to 208,940. Overall, the treatment capacity of facilities located in New York City is expected to grow significantly.[10]

Implementation of the mental health plan will be difficult, however. The Office of Mental Health is still working to identify the community-based service providers. Their hope is that nonprofit agencies will develop the capacity to play this role. That effort is complicated in New York City by the high cost of making physical facilities available. Many nonprofit agencies are reported to encounter trouble in finding New York City sites for purchase or leasing. This problem is a major obstacle to realizing the New York City component of the deinstitutionalization strategy.

The five-year capital plan for mental health is shown in Table 9.7. Significantly, over 80 percent of the total $1.2 billion is for rehabilitation of the large State hospitals. Even though the population of these institutions is expected to decline, their routine upkeep is an enormous cost. The remaining $174 million is capital support for community facilities. These monies are intended to help contractual providers with the acquisition, construction, and rehabilitation of service sites. Whether

TABLE 9.7
New York State Five-Year Capital Plan for Mental Health Facilities (in millions of dollars)

	Amount	Percentage
Maintenance and Improvement of Existing Facilities	$974.8	83.2%
Capital Support for Community Facilities	173.6	14.8
Other	23.3	2.0
Total	1,171.7	100.0

SOURCE: See Table 9.1.

this allocation will be sufficient, especially given the cost of New York City facilities, is an open question.

Environmental Protection

The five-year capital plan for the Department of Environmental Protection consists of two major areas, sewage treatment and hazardous waste clean-up. These two areas constitute nearly 70 percent of the five-year plan total of $1.2 billion. Most of the remaining funds are for upstate-oriented programs such as forestry, land preservation, and wildlife management. Significantly, as seen in Table 9.8, the 1986 Environmental Quality Bond Act, adopted by the voters subsequent to the five-year plan, may add up to another $4 billion for hazardous waste clean-up.

Sewage Treatment. The federal government has long-established leadership in the field of sewage treatment. Starting in the early 1970s, Congress mandated that local governments end the discharge of raw sewage into their waterways. To reach this goal, the federal government provides 55 percent of the cost of these projects and requires matching shares of 30 percent from the states and 15 percent from localities. The State of New York has funded its portion of the program with monies from the 1965 and 1972 bond acts.

The City of New York is close to reaching its mandated objectives and is ahead of many upstate localities in sewage treatment construction. The City expects by 1989 to complete a 15-year effort to construct and upgrade a network of 14 sewage plants. At that point the City expects to provide full wastewater treatment to all of its sewage discharge. Approximately $150 million of the $566 million of the State monies shown in Table 9.8 will go to the City for this purpose.

Despite this progress, however, the City confronts a unique sewage problem. Most sanitary sewers in New York City also serve as storm sewers for rainwater. Consequently, during inclement weather, raw sewage frequently will flow past holding tanks at the treatment plants. The City is under federal pressure to correct this problem. It has begun preliminary studies which suggest a potential cost of several hundred million dollars. The extent of federal and State aid for any such effort is an open question.

Hazardous Waste Clean-Up. The Department of Environmental Conservation has identified about 1,200 sites in New York State as contaminated with inactive hazardous wastes—mostly from industrial polluters. The department estimates that approximately 500 are serious

TABLE 9.8
New York State Capital Plan for Environmental Conservation (in millions of dollars)

	Total Appropriation		Funding Sources			
	Amount	Percentage	Federal Aid	General Obligation Bonds	Current Revenues	Other
FIVE-YEAR CAPITAL PLAN						
Sewage Treatment	$566.1	48.1%	—	$566.1	—	—
Hazardous Waste						
Clean-Up	253.4	21.5	95.4	—	1.1	156.9[a]
Other	357.8	30.5	25.5	249.1	81.5	1.7
Total	1,177.3	100.0%	120.9	815.2	82.6	158.6
1986 ENVIRONMENTAL BOND ACT						
Hazardous Waste						
Clean-Up	4,000.0		700.0	1,200.0	—	2,100.0
Other	250.0		—	250.0	—	—

SOURCE: See Table 9.1.

[a]Private funds generated from fees against industry polluters.

enough to require remediation. This condition looms as one of the State's most pressing environmental problems.

The State's five-year plan includes $253 million for hazardous waste clean-up. The State has put few of its own resources into the effort and is relying primarily on funds from the "Federal Superfund" and from fees on industry polluters. Estimates from the department indicated that, given such level of funding, it would take over 40 years to completely clean the 500 sites.[11]

The 1986 bond act is expected to accelerate the clean-up program greatly. It provides $1.2 billion from State general obligation bonds that will serve as matching funds to yield another $700 million in federal aid and $2.1 billion in industry fees. Funding of this magnitude will allow clean-up of the 500 sites in between 10 and 15 years.

The New York City share of the program is difficult to determine at this point. There are only 23 sites identified in the city: 8 each in Brooklyn and Staten Island, 5 in Queens, and 2 in the Bronx. Ironically, many industrial polluters in the city, in past years, apparently dumped waste into the sewer system. This practice thus kept the city from developing the more numerous sites that plague upstate. However, the sites which do exist in the city are large and complicated. Especially troublesome are the former municipal landfills at Edgemere in Queens, Brookfield in Staten Island, Pennsylvania and Fountain avenues in Brooklyn, and Pelham Bay in the Bronx. The clean-up expense at these locations is expected to be many times greater than the statewide average of $8 million. Thus, the cost for New York City will constitute a sizable portion of the $4 billion total.[12]

Highways and Bridges

The capital allocation for the Department of Transportation dominates the State's five-year plan, accounting for $9.3 billion, or 53 percent of the total. The use of these funds is shown in Table 9.9. Nearly $8.5 billion, over 90 percent of the Transportation allocation, is for highway and bridge repair. The remaining funds are for a variety of programs that include the upstate bus systems, the state's rail freight network, airport facilities, canal projects, and port development.

The need for extensive funding of highway and bridge work is explained by the size of the State's road network. As shown in Table 9.10, State government is responsible directly for 16,402 highway miles and 7,272 bridges statewide. This system encompasses most of the limited access highways and other major arteries in the state. Because of New York City's relatively limited geographic territory, only 284 of the highway miles and 579 of the bridges in the State system are located in

TABLE 9.9
New York State Five-Year Capital Plan
for Department of Transportation (in millions of dollars)

	Amount	Percentage
Highways and Bridges	$8,480.7	91.6%
Mass Transportation		
and Rail Freight	354.7	3.8
Airport or Aviation Program	109.4	1.2
Canals and Waterways	35.0	0.4
Port Development	38.5	0.4
Maintenance Facilities	119.8	1.3
Other	118.1	1.3
Total	9,256.2	100.0

SOURCE: See Table 9.1.

TABLE 9.10
Highways and Bridges, Statewide and New York City

		New York City	
	Statewide	Number	Share of Statewide
State Highway Miles	16,402	284	1.7%
Local Highway Miles	93,532	5,815	6.2
State Bridges	7,272	579	7.8
Local Bridges	12,320	1,401	11.4

SOURCES: State Department of Transportation, *1985 Highway Mileage Report,* April 1986; and *Bridge Inventory and Inspection System Report,* May 1986.

the city. Local governments statewide are responsible for another 93,532 road miles and 12,320 bridges. Of that total, 5,815 road miles and 1,401 bridges are in New York City, with City government as the responsible party.[13]

Highway and bridge conditions in New York suffered from neglect during the 1960s and 1970s. The State estimates that 11 percent of its highway surfaces and 15 percent of underlying roadbeds are in poor condition. Nearly 30 percent of the State bridges are in need of major repair.[14] In New York City, local officials acknowledge that, until recent years, work on City-managed roadways occurred at only one third to one half the desired cycles of reconstruction and resurfacing. Approximately one half of the City's local bridges are rated in "poor" or "fair" condition, indicating the need for major rehabilitation.[15]

Federal assistance is a dominant force in State and local highway repairs. The federal government provides money in some 20 different categories of aid.[16] It funds about 75 percent of the work on the State system. Moreover, it gives money to the State, with various matching requirements, through which the State can assist in the local government efforts. The distribution of those monies is governed by formulas which take into account population, mileage, road conditions, and other factors. The five-year plan assumes that $5.7 billion in federal highway assistance will flow to New York State over the period. (See Table 9.1.) That aid establishes the framework in which the State will use nearly $3 billion of its own resources.

State transportation officials estimate that approximately $1.5 billion—of the total $8.5 billion statewide program—will be designated for New York City projects, although a precise breakdown of this funding is not available.[17] The City's ten-year plan is to receive $962 million in federal and State aid for locally managed work in the fiscal 1987–1991 period. Presumably, the balance of the $1.5 billion, or something over $500 million, will be spent directly by the State on its own highways and bridges in the city. Given the relatively small percentage of the total statewide highway mileage and bridges located in the city, the funding level in the State plan suggests relatively good treatment for the City. (Or, perhaps, inaccurate estimates of spending in New York City by the State officials.)

What will the program accomplish in New York City? Again, details are not available from the State. However, their list of projects includes work on arteries such as the FDR Drive, the Hutchinson River Parkway, and the Clearview, Cross Bronx, Bruckner, Brooklyn-Queens, Van Wyck, and Long Island expressways. The City's ten-year plan calls for it to achieve optimal cycles of reconstruction on local roadways, ranging from 40 to 60 years depending on the type of thoroughfare. Moreover, the City intends to upgrade all of its bridges from the "poor" or "fair" condition rating.

One major issue confronting the highway program is to identify a replacement funding source for the 1983 bond issue. Approximately $1 billion of the State's resources in the five-year plan stem from this referendum. However, most of the bond issue funds will be gone by fiscal 1988–1989. The last two years of the plan include only enough State current revenues to prevent any loss of federal aid. The initiation of new construction will slow in fiscal years 1989–1990 and 1990–1991.

The Department of Transportation is expected soon to release a special report on financing of road work in the 1990s. It will include an assessment of need to provide the background for funding decisions. One possibility is another bond issue. However, there may be political reluctance to ask the voters to again approve a highway bond issue. Another option is a special revenue source, perhaps related to new taxes or charges on motorists. A special revenue of this kind also may be necessary to deal with the capital needs of New York City's mass transit system.

Mass Transit

Mass transit makes the single largest claim on public capital resources in New York City. The Metropolitan Transportation Authority (MTA) entered the 1980s with its equipment and facilities in abysmal condition. This situation led the MTA leadership, with the approval of the State Legislature, to mount an $8.5 billion program of capital renewal for the years 1982 through 1986. Subways and buses were allocated $6.3 billion and the commuter railroads $2.2 billion. These funds started a long-term effort of purchase and repair for the MTA's rolling stock, track, and other physical components.

Table 9.11 outlines how the five-year program was financed. Over $4 billion, or 47 percent of the total, came through direct grants from the federal, State, and City governments and from the Port Authority. The second major source was debt: $1.1 billion in bonds issued against bridge and tunnel revenues, $667 million issued against special State appropriations, and $1.9 billion issued or to be issued against general MTA revenues. A third significant source was $443 million from the sale and leaseback of MTA equipment to private corporations buying tax write-offs for depreciation.

Significantly, however, the 1982–1986 funding sources are not easily replicated. Federal grants are likely to be cut. The so-called safe-harbor leaseback provision has been eliminated from federal tax law. New MTA revenue bonds would place undue pressure on the farebox.

These funding obstacles come at a time when the MTA is projecting a high and sustained level of capital need. The goal of restoring the system to a "state of good repair" is far from achieved. In early 1986, the MTA outlined a long-term program of capital spending which exceeded its expiring five-year plan. The Authority has expressed the desire for annual capital commitments which grow from $1.5 billion in 1987 to $2.5 billion by 1996. This program requires funding sources of $8.6 billion in the five-year 1987–1991 period. Subways and buses would receive $6.7 billion and commuters railroads $1.9 billion.

Some new sources of capital support were available to the MTA in the 1987–1991 period. (See Table 9.12.) The Westway trade-in is expected to generate $900 million in federal funds. The Municipal Assistance Corporation will provide $275 million from its extra resources. Sale of the MTA-owned Coliseum property will generate $466 million. There is $1.1 billion in unused funds from the 1982–1986 plan. Less certain, but

TABLE 9.11

*Metropolitan Transportation Authority Funding Sources for
1982–1986 Capital Program (in millions of dollars)*

Source	Transit Authority	Commuter Railroad	Total
Grants			
Federal	$2,040[a]	$526	$2,566
State[b]	379	337	716
City	639	—	639
Port Authority	92	—	92
Total	3,150	863	4,013
Debt			
Triborough Bridge and Tunnel Bonds	646	430	1,076
Service Contract Bonds	434	233	667
Revenue Bonds	1,546	351	1,897
Port Authority Bonds	—	56	56
Parking Bonds	—	30	30
Total	2,626	1,100	3,726
Other			
Safe Harbor Leases	344	99	443
Conn. Federal Funds	—	68	68
Other	226	45	271
Total	570	212	782
Grand Total	6,346	2,175	8,521

SOURCE: Metropolitan Transportation Authority.

[a]Includes $37 million in federal aid to the City re-allocated to the Transit Authority.

[b]Includes both direct State grants and surplus funds from the service contract appropriations.

not unrealistic, is the assumption that the federal government will provide $1.9 billion in reduced but sustained assistance over the five-year period. Even with these substantial resources, however, the MTA still required large additional sums to carry out its entire capital plan.

The problem of how to meet the MTA's needs was left to the governor and legislature to resolve. This burden is a legacy of the basic 1968 decision to organize mass transit as a State function in the New York City region. The funding dilemma compelled a special session of the legislature in December 1986. Some decisions were reached without major controversy. The legislature agreed to provide general State revenues to finance another $765 million in debt for the MTA over the five-year period. It also consented to toll increases for Triborough Bridge and Tunnel Authority facilities in order to issue $1.1 billion in new revenue bonds. In light of these actions, the City agreed to double its annual contribution to nearly $200 million per year.

TABLE 9.12

Metropolitan Transportation Authority Funding Sources for 1987–1991 Capital Program (in millions of dollars)

Source	Transit Authority	Commuter Railroads	Total
Federal	$1,480	$395	$1,875
City	960	—	960
State-Supported Debt	500	265	765
TBTA Toll Bonds	650	434	1,084
Westway Trade-in	900	—	900
Sale of Coliseum	418	48	466
Municipal Assistance Corporation	275	—	275
Carryover from 1982–1986 Plan	825	192	1,071
New Revenue Source	371	316	687
Other	280	306	586
Total	6,659	1,956	8,669

SOURCE: Metropolitan Transportation Authority, staff submission to the MTA board, January 9, 1987.

Even with these measures, however, the MTA still found itself short $687 million for its five-year plan. Proposals to fill this gap caused great rancor in the special legislative session. Governor Cuomo initially recommended a 5-cent-a-gallon surcharge to the gasoline tax for motorists in the MTA region. This idea was rejected because of strong opposition by suburban legislators, especially in the Senate. Because two thirds of the proposed new revenues would come from suburban motorists, their legislators complained of an unfair subsidy of New York City needs. Efforts to develop alternative tax proposals met with similar objections. The special session ended without agreement on a new revenue source.

The dispute continued into the regular 1987 session. Finally, the legislative leaders agreed to raise more funds for transit through elimination of certain tax credits previously available to banks. The idea of asking motorists to subsidize transit needs was abandoned, even though the final agreement also included funding for Long Island highway needs. The entire episode left an unusual degree of city-suburban tension over MTA issues. The implications of this tension in the future remain to be seen.

STATE REGULATORY IMPACT ON CITY CAPITAL COSTS

State government has regulatory authority in significant areas such as the environment, health, and public safety. These regulations impose heavy capital costs upon the City in water supply, waste disposal, and public hospitals.

Water Supply

Municipal water supplies must meet standards imposed by the State Department of Health. In recent years residential and commercial development in northern Westchester County has posed threats to the quality of supplies from the City's Croton reservoir system. To assure compliance with State standards, the City is now installing a filtration system for the Croton water supplies. The cost of this effort is estimated at $320 million.[18]

In addition, there is a potential threat to the City's much larger Catskill and Delaware reservoir systems. These extensive facilities, located further upstate, provide 90 percent of the City's total supply. Some State officials believe that development in the vicinity of these reservoirs may eventually require filtration measures similar to the Croton projects.[19] The cost to the City could be in excess of $2 billion. This issue may create future tensions between State and City officials.

Waste Disposal

Sanitary landfilling has been the primary method used by local governments in New York State for solid waste disposal. In recent years, however, the State has toughened the standards for landfill operation. Such regulations reduce the capacity of landfill sites and shorten their periods of use.

The City gradually has closed its network of landfill sites. Its only remaining facility is the Fresh Kills landfill on Staten Island. The City is seeking to extend the useful life of Fresh Kills to its maximum capacity. Part of that effort requires compliance with State environmental codes. The cost of that compliance is estimated at $330 million.[20]

The City's long-range proposal for waste disposal is to construct, with the aid of private firms, a network of eight garbage-to-steam plants. This process of "resource recovery" involves high-temperature burning, which many environmental groups believe will produce dioxins and other air pollutants. The ultimate decision on the safe operation of the plants will rest with State officials. The City's design for the plants includes extensive scrubbers intended to meet State standards. This effort at the prevention of air pollution explains some of the high $3.8 billion cost for waste disposal plant construction.

Hospitals

State codes establish standards for hospital facilities in such areas as patient space, air and light, and fire safety. At present five hospitals run by the City's Health and Hospitals Corporation fall short of State code compliance: Kings County, Bronx Municipal, Queens, Elmhurst, and Coney Island. The ten-year plan includes $869 million for the reconstruction of those facilities.[21] Much of that reconstruction is compelled by the State codes.

SUMMARY

Like other municipalities in the state, the City of New York supports most of its capital program with local resources. The responsibility for basic infrastructure and operating facilities is expected to cost the City over $24 billion in the next ten years. The State assists the City in only two main areas—highway repair and sewage treatment—largely as a result of requirements for State matches to federal aid. Regulatory actions by the State increase City capital costs in three functions: water supply, waste disposal, and hospitals.

The State's most important role in capital development in New York City stems from those functions for which State agencies are the primary service provider. The State has assumed a heavy burden for rebuilding the City University. It also will pay the cost for hazardous waste clean-up in New York City. Both of these commitments reflect an effort to treat the city in a fashion comparable to upstate regions.

Provision of correctional and mental hygiene services to New York City residents presents the State with a special problem. Much of the statewide demand for these services comes from city residents. However, higher facility costs in the city make it difficult to provide those services within city boundaries. Consequently, New York City residents are obliged to use facilities located upstate. Movement towards community-based alternatives in both corrections and mental hygiene may offer some improvement to the current situation.

The State's largest capital funding problems exist in highway repair and mass transit. Both functions have enormous ongoing costs without clear or adequate means of support. Highways are predominantly an upstate need; mass transit is predominantly a need of the New York City region. This situation creates the opportunity for a political accommodation to provide new capital sources for both functions.

NOTES

1. The multi-year projections of capital expenditures in this essay all reflect annual adjustment for inflation as determined by the responsible State and City agencies.

2. New York State, Chapter 837, Laws of 1983. The legislation is known commonly as the "capital planning bill."
3. New York State, *Five-Year Capital Plan, Fiscal Years 1986–87 through 1990–91*, no date.
4. The total appropriations number in the plan is $19.7 billion. However, this amount includes $2.1 billion in bond proceeds appropriations which are pass-through accounts that represent a double-counting with general obligation bonds. Thus, the appropriation number for actual project work is $17.6 billion.
5. New York City, Office of Management and Budget, *Ten-Year Capital Plan, Fiscal Years 1987–1996*, May 1986. The dollar numbers in the ten-year plan are "commitments," which represent the final approval for a capital project to start.
6. New York State, *Five-Year Capital Plan*, p. 68.
7. New York State, *Five-Year Capital Plan*, p. 28.
8. Cost estimates provided by the State Office of General Services.
9. Richard McGahey, *New York State Project 2000: Corrections and Criminal Justice* (Albany: Nelson A. Rockefeller Institute of Government, State University of New York, June 1986).
10. For details, see Office of Mental Health, *Five-Year Comprehensive Plan for Mental Health Services, 1985–1990*, February 15, 1986.
11. Estimates provided in New York State, *1986–87 Executive Budget Briefing Book*, January 1986.
12. Information provided by Department of Environmental Conservation staff.
13. Of the total 1,402 local bridges in New York City, only 852 are highway-related structures. The remainder are rail, park, and other bridge types.
14. New York State, *Five-Year Capital Plan*, p. 76.
15. See the Citizens Budget Commission, *New York City's Ten-Year Plan for Capital Development* (New York: Citizens Budget Commission, November 1983).
16. See the U.S. Department of Transportation, Federal Highway Administration, *Financing Federal Aid Highways*, September 1983.
17. Statement based upon interviews with Department of Transportation officials.
18. New York City, *Ten-Year Capital Plan*, p. 18.
19. See the Citizens Union Foundation, *Thirsty City: A Plan of Action for New York City Water Supply* (New York: Citizens Union, 1986).
20. New York City, *Ten-Year Capital Plan*, p. 59.
21. New York City, *Ten-Year Capital Plan*, p. 40.

10

HUMAN RESOURCES MANAGEMENT

❧

Raymond D. Horton
and
David Lewin

AMERICAN governments allocate the largest share of their financial resources to their employees; in return, they deliver the overwhelming share of society's public services. Government employees thus play an important role in determining the cost and effectiveness of the public sector. Despite its importance, human resource management typically takes a back seat to other concerns among students of government. For example, financial management receives far more attention than human resource management. The simplest explanation for this bias is that the management of money is both easier to study and more amenable to change than the management of people.

The bias against the study of human resource management holds true in New York as well as nationally. For this reason, an essay on State-City relations in human resource management must build upon underdeveloped conceptual and empirical bases. The first two sections of this essay deal with human resource management in theory and in practice, respectively. The final section identifies several issues the resolution of which would advance the study and practice of human resource management in New York State and New York City.

HUMAN RESOURCE MANAGEMENT IN THEORY

Four sets of activities—staffing, compensation, personnel administration, and productivity—constitute the basic components of human resource management. Because these activities are interdependent, they may be conceptualized in systemic terms. A model appropriate for studying and evaluating human resource management in government may be developed by drawing upon both presumed and observed behavior in the private sector.

Staffing

In theory, the amount of labor an organization employs is determined by the principle of declining marginal utility: staffing will be at a level where the cost of adding an additional worker equals the organizational benefits of doing so. In a turn-of-the-century (and perhaps also a mid-1980s) New York sweatshop, where garment workers produced standardized products through standardized procedures in a highly competitive industry, managers (who were often owners) could determine and implement their staffing needs with relative ease. Subsequent changes in industrial organization and ownership, government regulation, and labor relations made performance of this managerial function more difficult for private firms. In governments, where benefits are harder to value, the principle of declining marginal utility is even more difficult to apply.

Nevertheless, the ability of public organizations to avoid under- or overutilization of labor remains an important determinant of their success. Governments unable to employ enough staff will experience difficulty providing constituents with services of the desired level and/or quality; long "customer" queues at vehicular registration offices or inadequate nursing care in public hospitals are only two manifestations of insufficient staffing. Governments that employ too many workers will experience difficulty providing constituents services at the desired cost; high taxes result from such overstaffing. The consequences of inappropriate staffing may not threaten the existence of a particular government, as they might a firm, but this does not mean that the citizenry is without means to protect its interests. It can elect new management or purchase services from other providers, including private firms or another government.

In addition to facing the problem of applying marginal analysis to service benefits which are hard to value, public managers determine staffing policy within the context of a larger budgetary process. Staffing is an important part of the budgetary process because employment levels are one of the few variables public managers can manipulate to reconcile available financial resources with preferred policies. But public budgetary processes are not models of "rational" decision making in the sense implied by the principle of declining marginal utility.

A basic reason for this is ambiguity of goals and fragmentation of authority. Public budgeting is an ongoing process featuring multiple actors with different values and multiple forums within which to assert them. For example, budgetary "managers" include legislators as well as executives.

Elected chief executives and their appointees may develop a coherent staffing policy while formulating a budget, but they cannot guarantee that legislators will embrace it, particularly when partisan or ideological differences divide the two branches of government. In short, staffing decisions result from a complex bargaining process, the outcome of which may bear only scant resemblance to those resulting from marginal utility analysis.

A second reason staffing decisions are difficult for public managers to reach systematically is that officials of other governments frequently intervene in these decisions. Intergovernmental mandates represent vertical fragmentation of authority that may be more important than horizontal fragmentation in determining staffing or other human resource management policies.

A third factor potentially complicating a government's ability to fashion appropriate staffing policies is the set of other human resource management policies. To repeat, the various human resource management functions are interdependent. Goals in one aspect of human resource management, such as staffing, may be frustrated by policies in another, such as compensation.

Compensation

In theory, compensation will be at a level sufficient to enable organizations to maintain a workforce large enough and skilled enough to produce its goods or services. Governments that pay too little may anticipate attracting an inadequate workforce in terms of numbers and/or quality, thereby disappointing citizens with respect to service delivery. Governments that pay too much will attract a sufficient supply of workers and may provide adequate or even high-quality services, but they risk public disapproval for "charging" too much for their services through high taxes.

Because resources are scarce, compensation competes with other purposes of public expenditure, including staffing. The compensation-employment tradeoff obliges public managers to reconcile the competing demands of spending for staff and spending for compensation. Were such decisions reached under conditions of perfect competition, the optimal tradeoff would be readily achieved: The "invisible hand" of the market would recognize the interdependence of staffing and compensation and determine the appropriate level of each.

For several reasons, however, determining employee compensation is difficult for public managers. One reason, again, is intraorganizational fragmentation of managerial goals and authority. Collective bargaining, now a widespread process for determining public sector compensation in the United States, not only provides organized employees a direct, formal role in determining their compensation but, at the same time, reorders the roles of public managers. The influence of legislators, personnel administrators, and budget officials has been reduced; that of labor relations negotiators has been enhanced. In general, the evolution of collective bargaining in the public sector has decreased management power over compensation.[1]

A distinctive characteristic of public sector bargaining, related to the fragmentation of managerial authority, is its multilateral as opposed to bilateral nature. A given government may provide multiple forums for determining the terms and conditions of employment, but the American brand of federalism also invites managers and union representatives alike to contest labor-related policies in the forums of other governments. Because localities are "creatures" of states, intergovernmental influence on compensation decisions typically runs from the state to the locality. However, compensation decisions of state governments may be affected by the compensation decisions of a large locality within the state.

Collective bargaining has complicated management's compensation decisions; it also has complicated the making of the compensation-employment tradeoff. Whereas budget officials previously dominated both staffing and compensation policies, their influence over the latter has been reduced by collective bargaining. The tension between budgeters and labor negotiators has become one of the major administrative conflicts of contemporary state and local government.

Personnel Administration

Personnel administration involves dual, and in many respects competing, purposes. On the one hand, personnel administration may be viewed as a subsystem of human resource management intended to augment compensation as a means of maintaining a quality workforce. Each of its components, including recruitment, selection (both for new hires and promotions), training, and discipline, is intended to improve the capacity of a given workforce to perform the tasks assigned it. Ensuring that a sufficiently large pool of applicants competes for public positions, hiring and promoting the "best and the brightest," adding to the skills of the workforce through education, and sanctioning poorly performing employees will, in theory, create a more qualified "stock" of human resources; this, in turn, will make it possible for employers to provide more and better services than otherwise would be the case.

On the other hand, personnel administration may serve the equity needs of workers more than the efficiency needs of managers. Indeed, civil service systems, a particular form of personnel administration, were initiated largely in response to "arbitrary" managerial behavior thought not to be conducive to developing a public workforce of high quality. Winnowing the pool of applicants for civil service positions, selecting the "best and the brightest" on the basis of written examinations graded to several decimal points, training all rather than a chosen few, and limiting the ability of managers to punish (and reward) individual workers are policies that many believe make the civil service fairer and civil servants more productive.

The difficulty in reconciling these conflicting goals has caused many personnel administrators to be shorn of responsibility for certain functions. The most important example—wage determination—was mentioned earlier, but other functions that have been transferred include job classification, the formulation and administration of examinations, training, and employee discipline. Once again, then, the responsibility for important aspects of human resource management is divided among various decision centers within a single government whose goals for personnel administration may vary. Personnel directors want to hire from their lists before high scorers take other jobs; budget directors sometimes do not want to hire at all in order to ease a fiscal problem through attrition; line managers or political "bosses" frequently want new hires, but not from competitive lists.

Once again, the way in which a given government conducts personnel administration may draw the attention of managers of other governments. Local personnel administration typically is regulated by state laws, and the federal government maintains legislative and judicial involvement in state and local personnel administration. Thus, it is not uncommon for municipalities to administer civil service examinations for a given position, but for the examination to have been prepared by a state personnel agency in keeping with federal mandates.

Productivity

Typically, public sector productivity programs seek to improve efficiency (usually defined as reducing unit costs) in order to make it possible for governments to offer the same services with fewer employees (and thus lower costs). The "savings" generated by increased productivity may permit tax reductions or may be reinvested to improve services. The substitution of capital for labor, the rationalization of work procedures, the creation of incentives to stimulate harder or better work, and the formation of joint labor-management committees to confer about "the workplace" represent different kinds of productivity programs. Other kinds of initiatives, lumped under the rubric "privatization," represent an attempt by public managers to avoid personnel utilization issues either by selling or contracting out. While they fall outside the scope of this essay, threats to privatize public functions may lead to altered utilization of the public workforce.[2]

The processes by which public managers seek to improve productivity are necessarily complex. Because "better" utilization implies "different" behavior, it is subject to the countervailing forces of bureaucratic inertia. It should be emphasized that management as well as labor sometimes is a source of support for the status quo. For example, many line agency managers may not share the budget director's interest in doing "the same for less."

For these reasons, managerial initiatives to improve productivity through different modes of workforce utilization frequently die at their own hands. When they do not, the employees whose behavior is threatened usually are able to be heard—within one or another of "their" governments. Collective bargaining and electoral politics are among the local forums available to employees seeking to prevent productivity initiatives, but if these do not suffice, officials of other governments may be called on to regulate local utilization of the workforce.

In summary, all organizations engage in a series of activities involving their employees. These activities—staffing, compensation, personnel administration, and productivity—are interdependent. In public organizations, however, these human resource management policies are determined by multiple actors who tend to be politically independent. Creating integrated human resource management policies is a particularly difficult task for officials of state and local governments. In this light, it is appropriate to ask, "How do the governments of New York State and New York City manage their workforces?"

HUMAN RESOURCE MANAGEMENT IN PRACTICE

Human resource management policies reflect broader concerns than those of "rational" managers. Making the most of the available workforce is only one of public officials' many concerns. In short, public human resource management systems are "open" rather than "closed." This means that the "environment" within which human resource management is practiced influences such policies.

Environmental Characteristics

While the concept of systemic environment is open-ended, the relevant literature suggests that some environmental characteristics are more significant than others to the management of human resources. First, the literature of American federalism suggests that there is substantial interdependence among the three levels of government—federal, state, and local.[3] While the relationship of the federal government to subnational governments has changed in fundamental ways since the eighteenth century, the relationship between state and city governments over human resource management has been quite stable. Underlying this relationship is the notion that cities, being "creatures" of states, are prevented from achieving "home rule" by state intervention. The city-as-creature-of-the-state principle is an important aspect of the environment of human resource management.

Second, since human resource managers manage people, the number of people they have to manage would seem to be an important factor influencing their behavior. While many things can affect the size of public workforces, the financial condition of governments is perhaps the most important factor. The growing literature examining the relationship between organizational finances and organizational management strongly suggests that organizations are managed differently under conditions of growth than under conditions of retrenchment.[4] This proposition extends to human resource management as well as to budgeting and other managerial functions.

Third, state and local political systems exhibit distinctive power relationships that influence a variety of decisions including human resource management policies.[5] Staffing, compensation, personnel administration, and productivity decisions involve multiple actors, groups, and agencies with their own agendas. These political forces intrude on human resource management just as do government finances and relationships with other governments.

Intergovernmental Relations. As noted earlier, analyses of state-city relationships emphasize the importance of state regulations or interventions on the operations of localities. This is certainly the case in New York. State policies shape the process by which the City's policies are reached, and in some instances specify the outcomes as well. For example, State laws and the State constitution prescribe, often in great detail, the operation of the City's civil service system; certain of the City's commissioners must deploy the workers in their agencies in accord with duty charts mandated by State laws; the State mandates specific elements of City employee compensation, particularly pension benefits.

However, this view of the intergovernmental aspects of human resource management is inadequate in two important respects as it applies to New York State and New York City. First, the State's role in the City's human resource management system is more dynamic than the "top-down" conceptualization suggests. The State's involvement ebbs and flows and takes various forms over time in response to changing financial and political circumstances. During the late 1960s, State officials attempted to ensure that the City's collective bargaining practices reached the "substantial equivalence" standard embodied in the State's Taylor Law, but they encountered resistance from the City (which already had a more developed collective bargaining system than the State) and withdrew to Albany to focus their energies on their own emerging labor relations problems. However, when the City experienced its fiscal crisis several years later, the State quickly intervened in the City's collective bargaining system by empowering the newly created Emergency Financial Control Board to disapprove labor contracts. Later, as the financial emergency eased, the State returned to a "hands-off" posture in local collective bargaining. The fiscal crisis also caused the State to alter its interventions in City compensation policies. Prior to the fiscal crisis, the State legislature frequently mandated pension benefits the City had opposed successfully in collective bargaining with municipal employee unions. During the fiscal crisis, the legislature responded by passing a "two-tier" pension system which reduced benefits for new workers; after the fiscal crisis passed, the legislature again began to liberalize the pension benefits of City employees.

Second, the city-as-creature-of-the-state interpretation obscures the fact that human resource management by the State is affected by developments in New York City. For example, the City's fiscal crisis led to State assumption of the senior colleges of the City University of New York, resulting in an expansion of the State workforce of approximately 15,000. Similarly, the City's collective bargaining settlements are watched carefully by those who negotiate the State's labor contracts, because the City's settlements serve as important reference points for evaluating how well negotiators of State contracts perform. Also, the strategies City employees use to adapt the local personnel and management systems to their needs become models for State employees who have not yet gained as much experience in these aspects of human resource management as have City workers.

Finances. As noted earlier, human resource management is affected by the financial condition of the organization. Organizations with more or less stable finances face different (and in general less difficult) human resource management problems than organizations with expanding or contracting resources.

The finances of both the State and City have been highly unstable in the period since 1970. Swings in the resources available to both governments have affected the number of employees to be managed in each, as well as the nature of the problems entailed in their management. During the first half of the 1970s, each government grew rapidly. In the second half of the 1970s, the State's spending was nearly stable and City spending fell nearly one tenth. Between 1980 and 1985, the State returned to rapid fiscal expansion and placed a high priority on adding staff. The City's fiscal retrenchment did not end until 1983, but since then it, too, has been expanding its spending rapidly—initially to restore salaries to pre-fiscal crisis levels and more recently to build up its workforce.[6]

The effects of financial instability were felt more heavily in the City than in the State. This reflects an intrinsic difference between the two governments, indeed between city and state governments generally. Because of their basic function—delivering services—local governments are more labor intensive than state governments, the basic functions of which include financing local governments as well as delivering services. And since city governments devote a larger share of their resources to their employees, human resource management in localities is affected more directly by financial instability than in state governments.

Politics. There are notable differences in the politics of the City and State that bear on the conduct of human resource management in each government. In the City, the politics of human resource management is dominated by two actors—the mayor and civil service unions. Their relative influence over human resource management policies may change from time to time, but they are the key players at all times. Management is more divided and civil service unions less influential in the State.

The greater centralization of management power within "officialdom" in the City results from the fact that the City's legislative branch—the City Council and Board of Estimate—has limited influence over the budget or administration of City government; moreover, the administrative agencies most involved with human resource management—the Office of Management and Budget, the Office of Municipal Labor Relations, and the Department of Personnel—are firmly under the control of the mayor.

The distribution of political influence over human resource management in New York City has changed since the introduction in the early 1960s of collective bargaining.[7] The new system reduced the role of the City's legislators and, more important, reduced the influence of the City's Personnel Department, which had played a central role in wage determination and personnel administration. The mayor's Office of Labor Relations (later Office of Municipal Labor Relations) became the chief executive's bargaining arm and gradually took over many of the Personnel Department's functions as the scope of bargaining extended beyond compensation to include personnel administration. The Office of Management and Budget, still the most important of the mayor's staff agencies, also increasingly defers to the Office of Municipal Labor Relations in collective bargaining.

The centralization of management authority under the mayor reflects the growing strength of civil service unions in New York City. These unions long have been influential in municipal affairs, but the introduction of formal collective bargaining strengthened them by weeding out many of the smaller unions and by giving those fewer but larger unions that remained both more security and a new forum—collective bargaining—for asserting their broad-ranging interests. Collective bargaining with the mayor's negotiators—and frequently with the mayor himself—was a means not only of establishing compensation, but of resolving matters involving personnel administration, agency work rules, and even agency staffing. The fiscal crisis reduced union influence in certain matters, but at the same time helped reduce conflict among municipal unions; with the passage of the fiscal crisis in the 1980s, their influence over collective bargaining has increased despite signs that the solidarity induced by the fiscal crisis is diminishing.[8]

The State's power structure reflects a stronger legislative presence as well as more competition among the agencies involved in human resource management. The State Senate and Assembly play a far more influential role in State finances and administration than the City's legislative bodies. Moreover, the State's Division of the Budget, Governor's Office of Employee Relations, and Department of Civil Service share authority in human resource management more than their counterparts in the City. Each contests the others for influence in human resource management, and to date governors have not intervened to create a more settled administrative process.

This fragmentation of authority may reflect the fact that the State's civil service unions are not as influential as the City's. The era of "modern" public sector labor relations began earlier in the City than the State, and the State's transition from a civil service to a collective bargaining system has been slower. The State's civil service unions were "company" unions long after the City's unions had acquired their own identity as aggressive and sometimes militant advocates. While the State unions are gaining a different identity, they do not yet compete with public officials with the same purposiveness as the City's unions.

The outstanding example of political interdependence between the State and City human resource management systems involves the City's unions and the State legislature. In addition to being actively involved in local elections for State legislative positions, the City's major unions support "upstate" candidates as well; moreover, such support is not limited to Democrats. Their ability to relate to State legislators provides the City's unions with the proverbial "two bites at the apple." On occasion, they are able to win through the State legislature what they are unable to realize in their negotiations with City officials. However, their ability to execute "end runs" is limited to certain issues and waxes and wanes over time. Mayors have their own involvements with State legislators, primarily Democrats from the city, and they are able to mobilize local constituencies, particularly the media, when the City's unions attempt to exploit their Albany connections. Nevertheless, there are times when upstate Republicans and downstate Democrats join with the City's organized bureaucracy to define or defend the City's human resource management system.

Staffing

The budgetary process largely determines the size of the public workforce. Those who perform this function do not start from scratch each year. The dominant theory of public sector budgeting holds that the application of decision routines and rules simplifying the process leads to incremental budgeting; that is, new budgets reflect minor adjustments to the prior year's pattern of resource allocation.[9]

There is substantial evidence, however, that budgeting in the City has not conformed to the incremental theory.[10] Consider how staffing has fared in the competition for public expenditure in the State and the City.

Budgeting and Staffing. If the priority attached to staffing is constant over time, then changes in public employment will move in parallel with changes in public expenditure. However, if the workforce expands more rapidly than spending (or during retrenchment declines less rapidly), then staffing has been assigned a relatively high priority in the budgetary process; and if staff increases less rapidly than spending (or during retrenchment declines more rapidly), then staffing has been accorded a relatively low priority.

Table 10.1 shows expenditures (adjusted for price changes) and employment in the State and the City for the 1970–1985 period. For the overall period, the State's workforce grew 39 percent, or from an employment base of 146,223 in 1970 to 202,897 in 1985; by contrast, the City's workforce fell 9 percent from 275,211 in 1970 to 251,720 in 1985. The different staffing policies of the two governments reflected their different financial fortunes during this period. The State's budget increased 52 percent, while the City's increased 19 percent. However, their "purchasing power" was not the only factor driving their employment levels, as a more detailed look at expenditure and employment trends reveals.

State spending exhibits considerable volatility, with two periods of rapid growth bracketing a period of slow growth. Changes in staffing levels, however, do not mirror overall expenditure trends. During the 1970–1975 period the State placed a relatively low priority on workforce expansion; expenditure growth of 24 percent yielded only a 3 percent expansion in the workforce. In the second half of the 1970s, however, the State accorded expansion of its staff a high priority. While financial resources rose by 2 percent, employment rose by 11 percent. In the period between 1980 and 1985, State expenditures and employment rose nearly in tandem and substantially.

Like the State, the City placed a low priority on staffing in the first half of the 1970s; despite a 23 percent increase in expenditure, the number of City employees increased only 4 percent. The City's spending fell 10 percent in the 1975–1980 period, and again staffing was a low priority. The City's workforce fell 20 percent, twice the percentage decline in expenditures. However, in the 1980–1985 period the City placed a relatively high priority on increasing its workforce. A 7 percent spending increase was used to increase staffing 10 percent.

Intergovernmental relationships as well as financial conditions influence the size of a government's workforce. Before discussing the impact of State policies on City staffing, it is important to consider the ways in which the State's budgeting and staffing policies are affected by developments in localities in general and in New York City in particular.

While the State's 200,000-plus workforce attests to its extensive service-delivery responsibilities, the bulk of State expenditure is devoted to aid to localities rather than direct services. Thus, in effect, local government officials and State workers are the two major competitors in the allocation of the State budget. When localities are able to increase their share in the form of aid, less money is available for State operations and staffing; when the State accords a higher priority to its own

TABLE 10.1

Expenditures and Employment in New York State and New York City, Fiscal Years 1970, 1975, 1980, and 1985 (in thousands of 1970 dollars)

Item	Amount				Percentage Change			
	1970	1975	1980	1985	1970–1975	1975–1980	1980–1985	1970–1985
Expenditures								
State	$7,762	$9,624	$9,801	$11,761	24.0%	1.8%	20.0%	51.5%
City	6,154	7,587	6,844	7,290	23.3	(9.8)	6.5	18.5
Employment								
State	146,223	150,227	166,227	202,897	2.7	10.7	22.1	38.8
City	275,211	285,856	228,874	251,720	3.9	(19.9)	10.0	(8.5)

SOURCES: New York State expenditure data provided by New York State Division of the Budget; New York City expenditures are operating budget totals from annual editions of the *Comprehensive Annual Report of the Comptroller* adjusted to reflect reporting practices that removed State and federal Medicaid expenditures from the City's operating budget. New York State employment data from U.S. Bureau of the Census, *Public Employment,* series GE78, no. 2 (Washington, DC: U.S. Government Printing Office, 1969, 1974, 1979, and 1984); and New York City employment data from New York State Financial Control Board and New York City Office of Management and Budget. Constant dollar adjustments made on the basis of the Consumer Price Index for all Consumers (CPI-U) in the New York–Northeastern New Jersey area.

NOTE: State and City expenditures exclude capital disbursements.

279

operations in the division of its budget, expansion of the State workforce is more likely. In recent years, local assistance has grown as a share of total State expenditures, though the overall rate of increase in State spending has enabled its direct operations budgets to grow substantially in absolute terms.[11]

The City has exerted an even more direct impact on the State budget and workforce. One consequence of the New York City fiscal crisis was State assumption in the 1978–1982 period of functions previously performed by the City, including phased takeovers of the senior colleges in the City University of New York and the City's court system. While the specific number of employees thus transferred from the City to State payrolls cannot be identified precisely because of the phased nature of the takeovers, as many as 20,000 of the 50,000-person increase in State employment between 1975 and 1985 may be attributable to State assumption of these two functions.

This "exchange" between the State and City governments is only one element in a complex system of intergovernmental relationships that also affects the City's budget and staffing policies. The centerpiece in that system is a series of aid programs which transfer funds from the State to the City. The City's $21.5 billion 1987 expense budget includes some $4.8 billion in such transfers (as well as an estimated $2.6 billion in federal aid). While $700 million of the State aid is transferred with "no strings" attached, the City must spend the remaining $4.1 billion in accordance with purposes spelled out by the State legislature. These restrictions include most of the "mandate millstones" that City officials attempt to have lifted in their ongoing relationships with State officials. Additional mandates are imposed independently of State aid programs in those instances where the State requires the City to perform certain functions but provides no financial support. By the City's count 48 separate State mandates and an additional 25 federal mandates require City expenditures in excess of $3 billion annually.[12]

Determining the staffing impacts of State aid programs is difficult, because it is unclear whether the State aid "substitutes" for City funds that otherwise would be expended or "stimulates" added City spending. While City officials emphasize the stimulative as opposed to substitutive effects on local spending and, by extension, employment, their effects cannot be estimated precisely. Presumably, the effects are twofold. First, the magnitude of the aid strongly suggests that some increase in aggregate City employment results. Second, the aid probably skews the distribution of the City's workforce. Some programs require matching local expenditures which, in the absence of the programs, probably would be used to support added staff in the so-called essential services such as police, fire, and sanitation.

This review of staffing trends since 1970 suggests that a number of factors influence the size of the State and City workforces. The financial circumstances of each government are important, but employment trends do not "fit" closely with spending trends. Apparently, each government changes the importance it places on staff as opposed to other purposes of expenditure. The State and the City do not reach their staffing decisions entirely independently; the policies of one government affect the policies of the other. While the dependence of the City on the State dominates the attention of analysts and policymakers, State spending and staffing decisions also are affected by developments among the State's local governments, particularly New York City.

Comparative Analysis. The trend data examined above show how— and suggest why—the size of the State and City workforces has changed over time; comparative data are helpful in appraising whether the State and the City are staffed appropriately. However, three issues complicate the conduct and interpretation of comparative research. First, governments differ in their scale, the functions they perform, and the number and political values of their citizenry. It is difficult to "control" for such differences. Second, it is hard to acquire reliable data for a large number of governments. Comparative research necessarily relies on data of uncertain accuracy. Finally, findings based on comparative research are difficult to interpret. A government that is "understaffed" in comparison to others may have a more skilled, more productive workforce. If so, is it really understaffed?

With these caveats in mind, are the New York State and New York City workforces similar in size to those of comparable governments? The data required to study that question are published by the U.S. Bureau of the Census.[13] The comparative State data used cover 11 state governments that served populations of more than 5 million in 1980, and that include one city with a population of at least 350,000; the comparison group of big-city governments include 17 serving populations in 1980 of at least 500,000. To adjust for differences in population size, staffing was measured on the basis of the number of employees per 10,000 residents; to control for differences in the functions among these governments, a particularly notable problem at the city level, only "common" functions performed by all governments in the comparison group were included.

The comparative analysis of state governments is summarized in Table 10.2. In 1985, the State of New York employed 114.4 workers per 10,000 population in the functions common to the ten governments in the comparison group, fully 21 percent more than the average for other state governments. This stands in sharp contrast to the experience in 1970, 1975, and 1980, when the State's staffing ratios were either slightly

TABLE 10.2

Employees per 10,000 Population in New York State Government Compared with the Average for Selected State Governments: Fiscal Years 1970, 1975, 1980, and 1985*

Function	1970 New York	1970 Others	1975 New York	1975 Others	1980 New York	1980 Others	1985 New York	1985 Others
Higher Education	16.05	27.76	16.62	32.86	15.36	35.37	23.20	34.25
Welfare	1.03	3.95	0.87	7.67	1.84	8.57	3.84	7.80
Hospitals	33.19	19.40	33.30	20.36	39.82	22.78	40.75	19.92
Health	3.04	2.11	4.69	3.49	4.54	4.70	4.73	4.47
Highways	9.21	12.18	9.80	10.65	8.66	9.21	8.15	8.19
Police	2.36	2.48	2.56	3.11	2.58	3.09	2.99	3.22
Correction	5.03	3.89	5.48	5.17	5.59	6.38	12.63	8.46
Financial Administration	7.36	4.02	6.38	4.37	6.31	4.85	7.22	4.24
General Control	2.55	1.59	3.13	2.73	9.39	4.18	10.88	4.33
Total	79.81	77.38	82.83	90.41	94.09	99.13	114.39	94.88
Ratio of New York to Others	1.03	—	0.92	—	0.95	—	1.21	—

SOURCES: U.S. Bureau of the Census, *Public Employment*, series GE78, no. 1 (Washington, DC: U.S. Government Printing Office, 1969, 1974, 1979, and 1984).

*Other State governments include California, Florida, Georgia, Illinois, Massachusetts, Michigan, New Jersey, Ohio, Pennsylvania, and Texas.

above (1970) or below the average elsewhere (1975 and 1980). A combination of rapid growth in New York and a reduction in the other states between 1980 and 1985 accounted for the State moving from slightly below average to substantially above average. The bulk of the State's adjusted employment growth in that period was concentrated in two areas—higher education (reflecting in part the aforementioned assumption of responsibilities previously performed by the City) and corrections. Virtually all of the difference between New York's overall level and the average in the other states results from employment in the hospitals function.

New York City also employs substantially more persons, adjusted for population, than its counterparts—24 percent more in 1985. (See Table 10.3.) Unlike the State, however, its relative staffing level fell in the 1970–1985 period. In 1970, the City's adjusted staffing level was 46 percent above average. In the 1970s, reflecting its fiscal problems and steady staffing growth in other cities, the City's staffing declined almost to the big-city average, but in the first half of the 1980s it increased again. Whereas the State's comparatively high staffing can be explained on the basis of one function, the City's staffing reflects above-average levels in all but one—namely, parks and recreation. In one area—sanitation— the City's adjusted staffing level is more than twice the big-city average; however, this discrepancy may be explained in part by the fact that some other cities contract out certain sanitation activities.

As noted earlier, interpretation of these findings is complicated. First, the data reflects the Census Bureau's collection and presentation procedures, which do not conform to the conventions of the specific governments involved in all cases. It is unlikely, however, that these variations explain the disparities of over 20 percent for the State and the City. Second, staffing levels must be considered with reference to the quality and productiveness of the workforce. One interpretation of Tables 10.2 and 10.3 is that the quality and productivity of the State and City workforces are lower than in other governments—that is, each must "overstaff" in order to produce services of comparable level and quality. Another interpretation, of course, is that the State and City workforces are of roughly comparable quality and productiveness, but because of their size produce above-average services. New Yorkers may expect and be willing to pay for more or better services than citizens elsewhere.

Compensation

Collective bargaining is the dominant process for determining the compensation of State and City employees. However, some employees of each government are excluded from bargaining by dint of the managerial

TABLE 10.3

Employees for Common Functions per 10,000 Population in New York City Government Compared with the Average for Selected City Governments: Fiscal Years 1970, 1975, 1980, and 1985*

Function	1970 New York	1970 Others	1975 New York	1975 Others	1980 New York	1980 Others	1985 New York	1985 Others
Highways	7.12	7.15	9.03	7.89	9.46	8.77	10.44	7.97
Police	47.09	29.66	47.39	33.90	40.23	35.72	43.96	33.92
Fire	19.44	16.09	18.35	17.28	17.47	17.42	19.14	16.84
Sanitation	19.76	9.56	15.86	8.60	16.18	8.56	16.60	6.85
Parks and Recreation	12.60	9.86	8.21	9.74	7.79	11.70	6.21	9.17
Financial Administration and Control	16.52	11.60	19.10	14.22	12.38	15.65	16.59	16.52
Total	122.53	83.92	117.94	91.63	103.51	97.82	112.94	91.27
Ratio of New York to Others	1.46	—	1.29	—	1.06	—	1.24	—

SOURCES: U.S. Bureau of the Census, *City Employment*, series GE78, no. 2; and *Local Government Employment in Selected Metropolitan Areas*, series GE78, no. 3 (Washington, DC: U.S. Government Printing Office, 1969, 1974, 1979, and 1984).

*Other city governments include Los Angeles, San Diego, San Francisco, Jacksonville, Honolulu, Chicago, Indianapolis, Baltimore, Boston, Detroit, Cleveland, Columbus, Philadelphia, Dallas, Houston, San Antonio, and Milwaukee.

or confidential nature of their jobs, and a few components of the compensation package of those who are represented by unions are determined by legislation rather than contract. For most workers, however, collective bargaining is *the* process by which their compensation is established. While collective bargaining performs a similar function in the State and the City, their respective bargaining processes differ in important ways.

The Development of Collective Bargaining. The differences between the State and City collective bargaining systems reflect the fact that the City already had a well-developed system by the time the State entered the "modern" era of public sector labor relations. History has narrowed but not eliminated these differences.

The State entered the modern era in 1967 when Governor Nelson A. Rockefeller signed the Public Employees' Fair Employment Law (more commonly known as the Taylor Law).[14] This law, which applied to employees of local governments as well as the State, permitted employees to bargain collectively over the terms and conditions of their employment, created an agency to determine bargaining units and to help resolve bargaining impasses (the Public Employment Relations Board, or PERB), and continued the prohibition of public employee strikes contained in earlier legislation. While the Taylor Law permitted localities to develop their own collective bargaining laws, it required that they be "substantially equivalent" to the overarching State law. The City, however, was expressly exempted from that mandate in recognition of its "unique" situation.

The City did have a unique labor relations system, at least among New York's governments.[15] Its formal commitment to collective bargaining predated the State's by almost a decade; moreover, the political setting of labor relations was different.

Mayor Robert F. Wagner introduced the City to collective bargaining with his Executive Order 49, which was promulgated in 1958. New York City at that time had a reputation of being a "union town." While its private unions were largely responsible for that appellation, the City's public employees had a long history of organization and political involvement. Wagner had close relationships with organized labor in general, but those with the City's civil service union leaders became increasingly important in the late 1950s as his support within the local Democratic party began to erode. Executive Order 49, signed shortly after he began his second term, helped solidify Wagner's support among municipal employees which, in turn, was crucial to his reelection to a third term in 1961. Despite Wagner's close political ties with municipal union leaders, he implemented the new collective bargaining system slowly and was able to keep control of it throughout his second and most of his third term. By all accounts he was a skilled negotiator able to maintain close personal and political relationships with civil service union leaders, notwithstanding his protagonistic role as the City's chief negotiator.

In 1965, late in his third term, Wagner was unable to settle a bitter strike in the City's Welfare Department through friendly persuasion and ultimately was forced to appoint an impartial arbitration panel. That panel not only sided with the striking unions in recommending a settlement, but as part of the settlement also recommended that another tripartite panel be created to reconsider the City's seven-year-old collective bargaining program. The second tripartite panel concluded that the core problem in the City's labor relations program was that its administration was too "political," and it recommended creation of an "impartial" agency composed of management, labor, and third-party or neutral representatives to administer the City's program and to assist in the resolution of negotiating impasses.

This approach to collective bargaining was accepted by Wagner's successor, John V. Lindsay, who in 1965 had campaigned against Wagner's personal style of negotiating with the City's "power brokers" and had suffered a transit strike during his first two weeks in office that helped convince him of the virtues of a "professionalized" and "depoliticized" collective bargaining system. The City took the first step in 1966 by creating the Office of Labor Relations (OLR) to act as its negotiating arm, and the second in 1967 by chartering a tripartite Office of Collective Bargaining (OCB) to administer a new collective bargaining program and to provide assistance when negotiations reached impasse.

Thus, by the time the Taylor Law was enacted, the City already had nearly a decade of experience with collective bargaining and already had rejected a "management-dominated" model in favor of one in which management and labor had equal standing. The State's new program differed from the City's in several respects: the State's administrative agency—PERB—was led if not controlled by the governor, while the City's OCB was dominated by impartial "third parties"; the State's scope of bargaining was defined more narrowly than the City's; the State law gave the legislature the ultimate authority to resolve bargaining disputes, while the City's law contained no "finality" procedure; the State required contracts to be resolved prior to budget submission dates, while the City's did not.

These formal discrepancies were troublesome to State officials, and in 1969 the Taylor Law was amended in an attempt to bring the City under the same "substantial equivalence" standard that applied to other localities. The City strongly resisted the State's attempt to bring its program into conformance. Ultimately, the City adopted a finality procedure that met the State's mandate by granting the OCB the authority to resolve impasses by binding arbitration, but it did so in a way that kept control within the City's labor relations establishment and out of the hands of the City Council.[16]

During the first half of the 1970s, the State essentially gave up its attempt to regulate labor relations in the City and focused its energies on implementing the Taylor Law for its employees and regulating nascent bargaining programs in localities other than New York City. The governor's Office of Employee Relations (OER), created in 1969 to negotiate on behalf of the State, had a much easier time than its City counterpart during this period. The State's PERB, with the benefit of observing what was going on in the City, determined in 1969 that there would be only five bargaining units for State employees. In the representation elections that followed designation of the bargaining units, one union, the Civil Service Employees Association (CSEA), won four of the five contests. The CSEA had been the dominant organization among State employees for decades, but it was not a "union" in the meaning of the word in the City. Its members included both State and local government employees, which meant that it had a divided focus; beyond that, it had never engaged in the kinds of activities that were characteristic of the City's unions. For example, it had never negotiated a labor contract, had never involved itself in electoral politics, and had never struck.

The contrast with the City's collective bargaining system during the first half of the 1970s could not have been more sharp. There were scores of bargaining units in the City, dozens of different unions represented workers, and intraunion and interunion conflict was great. This environment meant that civil service union leaders were under great pressure not to be outdone at the collective bargaining table. Bargaining was a nonstop process for the OLR, punctuated by strikes and frequently culminating in impasses that had to be resolved by binding arbitration conducted under the auspices of the OCB. The State had its conflicts, but they were minor compared with the City's. The CSEA's status as bargaining representative for the four units it controlled was challenged, unsuccessfully, in 1972; later that year, employees in one of the units it represented engaged in a short strike.

In the second half of the 1970s, the bargaining process changed in each government. Fiscal problems were the major agent of change both in the State and in the City, but they affected the two differently. The New York City fiscal crisis helped stabilize municipal labor relations; the State's fiscal problems had the opposite effect. The gravity of the City's fiscal crisis caused the City's union leaders to form a coalition for purposes of collective bargaining, to eschew strikes, and to negotiate settlements without relying on the OCB.[17] These settlements included "givebacks" of work rules and other benefits previously won at the bargaining table, but most significantly they resulted in a wage freeze (indeed, in a real wage cut). As Table 10.4 shows, City employees received no general wage increases in fiscal years 1977 and 1978, and the scheduled increase in 1976 was deferred. These outcomes stand in marked contrast to the record in the City during the first half of the 1970s, when general wage increases were in the 6 to 10 percent range.

In contrast, State labor relations were destabilized by the fiscal crisis, though other factors contributed as well. State negotiators took a hard bargaining position in the 1975 round of negotiations. To some extent, the State's position was shaped by its concern over the City's finances and labor relations. Governor Hugh Carey knew that wage restraint in the City would be hard to realize if it were not achieved in the State. When

TABLE 10.4

Range of General Wage Increases of State and City Employees: Fiscal Years 1970–1987[a]

Fiscal Year	State	City
1970	5.0%	7–9%
1971	7.5	8–10
1972	6.0	7–9
1973	3.5–4.0	7–9
1974	4.8–6.5	6–8
1975	5.5–7.0	8
1976	0–6.0	6[b]
1977	0	0
1978	8–10.5	0
1979	5.0–6.5	4
1980	7.0–8.5	4
1981	7.0	8–9
1982	5.0–7.0	8
1983	7.0–9.0	8
1984	8.0–10.0	7–8
1985	8.0–10.0	5–6
1986	4.0–5.0	5–6
1987	5.0–5.5	6–6

SOURCES: State data from Governor's Office of Employee Relations; City data from Office of Municipal Labor Relations.

[a]Excludes certain negotiated payments not related to changes in the basic salary rate, such as cost-of- living adjustments.

[b]Increase deferred for some City employees.

negotiations stalled at the State level, the legislature imposed a settlement that provided a $250 "bonus" instead of a general salary increase. And in 1976, State employees again received no general wage increase.

These outcomes, deeply resented by State employees, had important effects on the State's collective bargaining system. First, they strengthened the hand of insurgent union leaders who were attempting to obtain a role in the State's collective bargaining system. The CSEA, the lead union in the State, particularly was affected. Its competitors seized on the 1975 and 1976 wage freeze to support their claim that the CSEA was a "company" union. In 1978, the CSEA lost an important representation election for the 45,000-member unit of professionals, scientists, and technical employees to the Public Employees Federation (PEF). In subsequent years other unions gained footholds among groups of State workers through representation elections and the designation of additional bargaining units by PERB. Second, the State's civil service unions began to emulate the City's unions by entering the arena of electoral politics. While they operated cautiously at first, their influence was being felt in State elections by the late 1970s. Third, some State civil service unions were successful in expanding the scope of bargaining beyond compensation issues to include agency policies and work rules.[18]

The 1980s, in general, have been a relatively calm period for labor relations in the State and the City. With their fiscal problems behind them, both governments have focused on expanding employment and restoring the reductions in real earnings their employees suffered during the lean years of the 1970s. The expansionary period in the city has coincided with a gradual splintering of the practice of coalition bargaining, but conflict within the municipal union movement and between civil service leaders and City negotiators has not approached earlier levels. During the first half of the 1980s, the City's employees generally received wage increases substantially in excess of changes in consumer prices. State labor relations evidenced similar stability. Conflict within its civil service unions receded with PEF joining the CSEA as a major actor and several smaller unions becoming more secure in their units. As in the City, wage settlements for State workers also have increased faster than prices.[19]

While the developmental gap between the State and City collective bargaining systems has narrowed, important differences remain. First, the State excludes a larger share of its employees from collective bargaining on the basis that they hold managerial or confidential positions, and it does not set managerial salaries on the basis of bargaining settlements to the same degree as the City.

Second, the State has a much simpler bargaining structure. While the number of bargaining units in the State has grown to 11 from the original 5, the City has more than 100; in addition, the State's OER must negotiate with only 6 different unions, including CSEA, which represents about one half of the State's organized employees, and PEF, which represents about one quarter.[20] The City's OLR, in contrast, not only must negotiate a larger number of contracts, but it must do so with a larger number of unions. This difference has an important indirect affect on wage outcomes (discussed below).

Third, bargaining and budgeting are better integrated in the State than in the City. Each system typically negotiates multi-year contracts, which eases the integration problem somewhat, but unlike the City the State generally produces its labor contracts "on time." The City, for example, did not complete its contracts for the 1984–1987 round until the beginning of fiscal year 1986.

Fourth, the scope of collective bargaining is broader in the City than in the State. In part, this reflects the fact that the State's PERB has defined the scope of bargaining more narrowly than the City's OCB; more important, however, is that both City officials and union leaders have sought to use collective bargaining as a forum for resolving issues involving personnel administration and productivity improvements. Once included within the scope of bargaining, these so-called noneconomic issues are difficult to exclude.

Fifth, wage outcomes exhibit less variability in the City than in the State. In part, this reflects the difference in bargaining structure noted above. The greater labor relations workload in the City leads its negotiators to use simplifying decision rules, including pay parity for uniformed employees and pattern bargaining within the civilian group. Frequently, all municipal employees receive the same percentage raises.

Comparative Analysis of Compensation. Data are available on the average monthly earnings of employees in the same set of state and local governments used for the staffing comparisons. Adjustments to the data were made for variations and changes in the cost of living. (See Tables 10.5 and 10.6.)

For State employees, the average salary is in line with the average of employees in the ten other state governments. New York State pays above-average salaries in certain areas (health and welfare in particular) and below-average salaries in others (most notably highways), but the weighted average in 1985 ($620 a month in 1970 dollars) was only 1 percent higher than the weighted average for the ten other state governments.

State workers were paid well below the average in 1970 and saw their real earnings decline over the 1970–1980 period. It took a sharp increase in the 1980–1985 period coupled with slow growth elsewhere to restore

TABLE 10.5

Average Monthly Paycheck of New York State Employees Compared with the Average for Employees of Selected State Governments: Fiscal Years 1970, 1975, 1980, and 1985* (in 1970 dollars)

Function	1970 New York	1970 Others	1975 New York	1975 Others	1980 New York	1980 Others	1985 New York	1985 Others
Higher Education	$678.24	$707.74	$702.29	$733.76	$625.72	$672.44	$714.94	$688.07
Welfare	641.08	573.93	647.04	565.03	543.61	549.50	660.12	547.24
Hospitals	484.46	499.89	545.69	531.39	471.95	487.14	546.92	514.34
Health	594.84	665.72	656.65	712.89	586.46	594.90	709.77	578.23
Highways	592.78	607.52	575.30	642.95	506.35	616.62	564.70	628.17
Police	668.18	666.17	717.87	709.95	669.67	673.96	701.32	681.03
Correction	610.71	625.04	636.94	656.57	601.05	591.54	584.31	561.65
Financial Administration	532.37	569.09	563.32	614.48	538.64	565.73	530.45	574.56
General Control	797.44	800.06	705.43	788.29	763.60	687.63	758.52	732.18
Weighted Average	569.96	623.63	606.68	655.83	553.93	602.73	620.05	617.70
Ratio of New York Average to Others	0.91	—	0.93	—	0.92	—	1.01	—

SOURCES: U.S. Bureau of the Census, *Public Employment*, series GE78, no. 2 (Washington, DC: U.S. Government Printing Office, 1969, 1974, 1979, and 1984).

*Amounts are adjusted for differences in consumer prices as reported by the U.S. Department of Labor, Bureau of Labor Statistics.

TABLE 10.6
Average Monthly Paycheck of New York City Employees
Compared with the Average for Employees of Selected City Governments: Fiscal Years 1970, 1975, 1980, and 1985* (in 1970 dollars)

Function	1970		1975		1980		1985	
	New York	Others	New York	Others	New York	Others	New York	Others
Highways	$656.80	$651.67	$572.04	$671.34	$492.47	$610.71	$642.79	$637.43
Police	709.01	769.81	718.94	786.28	648.89	798.08	761.34	752.20
Fire	784.52	840.33	831.58	841.60	740.68	824.30	885.69	807.03
Sanitation	677.87	621.60	780.63	644.95	677.63	595.56	679.01	571.33
Parks and Recreation	421.82	518.48	538.13	561.57	483.60	482.73	545.49	532.58
Financial Administration and Control	717.77	678.64	596.05	698.13	609.10	643.92	561.65	642.19
Weighted Average	684.57	717.93	701.02	737.86	637.39	711.02	718.14	699.01
Ratio of New York Average to Others	0.95	—	0.95	—	0.90	—	1.03	—

SOURCES: U.S. Bureau of the Census, City Employment, series GE78, no. 2; and Local Government Employment in Selected Metropolitan Areas, series GE78, no. 3 (Washington, DC: U.S. Government Printing Office, 1969, 1974, 1979, and 1984).

*Amounts are adjusted for differences in consumer prices as reported by the U.S. Department of Labor, Bureau of Labor Statistics.

average State salaries to their 1970 levels and to close the difference with other state governments.

The picture for City employees in many ways is comparable. In 1970, their average salaries were lower than the average in the 17 other city governments, and in the 1970s they declined in both relative and absolute terms. In the 1980–1985 period, however, the average salaries of City employees rose sharply while the average fell elsewhere. As a result of these trends, the average salary of a City employee was 3 percent higher than the combined average in the other cities in 1985.

While the average earnings of State and City employees are in line with those of their counterparts in similar governments, there is a substantial difference between salaries and total compensation. In 1983, the last year for which data are available, the cost of providing fringe and pension benefits amounted to 22 percent of the salaries of state and local employees nationwide.[21] A comprehensive comparative analysis of compensation should consider fringe and pension benefits as well as salaries.

Unfortunately, comparative data on pension and fringe benefits for the 1970–1985 period do not exist. The limited available data suggest that State employees receive above-average fringe and pension benefits. The national Census Bureau survey found that in 1983 the cost of fringe and pension benefits of New York State employees was 27.1 percent of earnings compared with an average of 22.9 percent for the ten other state governments and 21.9 percent for all states. Similar data for city governments are not available. However, a 1981 study of municipal employee compensation in the 12 largest U. S. cities found that the cost of nonsalary benefits in New York City was above average for some groups of employees and below average for others.[22]

Personnel Administration

The foundation of modern public sector personnel administration is the merit system, which was introduced in New York by the 1894 Constitutional Convention. But today personnel administration extends far beyond the activities required to ensure that the civil servants are hired on the basis of qualification rather than "pull." However, the most salient contemporary issues involve an institutional legacy from the time when personnel administration *was* the merit system.

In New York implementation of the merit system was to be achieved through a centralized administrative structure. The legal framework was spelled out in the State constitution and defined further by State statute. These mandates, which applied to all governments in the State, would be enforced by a State Civil Service Commission; local governments could create their own civil service commissions, but they would be bound by State rules. Eventually, administrative reality required that operating units be grafted onto the commissions. The Department of Civil Service was created to administer the civil service system for the State government; the Department of Personnel was created for a similar reason in the City of New York. Nevertheless, these operating units were considered part of the centralized structure; their heads also were the heads of the respective civil service commissions.

Today, however, personnel administration within the State and City is fragmented. At the State level, the players include the Civil Service Commission, the Department of Civil Service (and its semi-autonomous Division of Classification and Compensation), the governor's Office of Employee Relations, and the State Division of the Budget. There are fewer players within the City: the Personnel Department, the Office of Municipal Labor Relations, and the Office of Management and Budget. In both governments the fragmentation has resulted from the need to conduct collective bargaining, prepare annual budgets, and conform to State Civil Service law.

Demise of the Personnel Department. The New York City Personnel Department faced a basic conflict in its mission from the time of its inception in 1954. As noted earlier, it was part of the administrative apparatus of State centralization created to protect the merit system— that is, to protect civil servants from arbitrary behavior by elected officials. At the same time, the Personnel Department was created to help the mayor achieve more effective (or modern) management.[23] Wearing one hat, the director of the Personnel Department was responsible for making the civil service system more responsive to the mayor and his appointees; wearing another hat, the chairman of the City's Civil Service Commission was responsible for protecting the civil servants from the mayor and his appointees.

Its ambiguous nature gave the department a weak voice in the mayor's "kitchen cabinet." Initially its major adversary within the mayor's circle was the Bureau of the Budget (later, Office of Management and Budget).[24] Budget officials often preferred that those who had passed civil service examinations not be appointed promptly, in order for the City to save money from "accruals." Personnel officials preferred to see those appointments made promptly, perhaps because delay lowers the quality of appointees as the best (highest-scoring) applicants accept other positions. The personnel directors more often lost than won arguments with the budget director (or, put differently, usually failed to convince the mayor that enhancing the quality of the workforce was more important than competing priorities).

In the late 1960s, the Department of Personnel lost influence to another overhead agency, the newly created Office of Labor Relations (later, Office of Municipal Labor Relations). Not being able to make appointments in a timely fashion was bad enough for the Personnel Department, but losing its role in wage determination was even worse. In addition, the City's labor negotiators sometimes agreed with the union position that certain rules and procedures of personnel administration were negotiable. Trading some of the Personnel Department's influence for lower wages and labor peace was, from the perspective of the City's labor negotiators, highly desirable.

By the mid 1970s, the inability of the Department of Personnel to perform its initial mission was well recognized; charter revision proposals in 1975 removed most of the Personnel Department's remaining functions and assigned them to the operating agencies.[25] The reform was not implemented, largely because the fiscal crisis diverted officials' attention. But the department was moribund during the fiscal crisis. At a time when the City's employees were being cut in pay and reduced in number, the Personnel Department was a silent bystander whose role was limited to issuing "pink slips."

The resumption of growth in the 1980s has not revived the Department of Personnel. It functions at a minimal level, some say with a primary goal of facilitating the appointment and retention of employees on a "provisional" basis (hardly a role in keeping with protection of the merit concept). One of its few remaining functions—administering civil service entrance and promotional examinations—is frustrated by allegations, many of them upheld in court, that the examinations do not test quality. Top appointments within the department have been made on the basis of patronage rather than professionalism.

In retrospect, it seems almost inevitable that the Personnel Department would fail. Its role was ambiguous; it could not defend its functions from budget and labor relations officials, and mayors never came to its rescue. Nor did State officials, despite the original conception that the State was the ultimate guarantor of the merit system. As in the case of collective bargaining, the State has permitted the City to practice home rule.

Future of the Department of Civil Service. In January 1985, Governor Cuomo asked the president of the Civil Service Commission (also head of the Department of Civil Service) to report on the future of the State's civil service system. "By next year," the governor said, "I expect to have a blueprint for revitalizing the civil service system."[26] In January 1986, the governor received his blueprint from the president of the commission, Karen S. Burstein.[27]

The Burstein report is a clarion call for overcoming current fragmentation in State personnel administration. It traces in detail the division of responsibilities among the Civil Service Commission, the Department of Civil Service, the department's Division of Classification and Compensation, the Division of the Budget, and the Office of Employee Relations. Conflicts among these agencies ensure that the personnel system serves neither the chief executive's interests nor those of civil servants. To overcome the fragmentation, the report recommends creation of a Division of Human Resources that would include the Department of Civil Service, the Division of Classification and Compensation, and the Office of Employee Relations; the new entity would be headed, like the Division of the Budget, by a gubernatorial appointee.

Had New York City's mayors asked the director of personnel to conduct a similar study two decades ago, the report would have painted a picture similar to that drawn by Burstein: the Personnel Department, like the Department of Civil Service, caught between its responsibilities to civil servants and to management; the Bureau of the Budget, like the Division of the Budget, successfully intervening in personnel administration when financial issues were at stake; the Office of Labor Relations, like the governor's Office of Employee Relations, displacing traditional civil service rules with new collective bargaining provisions; unionized City employees, like unionized State employees, using collective bargaining to "short circuit" established personnel procedures. Is the New York City experience a preview of developments in the State?

The pros and cons of reorganizing in the fashion proposed by the Burstein report are not clear. Continuing the present system of overlapping administration frustrates coordination and planning but avoids open conflict within the governor's overhead agencies. Creating a Division of Human Resources, even if feasible politically, would not necessarily overcome problems of coordination (or so the evidence of "superagencies" suggests). A third option, maintaining the current institutions but clarifying their responsibilities, would be an intermediate step.

Productivity

The City's involvement in formal "productivity" programs dates from 1970 and has taken many twists and turns since. The State's programmatic efforts are newer and narrower, reflecting differences in the nature of service delivery in the two systems and in the influence of those who actually do the "delivering." If the New York City experience might inform State officials of what not to do in the area of personnel administration, its experience with productivity programs suggests some options for State officials to consider.

The City's Experience. The City first approached the problem of increasing the productivity of the workforce during Mayor John V. Lindsay's second term. Its first programmatic model focused on collective bargaining. The City developed an explicit policy whereby it would use collective bargaining to "buy back" managerial prerogatives in return for salary "premiums." In three of its most labor-intensive agencies—the Departments of Police, Fire, and Sanitation—the City sought to increase output per employee and to "share the gain" with the unionized employees. While some changes in work rules were achieved, the City's share of the gain was small.[28]

Lindsay's successor, Abraham D. Beame, continued the City's focus on labor-management relations as the key component of its productivity program, but he redefined the process and purpose of the program. Instead of seeking to buy "givebacks" during wage bargaining, the City set up joint labor-management committees with four of the largest civil service unions. In addition, a Productivity Council was created to resolve conflicts that might arise at the agency level. Beame's approach was designed to improve productivity through cooperation between management and labor; indeed, the first (and only) report of the Productivity Council emphasized that adequate management ("lacking in almost every City agency") was the major impediment to increased productivity.[29] When the fiscal crisis occurred, the unions withdrew from the Productivity Council.

The same actors came together shortly thereafter in another form of labor-management interaction. The State's Emergency Financial Control Board in 1976, during the depths of the fiscal crisis, issued wage policy guidelines. It said, in essence, that general wage increases were prohibited, but cost-of-living-adjustments could be paid provided there was a quid pro quo. The board also created a Joint Labor-Management Committee on Productivity, which was to develop productivity programs that could be used to fund cost-of-living adjustments. In practice, it served to muster evidence that cost-of-living adjustments were justified by productivity savings.[30]

Under Mayor Koch, the City dropped the pretense of justifying cost-of-living adjustments and resumed the joint labor-management approach initially pursued by Beame. In 1979, pursuant to an agreement by which the federal government guaranteed City bonds, a second Productivity Council was created and charged with developing and implementing methods to improve the productivity of City operations. In addition, the Control Board was required to report annually on the record of accomplishment of the new Productivity Council. The annual reviews of the City's Productivity Council focus more on the process than the outcome of its deliberations. Its success, the reviews suggest, lies in affecting the "quality of life" in the workplace.

However, the annual reviews demonstrate that one aspect of the productivity program has produced tangible gains. Since the late 1970s, the City has incorporated within its financial plan a Program to Eliminate the Gap (PEG). The "gap" for planning purposes is the difference between estimated revenues and expenditures for the coming fiscal year, and it is "filled" by a combination of anticipated increases in intergovernmental aid and by actions the City itself will take. In addition to increasing revenues and cutting services, there is a third category of City actions, Productivity and Management Initiatives. While the estimates of these savings vary considerably depending on who is doing the estimating, the cumulative savings from productivity initiatives probably approached $500 million in the 1982–1986 period. The details of these savings suggest that the bulk of the gains derived from management initiatives rather than the efforts of the labor-management committees.[31]

The management-initiated programs have followed several approaches. One largely unsuccessful route has been to try to increase the number and authority of managers by modifying the civil service system. Efforts to gain support for such legislation in the State legislature have been futile, largely because of opposition from the civil service unions. A second approach focused on development of a Managerial Service; it was ratified in the 1975 charter reforms but, like the requirement to decentralize personnel administration to the operating agencies, was not fully implemented because of the onset of the fiscal crisis.

Of more significance are the City's efforts to develop an information system that could provide overhead and line agencies with common information about the costs and accomplishments of municipal agencies. In 1977, the City created the Office of Operations and assigned it the responsibility of preparing the *Mayor's Management Report*. In addition to its statistical and reporting functions, the Office of Operations has worked closely with the Office of Management and Budget and with line agencies in seeing that the latter meet their commitments under the annual PEG.

In summary, the City has engaged in considerable experimentation in the area of productivity in the last two decades. Its attempts to use the collective bargaining process as a forum to extract givebacks have not, in general, been successful, but labor-management committees at the agency level generally have improved working conditions, if not productivity. As a result of the fiscal crisis, the City developed a more management-oriented productivity program designed to yield recurring savings helpful in closing its annual budget gaps. This PEG program produced tangible savings, particularly during the period of retrenchment.

The State's Experience. Compared with the City, the State has less extensive experience with explicit productivity programs. Like the City, the State has supported the use of joint labor-management committees to improve the quality of work life at the agency level, but State negotiators have been reticent to tie wage bargaining to productivity improvements. As noted earlier, the State generally has kept work rules outside the scope of bargaining.

The State's major effort is a relatively new, management-oriented productivity program. In 1983, Governor Cuomo created by executive order the Office of Management and Productivity (OMP), which is headed by a director who serves as a special assistant to the governor. It is not, however, an agency with equal authority to the Division of the Budget, the Office of Employee Relations, or even the Department of Civil Service. It serves primarily as an "in-house" management consulting team.

The 1984 and 1985 annual reports of the Governor's Management and Productivity Programs describe a wide range of activities conducted by the OMP, but they do not demonstrate that the OMP has established a strong base within line agencies. Its major accomplishments cited in the 1985 report are a paperwork reduction program saving $2.9 million; a printing management program estimated to save $8 million to $10 million over five years; changes in the State's mailing operations with savings similar to those estimated for the printing management program; new management controls over the State's vehicular fleet that will save an estimated $740,000 annually; and inauguration of the Governor's Productivity Awards Program, which produced 135 nominees who identified $5.8 million in potential savings.[32]

With a core staff of 15 professionals, supported by loaned personnel from the agencies and from the private sector, the OMP will find it hard to achieve significant productivity gains. Moreover, there is little evidence that the State is prepared to incorporate productivity-generated savings into its budgetary process (as the State required of the City during the fiscal crisis).

One important way in which the State's approach compares favorably with the City's is the State's serious efforts, through the Office of Employee Relations, to develop a management "cadre." The 12,000-plus State employees who are excluded from collective bargaining by dint of their managerial/confidential status receive substantial training. The OER spends four times more on training this group than on its other activities, including negotiating labor contracts. The City, by contrast, does very little management training.

The State is moving slowly to develop productivity initiatives, relying primarily on a management-oriented approach rather than collaboration with unions. This may be the most appropriate strategy, given the nature of the State's collective bargaining system. However, to strengthen its productivity programs, the State may have to involve the civil service unions more prominently.

BRIDGING THEORY AND PRACTICE

The first section of this essay offered a conceptual framework that stressed the interdependence of staffing, compensation, personnel administration, and productivity policies. The second section reviewed the practices of New York State and New York City government in each of these areas. This section assesses these practices with standards derived from the theoretical framework and discusses how to bridge the gap between theory and practice.

Staffing

The comparative analysis in this essay indicated that the State employs about one fifth more workers than the average in other large states and the City about one fourth more workers than the average in other large cities (after adjusting for differences in populations served and functions performed). The State's relatively high staffing level is a product of the 1980s and results primarily from unusually high staffing in just one function—hospitals.[33] By contrast, the City's abnormal staffing level is of longer duration and is evident in nearly all functions.

Thus, one issue that should be of concern to State and City officials is whether they are maintaining larger workforces than is desirable. The fact that the State and the City maintain large staffs relative to their counterparts does not, perforce, mean that these are inappropriate policies for the two governments. Specific conditions may justify their decisions to maintain unusually large workforces: New Yorkers may demand, be willing to pay for, and receive better services than residents of other states and cities; the problems to which the State and the City must respond may be considerably greater; the quality of the State and City workforces may be so low relative to the staffs of other governments that higher staff levels are required to produce comparable services; the quality of the State and City managers may be so poor relative to other jurisdictions that it takes more workers to produce services of acceptable level and quality. These possibilities should be considered carefully before actions are taken to alter current staffing policies.

Compensation

The comparative data indicate that the average salary of State employees in 1985 was 1 percent above the relevant norm; that of City employees was 3 percent above the norm. The limited data on fringe and pension benefits suggest that State and City employees also do slightly better than their counterparts elsewhere in these forms of compensation.

Does this suggest that State and City compensation policies should seek to reduce the relative pay and benefit levels of public employees? Not necessarily. Again, a series of issues should be considered before this action is taken. Given the limited data on nonsalary benefits, is it indeed true that the compensation of State and City employees is above average? Is the nature of private labor markets (in New York City and in the locations throughout the rest of the state where State employees are concentrated) such that the State and the City must pay higher salaries and benefits in order to compete successfully for qualified workers? Would better pay and benefits improve the quality of the two workforces?

The answer to these questions is likely to be, "It depends on what employees you are talking about." The workforces of the State and the City are not undifferentiated masses with little or no variation around the means of their compensation, skills, and relative supply. In order for managers to use compensation policy as a tool for improving the quality and productivity of the workforce, they must be able to discriminate among employee groups. This is difficult to accomplish through collective bargaining. The State's formal bargaining structure discourages "fine-tuned" compensation policies because it has a relatively small number of bargaining units. The larger number of smaller units in the City would seem to encourage greater diversity in wage outcomes; however, the simplifying rules for wage allocation discussed earlier—pay parity and pattern bargaining—make collective bargaining a blunter policy tool in the City than the State.

Personnel Administration

Personnel administration provides opportunities for improving the quality of the State and City workforces independently of compensation policies. Consider that in the next three decades nearly all of the State and City employees will "turn over." In the next decade alone, assuming no growth in the size of the two workforces and continued turnover rates of

8 percent annually, the two personnel systems will have the opportunity
to hire approximately 400,000 people. In addition, the two personnel
systems will have the opportunity to train one-half million employees, to
prepare them for promotions, and to weed out those who should not
work for the State or the City. If the core functions of personnel
administration are performed well, the State and City workforces will be
more productive by reason of these activities alone; if they are poorly
performed, then whatever benefits may be realized from better staffing,
compensation, and productivity policies will be minimized if not
eliminated.

While the State and the City face similar opportunities through
personnel administration, they have dissimilar capacities. Relative to the
State, the City is severely disadvantaged. The City's Department of
Personnel, which bears the primary responsibility for personnel administration, functions at a minimum level. This situation has been caused by
the decisions of New York City's mayors from Wagner to Koch to
withhold support for the Personnel Department when its role was
threatened. Rebuilding the department may no longer be a viable option.

The State's personnel administration system is characterized by fragmentation among numerous agencies, a recognized problem that has not
been solved. One proposal is to create a Division of Human Resources of
equal standing, at least in name, with the Division of the Budget. Another
option is to continue to muddle through with the current system. Still
another is to define clearly which agencies are responsible for specific
functions.

A number of relevant questions should be considered by State officials.
Apart from the fragmentation of responsibility, is there evidence that the
State's personnel system is not yielding an appropriately skilled work-
force? What does the New York City experience imply about personnel
administration in the State? What does it indicate about the future of
State "civil service" agencies?

Productivity

The programmatic efforts of the State and the City to increase the
productivity of their respective workforces are relatively new, particularly for the State. The State has eschewed the City's practice of
attempting to improve productivity through joint labor-management
interactions in favor of improving the quality of managers; in addition,
it has not integrated its productivity efforts into the budgetary process as
much as the City. The City's programmatic efforts to increase productivity are better defined, largely because the fiscal crisis made these
activities essential.

A common, and probably valid, presumption is that each government could do significantly more to improve the utilization of its workforce. Increased output per employee would make it possible to reduce staffing and taxes or to provide better services. Officials of both governments, however, are chary about relying heavily on productivity programs as a primary mechanism for service improvement. They are under pressure to provide evidence that services are being improved, and the gains seem easier and surer if more workers are hired than if greater productivity is sought from the current workforce.

Concluding Observations

The State and City workforces are managed in a large setting that makes the development of integrated human resource policies difficult. Political power is fragmented within each system; the relationships between the State and the City, formal and informal, add a vertical dimension to fragmentation. The relationship between the State and the City is more subtle than is commonly recognized. The State intervenes in several ways that make it difficult for the City to manage its workforce effectively; at the same time, aspects of the City's human resource management system, personnel administration particularly, could benefit from greater State involvement.

One step each government should take is to devote greater resources to consideration of the issues identifed in this chapter. The fruit of expanded analysis is not likely to be reorganization that comports with a "systems" view of human resource management; nor is this required to begin developing more integrated policies. What is required is that "budget" and "labor relations" and "personnel" officials, and the chief executives who appoint them, better understand how their behavior affects human resources management.

NOTES

1. The view that collective bargaining increases the power of organized civil servants was expressed first in Harry Wellington and Ralph K. Winter, *The Unions and the Cities* (Washington, DC: Brookings Institution, 1971). That view was eroded by the period of urban fiscal stress in the 1970s, which prompted renewed scholarly interest in the issue of labor power. For reviews of the more recent literature and critiques of the Wellington-Winter thesis, see David Lewin, "Public Employee Unionism and Labor Relations in the 1980s: An Analysis of Transformation," in Seymour Martin Lipset, ed., *Unions in Transition* (San Francisco: Institute for Contemporary Studies, 1986), pp. 241–264; and Raymond D. Horton, "Fiscal Stress and Labor Power," *Proceedings of the*

Thirty-Eighth Annual Meetings, Industrial Relations Research Association, 1986, pp. 304–316.

2. An outstanding example of the "threat to privatize" leading to innovation in public sector service delivery is the New York City Sanitation Department, where long-standing union opposition to two-man refuse collection trucks was dropped shortly after the City announced its intention to solicit bids from private contractors to collect refuse in selected areas of New York City. See David Lewin, "Technological Change in the Public Sector: The Case of Sanitation Service," in Daniel B. Cornfield, ed., *Workers, Managers and Technological Change* (New York: Plenum, 1986), pp. 281–309.

3. The classic formulation is that American federalism is like a "marble cake" rather than a "layer cake," characterized by interdependence instead of separateness. See Morton Grodzins, "The Federal System," in *Goals for Americans* (New York: American Assembly, 1960), p. 265.

4. Charles Brecher and Raymond D. Horton, "Retrenchment and Recovery: American Cities and the New York Experience," *Public Administration Review* 45 (March-April 1985):267–274.

5. The general proposition is presented in Theodore Lowi, *The End of Liberalism* (New York: Norton, 1969). An early application of Lowi's thesis to public sector bargaining may be found in Raymond D. Horton, *Municipal Labor Relations in New York City: Lessons of the Lindsay-Wagner Years* (New York: Praeger, 1973).

6. For detail, see Citizens Budget Commission, "The City of New York's 1987 Executive Budget" (New York: CBC, June 1986).

7. For a review of the pre- and post-bargaining situation, see Horton, *Municipal Labor Relations in New York City*; for a review of the impact of the fiscal crisis, see Raymond D. Horton, "Economics, Politics, and Collective Bargaining: The Case of New York City," in A. Lawrence Chickering, ed., *Public Employee Unions: A Study of the Crisis in Public Sector Labor Relations* (San Francisco: Institute for Contemporary Studies, 1976), pp. 183–203; for a larger view of the influence of public sector unions on the politics of New York City, see Martin Shefter, *Political Crisis/Fiscal Crisis: The Collapse and Revival of New York City* (New York: Basic Books, 1985).

8. For analyses of the rise and decline of coalition bargaining in New York City, see David Lewin and Mary McCormick, "Coalition Bargaining in Municipal Government: New York City in the 1970s," *Industrial and Labor Relations Review* 34 (January 1981):175–190; and Horton, "Fiscal Stress and Labor Power."

9. The classic explanation of this view is Aaron Wildavsky, *The Politics of the Budgetary Process* (Boston: Little, Brown, 1964). The Wildavsky thesis has come under increasing scrutiny from analyses of all levels of government. For a current review of the literature, see Lance T. Leloup, "From Microbudgeting to Macrobudgeting: Evolution in Theory and Practice," in Irene Rubin, ed., *New Directions in Budget Theory* (Albany: State University of New York Press, 1988), pp. 19–42.

10. Charles Brecher and Raymond D. Horton, "Community Power and Municipal Budgets," in Irene Rubin, ed., *New Directions in Budget Theory* (Albany: State University of New York Press, 1988), pp. 148–169.

11. Cynthia Green, "The State Budget: What Are Governor Cuomo's Priorities?" *Citizens Budget Commission Quarterly* 6 (Spring 1986): 7–8.
12. New York City, Office of Management and Budget, "The Mandate Burden 1980–1985: Has It Changed?" December 1985.
13. U.S. Bureau of the Census, *Public Employment*, series GE78, no. 1, and *City Employment*, series GE78, no. 2 (Washington, DC: U.S. Government Printing Office).
14. For a review, see Robert D. Helsby and Thomas E. Joyner, "Impact of the Taylor Law on Local Governments," in Robert H. Connery and William V. Farr, eds., *Unionization of Municipal Employees* (New York: Academy of Political Science, 1970), pp. 29–42.
15. Unless otherwise noted, the material on the development of the City's formal collective bargaining system is drawn from Horton, *Municipal Labor Relations in New York City*.
16. This discussion of the State's attempt to conform the City's labor relations system to the State's Taylor Law is based on various memoranda from State officials and responses thereto by City officials provided by the New York City Office of Collective Bargaining.
17. Lewin and McCormick, "Coalition Bargaining."
18. See Interview with Meyer S. Frucher in Gerald Benjamin and T. Norman Hurd, eds., *Making Experience Count: Managing Modern New York in the Carey Era* (Albany: Rockefeller Institute, 1985), pp. 147–174.
19. Citizens Budget Commission, "Toward A Responsible Municipal Wage Policy" (New York: CBC, July 1984).
20. Data on the State's bargaining structure provided by the governor's Office of Employee Relations.
21. U.S. Bureau of the Census, *Finances of Employee-Retirement Systems of State and Local Governments in 1983–1984* (Washington, DC: U.S. Government Printing Office, 1984).
22. Elizabeth Dickson and George E. Peterson, *Public Employee Compensation: A Twelve City Comparison*, 2nd ed. (Washington, DC: Urban Institute Press, 1981).
23. The creation of the Personnel Department followed separate recommendations of the mayor's Committee on Management Survey (1952) and the Josephs Commission on the Government of New York City (1954).
24. The discussion of the Personnel Department relies heavily on David Stanley, *Professional Personnel for the City of New York* (Washington, DC: Brookings Institution, 1963); and Wallace Sayre and Herbert Kaufman, *Governing New York City*, 2nd ed. (New York: Norton, 1965).
25. See State Charter Revision Commission for New York City, "Personnel Reforms for New York City" (Albany: SCRC, January 1975).
26. Governor Mario M. Cuomo, "Message to the Legislature," January 4, 1985.
27. Karen S. Burstein, *Report to Governor Mario M. Cuomo on Civil Service Revitalization*, January 1986.
28. This review of the New York City experience relies heavily on Mary McCormick, "Productivity Programs and Issues," in Raymond D. Horton and Charles Brecher, eds., *Setting Municipal Priorities: 1980* (Montclair, NJ: Allanheld, Osman, 1979), pp. 171–194; and Raymond

D. Horton, "Human Resources," in Charles Brecher and Raymond D. Horton, eds., *Setting Municipal Priorities: 1986* (New York: New York University Press, 1985), pp. 185–191.

29. City of New York, Productivity Council, *Improving Productivity in Municipal Government: A Labor-Management Approach*, October 1975, p. 5.
30. McCormick, "Productivity Programs," pp. 182–187.
31. New York State Financial Control Board, *New York City Productivity Program*, 1980–1985 annual reviews.
32. Executive Chamber, Office of Management and Productivity, *1985 Annual Report, Governor's Management and Productivity Program*, January 1986, pp. 6–14.
33. There was considerable disagreement among those interviewed for this study about why employment in this function remains so high, particularly in light of the State's "deinstitutionalization" policy that has reduced dramatically the population in mental hospitals. Union pressure is one theory advanced to explain why employment declines have not mirrored inpatient declines more closely. Another is community pressure exerted through the State legislature. State mental health (and prison) facilities are important sources of employment in many upstate communities; thus, legislators are under pressure to protect these jobs regardless of State policies that might argue for reduced employment.

11

EDUCATION

❧

Robert Berne

T HE RESPONSIBILITY for public primary and secondary (K–12) education rests with state governments, which in turn delegate the delivery of education services to local school districts within their states. This seemingly straightforward arrangement defines the local-state government relationship as a crucial part of the structure of K–12 education, because all state governments maintain extensive control over their local school districts. Added to this structural element is the intergovernmental nature of financing; nationally, 45 percent of school district general revenues were from state sources, 48 percent from local sources, and 7 percent from federal sources.[1] Thus, the critical question in K–12 education is not *whether* the city-state relationships are important, but *which* are the most important.

K–12 education organization and finance in New York State are typical of those in other states in a few respects. There are 735 school districts in New York State, of which New York City is one. But New York City has a higher proportion of the students in its state than every other school district in the country except Honolulu. In fact, there are more students in the New York City school district than in 37 states![2] New York State is considerably below the national average in the state

---

NOTE: Partial support for this essay was provided by the Exxon Education Foundation.

share of financing, with 41 percent from state sources, 54 percent from local sources, and 5 percent from federal sources.[3]

The responsibilities of New York State's school districts are specified in the State's education laws. These laws differentiate between city and noncity school districts in the state in terms of the structure and responsibility of the governing board and the way in which the district's budget is determined. The State laws also have separate sections that pertain to "city" school districts and "large-city" school districts; the latter category includes Buffalo, Rochester, Syracuse, and Yonkers. Finally, separate sections of the law apply only to New York City.

An important difference among district types is the selection process for members of the Board of Education. The law specifies a seven-member appointed board in New York City, with each borough president entitled to one appointment and the mayor entitled to two. Yonkers also has an appointed board (nine members), but Buffalo (nine members), Rochester (seven members), and Syracuse (seven members) have elected boards. The locus of power in the education area is dependent on these arrangements.

In all school districts in the state, there is a direct relationship between the governing board and the schools in the district. Since 1969, New York City has had 31 or 32 (the current number) community school districts that have major responsibilities for elementary and junior high schools in their boundaries. But the responsibility is shared between the central board and the community school districts on matters such as curriculum, staffing qualifications, and capital construction.

There are also significant differences among New York State's school districts in budgeting procedures and responsibilities. Noncity school districts have independent taxing power that is subject to voter approval. The school districts in cities with populations under 125,000 are independent taxing entities, with most of the power for budgeting resting with the Board of Education. Although these city school districts must adhere to public hearing requirements, voter approval of the budget is unnecessary. The school districts in Buffalo, Rochester, Syracuse, Yonkers, and New York City are called "dependent" school districts because their budgets are submitted by the boards to the city government as part of the municipal budgeting process. Thus, in many ways, these city governments treat the school district as another city department, and school taxes are not separated from city taxes.

The most salient difference between New York City and other New York State districts is the characteristics of their students. New York City's public school population is predominantly "minority" compared with a "nonminority" rest of the state.[4] Moreover, as pointed out by Katherine Trent and Richard D. Alba, the incidence of poverty among children is uniformly higher in New York City than in the rest of the state for all racial and ethnic groups.[5] Finally, statewide 83 percent of the students with limited English proficiency and 40 percent of the handicapped pupils were in New York City, well above the New York City share of enrollment—36 percent.[6]

The objective of this essay is to investigate the nature and results of a subset of the important city-state relationships in the area of K–12 education. The remainder of the essay is organized into five sections. The first section compares city-state school finance relationships for New York City and 22 other large U.S cities. Financing also is the principal concern of the second section, which examines trends in revenues and expenditures within New York State and documents some of the special difficulties facing New York City. The third section examines staffing and salary trends for teachers in New York City and New York State. Schooling output data for New York City and New York State are compared in the fourth section and related to the findings on staffing and resources. Issues for future consideration are presented in a concluding section.

NATIONAL COMPARISONS

Although the core issues in this essay are the New York City–New York State relationships in K–12 education, initially it is useful to determine how this relationship compares with other big-city-state relationships. Data on population, enrollment, and current operating expenditures were gathered for New York City and New York State, and for the 25 next largest U.S. cities and their respective states.[7] Because of organizational issues, Phoenix, Honolulu, and Washington, DC, were excluded, so the comparison is limited to 23 of the 26 largest cities.[8] (See Table 11.1.)

The population data document New York City's unusually large share of the state's population: over 40 percent. Chicago is the only other city with more than 20 percent of its state's population. New York City has slightly more than one third of the public K–12 pupils in the state, again a substantially larger share than any other city.

Most large cities have a smaller share of public K–12 enrollment than of total population statewide. This is due to the cities' greater usage of private schools and smaller share of the total population of school age compared with the rest of their respective states. For example, in New York City 24 percent of K–12 enrollment is in private schools compared with 16 percent statewide; 18 percent of the population are in the

TABLE 11.1

Population, Enrollment, and Current Operating Expenditures for Large U.S. Cities and Their States

		Population (in thousands) (1982)	Enrollment (in thousands) (1983–1984)	Current Operating Expenditures (COE) (in thousands) (1983–1984)	Per Pupil COE (1983–1984)	Per Pupil COE (1982–1983)
(1)	New York City	7,086	923.7	$3,533,439	$3,825	$3,422
	New York	17,567	2,674.8	11,305,391	4,227	3,806
	City/State	40.3%	34.5%	31.3%	90.5%	89.9%
(2)	Los Angeles	3,022	549.2	$1,784,974	$3,250	$3,011
	California	24,697	4,089.0	12,062,874	2,950	2,800
	City/State	12.2%	13.4%	14.8%	110.2%	107.6%
(3)	Chicago	2,997	434.0	$1,346,803	$3,103	$2,979
	Illinois	11,466	1,853.3	5,188,711	2,800	2,689
	City/State	26.1%	23.4%	26.0%	110.8%	110.8%
(4)	Houston	1,726	189.5	$500,225	$2,640	$2,597
	Texas	15,329	2,989.8	7,525,568	2,517	2,376
	City/State	11.3%	6.3%	6.6%	104.9%	109.3%
(5)	Philadelphia	1,665	202.5	$647,688	$3,199	$2,750
	Pennsylvania	11,879	1,738.0	5,418,187	3,117	2,823
	City/State	14.0%	11.6%	12.0%	102.6%	97.4%
(6)	Detroit	1,139	210.3	$608,885	$2,895	$2,722
	Michigan	9,116	1,735.9	5,213,599	3,003	2,703
	City/State	12.5%	12.1%	11.7%	96.4%	100.7%
(7)	Dallas	944	127.2	$386,776	$3,041	$2,767
	Texas	15,329	2,989.8	7,525,568	2,517	2,376
	City/State	6.2%	4.3%	5.1%	120.8%	116.5%
(8)	San Diego	916	108.6	$349,167	3,214	$2,996
	California	24,697	4,089.0	12,062,874	2,950	2,800
	City/State	3.7%	2.7%	2.9%	108.9%	107.0%

TABLE 11.1 (continued)

	Population (in thousands) (1982)	Enrollment (in thousands) (1983–1984)	Current Operating Expenditures (COE) (in thousands) (1983–1984)	Per Pupil COE (1983–1984)	Per Pupil COE (1982–1983)
(10) San Antonio	819	59.7	$139,961	$2,343	$2,234
Texas	15,329	2,989.8	7,525,568	2,517	2,376
City/State	5.3%	2.0%	1.9%	93.1%	94.1%
(12) Baltimore	774	116.9	$334,568	$2,863	$2,543
Maryland	4,270	683.5	2,229,437	3,262	2,942
City/State	18.1%	17.1%	15.0%	87.8%	86.4%
(13) Indianapolis	708	58.4	$162,655	$2,785	$2,480
Indiana	5,482	984.4	2,323,009	2,360	2,146
City/State	12.9%	5.9%	7.0%	118.0%	115.6%
(14) San Francisco	692	59.3	$174,922	$2,950	$2,901
California	24,697	4,089.0	12,062,874	2,950	2,800
City/State	2.8%	1.5%	1.5%	100.0%	103.6%
(15) San Jose	659	30.9	$86,076	$2,790	$3,040
California	24,697	4,089.0	12,062,874	2,950	2,800
City/State	2.7%	0.8%	0.7%	94.6%	108.6%
(16) Memphis	646	109.0	$229,747	$2,107	$1,974
Tennessee	4,656	822.0	1,488,447	1,811	1,737
City/State	13.9%	13.3%	15.4%	116.4%	113.6%
(18) Milwaukee	632	81.2	$346,549	$4,268	$3,869
Wisconsin	4,645	774.7	2,610,088	3,369	2,993
City/State	13.6%	10.5%	13.3%	126.7%	129.3%
(19) Columbus	571	68.4	$228,203	$3,338	$3,007
Ohio	10,772	1,827.3	5,338,830	2,922	2,589

TABLE 11.1 (continued)

	Population (in thousands) (1982)	Enrollment (in thousands) (1983–1984)	Current Operating Expenditures (COE) (in thousands) (1983–1984)	Per Pupil COE (1983–1984)	Per Pupil COE (1982–1983)
(20) New Orleans	565	86.6	$223,754	$2,585	$2,417
Louisiana	4,383	800.2	1,861,146	2,326	2,322
City/State	12.9%	10.8%	12.0%	111.1%	104.1%
(21) Boston	561	55.6	$253,863	$4,565	$4,925
Massachusetts	5,750	878.8	2,819,770	3,209	2,979
City/State	9.8%	6.3%	9.0%	142.3%	165.3%
(22) Cleveland	559	75.7	$335,714	$4,433	$3,669
Ohio	10,772	1,827.3	5,338,830	2,922	2,589
City/State	5.2%	4.1%	6.3%	151.7%	141.7%
(23) Jacksonville*	556	98.5	$268,764	$2,727	$2,510
Florida	10,466	1,495.6	4,462,440	2,984	2,707
City/State	5.3%	6.6%	6.0%	91.4%	92.7%
(24) Denver	506	60.0	$213,924	$3,563	$3,346
Colorado	3,071	542.2	1,600,064	2,951	2,797
City/State	16.5%	11.1%	13.4%	120.7%	119.6%
(25) Seattle	490	43.9	$166,174	$3,785	$3,383
Washington	4,276	736.2	2,181,560	2,963	2,683
City/State	11.5%	6.0%	7.6%	127.7%	126.1%
(26) Nashville-Davidson	455	64.2	$158,439	$2,466	$2,337
Tennessee	4,656	822.0	1,488,447	1,811	1,737
City/State	9.8%	7.8%	10.6%	136.2%	134.5%

SOURCES: Population data from U.S. Bureau of the Census, *Statistical Abstract of the United States: 1985* (Washington, DC: U.S. Government Printing Office, 1986); enrollment data are unpublished figures from U.S. Department of Education, Center for Statistics; current operating expenditures from U.S. Bureau of the Census, *Finances of Public School Systems in 1983–84* (Washington, DC: U.S. Government Printing Office, 1985); and *Finances of Public School Systems in 1982–83* (Washington, DC: U.S. Government Printing Office, 1984).

*Indicates county school district for Jacksonville.

5-to-17-year-old age group in New York City compared with 20 percent statewide.[9]

The per pupil current operating expenditure data show that New York City spends about 90 percent of the statewide average.[10] Given what is known about greater educational needs and higher prices in cities compared with the remainder of their respective states, this is surprising. Not only is it surprising, but it is also unusual. Only three cities besides New York City—San Antonio, Baltimore, and Jacksonville—had lower per pupil current operating expenditures in both years examined than their respective states, and only Baltimore's ratios were consistently lower than New York City's.[11] Most of the other 19 large cities had per pupil current operating expenditures that exceeded the average in the entire state by a considerable margin.

Thus, the low spending identified here for New York City, and analyzed further in the next section, is not typical of other large cities in the United States. Public school children in New York City do not receive as high a level of resources, measured in dollars, as the average pupil in New York State, and this treatment is not typical of other large cities in the nation. Is this a recent phenomenon in New York State, and can we understand why this occurs? To answer these questions, a more detailed analysis of K–12 education finance in New York State is presented.

FINANCING PUBLIC K–12 EDUCATION IN NEW YORK CITY AND NEW YORK STATE

The task at hand is to understand how New York City has fared compared with the rest of the state as a result of local, State, and federal funding. Of course, the "rest of the state" is heterogeneous and comprises various urban and rural areas, including the downstate counties of Nassau, Suffolk, and Westchester; upstate cities such as Buffalo, Rochester, Syracuse, and Albany; and hundreds of other local school districts. Nonetheless, the rest of the state is useful as a reference point as long as its internal diversity is recognized.

The data reported earlier showed that slightly over one third of all public K–12 pupils in New York State were enrolled in New York City. Table 11.2 shows that the New York City share recently climbed to almost 36 percent, a high for the 20-year period examined. The City's enrollment has either declined less or grown more rapidly than enrollment in the rest of the state in 11 of the 12 years since 1975 and for all of the last 8 years. Thus, since 1975 the previous trend of a decline in the City's share of enrollment has been reversed.

TABLE 11.2
Public K–12 Enrollment in New York City and Rest of State, 1966–1986

Year	Public K–12 Enrollment in New York City	Public K–12 Enrollment in Rest of State	Public K–12 Enrollment in New York State	Percentage Shares		Percentage Changes	
				New York City	Rest of State	New York City	Rest of State
1966	1,060,054	2,116,520	3,176,574	33.4%	66.6%		
1967	1,077,845	2,171,034	3,248,879	33.2	66.8	1.7%	2.6%
1968	1,100,222	2,225,255	3,325,477	33.1	66.9	2.1	2.5
1969	1,116,711	2,280,702	3,397,413	32.9	67.1	1.5	2.5
1970	1,113,826	2,328,983	3,442,809	32.4	67.6	-0.3	2.1
1971	1,135,298	2,353,947	3,489,245	32.5	67.5	1.9	1.1
1972	1,140,349	2,363,510	3,503,859	32.5	67.5	0.4	0.4
1973	1,122,788	2,351,604	3,474,392	32.3	67.7	-1.5	-0.5
1974	1,099,280	2,329,011	3,428,291	32.1	67.9	-2.1	-1.0
1975	1,094,859	2,306,777	3,401,636	32.2	67.8	-0.4	-1.0
1976	1,096,460	2,285,909	3,382,369	32.4	67.6	0.1	-0.9
1977	1,074,851	2,232,380	3,307,231	32.5	67.5	-2.0	-2.3
1978	1,033,813	2,155,968	3,189,781	32.4	67.6	-3.8	-3.4
1979	996,577	2,064,334	3,060,911	32.6	67.4	-3.6	-4.3
1980	960,242	1,975,522	2,935,764	32.7	67.3	-3.6	-4.3
1981	941,159	1,897,234	2,838,393	33.2	66.8	-2.0	-4.0
1982	920,911	1,827,486	2,748,397	33.5	66.5	-2.2	-3.7
1983	914,782	1,768,816	2,683,598	34.1	65.9	-0.7	-3.2
1984	921,131	1,718,743	2,639,874	34.9	65.1	0.7	-2.8
1985	927,301	1,682,687	2,609,988	35.5	64.5	0.7	-2.1
1986	931,246	1,674,117	2,605,363	35.7	64.3	0.4	-0.5

SOURCE: New York State Education Department, Information Center on Education.

Expenditures

The analysis in this section uses the most appropriate measure of public K–12 education expenditures that is available in a comparable fashion over the time period under study: approved operating expenses (AOE) per pupil.[12] As shown in Table 11.3, AOE per pupil in New York City consistently has been lower than AOE per pupil in the rest of the state for the most recent 7 years, 1979 through 1985.[13] During the previous 13 years, AOE per pupil in New York City was usually near or above the figure in the rest of the state. Clearly, in recent years the pupils in the New York City public schools have not had the same level of resources devoted to them as the average pupil in the rest of the state.

The lower AOE per pupil in New York City is especially alarming because there are several reasons why *higher* expenditures per pupil in New York City compared with the rest of the state may be a reasonable expectation; it certainly held true for almost all of the cities examined in the first section. The two principal reasons are the higher prices in New York City compared with the rest of the state and the difficulty of educating the higher proportions of disadvantaged, foreign language, and handicapped pupils in New York City. Techniques are available to adjust the per pupil expenditure comparisons to take these factors into account, at least in an approximate way.

A price index for certain school inputs, calculated for one year— 1978—indicates that these prices were about 11 percent higher in New York City than in the rest of the state.[14] Assuming that these price differences represent differences for all educational inputs, and that the price differences estimated in 1978 hold for all years, "price-adjusted AOE per pupil" can be calculated. These data, displayed in Table 11.3, show that price-adjusted AOE per pupil in New York City have been consistently and substantially below those in the rest of the state for almost the entire 20-year period. In recent years the New York City figure has been only 86 percent or less that of the rest of the state.

A second adjustment for different types of pupils, who are agreed upon as being more costly to educate, reduces the expenditure levels for New York City even farther below the level in the rest of the state.[15] For the past seven years, with adjustments for prices and pupil needs, New York City per pupil expenditures have been about two thirds to three quarters of the levels in the rest of the state. In addition, there has only been minor improvement since 1980—the low point in the time series.

After its fiscal crisis, New York City had to manage with less; education provides a dramatic example. An analysis of revenue trends provides some understanding of why this has occurred.

TABLE 11.3

Approved Operating Expenses per Pupil in New York City and Rest of State, Unadjusted, Price-Adjusted, and per Weighted Pupil, 1966–1985

Year	Per Pupil AOE for K–12 in New York City	Per Pupil AOE for K–12 in Rest of State	Ratio of per Pupil AOE in New York City to Rest of State	Price-Adjusted per Pupil AOE for K–12 in New York City	Ratio of Price-Adjusted per Pupil AOE in New York City to Rest of State	Ratio of AOE per Weighted Pupil in New York City to Rest of State Without Price Adjustment	Ratio of AOE per Weighted Pupil in New York City to Rest of State With Price Adjustment
1966	$736	$690	1.07	$663	0.96	0.93	0.84
1967	792	766	1.03	714	0.93	0.90	0.81
1968	775	839	0.92	699	0.83	0.80	0.72
1969	925	947	0.98	834	0.88	0.85	0.76
1970	983	1,015	0.97	886	0.87	0.84	0.76
1971	1,182	1,137	1.04	1,066	0.94	0.90	0.81
1972	1,154	1,217	0.95	1,040	0.85	0.82	0.74
1973	1,299	1,308	0.99	1,171	0.90	0.86	0.78
1974	1,625	1,415	1.15	1,465	1.04	1.00	0.90
1975	1,879	1,585	1.19	1,694	1.07	1.03	0.93
1976	1,754	1,711	1.03	1,581	0.92	0.89	0.80
1977	1,880	1,842	1.02	1,695	0.92	0.89	0.80
1978	2,100	1,988	1.06	1,893	0.95	0.92	0.83
1979	1,962	2,158	0.91	1,769	0.82	0.79	0.71
1980	2,145	2,496	0.86	1,934	0.77	0.75	0.67
1981	2,539	2,781	0.91	2,289	0.82	0.79	0.72
1982	2,882	3,158	0.91	2,598	0.82	0.79	0.71
1983	3,360	3,503	0.96	3,029	0.86	0.83	0.75
1984	3,649	3,836	0.95	3,289	0.86	0.83	0.75
1985	3,904	4,216	0.93	3,519	0.83	0.80	0.73

SOURCE: New York State Education Department, Information Center on Education, *Annual Education Summary*, 1965–1966 through 1984–1985.

NOTE: For explanations of the price index and pupil weightings, see text.

Revenues

The shares of total revenues from local, state, and federal sources for New York City and the rest of the state are presented in Table 11.4. The federal share is consistently higher in New York City than in the rest of the State, but both experienced a drop in the federal share since 1980.[16] In New York City, the federal share dropped from a high of nearly 12 percent in 1980 to under 6 percent in 1985. Even with this drop, however, the federal share for New York City is substantially higher than the federal share for the rest of the state throughout the period.

Since 1974, the local share in New York City has declined while the State share has risen, about 10 percentage points in both cases. For the rest of the state, the local share rose and the State share fell from 1966 through 1978, about 8 percentage points in both cases. There have not been major changes in the State and local shares for the rest of the state since 1978.

It is also important to examine per pupil State aid in dollar terms. (See Table 11.5.) While per pupil State aid in New York City consistently has increased more rapidly than in the rest of the state, by 1985 it still was only 85 percent of the level in the rest of the state (77 percent after adjustments for price differences). Thus, the lower level of per pupil State aid in New York City is one reason why per pupil expenditures are lower in New York City. In fact in 1985, the $329 dollar difference in State aid per pupil between New York City and the rest of the state almost exactly equals the dollar difference in per pupil expenditures.

Local revenues are the other major source of funding. (See Table 11.6.) Although somewhat erratic, the overall trend in the ratio of per pupil local revenues in New York City to the rest of the state has been downward over the 20-year period. However, prior to 1982 per pupil local revenues were not a cause of lower expenditures in New York City. The most recent figure for New York City in 1985 is 88 percent of the level in the rest of the state, but other factors must be considered before reaching the conclusion that local revenues in New York City are "too low" after 1982.

Since local revenues are primarily property taxes, it is useful to examine the value of property on a per pupil basis.[17] These data also are presented in Table 11.6. The trend parallels the local revenue trend with New York City beginning the 20-year period about 60 percent above the level in the rest of the state, but by the end of the period the value of property per pupil was higher in the rest of the state than in New York City.

It is rarely the case that school districts of varying local wealth raise the same amounts of local revenues. Districts with higher property values

TABLE 11.4

Sources of Public K–12 Revenues, New York City and Rest of State, 1966–1985

Year	New York City				Rest of State			
	Total	Local	State	Federal	Total	Local	State	Federal
1966	100.0%	65.7%	30.7%	3.6%	100.0%	46.8%	50.5%	2.7%
1967	100.0	61.2	30.9	7.9	100.0	45.5	50.9	3.6
1968	100.0	63.2	33.1	3.6	100.0	46.1	51.0	2.9
1969	100.0	56.2	39.8	4.4	100.0	45.6	51.7	2.8
1970	100.0	54.3	38.3	7.5	100.0	48.3	49.1	2.6
1971	100.0	55.6	32.7	11.6	100.0	47.8	49.7	2.5
1972	100.0	57.8	32.2	10.0	100.0	49.3	47.3	3.4
1973	100.0	59.7	31.7	8.6	100.0	51.2	45.8	3.0
1974	100.0	65.7	28.3	6.1	100.0	52.4	44.5	3.1
1975	100.0	61.9	29.4	8.7	100.0	51.7	45.3	3.0
1976	100.0	60.8	31.3	8.0	100.0	52.6	44.8	2.6
1977	100.0	60.4	31.9	7.8	100.0	54.3	43.2	2.6
1978	100.0	61.5	29.9	8.7	100.0	55.3	41.6	3.1
1979	100.0	57.2	33.0	9.7	100.0	54.9	41.5	3.6
1980	100.0	55.8	32.4	11.8	100.0	55.0	41.6	3.4
1981	100.0	55.8	35.0	9.2	100.0	55.3	41.5	3.2
1982	100.0	58.3	34.5	7.2	100.0	56.2	41.2	2.6
1983	100.0	56.8	37.0	6.2	100.0	56.1	41.7	2.2
1984	100.0	58.7	34.9	6.5	100.0	56.4	41.5	2.1
1985	100.0	54.5	39.8	5.8	100.0	55.7	42.2	2.1

SOURCE: New York State Education Department, Information Center on Education, *Annual Education Summary*, 1965–1966 through 1984–1985.

TABLE 11.5

State Aid and Price-Adjusted State Aid per Pupil, New York City and Rest of State, 1966–1985

Year	Per Pupil State Aid			Per Pupil Price-Adjusted State Aid in New York City	Ratio of Price-Adjusted per Pupil State Aid in New York City to Rest of State
	New York City	Rest of State	Ratio of New York City to Rest of State		
1966	$291	$453	0.64	$262	0.58
1967	325	508	0.64	293	0.58
1968	375	549	0.68	338	0.62
1969	492	630	0.78	444	0.70
1970	505	642	0.79	455	0.71
1971	536	733	0.73	483	0.66
1972	527	752	0.70	475	0.63
1973	565	770	0.73	509	0.66
1974	604	814	0.74	545	0.67
1975	725	926	0.78	654	0.71
1976	734	991	0.74	662	0.67
1977	780	1,014	0.77	703	0.69
1978	823	1,063	0.77	742	0.70
1979	945	1,180	0.80	852	0.72
1980	1,055	1,311	0.80	951	0.73
1981	1,217	1,482	0.82	1,097	0.74
1982	1,375	1,645	0.84	1,240	0.75
1983	1,542	1,829	0.84	1,390	0.76
1984	1,609	1,975	0.81	1,451	0.73
1985	1,889	2,218	0.85	1,703	0.77

SOURCE: New York State Education Department, Information Center on Education, *Annual Education Summary*, 1965–1966 through 1984–1985.
NOTE: For explanation of price index, see text.

TABLE 11.6
Local Revenues, Full Value of Property, and Local Tax Effort, New York City and Rest of State, 1966–1985

Year	Per Pupil Local Revenues			Per Pupil Full Value of Property			Local Education Revenues as a Percentage of Full Value of Property		
	New York City	Rest of State	Ratio of New York City to Rest of State	New York City	Rest of State	Ratio of New York City to Rest of State	New York City	Rest of State	Ratio of New York City to Rest of State
1966	$621	$420	1.48	$40,784	$25,841	1.58	1.52%	1.62%	0.94
1967	643	454	1.42	$41,140	25,971	1.58	1.56	1.75	0.90
1968	716	497	1.44	41,258	26,030	1.59	1.74	1.91	0.91
1969	703	556	1.26	42,259	26,620	1.59	1.66	2.09	0.80
1970	716	632	1.13	44,240	27,452	1.61	1.62	2.30	0.70
1971	911	706	1.29	46,712	29,958	1.56	1.95	2.35	0.83
1972	946	783	1.21	50,513	32,427	1.56	1.87	2.41	0.78
1973	1,066	860	1.24	55,578	35,851	1.55	1.92	2.40	0.80
1974	1,405	960	1.46	61,811	40,099	1.54	2.27	2.39	0.95
1975	1,528	1,056	1.45	65,094	46,890	1.39	2.35	2.25	1.04
1976	1,427	1,164	1.23	66,965	51,787	1.29	2.13	2.25	0.95
1977	1,477	1,275	1.16	69,410	57,380	1.21	2.13	2.22	0.96
1978	1,695	1,413	1.20	74,903	63,854	1.17	2.26	2.21	1.02
1979	1,637	1,562	1.05	78,232	71,574	1.09	2.09	2.18	0.96
1980	1,816	1,736	1.05	82,819	80,103	1.03	2.19	2.17	1.01
1981	1,939	1,976	0.98	88,880	88,344	1.01	2.18	2.24	0.98
1982	2,323	2,242	1.04	95,159	97,275	0.98	2.44	2.30	1.06
1983	2,365	2,458	0.96	96,865	102,237	0.95	2.44	2.40	1.02
1984	2,709	2,689	1.01	101,921	108,006	0.94	2.66	2.49	1.07
1985	2,588	2,930	0.88	106,679	120,760	0.88	2.43	2.43	1.00

SOURCES: New York State Education Department, Information Center on Education, *Annual Education Summary*, 1965–1966 through 1984–1985; property value data from New York State, Office of the State Comptroller, "Financial Data for School Districts," various years.

per pupil can raise greater local revenues with less "effort" than districts with lower values, where effort is measured by the ratio of local revenues to the local ability to pay, in this case full value of property. Rather than judging local revenues in terms of dollars per pupil, it is more meaningful to compare revenue effort; that is, ratios of local revenues to property value (also shown in Table 11.6).[18] Since 1975, the revenue efforts in New York City and the rest of the state have been comparable, with some year-to-year variations. Using this standard, only if New York City is expected to exert a greater revenue effort than the rest of the state can it be concluded that the gap in per pupil expenditures should be closed by greater local effort on the part of New York City. Thus, the major source of the lower per pupil expenditures in New York City is the State aid system.

State Aid

One way to assess State aid in New York City and the rest of the state is to compare New York City's share of State aid with its share of enrollment. (See Figure 11.1.) Over the past 20 years, New York City's

FIGURE 11.1

New York City's Share of State Aid and Enrollment,
K–12 Education

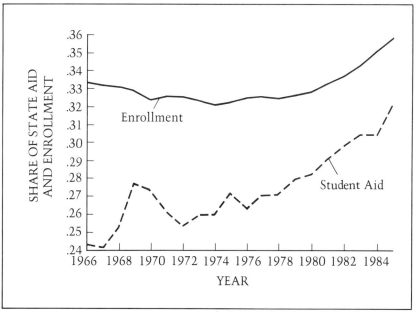

share of State aid has lagged considerably behind its share of enrollment. This was justified in the past by New York City's greater wealth, measured in property value. More recently, New York City is less wealthy than the rest of the state. When New York City's higher prices and pupil needs are added to the equation, it is difficult to justify the continued lower aid in New York City.

There are alternative ways to answer the question of why New York City's State aid is low. One approach is to focus on the political process that determines the aid distribution. The actual aid distribution is part of the budgetary process that involves the governor and his staff, the legislature and its staff, and the myriad interest groups affected by education finance.[19] What results from this process is an aid distribution for all 735 school districts in the state, including New York City. A second approach is to analyze the detailed components of this State aid formula to determine which elements work to the disadvantage of New York City.

The answer to the question "Why?" depends on both the political process and the aid distribution mechanisms, because there is an interaction between the two until the final distribution is agreed upon. But the relative utility of these two approaches depends on the reason that the question is asked. In cases where the focus is on the assessment of equity of the aid distribution system across the entire state, the emphasis may be on the aid distribution mechanisms; when the concern is how one large district fares relative to the rest of the state, then it is appropriate to begin with an examination of the political process.

Several observers of the process of education aid distribution in New York State have concluded that one of the first areas where agreement is sought is the share of State aid that will go to New York City. For example, commenting on the 1983–1984 aid distribution, Joan Scheuer writes that the legislature

> continued existing law with a relatively small increase in ceilings, even declining to reduce aid allocations for the few most wealthy districts. Instead of permitting the formulas to determine the distribution of aid freely and fully, the legislature agreed on a school aid increase of $203 million for the 1983–84 school year, and then made sure that New York City's share of total funds distributed remained close to 30 percent. Once again, the formulas were fine-tuned to meet this overriding political priority.[20]

Or consider the recent *New York Times* editorial, which stated,

> State school aid is supposedly distributed on the basis of complicated formulas that take into account each district's relative wealth and special needs. In

practice, the legislators first determine the city's share of state aid, then adjust the formulas to fit. Upstaters wield the upper hand, permitting the city only 31.5 percent of the state's education funds, though it has 35 percent of student enrollment—a current shortfall of $334 million.[21]

Finally, in an analysis of the politics of state aid distributions in New York State, Stanley Moses and Edwin Margolis conclude that:

> The amount of education aid for New York City is the key decision which drives the rest of the allocation. This decision is determined early in the game, as it is necessary for the two leaders [of the legislature] to agree on the New York City share before staff technicians can allocate the agreed on increase among the various components of the formula. The agreed upon city-state division is transmitted to their legislative staff technicians who fine-tune the formula so that the mathematical outcome results in the disbursement of the predetermined city and state shares. This distribution then drives the other elements of the state aid formula.[22]

If these observers are correct, the relationship plotted in Figure 11.1 is determined by legislative negotiation. Consequently, if New York City's share of State aid is to rise to a level that ameliorates some of the problems identified earlier, it will require a legislative initiative that runs counter to prevailing practices. But New York City's share of State aid is increasing faster than its increase in enrollment (see Figure 11.1), and per pupil State aid in New York City relative to the rest of the state is now higher than at any time during the last 20 years. An extrapolation of the most recent trends would work to New York City's advantage.

Although an extensive analysis of the circumstances that led to New York City's original relatively low level of State aid and the recent improvement in its treatment is beyond the scope of this essay, certain explanations are suggested by the fiscal and political data. First, as shown in Table 11.6, in the late 1960s New York City was substantially wealthier than the rest of the state judging by per pupil value of property. In a school finance system with an "equalizing" objective, higher wealth school districts have a weaker claim on resources. Second, 20 years ago there was less sensitivity to and fewer claims for additional resources for the educationally disadvantaged and the handicapped. Since New York City has a disproportionate share of these groups, its relative share of State aid should increase as more funding is directed to these areas.

These are rational explanations for New York City's low position 20 years ago and relative progress since, but they ignore the legislative dynamics discussed above. The process by which New York City's share of State aid is determined in the legislative deliberations describes how, rather than explains why, the New York City share is at a particular level. The composition of the legislature is a logical place to begin to answer the question "Why?"

The Legislature. Gerald Benjamin's essay in this volume describes and documents the significant changes in the State legislature since the early 1960s. Both party domination and geographic distribution have changed, particularly for New York City relative to the rest of the state. In 1963, the Republicans controlled both the Assembly and the Senate and, what may be more significant, they had at least 50 percent of the membership in both houses without the Republicans from New York City. From a political perspective, a relatively low level of State aid for New York City was consistent with this distribution.

By 1975 the situation had changed significantly. In the Assembly the Democrats had the majority, but this majority required significant non-New York City participation. Moreover, it was the growth in the number of non-New York City Democrats that permitted the Democrats to take control. In the Senate the Republicans still had a majority, but this required New York City's six Republican senators. Thus, the Democrats gained in the Assembly and this presumably benefited New York City, and the New York City Republican senators also had the potential to play a crucial role. In sum, there were political gains for New York City, and this is consistent with the trends in aid distribution.

The changes in the Senate from 1975 to 1985 were small. The Republicans still had a majority, but not without some New York City participation. In the Assembly, the Democrats had strengthened their majority, and New York City Democrats were about 38 percent of the Assembly, almost the same share as earlier.

These numbers do not tell the entire political story. New York City's gain in aid also was helped by the leadership positions assumed by New York City's legislators. As Benjamin suggests, more of the influential positions in the legislature now seem to be held by New York City representatives, although the detailed analysis of these changes remains a topic for future research. Also, the political trading between parties, houses, and legislators and the executive should be investigated further to determine the degree to which the trends in education aid are the result of a larger set of issues. Nonetheless, the results of this initial political analysis are consistent with New York City's relative gains.

The Distribution of State Aid. Since the multiple State aid programs are the vehicles by which allocation decisions are implemented, it is useful to assess the recent distribution among programs. Owing to the complexity of New York State's aid system, only the most critical features are discussed here.[23]

Table 11.7 presents the State aid distributions by program for fiscal years 1984–1987. The single largest category is operating aid, which is distributed under a "percentage equalizing" formula that distributes more aid to districts with lower ability to pay. In 1987 operating aid was 61 percent of total aid, down from 67 percent in 1984. The other major categories include transportation aid, aid for handicapped pupils, construction aid, supplemental (operating) aid, aid to Boards of Cooperative Education Services (BOCES), aid to small city districts, high tax aid, excellence in teaching aid, and textbook aid. In addition, there are numerous other special purpose aid programs, many of which have grown substantially.

Table 11.8 displays New York City's percentage of each program. Most aid mechanisms fall into one of three groups. First are those for which aid is allocated to New York City similarly to total aid. Operating aid, excellence in teaching, supplemental support aid, and transportation are examples. Second, several programs, such as high tax aid, BOCES aid, and aid to small cities, provide no aid to New York City. Third, programs such as early grade intervention, limited English proficiency, attendance improvement—dropout prevention, special services, and handicapped aid are allocated to New York City in greater proportions than enrollment figures alone would justify. Some of the programs in this latter category have increased very rapidly. Thus, there has not been a simple plan to increase the share of aid in New York City, but, instead the complexity has persisted, and through both operating and nonoperating aid New York City has gained relative to the rest of the state.

TEACHERS IN NEW YORK CITY
AND NEW YORK STATE

Public K–12 education revenues are expended on a variety of items, but the single most important category is teachers. Personal services were 55 percent of all educational expenditures in 1984, and employee benefits accounted for an additional 20 percent. Teachers constitute 86 percent of all personnel.[24] In addition, recently there has been significant discussion and debate over aspects of the teaching profession including certification, education, and compensation.

A basic question is whether the expenditure differences between New York City and the rest of the state documented previously are evident in the deployment of teachers. Data on total professional staff and classroom teachers in New York State and New York City are presented in Table 11.9.[25] The statewide peak in number of personnel was in 1975, after which there was decline through 1983. The most prominent trend in New York City is the drop in total professional staff and classroom

TABLE 11.7
New York State Education Aid, Fiscal Years 1984–1987
(millions of dollars)

Category	1983–1984	1984–1985	1985–1986	1986–1987
Operating	$3,251.0	$3,538.8	$3,786.6	$4,046.4
Excellence in Teaching	0.0	0.0	0.0	90.9
Early Grade Intervention	0.0	0.0	13.0	13.0
Supplemental Support Aid	0.0	0.0	103.1	189.2
Low Income Supplemental School Aid Transition	0.0	0.0	5.4	0.0
Speech Therapy	0.0	0.0	0.0	4.6
Educationally Related Support Services Aid	0.0	0.0	0.0	8.5
High Tax	30.9	56.2	65.8	104.6
Transition Aid	0.0	0.8	2.0	0.0
Diagnostic	9.3	9.3	9.4	9.5
Gifted and Talented	4.3	9.8	9.8	13.3
Limited English Proficiency	5.2	11.8	12.9	16.7
Attendance Improvement—Dropout Prevention	0.0	27.1	27.1	37.1
Employment Preparation Education	0.0	5.8	12.0	12.0
Handicapped—Public	375.1	447.9	497.9	547.7
Handicapped—Private	33.3	35.8	36.4	40.1
Low Income	23.2	23.0	0.0	0.0
Special Services	32.8	44.1	57.3	64.9
Reorganization Incentive	3.6	4.4	4.5	4.4
Board of Cooperative Educational Services (BOCES)	127.2	134.5	150.3	158.1
Transportation	517.4	567.1	613.1	635.3
Building (excluding Bond Anticipation Notes)	200.9	201.2	207.9	216.9
Computer Hardware	0.0	10.1	11.3	11.3
Library Materials	0.0	0.0	6.3	6.2
Vocational Education Equipment	0.0	0.0	0.0	3.3
Textbook (including Lottery)	64.9	78.9	78.1	77.7
Software	0.0	8.0	9.5	9.4
BOCES Excellence in Teaching	0.0	0.0	0.0	4.5
Declassification Support Services	0.0	0.0	0.0	0.2
Incarcerated Youth	0.0	0.0	0.0	5.6
Building Bond Anticipation Notes	25.8	35.0	40.0	40.6
Special School Districts	0.7	0.7	0.7	0.
County Vocational Education Extension Boards	0.2	0.2	0.2	0.
Section 4407 Deduction	(6.0)	(7.0)	(7.0)	(7.
Reorganization Study Grants	0.0	0.0	0.5	0.
Categorical Reading	22.8	23.8	23.8	34.
Mentor—Interns	0.0	0.0	0.0	4.
Improved Pupil Performance	10.8	10.0	10.0	20.
Magnet Schools	8.5	13.5	18.5	25.

TABLE 11.7 *(continued)*

Category	1983–1984	1984–1985	1985–1986	1986–1987
Comprehensive Instructional Management Systems	$0.0	$5.0	$5.0	$5.0
Asbestos Project—Public	2.0	1.8	1.8	1.8
Asbestos Project—Nonpublic	0.0	0.0	2.0	2.0
Education of Office of Mental Health or Office of Mental Retardation Pupils	12.0	15.0	15.0	18.0
Aid to Small City Districts	57.2	78.6	95.6	104.1
Refund Credit	(4.0)	(4.0)	0.0	0.0
Bilingual Education	1.6	1.9	3.0	4.0
Adult Education	1.7	0.0	0.0	0.0
Special Category Projects	7.0	7.0	8.0	10.0
Prior-Year Adjustments	23.0	42.4	21.2	16.0
Prior-Year Adjustments BOCES	0.0	0.0	1.6	0.0
Total	$4,842.1	$5,438.4	$5,959.4	$6,609.8

SOURCE: Unpublished data provided by the Education Unit, New York State Division of the Budget.

teachers between 1975 and 1977 when, because of the fiscal crisis, the two categories declined 24 and 21 percent, respectively. The increase between 1983 and 1986 for New York State is explained almost entirely by the increase in New York City.

A more useful way to examine staffing trends is with ratios of pupils to staff, shown in Table 11.10. Prior to 1976, pupil-staff ratios were similar in New York City and the rest of the state. After the teacher layoffs in New York City during 1976 and 1977, the ratios became 23 percent higher in New York City than the rest of the state; most of the ground lost during those two years has not been made up. The most recent data show that in 1986 pupil-teacher ratios were 16.5 in New York City compared with 14.1 in the rest of the state. Simultaneously over the entire period, however, pupil-staff ratios have been declining, primarily because of enrollment decline. The 1986 ratios are the lowest ever for New York City and the rest of the state. Thus, the relationship between funding and enrollments has permitted systematic class size decline in the entire state, including New York City, but New York City has more pupils per staff member than the rest of the state, where the educational needs are less severe.

Aside from their absolute numbers, there is heightened concern over the quality of teachers. A wide range of factors determine an individual's career selection, but recently attention has focused on the role of salaries in teacher recruitment. The Carnegie Task Force on Teaching as a

TABLE 11.8
New York City Share of State Education Aid by Program, Fiscal Years 1984–1987

Category	1984	1985	1986	1987
Operating	30.4%	31.6%	32.6%	33.1%
Excellence in Teaching	NA	NA	NA	34.1
Early Grade Intervention	NA	NA	86.3	86.3
Supplemental Support Aid	NA	NA	26.0	33.9
Low Income Supplemental School Aid Transition	NA	NA	0.0	NA
Speech Therapy	NA	NA	NA	35.2
Educationally Related Support Services Aid	NA	NA	NA	30.9
High Tax	0.0	0.0	0.0	0.0
Transition Aid	NA	0.0	0.0	0.0
Diagnostic	33.3	35.4	36.1	36.7
Gifted and Talented	31.5	33.1	33.6	34.2
Limited English Proficiency	84.1	83.9	82.9	82.7
Attendance Improvement— Dropout Prevention	NA	79.8	80.1	80.4
Employment Preparation Education	NA	38.2	37.5	37.5
Handicapped—Public	40.6	41.6	40.8	41.3
Handicapped—Private	44.5	41.9	38.4	34.9
Low Income	24.1	26.0	NA	NA
Special Services	80.7	80.0	80.8	79.9
Reorganization Incentive	0.0	0.0	0.0	0.0
Board of Cooperative Educational Services (BOCES)	0.0	0.0	0.0	0.0
Transportation	34.1	32.9	32.9	33.4
Building (excluding Bond Anticipation Notes)	18.2	19.0	19.0	20.1
Computer Hardware	NA	31.2	33.0	34.2
Library Materials	NA	NA	38.6	39.3
Vocational Education Equipment	NA	NA	NA	0.0
Textbook (including Lottery)	40.4	39.2	39.7	40.2
Software	NA	38.4	38.6	39.2
BOCES Excellence in Teaching	NA	NA	NA	0.0
Declassification Support Services	NA	NA	NA	50.0
Incarcerated Youth	NA	NA	NA	76.0
Building Bond Anticipation Notes	0.0	0.0	0.0	0.0
Special School Districts	0.0	0.0	0.0	0.0
County Vocational Extension Boards	0.0	0.0	0.0	0.0
Section 4407 Deduction	45.9	43.6	43.6	43.6
Reorganization Study Grants	NA	NA	0.0	0.0
Categorical Reading	17.9	21.1	21.1	31.8
Mentor—Interns	NA	NA	NA	31.8
Improved Pupil Performance	36.3	37.5	37.5	47.3

TABLE 11.8 *(continued)*

Category	1984	1985	1986	1987
Magnet Schools	11.8	11.2	11.8	8.5
Comprehensive Instructional Management Systems	NA	44.0	44.0	44.0
Asbestos Project—Public	57.7	39.4	39.4	39.4
Asbestos Project—Nonpublic	NA	NA	40.0	40.0
Education of Office of Mental Health or Office of Mental Retardation Pupils	0.0	16.7	16.7	16.7
Aid to Small City Districts	0.0	0.0	0.0	0.0
Refund Credit	0.0	0.0	NA	NA
Bilingual Education	66.7	63.9	63.7	63.8
Adult Education	12.6	NA	NA	NA
Special Category Projects	0.0	32.1	32.1	32.1
Prior-Year Adjustments	16.4	64.6	48.2	31.3
Prior-Year Adjustments BOCES	NA	NA	0.0	NA
Total	29.9%	31.4%	31.7%	32.3

SOURCE: See Table 11.7.

NOTE: NA = not applicable.

TABLE 11.9

Teachers and Professional Staff, 1971–1986

	New York State		New York City	
Year	Total Professional Staff	Total Classroom Teachers	Total Professional Staff	Total Classroom Teachers
1971	213,166	185,223	71,190	63,191
1972	213,544	185,325	66,596	59,216
1973	213,718	186,943	67,334	60,683
1974	215,887	187,956	67,367	60,589
1975	222,340	190,481	72,730	61,970
1976	210,631	182,772	61,231	54,161
1977	199,594	173,975	55,484	48,931
1978	203,138	175,879	59,110	50,580
1979	203,619	176,141	61,691	52,537
1980	201,811	172,803	61,165	50,178
1981	196,657	169,189	56,999	47,826
1982	195,726	168,516	58,893	49,598
1983	193,362	167,172	58,412	49,237
1984	196,637	168,944	62,983	52,604
1985	198,775	171,093	63,556	53,840
1986	203,376	175,256	66,323	56,424

SOURCE: New York State Education Department, *Annual Educational Summary*, various years.

TABLE 11.10

Pupil–Professional Staff and Pupil–Teacher Ratios, 1971–1986

Year	Rest of New York State		New York City		New York City Compared with Rest of State	
	Total Professional Staff	Total Classroom Teachers	Total Professional Staff	Total Classroom Teachers	Total Professional Staff	Total Classroom Teachers
1971	16.58	19.29	15.95	17.97	0.962	0.931
1972	16.08	18.74	17.12	19.26	1.065	1.028
1973	16.06	18.63	16.67	18.50	1.038	0.993
1974	15.68	18.29	16.32	18.14	1.041	0.992
1975	15.42	17.95	15.05	17.67	0.976	0.984
1976	15.30	17.77	17.91	20.24	1.170	1.139
1977	15.49	17.85	19.37	21.97	1.251	1.230
1978	14.97	17.21	17.49	20.44	1.168	1.188
1979	14.54	16.70	16.15	18.97	1.111	1.136
1980	14.05	16.11	15.70	19.14	1.118	1.188
1981	13.58	15.63	16.51	19.68	1.215	1.259
1982	13.36	15.37	15.64	18.57	1.171	1.208
1983	13.11	15.00	15.66	18.58	1.195	1.239
1984	12.86	14.77	14.63	17.51	1.137	1.185
1985	12.44	14.35	14.59	17.22	1.172	1.200
1986	12.22	14.09	14.04	16.50	1.149	1.172

SOURCE: See Table 11.9.

Profession, which recommends significant restructuring of the teaching profession, specifically claims:

> Teaching must offer salaries, benefits, and working conditions competitive with those of other professions. Assuming that a better than average level of intellectual ability is desired in the teaching work force, the schools will be competing for talent with a wide range of enterprises that, in many instances, are prepared to bid up salaries until they get the people they believe they need to prosper as an organization.
>
> To attract such people, districts will have to pay salaries at least equal to those offered in the mid-range of the wage scale for occupations requiring comparable education, roughly equivalent to what accountants are paid today.[26]

Several states, including New York and New Jersey, have already implemented special plans directed at improving teacher salaries, but considerably more would have to be done to implement the Carnegie Task Force's recommendations.

Although a complete analysis of the quality of teachers in New York City and the rest of the state is beyond the scope of this essay, it is instructive to compare salaries for New York City's teachers with those for relevant reference groups. (See Table 11.11.) Although teachers' salaries in New York City were consistently higher than in the rest of the state between 1971 and 1986, a post-fiscal crisis decline is apparent. Salaries in New York City fell from 15 to 5 percent above the statewide average between 1975 and 1979. Even by 1986 New York City had not returned to previous relatively high salary levels. New York City's relative disadvantage compared with the neighboring counties is also clear from the table, and the most recent differences are substantial.

One potential problem with comparisons that include all teachers is that there are no controls for differences in years of experience and education levels that are incorporated in teacher salary scales. One method of controlling for these factors is to compare salaries for teachers with similar years of experience and education levels. Table 11.12 presents one such comparison, at a point near the beginning of teachers' careers: a bachelor's degree with one year of experience. This point on the salary scale is particularly important because beginning teachers will use salaries in determining where they take their first job. Moreover, with a "mature" teacher population, New York City, like much of the nation, faces significant retirements in the coming years and this will increase the demand for new teachers.[27] In 1971, the salary for these teachers in New York City was higher than in the rest of the state and in the three

TABLE 11.11
Median Teacher Salaries in New York City and State, 1971–1986

Year	Total State	New York City	Nassau	Suffolk	Westchester
Dollar Amount					
1971	$10,600	$11,000	$12,481	$11,040	$11,775
1973	12,400	13,750	NA	NA	NA
1975	14,690	16,850	17,287	15,543	16,445
1977	17,150	19,200	20,719	18,465	20,125
1979	18,500	19,500	22,815	21,000	22,660
1981	21,289	22,566	25,879	24,100	26,228
1983	24,974	26,572	30,400	28,250	30,450
1985	28,380	30,706	35,000	33,651	35,960
1986	30,631	33,777	37,860	36,086	38,302
Salary of New York City Teachers Compared with					
1971	1.038	1.000	0.881	0.996	0.934
1973	1.109	1.000	NA	NA	NA
1975	1.147	1.000	0.975	1.084	1.025
1977	1.120	1.000	0.927	1.040	0.954
1979	1.054	1.000	0.855	0.929	0.861
1981	1.060	1.000	0.872	0.936	0.860
1983	1.064	1.000	0.874	0.941	0.873
1985	1.082	1.000	0.877	0.912	0.854
1986	1.103	1.000	0.892	0.936	0.882

SOURCE: New York State Education Department, Information Center on Education.

NOTES: "Total State" includes New York City. NA = not available.

TABLE 11.12

Median Salary for Teachers with a Bachelor's Degree and One Year's Experience, 1971–1986

Year	Total State	New York City	Nassau	Suffolk	Westchester
Dollar Amount					
1971	$8,300	$8,450	$8,198	$8,100	$8,100
1973	9,191	8,994	NA	NA	NA
1975	9,200	9,188	10,135	10,128	10,223
1977	9,575	9,700	11,375	11,000	11,481
1979	10,036	9,700	12,399	11,922	12,547
1981	10,981	10,141	13,014	13,125	13,994
1983	12,571	12,571	14,077	14,837	16,288
1985	14,527	14,527	17,786	16,809	17,598
1986	18,500	18,500	18,835	18,000	19,819
Salary of New York City Teachers Compared with					
1971	1.018	1.000	1.031	1.043	1.043
1973	0.979	1.000	NA	NA	NA
1975	0.999	1.000	0.907	0.907	0.899
1977	1.013	1.000	0.853	0.882	0.845
1979	0.967	1.000	0.782	0.814	0.773
1981	0.924	1.000	0.779	0.773	0.725
1983	1.000	1.000	0.893	0.847	0.772
1985	1.000	1.000	0.817	0.864	0.825
1986	1.000	1.000	0.982	1.028	0.933

SOURCE: New York State Education Department, Information Center on Education.

NOTES: "Total State" includes New York City. NA = not available.

TABLE 11.13

Median Salary for Teachers with a Master's Degree or Equivalency and Five Years' Experience, 1971–1986

Year	Total State	New York City	Nassau	Suffolk	Westchester
Dollar Amount					
1971	$9,950	$10,200	NA	NA	NA
1973	11,200	11,150	NA	NA	NA
1975	13,350	13,879	$13,700	$13,820	$13,495
1977	13,350	14,350	15,331	14,719	15,412
1979	13,500	13,350	16,501	16,174	16,627
1981	14,610	14,658	17,884	17,311	18,344
1983	17,299	17,742	19,646	19,615	20,989
1984	19,318	20,665	21,358	21,304	22,475
1985	19,828	20,192	23,010	22,508	24,382
1986	22,343	22,731	24,728	23,763	26,374
Salary of New York City Teachers Compared with					
1971	1.025	1.000	NA	NA	NA
1973	0.996	1.000	NA	NA	NA
1975	1.040	1.000	1.013	1.004	1.028
1977	1.075	1.000	0.936	0.975	0.931
1979	0.989	1.000	0.809	0.825	0.803
1981	1.003	1.000	0.820	0.847	0.799
1983	1.026	1.000	0.903	0.905	0.845
1984	1.070	1.000	0.968	0.970	0.919
1985	1.018	1.000	0.878	0.897	0.828
1986	1.017	1.000	0.919	0.957	0.862

SOURCE: New York State Education Department, Information Center on Education.

NOTES: "Total State" includes New York City. NA = not available.

neighboring counties. By 1981, however, New York City's relative position had slipped to less than 80 percent of the levels in the three neighboring counties. New York City has made progress in offering competitive beginning salaries since 1981, and this could help improve the relative quality of New York City's new entrants.

Table 11.13 presents salaries for teachers with five years of experience and either a bachelor's degree and 30 credits or a master's degree. The familiar pattern of relative decline after the fiscal crisis is evident, although there was some recovery in the most recent years. But these figures point out that changing starting salaries are not enough. If the entire salary schedule in New York City is to become more competitive with teachers' salaries in neighboring counties, additional resources will be required.

Thus, in terms of the most critical educational input—teachers— New York City is at a disadvantage on two counts. First, compared with the rest of the state New York City has more pupils per teacher. Second, relative to three neighboring counties, New York City has been at a disadvantage in terms of salaries since the fiscal crisis. However, there are signs of improvement as teachers' salaries in New York City have recently risen relative to the three neighboring counties.

SCHOOL OUTPUTS

A complete analysis of the outputs and outcomes of schooling in New York City and New York State would require examination of variables such as scores on achievement tests, dropout rates, SAT scores, attendance rates, and post-high school college and employment patterns. This is not possible within the scope of this essay. Nevertheless, some analysis is important. This assessment is limited to reading and mathematics achievement tests administered statewide since the 1960s. Performance on reading and mathematics achievement tests is not the *sole* criterion for evaluating schools; however, there is something wrong when schools cannot teach these basic skills to a broad spectrum of the student population.

For over 20 years, the New York State Education Department has overseen the administration of standardized achievement tests, known as "PEP" tests, in reading and mathematics for third and sixth graders throughout the state.[28] Data are available on the percentage of pupils in New York State and New York City who score below a State-determined level that demarcates the point below which a pupil needs remedial instruction.

Before these scores are compared for New York City and New York State, some cautionary notes are in order. First, the specific form of the test and the score indicative of a need for remedial help have changed over time. Thus, although the city-state comparison in a particular year is valid, the year-to-year changes must be scrutinized with knowledge of these test and scoring changes. Second, there have been changes in the way the test results have been reported over time. For example, prior to 1983, the results for handicapped pupils who took the tests were reported in the summary data.[29]

Third, the results of the tests reflect the performance of the schools *and* the background of the pupils. The achievement score for a single subject and grade is affected by both what the students bring to school in terms of preparation and ability and what is taught in school, and therefore it should be interpreted in the context of the relevant pupil populations. As indicated by the poverty and limited English proficiency data discussed earlier, pupils in New York City are different from those in the rest of the state. Finally, there are differences between New York City and the rest of the state in the percentage of enrolled pupils who take the test. Not only is attendance lower in New York City but some limited English speaking and handicapped pupils do not take the test, and there is a higher proportion of these pupils in New York City.

With all these cautions, is it still worth examining the data? The answer is yes, because there is a scarcity of any data that compare New York City with the rest of the state over a significant time period. Whether the achievement scores of pupils in New York City have improved relative to the rest of the state is a question worth answering, even if imperfectly.

The results of the achievement tests for third grade reading for school years 1967 to 1986 are reported in Table 11.14. A significant change in the form of the test and the cutoff occurred in 1983, and this is obvious in the data. Even without this testing change, the interpretation of these figures is not simple. Should the *relative* percentages in New York City and the rest of the state be compared (for example, twice as many were below the cutoff and now three times as many are below) or the *absolute* difference between the percentages be compared (for example, there was a 20 percentage point difference between the two groups; now there is a 15 percentage point difference)? The answer depends on the values of the interpreter, and there is no one "correct" answer. To illustrate this point, what if at one time the percentages of pupils falling below the statewide minimum were 50 and 25 percent in two respective jurisdictions, and were 25 and 12.5 percent at some later point in time? Would the worse off jurisdiction have gained compared with the better off one over the period? The answer is yes in absolute percentage points (25 percentage point difference in the earlier period and 12.5 in the later period) but no in relative terms (twice as many pupils falling below in both periods). For some observers, the absolute progress of the worse off district would have them conclude that they were not as worse off in the later period. To see this argument more clearly, substitute 8 and 4 percent in the later period and then make the judgment. Influencing this comparison is the fact that the scope of the problem is not as severe in the later time period, or, in other words, each percentage point has more "meaning" at the higher levels. However, since some observers would still focus on the relative comparisons, both should be examined.

The lower panel of Table 11.14 displays several variables that can help interpret the trends in the percentage of pupils below the statewide minimums. The first two data columns compare the percentages below the statewide minimum in relative terms by dividing the percentage in New York City by either the statewide percentage (NYC/NYS) or the percentage in New York State without New York City (NYC/NYS-NYC). The third data column is the absolute percentage point difference between New York City and the rest of the state. The final three data columns are the ratios of test takers to enrollment for New York State, New York City, and the rest of the state, respectively, for years when these data are reported. New York City's attendance to enrollment ratio is consistently in the mid to high 80 percent levels, while the rest of the state is consistently in the high 90 percent levels. Some of this difference is due to the higher percentage of non-English speaking and handicapped pupils in New York City who are excused from the test, but some of the difference is also due to the lower attendance rates in New York City.

How has New York City fared relative to the rest of the state in third grade reading achievement? Since a change in the form of the test occurred in 1983, the 1967 to 1982 period is examined first. The most striking trend over this period is the relatively consistent and dramatic decline in the *absolute* percentage point difference in pupils below the statewide minimum in New York City and in the rest of the state. In 1967 there was close to a 30 percentage point difference that had been reduced to about 16 percent by 1982. In relative terms, New York City was not better off, with about three times as high a percentage below the statewide minimum at the beginning and end of the period. This is where a judgment must be introduced, however, and most (but not all) observers would probably conclude that New York City is *relatively* better off in 1982 when 24.5 and 7.8 percent are below the minimum in New York City and the rest of the state, respectively, compared with 1967 when 46.5 and 16.8 percent were below the minimum in New York City and the rest of the state, respectively.

TABLE 11.14

Third Grade Reading Scores, 1967–1986

	All New York State		New York City		New York State Without NYC	
	Below State Minimum					
Year	Number	Percentage	Number	Percentage	Number	Percentage
1967	64,125	26.2%	36,178	46.5%	27,947	16.8%
1968	65,170	26.3	36,279	46.5	28,891	17.1
1969	60,295	24.6	31,178	42.8	29,117	16.9
1970	66,788	25.9	36,612	46.4	30,176	16.9
1971	68,722	26.7	37,089	46.5	31,633	17.8
1972	69,408	26.6	37,841	45.4	31,567	17.8
1973	63,667	24.7	33,925	41.7	29,742	16.9
1974	60,868	24.7	33,309	42.3	27,559	16.4
1975	53,071	22.6	28,503	38.2	24,568	15.3
1976	45,797	20.7	25,464	37.6	20,333	13.3
1977	39,965	19.0	21,669	34.5	18,296	12.4
1978	35,595	16.9	19,278	30.9	16,317	11.0
1979	31,367	14.8	17,693	28.1	13,674	9.2
1980	24,964	12.5	13,646	22.5	11,318	8.2
1981	22,599	12.6	13,078	23.3	9,521	7.8
1982	22,831	13.3	13,840	24.5	8,991	7.8
1983	NR	24.4	NR	43.8	NR	14.5
1984	NR	22.8	NR	41.9	NR	13.0
1985	NR	22.1	NR	41.8	NR	11.4
1986	NR	20.9	NR	39.6	NR	10.3

TABLE 11.14 (continued)

Year	Percentage Below Minimum		Absolute Percentage Points NYC Below Rest of State	Test Takers/Attendance Ratios		
	NYC/NYS	NYC/NYS-NYC		NYS	NYC	NYS-NYC
1967	1.775	2.778	29.8	96.4%	91.1%	99.1%
1968	1.766	2.728	29.5	93.2	90.1	94.7
1969	1.742	2.537	26.0	92.4	83.9	96.6
1970	1.790	2.749	29.5	94.4	87.7	97.7
1971	1.739	2.605	28.6	94.0	88.2	96.9
1972	1.705	2.551	27.6	95.0	90.0	97.6
1973	1,687	2,470	24.8	96.0	91.8	98.1
1974	1.714	2,577	25.9	93.8	86.0	97.9
1975	1.690	2.491	22.9	95.9	90.9	98.3
1976	1.815	2,836	24.3	94.3	86.9	98.0
1977	1.818	2.787	22.1	94.2	86.1	98.1
1978	1.831	2.813	19.9	94.3	86.5	98.1
1979	1.896	3.055	18.9	93.3	83.8	98.0
1980	1.791	2.745	14.3	94.8	87.6	98.3
1981	1.845	3.006	15.5	94.4	87.1	98.2
1982	1.846	3.148	16.7	94.2	87.4	98.0
1983	1.795	3.028	29.3	NA	NA	NA
1984	1.838	3.222	28.9	NA	NA	NA
1985	1.891	3.678	30.4	NA	NA	NA
1986	1.895	3.839	29.3	NA	NA	NA

SOURCE: New York State Department of Education, Bureau of Elementary and Secondary Testing Programs.

NOTES: NR = not reported; NA = not applicable.

339

In 1983 the State's judgment about what constitutes the acceptable minimum increased substantially simultaneously with a change in the form of the test. This increased the percentage of pupils below the statewide minimum in both New York City and the rest of the state. The result is that New York City's relative and absolute positions compared with the rest of the state in 1986 are close to the worst they have been during the entire time period. Also, New York City's relative performance was not changing appreciably relative to the rest of the state during both the 1980–1982 and the 1983–1986 periods.

Sixth grade reading scores are displayed in an identical format in Table 11.15. Changes in the test and the minimum occurred in 1980, 1982, and 1986. In addition, there appears to be a problem in the 1982 data with the number actually or reportedly taking the test in New York City.[30]

The data suggest that performance in New York City has not gained substantially compared with the rest of the state over most of the period. The results for 1986 show some improvement for New York City relative to the rest of the state, but with only one data point and a new form of the test, any generalization should be avoided.

The overall trends in mathematics achievement in both third and sixth grades are similar to those in reading achievement. (See Tables 11.16 and 11.17). For the third grade, the form of the test and the statewide minimum were changed in 1983 and 1986. Between 1967 and 1982 the trend was a reduction in percentage below the minimum in the entire state, with the *absolute* difference between New York City and the rest of the state in the percentage below the statewide minimum also declining over the period. A similar trend was not evident in the *relative* difference which declined from 1967 to 1973, but was higher from 1978 to 1982. The data from 1983 to 1986 do not show appreciable changes in the absolute differences between New York City and the rest of the state, although the relative differences have become quite large.

For sixth grade mathematics, the form of the test and the statewide minimums also were changed in 1983 and 1986. In *absolute* terms New York City began and ended the entire period at roughly the same level relative to the rest of the state. In *relative* terms there has been some slippage for New York City compared with the rest of the state in the most recent years.

Before summarizing these trends, what about the current situation? The most recent (1986) data for the percentage of pupils below the statewide minimums are:

Grade Subject	New York City	Rest of the State
Third Reading	39.6%	10.3%
Sixth Reading	36.7	13.6
Third Mathematics	31.6	4.5
Sixth Mathematics	36.5	8.6

The results are quite consistent and if the statewide minimums are valid numbers, then the pupils leaving the third and sixth grades in New York City are far likelier to be in need of remedial attention than the pupils in the rest of the state. Do differences such as these argue for change in the State education system? While many agree that they do, the concluding section of this essay considers why consensus on the nature of the change is not a simple matter.

The trends in achievement scores are more clear-cut for the sixth grade than for the third grade. For sixth grade reading and mathematics achievement scores over the 1967–1986 period, generally between two and three times the percentage of pupils are below the statewide minimums in New York City than in the rest of the state. The absolute difference in pupils below the statewide minimum is consistently in the 25 to 30 percentage point range. Thus, for the most part sixth grade output measures in New York City relative to the rest of the state have not changed dramatically over the past 20 years.

For third grade reading and mathematics achievement scores, there was a decline in the absolute percentage point difference in pupils below the statewide minimum for New York City and the rest of the state between 1967 and 1982. However, the new test and the more stringent cutoff implemented in 1983, which created much larger percentage point differences, raises questions about the validity of the improving trends. Such a drastic, unfavorable change after the implementation of the new test and cutoff would not have occurred if the previous assessment standards were valid. The most recent test results paint a picture very similar to the situation in the early 1970s in terms of absolute differences between New York City and the rest of the state. However, it is likely that expectations and the statewide minimums are more demanding in the 1980s than they were in the 1960s.

CONCLUSIONS

In many ways, public K–12 education in New York City is different from public education in other large cities. National comparisons show that while most major cities spend more per pupil than the statewide

TABLE 11.15

Sixth Grade Reading Scores, 1967–1986

| Year | Below State Minimum | | | | | |
| | All New York State | | New York City | | New York State Without NYC | |
	Number	Percentage	Number	Percentage	Number	Percentage
1967	59,449	26.2%	32,391	44.8%	27,058	17.5%
1968	61,655	26.6	32,371	44.2	29,284	18.5
1969	60,373	25.8	28,876	42.9	31,497	18.9
1970	69,671	28.4	34,739	47.7	34,932	20.3
1971	75,469	30.1	37,887	50.3	37,582	21.5
1972	76,426	30.4	37,110	49.7	39,316	22.3
1973	75,667	29.8	35,714	48.1	39,953	22.3
1974	75,875	30.2	37,064	50.6	38,811	21.8
1975	76,750	30.6	36,845	49.8	39,905	22.5
1976	73,153	29.7	34,625	49.0	38,528	22.0
1977	67,365	28.9	31,931	47.4	35,434	21.4
1978	60,895	27.8	29,187	45.9	31,708	20.4
1979	52,445	25.3	25,124	41.7	27,321	18.6
1980	81,135	40.1	36,394	60.4	44,741	31.5
1981	78,532	38.3	36,899	60.4	41,643	28.9
1982	65,377	30.3	37,210	52.3	28,167	19.5
1983	NR	23.8	NR	43.2	NR	15.5
1984	NR	22.5	NR	40.0	NR	14.7
1985	NR	21.7	NR	41.1	NR	12.5
1986	NR	21.2	NR	36.7	NR	13.6

TABLE 11.15 (*continued*)

Year	Percentage Below Minimum		Absolute Percentage Points NYC Below Rest of State	Test Takers/Attendance Ratios		
	NYC/NYS	NYC/NYS-NYC		NYS	NYC	NYS-NYC
1967	1.709	2.557	27.3	97.3%	93.1%	99.3%
1968	1.660	2.389	25.7	92.7	90.2	93.9
1969	1.663	2.270	24.0	91.5	81.9	96.1
1970	1.680	2.356	27.5	94.3	87.8	97.3
1971	1.668	2.341	28.8	94.0	88.5	96.6
1972	1.634	2.233	27.5	94.2	88.5	96.8
1973	1.614	2.162	25.9	95.7	90.9	97.8
1974	1.676	2.321	28.8	92.8	82.5	97.7
1975	1.631	2.214	27.3	96.0	91.6	97.9
1976	1.647	2.228	27.0	94.1	85.8	97.9
1977	1.639	2.216	26.0	94.2	86.6	97.7
1978	1.652	2.252	25.5	94.5	87.5	97.7
1979	1.649	2.247	23.2	93.3	84.2	97.7
1980	1.505	1.917	28.9	95.0	88.5	98.1
1981	1.579	2.091	31.5	94.7	88.1	97.8
1982	1.725	2.683	32.8	98.0	98.4	97.8
1983	1.815	2.788	27.7	NA	NA	NA
1984	1.778	2.714	25.3	NA	NA	NA
1985	1.894	3.278	28.6	NA	NA	NA
1986	1.731	2.708	23.1	NA	NA	NA

SOURCE: New York State Department of Education, Bureau of Elementary and Secondary Testing Programs.

NOTES: NR = not reported; NA = not applicable.

TABLE 11.16
Third Grade Mathematics Scores, 1967–1986

	Below State Minimum					
	All New York State		New York City		New York State Without NYC	
Year	Number	Percentage	Number	Percentage	Number	Percentage
1967	62,610	25.7%	41,903	54.4%	20,707	12.4%
1968	60,525	24.6	39,378	50.8	21,147	12.5
1969	51,869	21.3	30,379	42.7	21,490	12.5
1970	56,725	21.9	35,714	44.7	21,011	11.7
1971	53,189	20.9	30,445	39.4	22,744	12.8
1972	53,706	20.8	31,660	38.7	22,046	12.5
1973	49,374	19.3	28,345	35.5	21,029	12.0
1974	48,172	19.8	29,057	38.2	19,115	11.4
1975	41,994	18.1	24,689	34.1	17,305	10.8
1976	35,352	16.3	20,489	32.1	14,863	9.7
1977	29,932	14.6	16,199	27.7	13,733	9.3
1978	30,639	14.6	18,435	29.9	12,204	8.2
1979	26,016	12.4	15,981	26.1	10,035	6.8
1980	22,310	11.3	13,609	23.0	8,701	6.3
1981	24,508	13.5	17,302	29.2	7,206	5.9
1982	20,344	11.9	13,235	23.7	7,109	6.2
1983	NR	21.4	NR	39.2	NR	12.4
1984	NR	20.0	NR	38.5	NR	10.5
1985	NR	18.3	NR	37.0	NR	8.2
1986	NR	14.3	NR	31.6	NR	4.5

TABLE 11.16 (continued)

Year	Percentage Below Minimum		Absolute Percentage Points NYC Below Rest of State	Test Takers/Attendance Ratios		
	NYC/NYS	NYC/NYS-NYC		NYS	NYC	NYS-NYC
1967	2.116	4.373	41.9	96.0%	90.3%	99.0%
1968	2.070	4.062	38.3	92.8	89.5	94.4
1969	1.999	3.412	30.2	91.6	82.1	96.2
1970	2.039	3.805	33.0	94.8	88.9	97.7
1971	1.885	3.070	26.6	93.0	85.3	96.8
1972	1.866	3.109	26.3	94.3	88.3	97.4
1973	1.837	2.965	23.5	95.4	90.2	97.9
1974	1.929	3.342	26.7	92.7	83.2	97.7
1975	1.882	3.141	23.2	94.7	88.4	97.9
1976	1.968	3.302	22.4	92.5	82.0	97.7
1977	1.906	2.975	18.4	92.0	80.1	97.8
1978	2.050	3.636	21.7	93.8	85.4	97.9
1979	2.105	3.863	19.4	92.3	81.3	97.7
1980	2.031	3.643	16.7	94.0	85.5	98.1
1981	2,164	4.958	23.3	95.9	92.0	97.9
1982	1.990	3.833	17.5	93.7	86.5	97.6
1983	1.832	3.154	26.8	NA	NA	NA
1984	1.925	3.660	28.0	NA	NA	NA
1985	2.022	4.501	28.8	NA	NA	NA
1986	2.210	7.096	27.1	NA	NA	NA

SOURCE: New York State Department of Education, Bureau of Elementary and Secondary Testing Programs.

NOTES: NR = not reported; NA = not applicable.

TABLE 11.17
Sixth Grade Mathematics Scores, 1967–1986

Year	All New York State		New York City		New York State without NYC	
	Number	Percentage	Number	Percentage	Number	Percentage
			Below State Minimum			
1967	57,579	25.5%	33,733	46.6%	23,846	15.5%
1968	63,235	27.4	35,852	49.1	27,383	17.3
1969	61,623	26.6	30,385	46.4	31,238	18.8
1970	72,142	29.4	37,295	51.1	34,847	20.2
1971	79,440	31.8	40,170	53.5	39,270	22.5
1972	79,356	31.8	36,913	50.6	42,443	24.1
1973	80,559	31.9	36,889	50.3	43,670	24.4
1974	84,265	33.8	38,650	53.7	45,615	25.7
1975	85,501	34.3	38,826	53.4	46,675	26.4
1976	81,560	33.3	37,018	52.8	44,542	25.5
1977	75,699	32.5	34,668	51.4	41,031	24.8
1978	68,682	31.4	31,338	49.6	37,344	24.0
1979	61,412	29.6	29,767	49.1	31,645	21.6
1980	56,347	27.9	27,588	45.9	28,759	20.3
1981	55,422	26.9	28,233	45.7	27,189	18.8
1982	57,992	27.2	29,851	45.0	28,141	19.2
1983	NR	24.3	NR	43.3	NR	16.3
1984	NR	22.5	NR	41.2	NR	14.2
1985	NR	20.3	NR	40.0	NR	11.1
1986	NR	17.8	NR	36.5	NR	8.6

TABLE 11.17 (continued)

Year	Percentage Below Minimum		Absolute Percentage Points NYC Below Rest of State	Test Takers/Attendance Ratios		
	NYC/NYS	NYC/NYS-NYC		NYS	NYC	NYS-NYC
1967	1.831	3.007	31.1	97.1%	93.0%	99.1%
1968	1.794	2.833	31.8	92.4	89.9	93.6
1969	1.747	2.473	27.6	90.6	79.6	95.8
1970	1.738	2.528	30.9	94.3	88.0	97.2
1971	1.682	2.380	31.0	93.8	88.1	96.5
1972	1.589	2.101	26.5	93.5	86.6	96.7
1973	1.578	2.065	25.9	95.3	89.8	97.7
1974	1.588	2.087	27.9	92.1	81.2	97.4
1975	1.558	2.022	27.0	95.3	90.1	97.6
1976	1.586	2.074	27.4	93.7	85.1	97.6
1977	1.581	2.073	26.6	94.1	86.7	97.5
1978	1.578	2.063	25.6	94.2	86.9	97.5
1979	1.658	2.276	27.5	93.4	84.8	97.5
1980	1.645	2.263	25.6	94.9	88.3	98.1
1981	1.699	2.425	26.9	95.1	89.1	97.9
1982	1.652	2.344	25.8	95.0	88.5	98.2
1983	1.782	2.658	27.0	NA	NA	NA
1984	1.831	2.909	27.0	NA	NA	NA
1985	1.970	3.588	28.9	NA	NA	NA
1986	2.051	4.257	27.9	NA	NA	NA

SOURCE: New York State Department of Education, Bureau of Elementary and Secondary Testing Programs.

NOTES: NR = not reported; NA = not applicable.

average, this relationship is reversed for New York City and New York State. A more detailed analysis of expenditures per pupil in New York City and the rest of the state documented lower spending in New York City since 1978. When adjustments are made for different prices and student needs, the differences in the most recent years are about 20 percent. These lower levels of resources make a powerful statement about how New York City stands in the State's system of public K–12 education.

A substantial part of the disparity between New York City and the rest of the state can be traced to the State aid system. New York City's share of State aid is lower than its share of statewide enrollment. This gap has narrowed over the past 20 years, and a critical question is whether the trend toward greater State aid for New York City will continue to the point where expenditures per pupil there are comparable to those in the rest of the state.

A post-fiscal crisis decline in New York City's status relative to the rest of the state is evident in the ratios of teachers and professional staff to pupils. Teacher layoffs increased New York City's ratios of pupils per teacher (and professional staff) relative to these ratios in the rest of the state, and class size has remained larger in New York City than in the rest of the state from the mid 1970s to the present. More positive is the overall reduction in the ratio of pupils to teachers in both New York City and the rest of the state throughout this period.

In relation to the neighboring counties, teacher salaries declined in New York City during the period after the fiscal crisis. Most recently there has been some improvement in New York City's relative position for starting teachers, but it will be important (and costly) for this recent change to spread to teacher compensation across the salary scale.

Because of the numerous changes in tests and statewide minimums, it is not possible to draw definitive conclusions on trends in reading and mathematics achievement over the past 20 years. The evidence indicates that there may have been some progress in New York City relative to the rest of the state in the third grade results, at least through 1982, but the most recent data suggest that New York City is still far behind the rest of the state. The significant disparity between New York City and the rest of the state is apparent through the 20 year period for the sixth grade results in reading and mathematics, although there were some promising results in 1986.

The disparity in achievement scores between New York City and the rest of the state can be viewed in at least two ways. First, from a pupil perspective, the fact that about 36 percent of third and sixth grade pupils are below statewide minimums (indicating that they may not reach minimum competency levels by high school) compared with about 9 percent in the rest of the state is an unsatisfactory situation. Simply stated, children should be able to leave schools better prepared. Second, from an education production perspective, given the resources available to the schools and the background and abilities of the students, it is not easy to conclude whether or not the schools in New York City are doing well or poorly. It may be that with the pupil population and available resources the schools are doing as well as can be expected. Not only are these two points not contradictory, but a conclusion on the second point is necessary in order to make progress on the first point. The difficulty in knowing how well the schools are doing given their task and resources is indicative of the absence of a "quick fix" to provide the educational outcomes that all children deserve.

Given the current authority and organizational structure in public K–12 education, the pressing issue is who is responsible for the present state of affairs in New York City. Taking elementary education as an example, each school has some responsibility for its own situation, but until recently the school has not typically been used as the policy relevant decision point in elementary education.[31] Each school is expected to make the most of its available resources and student population, but schools have not been evaluated in this manner. In New York City the community school district is responsible for elementary education in its geographic jurisdiction, but the division of responsibilities for elementary education between the Board of Education and the community school district is not absolute. At the top of the formal hierarchy is the Board of Regents and State Department of Education who have overall responsibility for education in the state. Standing somewhere on the sidelines (depending on the particular issue) are the governor and mayor, and setting many of the rules is the legislature. Clearly, there is no *single* button to push to move the system in a positive direction, but instead a series of players, each with somewhat different agendas and perspectives. Perhaps it will be necessary for one of the players to take on the dominant role if significant progress is to result. The Board of Education and the chancellor are the most obvious sources of leadership, but their authority over elementary schools is complicated by the decentralized system.

The size of New York City as a school district, the presence of community school districts, the power of the mayor, and the legislative politics create a different education decision process for New York City than for any other school district in the state. The solutions to the financial problems documented in this essay are probably easier to identify than the solutions to other educational problems. But both New York City and New York State operate in a world of scarce resources, so that more money for education in New York City usually means less money for other services in New York City or less money for other services in the state. The key financial decision point is the budget process where both the legislature and governor have some leverage, but in the past the legislature has altered school financing proposals put forward by governors and the Board of Regents to treat New York City and other districts more equitably.

While the solutions for the educational problems are more elusive, apparently there will be more active participants in the process. New York City's chancellor has issued reasonably strict standards to apply to individual schools; the State Education Department is identifying schools that do not meet certain criteria; New York City is reducing class size in the lower grades, has expanded the all-day kindergarten program, and is now developing a program for 4-year-olds; specific components of school aid have been set aside for teachers' salaries, early grade intervention, and dropout programs; and the Board of Regents is implementing a comprehensive action plan. A board-level review of the community school districts and an assessment of the school system's capital needs are now being planned. These are promising trends, but there is a long way to go.

NOTES

1. See U.S. Bureau of the Census, *Finances of Public School Systems in 1983–84* (Washington, DC: U.S. Government Printing Office, December 1985). Fiscal 1984 is the most recent year for which national data are available. In the census data the federal share includes federal aid *redistributed* by the state. The state share has been about 45 percent since 1980; however, the federal share has declined from 8.9 percent in 1980 and the local share has increased.
2. Data from U.S. Department of Education, Center for Statistics; enrollment for fall 1983.
3. Data from U.S. Bureau of the Census, *Finances of Public School Systems in 1983–84*. These figures differ somewhat from the more detailed data from New York State examined later in the essay.
4. In 1985–1986, enrollment in public schools in New York City was 22 percent white, non-Hispanic, while the comparable figure for the rest of the State was 86 percent. Data from the State Education Department, Information Center on Education, *Racial/Ethnic Distribution of Public Students and Staff*, 1986, table 1.
5. See Katherine Trent and Richard D. Alba, "Population," in this volume.
6. Data from the New York State Education Department, Information Center on Education; figures for Fall 1986.
7. It is worth emphasizing that the data in Table 11.1 are being used for *national* comparisons. Census data are rarely as accurate as data gathered at the state level; however, comparability is sacrificed when interstate comparisons are made using state level data. The validity and comparability of the census data are sufficient to identify general relationships at

the national level. More detailed state data are used for New York City—New York State comparisons later in this essay.

8. Phoenix was excluded because the school district organization prevents city-state comparisons; Washington, DC, has no state government counterpart; and Honolulu is part of the single school district that covers Hawaii.

9. Data from the 1980 census, as reported in U.S. Bureau of the Census, *County and City Data Book, 1983* (Washington, DC: U.S. Government Printing Office, 1983). For additional information on private schools in New York City, see Robert Berne, "Education," in Charles Brecher and Raymond D. Horton, *Setting Municipal Priorities, 1986* (New York: New York University Press, 1985).

10. Current operating expenditure excludes capital and debt service expenditures and also excludes payments made by a school district to another level of government.

11. During the late 1970s and early 1980s, both the Maryland and New York State school finance systems were challenged, in part on the basis of the treatment of Baltimore and New York City, respectively. Neither case was successful. For more details on the case in New York State, see Joel S. Berke, Margaret E. Goertz, and Richard J. Coley, *Politicians, Judges, and City Schools: Reforming School Finance in New York* (New York: Russell Sage Foundation, 1984).

12. As defined by New York State, approved operating expenses (AOE) are the day-to-day operating expenses of the schools funded from *state* and *local* sources. Excluded are expenses for building construction, transportation of pupils, payments made to purchase services from a Board of Cooperative Educational Services (BOCES), tuition payments to other districts, and expenses for programs that do not conform to law or regulation. Also excluded are all expenses funded by federal aid, proceeds from borrowing, and state aid for a few experimental programs and for textbooks. For a more precise definition of AOE, see New York State Education Department, Form SA 122, and the *Annual Financial Report*, ST- 3.

13. Throughout this chapter, a school year such as 1984—1985 is referred to by the latter year, in this case 1985.

14. For more details on this price index, see Wayne Wendling, "Cost of Education Indices," discussion paper prepared for the New York State Special Task Force on Equity and Excellence in Education, Education Commission of the States, Denver, Colorado, October 23, 1979.

15. The weights, defined as the extra cost of educating a pupil in a particular category, were developed for the New York State Special Task Force on Equity and Excellence in Education. The weights are as follows: handicapped pupils in special classes = 2.00; handicapped pupils in resource rooms = 1.00; speech-impaired pupils = 0.15; pupils with special education needs = 0.35; bilingual pupils = 0.40. Using these weights and the data for pupils in these categories for one year, pupil weights were calculated for New York City and the rest of the State and applied to all years in the time series. For more details on the weightings, see New York State Education Department, "Providing State Aid for the Education of Children with Handicapping Conditions Based on a Study of Program Costs," a report required by Chapter 789 of the Laws of

1978, pt. 2, November 1979; and J. M. Gaughan and R. J. Glasheen, "Study on Special Pupil Needs, Interim Report," New York State Special Task Force on Equity and Excellence in Education, November 1979. The weightings used in this analysis are slightly different from the weights currently used in New York State school finance laws. The differences should not have any effects on the conclusions.

16. Federal aid is often excluded when analyzing the finances of public K–12 education because federal aid is viewed as supplementing rather than supplanting state and local revenues. In practice some federal aid replaces state and local revenues.

17. Property values, though "equalized," are subject to numerous planned and unplanned complications that make them less than perfect measures of property wealth. Foremost among the issues is the lag that is incorporated in the property assessment and equalization procedures. Nonetheless, the State's education finance system uses this measure and it is probably the best measure available. For a discussion of the problems related to lags in the current procedures, see Robert F. Jones, "Equalization Rates: The Argument for a More Current Value Standard" (Albany: New York State Board of Equalization and Assessment, January 29, 1985). This report indicates that the growth of full value of property in New York City has exceeded the statewide average in the most recent period although this is not yet reflected in the equalized values.

18. This entire analysis assumes that the local revenues for education in New York City are generated from the property tax. Since New York City's local contributions to education come from the general fund it is impossible to attribute specific revenue sources such as the property, sales, and income taxes to a particular function. The assumption is used to compare New York City with other districts in the state.

19. For a review of this process, see Susan Fuhrman, "Politics and Process of School Finance Reform," *Journal of Education Finance* 4, no. 2 (Fall 1978):158–178.

20. Joan Scheuer, "The Equity of New York State's System of Financing Schools: An Update," *Journal of Education Finance* 9, no. 1 (Summer 1983):95.

21. *New York Times*, March 26, 1986, p. A22.

22. Stanley Moses and Edwin Margolis, "Why Equal Education Opportunity Cannot Be Achieved in New York," *New York Affairs* 9, no. 3 (1986): 111–121.

23. For more details on the aid system, see the publications of the Education Unit, New York State Division of the Budget, "Description of New York State Aid Programs," published annually; and Joan Scheuer, *State Aid for City Schools: A Handbook for Policy Makers* (New York: New York City Board of Education, January 1985). Also see the publications of the New York State School Boards Association.

24. Data from the State Education Department, Information Center on Education, *Annual Educational Summary, 1983–84*, pp. 8 and 27.

25. Professional staff who are not teachers are those who spend more than 50 percent of their time at professional nonteaching duties. They include principals, assistant principals, guidance counselors, and others.

26. Carnegie Task Force on Teaching as a Profession, *A Nation Prepared: Teachers for the 21st Century*, May 1986, p. 99.

27. See Constancia Warren, "Teaching in New York City, 1986: A Profession in Crisis," unpublished paper, April 1986, pp. 6–7, for a discussion of the "aging out" of New York City's teachers.
28. These tests are given to private and public school pupils; however, only the results for public school pupils are reported in this essay.
29. Not all handicapped pupils took the standardized tests. But in 1981–1982, for example, 7,976 handicapped pupils took the third grade reading test, 3,008 of whom were in New York City.
30. In 1982 the State Education Department reports that 71,182 pupils took the test in New York City. This compares with 61,058 in 1981 and 55,874 in 1983. The unusual increase in 1982 raises some question about the figure.
31. Recent initiatives of the chancellor regarding standards and other issues such as tenure for principals are related to school-based accountability.

12

HEALTH CARE

Kenneth E. Thorpe

H EALTH care is a major industry in New York State, accounting
for 8 percent of all private sector jobs and generating over
$35 billion in expenditures.[1] New Yorkers spend more per
capita on health care than people in every state except
Massachusetts. Health care spending in New York City is especially high,
totaling $2,200 per capita in 1984, 52 percent above the national
average.[2] The State of New York and the City of New York account for
a substantial share of this health care spending. Fiscal year 1984 spending
under the State's Medicaid program, which pays for care to the poor,
totaled $6.4 billion, with $4.3 billion spent in New York City alone. In
addition, the City of New York contributed $598 million of local revenue
in a recent year to help support the Health and Hospitals Corporation
(HHC), which operates municipal hospitals.[3]

Clearly, the State and City governments have major roles in forging
health policy. To provide an understanding of the State-City relationships in developing health policy, this essay will focus on one component:
hospital rate setting. The focus on hospital policy is not myopic,
however, as over $12 billion, or 37 percent of all New York State health
care spending, flows through hospitals each year.[4] It is also hospitals, and
the private companies selling and purchasing hospital insurance, who are
the most active political actors in this arena of public policy.

To provide the necessary background for understanding health policy in New York State and New York City, the first section describes relevant features of the industry statewide and highlights distinguishing features of health care in New York City. The second section analyzes the State-City interactions during a three phase history of expanded State regulation of hospital payments—the immediate post-Medicaid period, the fiscal crisis era, and the current stage of State experimentation with comprehensive regulations. The conclusion of the essay considers more explicitly the implications of State hospital payment policy for the City of New York and its health care programs.

HEALTH AND HEALTH CARE IN NEW YORK CITY AND NEW YORK STATE

Health policy in New York State is shaped, in part, by the characteristics of the state's population and health care sector. These characteristics include the health status of the population, the supply of health facilities and providers, and patient utilization patterns.

Health Status

Several indicators suggest that the health status of New York City residents is worse than that of residents of either the rest of the state or the nation as a whole. (See Table 12.1.) Most notably, the mortality rate (deaths per 100,000 population) is significantly higher in New York City, totaling 1,050 compared with the national average of 870 and the statewide average of 960. The largest contributor to the relatively high mortality rate in the city is the large number of deaths from ischemic heart disease. The incidence of heart disease in New York City is significantly higher than in other major metropolitan areas as well as higher than in the rest of New York State. The higher mortality rate from ischemic heart disease reflects, in part, New York City's relatively larger population of elderly.

Infant mortality is also significantly higher in New York City, totaling 13.6 deaths per 1,000 live births. This compared with 10.9 and 10.6 at the state and national levels, respectively. The infant mortality rate in New York City remains higher than either the state or national average, though the difference has narrowed over time. While the exact relationship between prenatal care and birth outcomes remains unknown, a portion of the relatively higher infant death rate is probably the result of fewer New York City women receiving adequate prenatal care. Nearly

TABLE 12.1

Health Status Indicators for New York City, New York State, and the United States

	United States	New York State	New York City
Total Deaths per 100,000 Population[a]	870	960	1,050
Deaths from Heart Disease per 100,000 Population[a]	330	410	470
Infant Deaths per 1,000 Live Births[b]	10.6	10.9	13.6
Percentage of Mothers Receiving Late or No Prenatal Care[c]	5.6	9.2	17.5
Number of AIDS Cases[d]	28,000	10,000	9,000

SOURCES: United Hospital Fund, *Health and Health Care in New York City, 1986* (New York: UHF, 1986); and New York City Department of Health, unpublished data.

[a]Death rates are based on 1984 data and not adjusted for age.

[b]Based on 1984 data.

[c]U.S. figure is for 1984; New York figures are for 1985.

[d]Cumulative cases to 1985.

one woman in five in the city received inadequate prenatal care compared with nearly one woman in ten at the state level.

In addition to its significantly higher infant and overall mortality rates, New York City has a greater incidence of communicable diseases. Most notable has been the tremendous rate of growth in Acquired Immune Deficiency Syndrome (AIDS) cases. New York City residents accounted for over one case in three of AIDS reported nationally by 1985, and 90 percent of all cases in New York State.

Health Services Supply

Ironically, while many health status indicators for New York City are worse than the comparable state or national figures, health care providers are abundant in the city. New York City and New York State have a substantially larger supply of physicians than nearly any other city or state in the country. As of 1984, over 3 physicians per 1,000 population practiced medicine in New York City.[5] In contrast, 30 percent of all counties in New York State had fewer than 1 physician per 1,000 population. On the average, 2.5 physicians for each 1,000 residents practiced in New York State, while the national average totaled 1.7 physicians per 1,000 population.

Despite the aggregate surplus, physician location decisions do not necessarily match health care needs. Physicians selectively locate in high income areas, leaving portions of the city underserved. For instance, within New York City physician/population ratios range from 7.4 per 1,000 residents in Manhattan to 1.8 in Brooklyn.[6]

New York State and New York City also have relatively generous supplies of hospital beds. General care hospital beds per 1,000 population in New York City and statewide totaled over 4.5 compared with 4.3 nationally.[7] The average size of a hospital in New York City is substantially larger than the state or national averages. Average number of beds per hospital in the city totaled 405—over twice the national average and 100 beds greater than the statewide average. Growth in the average size of New York City hospitals is related to recent closures among small proprietary and municipal hospitals.

New York City accounts for the largest concentration of academic medical centers and specialty hospitals in the United States. Patients throughout the country, and in some cases the world, are attracted to the specialized care available in New York City. About 100,000 patients annually, over 10 percent of all admissions in city hospitals, are not New York City residents.[8]

New York City also has the largest concentration of teaching hospitals in the country. While the city accounts for 3 percent of the nation's population, the city's hospitals account for 10.5 percent of all residency positions.[9] Of the 70 general care hospitals in the city, 69 percent, compared with 9 percent nationally, are involved in teaching activity.

Finally, the City of New York operates the largest local public hospital system—the Health and Hospitals Corporation (HHC)—in the country. The HHC's 11 acute care and 4 long-term care facilities account for annual expenditures of over $2 billion.[10] The HHC accounts for 20 percent of New York City's inpatient admissions and 43 percent of hospital based ambulatory care visits.[11] The HHC is also a major source of local employment, with nearly 49,000 workers (including affiliated staff) in 1985.[12]

Utilization

New York City hospitals have traditionally experienced relatively high occupancy rates and long lengths of stay. Since 1980, occupancy rates in the city have been about 10 percentage points or more above the national average. In 1985 New York City hospitals had an average occupancy rate of 88 percent compared with 69 percent nationally.[13] However, the occupancy rates nationally have been declining steadily since 1980 while they have been nearly constant in New York City and New York State until very recently. A 1986 survey by the Greater New York Hospital Association indicated a recent decline in medical/surgical occupancy rates of the city's voluntary hospitals to 80 percent.[14] Despite this short-term decline in hospital utilization, the rapidly growing AIDS population may increase the demand for hospital beds. This recent trend has generated debate regarding the "appropriate" number of beds needed in New York City.

An abundant bed supply and high occupancy rates suggest unusually high demand for hospital care in New York City. In fact, total hospital days per 1,000 population in the city was 1,416 in 1985, significantly above the national average yet lower than the statewide figure of 1,442. (See Table 12.2.) The rate of hospital admissions in New York City also exceeds both the national average and state average.[15] New York City hospitals have long lengths of hospital stay, 2 to 3 days longer than the national average. According to the latest data available, length of stay nationally was 7.3 days whereas in New York City it totaled 9 days.[16] A number of factors account for the differences in hospital utilization patterns including the relative lack of off-sight ambulatory care services in New York City, the State's relatively high payments for hospitalized Medicaid patients (especially those awaiting placement in long-term care facilities), and New York State's relatively late movement onto Medicare's hospital case payment system. The large volume of patients in hospitals waiting for placement in long-term care facilities explains much of the observed longer lengths of stay in New York City. Indeed, one

TABLE 12.2

Patterns of Hospital Utilization in New York City,
New York State, and the United States, 1985

	United States	New York State	New York City
Hospital Beds per 1,000 Population	4.3	4.6	4.5
Average Occupancy Rate	69.0	86.0	87.0
Hospital Days per 1,000 Population	1,097	1,442	1,416
Average Length of Stay	7.3	9.6	8.9
Hospital Admissions per 1,000 Population	150.2	149.8	158.2

SOURCE: American Hospital Association, *Annual Survey of Hospitals* (Chicago: AHA, 1985).

recent study indicated that the hospital backlog problem was the most important determinant of New York City's relatively long length of stay.[17]

Spending

Expenditures for personal health care services in New York State and New York City are substantial, exceeding $30 billion and $15.5 billion, respectively, in 1984.[18] This is equivalent to nearly $2,200 per New York City resident, far in excess of the state per capita average of $1,700 and national average of $1,446. High spending levels reflect, in part, greater underlying demand for care—stimulated through a larger need for services, the substantial financial commitment made by the State and City through the Medicaid program, and the large concentration of academic medical centers and public hospitals.

However, higher spending for hospital care in the city is also related to higher unit costs of services. Hospital expenses per admission in the city hospitals are 23 percent higher than the statewide average of $3,930, although they are similar to expenses in other major northeastern cities.[19] In 1985, expenses per admission in general care hospitals in the city averaged $4,818, ranking it only the sixth highest among the 20 largest cities.[20]

Higher costs in New York City relative to the state average reflect the significantly higher costs associated with graduate medical education, higher wage rates, and a more severely ill patient mix. These high costs, however, are predominantly concentrated in New York City's major academic medical centers and public hospital system. Unit costs in other hospitals in New York City are similar to those upstate.

In sum, more severe health care problems, the large scale of graduate medical training, the relatively large size of the public sector, and the high volume of hospital spending all distinguish New York City from the rest of the state. Thus, a key issue for State health policy is how to respond to these unique features. The ways in which State officials have been pressed to make adoptions and their responsiveness are examined in the next section, which focuses on State hospital payment policy since 1965.

STATE REGULATION OF HOSPITAL SPENDING

State government controls two policy levers which influence the level of hospital spending in New York State. First, the State can—subject to federal guidelines—determine eligibility requirements for its Medicaid program. The Medicaid program pays for health care services to persons receiving welfare and to persons not receiving welfare but whom the State defines as medically needy. State flexibility in shaping the Medicaid program was enhanced under the Omnibus Budget Reconciliation Act (OBRA) of 1981. The OBRA grants greater autonomy to states in defining eligibility for the medically needy. Moreover, the OBRA also provided increased state discretion in determining what services are provided and how they are paid.

Second, under State law, the State Health Department has the authority to regulate hospital payment rates by all private insurance companies. Private payers—predominantly Blue Cross—account for approximately 25 percent of all hospital revenue. Methods used to regulate Blue Cross rates have traditionally been tied to State Medicaid policies. The similarities in the Blue Cross and Medicaid reimbursement methodologies allowed the State to control approximately 40–45 percent of all hospital revenue.

Control over Medicaid eligibility has been used at different times to broaden or contract either the number of people eligible for Medicaid, the range of health care services offered to the poor, or both. In contrast, the Health Commissioner's power to set hospital payment rates has traditionally been used to moderate the level of hospital, and in particular Medicaid, spending.

The State's dual role as financier of Medicaid benefits and as hospital payment regulator creates the potential for conflict. As a promoter of public health, State officials are under pressure from numerous constituencies to expand the pool of those eligible for Medicaid and the range of services available to them. Broader coverage, it is argued, leads to better health outcomes. On the other hand, increased Medicaid coverage often comes with a sizable price tag, one which must compete with other spending (or tax reduction) priorities pursued by State leaders.

The broad powers of the State officials to determine how much is spent on hospital care also makes them the focal point for interest group conflict. Various interest groups appeal to State officials to exercise their regulatory powers in different directions. The hospital industry—primarily through its lobbying group, the Hospital Association of New York State (HANYS)—has traditionally noted the deficit position of its member hospitals in an appeal for an increased State fiscal commitment to the hospital sector. Unions—in particular Local 1199 of the National Union of Hospital and Health Care Employees (AFL-CIO), representing workers in some 30 New York City voluntary hospitals, and District Council 37 of the American Federation of State, County and Municipal Employees (AFSCME), representing municipal hospital employees—have concurrently sought increases in wages and employment levels.

The leaders of the City of New York also are bargainers in this process, although their interests are somewhat schizophrenic. Municipal officials have an interest in Medicaid policy decisions, because the City finances from local taxes over one fourth of the $4.8 billion of Medicaid spending in New York City. Medicaid policy decisions also influence the need for City tax levy contributions to the HHC. Expanded Medicaid coverage has reduced the percentage of the HHC's budget which the City must finance from local tax sources.[21]

Moreover, Medicaid policy decisions also influence utilization patterns in the city and, in particular, in HHC hospitals. Expanded Medicaid coverage provides the poor with wider discretion when selecting hospitals, which has historically reduced the share of services accounted for by the public sector.[22]

The special characteristics of New York City are an important influence on State policymaking. State initiatives have been responsive to significant changes in New York City. Two patterns of response can be identified. First, rapid growth in Medicaid expenditures has been followed by regulatory efforts to moderate spending; these efforts, in turn, have been followed by strong political pressures to expand hospital revenues. As will be described below, the reductions in spending have been accomplished by failing to adjust Medicaid eligibility limits for inflation combined with expansion of the State Health Department's control over hospital revenues. The resulting reduced Medicaid spending has been associated with larger hospital deficits, labor retrenchment, and increased demands on the HHC. Opposition to Medicaid cutbacks by labor unions, HANYS, and public interest groups has led to policy innovations that respond to these groups' desires.

Impact of Medicare and Medicaid

The passage of federal Medicare and Medicaid legislation in 1965 was a watershed for health care financing policy. New York State enacted its Medicaid program in 1966, with eligibility defined to include one quarter of the city's population.[23] In addition to the nearly 2 million individuals covered by Medicaid, the Medicare program provided federally financed benefits for an additional 900,000 elderly persons in New York City. City officials viewed the new programs as a financial boon; Medicaid and Medicare would allow them to reduce the local tax share of financing for indigent care as well as provide new funds for needed capital improvements.

While the new federal and State programs increased access to mainstream medical care for millions of poor New Yorkers, they also fueled the growth in health care spending. The initial generosity of New

York's Medicaid program created expenditure growth substantially higher than originally anticipated or budgeted. It also created an initial level of expectations by the poor and their advocates which made program revisions politically unpopular.

Nevertheless, rapid growth in State Medicaid spending, particularly in New York City, generated two important policy responses by the State. First, in 1968 and 1969, eligibility requirements for Medicaid were tightened. This reduced the number of eligibles by 390,000—a 14 percent reduction—statewide between 1969 and 1972. Most of the reduction in Medicaid eligibles occurred in New York City, where the number declined by 420,000—a 22 percent reduction. (See Table 12.3.) Second, Chapter 957 of the New York State Laws of 1969 was passed, allowing the health commissioner to establish Medicaid payment rates for hospitals that are related to the cost of the efficient production of services. In addition, the commissioner was given a similar mandate for

TABLE 12.3

Medicaid Enrollees and Expenditures in New York State and New York City, 1968–1985 (dollars in thousands)

	New York State		New York City	
	Enrollment*	Expenditures	Enrollment*	Expenditures
1968	2,688,307	$1,036,703	1,742,873	$697,360
1969	2,719,835	1,028,726	1,903,810	692,511
1970	2,342,128	1,030,761	1,499,371	666,092
1971	2,495,370	1,590,880	1,618,204	1,128,609
1972	2,330,432	1,828,599	1,483,890	1,306,359
1973	2,094,738	1,902,768	1,364,178	1,335,531
1974	1,819,943	2,120,816	1,158,787	1,482,055
1975	2,268,708	2,772,244	1,430,510	1,967,105
1976	2,229,809	2,919,871	1,393,415	2,047,233
1977	2,100,068	2,670,872	1,310,021	1,814,872
1978	2,006,935	2,810,960	1,262,287	1,843,047
1979	1,919,740	3,204,148	1,204,221	2,117,538
1980	1,954,003	3,728,340	1,189,085	2,458,446
1981	1,982,158	4,438,414	1,204,894	2,938,035
1982	1,915,885	5,024,064	1,220,853	3,311,635
1983	2,010,809	5,662,186	1,246,647	3,757,816
1984	2,069,753	6,413,015	1,290,317	4,273,676
1985	2,093,615	6,948,646	1,313,182	4,664,640

SOURCES: New York State Department of Social Services, personal communication; and *Annual Report, Statistical Supplement* (Albany: NYS DSS, 1981, 1984, and 1985).

*Total monthly average number of enrollees.

Blue Cross rates, which effectively coupled Medicaid and Blue Cross payment rates. Chapter 957 empowered the State health commissioner with substantial control over hospital revenues through enhanced rate setting powers. Expanded regulatory power at the State level was opposed by HANYS, citing the State's conflicting role as payer and regulator. However, the State legislature was not swayed by these arguments, probably because of the extreme budget pressure caused by enlarged Medicaid spending.

The rules and regulations developed under Chapter 957 provided the foundations of New York's current regulatory apparatus. As noted above, only those costs reasonably related to the efficient production of services (as interpreted by the State Health Department) were recognized in the payment formula. The tremendous variation in costs across the state—in part stemming from the unique characteristics of the hospitals in New York City—presented special challenges.

Under the previous payment system, Medicaid and Blue Cross payments to a hospital were based on the past costs incurred by that individual hospital. However, Chapter 957 established a payment system where rates were set by comparing each hospital's costs with those of a larger peer group. Given the substantial variation in cost between New York City and upstate hospitals, the new payment system could have redistributed large sums of Medicaid and Blue Cross revenue from New York City to other areas. To avoid penalizing New York City hospitals for any justifiable higher unit costs, the State Health Department grouped hospitals based on their bed size, teaching status, auspice, and geographic location. These "peer groupings" ensured that New York City's municipal and large teaching hospitals would not be compared with smaller and less costly upstate hospitals. The use of these peer groups was an important policy decision; it locked into place the earlier payment differences among New York City hospitals and between city and upstate hospitals created under cost-based reimbursement.

Over time, the payment rate-setting process became quite complex. Once hospitals were grouped, costs exceeding 10 percent of the group average were disallowed. Payments for a new year were determined by applying a trend factor to reflect inflation in input prices. Later, penalties against hospitals with abnormally high lengths of stay or low occupancy rates were added.

The introduction of payment controls at the State level reduced the City's autonomy in health care spending decisions. Prior to the enactment of Medicare and Medicaid, the City purchased care for its indigent patients from voluntary hospitals and through its municipal system with program and appropriation decisions made through the City budget process. After 1966, the State—through Medicaid rate-setting decisions—assumed a central role in defining the size and composition of the City's Medicaid budget and its municipal hospital care spending levels.

Fiscal Crisis Era

Events in New York City were also largely responsible for a second wave of major State policy innovations. During the summer of 1974, the New York State Assembly uncovered numerous improprieties in the city's nursing home industry. The scope of the Medicaid nursing home scandal was far-reaching, ranging from fraud to unacceptable levels of care. The scandal generated substantial political attention, resulting in the creation of a special Moreland Act Commission.

Nearly coincident with the nursing home scandals was the fiscal crisis in New York City. In 1975, New York City was on the brink of bankruptcy, reeling from sizable budget deficits and cut-off from access to credit markets. As these events developed, Governor Hugh Carey in 1976 delivered the State's first "Health of the State" message. He promised sweeping policy changes aimed at rationalizing and streamlining the health care system.

A major policy change, Chapter 76 of the laws enacted in 1976, grew out of this turbulent time. Chapter 76 gave increased rate-setting powers to the State officials. The State budget director was given authority to approve Medicaid rates determined by the prospective payment formula, but subject to the State's fiscal health. The Health Department's regulatory arm was strengthened further when the director of the Office of Health Systems Management (OHSM), the unit responsible for rate-setting, was given cabinet level status.

The New York City fiscal crisis was directly responsible for two major regulatory changes designed to reduce State, and especially City, Medicaid spending. First, income limits for Medicaid eligibility were not updated despite rapid inflation during this period. This resulted in a reduction in the proportion and number of poor covered by Medicaid. Between 1976 and 1979, the number of Medicaid beneficiaries fell by 215,000—a 21 percent reduction—in New York State. (See Table 12.3.) Second, the "bindingness" of the payment scheme was increased. Disallowances for costs for ancillary services greater than the peer group mean were added. Moreover, routine service costs were disallowed if they exceeded the peer group average. (Previously, they could be up to 10 percent above average.) Hence, any costs—either routine or ancillary—exceeding the peer group mean were not recognized in the State payment formula.

Control by the State Health Department over future levels of hospital spending was also enhanced. Prior to 1976, yearly increases in Medicaid hospital payments were linked to an index of wages for occupations outside the hospital industry. Moreover, wage settlements negotiated between the voluntary hospitals and their unions were often paid in future years through special rate appeals. This practice significantly enhanced the bargaining power of the hospital unions. However, during the fiscal crisis, the State adopted an alternative wage trend factor for New York City hospitals and extended it to Blue Cross payment rates as well as Medicaid. (Wage indexes used for upstate hospitals were not altered at this time.) The new index limited annual rate increases to the rate of increase obtained in collective bargaining agreements in the hospital industry outside New York City. Use of the new index was opposed by Local 1199 because it would inhibit "market" oriented wage settlements.

As a result of these significant regulatory changes, statewide Medicaid spending *decreased* about $100 million, or about 4 percent, between 1976 and 1978. (See Table 12.3.) In contrast, spending for Medicaid increased 13 percent nationally over the same period.[24]

One result of the reduced Medicaid spending was a deterioration in the fiscal health of the state's hospitals. Hospitals in New York City suffered disproportionately because they relied more heavily on Medicaid payments than upstate hospitals. By 1980, the average voluntary hospital in the state incurred an operating loss of 3.1 percent of assets.[25] These large operating losses occurred during a period when the typical hospital nationally enjoyed a 2.1 percent operating surplus. Other measures of fiscal health—including current ratios, equity financing ratios, and total margin ratios—all painted the same picture; the financial condition of New York State hospitals, especially those in the city, was well below the national standard and had deteriorated progressively from 1977 to 1980.

The State's response to the fiscal crisis also had a dramatic impact on New York City's spending for health care. Tightened Medicaid eligibility policies increased the city's uninsured poor population, generating a $130 million increase in City tax levy spending between 1976 and 1980.[26] At the same time, Medicaid revenues received by the HHC decreased from $495 million to $397 million.[27]

Hospitals responded to revenue reductions in a number of ways. Staffing at many hospitals, especially in New York City, was reduced, often quite sharply. Personnel reductions were especially evident in the municipal hospital system, as HHC employment was reduced 17 percent between 1975 and 1978.[28] Recent studies indicate that tightening of the regulatory constraints also had a significant retarding effect on the diffusion of new technology among New York State hospitals.[29] Finally, a number of politically controversial hospital closings occurred, disproportionately in New York City. Indeed, 9 of the city's 58 voluntary hospitals ceased operation, while 3 of the HHC hospitals also closed.[30] Hospital closures and efforts to close beds resulted in a significant reduction in bed capacity, which was sought by the State Health Department. The contraction was especially severe in New York City as over 4,500 beds, accounting for 11 percent of all beds, were closed between 1975 and 1979. The bed complement was reduced by over 1,000 in the HHC hospitals alone. In contrast, total beds outside New York City increased by nearly 300 over the same time period.[31]

In addition to reducing hospital spending, the State and City also sought to limit their long-term care expenditures under Medicaid by shifting a portion of these costs to the federal government. The "Medicare maximization" effort sought to increase federal Medicare payments for skilled nursing facility (SNF) care previously financed under the Medicaid program.[32] A central component of the maximization effort was to require all SNF facilities to obtain accreditation for Medicare long-term care reimbursement. This effort to shift a portion of State and City Medicaid costs to the federal Medicare program enjoyed some success. The number of Medicare-covered SNF days increased 36 percent and federal reimbursement jumped 71 percent between July 1975 and June 1978.[33]

In sum, the events evolving from the New York City fiscal crisis had a profound impact on the State health policy. The ascendancy of a liberal Democratic governor combined with the events in the city shifted power to the State. Chapter 76 of 1976 increased the scope and bindingness of regulations. Hospital rate-setting controls were expanded and tightened, with the expressed goal of significantly reducing Medicaid spending. Hospital utilization controls were extended to include on-site inspection at hospitals—predominantly in New York City—with heavy Medicaid caseloads. Strict certificate-of-need (CON) requirements evolved requiring very formalized demonstrations of "need" before capital expenditures could occur. The CON and health planning process was unique in New York State since the State legislature granted the health commissioner power to revoke the operating license of any hospital's operating certificate unless a demonstrable "public need" existed. These regulations were effective; over 6,000 beds were eliminated and 28 hospitals were closed during the 1974–1980 period.[34]

These State efforts to reduce Medicaid spending created considerable unrest in the hospital industry and among commercial insurance companies. Mounting hospital deficits increased tension between HANYS and State Health Department leaders. Commercial insurance companies, citing a growing unfavorable gap between regulated Blue Cross hospital payments and the rates the commercials were obligated to pay, began to withdraw from the New York State insurance market. Finally, growth in the number of fiscally distressed hospitals placed the State at increasing risk for assuming the debts of some large New York City voluntary hospitals. This broad alliance of adversely affected groups created an environment conducive to policy change.

The New York Prospective
Hospital Reimbursement Methodology

While the State policies emanating from the New York City fiscal crisis solved the budgetary problems of the late 1970s, they proved to be stop-gap solutions. Failure to update Medicaid income eligibility limits and stringent control over hospital revenues contributed to serious hospital financial difficulties. With fewer Medicaid-covered poor patients, the volume of uncompensated care provided by the city's voluntary hospitals grew. The combined impact of fewer paying patients and strict payment limitations for Medicaid and Blue Cross patients forced many hospitals to dip into their endowments.

While the fiscal conditions of hospitals across the state deteriorated during the mid to late 1970s, conditions among city hospitals were especially distressed. Operating losses had increased, reaching 3 percent of total assets by 1977 and 1978.[35] Many hospitals in the city faced severe fiscal problems, with a number of institutions on the brink of bankruptcy.

Attempts by hospitals to escape the influence of the State's new regulatory vigor were numerous and diverse. Hospitals attempted to compensate for their financial shortfalls by adjusting their price (charge) schedules for patients with commercial health insurance. Rapid rise in hospital charges to charge paying patients created a significant divergence between hospital charges paid by commercial payers and rates paid by Medicaid and Blue Cross plans. The differential exceeded 100 percent of the Medicaid rate in some areas. Because of the aggressive pricing policies pursued by some hospitals, many commercial payers refused to write new health care insurance policies in New York State.

A few upstate hospitals also attempted to raise additional revenues by canceling their contracts with Blue Cross plans and subsequently billing Blue Cross patients full price. The difference between individual charges and regulated Blue Cross payment rates were substantial, potentially exposing fully insured patients to new financial risk.

The mounting differential between hospital costs and charges forged an alliance between the Health Insurance Association of America (HIAA), which represents a national cross-section of commercial insurers, and Local 1199 to limit the differential. These parties were interested in promoting "equity" in payment rates by third-party payers. The State legislature responded to these pressures and enacted the Charge Control Act in 1978. This act limited the annual rate of increase in hospital charges to the rate of increase in the price index used to adjust Medicaid rates.

The bleak financial picture of many hospitals, particularly the voluntary sector in New York City, mounting charge/cost differentials, and a rapidly rising volume of uncompensated care generated enormous pressure from HANYS and the HIAA for legislative reforms. The response to these widespread demands was Chapter 520 of the Laws of 1978. It created a special Council on Health Care Financing, which was directed to develop a new system for financing general care hospitals in the state. The council was guided by the chairman of the Senate Health Committee, with his counterpart in the Assembly acting as vice-chairman. Gubernatorial appointments to the council represented the relevant groups, including Blue Cross, commercial payers, Local 1199, hospital administrators, and the HHC.

In its deliberations, the council noted a number of shortcomings with the existing financing system. Medicaid rates, and hence hospital revenues, were not predictable, inhibiting hospital financial planning. Moreover, hospitals in the state were paid according to numerous different methods, including prospective payments for Medicaid and Blue Cross, charges for commercial insurers, and retrospective costs for Medicare. These methods created widely different payment rates for hospital care. Because of these payment differentials, hospital leaders and State policymakers were attracted to the concepts of uniformity in payment methods and revenue predictability.

Another central concern of the council was the financing of uncompensated care. Since 1974, a portion of hospital bad debt and charity care had been financed by Blue Cross. The legislature required allowances for ambulatory and emergency care losses in the Blue Cross payments to voluntary hospitals. However, since federal laws precluded Medicare and Medicaid payments for uncompensated care to patients not covered by these programs, Blue Cross was the only third-party payer which included the allowances in its payments. Yet, the volume of uncompensated care was substantial and growing, exceeding $220 million among the city's voluntary hospitals by 1981.[36] The council concluded that any solution to the uncompensated care problem required broader financial participation than only Blue Cross plans.

Based largely on the recommendations of the Council on Health Care Financing, State officials ultimately developed an innovative set of regulatory policies. These policies represented a compromise between the Health Department, HANYS, Blue Cross, the Federal Health Care Financing Administration (HCFA), and commercial payers.

Two major components of the new proposal were novel. First, it authorized the State Health Department to determine payment rates to hospitals from *all* revenue sources. Since the plan included regulation of Medicare rates, a special waiver of federal regulations was required from HCFA. Second, it expanded the State's role to include assessing and collecting payment surcharges and redistributing these funds to financially distressed hospitals and hospitals with large volumes of uncompensated care. These powers changed the focus of State health regulation from cost control to a "public finance" role, which redistributed hospital revenues to further broader health policy goals.[37]

The proposed redistribution of hospital revenue based on bad debt and charity care burdens created the potential for serious conflict between upstate and New York City hospitals as well as between the voluntary and municipal sector within New York City. A disproportionate share—over two thirds in 1981—of the total volume of uncompensated care occurs in New York City.[38] The concentration of uncompensated care and voluntary hospital fiscal distress in New York City could lead to a significant redistribution of revenue from upstate hospitals to institutions in the city. Moreover, because of the substantial volume of uncompensated care provided by HHC hospitals, equal distribution of pool monies would greatly benefit the public sector. While the HHC argued that it should be treated on a basis equal to voluntary hospitals for receiving funds for uncompensated care, the voluntary hospitals and some State officials argued that equal treatment of the municipal system would simply allow the City Office of Management and Budget (OMB) to substitute the New York State raised revenues for City tax levy payments without increasing HHC's budget. The final agreement largely accommodated the voluntary sector by limiting the amount of payments available for public hospitals and concentrating the new revenues among private hospitals.

In 1982, the HCFA approved the State's proposed three-year, experimental program known as the New York Prospective Hospital Reimbursement Methodology (NYPHRM). Approval of the experimental program did not come without strings, however. Of special concern to HCFA was limiting Medicare's role in financing uncompensated care provided to non-Medicare patients. However, New York State officials were convinced that NYPHRM would save Medicare money, even with Medicare's additional payments into the proposed bad debt and charity care pools. To secure federal participation in NYPHRM, State officials agreed that should the rate of increase in Medicare spending in New York State over the three-year period exceed the national average for Medicare, the State would repay the difference to HCFA.

NYPHRM was implemented in January 1983. Its two major components were a uniform, prospective system to determine per diem hospital payments for all third-party payers and the levying of surcharges on hospital revenues in order to create new revenue "pools" that are redistributed to hospitals providing uncompensated care. The surcharges were substantial, amounting to over $400 million by 1985. Also, the pools were regionally limited to avoid substantial shifts of funds across the state and especially from upstate to New York City. Finally, voluntary and major public hospitals were treated differently under the pool distributions.

The specifics of the redistribution plan included the creation of four different pools:

1. Bad Debt and Charity Care Pool. Eight regional pools were established. The regions were the six Blue Cross plan regions, except Blue Cross of Greater New York, which was subdivided into the three separate areas—northern metropolitan, New York City, and Long Island. The pools were funded by a surcharge averaging 2 percent statewide in 1983 and rising to 4 percent in 1985. Within each region, hospitals received payments from the pool in proportion to their cost for uncompensated care. Payments into the eight pools totaled $154 million in 1983, $252 million in 1984, and $364 million in 1985.[39]

HHC and other large public hospitals were placed in a separate category within their region. Their uncompensated care was only partly financed using a different distribution principle. The share of total resources from the pool allocated to the local public hospitals depended upon their proportion of statewide inpatient costs. This adjustment ensured that public hospitals—dominated by the HHC—would receive less from the pools than if they were treated the same as voluntary hospitals.

2. Financially Distressed Pool. A surcharge of .33 percent was levied to establish regional distressed hospital pools (the regions are the same as those for the bad debt and charity care pool). These pools were used to distribute monies to private hospitals experiencing severe financial difficulties. To become eligible, hospitals are required to demonstrate severe financial hardship resulting from insufficient funds to finance uncompensated care. Approximately $21 million annually was collected and distributed from this pool.[40]

3. Discretionary Allowances. Discretionary allowances ranging from 1 to 2 percent for private hospitals and up to 3 percent for public hospitals were included. Acceptable uses of these funds included the retirement of short-term debt, offsets of reductions in revenues resulting from the State's charge control limitation, meeting costs of uncompen-

sated care not met through the bad debt and charity care pool, and
needed improvements of current ratios.

4. Transitional Allowances. An additional .25 percent was added to
each payer's per diem for private hospitals, amounting to about $17
million statewide. This allowance was designed to assist private hospitals
negatively impacted by the inclusion of Medicare in the NYPHRM.

The remaining components of the payment system were similar to
those existing prior to NYPHRM. To ensure that costs reflected the
"efficient production of services," hospitals were peer grouped with costs
in excess of 7.5 percent of the group average routine costs and 5 percent
of ancillary costs per discharge not included in the payment formulas. By
this time, the peer grouping process had become very sophisticated. A
complicated "seed clustering" method taking into account 15 different
hospital characteristics was used. Since the resulting "peer groups" were
small, use of numerous hospital characteristics limited cost disallowances
for high-cost hospitals—especially the HHC and New York City
academic medical centers. The new NYPHRM grouping process included
an expanded set of characteristics such as length of stay, physician
practice patterns, occupancy rates, bed size, and case mix to group
hospitals. While the use of an expanded set of grouping variables aided
high-cost New York City hospitals, it further isolated the HHC hospitals
and downstate academic hospitals as facilities requiring special consideration under State regulations.

NYPHRM achieved many of its intended goals. The all-payer
approach combined with the revenue redistribution pools directed funds
to weaker voluntary institutions serving the uninsured and thereby
stabilized the local hospital system. By design, HHC facilities garnered
fewer fiscal benefits under the new system. HANYS has estimated that
under NYPHRM the financial condition of New York State hospitals
improved, with a reduction in annual operating losses of $70 million
in NYPHRM's first year.[41] Moreover, HANYS estimated that without
NYPHRM's special revenue pools, hospital losses in the state would have
increased 7 percent to $606 million in 1983 and to $838 million by 1984.
In contrast, actual losses statewide (including the HHC) totaled $588
million in 1984. In sum, the NYPHRM stabilized a shaky hospital system
by redistributing income to weak and marginal institutions—especially
voluntary hospitals in New York City—while concurrently moderating
growth in total hospital expenditures.

Despite these favorable results, there was some discontent with
NYPHRM. One problem was the persistent volume of rate appeals.
While appeals have been common in all state hospital rate-setting

systems, the uniform rules of NYPHRM were touted as able to make appeals far less frequent. However, in practice hospitals were quick to challenge their peer grouping and, as a result, the rate promulgated for them by the State Health Department. The large volume of appeals created a significant backlog in the Office of Health Systems Management, creating additional antagonism between the Health Department and the hospital industry, especially the upstate hospitals that had always been reluctant to delegate additional authority to the health commissioner. On its part, the State Department of Health became increasingly concerned with the growing divergence between the New York State and the national average lengths of stay. While the length of stay for New York State Medicare patients fell over the three years of NYPHRM from 14.2 to 13.4 days, the comparable national average fell to 8.4 days, resulting in a full 5-day differential.[42] It became clear that the per diem payment principle under NYPHRM provided few incentives for hospitals to reduce hospital stays.

Another problem under NYPHRM was the strong tension created between the State's need to curb hospital expenditures and the wage demands of unionized hospital workers, especially those of voluntary hospital employees in New York City represented by Local 1199. These tensions erupted in a bitter 47-day strike by Local 1199 beginning in July 1984.

Earlier in 1984 State officials calculated that average hospital payments in the coming year would rise by 5 to 7 percent. This rate of increase would enable the State to meet its earlier noted commitment to the federal government to keep Medicare payments in New York State below the national average and avoid having the State pay penalties to HCFA. However, this rate of increase was not sufficient to enable hospitals to meet the wage demands of their workers. The workers went on strike seeking a larger increase, and the hospitals took the position that approval of a higher payment rate from the State was necessary to reach a settlement. In effect, NYPHRM put the governor in the difficult political position of being an involved party to hospital collective bargaining. Voluntary hospital labor relations have remained problematic since the 1984 strike, which was settled only after State officials agreed to modify payment levels to take into account new bargaining settlements.

Perhaps the most troublesome criticism of NYPHRM emerged in 1985 after the federal government changed its payment rules under Medicare. A series of simulations conducted by HANYS revealed that hospitals in New York State would receive, at a minimum, $175 million in additional revenue should they move to Medicare's new diagnosis-related grouping (DRG) payment system rather than continue under

NYPHRM.[43] Much of the expected "windfall" stemmed from Medicare's generous recognition of indirect teaching costs and large expected payments for cases called "outliers." Moreover, the cost per case among upstate hospitals was slightly lower than the average cost among their national reference group; this suggested especially large revenue windfalls for these hospitals under the Medicare DRG system. Thus, while many recognized the stabilizing aspects of NYPHRM, the opportunity to receive additional Medicare revenue was a powerful enticement for the hospital industry.

This is not to say, however, there was no dissention. Shifting from NYPHRM to Medicare's new payment system also meant losing Medicare's substantial contributions to the bad debt and charity care pools. This prospect alarmed some regional hospital associations, the HHC, and other hospitals in New York City that relied heavily on these payments. Despite these internal disagreements, HANYS supported the governor's decision not to seek an extension of the Medicare waiver and thus to end the innovative three-year experiment. As a result, hospitals in New York State entered Medicare's case payment system in January 1986.

The stabilizing effect of NYPHRM on the New York State hospital industry was a double-edged sword. On one side, it accomplished its goals of containing costs while redistributing revenues to fiscally distressed hospitals. On the other side, the highly regulatory approach insulated New York hospitals from changes in the health care industry occurring outside the state and making other institutions become more competitive in their strategies. Once the New York State hospital system was stabilized, external events raised questions about the desirability of maintaining the existing hospital practices and infrastructure.

Mounting competition among insurance plans, combined with the introduction of Medicare's DRG system, brought dramatic management, utilization, and financial changes to hospitals outside the state. Efforts by private insurance companies and employers outside New York State to limit health care costs expanded. Reliance on competitive rather than regulatory approaches became dominant. These competitive approaches to reducing costs focused on reducing hospital and physician utilization rather than regulating payment rates to providers. As a result, dramatic changes in the structure of the hospital industry (which New York State hospitals had been insulated from under NYPHRM), including large reductions in hospital utilization and increased use of ambulatory facilities, transpired. Yet, clearly New York State hospitals would eventually feel the impact of these increased competitive pressures.

In a 1987 program bill, Governor Mario Cuomo expressed an intention to make broader use of the health commissioner's regulatory authority to pursue a wider range of health policy goals. Successful use of the State's payment system to finance uncompensated care under NYPHRM generated interest in using hospital payment policies to achieve other goals. In particular, the governor's original proposal would expand the State's influence over the hospital industry through prospective payment of capital funds and tightened control over graduate medical education expenses. Indeed, these proposals would broaden the use of the hospital payment system to achieve State health manpower and capital planning goals. Three major proposals are:

1. Moving to a Per Case Payment System for All Hospital Payments. This proposal would shift hospital payment to a per case payment system for all third-party payers. The revenue pools used to finance uncompensated care would be retained.

The proposal to shift all (non-Medicare) payers to a per case payment system impacts New York City, but the ultimate effect depends less on the move to case payment per se than on the design of the system. In particular, the impacts of a case payment system on the HHC and voluntary hospitals depend crucially on the groups used to determine the payment rates for individual hospitals. For instance, because of their relatively high costs, grouping all downstate hospitals to set payment rates would significantly disadvantage the HHC hospitals and major academic medical centers. Even after accounting for wage and case mix differences, Medicaid cost per case among the HHC hospitals is 28 and 117 percent higher than upstate teaching and nonteaching hospitals, respectively. (See Table 12.4.) While the HHC Medicaid costs per case are about 13 percent higher than New York City's major academic medical centers, costs for HHC Blue Cross patients (which account for only 5 percent of HHC patient care revenues) are 4.6 percent lower. The substantial variation in costs among HHC and New York City's major academic medical centers will most likely continue to be recognized in any future payment system. Specific details of the proposed case payment system are currently being developed.

2. Modifying Payment for Graduate Medical Education. The State Health Department has proposed that all current direct (physician and resident salaries) and indirect teaching costs be identified, the necessary funds pooled regionally and reallocated to achieve the goals enunciated in the *Report of the Commission on Graduate Medical Education.*[44] Briefly, these are to reduce first year residency appointments by 30 percent over the next five years; to limit the hiring of foreign medical graduates in residency programs; to encourage balanced inpatient and outpatient experience for residents in general internal medicine, pediat-

TABLE 12.4

Operating Cost per Discharge, New York City
and Upstate Hospitals, by Payer, 1985

	Medicaid	Blue Cross
New York City		
Nonteaching Hospitals	$1,453	$1,640
Major Public Hospitals	3,162	2,572
Major Academic Centers	2,795	2,691
Other Teaching Hospitals	2,462	2,356
Upstate		
Nonteaching Hospitals	1,340	1,516
Teaching Hospitals	1,722	1,777

SOURCE: New York State Department of Health, Office of Health Systems Management.

NOTES: All figures exclude outlier costs. Outlier days were defined using Medicare's length of stay trim points. See *Federal Register*, June 10, 1986. Cost per discharge is standardized for Medicaid and Blue Cross case mix and regional wage index.

rics, obstetrics/gynecology, and family medicine; and to redistribute residents from subspecialties to primary care specialties.

The HHC facilities appear most at risk under the proposed restrictions on the hiring of foreign medical graduates (FMG) for residencies owing to their disproportionate reliance on FMGs. In 1985 nearly 300 of the 553 residency positions available in HHC hospitals were filled by FMGs. This substantially exceeds the proportion—about 26 percent—of FMGs in other graduate programs in New York State.[45] Phasing out FMGs for residency positions in the state would clearly provide a short-run burden on the HHC facilities as they attempt to find suitable replacements.

The other major proposals for graduate medical education would also have a dramatic impact on the organization of New York City hospitals. Reducing the number of residency positions and altering their specialty mix would shift the focus of training to ambulatory and long-term care sites. While the "indirect" costs associated with graduate training would fall, the focus on primary care might slow the rate of technological advancement in subspecialties. Moreover, since Medicare reimburses teaching hospitals based on resident to *bed* ratios, New York's proposals may directly conflict with financial incentives favoring inpatient care in the HCFA payment formula.

3. Use of Prospective Capital Reimbursement. Traditionally the State has authorized payment of capital costs (depreciation and interest) under Medicaid and Blue Cross on the basis of actual expenditures by the hospital. Proposed changes in this system are largely a response to recent federal proposals to provide a fixed percentage add-on for capital payments under Medicare. The proposed add-on would equal the national average ratio of capital to operating expenses. This federal approach significantly disadvantages New York State and particularly New York City hospitals requiring significant upgrades in their physical plants. Many New York City hospitals—including the HHC hospitals—have recently planned or undertaken major capital renovations. Since depreciation and interest expenses are relatively high in the initial years of major capital projects, capital expenses for new projects would substantially exceed the fixed percentage proposed by HCFA. As a result, financing new capital projects aimed at offsetting years of structural neglect in the hospital industry—a major outcome of New York State's tight regulatory policies—would become nearly impossible.

While not proposed in the governor's 1987 program bill, the State is considering a pool to finance new capital projects. This capital pool would expand further the State Health Department's ability to control growth in total health care spending while simultaneously using the payment system to achieve broader goals. Given the concentration of uncompensated care, graduate medical education, foreign medical graduates, and needed new capital projects in New York City, these proposals could significantly alter the existing distribution of health care spending between New York City and the rest of the state and between the voluntary and public sectors within the city.

The sweeping nature of these proposed regulatory changes met some resistence from the legislature as well as HANYS. A less dramatic change was proposed by the legislature during the 1987 session. The bill finally passed established a case payment system for all non-Medicare payers. Payment rates under the system, however, would be primarily based on each hospital's historical costs rather than the pure pricing system desired by the State health commissioner and the governor. Moreover, other issues, such as the financing of capital and graduate medical education, were not addressed in the legislature's bill. The governor, citing the apparently higher costs of the legislature's bill and its failure to move quickly to a pricing system, vetoed the bill. Ultimately, another compromise bill was developed to move all-payers to the case payment system. The agreement avoided a potential override of the governor's veto by the legislature.

The compromise increased the pricing component of the case payment rates to 55 percent in the third year. While some discretion was left to the State health commissioner to develop appropriate peer groups, it was generally agreed that New York City's major academic medical centers and the HHC hospitals would form their own peer groups. This decision would limit the extent of revenue redistribution among high- and low-cost facilities. The agreement also called for some limited pilot projects to provide health care for uninsured individuals using negotiated payment rates. However, changes in the methods for financing graduate medical education and capital were not addressed.

CONCLUSION

State and City health care policies and spending priorities are inextricably linked through the Medicaid program and New York City's municipal hospital system. Since its enactment in 1965, significant State policy innovations have changed the Medicaid program. The three major changes were the introduction of prospective rate reimbursement in 1969, eligibility and expenditure cutbacks following the nursing home and fiscal crises in New York City in the mid 1970s, and the development and evolution of NYPHRM to deal with the consequences of Medicaid cutbacks on the hospital industry.

The most significant trend in State health policy over this period was its increased control over the scale and distribution of hospital revenues across the state. Indeed, the primary functions of State regulation have expanded from simple concern over Medicaid expenditure growth to active use of hospital payment policy to pursue broader policy goals. This expansion of State powers has assumed an important role in determining the size, shape, and composition of both the voluntary and municipal health care sectors in New York City. Increased control over the level and distribution of hospital revenue by the State Health Department has reduced considerably the autonomy of the City in setting policy both for its own municipal hospitals and for the voluntary sector. Recently, expanded Medicaid coverage combined with partial payments of uncompensated care have, at least in the short run, increased the economic attractiveness of poor patients admitted to voluntary hospitals. In this and other more direct ways, increased State authority over the size and distribution of hospital revenue has increasingly forced the HHC to lobby actively for its fair share of revenues.

A second observation concerns the pattern of Medicaid policy choices historically pursued by the State. This pattern was established in 1966 when New York State introduced its relatively generous Medicaid program. Rapid growth in Medicaid spending in the late 1960s was quickly followed by eligibility restrictions and the nation's first prospective rate-setting system. Legislative authorization of increased rate-setting powers to the health commissioner was explicitly designed to reduce State and City Medicaid spending. Despite these new regulatory powers, hospital expenditures continued to expand at rates exceeding Medicaid and Blue Cross revenue growth, creating mounting hospital operating deficits. Hence, even before the fiscal crisis in 1975, the pattern of relaxed Medicaid policy which generated cost growth followed by a period of Medicaid cutbacks leading to worsened hospital fiscal conditions was established.

State Medicaid policy came full circle with the events surrounding the introduction of NYPHRM. Those adversely affected by Medicaid eligibility restrictions and increased regulatory vigor created significant pressures for reform. The final product of this process was NYPHRM: an all-payer system designed to control total expenditure growth while redirecting revenues to voluntary hospitals disadvantaged from previous Medicaid cutbacks.

The design of NYPHRM highlighted the different hospital constituencies across the state and within New York City. The tremendous variation in unit costs within the state led to a sophisticated process for grouping hospitals in order to determine their payment rates. This grouping procedure ensured that relatively high-cost facilities—such as the HHC hospitals and academic medical centers in New York City—would not be highly penalized.

A major goal of NYPHRM was to finance otherwise uncompensated care. Since uncompensated care incurred by the HHC hospitals was commonly perceived as already "compensated" through New York City's tax levy contributions, arguments by the HHC for equal treatment under NYPHRM revenue pools were ultimately rejected. While the HHC and the City of New York received some benefits through the revenue pools, the city's voluntary hospitals were the largest winners.

In sum, the past quarter century has witnessed an unprecedented expansion of State control over the health care industry. While this expansion has partly been a shift of control from the local to the state level, it has more importantly been an expansion of public sector financing and regulation into an arena previously left primarily to the private sector. In exercising this vastly expanded authority, officials of the State of New York have had to recognize the tremendous diversity of hospitals within the state in terms of ownership, teaching mission, patient population, and unit costs. Simple uniform policies could not be applied to so diverse an industry without severe inequities; consequently, a highly complex regulatory system has evolved. But the nature of the complexity has often served the interests of New York City institutions well.

NOTES

1. United Hospital Fund, *Health and Health Care in New York City, 1986* (New York: UHF, 1986).

2. United Hospital Fund, *Health.*
3. Charles Brecher, Kenneth Thorpe, and Cynthia Green, "The New York City Health and Hospitals Corporation," in Stuart Altman, Charles Brecher, Mary Henderson, and Kenneth Thorpe, eds., *Competition and Compassion: Conflicts Roles for Public Hospitals* (Ann Arbor: Health Administration Press, 1988).
4. New York State Department of Health, Office of Health Systems Management, unpublished data.
5. New York State Department of Education, *Physician Manpower Survey* (Albany: New York State Department of Education, 1982).
6. New York State Department of Education, *Physician Manpower Survey.*
7. United Hospital Fund, *Health.*
8. United Hospital Fund, *New York's Role as a Center for Health Care: An Analysis of Nonresident Patients* (New York: UHF, 1986).
9. New York State Department of Health, *Survey of Unlicensed Physicians* (Albany: Department of Health, 1984).
10. Brecher et al., "New York City Health and Hospitals Corporation."
11. United Hospital Fund, *Health.*
12. Brecher et al., "New York City Health and Hospitals Corporation."
13. United Hospital Fund, *Health.*
14. Greater New York Hospital Association, *Skyline News,* July 14, 1986.
15. American Hospital Association, *Annual Survey of Hospitals, 1984* (Chicago: AHA, 1985).
16. American Hospital Association, *Annual Survey.*
17. James Knickman and Ann Marie Foltz, "A Statistical Analysis of Reasons for East-West Differences in Hospital Use," *Inquiry* 22(1985):45–58.
18. United Hospital Fund, *Health.*
19. American Hospital Association, *Annual Survey.*
20. American Hospital Association, *Annual Survey.*
21. Brecher et al., "New York City Health and Hospitals Corporation."
22. Brecher et al., "New York City Health and Hospitals Corporation."
23. New York State Department of Social Services, *Annual Report* (Albany: NYSDSS, 1987).
24. R. Gibson, "National Health Expenditures, 1978," *Health Care Financing Review* (Summer 1979):1–30.
25. Charles Brecher and Susan Nesbitt, *The Financial Condition of New York City Voluntary Hospitals II* (New York: Commonwealth Fund, 1985).
26. Brecher et al., "New York City Health and Hospitals Corporation."
27. Brecher et al., "New York City Health and Hospitals Corporation."
28. Brecher et al., "New York City Health and Hospitals Corporation."
29. Brecher and Nesbitt, *Financial Condition.*
30. Brecher et al., "New York City Health and Hospitals Corporation."
31. American Hospital Association, *Annual Survey,* various years.
32. P. Bulgaro and A. Webb, "Federal-State Conflicts in Cost Control," in A. Levin, ed., *Regulating Health Care: The Struggle for Control* (New York: Academy of Political Science, 1980), pp. 92–110.
33. Bulgaro and Webb, "Federal-State Conflicts."
34. New York State Department of Health, Office of Health Systems Management, unpublished data; and American Hospital Association, *Annual Survey.*
35. Brecher and Nesbitt, *Financial Condition.*

36. New York State Department of Health, Office of Health Systems Management, unpublished data.
37. For other examples, see R. Posner, "Taxation by Regulation," *Bell Journal of Economics and Management Science* 2 (Spring, 1971):22–50.
38. New York State Department of Health, Office of Health Systems Management, unpublished data.
39. Council on Health Care Financing, *Report of the New York State Council on Health Care Financing* (Albany: Council on Health Care Financing, March 31, 1986).
40. Ibid.
41. Hospital Association of New York State, *Fiscal Pressures Survey, 1984* (Albany: HANYS, 1985).
42. American Hospital Association, *Annual Survey.*
43. Hospital Association of New York State, *Modelling Alternative Reimbursement Systems* (Albany: HANYS, 1985).
44. New York State Department of Health, *Report of the New York State Commission on Graduate Medical Education* (Albany: NYSDH, February 1986).
45. New York State Department of Health, *Report.*

13

MENTAL HEALTH AND MENTAL RETARDATION SERVICES

❧

Barbara B. Blum
and
Susan Blank

NEW YORK State's mental health and mental retardation agencies serve an estimated 500,000 mentally ill and 100,000 mentally retarded citizens a year.[1] Over the past two decades, both of these systems have undergone dramatic transformations. One indication of the change is that 20 years ago, the two systems were one: The separate State agencies that are today responsible for the mentally ill and mentally retarded were in the 1960s a single Department of Mental Hygiene serving both groups.

It was largely deinstitutionalization, the policy to care for as many mentally disabled citizens as possible in the community rather than in large institutions, that prompted the formation of a separate State mental retardation agency. Most other recent changes in the two systems also stem from deinstitutionalization.

While deinstitutionalization has been the single most important influence on both systems, each has responded differently. This essay identifies the two sets of responses and examines how each has shaped and been shaped by relationships between New York State and New York City. The first section briefly discusses the history of mental health services. The second section traces the more recent change from a system dominated by large State institutions directed by a single State agency to today's more complex situation. This section also considers how and why deinstitutionalization in New York City proceeded along different paths in the fields of mental health and mental retardation. The third section explores the key issues that currently dominate City-State relationships in both mental health and mental retardation services. Most of the discussion is devoted to mental health, where deinstitutionalization has left a legacy of multiple City-State conflicts. The concluding section speculates on the future dynamics in the two delivery systems.

HISTORICAL BACKGROUND

New York State's mental health and mental retardation systems originated in the nineteenth century. With its crusades against poorhouses and its Commissions on Lunacy and for the Feeble Minded, that era may seem remote from today's mental health issues, but in some respects the distance traveled has been more circular than linear. Three themes from these early years still echo.

One is that the system is driven by episodic reforms. The state's earliest mental hospitals were created in response to a belief that the insane did not belong in poorhouses but should be cared for in therapeutic institutions. By 1856, after the investigations of Dorothea Dix had widely publicized the abuses of the poorhouse system, 10 of the state's 50 counties had separate asylums for the insane. Further investigations of conditions in the poorhouses led in 1869 to the founding of New York State's Willard Asylum for the Chronically Insane and to the groundbreaking Willard State Care Act, which gave the State responsibility for care of the mentally ill.[2]

However, once the principle of State responsibility had been embodied in law, there followed a 20-year period of significant backsliding. In 1890 the insane in fully one third of the state's counties remained in workhouses or in county asylums closely associated with them. The State once again began a process of reform. In 1890 a new State Care Act was enacted to restore and fortify the Willard Act requirements by completely abolishing the poorhouse system of care for the insane. Ironically, the nineteenth century calls for State institutions to assume a larger role in caring for the mentally ill were interwoven with sharp criticism of those facilities. Founded with hopes for establishing order and effecting rehabilitation, many of them had degenerated into grim caretaker institutions.[3]

With a new State Care Act in place and with the gradual growth of authority of a three-member State Commission on Lunacy, which during the 1890s was given responsibility for supervising the State institutions, the change to State responsibility took root. Not until 1954 were localities again given a significant role in caring for the mentally ill.

Another early theme echoed today is skepticism about the appropriateness of acute and chronic classifications of patients as a way of organizing services. The Utica Asylum had been established by the State in 1848 to care for the acute mentally insane; the Willard Asylum was created for the chronically insane, and the Willard Act of 1869 directed the State to assign patients to one or the other institution based on their condition. During the 1880s, State Commissioner Stephen Smith voiced concern about the artificial separation of care for the two categories of patients. He feared that an institution caring only for the chronically ill would be more prone than a mixed facility to warehouse, rather than treat, patients. He also might have reasoned that an institution without chronic patients would be more likely to be held to the very difficult standard of cure, as opposed to caretaking, and would hence be more difficult to operate. Both attitudes were pervasive among mental health professionals of this era.[4] In any event, the separation was abolished in 1890 by legislation that required State institutions to accept either type of patient.

A third recurring theme is that of shared and sometimes overlapping responsibility between different State agencies. In the early 1870s, for example, before a state commissioner had been appointed, the State Board of Charities—a body that had originally been established to care for Civil War orphans—investigated the treatment of the insane. Later, when the new three-member Commission on Lunacy was in its early stages, there was confusion about the role of that group vis-à-vis that of the State Board of Charities. To which body, asked the state asylums, were they accountable for regulation and direction? The issue was resolved in favor of the commission, but this was not the last time there were questions about decision-making powers in the system.

DEINSTITUTIONALIZATION AND ITS CONSEQUENCES

From the turn of the century through the mid 1950s, New York State's mental health and mental retardation services followed a developmental path typical of most social service systems during this period—increased professionalization of staff, institutionalization, and growth. By 1927 the three-member Commission on Lunacy had evolved into the State Department of Mental Hygiene. Its institutions expanded continuously. In 1955, the State mental health institutions held over 93,000 patients, more than twice as many as any other state.[5]

Like the mentally ill, most mentally retarded citizens were cared for in large custodial State institutions, with a much smaller number in family care situations. At their highwater mark in 1967, the State's institutions for the mentally retarded held over 27,000 individuals.[6]

The next 25 years witnessed a reversal of this trend. By 1975, the number of patients in the State's mental institutions had dropped from their 1955 peak to under 33,000; by 1985 they numbered less than 21,000. (See Table 13.1.) The changes affected all areas of the state. In New York City institutions, the number of residents in 1985 was less than one third of what it had been 30 years earlier. Similarly, the number of mentally retarded in State facilities was halved between 1975 and 1985. (See Table 13.2.)

The change has been driven by the policy of deinstitutionalization, which sought to release from large State facilities all patients who could be cared for in the community and to avoid the admission of new patients who could be better served outside these facilities. Some 30 years after the movement began, deinstitutionalization remains the central issue of State-City relations in the mental health field.

Beginnings in the 1950s and 1960s

Interest in providing more treatment for mental illness in smaller community settings emerged in the 1950s. Just as New York State led other states by assuming responsibility from localities for the mentally disabled in the nineteenth century, so it was at the cutting edge of the twentieth-century movement for more local involvement. The State's Community Mental Health Services Act of 1954 established community mental health boards in each county and in New York City to oversee the delivery of services to the mentally disabled in community settings. Half of the expenditures of the boards were reimbursed by the State, a funding arrangement which has continued to the present.

Counties throughout the state took advantage of this State assistance to expand their community services. Nevertheless through 1965, the State did comparatively little to reduce its inpatient population—a 9.4

TABLE 13.1
Residents in New York State Psychiatric Hospitals, 1955–1985

Psychiatric Center Location	1955	1965	1975	1985
New York City	13,358	16,567	4,061	4,419
Rest of State	79,956	68,919	28,873	16,065
Total	93,314	85,486	32,934	20,484

SOURCE: New York State Office of Mental Health.

TABLE 13.2

New York State Developmental Center Census, 1975–1986

Year*	Census
1975	20,062
1976	19,160
1977	18,438
1978	16,441
1979	15,578
1980	14,403
1981	13,339
1982	12,420
1983	11,792
1984	11,215
1985	10,681
1986	9,956

SOURCE: New York State Office of Mental Retardation and Developmental Disabilities.
*As of March 31.

percent decrease as opposed to up to 30 percent in other states—and efforts to modernize hospitals were largely ineffective. In part New York State's lackluster record during this period resulted from an inability of the Department of Mental Hygiene to exercise strong authority over individual State mental institutions. During the 1950s and early 1960s these institutions were "feudal baronies" led by directors who were subject to very little control from an understaffed State Mental Hygiene Department.[7]

Under a new commissioner, who took office in 1960, the State department was reorganized to assert more authority over hospital operations. The staffing levels of the department were increased, new controls were exercised over budgets of the State hospitals, and more attention was devoted to reforming their custodial approach to patient care. Also, in response to pressure from the New York State Association for Retarded Children, which claimed that the special interests of the retarded were being lost in the department, a separate division of Mental Retardation was established.[8]

In 1964, the federal Community Mental Health Act provided federal funding to establish a network of community mental health centers. Through that legislation, the New York City Community Mental Health Board acquired new resources and expanded its activities. While other communities eventually availed themselves of these funding opportunities, New York City was particularly early and active in creating new services. By 1986, New York City was the home of 14 federally designated Community Mental Health Centers (CMHC). Of this group, five were established before 1970. Among the 28 designated centers in the rest of the state only two were established before 1970.[9]

In 1969 the board became the Department of Mental Health and Mental Retardation (NYC DMH & MR), a full-fledged municipal department. (The department was also responsible for alcoholism services, and in 1979 its name was changed to the New York City Department of Mental Health, Mental Retardation and Alcoholism Services—NYCDMHMR & AS.) A commissioner was vested with policymaking authority for the department, while the former board, renamed the Community Services Board, assumed an advisory role. This was a departure from the practice in most other areas of the state, which continued to use boards rather than departments.

The first response of both the New York City Community Mental Health Board and its successor agency to new federal funds was to expand services in existing institutions. Gradually, however, City officials began to examine the allocation of mental health services among New York City's various communities.[10] The pattern was clear. Manhattan had the largest number of both voluntary nonprofit agencies and prestigious medical schools affiliated with hospitals; consequently, that borough received the largest share of mental health dollars. In 1958, with one half Brooklyn's population, Manhattan received more than twice as much funding for mental health services. The boroughs of Queens, Staten Island, and the Bronx were similarly underfunded.[11]

As the City began to confront these imbalances, the State Department of Mental Hygiene was considering the characteristics of former New York City residents in its institutions, many of which were distant from the city. One analysis showed that, perversely, whites were more likely to be placed in State facilities in New York City or close by, while blacks and Hispanics, with lower average incomes and thus less access to transportation, were more likely to be assigned to the more distant hospitals.

Faced with such information, the State realized that it shared with the City an interest in reaching mentally ill minority group members, many of whom were outer borough residents, in facilities closer to their homes. The State and City mental health agencies joined forces to advocate for the creation of community services in the outer boroughs. Three new centers were established with federal funds in Brooklyn, one in Staten Island, and three in the Bronx. Concurrently, the City allocated local tax funds to develop nine smaller new outpatient clinics in disadvantaged areas such as Far Rockaway and East New York. Ultimately the City established 14 new Community Mental Health Centers.

One key limitation on the extension of services beyond Manhattan was that NYC DMH & MR had few links with the voluntary agencies that could help to provide and plan services in the outer boroughs. As a first step toward remedying that situation, the agency in the late 1960s established federations—now known as councils—of private mental health and retardation agencies in each borough to provide advice. Later, the citywide Federation Executive Committee was established to perform the same functions for issues that crossed borough lines.

The interest of the Community Mental Health Board and of its successor agency in serving the mentally retarded did not develop at the same pace as its commitment to the mentally ill. Until 1966, no contract with a voluntary agency for services to the retarded had been approved by the board. As a result, parent groups and agencies serving mentally retarded persons had become active advocates for change.

After John V. Lindsay was elected mayor in 1965, he appointed a committee to provide advice on how to enhance services for the retarded. The committee's recommendations were wide-ranging, but they stressed using State mental health funds for community services. This was achieved in 1968. To stimulate expansion of services for the retarded, the mayor in 1967 appointed an assistant commissioner to supervise mental retardation planning and program development. On the whole, however, the City remained less active in this area than in mental health. City tax levy dollars were still not readily available to match the State funds. Instead, most of the matching funds were provided by philanthropic contributions from voluntary agencies, which had a long-standing interest in serving the mentally retarded.

Deinstitutionalization in the 1970s

Mental Health. As the newly vitalized State Department of Mental Hygiene of the mid 1960s sought to gain greater control over the State institutions, it became increasingly interested in the release of mental patients to community care.[12] In the late 1960s, the associate commissioner of the department's Hospital Division was a strong proponent of the view that large numbers of individuals did not need institutionalized care and would be better off in their communities. His point of view eventually was accepted by the commissioner and plans were developed for large-scale discharges.

The first set of discharges—at Bronx State Hospital in 1968—typified the pattern at many institutions over the next decade. The commissioner and his staff, having determined that elderly patients on the back wards—many of them there for years—were inappropriate for State hospital care, moved them out by bus to the Upper West Side of Manhattan. Large numbers of these patients were housed in Single Room Occupancy buildings (SROs) with few amenities. For their support the

State relied primarily on funds from the Aid to the Disabled Program administered through the City's Human Resources Administration. Concurrently, Bronx State closed admissions to patients over age 60.

New York City officials and particularly staff at NYC DMH & MR protested the State plan to discharge patients before community services were developed for their resettlement, but the pleas were ignored. With the conviction that such services would never be developed until the pressure of large numbers of discharges forced the City into action, the State commissioner seemed honestly to believe that the change would be beneficial to patients.

As is often true when major institutional change is effected, the personal enthusiasm of individuals for the new policy was consistent with larger social forces. Besides the appeal of community-based service models that had emerged in the 1950s and 1960s, four other factors helped create a favorable climate for deinstitutionalization.

First, beginning in the 1950s, the development of psychotropic drugs made it feasible to control some of the more extreme symptoms of mental illness that posed a major obstacle to the mentally ill living among their neighbors. Second, the inadequacy of the State institutions helped to make community residence and treatment an appealing alternative. Generally, the twentieth-century growth in the size of State institutions had not been accompanied by commensurate advances in humane or effective care.

Third, deinstitutionalization was encouraged by a series of court decisions establishing the rights of the mentally disabled. In the most well-known case, *Wyatt* v. *Stickney*, a federal judge, having determined that constitutional due process required adequate and effective treatment in the case of involuntary commitment, set minimum requirements for Alabama's mental health system centering on the physical plant, staffing ratios, prohibition of unpaid work, and the selection of the least restrictive treatment setting.[13]

Finally, deinstitutionalization was greatly accelerated by resources from two federal programs; Medicaid and Supplementary Security Income (SSI). The Medicaid program supported community care for the mentally ill, but did not fund care for adults aged 22–64 in mental institutions. Moreover, New York State's Medicaid funding formula called for the State and locality to divide costs not covered by the federal government. In contrast, care in State institutions was funded exclusively from State tax dollars. Thus, for the State to place an adult patient in a community facility that accepted Medicaid patients, rather than in a State institution, meant that it would enjoy a substantial funding advantage. Hence, while Department of Mental Hygiene officials may have initiated deinstitutionalization in the belief that it would be advantageous to the patients, the shift to community care also reduced the State's financial burden.

SSI, enacted in 1972, allowed for support of the aged, blind, and disabled in the community at 50 percent federal reimbursement. Like Medicaid, it made available to New York State a new source of federal money that could be tapped for individuals in the community. One measure of the importance of these new sources of funding is that in 1980 they jointly constituted the State's largest single source of support for mental health services.[14]

As a result of deinstitutionalization, discharges from State hospitals increased well into the 1970s, and admissions were tightened. Increasingly, discharged patients in New York City were referred not only to SROs but to Private Proprietary Homes for Adults (PPHAs). These facilities, which had higher SSI reimbursement rates than independent living situations, had been developed initially to house elderly people in need of some assistance in the activities of daily living. The homes responded to the influx of the mentally ill by expanding capacity rapidly, but the State standards for licensure were not amended to respond to the service needs of the mentally ill. Their staffing levels were too low, procedures for dealing with medications were not in place, and program activities were not designed to engage disturbed individuals. Many investigations ensued, but remedial action to strengthen PPHA programs and limit access to those who could function in those settings was not fully effected until 1979.

In the late 1970s, SROs, which had continued to house large numbers of the discharged mentally ill, were increasingly converted into luxury residences. When some action was taken to restrict such conversions, it was insufficient to stem the tide of homelessness that began to sweep over New York City. In 1986 the Coalition for the Homeless estimated that there were 60,000 homeless people in the city, with some 20 percent of the single homeless individuals suffering from mental disabilities. While others believe these estimates are high, virtually all observers agree that homelessness among the mentally disabled is a matter of grave concern.

As it became clear that available community mental health facilities were inadequate to meet the demands of the newly discharged patients, the State psychiatric hospitals developed after-care clinics which were intended to provide follow-up assistance. However, because these clinics often were not easily reached by public transportation and because their staffing levels were too low to allow for outreach activities, they did not provide an effective solution to the problems of many dischargees, some of whom were at times disoriented, unable to keep appointments or to recognize the need to renew prescriptions for medications to help them function.

Mental Retardation. While deinstitutionalization was in full force for New York's mentally ill by the early 1970s, it was not until midpoint in the decade that it became important for the mentally retarded. It was initiated by a different constellation of forces than those predominating for the mentally ill, it proceeded differently, and it had far more satis-factory outcomes.

By the 1960s, conditions in institutions for the retarded, as in those for the mentally ill, were widely criticized. Facilities were often old and overcrowded, frequently unsanitary and dangerous, and inadequately staffed. Any efforts at systematic programming were impeded by the wide variety of medical disabilities among residents and by their equal-ly wide range of ages. Over the years, politicians had periodically ex-posed the worsening conditions at these institutions, particularly at the Willowbrook facility on Staten Island. Visiting there in 1965, Sena-tor Robert Kennedy described the institution as "less comfortable and cheerful than the cages in which we put animals in a zoo."[15] Wil-lowbrook, however, remained seemingly impervious to change.

In 1972, television reporter Geraldo Rivera filmed Willowbrook and its residents and aired the clips. The resulting publicity was sufficiently strong to generate a class action suit in federal court. Willowbrook parents claimed that their children had the right to receive adequate care so long as they remained in the institution. The litigants also claimed that they had the right to be returned as promptly as possible to the community. In 1975 a consent decree granted relief for the plaintiffs. The decree was remarkable in the detail in which it spelled out the criteria for assessment of service needs, provision of services, due process for both client and family, and the eventual closure of Willowbrook.

The judgment set in motion a large-scale initiative for the discharge of mentally retarded clients. At the time of the litigation in 1972, Willow-brook's population was 5,400. By 1982, 2,600 of these clients had been placed in community residences; by mid 1986, only 250 of the 1976 Willowbrook residents remained in that institution.[16]

Especially in the years immediately following the consent decree, Willowbrook was the centerpiece of the State's deinstitutionalization efforts. However, while they were most heavily focused on this one New York City institution, the efforts ultimately reshaped the entire system. As illustrated in Table 13.3, the State was making community place-ment for nonclass members throughout the period following the consent decree.

To effect the change at Willowbrook, the Office of Mental Hygiene created a special cadre of staff called the Metropolitan Placement Unit (MPU). Its charge was to develop appropriate services and group homes for the Willowbrook class. MPU staff gathered information on the types

TABLE 13.3

*Statewide Community Placements of Mentally Disabled,
Fiscal Years 1976–1986*

Fiscal Year	Willowbrook Class	Nonclass	Total
1976	142	841	983
1977	237	505	742
1978	463	574	1,037
1979	434	941	1,375
1980	387	996	1,383
1981	264	974	1,238
1982	215	1,226	1,441
1983	118	1,263	1,381
1984	164	989	1,153
1985	186	1,136	1,322
1986	344	1,065	1,409
Total	2,954	10,510	13,464

SOURCE: New York State Office of Mental Retardation and Developmental Disabilities.

of residences and services that would be needed to place residents; pioneered the use of a newly developed instrument to replace the IQ, which had proven useless in measuring the capabilities of the mentally retarded; and expanded or created day programs for a group of clients who were considerably more disabled than former participants in such programs.

The biggest challenge for MPU, however, was to open group homes. In 1976 there were only three group residences for the retarded in New York City. Thus, the court's deinstitutionalization goal required that such facilities be created on a scale never before attempted. The challenge entailed recruiting agencies to operate the homes, addressing community opposition, meeting building codes, accommodating homes to special disabilities of residents, and training staff.

Despite some staffing difficulties and despite larger questions about the costs entailed for placement of the most disabled, the Willowbrook experience has generally received high marks. What accounts for the striking contrast between the outcomes of New York State's deinstitutionalization for the mentally retarded and the mentally ill? A good starting point for answering the question is to consider the difference between the origins of the two policies.

Cost-saving considerations figured prominently in the decision to deinstitutionalize the mental health system. For officials involved in implementing the Willowbrook policy, these factors were clearly secondary to clients' well-being. One aspect of MPU's funding policies illustrates the point: In the early stages of deinstitutionalization, agency officials were reluctant to use Medicaid funds to resettle clients in facilities that met that program's standards for "intermediate care facilities," in part because the procedures for licensing such facilities were time-consuming, but also in part because they feared that requiring group homes to meet the Medicaid requirements would medicalize services and give them an overly institutional style. Only in 1978, when the State Division of the Budget placed more stringent limitations on MPU's spending of other funds, did the unit encourage group homes to conform to Medicaid criteria for intermediate care facilities. Because at that point the homes had already developed their own operating style, they were able to adapt to the Medicaid standards without sacrificing a quality of care that MPU deemed important.[17] Thus, while MPU officials were pragmatic enough to turn to a potentially useful but problematic source of support when they felt it was necessary, their initial impulse was to reject such funding partly on the grounds that it might undermine the kind of services they wished to offer clients.

In some measure, then, it was because the impulses behind the deinstitutionalization of Willowbrook were more clearly reform-minded that officials translated the concept of community care into a far more detailed and specific system of services than was the case for mental health. But differences in motivation alone cannot account for differences in outcomes. The quality of leadership involved in implementing each of the two policies were also important.

Governor Carey, who took office in the midst of the Willowbrook controversy, had a long-standing interest in the mentally retarded. While a congressman, he had drafted and sponsored the first bill providing federal funds for special education. According to his budget director, when he was governor, Carey favored the mental health and retardation agencies over most other departments, protecting their programs from austerity measures.[18] In reflecting on his early plans for his governorship, Carey cited Willowbrook as one of the major problems he faced at the outset of his term, and one about which he needed to find "some way to deal with immediate conditions through extraordinary means."[19] In keeping with these impulses, Carey provided strong backing for the Willowbrook consent decree and devoted staff energy to implementing it. Thus, the governor during the Willowbook experience seized an opportunity to direct political forces into channels of reform where they otherwise might not have flowed so readily.

Another critical difference between the two deinstitutionalization experiences lay in the means available to officials to carry out the policies. While court decisions figured in the development of both policies, the decisions that helped to spark deinstitutionalization for the mentally ill articulated only broad guidelines for action. In contrast, the Willowbrook consent decree was explicit in defining the quality of community care to be offered to clients.

To ensure that such care was available, the State devoted relatively generous resources to establishing group homes, and this is arguably the most important factor for the success of the policy. There was a precipitous jump in the support available to place Willowbrook class members in a group home after the decree. The bare statistics delineating the change—from $9,000 annually before 1975 to between $25,000 and $50,000 per client annually shortly thereafter[20]—are somewhat misleading in that the clients placed in the three group homes that operated before 1975 were able to function with much less support than individuals who were placed after extended stays in Willowbrook. Nevertheless, a large part of the increase reflects the infusion of new State support, which allowed MPU to write generous contracts with voluntary providers.

The extent of State generosity in funding is documented in Table 13.4. State appropriations for directly provided mental retardation services

TABLE 13.4

State Appropriations for Mental Retardation Services, Fiscal Years 1975–1987 (in millions)

Fiscal Year	Direct Services	Local Aid
1975	$296.8	NA
1976	325.3	NA
1977	345.0	NA
1978	368.1	NA
1979	492.9	$73.3
1980	530.2	86.6
1981	498.1	109.6
1982	611.7	174.9
1983	619.3	187.9
1984	643.2	204.5
1985	703.1	232.7
1986	775.8	262.9
1987	811.3	302.6

SOURCE: New York State Office of Mental Retardation and Developmental Disabilities.
NOTES: Figures since fiscal year 1978–1979 are appropriations for NYS OMRDD. Figures for earlier years reflect reported appropriations only for mental retardation services within the Department of Mental Hygiene. NA = not available.

increased almost threefold over the 1975–1987 period, and local aid appropriations rose more than fourfold between 1979 and 1987. Although the increases were significant, it should be noted that as a proportion of the State budget, the appropriations were not large enough to cause alarm among the voting public or elected officials. The relatively small number of mentally retarded clients minimized the impact of significant increases in per client expenditures on the State budget, and this facilitated efforts to implement deinstitutionalization.

Another difference between the deinstitutionalization experiences of the mentally ill and the retarded is the nature of the definitions commonly applied to the two disabilities. Mental illness is often conceived of in terms of a medical model that dictates treatment for illness in a special facility, followed by release to independent living once symptoms abate. For the mentally retarded, however, the State held much more closely to the traditional notion of "asylum" — continuous care for a chronic condition, the difference being that it was now to be provided in a community group home rather than in a large institution. As misguided as it may have been to release highly disoriented mentally disabled individuals to live in the community without enough support, it was unthinkable to follow such a course with the retarded, who are more obviously unable to function under these conditions.

Partly because this need for continuous care for the mentally retarded is well recognized, parents of the retarded have consistently been active in demanding improved services for their children. For example, parents are an important constituency within the Association for Retarded Children (ARC), which during the 1960s advocated the creation of a separate division for mental retardation within the Department of Mental Hygiene. With the development and implementation of the Willowbrook consent decree, parental involvement from ARC and other organizations intensified. Fortifying the interest of the governor and the courts in providing quality community services, parents constituted another pressure group that helped to make deinstitutionalization a more effective policy for the mentally retarded than for the mentally ill.

More Recent Changes

Mental Health. As deinstitutionalization hit full stride, localities felt increased pressure to serve the mentally ill who had either been discharged from State institutions or who had never been admitted under more stringent criteria. To help the localities cope, funding for community services was expanded. Statewide local aid for mental health increased from $80 million in 1975 to $285 million in 1987. (See Table 13.5.)

Not only did the State add to existing aid packages, but it also created new funding mechanisms targeted to the deinstitutionalized. In 1974, in a program known as Chapter 620, the State agreed to reimburse fully both City and voluntary service providers for the cost of mental health services for individuals who had been in State institutions for five or more years as of January 1, 1969. In 1979 the State enacted the Community Support Services (CSS) program, which provides funds, again at 100 percent of costs, for the treatment of the chronically mentally ill, either in outpatient clinics of State psychiatric facilities or in the voluntary sector. Except for a small group of clients made eligible by residence in certain kinds of congregate care facilities, CSS funds are reserved for individuals who have been institutionalized. In 1983, in the Medicaid Overburden Legislation, the State agreed to reimburse localities fully for Medicaid expenses incurred for certain categories of the mentally disabled. The basic mental health local assistance program, however, continues to account for most State funding of City services. For example, in 1985–1986, this program accounted for 17 percent of NYC DMHMR & AS's budget, while CSS and Chapter 620 were together only 5 percent.[21]

In a separate response to the needs of the mentally ill, the State in 1972 initiated its own community residence program, in which it contracts with voluntary providers to establish community homes of no more than 24 residents. The State pays for a portion of the developmental, rental, and operating costs of these facilities, with the balance supported by user fees. Contracts are managed by the New York State Regional Office of Mental Health.

TABLE 13.5

Local Aid Expenditures for Department of Mental Hygiene, Fiscal Years 1955, 1965, 1975, and 1987

	1955	1965 Amount	1965 Percentage	1975 Amount	1975 Percentage	1987 Amount	1987 Percentage
Total New York	$116,486	$15,756,464	100%	$80,089,686	100%	$285,397,000	100%
City	NA	10,648,132	68	42,284,490	53	152,857,033	54
Rest of State	NA	5,108,332	32	37,805,196	47	132,539,967	46

SOURCE: New York State Office of Mental Health.

NOTE: Includes expenditures for Mental Health, Alcoholism, Drug Abuse, and Mental Retardation; discrete expenditures for mental health are not available for these years. NA = not available.

One other funding arrangement proposed by the State during this period was entertained but ultimately rejected by New York City—and indeed by all but five counties in the state. This was the Unified Services Funding proposal, offered in 1974 as an alternative to local assistance funding. Under this plan, New York City would have shared the costs of local mental health operations with the State based on a formula calculated according to population. The formula would have granted the City significantly more than the 50 percent reimbursement under the existing local assistance program, but in return the City would have had to assume a share of the costs for its residents housed in State facilities. The plan also would have entailed joint State-City planning for delivery of services.[22] The City rejected Unified Services after a determination that its local assistance formula would have meant the assumption of a greater fiscal burden than the existing funding structure.[23]

A substantial portion of the expanded resources devoted to the City during the 1970s was funneled into voluntary and municipal hospitals. In connection with the growing complexity of service provision in New York City, it is important to bear in mind the size and scope of its municipal hospital system operated by the Health and Hospitals Corporation (HHC). With 11 municipal hospitals the HHC maintains a far more elaborate service configuration than the single county hospital that typically serves the mentally ill in other large municipalities. Thus, to the extent that the individual municipal hospitals vary in their policies and practices, the City and State agencies must relate to a wider range of actors than is the case in smaller communities. At the same time, the agencies must negotiate changes in hospital policies not just with a few institutions, but with a central bureaucracy representing the potentially different interests of many hospitals.

Mental Retardation. Like the mental health bureaucracy, the mental retardation structure was reshaped and expanded by deinstitutionalization. To help make the Department of Mental Hygiene more responsive to the consent decree, Governor Carey appointed in 1975 the politically skillful Thomas Coughlin, a former state trooper who is the parent of a mentally retarded daughter and who had been a local director of the Association for Retarded Citizens in northern New York, as the department's deputy commissioner for the Division for Mental Retardation. By 1978, the division had acquired enough power—in part because of pressure from Willowbrook parents—to become an independent department, with Coughlin as its first commissioner. In one important respect, this change signaled a departure from the previous leadership structure. By law, the commissioner of the State Mental Hygiene

Department must be a psychiatrist. With the creation of the new department, authority was vested in an official who was by background apt to be more focused on developmental disability issues.

The new Office of Mental Retardation and Developmental Disabilities (NYS OMRDD) was put on an equal standing with the Office of Mental Hygiene (now renamed the New York State Office of Mental Health— NYS OMH—with a third agency, the Office of Alcoholism and Substance Abuse, also placed at the same level). The MPU director, serving as an assistant commissioner of the new NYS OMRDD, assumed oversight responsibility for New York City's developmental disability centers.

In 1978, the State legislature passed the Site Selection Law. Declaring that the State was to provide a residential setting for the mentally disabled that was as free of restrictions as possible, the legislation established procedures for establishing community residences to meet this "least restrictive" stipulation. The procedures, which permit community residents to have a voice in the site selection process, are designed to defuse conflict so that residents and advocates for the disabled do not become locked in irreconcilable differences. The New York State Committee on Mental Hygiene and Addiction Control, which was largely responsible for the legislation, claims that over the past eight years it has proven highly effective. The committee points out that during that period most community residences have been established without court challenges.[24]

Another step taken during this period was State assumption of the local share of Medicaid and SSI costs to support intermediate care facilities for the retarded. This change predated by a decade the Medicaid Overburden legislation, which essentially attempts to accomplish the same purpose in the mental health field.

In developing day treatment services and group homes for New York City's mentally retarded, MPU worked directly with a range of voluntary agencies. As the MPU became a presence in the city, there was some degree of concern from NYC DMHMR & AS that MPU could intrude on the City's efforts to work with the voluntary agencies or that it could disrupt the planning and consulting mechanisms that the agency had developed through its borough federations. To address these concerns, MPU attempted to keep the agency informed of its plans, so that the City would be aware of any new demands being placed on the voluntaries by the State. After the formation of NYS OMRDD, a joint NYS OMRDD/ NYC DMHMR & AS deputy commissioner was appointed and charged with furthering coordination between the two agencies. Nevertheless, the lead role for serving the mentally retarded of New York City was clearly the State's. The City had not been named in the Willowbrook suit nor was it required to finance the changes the State was now undertaking. Thus, in this major initiative, New York City remained the State's cooperative, interested, but largely junior, partner.

CITY-STATE RELATIONSHIPS IN THE 1980S

The two different experiences with deinstitutionalization have left New York City's and New York State's mental health and retardation service delivery systems in two distinctly different positions. In 1984 NYS OMRDD issued a booklet entitled *A Decade of Triumph and a Future of Hope: Services to Developmentally Disabled Persons in New York State.* Among the achievements cited in the publication are a record of deinstitutionalization that exceeds that of all other states, a reliance on institutional beds that has dropped by 50 percent, nationwide leadership in the number of clients living in small group settings, and minimal use of skilled nursing facilities which are considered inappropriate for clients who do not require medical treatment.[25] According to a recent study of state expenditures for mental retardation and developmental disabilities, New York moved from forty-second among the states in the proportion of resources spent on community services in fiscal year 1977 to eighteenth in fiscal year 1984.[26]

Even allowing for the hyperbole that inevitably characterizes an agency's report on its own programs, NYS OMRDD has a sound basis on which to claim significant accomplishment. By contrast, it is difficult to envision NYS OMH publishing a report with a title similar to that chosen by NYS OMRDD. When the NYS OMH commissioner addressed the State's public health association in 1984, the title of his remarks was "Mental Health Treatment: Have Two Decades Made a Difference?"

Recently the national Public Citizen Health Research Group released a report, *Care of the Serious Mentally Ill: A Rating of State Programs.*[27] The first analysis of its kind, it made comparative assessments of the quality of mental health services delivered by all 50 states. In the rating of states by quality of inpatient and outpatient programs combined, 17 states ranked more favorably than New York. While acknowledging that in a state the size of New York, there are many "bright spots" in its care system, the study concluded that on the whole, New York's problems outweigh its progress.

Undoubtedly, many familiar with New York's mental health system would dispute the study's final judgment, and it is beyond the scope of this essay to assess its accuracy. However, most actors in and observers of New York State's system would not dispute the conclusion that the system continues to face major problems. This section examines those problems and considers the less complicated set of State-City interactions that characterize mental retardation services.

Mental Health

Responsibilities for Acute and Chronic Care. The current division of responsibility between New York City and New York State for care of the mentally ill does not result from conscious decisions about which level of government can best handle which functions, but is the outcome of a series of historical forces and arrangements. For example, both City and State have been responsible for residential care for many decades— the City in its municipal hospitals and the State in its institutions. But before the onset of deinstitutionalization, the question of which facility a patient belonged in was not troublesome because City hospitals could more readily transfer patients to the State institutions, with their relatively flexible admissions policies. What was once a fairly open door to the large institutions has closed considerably, causing growing pressure on the municipal hospitals. While the city's supply of acute psychiatric beds has increased, it has not kept pace with demand. Psychiatric services in municipal hospitals now operate at between 90 and 100 percent of capacity.[28]

With this new strain on hospital facilities, the distinction between the traditional responsibilities of City and State—acute versus chronic care—takes on greater importance. It raises the same issue addressed by the commissioner of lunacy in the late nineteenth century—whether it is appropriate to transfer patients from one system to another as they move from one phase of mental illness to another.

Assuming that the distinction is a useful one, the transfer from one system to the other should be smooth. Yet it is not, and there is a blurring of accountability between the two levels of government. For example, HHC officials point out that routinely there are patients awaiting transfer in the municipal psychiatric facilities no longer in crisis who take up beds needed by other individuals who have legitimate acute care needs.

Recently the City and the State drafted Uniform Admission Guidelines that spell out the kinds of conditions that each institution should treat. The State also has worked with the City to develop special arrangements to ease the worst overcrowding. One such arrangement, the Brooklyn Plan, is a permanent system-wide change. This agreement among the major inpatient providers—voluntary, municipal, and State—in the borough divides responsibilities for patient care among three catchment areas, one served by a municipal hospital and two by State pyschiatric centers. Each facility is responsible, with the aid of the appropriate voluntaries, for all care, both acute and chronic, in its area.[29]

In addition to the Brooklyn Plan, the City and State have developed three arrangements, now viewed as temporary measures: First, there are "Special Assessment Teams," a group of OMH and HHC officials who visit municipal hospitals to try to effect appropriate transfers for hard-to-place patients. Second, there is "the Tripwire Agreement," a plan that allows transfer of patients from North Central Bronx and Harlem hospitals to selected State facilities on weekends if these municipal facilities are at 100 percent of inpatient capacity.[30] Finally, a new weekday arrangement broadens the Tripwire arrangement. Under this plan, State institutions—primarily in Rockland County—agree to consider taking acute care patients when municipal hospitals are unable to place patients from their psychiatric emergency rooms elsewhere in their own system or in the voluntaries because they are at capacity.[31]

Nonetheless, transfers of acute patients from City to State facilities, even under emergency mechanisms, cannot be automatically assumed. Sometimes patients are unwilling to be sent to State facilities and use legal challenges to avoid the shift. Sometimes hospital staff are reluctant to use State facilities for patients, particularly when, as is often the case, they have alcohol- or drug-related difficulties. In turn, State facilities may hesitate to accept such patients, fearing that the individuals will require more medical attention than the facilities can offer.

The last reaction underscores another question about State responsibilities: Are State institutions appropriate for acute care? In a sense, the State has backed into the role of providing such care, in 1984 accounting for over 13 percent of all acute psychiatric beds in New York City.[32] With the exception of the Brooklyn agreement, the State's assumption of authority for acute care has thus far been not so much consciously chosen as developed on an ad hoc basis in response to pressing needs elsewhere in the system.

Although responsibility for chronic care has been the State's primary role throughout the twentieth century, the nature of the role has shifted considerably. Two facts about patients in the system delineate the change. First, their median length of stay in State institutions is markedly shorter—six years in 1970 versus 30 days for a newly admitted patient in 1983.[33] Second, in a pattern known as the "revolving door syndrome," patients are apt to return for care. For example, a study of 119 chronic mental patients discharged from institutions and followed between 1977 and 1979 found that their one-year rehospitalization rate was 58 percent.[34] The OMH reports that in 1965 only 36 percent of patients in New York City OMH facilities were readmissions, but the proportion in 1985 was 71 percent. (Patterns upstate were similar.) The extent of the State's responsibility for the mentally ill when they are not under this increasingly short-term care remains a critical issue. It is particularly critical in New York City, given the changing nature of its mentally ill population. The city's population is markedly younger than it was in previous eras, and young adulthood is typically the time for the onset of schizophrenia. Greater availability of drugs and alcohol have made this same population more subject to substance abuse. With more widespread agreement that "the phasedown of the asylum will not eliminate chronicity,"[35] State and City must grapple with the issue of how to provide continuous care for a population which, if anything, poses more challenges than the mentally disabled of the 1960s.

Responsibilities for Post-State Hospital Care. State responsibilities for the mentally ill extend beyond the walls of residential institutions. The State's mental hygiene legislation charges both the State and its localities with the planned care, rehabilitation, and treatment of the mentally ill. In a class action suit, *Klostermann* v. *Cuomo*, the New York State Court of Appeals ruled that homeless, formerly institutionalized defendants have the right to sue the City and the State for residential services after they have left a State institution. It is unlikely that the courts will soon be involved with deinstitutionalization issues in the mental health field with anything like the level of detail entailed in the Willowbrook consent decree. Among other reasons, the Supreme Court's 1982 ruling in *Pennhurst State School* v. *Halderman* has been widely interpreted as a reluctance to become heavily involved in specifying the quality of conditions in state institutions.[36] Nevertheless, the preliminary ruling in the *Klostermann* case suggests that courts in New York State may in the future take a more active role in defining the State's obligations.

Since 1982 NYS OMH has had a comprehensive discharge policy, which replaces numerous individual policy directives developed since the mid 1970s and which details how its institutions are to plan post-treatment care for dischargees. Planning is to involve staff at the State institution, community mental health staff, and, as needed, staff from the Department of Social Services. Once a patient is discharged, State hospital staff are to monitor the provision of community mental health services by ascertaining within 30 days that the individual has kept the first appointment for care. (State staff are not responsible for monitoring the provision of other services specified in the plan.) The community mental health agency may be equipped to take on the tasks of further follow-up when an appointment is missed, but if the agency does not define such follow-up as part of its responsibilities, the State institution is expected to do so.[37]

Implementing this policy, especially in a New York City facility, poses a number of difficulties. Limited resources within the institution may mean that care for newly admitted patients, especially those in acute stages of illness, places burdens on staff who are responsible for both this activity and after-care planning. Also, while staff search for appropriate post-institutional services, the patients—many of them young adults, who are less passive and compliant than the patients who used to dominate the institutional population—may decide to leave of their own accord. In this situation, the State institution is not responsible for monitoring subsequent activities. In cases where patients are discharged to after-care, these same young adults are apt to miss clinic appointments and disappear within the city, only to later reappear at the "revolving door" of the State institution for another bout of acute illness.

Discharged clients served by CSS program funds are assigned to a case manager. CSS, however, serves only a small proportion of the chronically mentally ill. Of the approximately 47,000 mentally ill New York City residents who meet CSS's eligibility criteria, the program treats an estimated 4,000–6,000 clients at any one time.[38] For the mentally ill treated by non-CSS-funded programs, the provision of consistent follow-up by one person depends on the policy of the particular agencies working with the dischargee. It is possible that the client will be referred to a range of providers for a range of services, with no central source of accountability.

Staff of the State institution may discharge patients to the care of their own outpatient clinics or to a City-sponsored facility. In the latter case, staff may perceive the transfer as not only from one *facility* to another but also as from one *system* to another. Thus, as they encounter problems with the quality of care at a particular City facility to which they plan to discharge patients, staff may conclude that they have less leverage than they would like in advocating improvements—simply because the facility is managed by another agency in which they have no standing.[39] This disjuncture can further complicate after-care planning.

Allocation of State Resources. Perhaps the most serious barrier to good community care in New York City is simply a lack of resources. Appropriate housing, to cite the most pressing need, is in critically short supply. A joint NYS OMH/NYC DMHMR & AS New York City Temporary Committee on Discharge Planning concluded in 1981 that "until such time as funds are made available for specialized housing, other solutions can only tinker with [discharge] problems.[40]

New York State, which spends more per capita on mental health services than any other state, has been widely criticized for spending a disproportionate amount of these funds on institutional care, thus diverting resources from community care.[41] As shown in Table 13.6, OMH local assistance allocated to the City for fiscal year 1987 was less than a third of expenditures for State psychiatric centers in 1985. One opponent of State spending priorities has pointed out that from 1967 to 1972, a period in which there was a precipitous decline in the population of State institutions, the State *increased* its annual funding to its facilities by $254 million, while boosting aid to localities by only $28 million.[42]

The institutions clearly needed improvement, but the continued investment in these facilities has been linked in the minds of many to the size and power of their workforce. The vast majority of NYS OMH's 37,000 employees work in its institutions. Most of these workers are represented by the Civil Service Employees Association (CSEA), which has been frequently charged with using political influence to maintain the existing distribution of resources.[43]

State and CSEA officials contend that the picture of politicians, bureaucrats, and the union collaborating to perpetuate institutions at the expense of community care is a distorted one. They point out that State OMH expenditures for community care are only a small percentage of a large and rapidly growing pool of funds supporting these services and that the entire range of State expenditures for community care should be compared with the institutional care budget. The other community care expenditures include Medicaid reimbursements, mental health services in generic health system programs, and other mental health programs. One estimate is that these programs add $650 million to the State's contribution to community care and that $120 million of the institutional budget was actually dedicated to community programs provided through these facilities.[44]

TABLE 13.6

New York State Expenditures
for Institutional and Community Mental Health Services

	Expenditures for Psychiatric Centers, Fiscal Year 1985	Assistance for Community Services, Fiscal Year 1987
Total	$1,447,554,814	$285,397,000
New York City	419,586,308	132,539,967
Rest of State	1,027,968,506	152,857,033

SOURCE: New York State Office of Mental Health.

NYS OMH and CSEA officials also argue that institutional staffing levels, which are approximately at the national average, are not excessive. A 1984 review of living conditions in nine predominantly urban State psychiatric centers by the New York Commission on the Quality of Care for the Mentally Disabled found serious deficiencies in all of the facilities.[45] While pointing to such deficiencies, CSEA at the same time recommends a significant retraining and redeployment of State psychiatric staff into the community.[46]

While seemingly contradictory, advocacy of current institutional staffing levels and retraining of those staff members for community work is a logically consistent position. There is a need to maintain a large institutional workforce, because there are inadequate community resources to care for many short-term patients. At the same time, there may be a scarcity of resources to develop community care, because staffing levels at the institutions must be maintained to serve current residents.

There also is the possibility of holding present patient/staff ratios within institutions constant, but of consolidating institutions to effect administrative and support staff savings. However, even though some institutions have periodically dipped to very low populations, there has been little consolidation of facilities. When asked about unsolved problems at the end of his tenure as commissioner of NYS OMH during the Carey Administration, James Prevost replied, "I was never able to close a State hospital."[47] Clearly, closing some of the rural institutions would cause significant employment problems in communities with few alternative sources of jobs.

Whatever the dynamics behind the current mix of institutional and community services, one clear indication that the balance must be redressed is that both NYS OMH and CSEA join other major parties in calling for a build-up of community care capacity. NYS OMH has recently begun a long-range planning process for the reconfiguration of the system by 1995. At that point, the goal is to have 10,000 community residence beds—up over 6,000 from the current level—with an additional 5,000 beds in larger Residential Care Centers for Adults, which so far are represented by only one center with 200 beds. At the same time, the system's long-term and short-term inpatient bed capacity would decrease from its current level of approximately 20,000 to 13,000.

There is further consensus that the need for community resources is particularly acute in New York City, where, although community services have expanded significantly in recent years, there is still less use of community services and family care than in the rest of the state. According to a 1981–1982 survey of patient characteristics, New York City led other regions around the state in clinical treatment per 100,000 patients, but was "relatively low in community residence and family care days."[48]

With State institutions concentrated upstate and the bulk of the mentally ill in New York City, the State is routinely accused of shortchanging city needs. For example, in testimony in public hearings on NYS OMH's 1985–1990 five-year comprehensive plan in October 1985, the NYC DMHMR & AS commissioner noted that an initial review of the State's plans by her department raised the possibility that the State was planning to reduce intermediate care capacity in New York City, thus worsening "the existing imbalances in New York City's service system."[49]

The State contends that the city is more generously served than is often acknowledged. NYS OMH points out that while a relatively small percentage of allocations for inpatient services went to New York City institutions, fully 50 percent of adult expenditures went to New York City *residents* (see Table 13.7), many of whom were in upstate facilities. Similarly, for children and youth inpatient services, the proportion was 62 percent for New York City residents. Of course, unless most of the large numbers of New York City residents served upstate prefer to be treated there, these figures also suggest that New York City residents cannot be served near their homes and that in this respect New York City is at a disadvantage compared with upstate communities.

TABLE 13.7

State Appropriations for Mental Health Services,
Estimated Allocations to New York City
and Rest of State Residents,* Fiscal Year 1987

	Adult and Forensic		Children and Youth	
	Amount	Percentage	Amount	Percentage
Inpatient				
New York City	$477,451,176	50.4%	$32,933,560	61.7%
Rest of State	470,436,804	49.6	20,417,420	38.3
Outpatient				
New York City	44,425,197	26.6	14,123,039	47.0
Rest of State	122,586,823	73.4	15,925,981	53.0
Total				
New York City	521,876,373	46.8	47,056,599	56.4
Rest of State	593,023,627	53.2	36,343,401	43.6

SOURCE: New York State Office of Mental Health.

*Based on county of residence for inpatient distribution and location of facility for outpatient distribution.

Although the State has extended various funding mechanisms—Chapter 620, CSS, and Medicaid Overburden—to localities to cope with mentally disabled institutional dischargees, these measures have been assailed frequently as too narrowly categorical to meet many needs. For example, New York City has a suit pending against the State charging that NYS OMH, NYS OMRDD, and the Department of Social Services, which jointly developed criteria to define which individuals would be eligible for 100 percent State reimbursement under the Medicaid Overburden Legislation, constructed an overly narrow definition of mental disability. Under these definitions, the City is obliged to continue to provide its 25 percent Medicaid share to large numbers of needy individuals.

In the years immediately preceding the Cuomo Administration, State local assistance for community services grew, but slowly. When the new governor took office, he proposed $13 million in statewide cuts in local assistance for outpatient services in psychiatric wards, on the grounds that the facilities would be able to cover those costs through a newly instituted bad debt and charity pool. The proposals drew sharp criticism from Mayor Koch and other local officials. The cuts were reduced to $6.2 million (with $3.9 million of them concentrated in New York City). The City compensated for the cuts by voting additional funds for psychiatric services in municipal and voluntary hospitals. In late 1983, the governor pledged to restore the cuts, saying that he had been mistaken in thinking that the bad debt pool could compensate for lost resources.[50]

While the State's improved fiscal picture facilitated this reversal, the protest elicited by the cuts suggests that by the early 1980s mental health services in New York City had reached enough of a crisis point to place local assistance politically off limits to significant budget cutting. Over the past several years, the legislature has consistently added support, in the range of $3 million a year, to NYS OMH's requests for local assistance. In the same vein, in contrast to its past policy of renting facilities for community residences, NYS OMH has begun to include proposals for community housing for the mentally ill in its capital budget. Also in recent years, the State's commitment to community residences in New York City has increased significantly from 982 to 2,020 beds between 1982 and 1986.[51]

Inter-Agency Relations. A criticism frequently leveled at current City-State funding arrangements is that they are highly fragmented. Each program has its own eligibility criteria, reimbursement levels, and reporting requirements, leaving many cracks into which clients can fall. Both a cause and a result of this fiscal fragmentation is the divided NYS

OMH/NYC DMHMR & AS structure. The fact that each agency has separate lines of accountability for resource allocation, service delivery, contract procedures, and quality control is one reason for the absence of comprehensive case management.

The dual-agency responsibility likewise impedes comprehensive planning. For example, in the testimony on NYS OMH's five-year plan and in similar testimony to the State legislature, the NYC DMHMR & AS commissioner pointed out that both this plan and the State's capital budget for construction of new facilities were not timed so as to benefit from input from the City's local planning process.[52]

Also, the fact that so many of the City's mental health services are delivered in municipal hospitals has a bearing on prospects for systematic planning. The HHC has little authority to solve problems on its own; for example, the State would have to give HHC approval to decertify medical beds and replace them with psychiatric beds. In other words, plans in an already complex environment must take into account a hospital system that has responsibility for the needs and priorities of the physically ill as well as the mentally disabled.

The former commissioner of NYS OMH concluded that one of the major unsolved problems of his tenure was a failure to develop a satisfactory working relationship with New York City.[53] Does this problem continue?

In her testimony on NYS OMH's five-year plan, the City commissioner, while praising some aspects of the document, was critical of many others. Such public voicing of dissatisfaction could lead to the conclusion that communications between the City agency and NYS OMH are as strained as they were in the past. Apparently, however, this is not the case. The New York City background of the current State commissioner (who was formerly the medical director of Bellevue Hospital's Department of Psychiatry) has improved City-State communications. Although there are no formal requirements to do so, the City and State commissioners consult regularly. The City commissioner credits her State counterpart with the broadening of the original "tripwire" capacities for institutional transfers. The improvement in communications between agencies fostered the establishment of a new joint City-State planning group.

Mental Retardation

As NYS OMRDD and City agencies seek to assist New York's developmentally disabled, they have encountered areas of conflict, centering on placements for individuals in special categories. Underlying these disputes is the fact that more people remain in need of placement than there are beds to accommodate them. NYS OMRDD has a waiting list of over 8,000 people and is seeking to increase community residential capacity from 15,000 to 21,000.[54]

When confronted with individuals they believe belong in NYS OMRDD facilities, municipal hospitals and agencies such as the Office of Special Services for Children (SSC) within the New York City Department of Social Services have an understandable interest in having them placed, especially in cases when such individuals will remain supported in part or in toto at City expense until placement is effected. Individuals who pose particular placement problems to SSC and HHC include the multiply disabled—with symptoms of both mental illness and mental retardation—and a group referred to as "aging out youths," young adults who have been living with parents who are now too old to care for them, or youths who were once placed in out-of-state group homes by SSC and who reappear in the city in need of assistance when they pass the age of eligibility for residence in those facilities.

In 1982, HHC signed an informal agreement, known as the Tripartite Agreement, with NYC DMHMR & AS, NYS OMH, and NYS OMRDD specifying that within set time limits, difficult-to-place individuals referred to City agencies and awaiting placement would be referred to NYS OMH if they tested with IQs above 70, to NYS OMRDD if they had scores below 50 or were members of the Willowbrook class, and that the case would be reviewed jointly by the two agencies if scores fell between 50 and 70. Although in force for some time, this agreement is no longer operative. According to the NYS OMRDD commissioner, the City wishes to revive and formalize the agreement, but he does not. Although he has been urged to do so by NYC DMHMR & AS and by NYS OMH, he is unwilling to renew without formal direction to do so from the legislature, because he believes that the policy should be subject to legislative review. More immediately, he believes that the agreement undercuts his agency's authority to make its own determination about how to prioritize waiting lists.

In a similar dispute, SSC and NYC DMHMR & AS have jointly brought suit against NYS OMRDD for more expeditious transfer of SSC clients to NYS OMRDD facilities. The City contends that NYS OMRDD has a responsibility for placement; the State holds that it has no absolute obligation to take any particular client before any other but that discretion is vested by the legislature in the department and its commissioner to set priorities for who is placed.[55]

Both the NYS OMRDD commissioner and City officials acknowledge that while each case of a difficult-to-place individual can pose a serious challenge to their agencies, the overall number of such cases is small. Leaving aside these conflicts, delineation of authority for mental retardation services between City and State appears to be far more clear-cut and less stressful than in the mental health field. The State is responsible for residential issues, and focuses to a lesser extent on day treatment and ancillary services. The City agency is concerned with nonresidential services.

Interestingly, this comparatively clear understanding of roles and responsibilities apparently owes little to the creation of informal channels of City-State communications. Commissioners of both NYS OMRDD and NYC DMHMR & AS report that they rarely consult with each other. The joint City-State departmental appointment instituted at the inception of NYS OMRDD no longer exists. The contrast between these dynamics and those in the mental health field, where communications are good but allocation of responsibility is highly problematic, suggests that interagency communication may be most needed in cases in which roles are least clearly defined.

Another issue for consideration is whether City and State will maintain their current balance of power in the future. One possible source of tension is the role of the borough councils of NYC DMHMR & AS. Representatives of individual State facilities sit on these councils, which are composed of provider and consumer representatives for mental health and retardation services, and representatives of the State regional office of NYS OMRDD attend their meetings. Their official function is to advise the City department on planning and service delivery, but unofficially, there is a potential for them to play a second role—to relate directly to the State.

NYC DMHMR & AS officials express concern about recent efforts of the State Office of Alcoholism and Substance Abuse (the counterpart agency to NYS OMRDD) to contract directly with two borough councils for services. Since the councils are intended to provide locally based planning consultation, they hold that this direct contact from the State creates a potential conflict of interest. No similar actions have been taken by NYS OMH or NYS OMRDD; commissioners of both agencies merely speak of their interest in "maintaining good relationships" with the councils. But the fact that the State agencies can—and do—relate directly to the councils raises the possibility that the councils could become an independent power base.

One can further speculate that for two reasons the likelihood of this happening is particularly great for NYS OMRDD. First, the relationship between NYS OMRDD and the City agency is not close. At the same time, the link between NYS OMRDD and the voluntary agencies that sit on the borough councils is historically strong. Furthermore, since the inception of local assistance, voluntary agencies have been allowed to contribute to the City's portion of the match, and this voluntary share has been particularly important for mental retardation services. Thus, while the City-State relationship in the mental retardation field is not as complex as for mental health, one cannot assume that it is either static or protected from new developments.

FUTURE TRENDS AND DIRECTIONS

Mental Retardation

NYS OMRDD was born out of the Willowbrook consent decree, and over the agency's eight-year history the task of complying with that mandate has been a major focus of its work. With the final disposition of the decree within reach, NYS OMRDD may be about to formulate new priorities. The tasks and responsibilities that have thus far occupied the agency will not evaporate when all the Willowbrook class members have been placed and the Willowbrook standards put in place statewide. There will remain an acute shortage of community placements and a need to monitor and improve the quality of existing group homes. Furthermore, the agency will continue to have responsibility for a network of developmental disability centers that have achieved at best a very uneven record of care.

Nevertheless, with one major stage of deinstitutionalization behind it, NYS OMRDD is committed to exploring new areas and intensifying its activities in others. The agency seeks to expand primary prevention and day services and to create new and better services for the multiply disabled.[56] Also, OMRDD has recently begun an effort to help the families of developmentally disabled individuals who are cared for at home.[57]

If the agency continues to move in new directions, the way in which it will relate to the City system—where officials also have an interest in day services and primary prevention activities and may have their own ideas about how to target services—remains an open question. One part of the answer may be in the level of interest officials at NYS OMRDD and NYC DMHMR & AS have in establishing better communications. Another key factor is resources: How much funding will the City, which is pressed on many mental health issues, devote to mental retardation services? The fiscal year 1987 City Budget increases the proportion of the local assistance match made up by its own tax levies—as opposed to that contributed by the voluntaries—from 36 to 41 percent. Trends in this direction, even modest ones, might signal a greater City stake in mental retardation services and could help to strengthen its role in planning. Another important question regarding funding is the future capacity of

NYS OMRDD to continue to obtain increased State funding for services for the mentally retarded once the consent decree era has ended.

Mental Health

If mental retardation services in New York State and New York City can be described as on the brink of a post-Willowbrook phase, perhaps the best analogue for summing up the state of mental health services is "post-Select Commission." The commission, composed of 19 members representing private and public interests in the field and appointed shortly after Governor Cuomo took office, was charged with conducting a comprehensive evaluation of the State's mental health needs and services. Intensive investigations and hearings were conducted over a 14-month period, culminating in the publication of the final report in November 1984. Among its key recommendations were the creation of regional local mental health management authorities, accountable to NYS OMH, responsible for administering mental health services to all but the currently institutionalized long-term patients in their regions; consolidation of existing funding streams to be followed by the establishment of a capitation system of financing for the local management authorities; continuation of NYS OMH's role as the provider of inpatient care in State institutions for the long-term population; and the reorganization of NYS OMH into discrete units responsible for provision of services in State psychiatric care centers, stimulation and balancing of community care, and regulation, funding, certifying and licensing of public mental health systems.

Governor Cuomo hailed the report as a "historic document in the annals of mental health policy."[58] However, the proposals have not been translated into legislation. Although the commission called for guarantees of job continuity and employment opportunities for the current mental health workforce, CSEA was widely accused of helping to block the commission's agenda. The union representative resigned from the commission shortly after the report was released, and CSEA issued a strongly worded report of its own opposing the recommendations.

The union was not alone in voicing doubts about the merits of the commission's recommendations. For example, the NYC DMHMR & AS deputy commissioner for operations also expressed uncertainty about the feasibility of a statewide capitation system, and the NYS OMH commissioner is opposed to the separation of the agency's functions recommended in the report.

Perhaps more significant than any one objection is that the recommendations were greeted with the inherent caution with which proposals for sweeping reform are frequently met. The reaction of Senator

Padavan, chairman of the Senate Committee on Mental Hygiene and Addiction Control, to the commissioner's report was that the recommendations were "unrealistic."[59] Other officials—for example, the NYS OMH commissioner and chairman of the State Commission on the Quality of Care—view the effort required to replace one major system with another as diverting too much attention from the task of devising more immediate solutions to service provision problems.

In a sense the Select Commission's recommendations were the second proposed systemwide reform that failed to materialize in the period following deinstitutionalization. The first was the Unified Services Plan, rejected by New York City and by most other counties. It is interesting to speculate whether the commission's recommendations would have been received in the same manner had they taken the form of a renewed call for a Unified Services plan—perhaps one with a different funding formula than that previously rejected by New York City. One advantage of such an approach is that its proponents could have answered some questions about feasibility by pointing to models already in existence.

It is widely acknowledged that Unified Funding is working successfully in the five counties in which it was adopted. According to the Rockland County commissioner of mental health, the use of this funding arrangement in this system (a system which won a 1983 Gold Achievement Award of the American Psychiatric Association) has led to a markedly better capacity to plan and provide comprehensive services.[60] Unified Services in Rockland County is administered by a county-wide Executive Committee with representatives from both State and county facilities. Reporting to the committee are 14 Work Groups, composed of agency representatives, which resolve service issues related to their area. The commissioner adds that his own strong differences of opinion with the director of the local State psychiatric center have not hindered the functioning of the county system.

Whether Rockland County's experience with Unified Services could be replicated in New York City is an open question. On the one hand, it may be too complex a change to impose on a mental health system of the scope of New York City's. On the other hand, the rejection of Unified Funding may have been a lost opportunity for the City.

Although the Select Commission's report has not led to major reorganization, the "post-Select Commission" period has witnessed several significant State and City efforts to explore aspects of the recommendations. The State legislature is considering consolidation of Chapter 620 and CSS funding, with expanded definitions of eligibility. The expansion of eligibility would mean that statewide an additional 25,000 people would be covered by the new program.

In New York City, the commission's report was apparently a catalyst for the creation of the Special Assessment Teams that have worked to resolve hard-to-place cases in City facilities. Another broader project which builds directly on the commission's recommendations is a NYC DMHMR & AS proposal for a demonstration project to the Robert Wood Johnson Foundation and the U.S. Department of Housing and Urban Development for a District Mental Health Services Management Project. Developed in consultation with NYS OMH officials, the proposal builds towards the division of New York City into 13 management districts, each of which would plan the full range of mental health services for the area.

A third recent development is the establishment of an informal planning body, composed of representatives from NYC DMHMR & AS, HHC, and NYS OMH, which has addressed both the City's short-term hospital bed crisis and NYS OMH's plan to reconfigure the mental health system by 1995. The planning effort was prompted by the City commissioner's critical testimony on the State's five-year plan, and by the onset of better communications that has been a feature of the tenure of the current State commissioner.

Whatever direction City and State planning takes for the balance of the 1980s, the issue of housing for the city's mentally ill will remain paramount. NYS OMH has recently developed a new arrangement for such housing, known as the Residential Care Centers for Adults, or RCCAs. RCCAs are extended-stay congregate residential programs for chronically mentally ill persons who require stable, long-term residential services and who are currently unserved by community residences or adult group homes. They offer services that enhance functional skills and are to be staffed more intensively than many community residences. Their scale, ranging from 25 to 200 beds, is expected to be greater than those of most community residence programs. One RCCA, equipped to house nearly 200 residents, now exists at Creedmoor Psychiatric Center, and a minimum of 300 RCCA beds are scheduled to open in New York City within the next two years.[61]

One controversy forming around the RCCAs is whether they will be satellite facilities for psychiatric centers or whether efforts will be made to link them firmly to the community. The director of the Coalition for the Homeless views them as a dubious substitute for community care; Senator Padavan and the NYS OMH commissioner cite them as a welcome addition to the State's repertoire of services. It is premature to make predictions on the outcome of the RCCA initiative, but if these facilities continue to engender controversy, the opponents seem less likely to be State versus City than government versus voluntary officials, with the government, both City and State, claiming that the RCCAs are an

appropriate mechanism for caring for the chronically mentally ill, and the
voluntaries countering that they could better assist these individuals in
smaller and more community-oriented facilities.

New York City's mental health system approaches the 1990s confronted with pressing problems. In a state where there is already
relatively generous public support for mental health services and many
other competing demands on funds, it may be unrealistic to expect a
major infusion of new tax support for mental health care. If this is true,
then the issue becomes: Can care be delivered differently within current
funding parameters? In this context additional constraints—especially
the needs and prerogatives of institutions that now deliver services—
become prominent. As this essay has suggested, recent attempts to effect
major changes in current institutional arrangements have been rejected.
The question still to be answered is whether a more incremental
approach to reform, which now appears to be taking shape within New
York State and New York City, can bring about the significant improvements that so many officials at both levels of government have called
for. This is a question of a quite different level of urgency than are the
issues for the future, however serious, that confront the State and the City
in the field of mental retardation.

NOTES

1. For information on the scope of the mental health system, see Jerome M.
   Goldsmith, *Final Report of the Governor's Select Commission on the
   Future of the State-Local Mental Health System* (Albany: the Commission, November 1984). Information on the scope of State mental
   retardation services was supplied by the Office of Public Information,
   New York State Office of Mental Retardation and Developmental
   Disabilities.
2. Much information in this section is from an unpublished document on the
   history of the New York State Department of Mental Hygiene, compiled
   by Librarian Dorothy Butch, New York State Library, Albany, New
   York.
3. David J. Rothman, *The Discovery of the Asylum: Social Order and
   Disorder in the New Republic* (Boston: Little, Brown, 1971), pp.
   263–287.
4. Rothman, *Discovery of the Asylum*, pp. 274–278.
5. Robert Connery and Gerald Benjamin, *Rockefeller in New York:
   Executive Power in the State House* (Ithaca: Cornell University Press,
   1979), p. 167.
6. Information from the Office of Public Information, New York State
   Office of Mental Retardation and Developmental Disabilities.
7. Connery and Benjamin, *Rockefeller*, p. 167.
8. Connery and Benjamin, *Rockefeller*, pp. 171–172.
9. Unpublished information supplied by the New York State Office of
   Mental Health.

10. Unless otherwise noted, information on the activities of DMHMR & AS during the 1960s and early 1970s are based on the recollections and knowledge of Barbara B. Blum, who served as a member of the Community Mental Health Board in 1967, as deputy director of the New York City Community Mental Health Board, 1968–1969, and as deputy commissioner of NYC DMHMR & AS, 1969–1970.
11. New York City Department of Mental Health and Mental Retardation Services, "Budget Preview Submission, 1970–1971."
12. Many of the details on the way in which deinstitutionalization for the mentally disabled and retarded proceeded from the late 1960s through the late 1970s in New York State are based on the recollections and knowledge of Barbara B. Blum, who served as the following during this period: metropolitan director, New York State Board of Social Welfare, 1974–1976; director of the Metropolitan Placement Unit; New York State Office of Mental Hygiene, 1976–1977; and commissioner, New York State Department of Social Services, 1977–1982.
13. Tom Christoffel, *Health and the Law: A Handbook for Health Professionals* (New York: Macmillan, 1982), p. 378.
14. Morris Cohen, "Financing Mental Health Care in New York State," information prepared for New York State Office of Mental Health, September 1983, p. 4.
15. David J. Rothman and Sheila M. Rothman, *The Willowbrook Wars: A Decade of Struggle for Social Justice* (New York: Harper & Row, 1984), p. 23.
16. Information supplied by the commissioner of the New York State Office of Mental Retardation and Developmental Disabilities.
17. Rothman and Rothman, *Willowbrook Wars*, pp. 308–310.
18. Gerald Benjamin and T. Norman Hurd, *Making Experience Count: Managing New York in the Carey Era* (Albany: Nelson A. Rockefeller Institute of Government, 1985), p. 67.
19. Benjamin and Hurd, *Making Experience Count*, p. 4.
20. Rothman and Rothman, *Willowbrook Wars*, p. 157.
21. New York City Department of Mental Health, Mental Retardation and Alcoholism Services, "District Mental Health Services Management Project," proposal submitted to the Robert Wood Johnson Foundation/U.S. Housing and Urban Development Department Program for the Chronically Mentally Ill, May 15, 1986, p. 14.
22. Frank Padavan, *The Mentally Ill Homeless: Shelters Become Sanctuaries for the Victims of Neglect* (Albany: New York State Senate Committee on Mental Hygiene and Addiction Control, January 1985), p. 6.
23. Information on why New York City rejected Unified Services from interviews with Clarence Sundram, chairman of the New York State Commission on Quality of Care for the Mentally Disabled, and Judge Arthur Jurow, former first deputy commission, NYC DMHMR & AS.
24. New York State Senate Committee on Mental Hygiene and Addiction Control, *After Eight Years: An Analysis of the Use, Impact and Effectiveness of the 1978 New York State Site Selection Law Governing Community Residences for the Mentally Disabled*, May 1986.
25. New York State Office of Mental Retardation and Developmental Disabilities, *A Decade of Triumph and a Future of Hope: Services to Developmentally Disabled Persons in New York State*, July 1985, p. 9.

26. David Braddock, Richard Hemp, and Ruth Howes, *Public Expenditures for Mental Retardation and Developmental Disabilities in the United States* (Chicago: Institute for the Study of Developmental Disabilities, University of Illinois at Chicago, December 1984), p. 23.
27. E. Fuller Torrey and Sidney M. Wolfe, *Care of the Serious Mentally Ill: A Rating of State Programs* (Washington, DC: Public Citizen Health Research Group, 1986).
28. Goldsmith, *Final Report*, p. 52.
29. Goldsmith, *Final Report*, p. 52.
30. Goldsmith, *Final Report*, pp. 54–55.
31. Information on this arrangement from Edith Cresmer, director of Planning and Program Development, HHC Office of Mental Hygiene Services.
32. Dick Netzer, "The Report of the Subcommittee on the New York City Psychiatric Bed Crisis," Appendix F in Goldsmith, *Final Report*, pp. 51–52.
33. Steven E. Katz, Edwin S. Robbins, Albert Sabatinie, Marvin Stern, and Lillian Robbins, "Who Will Treat the Impoverished Mental Patient?" *New York State Journal of Medicine* 83, no. 5 (April 1983):709.
34. Carol L. M. Caton, "The New Chronic Patient and the System of Community Care," *Community Psychiatry* 32, no. 7 (July 1981), pp. 475–478.
35. Caton, "New Chronic Patient."
36. 451 U.S. 1; Kenneth R. Wing, *The Law and the Public's Health*, 2nd ed. (Ann Arbor: Health Administration Press, 1985), pp. 65–66.
37. Information from Elizabeth Salerno, director of the Bureau of Regulations and Standards, NYS OMH Program Division.
38. Governor's Program Bill Memorandum, "An Act to Amend the Mental Hygiene Law in Relation to the Establishment of a Community Support Services Program under the Jurisdiction of the Commissioner of Mental Health," 1986, p. 4.
39. It is interesting to note that the authors encountered evidence both of municipal hospital staff's reluctance to send patients to State facilities and, conversely, of State staff who hesitate to place patients in City care.
40. New York State Office of Mental Health, "Committee Report to the Commissioner of Mental Health on the Need for Discharge Planning and Follow-Up Services for Patients Released from Facilities Licensed or Operated by the Office of Mental Health," December 1982, Appendix.
41. Torrey and Wolfe, *Care of the Serious Mentally Ill*, pp. 61–62.
42. George L. Jurow, "The Public Sector as Provider in Distress: The Crisis in New York State's Mental Hygiene System," paper presented at a special session of the annual meeting of the American Public Health Association, Detroit, October 21, 1980, p. 5.
43. "Mentally Ill Fall Through Cracks in System," *Albany Times Union*, April 20, 1986.
44. *New York Times*, November 9, 1985, p. A26, letter from Steven E. Katz, commissioner of New York State Office of Mental Health.
45. New York State Commission on Quality of Care for the Mentally Disabled, *A Review of Living Conditions in Nine New York State Psychiatric Centers*, December 1984.
46. Civil Service Employees Association, *Compassion and Care: CSEA and AFSCME's Recommendations to Governor Mario M. Cuomo and a*

Report on the Select Commission on the Future of the State/Local Mental Health System, November 1984, p. 26.

47. Quoted in Benjamin and Hurd, *Making Experience Count,* p. 208.
48. See Goldsmith, *Final Report,* p. 10.
49. Sara L. Kellermann, "Reform of the Community Based Mental Health Service," testimony submitted to the public hearings sponsored by the Assembly Standing Committees on Ways and Means and Mental Health, Mental Retardation and Developmental Disabilities, Alcoholism, and Substance Abuse, New York, October 24, 1985.
50. "Cuomo Promises to Restore Cuts in Funds for Mental Clinics Across State," *New York Times,* December 9, 1983, p. B1.
51. Goldsmith, *Final Report,* p. 15.
52. Kellerman, "Reform."
53. Benjamin and Hurd, *Making Experience Count,* p. 208.
54. New York State Office of Mental Retardation and Developmental Disabilities, *A Decade of Triumph,* pp. 9, 10.
55. Information on this case supplied by Michael Sparer, New York City Law Department, and Alan Adler, Deputy Counsel for Litigation, NYS OMRDD.
56. New York State Office of Mental Retardation and Developmental Disabilities, *A Decade of Triumph,* p. 2.
57. Hellis Shaw and Richard Johnson, "Family Support Services: Expanding Alternatives for Families with Developmental Disabilities" (Albany: New York State Office of Mental Retardation and Developmental Disabilities, October 1985).
58. Quoted in *New York Times,* "Revamping Care of the Mentally Ill," November 18, 1984, p. A43.
59. Quoted in *New York Times,* "Revamping Care of the Mentally Ill."
60. This information is based on the authors' interview with Dr. Bertram Pepper, Commissioner, Rockland County Department of Mental Health.
61. New York City Department of Mental Health, Mental Retardation and Alcoholic Services, "District Mental Health Services Management Project," p. 11.

14

SOCIAL SERVICES

❧

Irene Lurie
and
Mary Jo Bane

NEW YORK City is home to more poor people than any other city or county in the nation. About one fifth of the city's residents and one third of its children live in poverty. The city contains 40 percent of the state's population, but 60 percent of its poor.

To help meet their needs, the City of New York administers the nation's largest public assistance program, providing cash support to 1.4 million people. Two thirds of the state's public assistance recipients live in the city, receiving a similar share of public assistance payments. An even larger share of statewide expenditures for child protective services, foster care, and other social services are directed at New York City residents. In 1984, statewide expenditures for cash assistance and social services totaled $4.2 billion, with New York City accounting for $2.8 billion, or two thirds.[1]

The severity of poverty in New York City, the magnitude of programs to alleviate it, and the institutions established to serve the city's disadvantaged residents profoundly affect New York State social welfare policies. The State sets the parameters within which the City assists the disadvantaged, but its legal authority over lower levels of government is in practice constrained by the realities of the New York City situation. This City-State relationship has evolved over more than a century. Conflict over the powers and responsibilities of the State and its localities has influenced strongly this evolution. In 1941, a history of public welfare in New York State noted that "nearly every extension of state supervision over welfare institutions and agencies throughout the state's history encountered either active opposition or failure to co-operate on the part of some local authorities, an attitude usually justified in the name of 'local autonomy' or 'home rule.' "[2]

This essay addresses several questions about the interaction between the City and the State over social services, focusing on the period since the City's fiscal crisis. What is the nature of City-State interaction when the legally subordinate level of government is responsible for the predominant share of service delivery, clients, and costs? How is responsibility and influence divided between the two governments? How does the concentration of poverty in the city and the nature of the City's service delivery system influence State policy?

The first section of this essay provides a brief overview of the formal structure of social service programs in the city and the state. The second section details the State's largely successful recent efforts to exercise greater control over public assistance programs. The third section presents a detailed analysis of child welfare services and changes in these services following the Child Welfare Reform Act of 1979. These case studies provide a basis for identifying more general features of the State-City relationship in social services in the final section.

PROGRAM STRUCTURE

The 1935 Social Security Act, together with its amendments and accompanying regulations, establishes the basic structure of public assistance and social services programs in New York and other states. New York's response to federal law, written into its constitution in 1938, gives the State an affirmative duty to aid the needy: "The aid, care and support of the needy are public concerns and shall be provided by the state and by such of its subdivisions, and in such manner and by such means, as the legislature may from time to time determine."[3] State legislation has taken full advantage of federal support for programs for the needy and committed generous amounts of State and local resources to them.

Federal law requires that a single state agency be given the authority to either "administer" or "supervise" the administration of public assistance programs. New York and 17 other states are the minority that have chosen to supervise these programs, leaving their administration to local government. The New York State Department of Social Services

(DSS) is the single state supervisory agency. Administrative responsibility is lodged with the State's 57 counties and New York City, which constitute the 58 local social services districts. Because the distinction between "administration" and "supervision" is conceptually blurred, the division of responsibility varies from one program to another, has changed over time, and is a source of tension between localities and the State.

The broad division of responsibility between the State and the local districts is laid out in State Social Services Law. The basic responsibility for care and assistance lies with local districts, growing out of a long tradition of local county farms, outdoor relief programs, and "child saving" activities. Current law reflects this tradition: "Each public welfare district shall be responsible for the assistance and care of any person who resides or is found in its territory and who is in need of public assistance and care which he is unable to provide for himself."[4]

With passage of the Social Security Act and the 1938 amendment to the State constitution, however, the State assumed new responsibilities for funding and supervising the local districts. The law now gives the DSS commissioner the powers to:

Determine the policies and principles upon which public assistance and care shall be provided within the state

Supervise all social services work

Distribute, reimburse and grant the funds appropriated by the legislature

Withhold or deny state reimbursement, in whole or in part, from or to any social services district or any city or town thereof, in the event of the failure of either of them to comply with law, rules or regulations of the department relating to public assistance and care of the administration thereof.[5]

Basic policy is set by the State through legislation and regulations, which establish uniform benefit levels, eligibility rules, and procedures for providing support and services. The State's legal authority to regulate the manner in which these funds are spent, and to withhold reimbursement if regulations are not complied with, gives the State considerable power over local district policies. However, for reasons discussed below, the State has not always chosen to exert its full power.

Local governments in New York State play a greater role in the financing of public assistance than in most other states. New York is one of only ten states that require local governments to finance a share of public assistance costs. Historically, the federal government has financed 50 percent of Aid to Families with Dependent Children (AFDC) payments with an open-ended matching grant. The State and the localities have each financed 25 percent of AFDC and have shared equally in financing Home Relief, which receives no federal support. While in recent years both the federal and State shares have increased slightly, local governments still bear an unusually high proportion of public assistance costs compared with other states. Financing of social services is more complicated, because the percentage shares vary with the type of service and because federal funds under the Social Services Block Grant (Title XX) are subject to a ceiling.

In the division of responsibility between the State and its localities, there are significant differences between public assistance and social services. The State, over the past 15 years, has assumed increased authority over public assistance programs. In contrast, social services remain controlled primarily by the counties and by public and private organizations within New York City. The different outcomes of efforts to alter the distribution of authority in public assistance and in foster care, the largest single social service program, are described in the next two sections.

PUBLIC ASSISTANCE

Until 1969, local districts had considerable discretion in determining the amount of the public assistance payment and in setting conditions for its receipt. Concerns about lack of uniformity in eligibility determination and benefit levels and about infringement upon the legal rights of welfare recipients, nationwide as well as in New York, led to amendments in federal law establishing more uniform and equitable rules and strengthening the legal safeguards of recipients. In response, New York State established a uniform schedule of grants and allowances for all local districts in 1969. Responsibility for setting the basic benefit rested with the State Board of Social Welfare which, while appointed by the governor, had semi-autonomous status.

Greater exercise of the State's authority began in 1971, when responsibility for setting the basic benefit was shifted from the Board of Social Welfare to the legislature. Furthermore, the board's power to set other public assistance policy was transferred to the DSS commissioner and authority to appoint the commissioner was taken from the board and given to the governor, thereby strengthening his control over policy and administration. State authority was further increased in 1973, when responsibility for administering the cash and services programs was transferred from city and town welfare departments to the counties, which identify more closely with the State. The administration of public assistance was separated from social service provision in the same year, which routinized public assistance eligibility determinations and made them more amenable to state-wide standardization.

The rapid growth in the public assistance caseload during this period, while hailed by some as the benefit of a more equitable and dignified system, was seen by others as evidence of widespread ineligibility and overpayments. Although both the City and the State took some action to improve program administration, "It was the fiscal crisis in New York City which provided the political framework and the impetus for a determined effort to reduce fraud and abuse."[6] The State, under some pressure from federal authorities, took the lead in "quality control," requiring recipients to respond to periodic questionnaires about changes in their need for welfare, strengthening the face-to-face recertification procedure, and extending the matching of welfare records against information on other sources of income such as Social Security and unemployment insurance and, eventually, wages.[7] While the City later increased its efforts to curb fraud and abuse, the fiscal crisis illuminated the State's vulnerability to lax administration by the City and encouraged the State to exercise its legal authority more fully.

A significant example of the increase in the State's control over local administration of public assistance is the Welfare Management System (WMS), a computerized information system. Since 1982, all upstate counties have determined eligibility and benefits using computers located in Albany; a separate but functionally equivalent system is being installed by the Human Resources Administration (HRA) in New York City. WMS leaves local districts with little discretion in deciding who is eligible for assistance and how much they receive. It is significant that New York City has its own system, which is being implemented more slowly than the system for the upstate counties, but HRA, too, will be more constrained by the uniform rules and procedures established in Albany.

With the implementation of standardized rules and benefit levels, quality control, and WMS, the differences between a State-supervised program and a State-administered program become subtle. One difference is that the State is prohibited from setting staffing requirements for the districts. Although it has the power to determine qualifications for local staff, it has no authority to regulate numbers of staff or staff workloads, and no authority over salaries. Thus, how many people to hire, what to pay them, and how to organize their work remain decisions of the local districts. In short, the State can mandate programmatic requirements but cannot ensure that localities devote sufficient resources to meet them.

The trend toward centralization is also reflected in greater State financing of programs whose nonfederal share had been divided equally between the State and the counties. In 1978–1979, the State assumed the full cost of supplementing the federal Supplementary Security Income (SSI) program for the aged, blind, and disabled. In 1981, the public assistance benefit was increased 15 percent by the addition of an "energy allowance" financed entirely by the State.

In sum, since 1969 the relationship between the State and the City has changed substantially in the public assistance arena. Although the purpose of WMS and other administrative changes was to increase uniformity and equity in dealings with clients and to improve program management, the result has been less discretion among local districts and, thereby, increased authority for the State. This outcome presents an interesting contrast to developments in the administration of child welfare programs, where similar state centralization has not occurred.

CHILD WELFARE PROGRAMS

New York State has been a pioneer in the provision of social services since the early nineteenth century and today maintains services that extend well beyond the requirements of the federal Social Security Act. State law requires that localities provide certain services to specified population groups, such as foster care for children. Localities must provide other services, such as day care and family planning, under certain specified conditions. They may choose whether to offer a third group of "nonmandated" services, such as employment services and services to victims of domestic violence.[8] Foster care is the single most costly social service, accounting for 43 percent of statewide social services expenditures.[9]

The Child Welfare Reform Act of 1979 significantly altered the State's programs for children in foster care or at the risk of being placed in care. It provides an illustration of recent State-City interaction in both policy formation and implementation.

Historical Background

Private philanthropic and religious organizations have long played a central role in caring for poor, orphaned, or neglected children in New York. In the early 1800s, in response to concern with the practice of indenturing children and the unhealthy conditions of almshouses, charitable organizations were founded to establish and operate orphanages. Private orphanages were common by 1850 and had become the favored alternative of philanthropic reformers over home relief, apprenticeship, and the almshouses. Many were established under religious auspices, especially the Catholic church.

Government began supporting the private orphanages almost from their founding. The State legislature authorized the City to provide funds to the Orphan Asylum Society in the City of New York, founder of the first orphanage in 1808, and made a grant to the society as early as 1811. In the following decades, private orphanages were established throughout the state with the support of both State and local funds.[10] By 1872, the State subsidized over 108 private orphanages through annual appropriations distributed to counties and through direct grants to specified institutions. Localities became a major funding source after 1874, when the State constitution was amended to prohibit, with certain exceptions, State aid to private agencies.[11]

Although orphanages were considered preferable to almshouses, sentiment began growing in the 1850s against the placement of children in institutions of any kind. The belief that children could be best raised in foster homes led to the organization within New York City of the Children's Aid Society, which led a movement to place children in families. However, increased placements of children in foster homes raised concern among Catholics, who were opposed to the placement of their children with Protestant families. In response Catholic groups organized their own child welfare agencies.[12]

Early public support of private agencies, and their organization by religious affiliation, established a pattern that continues in New York City today and that sets it apart from the rest of the state. The City did not open a municipal shelter for children until 1947. Voluntary agencies, the majority organized under three religious federations—Catholic Charities (Archdiocese of New York and the Diocese of Brooklyn), the Federation of Protestant Welfare Agencies, and the Federation of Jewish Philanthropies—continue to be the predominant providers of foster care. In 1976, there were over 80 voluntary foster care agencies serving New York City children.[13] These agencies no longer rely primarily on private contributions and donations, but typically receive 90 percent or more of their support from government.[14] Although voluntary agencies provide group care in other parts of the state, they are not involved in foster family care, which is administered directly by the counties. By the 1970s, 90 percent of the foster care children in New York City were served by voluntary agencies, compared with only 20 percent in the rest of the state.[15]

The private voluntary agencies in New York City wield considerable power, stemming from a variety of sources. Their religious affiliations bring them the support of organized religion, as well as moral authority. Socially and financially prominent individuals sit on their boards and social work professionals are among their staffs. Finally, and perhaps most important, the City does not have an independent capacity to provide foster care and is dependent upon them. These sources of power give the voluntary agencies political influence in the city and the state.

State oversight of the private organizations caring for children came hand-in-hand with its financial support. In 1867, a state supervisory body, the Board of State Commissioners of Public Charities, was established to visit and inspect all charitable institutions and to report annually to the State legislature. The board ultimately evolved into the State Board of Social Welfare, which had authority to visit and inspect all public and private foster care institutions receiving public funds. The board continued to perform this function until 1977, when all of its duties were transferred to the DSS.

The initial impact of the Social Security Act on foster care was limited because federal funding for foster care services was virtually prohibited. The private child welfare agencies, especially the Catholic agencies, feared that their financial arrangements with cities would be jeopardized by federal and state involvement and effectively lobbied Congress to limit the funding of child welfare services to rural areas where they were not active.[16] After this limitation was lifted in 1951, public provision of foster care services increased in most areas of the country other than New York City.

Federal amendments to the Social Security Act in 1958, 1962, and 1967 broadened funding for child welfare services and extended AFDC to many of the children in foster care. New York State and New York City took advantage of these liberalizations, expanding the AFDC—Foster Care caseload and thereby shifting some of their foster care costs to the federal government. The number of children in foster care also increased because of a combination of demographic factors, programmatic changes, and the view that some children would be better off if they were removed from their own homes. Between 1960 and 1970, the number of children in foster care in New York State rose from 37,489 to 50,932; after 1971, the number of foster care children began to decline, at least in part for demographic reasons.[17]

Pressures for Reform

While foster care had been viewed in the 1960s as a way of improving the lives of children by removing them from poor home environments, the increase in foster care children and expenditures helped send the pendulum swinging back. Observers began to argue that too many children were in foster care, citing evidence that children were removed from their homes unnecessarily and that insufficient efforts were made to return them home or to find permanent adoptive homes for them. A study in New York City estimated that 15 percent of the children placed in foster care could have remained at home if appropriate services for their families had been available.[18] Children were also staying in care for longer periods of time. Between 1973 and 1977, the average duration of a placement in foster care in New York State rose from 3.5 to almost 5 years.[19]

During the 1970s, dissatisfaction with the foster care system crystallized among at least one set of actors at each level of government: the U. S. Congress, the New York State Legislature, and the New York City Comptroller's Office and Board of Estimate. Foster care became a visible issue in Washington primarily through the efforts of Congressman George Miller of California, a state in which the foster care budget and caseload rivaled those of New York State.[20] Miller introduced legislation in 1977 that later became the Adoption Assistance and Child Welfare Act of 1980.

New York contributed in several ways to congressional legislation to reform the foster care system. First, the State was a big part of the problem. New York accounted for 20 percent of all children in federally assisted foster care and for 39 percent of all AFDC-Foster Care payments.[21] Second, several prominent studies on the outcomes of foster care and preventive services had been performed in New York. Third, the State and City reform efforts discussed below were the subject of congressional testimony and thus familiar to federal lawmakers; indeed, some observers believe that New York's Child Welfare Reform Act of 1979 was a model for the 1980 federal legislation.[22] (In contrast many knowledgeable New Yorkers argue that the prospect of federal legislation had little influence on the State's reform of its foster care program.)

In New York State, responsibility for supervising and administering foster care was fragmented. As of the mid 1970s, the DSS was responsible for supervising the local social services districts and administering federal and State funds. But DSS had little presence in New York City and chose not to exercise fully its supervisory authority. The State Board of Social Welfare, which at this time was independent of DSS, was responsible for licensing, visiting, and inspecting foster care agencies. It had an office in New York City, but no clear authority over the agencies' programs or performance.

Within New York City, Special Services for Children (SSC), a unit of the Human Resources Administration, administered foster care services. It assessed a child's need for foster care, arranged a placement with a voluntary agency, and reviewed periodic reports on each child sent by the voluntary agency. The Family Court was charged with determining whether a child should be placed in foster care and with reviewing the status of children who had been in care for a continuous period of two years. Formal contracts between the City and the voluntary agencies were negotiated by SSC and then approved by the Board of Estimate. The rate paid to the agencies for each day of care was set by SSC and the mayor's Office of Management and Budget; payments were made by the Comptroller's Office.[23]

At the state level, pressure for reform came primarily from the legislature, which in 1974 established the Temporary State Commission on Child Welfare. Chairing the commission and strongly influencing its views was Joseph R. Pisani, a Republican senator from Westchester. Pisani had the support of the upstate Republican majority in the Senate and could maintain some independence from political interests in New York City. He also had a long-standing interest in foster care, as both a sponsor of legislation in these areas and a private attorney in a well-publicized effort by a mother to regain custody of a child she had given up for adoption.

The commission, in a series of reports issued between 1975 and 1978, identified numerous problems in the foster care system. Financial incentives favored foster care over services to prevent the need for placement and to achieve a permanent home for children. Funds for foster care were open-ended at both the federal and state levels. In contrast, funds to prevent placement and to promote adoption were extremely limited.

The commission pointed to a wide range of administrative problems. While some of them occurred statewide, such as a lack of criteria for determining whether children and their families could benefit from foster care, many arose in New York City from the partnership between the City and the voluntary agencies. Often, once a City caseworker decided to place a child in a voluntary agency, the City lost control over the progress of the child. The voluntary agencies selected the child's placement; the majority of agencies participated in one of the three sectarian federations, each of which screened referrals from the City and either rejected them or referred them to a member agency. In many cases, children came directly to the voluntary agencies, with only after-the-fact approval of the placement by the City. After placement, the City caseworker often did not see the child again and relied on late or incomplete reports from the agency, the content of which was often unexamined or unchallenged by overworked City caseworkers, 80 of whom were responsible for overseeing approximately 20,000 children.[24] Because information about services provided to the child and the progress of the child toward achieving a permanent home was inadequate, agencies could not be held accountable for their performance.

Without this information the City was unable to control the voluntary agencies; the State, in turn, was unable to control the City. Although the State possessed the power to invoke sanctions such as withholding of

State aid, decertification, and revocation of licenses, it had not developed uniform criteria for performance and information needed for performance assessment. State action was also impeded by the division of responsibility between the DSS and the Board of Social Welfare. Hence, the commission argued that remedying the problems in foster care was "seriously obstructed by the lack of cooperation between State agencies themselves, between State agencies and their local government counterparts, and between local agencies, both public and private."[25]

In New York City government, dissatisfaction stemmed primarily from the lack of control and accountability in the foster care system. Criticism of the system was voiced by the Comptroller's Office, the Office of the City Council President, and the Board of Estimate. The Comptroller's Office, through a 1976 audit of five voluntary agencies and an examination of available case records, estimated that children were staying in foster care an average of 5.2 years, considerably longer than necessary, and that agencies showed a "pervasive lack of effective effort" to return them to their parents or place them in permanent adoptive homes.[26] The Comptroller's Office argued that this poor performance was due not to lack of resources, but to the structure of financing that reimbursed agencies for keeping children in care but offered almost no incentive for finding them a permanent home.

Special Services for Children (SSC) was found to be "rather ineffectual in its monitoring of the voluntary agencies,"[27] in part because its purchase of service contracts with the agencies "lacked teeth."[28] The audit found that SSC often deviated from its own guidelines in assessing agencies and that it was a "negligible factor" in agency case management.[29] Agencies ignored court orders, and SSC was sometimes aware of "agency flaunting of court orders."[30] The audit also revealed instances where City officials were members of agency boards of trustees, posing a possible conflict of interest.[31]

The Comptroller's Office recommended fundamental changes in the financing and administration of foster care, many of which were similar to reforms being considered by the Temporary State Commission. Some of these recommendations were aimed at the City, but others called for State action. Of particular interest is the suggestion that the DSS monitor SSC more closely and use its available fiscal sanctions.[32]

Another critic of the foster care system was the president of the City Council, whose office in 1978 undertook an analysis of the expenditures and performance of 53 voluntary agencies. This analysis found that poor agency performance could not be blamed on inadequate funds and concluded that SSC should strengthen its efforts to measure and improve its performance.[33] These allegations of poor performance reflected upon the Board of Estimate, which approves the City's contracts with the voluntary agencies and is thereby a primary link in the chain of accountability. In response to the various criticisms of the foster care system, the Board of Estimate passed a resolution in May 1979 requiring SSC to develop and implement a system for assessing the performance of the private agencies.

The Program Assessment System (PAS), developed by SSC during the following year, is a mechanism for monitoring the City's contracts with the voluntary agencies. The PAS is noteworthy because it was developed at the time of the passage of the Child Welfare Reform Act. Although the PAS differs fundamentally from the Act, both are designed to remedy many of the same problems. The near-simultaneous approval of both measures suggests that the Board of Estimate did not look to the State to solve these problems. The City could have asked the State to assume greater oversight of the voluntary agencies via the Board of Social Welfare's authority to license them. Instead, it pursued an independent course.

Passage of the Child Welfare Reform Act

The Temporary State Commission was successful in enacting legislation to remedy some of the problems it had identified, but it argued for a more radical approach that would eventually become the heart of the Child Welfare Reform Act of 1979. Because the act would significantly reorder the relationships among the State, the localities, and the voluntary agencies, all relevant actors sought to participate in the negotiations leading to the legislation.

In the words of one participant in these negotiations: "There were 100 authors of the Act. Everyone was co-opted by the inclusion of something they could support. The result was legislation that was a finely balanced package of carrots and sticks." The commission itself represented many of the key actors in the foster care system, including the Catholic, Protestant, and Jewish agencies, the Family Court, and upstate social services districts. Although both an assemblyman and a senator from New York City were on the commission, City government was not represented directly.

City officials did participate in the negotiations prior to the drafting of legislation, although they did not play an aggressive role. In the many public and private meetings intended to involve a broad spectrum of interest groups in the design of the reform, the City's opinions were solicited. However, the legislation was eventually drafted by its legislative sponsors and representatives from the State Division of the Budget and the DSS, with virtually no input from the City.

The position of the voluntary agencies during the negotiations cannot be characterized simply. Some agencies stood to lose more from the act than others. Variation in the quality of care provided by the agencies, while rarely mentioned explicitly, was a reality underlying the debate. Voluntary agencies have traditionally been reluctant to regulate themselves and representatives of some agencies were willing to give government more influence over their activities in order to promote the interests of the children in their care. Their representation on the commission enabled them to help shape the reforms, a prerequisite to getting their support for the legislation.

Provisions of the Child Welfare Reform Act

The Child Welfare Reform Act of 1979 fundamentally changed the foster care system. The purpose of the act is to discourage long-term stays in foster care that had become the norm and to encourage "permanency," either by keeping a child with his biological parents, by returning a child from foster care to his parents, or by promoting his adoption. Permanency is to be achieved by the provision of services—preventive services to reduce the need for foster care, services while in foster care to return the child to his parents, and adoption services when the child cannot be reunited with his biological parents.

Fiscal incentives for permanency are provided by restructuring State aid to local districts. Reimbursement to districts for foster care remains at 75 percent of their costs, but reimbursement is to be denied when care provided by the district is substandard or otherwise inappropriate. Reimbursements for preventive services, which had been limited to 50 percent of the districts' expenditures up to a small annual appropriation, are extended to 75 percent of expenditures for mandated services on an open-ended basis. Reimbursement for adoption services is also increased to 75 percent. Because the State now pays 75 percent of the cost of all mandated preventive and adoption services as well as foster care, local districts have no financial incentive to view foster care as the treatment of choice. Enriched funding for preventive services is the primary "carrot" in the act.

Local districts are to be held accountable for their efforts to promote permanency. Accountability is to be achieved through planning, the establishment of standards, the collection of information, utilization reviews of the performance of districts and agencies, and sanctions. Districts must develop plans for their child welfare services, which are to be reviewed by DSS and then either approved or disapproved. The State must develop regulations establishing preventive services program standards, standards for evaluating prospective adoptive parents, and standards for imposing the available sanctions.

Utilization Review standards are to be developed by DSS. These standards are used to determine whether the placement in foster care is necessary, the type of placement is appropriate to the child's needs, the agency is exercising diligent efforts to return the child home or find an adoptive home, and the required preventive services have been provided. For the first time, the State must set standards for the performance of the districts and agencies and will thereby be able to hold them accountable for their actions.

A Child Welfare Standards Advisory Council is established to advise the DSS in developing the Utilization Review standards. Its 15 members are appointed by the commissioner of DSS, to include representatives of local social services districts, voluntary sectarian and nonsectarian child care agencies, children's advocacy groups, groups concerned with the welfare of minority children, and representatives of professional organizations. It was created at the request of the New York State Association of Counties, which wanted local districts and other organizations to have some influence over the standards to be used in imposing the act's fiscal sanctions. The groups to be regulated wanted to be involved in drafting the regulations.

Case planning for each child is to be structured and documented by a new Uniform Case Record, which must include an assessment of the child's needs, his service plan, the types and dates of care and services provided, and historical and other relevant information. The record is the primary data source for the Child Care Review Service, a computerized information system to improve management and accountability.

The "stick" of the act is fiscal sanctions against the districts and the agencies. First, the State will not reimburse expenditures for services that are delivered in violation of statutory requirements such as periodic review of cases by Family Court judges. All cases are to be reviewed periodically to determine whether the required actions are being taken. Districts that are penalized under these "process reviews" must pass along the sanction to agencies to the extent that they are responsible for the penalty. The district and agencies must continue to care for the child if penalties are imposed.

A second type of sanction applies not to violations of the specific statutory standards but to districts delivering "inferior or inappropriate care or services."[34] To impose sanctions for these less precise reasons, a "utilization review" is to be performed on a sample of cases in each district using the standards described above. State funds are to be denied to each case found to be in violation of the standards. If more than 7.5 percent of the sampled cases violate the standards, funds are to be denied to the entire caseload in proportion to the extent that the violation rate exceeds 7.5 percent. Sanctions must be passed along to the voluntary agencies if they are responsible for causing the penalty, although they will still be responsible for the child. Districts and agencies are given the protection of an administrative hearing under all sanctions.

Implicit in these reforms is an increase in power of the State over the City. Prior to the act, the City lacked control over the activities of the voluntary agencies, which decided what placement and services were appropriate for each child. Because the City lacked power, the State's ability to supervise the City was limited as well. The act gives the State authority to define the appropriateness of the placement and treatment provided by the districts and the agencies and holds them accountable for their performance. This gives the State more formal influence over the City and, by empowering the City in its relationship with the voluntary agencies, may enable the State to exert this influence more effectively.

Writing the Regulations

The Child Welfare Reform Act was described by Barbara Blum, commissioner of DSS at the time of its enactment, as "the single most complicated piece of legislation to implement that I've ever seen."[35] Implementation of the act proceeded in two phases, each exhibiting a different form of State-City interaction. The first phase was the period of planning and policy formation, during which regulations were written specifying the meaning of and need for preventive services, the format and contents of the Uniform Case Record, and the standards for utilization review. This phase began in late 1979 and was largely completed by 1984. The second phase was the period of actual implementation.

State DSS generally took the lead in drafting the standards and regulations, which were then discussed by the Child Welfare Standards Advisory Council.[36] The council was appointed on schedule and expanded from 15 to 25 members to achieve wider representation. Approximately half of the council's members were from New York City, almost all representing private organizations. While many of the organizations based in the city represented statewide constituencies, there was some concern among council members that the New York City voluntary agencies were overrepresented.[37]

Local social services districts were represented on the 25-member council by two members in some years and three in others. Although the administrator of SSC was one of the representatives, the City maintained a low profile and made less effort than other districts to shape the regulations. In interviews, participants in the council's deliberations speculated about why the City played a small role. One argued that SSC did not recognize the extent to which the act gives the State influence over the City and the City did not take the State's new sanctioning authority seriously. Another pointed out that SSC was beset by crisis and by criticism from the mayor, City Council, and Board of Estimate, and therefore could not assign priority to the Advisory Council's activities.

While the council in many cases amended the standards drafted by DSS,[38] some were issued by DSS over the objections of the council. In a survey of its members in 1982, following its most intense period of deliberation, 64 percent of the respondents indicated that their advice was "at least somewhat effective" in influencing the final standards.[39] By implication, more than one third felt they had not been effective.

Implementation of the Reforms

In many respects, the most significant change in the act was expanded funding for preventive services. Effective April 1, 1981, State funding to support these services was increased from 50 to 75 percent of local expenditures.

Localities responded to the new formula as expected. Reimbursement claims for preventive services grew from $9.3 million in 1980 to $62.4 million in 1984, with claims from New York City rising somewhat more rapidly than in upstate areas.[40] However, it is not clear that all these expenditures reflect additional services. Some simply represented localities' efforts to obtain State funding for services affected by the funding cuts of the Reagan Administration beginning in 1981.

The accountability components of the Act have been implemented slowly and with difficulty. These components are interconnected. The Uniform Case Record (UCR) provides the information for the Child Care Review Service (CCRS) system, which is used in the process reviews described above. Poor performance in these reviews, in turn, leads to the denial of public funds to individual agencies. Because these provisions of the act must be implemented sequentially, delay in implementing one contributes to delay in implementing the next.

Despite a large-scale training effort, caseworkers throughout the state criticized the UCR as increased or duplicative paperwork, arguing that time devoted to it significantly interfered with their ability to serve their clients. In New York City, where SSC required its own forms in addition to the UCR, criticism of the UCR was voiced by the agencies, whose caseworkers had to fill them out, and by SCC. In response to criticism of the UCR in many districts of the state, and a recognition by DSS that some of these criticisms were valid, the State redesigned the UCR to make it shorter, clearer, and more useful as a case planning tool.

Resistance to the UCR took on an additional dimension in New York City. The voluntary agencies argued that government access to information in the record might limit families' participation in preventive services programs, and representatives of 40 agencies formed an ad hoc committee concerned with preserving the confidentiality of this information. These agencies refused to supply the City and the State with individually identifying case information, and 12 filed suit against the State and HRA contending that supplying this information would violate their clients' rights and jeopardize the effectiveness of preventive services. The consent decree issued by the U.S. District Court in July 1982 was a partial victory for the voluntary agencies; they must give the City personally identifying UCRs of preventive services clients when a child is referred to SSC for foster care or when abuse and neglect has been reported, but not otherwise.[41]

The CCRS is a computerized information system built largely upon data collected in the Uniform Case Record. Prior to the act, New York City led the State in using computers to help manage the foster care system. In cooperation with the voluntary agencies, the City contracted with a private organization, Child Welfare Information Systems (CWIS), for a computerized system to assist in billing for foster care and for tracking and analyzing case flow. Data from CWIS revealed inadequacies in the foster care system and helped support the case for the act. However, the City's experience with a computerized system did not translate into strong initiatives to implement the new CCRS.

Although there were delays throughout the state in designing the CCRS system, delays were substantially longer in New York City. The CCRS system was in place upstate by early 1982, but was not completely installed in the city until 1984. Entering data into the system required additional time and was impeded by a variety of problems. In New York City, the entry of information on the preventive services cases was impeded by the confidentiality lawsuit discussed above and did not occur until 1986. The system did not contain information on as many as 10 percent of the City's foster care cases as of 1985.[42]

The delays in New York City in implementing the UCR and CCRS can be attributed to a variety of factors: inadequate resources within HRA and SSC; problems of organization and management within these agencies; the assignment of low priority by City officials to the implementation of State law; pressure and resistance from the voluntary agencies; and difficulties with the structure of the act itself. The delays illustrate the inability of the State to impose its own timetable on the City. These delays should not, however, obscure the fact that the UCR and CCRS will significantly strengthen the control of both the City and State over the voluntary agencies and the foster care system.

Use of Sanctions

The DSS imposed sanctions gradually and, until recently, conservatively both in New York City and upstate. Gradual implementation of the sanction provisions has been unavoidable, since both the UCR and the CCRS are prerequisites for review and sanctions. The conservative interpretation of the act means that the first sanctions were small in dollar terms and illustrates the State's reluctance to take a heavy hand toward the local districts and the voluntary agencies. The act is perceived as punitive by some at the local level, and the State initially proceeded conservatively to blunt this perception and gain their cooperation.

Sanctions for failure to adhere to statutory requirements have not been imposed with full force. Only two of the six "process" requirements are being reviewed; CCRS cannot track two of the requirements and is not considered accurate enough in tracking the other two. Upstate, the dollar amount of sanctions imposed has been very small, although more than $1 million in sanctions were imposed on the City in 1984.[43]

Utilization reviews, which lead to the second category of sanctions, have been implemented gradually but with increasing stringency. The first utilization review of a sample of foster care cases took place in 1982 and resulted in $37,420 of sanctions, all upstate. The small amount of the sanctions, and the lack of any sanctions in New York City, has several explanations. The most obvious is that districts were notified in advance about the sample that would be audited and could attempt to bring these cases into compliance before the audit. The City was able to correct errors in the entire sample and achieved a zero error rate. Second, sanctions were imposed only from the date of the audit to the date the case was brought into compliance, not retroactively as permitted by the act. Third, several sanctionable items were waived "to accommodate administrative or logistical problems confronting the local districts."[44] A final shortcoming of the sanctioning process was that the regulations did not specify what corrective action needed to be taken to bring a case into compliance.

Regulations were amended effective mid 1984 defining corrective actions and making sanctions retroactive for a period preceding the audit. (The length of the retroactive period was subsequently reduced to soften the impact on localities.) The second round of utilization reviews began in August 1984, and districts were not notified of the sample in advance. With these more stringent procedures, substantial sanctions have been calculated for the City and smaller amounts for the upstate districts. The actual imposition of sanctions is pending the results of fair hearings requested by the City and some upstate counties.

No procedures have been developed so far to pass sanctions on to the voluntary agencies. Most of the sanctions calculated for the City are extrapolations from the sample and cannot be reliably identified with a particular agency.

The pending sanctions are interpreted by both the City and the State as a signal that times have changed. The State is willing to exert its authority over the City—to use its formal powers more aggressively to change the attitudes and procedures of the City and the voluntary agencies. But tempering this interpretation is the recognition that the full force of the State has not been brought down upon the City, because the State also bends to the City's concerns. These include not just the loss in funds but their impact on the morale of SSC, already weakened by rapid staff turnover, a shortage of personnel and foster care beds, and a critical press. The DSS recognizes that large sanctions against the City may be counterproductive in achieving the ultimate goal of improving the welfare of children.

Impact of the Act

The number of children in foster care has declined sharply, from 34,520 in 1980 to 26,471 in 1985, and average length of stay has dropped from 4.5 years in 1979 to 3.3 years in 1984. Between 1980 and 1984, expenditure claims for foster care rose only slightly, from $337.8 million to $348.6 million, which can be explained by inflation and an increase in the services given to troubled children. While the foster care caseload had begun falling prior to passage of the Child Welfare Reform Act, suggesting that other factors were at work, the more rapid drop after passage supports the hypothesis that the act contributed significantly to the decline in the caseload. Recently, the caseload in the city has risen, at least in part because of well-publicized instances of abuse and neglect by parents and efforts by the City to protect children by removing them from their homes. Explaining these trends is a study in itself and beyond the scope of this essay.

From the perspective of the State-City relationship, the act represents an assertion of the State's authority to supervise the administration of foster care services. The act gives the State new powers to influence the behavior of local districts and voluntary agencies: new funding streams, planning procedures, performance standards, information systems, and sanctions. The absorption of the Board of Social Welfare into the State DSS, just prior to the act, consolidated the State's authority and placed it squarely under the governor. Hence, in some respects, the State achieved the transfer of authority in foster care that it had achieved a few years earlier in public assistance.

Yet it can be argued that the State pulls back in its exercise of power and does not use the complete scope of its authority. The findings from utilization reviews indicate that the mandates of the act have not been fully implemented—or fully documented—by localities. Sanctions could be larger if the act were interpreted differently. But using all its power to deny funds to the localities could be counterproductive to the ultimate objective of helping children. Because services, unlike public assistance, must be provided locally and require considerable discretion and judgment on the part of the caseworker, the State would accomplish little good by severely cutting support to the localities and the private agencies.

RELATIONSHIP BETWEEN THE STATE AND THE CITY

Three questions can guide more general thinking about state-city relationships around social services: Who are the major actors? How do these actors relate to each other? What are the implications of this mode of relationship for policymaking and implementation?

Major Actors

The experience of passing and implementing the Child Welfare Reform Act, as described above, suggests that there were four major actors in policymaking for social services in New York: the City, the State, the federal government, and the voluntary agencies. Upstate counties also played a role in developing the act, primarily through the vehicles of the New York State Association of Counties and the New York Public Welfare Association.

Other experience suggests that policymaking around public assistance issues—for example, the development and implementation of work opportunities and requirements for recipients—also involves these four actors, although voluntary agencies are far less important and the federal government more important than in the case of foster care. To some extent, advocacy and legal services groups take the place of the voluntary agencies in policymaking for public assistance, usually playing the role of advocating for higher benefits and protections of clients' rights. They do not, however, have the strong self interest in the outcome as do the voluntary agencies in foster care.

Mode of Relationship

The relationships between the City and the State are best described in terms of negotiation and bargaining. Instances of negotiation and bargaining emerge regularly in the case study, around both the design of the policy and its implementation. The City and State would start from somewhat different positions—for example, on the timing of implementation of the CCRS or the documentation of case planning—but through a series of compromises and clarifications would reach an accommodation. This is in contrast to two other plausible models: hierarchy and cooperative problem solving.

There are, of course, elements of hierarchy in the relationships, with formal control flowing from the federal government, to the State, to the City, and finally to the voluntary agencies. As described above, State Social Services Law gives the State commissioner broad regulatory and supervisory authority over local social services districts, including New York City. The State has the authority to withhold its share of funds from New York City and, in cases where the State perceives violations of law, has the authority to take the City to court to enjoin its activities. In the area of foster care, the State has a statutory mandate to audit and review City operations and to levy fiscal sanctions for nonperformance. The State also has the weapon of publicity against the City: State reports on City operations are common and can be damaging.

It would appear then that formal authority rests with the State to define policy and to force the City to implement it, just as formal authority rests with the federal government to compel actions by the State. In fact, however, the State has held back from wielding its full authority, not only in the imposition of sanctions but also in other areas. Why does this happen? One possible explanation is that the City has considerable power against the State. The State does not have the resources to carry out its own directives and must rely on the City to provide them. The City can simply not obey the directives of the higher level of government and, though they would lose in any legal confrontation, could conceivably go undiscovered or hold out for quite long periods of time. This challenge to its authority could be a considerable embarrassment to the State, especially on issues where public opinion was on the side of the City. Thus, it is in both sides' interests to avoid confrontations. Positions that both sides can live with are worked out ahead of time, so that formal hierarchical authority does not have to be either exercised or challenged.

Relationships of negotiation and bargaining also contrast with cooperative problem solving. This pattern is followed occasionally when the two parties agree on positions and work together to formulate responses to issues. Cooperative problem solving is not the norm, however. Why not?

One reason has to do with differences in ideology or politics broadly defined. Even when they are of the same political party, the mayor and the governor often engage in a more or less friendly political rivalry. To some extent this is fed by differences in ideology, which are often exaggerated by the two commissioners. Since the late 1970s, the State DSS commissioner has generally been considered more "liberal" than the City's HRA commissioner. This often leads to policy differences, especially on public assistance issues. The City, for example, has been more eager to impose work requirements and to sanction clients for noncompliance than the State.

In addition, because the City is the actual operational entity, it tends to be more concerned with details of implementation and operations. Policy change—for example, to the UCR or to a new computer system for public assistance—is sometimes resisted by City officials because they feel (often correctly) that it is simply impossible to hire and train the personnel, work out the procedures, and institute the controls that would be necessary to make the policy work. The State is often less concerned with these issues and sometimes seems to feel that the City is using them as an excuse for avoiding policy change.

Finally, the City and the State sometimes differ over fiscal issues, and both often argue with the voluntary agencies over money. Who pays for what is quite complicated in social services and often difficult to figure out in individual cases. But since the City shares in the costs of virtually all social services programs, it often objects to policy change on fiscal grounds. The voluntary agencies, on the other hand, are often advocating for programs that cost more.

Thus, there are differences between the City and the State that preclude genuine cooperative problem solving. At the same time, the two often agree on goals, especially on broad goals like permanency for children. Even when they do not, it is in the interest of both sides to avoid confrontations and challenges to authority. Thus, a negotiations and bargaining mode develops that usually results in mutual accommodation.

Implications

What does this imply for how well policy is made and carried out in social services? Negotiation and bargaining inevitably result in somewhat messy policies that are not completely satisfactory to anyone. This mode of operation also implies that policy development may not be as smooth or as quick as one would like.

At the same time, the process of working through differences as policy is developed and implemented seems to result in policies that work reasonably well. Confrontations are in fact minimized; disputes are resolved within an agreed-upon framework.

There is always the danger, of course, that the interests of those who are not parties to the negotiations will be forgotten. It could be argued, for example, that neither the State nor the City represents particularly well the interests of the children and their parents. There are, to be sure, many other checks—the legislature, the courts, and the press, for example—but with two very strong powers coming to agreement, these checks may not be sufficient. In the case of the Child Welfare Reform Act, the interaction between the City and the State seemed to produce a reasonably good, but by no means perfect, outcome.

NOTES

1. New York State Department of Social Services, *1984 Annual Report, Statistical Supplement*, p. 1. Includes expenditures for local administrative costs and the Home Energy Assistance Program.
2. David M. Schneider and Albert Deutsch, *The History of Public Welfare in New York State, 1867–1940* (Chicago: University of Chicago Press, 1941), p. 132.
3. Article XVII, Section 1.
4. New York State Social Services Law, Section 62.
5. New York State Social Services Law, Sections 17 and 20.
6. Blanche Bernstein, *The Politics of Welfare* (Cambridge, MA: Abt Books, 1982), p. 26.
7. Bernstein, *The Politics of Welfare*, pp. 26–29.
8. New York State Department of Social Services, "Consolidated Services Plan for New York State for April 1, 1982 to September 30, 1984," p. 48.
9. New York State Department of Social Services, *1984 Annual Report, Statistical Supplement*, p. 1.
10. Schneider and Deutsch, *History of Public Welfare*, pp. 190–191.
11. Schneider and Deutsch, *History of Public Welfare*, p. 20.
12. Schneider and Deutsch, *History of Public Welfare*, p. 73.
13. New York City Comptroller's Office, "The Children Are Waiting" (New York: New York City Comptroller's Office, 1977), p. 1.
14. New York City Comptroller's Office, "The Children Are Waiting," p. 2.
15. New York State Temporary Commission to Revise the Social Services Law, "Foster Care: A Retrospective View," Study Report no. 9, November 1981, p. 12.
16. Gilbert Y. Steiner, *The Futility of Family Policy* (Washington, DC: Brookings Institution, 1981), p. 135.
17. New York State Department of Social Services, *Foster Care Trends in New York State* (Albany: New York State Department of Social Services, June 1982), p. 25.
18. Temporary State Commission on Child Welfare, "Foster Care Reimbursement: A New Approach" (May 1978), p. 3.
19. Temporary State Commission, "Foster Care Reimbursement."
20. Steiner, *Futility of Family Policy*, p. 145.
21. U.S. Department of Health, Education, and Welfare, National Center for Social Statistics, NCSS Report A-2 (December 1975) "Public Assistance Statistics," Table 7.
22. Welfare Research, Inc., "Child Welfare Reform Act: An Evaluation Report to the Division of the Budget on Impact and Implementation" (Albany: Welfare Research, Inc., October 1985), p. ix.

23. New York City Comptroller's Office, "The Children Are Waiting."
24. Temporary State Commission, "Foster Care Reimbursement," p. 23.
25. Temporary State Commission on Child Welfare, *The Children of the State II* (October 1976), p. 11.
26. New York City Comptroller's Office, "The Children Are Waiting," pp. 10–12, p. 18.
27. New York City's Comptroller's Office, p. 32.
28. New York City's Comptroller's Office, p. 31.
29. New York City's Comptroller's Office, p. 33.
30. New York City's Comptroller's Office, p. 35.
31. New York City's Comptroller's Office, p. 43.
32. New York City's Comptroller's Office, p. 42.
33. Office of the City Council President, *Good Money After Bad: An Analysis of Expenditures and Performance in Private-Sector Foster Care* (New York, Office of the City Council President, May 1979).
34. Temporary State Commission, *The Children of the State III* (March 1980), p. 32.
35. Gerald Benjamin and T. Norman Hurd, *Making Experience Count: Managing Modern New York in the Carey Era* (Albany: Rockefeller Institute of Government, 1985), p. 90.
36. Welfare Research, "Child Welfare Reform Act" (1985), p. 11.3.
37. Welfare Research, "Child Welfare Reform Act of 1979: An Evaluation of Planning and Implementation Activities" (Albany: September 1982), App. D.
38. Welfare Research, "Child Welfare Reform Act" (1985), p. 11.3.
39. Welfare Research, "Child Welfare Reform Act" (1982), App. D.
40. Welfare Research, "Child Welfare Reform Act" (1985), p. 14.12.
41. Welfare Research, "Child Welfare Reform Act" (1985), pp. 5.3–5.4.
42. Welfare Research, "Child Welfare Reform Act" (1985), pp. 6.3–6.7.
43. Welfare Research, "Child Welfare Reform Act" (1985), p. 7.6.
44. Welfare Research, "Child Welfare Reform Act" (1985), p. 7.10.

15

HOUSING

❦

Emanuel Tobier
and
Barbara Gordon Espejo

Government housing policies in the United States are best viewed as responses to developments within the private sector. There is widespread agreement that the major decisions about where people obtain housing, how much they consume, and the prices they pay should be determined by market forces. However, this commitment to the market is not consistently maintained. To the extent that the United States can be said to have a national housing policy, it is to encourage home ownership. The steadfast provision of substantial tax subsidies to homeowning, middle class households represents the heart of the national housing policy consensus. There is, by contrast, little agreement about what government should do when private housing markets produce unsatisfactory results, as is the case for the poor. In fact, this lack of consensus has allowed the Reagan Administration to curtail drastically long-standing federal housing subsidies to the poor.

In examining the evolution of housing program relationships between New York State and New York City one quickly becomes aware of a third player. What had been a duet became a trio in the 1930s. Subsequently, with few exceptions, the State and the City fashioned their housing programs in response to initiatives designed by the federal government. The latter's waning involvement has placed considerable pressure on the State to take on greater responsibilities.

445

This essay begins with a description of the key characteristics of New York City's housing market—highlighting the ways in which it differs from other parts of the state. The second section provides historical background on the development of the housing "problem" and early attempts to deal with it. The succeeding sections discuss six major housing programs or program types that have been of importance in New York City and in which the State has played an influential role. These are (1) rent regulation; (2) the Mitchell-Lama program; (3) the New York State Urban Development Corporation; (4) federal and State low-income housing subsidy programs, including public housing; (5) shelter allowances as part of the public assistance program; (6) tax subsidy programs. The concluding section raises some of the contemporary housing issues that seem likely to affect or be affected by State-City relations.

NATURE OF NEW YORK CITY'S HOUSING MARKET

New York City's housing market is strikingly different from those in other parts of New York State. Most significant is the extent to which housing in New York City is dominated by the private rental sector—that is, by relations between tenants and landlords. In 1900, 88 percent of New York City's families rented and only 12 percent owned. In the state's next five biggest cities (Buffalo, Rochester, Albany, Syracuse, and Yonkers) the combined margin of renters over owners was only two to one. In the balance of the state, owners predominated, 57 to 43 percent.[1]

For the nation and New York State, each subsequent decade, with the exception of the 1930s, saw an increase in the relative importance of homeownership. (See Table 15.1.) For the "big-five" cities, the share of homeownership peaked in 1960 at 45 percent and has since slipped gradually. New York City, starting from a much lower level, advanced to 24 percent in 1970 before retreating slightly in 1980.

Outside New York City, rental apartments tend to be in low-rise and modest-sized buildings. In contrast, 79 percent of all rental units in New York City are in structures with five units or more. The comparable figures for the big-five cities and the rest of the state are 43 percent and 37 percent, respectively. Approximately 80 percent of all rental units in buildings with 5 units or more in the state are located in New York City. However, since the 1960s, there has been a significant increase in the relative importance of larger buildings within the rental sectors outside New York City. This rapid growth in the number of voting tenants in Nassau, Suffolk, and Westchester counties created the political support for the initiation of rent regulation in these areas in the 1970s.

TABLE 15.1

*Selected Characteristics of Housing Units in New York State
by Part of State, 1930–1980 (percentage distribution)*

	1930	1940	1950	1960	1970	1980
New York State						
Occupied Units	100%	100%	100%	100%	100%	100%
Owner-Occupied	35	28	38	45	47	49
Renter-Occupied	65	72	62	55	53	51
Five Units or More	NA	38	36	35	34	33
New York City						
Occupied Units	100%	100%	100%	100%	100%	100%
Owner-Occupied	20	16	19	22	24	23
Renter-Occupied	80	84	81	78	76	77
Five Units or More	NA	60	60	61	61	60
"Big-Five" Cities						
Occupied Units	100%	100%	100%	100%	100%	100%
Owner-Occupied	44	33	44	45	43	42
Renter-Occupied	56	67	56	55	57	58
Five Units or More	NA	13	16	18	22	25
Rest of New York State						
Occupied Units	100%	100%	100%	100%	100%	100%
Owner-Occupied	58	50	65	73	73	72
Renter-Occupied	42	50	35	27	27	28
Five Units or More	NA	5	6	6	8	10

SOURCE: U.S. Census of Population, various years.
NOTE: NA = not available.

The City's position with regard to the possible range of housing programs has been influenced historically by the fact that so many of its residents are renters. Other jurisdictions, with their very different patterns of housing, have very different wish lists. This is doubly unfortunate since New York City's need for suitable government housing programs has escalated as the economic situation of its residents has deteriorated. In 1950 the median income of families in New York City was slightly above that for the entire state; by 1980 it had fallen to 17 percent below. Because of its increasing low-income component, New York City's housing market had suffered greatly in its ability to attract private capital.

In the 1950–1970 period incomes in New York State and New York City rose at a faster pace than either rents or house prices, and the proportion of income spent on housing fell. However, the incomes of renter households was increasing at a much slower rate than those of homeowners, and the rental sector became the part of the housing market that catered to lower income people. In the 1970s, however, incomes advanced less rapidly than either house prices or rents in both the state and the city. This disparity was most marked in the rental sector, which was the crucial one in New York City.

HISTORICAL ORIGINS OF NEW YORK CITY'S HOUSING "PROBLEM"

Early concerns about the housing "problem" in New York City revolved around issues of physical congestion and moral contagion.[2] The city's settlement pattern, from its seventeenth-century origins, was compact and intensive. The interdependencies created by many people living and working in a relatively small area led early on to government measures designed to regulate the character of housing and development. The nature of the city's housing market was transformed root-and-branch, in the decades before the Civil War, by massive industrialization. New York City became the nation's premier factory town, as it already was its leading center for shipping and finance. For most of the nineteenth century, because the means of transportation were slow and costly, blue collar families were compelled to live in an unprecedentedly concentrated fashion. As of 1900, close to 1.9 million people, out of a citywide population of 3.4 million, lived in Manhattan, the vast majority of them south of 59th Street. The turn-of-the-century Lower East Side achieved densities comparable today to Bombay, that symbol of Third World urban squalor.

In New York City, housing for working class families took the form of tightly packed multi-family tenements built to shabby standards. However, the forces which produced these wretched habitations were early and vigorously challenged. Government came under increasing pressure to intervene in the operations of the private market in working-class housing.

The idea of intervention, however, ran against the ideological grain of that age. Nevertheless, there were countervailing voices. Widespread housing deficiencies seemed to pose a threat to the social order. But before the 1920s, when greater activism became politically possible, government efforts to deal with problems of slum housing were confined to measures which mandated higher minimum standards of initial construction and maintenance. The major legislative landmarks for such actions, the Tenement House Acts of 1867 and 1901 and the 1916 Zoning Resolution, did not require dramatic improvements in existing housing; indeed, for them to have done so would have been out of character for reform efforts of this era.[3]

Competition among suppliers of housing was relied upon as the principal mechanism for upgrading the housing standards of the ordinary family. Governmentally mandated building, occupancy, and zoning codes only made back-sliding more difficult (though not impossible). For the most part these codified the results that markets would have produced. For the real wages of factory workers in New York City grew substantially, and this increased purchasing power attracted a host of new housing suppliers.[4] In fact the expansion of the rapid transit system, of all the activities supported by government, represented the single most powerful force in expanding the supply of affordable housing to the city's rank-and-file population, by bringing a vast acreage of low-priced sites into development.[5]

In the 1920s four measures were enacted that affected New York City's housing market: rent control, tax exemption, the State Housing Law of 1926, creating the state's first housing survey and providing for the establishment of "Limited Dividend Corporations," and the Multiple Dwelling Law of 1929. Inflation accelerated during World War I and its immediate aftermath. Rents (and house prices) rose especially rapidly because of the wartime slowdown in construction. In 1919 the number of apartment units completed in New York City was 1,624. By comparison, they had averaged 25,000 annually in the five years before the entry of the United States into the war in 1917.[6] The demand for housing in the city had slowed between 1914 and 1918 because of the cessation of European immigration to the United States, the major source of New York City's population growth over the preceding decades. Once the war ended, however, immigration soared. It was dominated by eastern European Jews who were disproportionately attracted to New York City where many of their compatriots had settled as part of the prewar migration.

The response of the political system to this tight housing market was to do something about the housing shortage. In 1920 the New York State legislature, with a Democratic governor, Alfred Smith of New York City, enacted a rent control law. While statewide in scope it was aimed mainly at New York City where over 60 percent of the state's rental housing was then located. The law provided that an agreement in which rent had been increased by more than 25 percent annually was presumptively unjust. However, rents stabilized in the mid 1920s. The legislature began to phase the program out, confining its scope to low-rent apartments. By 1928 only 20 percent of all rental units in New York City were subject to regulation. When the law expired in 1929, the City re-enacted it

450 THE TWO NEW YORKS

without substantial change. Shortly thereafter, it was struck down on the grounds that State action in this area preempted City action.[7]

Another measure passed in 1921 to stimulate residential construction inaugurated a policy of exempting new buildings from some part of local property taxation for a specified period. As constitutionally required, the law permitting New York City to exempt buildings from taxation was enacted by the State legislature as an amendment to the State's Tax Law. However, only New York City utilized the powers granted by this measure. The law was allowed to lapse in 1926.[8]

How significant was this measure in increasing the production and lowering the cost of housing? Over 750,000 dwelling units were completed in New York City between 1921 and 1930 including 310,000 one- and two-family houses and 455,000 units in multi-family buildings. Enthusiasts for tax-exemption programs have retrospectively credited this program with overcoming the city's housing shortage.[9]

Closer examination breeds skepticism about such sweeping claims. Tax savings to homeowners were significant, but savings to renters were very modest. The law exempted newly constructed one- and two-family dwellings from taxation for up to $5,000 and $10,000, respectively, in assessed value for a period of ten years. Apartments and multi-family dwellings received a maximum exemption of $5,000 per apartment or $1,000 per room, whichever was less. However, in 1923 the maximum exemption for a newly built multi-family dwelling was capped at $15,000, no matter how many individual apartments were involved.[10] The city's housing market during the 1920s probably owed its strength to more basic factors such as rapid population growth and expansion in real incomes.

The State Housing Companies Law of 1926 was the precursor of the 1950s Mitchell-Lama (or Limited Profit Housing Companies) program. Housing companies could be formed with the power of eminent domain and the potential for substantial reduction of real estate taxes at the discretion of the municipality in which they operated.[11] Limitations were placed on rentals to ensure that savings due to such assistance would be passed on to tenants. The program attracted few takers. Only 6,000 units were built under its auspices, virtually all in New York City.[12]

The Multiple Dwelling Law of 1929, which was enacted by the State over the City's opposition, revised the 1901 Tenement House Code, which had undergone continual revision since its original enactment.[13] While the Multiple Dwelling Law raised the minimum standards of new construction, it is unclear how many households previously able to afford apartments in newly constructed buildings were priced out of the market by its provisions. As real wages increased, working-class families could afford the better multi-family apartments being built in the Bronx, Brooklyn, and Queens. The concurrent depopulation of areas of first settlement such as the Lower East Side testified to the strength of working-class demand for newly built housing.

The possible long-term consequences of the Multiple Dwelling Law were overwhelmed by the impact of the Great Depression. After 1929 rates of new construction dropped sharply. Only 3,034 new units were completed in 1933 compared with 107,000 in 1927.[14] The vacancy rate for multi-family rental housing skyrocketed, reaching 15 percent by 1933.[15] Rents fell sharply, too. There was widespread distress as tax arrears mounted and banks foreclosed on thousands of properties no longer able to meet their mortgage payments.

Until the 1930s, housing policy was largely a state and local matter. Today's extensive intervention by the federal government in the housing market began in the 1930s as part of a larger effort to ameliorate the consequences of the Great Depression. In housing the federal approach was to create a supportive environment in which the private market could perform better, not to supplant it. The centerpieces of this effort were (1) the reorganization in 1933 of the nation's thrift institutions to allow them to operate more effectively as specialized residential mortgage leaders; and (2) the passage in 1934 of the National Housing Act, which established a government-backed insurance program to insure lenders of residential mortgages against the risk of default and to provide easier terms to borrowers. At first, insurance was available only for smaller owner-occupied units, but by 1937 it was extended to multi-family rental buildings. The low-rent public housing program, enacted in 1938, was the only program that sought in even a small way to replace private ownership. It provided capital subsidies to local housing agencies to build housing for low-income families.[16]

The revival of the national and New York economies in the late 1930s sparked a revival in new housing construction. Incomes and rents advanced and the rental vacancy rate fell to 7 percent by 1940, half its 1935 level. From just over 3,000 units in 1933, new units built reached 37,000 in 1941. Virtually all new construction was undertaken by private developers operating on an unsubsidized, fully tax-paying basis. Only 8 percent of the units completed in New York City between 1936 and 1941 were built in connection with a public housing program.[17] These involved federally financed units and units built under complementary State and City programs. An increasing proportion of this resurgent demand for housing, however, was for one- and two-family units which took advantage of the federal mortgage insurance program.

The entry of the United States into World War II forced a virtual halt to non-defense-related residential construction. As prosperity returned during World War II, households that had doubled up began to undouble. By the war's end, the city's rental vacancy rate had fallen to an extremely low level of 1 percent.[18]

RENT CONTROL

What is known today as "rent control" became effective in New York City in 1943 as part of a national system of wartime price controls. The federal government retained rent control in the years immediately after the war's end to allow new production to accelerate to meet the housing shortage that had developed during the depressed 1930s and the war years. There was, however, a progressive easing of constraints on rent increases, and private rental housing built after February 1, 1947, was excluded from control. However, individual states were allowed to continue controls. New York State exercised this option and enacted the Emergency Housing Act of 1950.[19]

In New York City from 1950 to 1962 rent control was administered by the State through the Temporary Rent Commission. The commission exercised similar responsibilities in other jurisdictions which exercised their local options under the State enabling law to continue the rent control program. In 1950 some 96 percent of all rental units in New York City were controlled, accounting for just under 80 percent of the city's total housing stock. Another 640,000 units elsewhere in the state were subject to rent control when this program was passed. Rental units built after February 1, 1947, were exempted from control in order not to discourage new construction. There were a number of grounds under which owners of controlled properties could obtain rent increases. The principal occasion was tenant turnover, at which time a 15 percent rent increase was allowed. In effect, turnover rates determined the rent levels of controlled units.

Rent control served the interests of existing tenants, particularly better-off ones who lived in prime neighborhoods, by providing them with spacious apartments at bargain rents. However, this was still not enough over the long run to curtail the exodus of the middle class. Middle-class families had to weigh cheap rents against prospects for capital appreciation and the tax advantages of owning. For many in the middle class, rental housing, even under the most advantageous rent controlled terms, had become an inferior good. In the long run, rent control also undermined the incentive of owners to maintain their properties. It did this by setting an arbitrary limit on the rents they could charge. Eventually this led to a situation in which housing occupied by the middle class was no longer attractive to them.

As the middle class moved from the city their place was taken by in-migrating, lower-income black and Puerto Rican households. Given the mechanics of the rent control system, in which the rate of turnover determined the rate at which rents increased, the fact that there was a replacement of a higher-income group by a lower-income group should have been of little importance to owners. In fact, they should have regarded the process favorably because of its positive short-run conse-quences for rents. However, as a consequence of racial and economic class change, owners raised the rate at which they discounted the present value of the rents to be expected from rent controlled housing and further reduced their investments and maintenance outlays. This problem cannot be blamed on the rent control program, but nevertheless it added to the adverse trends in the city's rental sector.

Between 1950 and 1962, when the State ran the program, rent control did not produce a visible crisis, just a slow crumbling. Disinvestment moved slowly, in part because of the gradual rate of inflation. Aggregate rents were advanced slowly — as permitted under the law — but the same was true for operating and maintenance costs, reflecting the modest rate of postwar inflation.

When instituted in 1950, rent control was viewed as a temporary measure, the need for which would disappear as the housing shortage that made it necessary was overcome. By the early 1960s rent control was no longer viewed as a temporary program in New York City. It had become a permanent part of the political landscape, ardently supported by a large and vocal constituency. However, its realm contracted outside New York City as more and more jurisdictions dispensed with it. By 1961 approximately 160,000 units in the rest of New York State were still rent controlled (most of them in Buffalo).[20] The comparable 1950 figure had been 640,000. Those running for office statewide or in New York City found it necessary to speak well of rent control. The program's politically sacrosanct status showed up clearly in the controversies which led to its transfer from the State to the City in 1962.

The mayoral election of 1961 pitted the Democratic incumbent Robert Wagner against Louis Lefkowitz, the State's lieutenant gover-nor. Wagner made rent control an issue, asserting that the Republicans in Albany had been lax in its administration and that recent changes "opened the door to the biggest rent gouge in the history of rent control."[21] In fact, these changes were much less drastic than Wagner's charges suggested. Nevertheless, Lefkowitz, supported by Governor Rockefeller, agreed to reverse them[22] and furthermore urged the transfer of the responsibility for rent control to New York City. Lefkowitz lost, but in 1962, a gubernatorial election year, Rockefeller pushed the enactment of the Emergency Housing Act of 1962, which in effect compelled New York City to take over the administration of rent control.[23]

This transfer heightened the program's susceptibility to political considerations and greatly reduced its ability to respond flexibly to changing economic conditions. The potential pro-tenant bias of the rent control program is obviously considerable in a city like New York where renters outnumber owners by a wide margin.

Unfortunately, from the point of view of the long-term physical well-being of the city's rental housing stock, this transfer occurred when inflation, and particularly the cost of operating multi-family housing, was rising rapidly. A wide gap opened between rents and the amounts owners needed to maintain housing services, triggering large scale capital flight from the city's renter housing sector.

Few observers fully foresaw the crisis in New York City housing during the last part of the 1960s. Extensive stretches of the city's residential fabric—in the South Bronx, Central Brooklyn, Upper Manhattan— literally went up in smoke. Owners were abandoning their properties. Moreover, the perimeters of these beleaguered neighborhoods were widening dramatically.

At issue was the ability of the private sector to function in an acceptable manner as a provider of housing for the city's low-income population. Historically, the largest part of the responsibility for housing the poor had fallen to private landlords. At the end of the 1960s, no more than 160,000 lower-income households lived in publicly owned or subsidized housing. A minimum of three to four times as many households with comparable incomes lived in privately owned units. The specter which haunted the city was the probable fate of poor tenants living in unsubsidized buildings.

Before this problem could be dealt with, other more politically salient housing matters pressed for solution. During the first half of the 1960s, New York City experienced an unusually high level of new construction.[24] Close to 250,000 new units were built, of which 70 percent represented privately owned and nonsubsidized construction. A major reason for this heightened activity was the passage in 1961 of a new zoning law to go into effect in 1964. Under its provisions the development capacity of sites was to be cut back significantly. Builders accelerated construction before the new law came into force. But as these new units entered the market, competition for tenants increased and, by the mid 1960s, owners of newly built apartment houses were offering substantial concessions. However, soon these additions were absorbed.

Vacancy rates, in the absence of new construction, fell once again to low levels and rents in the uncontrolled sector began to rise.

The rapidity with which rents rose was a function of two factors. First, new zoning laws discouraged construction by raising site acquisition costs. Second, higher rates of inflation pushed up rents. In response, the City, acting under powers given it by the 1962 Emergency Housing Act, enacted the rent stabilization program in 1969.[25] This measure placed 350,000 privately owned units built since 1947 under rent regulation. They represented the city's newest multi-family housing units. Their tenants were considerably better off than their rent controlled counterparts.

In essence, rent stabilization was created to shelter middle- and upper-income tenants from market forces. Its enactment abrogated a tacit agreement in effect since 1947 under which newly constructed apartment buildings were exempt from rent control. It was expected that this turnabout would have an adverse effect on the future willingness of developers to build unsubsidized rental housing in New York City. But 1969 was an election year and the incumbent mayor, John Lindsay, faced a tight race.

The maximum rents that stabilized owners could charge were determined under annual guidelines, issued by a Rent Guidelines Board (RGB), an independent body appointed by the mayor. The RGB's annual orders specified maximum rent increases expressed in percentage terms for tenants whose leases expire during a given year. In theory, these would be determined by an annual review of operating costs. However, this review was not to be conducted for individual buildings, but for the "class" of stabilized properties. Unlike the then-current rent control program, rent stabilization allowed for annual increases for existing tenants. This new form of rent regulation pointed the way to reform of the old rent control program, which by 1969 was widely viewed as a major contributor to the rapid decline of the city's older housing stock.

In 1970, the year *after* his re-election, Mayor Lindsay engineered a restructuring of rent control. Under this reform each of the city's then 1.2 million rent-controlled units was assigned a Maximum Base Rent (MBR) which took into account operating costs, financing charges, and a competitive return on investment.[26] The MBR was a moving target, readjusted periodically as costs rose.

For a high proportion of the units involved, the MBR was substantially above the current rent. To avoid tenant hardship apartments continuously occupied by the same household could be advanced toward their MBR at a maximum rate of 7.5 percent a year. Vacated units could be moved to their full MBR immediately.

The MBR program was quickly overwhelmed by events. The MBR program increased rents more rapidly than before, but housing costs were increasing at a much faster rate than before. Further reform of rent control was needed to deal with this problem, but Mayor Lindsay was unwilling to go beyond the limits of the new MBR program.

Consequently, in 1971 Governor Rockefeller, despite the objection of New York City politicians, obtained passage of the Vacancy Decontrol Law.[27] It returned rent control powers delegated to the City in 1962 to the State. It freed rent-controlled and rent-stabilized apartments from all controls when voluntarily vacated. Given normal rates of turnover, this law was designed to cause the City's two rent regulation laws, one only recently enacted, to wither away.

The increases on continuously occupied apartments through the MBR program and the increases made possible by vacancy decontrol enabled rents in New York City to rise rapidly in the first half of the 1970s. Unfortunately, that was not the case for the incomes of New York City residents. While the United States was prosperous during this period, New York City was in the grip of a severe local recession that began in 1969 and lasted well into the decade's second half.

Predictably, the reaction to these increases in rents was another major reform of the rent regulation laws. This came in 1974, which was (surprise) an election year. In December 1973, Rockefeller had resigned from the governorship leaving Malcolm Wilson, his lieutenant governor, to serve out the remaining part of his unexpired term. Wilson decided to run for governor on his own. His political career had been closely identified with suburban constituencies. To attract support from New York City voters and apartment house dwellers in other parts of the state, he supported the Emergency Tenant Protection Act (ETPA), which was passed in 1974.[28]

Under the ETPA, all units that had destabilized upon becoming vacant in the period between 1971 and 1974, were restabilized. Their future rents as well as those of continuously stabilized apartments would be determined by the Rent Guidelines Board. Units once rent controlled that had been decontrolled—under the short lived Vacancy Decontrol law—were stabilized as were all rent-controlled apartments that became vacant in the future. Continuously occupied rent-controlled units remained under the old rent control program with their rents set under the MBR program. This arrangement lacked any economic logic or purpose; its aim was purely political.

The ETPA set in motion a process by which the rent control and rent stabilization programs would in time be folded into each other, blurring the separate identities of the two programs with their heretofore different constituencies. Rent stabilization had been created in 1968 on behalf of

middle- and upper-income tenants. Rent-controlled housing meanwhile
had become dominated by low-income households. However, they were
now, under the ETPA, destined to become one. A decade later, 219,000
units remained under rent control; rent stabilization covered 946,000
units, two thirds of which were in buildings constructed before World
War II.

In 1983, with the passage of the Omnibus Housing Act (effective April
1, 1984), Governor Mario Cuomo reclaimed both the rent control and
rent stabilization programs.[29] Mayor Edward Koch strongly supported
this initiative. Having exercised direct responsibility for administering the
two rent regulation programs since the 1960s, City politicians had come
to regard it as a no-win situation. However, the governor may have
perceived some advantage from assuming responsibility for it. Tenant
advocacy groups throughout the state felt that their position would
receive more sympathetic treatment from the Cuomo administration than
they could get at the local level. So they lobbied hard (and successfully)
for this change. Landlord groups stood apart from the fray, maintaining that rent regulation was an inherently flawed policy and that it made
little difference which level of government was responsible for its
administration.

Another hypothesis, impossible to confirm, is that the leaders of the
Department of Housing and Community Renewal (DHCR), the State's
housing agency, wished to enhance their bureaucratic and political
standing by augmenting the agency's responsibilities. Previously, DHCR
administered rent control outside New York City under the ETPA. Under
that program, rent stabilization outside New York City was limited to a
few civil divisions in Nassau, Westchester, and Rockland counties which
elected to become subject to its regulations. There were 86,000 such units
in 1983.[30] In those communities which have rent control, including
Albany and Buffalo, vacated controlled units became stabilized. Thus, in
one fell swoop, as it were, DHCR increased its regulatory workload from
about 130,000 to 1.4 million units.

By intervening so boldly in the city's vast rent regulated housing
sector, the State has given many hostages to fortune. Whatever goes
wrong in this market the City will have the State to blame. And problems
are likely to be greatest in the oldest parts of the city's housing stock
which are either under the old rent control program or have, since 1974,
become part of rent stabilization.

The governor promised to unveil a plan for rent regulation for
consideration by the legislature in 1987, when both the rent control and
rent stabilization programs were to be renewed. But before Election Day
in 1986, Cuomo ruled out vacancy decontrol in any variant as a possible
policy option. This plus an earlier DHCR ruling to restrict rent increases

permitted in connection with building-improving capital investments
indicates that the tenant advocacy groups reckoned right.[31]

THE MITCHELL-LAMA PROGRAM

Few programs better illustrate the pitfalls of direct government
involvement as a provider of subsidized services for the middle class
than the 1955 Limited Profit Housing Companies Law (more familiarly
known as the Mitchell-Lama program after the legislators who introduced it). In addition to a State-financed component, operating throughout the state, it authorized separate programs to be funded by individual
cities. In the event, only New York City set up its own effort.[32]

The idea for the program came from Mayor Robert Wagner. The
objective of the program from Wagner's point of view was to stimulate
construction within New York City of housing affordable to middle-
income families to keep them from joining the exodus to the suburbs.
In Wagner's analysis, this could be done by subsidizing construction.
Moreover, a precedent, in the form of the 1926 Limited Dividend Companies Program, existed for reducing certain of the input costs of
construction and passing these savings on in the form of lower rents or
carrying charges to middle-income tenants.[33]

In the mid 1950s chances for getting a strengthened version of this
earlier measure seemed promising. The scope for savings on interest
charges was greater as higher postwar income tax rates increased the
advantage to investors of tax-exempt State and local securities sold to
finance mortgages. The wording of the State constitution, however,
stipulated that the legislature may supply housing funds only for slum
clearance, for low-rent housing, or for low-income persons. As this was
not the target of the Mitchell-Lama program, its enabling statute fudged
the issue by using language which talked of providing housing for
families who are in low-income groups who cannot afford to pay enough
to cause private enterprise to build a sufficient supply of adequate safe
and sanitary dwellings. This language enabled the courts to rule that such
families could also be in the middle-income group.

Fortunately, from the point of view of New York City-based advocates of the Mitchell-Lama program, Averell Harriman, a Democrat,
was elected governor in 1955. A New Deal liberal, Harriman supported
Wagner's proposal for middle-income housing. For the City, joining
forces with the State helped in meeting possible legal challenges to the
constitutionality of a middle-income program and provided another
source of financing for Mitchell-Lama projects in the city.

Developers under the program received low cost mortgages from the City or State financed by tax-exempt bonds. In addition, exemptions from normal property taxes were available. The developers submitted to supervision over tenant selection and schedules of rents or carrying charges. Generally speaking, if a tenant or a co-op purchaser had an annual income which was no more than 6 or 7 times, depending on household size, the required rent or carrying charges he or she was eligible for Mitchell-Lama housing. Required rents (or carrying charges) were those which were needed to cover operating costs, capital charges, and the sponsor's profit (set at 6 percent of equity investment). Tenants would be required to pay surcharges if their subsequent increases in income put them over the indicated income limit.

Enacted during Harriman's one-term incumbency, the State's Mitchell-Lama effort was vigorously expanded during the long reign of a Republican, Nelson Rockefeller. To Rockefeller, the Mitchell-Lama program, then just getting started, was not an ideological embarrassment, but a vehicle for solving housing problems. A task force on housing appointed by him in 1959 reported that there was a middle-class housing crisis in the state.[34]

One "problem" the task force recommended solutions to was the growing resistance by voters in State housing referendums to bond issues for housing subsidy programs. New York's State Constitution specifies that voters must approve by referendum the sale of any bonds whose repayment is pledged by the State's full faith and credit (so-called general obligation bonds). When the Mitchell-Lama program went into effect in 1955, gaining voter assent was viewed as a problem of little consequence. But it quickly became one. Before Mitchell-Lama's passage, voters in New York State referendums had typically approved housing propositions by a wide margin. In 1954, for example, 61 percent voted yes and 39 percent voted no on a housing bond issue. New York City voters tended to be more favorably disposed than upstaters; but even voters outside New York City produced favorable, if narrow, majorities.

However, in the first bond issue which involved borrowing for Mitchell-Lama purposes (as well as for the State-financed low-rent public housing program) the earlier margins of approval diminished considerably. In 1956, a $100 million bond issue for middle-income housing was rejected by the voters, and two years later, it passed by the narrowest of margins. New York City voters still were strongly in favor, but upstaters were now strongly in opposition. This trend continued for the balance of the decade. Given the demographic and voting power shift within the state from cities to suburbs, the handwriting was on the wall.

In 1962 Proposition Number 2, the Low Financing Experiment (LIFE)—technically not a bond issue—sought approval to divert $3

million annually from previously authorized funds to subsidize the rents
of low-income families living in middle-income housing projects. It went
down to defeat by a 64 to 36 percent margin and lost both in New York
City and upstate. Then in 1964 and 1965 in voting on propositions to
expand the state low-rent housing program, the strength of negative
upstate sentiment overwhelmed narrowly favorable New York City
majorities. Both went down to resounding defeats. Henceforth the
low-rent public housing program in particular, and low-income housing subsidies in general, would be reliant on federal programs and
funds. This also threatened to cut off further funds for Mitchell-Lama
and would in time have left it as a relatively small, strictly City
operation.[35]

The immediate question for Rockefeller was how to bypass voter
resistance in bond referendums. A way out of this impasse, suggested by
the task force, led to the creation in 1960 of the New York State Housing
Finance Agency (HFA), a public benefit corporation. Authorized by the
legislature with enormous and bipartisan margins, HFA could raise funds
through tax-free bonds and lend them at below-market interest rates as
mortgages to developers to build housing. The bonds were secured by the
housing and to be liquidated by rents (or carrying charges) from
operating these structures. HFA's bonds were technically not obligations
of the State, although borrowers expected them to be treated as such.
HFA was thus the first issuer of the so-called moral obligation bonds
which were used widely for the next decade and a half to finance public
and quasi-public capital expenditures in a wide variety of activities
within New York State.

Nevertheless, HFA's operating style was unadventurous. While the
City in its Mitchell-Lama program selected sites in marginal areas, the
State Mitchell-Lama program was much more careful. Private developers
originated projects and submitted applications to HFA for construction
and mortgage financing. HFA reviewed the project submissions and
DHCR evaluated their financial viability.[36]

Administration of the State Mitchell-Lama program was criticized in
the mid 1960s for being too risk-averse. It was charged with curtailing
the amount of housing that could have been built. During the first decade
of its existence, the State Mitchell-Lama program financed approximately 30,000 units, five sixths of which were located in New York
City.

The City's Mitchell-Lama program was administered by the municipal
Housing Development Administration (HDA). By the late 1960s the
30,000 units for which it had provided financing were occupied, and
commitments had been entered into for an additional 20,000 units. As its
borrowing and building costs began to escalate in line with the

increasingly inflationary trend in the economy, the City's Mitchell-Lama program confronted growing problems of marketability. Committed to building in marginal locations, in order to assist in the upgrading of deteriorating neighborhoods, the program's sponsors found it difficult to secure tenants who could pay the required rents, even with the granting by the City of virtually full property tax abatement and the use of mortgages with below market interest rates.[37]

Even more pressing at this point, however, were the problems posed by the nature of the Mitchell-Lama financing arrangements. The City had been borrowing short term in order to finance loans to Mitchell-Lama companies. As the short-term notes matured, they were rolled over. This practice was followed in the hope, doomed to disappointment, that long-term interest rates would fall substantially. It was also a device to keep the City from exceeding its constitutionally imposed housing purposes debt limit.

By 1970 the press of other financing requirements made it necessary for the City to refinance its short-term Mitchell-Lama debt into long-term bonds. In order to deal with the debt limit problem and to provide additional borrowing power to continue building, the City in 1971 obtained State legislation which created the New York City Housing Finance Development Corporation (HDC).

HDC, as a New York State public benefit corporation, was authorized to raise funds in the capital markets in order to finance the City's Mitchell-Lama program. Because it was a public benefit corporation, HDC was not bound by constitutional limitations on the amount of housing-related debt it could issue. Its bonds were ostensibly secured by City Mitchell-Lama project revenues. But ultimately they were backed by a particularly strong version of the State's "moral obligation" under which, all else failing, investors in HDC bonds had first call on the payments that the State makes to the City for any purpose.[38]

Between the late 1960s and the early 1970s pressure for more governmental action in assisting low-income housing intensified. At the federal level this led to the passage, as part of the 1968 Housing Act, of two major new federal subsidy programs. In New York, it led to the creation of the Urban Development Corporation which, as shall be discussed, was the chosen instrument for producing low-income housing in New York State. However, it also put pressure on the Mitchell-Lama agencies to shift from being almost wholly a financier of middle-income housing to taking an increasing position in the lower-income end of the market.

Prior to 1968 DHCR/HFA's modus operandi was to provide shallow off-budget subsidies for middle-income families in newly built multi-family apartment buildings. To house lower-income families, deeper subsidies would be required. For this clientele, the savings from tax-exempt bonds and exemptions from local property taxes were not enough. DHCR/HFA felt that undertaking this role, without explicit commitment for larger subsidies, would compromise its ability to tap the tax-exempt market to fund its ongoing middle-income program as well as the many other State-related facility funding efforts with which it was involved. However, the availability of new sources of subsidy from the federal 1968 Housing Act changed its position. High levels of production were maintained under the State and City Mitchell Lama programs through the mid 1970s, but increasingly they relied on federal subsidies to accommodate lower income families.

No additional commitments were allowed to be made under the State and City Mitchell-Lama programs after 1974. In that year 70 percent of the City's projects were in arrears on their mortgage payments. For political reasons, the City had been unwilling to raise rents and carrying charges enough to cover operating costs or, failing that, to foreclose the mortgages. The State's mortgage portfolio was in much better shape in that a much smaller percentage of its projects were in arrears. However, the State's program, as administered by the DHCR/HFA, had one huge problem to contend with—the mammoth 15,000-unit Coop City development in the North Bronx then in the midst of a long-running and, to DHCR/HFA, financially devastating rent strike.[39]

Approximately 73,000 units were constructed under the State's Mitchell-Lama program. Over 80 percent of these were in New York City. Only 12,000 units in total were built in all other parts of the state. Approximately one sixth of the State-funded Mitchell-Lama projects in the city were built for lower-income families (mainly through the use of federal housing subsidies). This share was even lower outside the city. The City's Mitchell-Lama program built 66,000 units, approximately 5,000 more than were put up in the city by the State. It was less of a middle income program, though, since close to a third of its units were for lower-income families.

After construction activity under the State's Mitchell-Lama program was terminated, DHCR continued to supervise the 113 projects—61 of them in New York City—for which HFA, its financing arm, had provided mortgages. HFA's portfolio, though in much better shape than its City counterpart, was not without its problems. Moreover, in working these out DHCR/HFA had time on its side. The State's fiscal problems were considerably less onerous than the City's and DHCR/HFA was not compelled, as HPD/HDC was, to have what was in effect a fire sale of its Mitchell-Lama properties to raise revenues. As of October 1985, eight HFA projects—all in New York City—were in arrears on their mortgages. These represent about 40 percent of the housing units and one third of the mortgage commitments made by HFA. Coop City alone accounts for nearly 60 percent of the units and over 80 percent of the total amount of debt service arrearages. However, HFA, within the last few years, excepting these eight troubled projects, has made considerable progress in reducing its risk exposure. In 1981 30 of its projects had debt service coverage ratios below 1.00. By 1985 this figure was down to 13.[40]

As of June 1974, the City had financed, through the HDC, $1.6 billion in loans under its Mitchell-Lama program. Of the 114 operating projects, 80 were in arrears on their mortgages. Since then, however, the City's mortgage exposure has been sharply reduced (but at a cost). The City was compelled by the fiscal crisis to sell off—or refinance—a substantial portion of its Mitchell-Lama debt. By early 1980, 87 Mitchell-Lama projects had gone through this process. In order to sell these mortgages the City took a substantial loss—an estimated 40 percent—as the mortgages were marketable only at sharp discounts from their nominal value. The face value of the bonds, however, which were initially issued to fund these mortgages, still remains a part of the City's long-term debt burden. The projects whose mortgages were refinanced are insured by the Federal Housing Administration to make them attractive to investors. As a result, rent and carrying charge determinations in these projects have to be approved by the federal government. The City now holds 57 Mitchell-Lama project mortgages. In the last few years the City has been more aggressive in increasing rents to meet higher costs and debt requirements. Only one is not paying debt service. However, more than a third still have accumulated arrears.[41]

While the City's HPD administers the Mitchell-Lama projects built under its auspices, HDC services the remainder of its mortgage portfolio. Like its State counterpart—HFA—HDC has focused its post-Mitchell-Lama efforts on selling tax-exempt bonds to finance new construction and substantial rehabilitation projects built under the federal Section 8 program.

THE URBAN DEVELOPMENT CORPORATION

The New York State Urban Development Corporation (UDC) was created by a midnight vote of the State legislature on April 9, 1968. This controversial law was signed the next day by Governor Rockefeller, in whose office it had been drafted.[42]

From the time he was first elected governor in 1958, Rockefeller made little effort to conceal his presidential ambitions. He was a leading member of the Republican Party's liberal/moderate wing, which then wielded enormous influence within its councils. In the 1960s—a period that combined rapid economic growth and intense civic and social unrest—success in presidential elections seemed likeliest to go to those who seemed capable of grappling with the problems of the cities where the issues of race, class, and poverty were concentrated. Large-scale housing subsidy programs were seen as part of the solution to such problems. This was the view not just of Democrats, who followed the lead of Presidents Kennedy and Johnson, but of Republicans like Rockefeller. The UDC was to be Rockefeller's vehicle for achieving this goal.

Rockefeller had initially requested that UDC be given a virtually unprecedented power for a public authority: the ability to override local zoning and building codes. Opposition to this was widespread. Some objected because it abridged the principle of home rule. New York's Mayor Lindsay opposed UDC on this ground. Others representing a broad range of white working-class and lower-middle-class communities—some Republican, some Democrat—were concerned over the possibility that UDC might use its powers to locate subsidized housing projects for lower income minority families in their communities.

The bill to establish UDC foundered in the 1968 legislative session. But just when it seemed dead, Rockefeller brought it to a vote in the turbulent days after the assassination of Martin Luther King, Jr. Although it passed the Senate, it was decisively rejected in the Assembly by a coalition of big-city Democrats and suburban Republicans. Rockefeller succeeded in reversing this vote by threatening members of his own party with political reprisals.

When UDC commenced operations in April 1968, it was unclear from where it would draw its funds and what the scale of its operations would be. It had only the same power as HFA to sell tax-exempt bonds and to secure local property tax exemptions. But it was supposed to aid low-income households requiring far greater subsidies than the middle income group served by the HFA. UDC's dilemma proved short-lived. The *deus ex machina* turned out to be a major new federal rental housing subsidy program, enacted as part of the U.S. Housing Act in August 1968, four months after UDC was formed.

UDC's career in low-income housing proved to be brief. It was very much Rockefeller's agency, but Rockefeller left office in December of 1973, a year before his term expired. From UDC's point of view, this could hardly have come at a worse time. In January 1973 the Nixon Administration abruptly declared a moratorium on all new commitments under existing housing subsidy programs. UDC had made sizable commitments premised on informal commitments from HUD. UDC's fast track development methods required the timely availability of subsidy funds from the federal government. UDC now faced a situation in which unless the moratorium ended, *and* HUD's informal commitments were formalized promptly, it would be overextended. By early 1974 UDC was in a fiscal bind.

As these developments became known, the financial community became alarmed. UDC's debt was not backed by the State's full faith and credit, but by a moral obligation. Governor Wilson tried to keep UDC's affairs under control, but his clout with the financial community was much weaker than Rockefeller's. Matters went from bad to worse after Hugh Carey, a Democrat, beat Wilson in the election in November 1974. The next few months were an awkward period of transition. The incumbent was unwilling to commit his successor, and the successor was uncertain as to what he could, or should, do.[43]

After taking office in January 1975, Carey reorganized UDC's operations and finances. Its top management was replaced, and a portion of its subsidized housing portfolio was assigned to the Project Finance Agency (PFA), which was created by the legislature to provide long-term financing needed to complete construction of UDC projects. The responsibility for supervising UDC-financed projects was given to the State's DHCR. A UDC subsidiary, the Mortgage Loan Enforcement and Administration Corporation, was formed to service the UDC/PFA mortgages that had been made to UDC's 112 projects. Virtually all were behind on their debt service. For practically all of the projects, difficulties were created by the discrepancy between slowly increasing tenant incomes and, hence, rent-paying capacity, and rapidly increasing operating costs. Two thirds of all UDC projects were still in arrears on their debt service in the mid 1980s.

UDC financed the construction of just under 32,000 units throughout the state. Of these, 49 percent were located in New York City and 51 percent in other parts of the state. UDC's efforts were much less New York City-centered than either the State-aided, low-rent public housing program or the State's Mitchell-Lama effort. Virtually all of UDC's projects, inside or outside New York City, were built with the use of federal funds.[44]

UDC's downfall during the 1973–1975 period was caused by its cash flow problems and by the sudden instability in its political environment. But its problems as a widely touted entrepreneurial State housing development agency reflect deeper forces. Its cash flow problems could have been dealt with, given a reasonable degree of political support. There was little reason to believe that Governor Carey would not be at least as sympathetic as his predecessor to an agency which was dedicated to providing low-income housing. Rather, the fundamental problem was the elimination of the federal program which made it possible for project sponsors to rent to low-income families. UDC viability depended upon federal support, and the decline of federal support was a fundamental problem.

FEDERAL HOUSING SUBSIDIES

The low-rent public housing program was created by the federal government in 1937, the last of the New Deal's major social welfare measures. It subsequently received only grudging support from either the President or Congress.

The principal public agency involved in the direct provision of housing services for low income households in New York City is the Housing Authority (NYCHA). The NYCHA was created in 1934 to operate housing for low income families. It was one of the first housing authorities in the United States. But its activity was minimal until the passage of the Federal Housing Act of 1937, which provided sizable federal funding of low-income housing. The NYCHA as of 1985 housed 172,000 families whose average income was just over $10,000. In addition, the NYCHA is responsible for administering the Federal Section 8 Existing Housing Certificate program in New York City. In total, the NYCHA is responsible for housing over 500,000 low-income New York City residents.[45]

The NYCHA's projects have been financed under three programs, each involving a different level of government. In each, long-term financing was raised through the sale of tax-exempt bonds to private investors. In the federal part, HUD is committed to annual subsidy payments to cover the difference between the rents paid by the low-income tenants and the cost of debt service and project operation. As originally conceived, tenant rents were to be high enough to meet operating costs. HUD's contribution would cover only capital charges. By the 1960s, however, tenant incomes in public housing projects, nationally as well as in New York City, were well below the levels needed to meet operating costs, creating a serious financial problem for local housing authorities. In 1970 the program was broadened to include an operating subsidy as well. Tenants were now expected to contribute a specified portion of their incomes for rent, and any additionally needed revenues to cover debt and operating costs are provided by the federal government.[46] In 1981 this proportion was raised from 25 to 30 percent.

Before 1938 the State was constitutionally prohibited from lending money or using its credit for housing. However, stimulated by the passage of the Federal Housing Act of 1937, the New York State

Constitutional Convention in 1938 authorized the legislature to ". . . provide . . . for low rent housing for persons of low income . . . or for the clearance, replanning, reconstruction and rehabilitation of substandard and insanitary areas or for both such purposes." The State legislature then enacted the Public Housing Law of 1939, the nation's first such state-assisted housing program. Projects built under this program were managed by local housing authorities (such as the NYCHA), but their construction was financed by the State and operating costs were subsidized through annual contributions. The subsidies from the State to the City in this program were somewhat less generous than those from the federal government to the City. It was intended to serve a slightly higher-income clientele than those in the federally aided program at commensurately higher rents and lower subsidy requirements.[47]

The 1938 New York State constitution also authorized the legislature to permit a city to (1) make loan and subsidy payments to a public corporation for housing purposes and to guarantee its obligations; (2) incur debt for housing purposes, beyond its normal debt limit, or not more than 2 percent of the average assessed valuation of the city's taxable real estate during the preceding five years; (3) to levy special excise taxes for loan or subsidy payments to a local housing authority. Acting under these provisions, the City of New York has funded projects through the NYCHA. All were exempt from real property taxes, on the same basis as the federal and State-funded components.

In 1964 the NYCHA had nearly as many State-aided units as federal ones — 45,800 for the former and 49,200 for the latter. Eighty percent of the units that were part of the State-aided low-rent public housing program were located within New York City. This, however, proved to be the high-water mark for the State program. Voters defeated housing propositions to authorize additional loan and subsidy funds in 1964 and 1965. Ultimately the State program in New York City reached its peak of close to 52,000 units in the early 1970s, but the federal component continued to grow and reached 100,000 units in 1976.

By the early 1960s construction under City-funded low-rent public housing projects amounted to 27,700 units. They served a lower-middle-income clientele and initially were not expected to require cash contributions from general revenues to cover their operating and debt charges. By the mid 1960s, however, subsidy payments were needed. Because other programs, like Mitchell-Lama, were serving this group, further production was halted.

In 1977 a window of opportunity opened for the NYCHA in the form of a federal housing bill which allowed it to transfer State- or City-

financed developments to the federal program. By 1985 only 13 percent
of the Housing Authority's 172,000 units were still the financial
responsibility of the State and the City. A decade earlier the comparable
figure had been 42 percent.[48]

Commitments for new production under the federal low rent public
housing program are no longer being made. The NYCHA's chief growth
sector in recent years was administering the federal Section 8 Existing
Housing Certificate program, but this has been phased out by the Reagan
Administration. Its successor, the Housing Voucher program authorized
in 1983, offers little promise in tight housing markets such as New York
City because of its funding limitations. The NYCHA with its vast domain
of low-income families is in a holding pattern.

Historically the State has taken a hands off position with regard to the
running of the NYCHA. While it subsidized a substantial number of
units that were part of the NYCHA's early operations, this type of
support has been considerably reduced since 1977 because of the
increased federal role. Basically, the NYCHA negotiates with the federal
agencies over tenant selection, rent, and maintenance practices. The
NYCHA's management is selected by the City's mayor and is, for all
practical purposes, answerable to him. A highly bureaucratized organization with a long and seemingly well-entrenched history, it has enjoyed
a good reputation as a manager of large-scale projects for low-income
households. But its provision of high-quality housing services through a
unionized civil service workforce does not come cheaply. As the federal
role in the low-income projects is cut back, the City will be forced to turn
to the State for the funding needed to keep its units within the low-
income market.

Until well into the 1960s the federal effort in providing low-income
housing subsidies was dominated by the public housing program. The
Federal Housing Act of 1968 introduced two new major housing subsidy
programs: Section 235 for low-income homeowners and Section 236 for
low-income renters. These programs enjoyed much higher early levels of
production than did the public housing program, but their successes led
quickly to their demise.

The 1968 Housing Act's subsidy programs, together with the passage
of federal tax shelter legislation in 1969, triggered a boom at the national
level in the construction of low-income housing. Between 1969 and 1973
commitments were made to fund approximately 600,000 units under the
Section 235 and Section 236 programs. By comparison approximately
900,000 units had been put into operation under the public housing
program over a 35-year period. Nor was this a partisan program.
Although it was the handiwork of a Democratic administration, it was

implemented aggressively during the first Nixon Administration. During this period both major parties shared a commitment to increase the supply of subsidized, low-income housing through new construction programs.

At the same time as these historically unprecedented commitments were being made by the federal government to finance the construction of housing for the poor, an even larger number of old but, given proper maintenance, still viable units were being abandoned by their owners in cities throughout the nation. In this context the question arose as to whether it would be less costly to shore up the older stock than to build new units. If that were possible, then more families could be served for the same amount of subsidy money. This led, at the federal level, to a search for a successor to Section 236. Before it was eliminated, however, 51,000 multi-family rental units were built in New York State under the Section 236 program. Of these, 52 percent were in New York City. As noted earlier, UDC played a major role in the Section 236 program, accounting for about 60 percent of its output.

The Section 8 program, the successor to Section 236, was created as part of the 1974 Housing and Community Development Act. The Section 8 program had two major components. One utilized the existing rental stock. Eligible households were those whose incomes were too low to enable them to pay the costs of renting units which met minimum physical standards. The difference between a household's rent-paying ability and the so-called fair market rent would be paid by the federal government. The other component resembled the Section 236 program in that it provided subsidies to newly built or substantially renovated units to cover the difference between the cost of the units developed and a fixed percentage of the tenants' incomes. However, Section 236 rental subsidies were restricted to less than 40% of the units in a project, and Section 8 rental subsidies could be used for 100% of such units.

The Section 8 program has been responsible for 94,000 newly constructed or substantially rehabilitated units in New York State. Of these, just under 80 percent have been in New York City. The existing Section 8 program has funded 172,000 units in New York State with slightly more than 80 percent in New York City.

With the advent of the Reagan Administration, the federal housing subsidy programs underwent a radical change. New commitments under the old subsidy programs were made sparingly. Since 1981 additions under these programs largely have reflected the completion of projects committed by the Carter Administration.

The centerpiece of the Reagan Administration's housing policies is a housing subsidy voucher that makes up the difference for eligible families

between 30 percent of their monthly income and reasonable rent levels
wherever they choose to live. Congress, anxious to trim the deficit, agreed
to end most subsidized construction and rehabilitation of low-rent
apartments and approved this housing voucher program in 1983. It has
started slowly. As of late 1986 a mere 12,000 families nationwide have
used vouchers to sign leases.

PUBLIC ASSISTANCE AND THE HOUSING MARKET

Public assistance, while not a housing program per se, plays an
increasingly important role in the low-income private rental market.
Administered in New York City by the New York City Human
Resources Administration (HRA) and in other parts of New York State
by county welfare departments under rules set by the State's Department
of Social Services (DSS), public assistance is part of a national program.
The federal government pays for 50 percent of the costs, with the State
and localities splitting the balance. The State, however, enjoys great
discretion in setting grant levels.

The welfare grant to an eligible family consists of a shelter allowance—to pay for housing—and a so-called basic allowance for non-
housing items. The shelter allowance is equal to the household's actual
rent within limits set by the State that vary according to the number of
persons in the household and geographical location.

The current shelter allowance system evolved from a major reform of
welfare grants in the early 1970s. In 1975 shelter allowance maximums
were set so that 95 percent of the rents then being paid would be under
the limit. At that time 50 percent of all public assistance households in
New York City paid rents which were at least 25 percent below the
maximum established by the State.[49]

However, high rates of inflation after 1975 soon made these ceilings
less generous. By 1983, 68 percent of all welfare households were paying
rents in excess of their shelter allowance; in 1975 the comparable figure
had been under 7 percent. In such circumstances, in order to meet their
rents a high proportion of welfare households were required to utilize
part of their basic grant. However, the real value of the basic grant,
which had been capped at its 1974 level, also had fallen greatly because
of inflation. Consequently, a growing portion of welfare tenants fell
behind in their rental payments.

The principal device available to assure that rent is paid and evictions
do not take place is the two-party check: that is, a check requiring
endorsement by both landlord and tenant. In 1975 fully 26 percent of the

City's welfare families were being issued two-party checks. However, federal regulations at the time limited such arrangements to 10 percent of all cases. The City was forced to reduce its use of two-party checks. Rent arrears increased sharply. In 1977 Congress raised the ceiling on two-party checks to 20 percent, and in 1981 the Reagan Administration secured passage of a measure which lifted all restrictions on the use of two-party checks. However, as a price for this victory it consented to administrative arrangements which guaranteed welfare clients a fair hearing before the two-party check status could be imposed. These have proven to be so onerous in practice that the incidence of two-party checks has failed to grow significantly. As of early 1985, only 14 percent of all welfare families in New York City, up from 10 percent two years earlier, were being sent two-party checks.[50]

The maximum shelter allowance was raised 10 percent by the State DSS in 1984. This led to a sharp decrease in the percentage of public assistance households with rents over the shelter maximum—from 68 percent in December 1983 to 29 percent in March 1984.[51] However, this improvement did not last long. Two years later, 58 percent of public assistance households had rents above the new shelter maximum.

There are about 400,000 households—about a million people—on public assistance in New York City. About three quarters of them receive shelter allowances; of these, nine out of ten live in private housing (the balance are in NYCHA apartments). The number of low-income persons whose housing expenses are paid for by this program are far greater than those living in any other kind of subsidized housing. However, the shelter allowances fall far short of what is needed to meet the cost of standard housing. The 1986 maximum shelter allowance for a three-person family was $244; Governor Cuomo in his 1987 Budget Message proposed an average 22 percent increase in the allowance. Yet the minimum rent required to keep a two-bedroom apartment in tolerably good working order on a fully taxpaying basis is around $475 a month.

The shelter allowance set by the State is inadequate throughout New York State in terms of its relationship to the cost of maintaining standard housing. But localities, including the City, also view shelter allowance increases as a mandated expense because they have to pay 25 percent of public assistance costs (except general assistance, where they have to pay 50 percent). In most states, the cost of public assistance is shared by the federal government and the state government. New York State's local governments have, as a result, mixed feelings about pushing for higher welfare allowances. The City, with about two thirds of the state's public assistance beneficiaries, has not resisted such increases, but neither has it sought them aggressively because of the costs involved.

TAX SUBSIDY PROGRAMS

The two major tax subsidy programs for housing are the so-called J-51 and 421 programs. Both are authorized in State law, but apply only to New York City (that is, to civil divisions having populations of 1 million or more). The 421 program, the younger of the two, was created in 1971. It comes in two versions: 421-a, the more important and controversial part, provides a variable exemption from local property taxes for a period of ten years to new multiple dwellings (rental, cooperative, or condominium); 421-b does the same for one- and two-family houses.

When 421 came into existence, new nonsubsidized multi-family building had fallen to pitiable levels in New York City. Fewer than 2,400 units in such structures were completed in 1970, a far cry from the 14,500 annual average of the 1951–1970 period. Restrictive zoning code changes, which came into force in the mid 1960s, had boosted land costs. The extension of rent regulation to post-1947 buildings via the 1969 Rent Stabilization Law had dampened developer interest in the New York City residential real estate market. Another reason the City successfully sought the 421 program at this time was its desire to stimulate a sagging local economy.

To qualify for the program owners of rental buildings must agree to be subject to rent stabilization after the first market rental of each apartment. Between 1972 and 1984, the latest year for which these data are available, 45,000 multi-family units were built under 421-a; 421-b added another 6,900. Virtually all of the multi-family units were built in Manhattan and catered to upper-middle-income or high-income residents. Developers under the 421 program assumed that their properties would be subject to stabilization only during the tax-exemption period. After ten years elapsed, full taxes were to be paid, and the developers expectation was that they would also then be free of any rent regulation. However, when sizable numbers of 421 buildings began to pass their tenth birthdays, legislation was enacted which kept their rental units under stabilization (with the exception of units which became vacant and/or condominiums or cooperatives).

The program began to draw increasing political fire by the late 1970s. Its many opponents claimed that the luxury developments involved would have been built without tax concessions; it was simply a giveaway of badly needed tax dollars. There was strong resentment against a program which provides tax subsidies to real estate developers to house high-income people in a city in which there was an increasing number of poor people. Mayor Koch opposed restrictions of the 421 program on the grounds that it was less a housing subsidy than an economic development measure. But local opponents, operating in the State legislature, curtailed the geographic area within which the program could operate, excluding virtually all of Manhattan.

The other major tax subsidy program is the J-51 program. It had modest aspirations when begun by the City with State approval in 1955. It provided tax benefits—through exemptions and abatements—to help offset the costs of installing central heating in multiple dwellings built before 1901. Upgrading took place with tenants in residence and the properties remained under rent control.

J-51's scope was expanded in the 1960s to encourage owners of rent-controlled multiple dwelling units built before 1929, not just before 1901, to upgrade their buildings. However, restrictions on the dollar amounts of improvements eligible for abatement and exemption greatly reduced J-51's value for more ambitious undertakings, such as major rehabilitation. But in the 1970s, in the context of the city's deepening economic crisis, J-51's nature changed. Dollar limits on benefits were dramatically raised. In 1976 even more restraints on J-51 were dropped. Benefits from J-51 were extended to residential conversions of nonresidential structures and single room occupancy hotels (SROs). Consequently, J-51 became an important element in Manhattan's upscale residential development, which suddenly began to show surprising strength.

Large numbers of new housing units were produced under the J-51 program after 1976. Between 1976 and 1982 an average of about 6,000 units annually came into being under its auspices. Its critics maintained that the City unnecessarily gave away tax revenues to owners who would have upgraded their properties without the benefits. In addition, J-51, even more than 421, was seen as a program which displaced lower-income households to provide housing for a higher-income group.

Largely in response to these criticisms, the State legislature in 1981 and again in 1983 placed major restrictions on the J-51 program. The 1981 measure excluded extensive portions of Manhattan from receiving benefits. The 1983 measure reduced the maximum post-rehabilitated values against which taxes could be abated or exempted. It also removed from the program conversions of SROs, which emerged as a highly charged emotional symbol of the plight of homeless people.

Initially, in authorizing the J-51 and 421 programs the State seems to have simply let the City do what it wanted with its own tax dollars. However, as opposition to the programs grew, the fact that State authorization was needed to continue the programs permitted their opponents, all of whom were from New York City, to use the State legislature as an effective forum for contesting a fundamentally local issue. It is unlikely that many upstate legislators cared deeply about the merits of the arguments involved in this fight between Mayor Koch and his opponents.

POLICY DIRECTIONS

There is little that the City or any locality in New York State can attempt as far as housing programs are concerned without the State's authorization. Therefore, the key policy questions are: "What housing policies and programs should have the highest priority?" Furthermore, "How might the State join forces with the City to carry out such initiatives as are called for?"

Since the advent of the Reagan Administration, the task of providing clear and credible answers to these questions has assumed greater urgency. There have been extensive reductions in federal expenditures on low-income housing subsidy programs. Given the extent to which the federal government has come to dominate this area, it is unrealistic to expect that additional resources that might be made available by the State or the City will compensate for lost federal housing dollars. Housing subsidy resources, increasingly scarce, will need to be carefully targeted.

Because its fiscal capacity is greater than localities' capacity, the State will be subjected to increased pressure to offset the declining federal role. However, the State's past performance in this area leaves a good deal to be desired. Its present "policy" toward housing amounts to little more than the sum of a number of unrelated programs operated by diverse agencies. These arrangements lack an underlying strategy.

In the past, the thrust of the State's involvement in housing was to augment the supply available to middle-income households. Its most active direct involvement with low-income federal subsidy programs through the UDC terminated in a debacle. And since the late 1970s the State has transferred an appreciable portion of the low-income housing originally built under its auspices to the federal government. The recent takeover by the State of rent regulation increases its involvement in housing for low income families, but it is still unclear how it will use these new powers.

The root problems besetting the low-income, private rental market are those created by poverty. In the long run, the way out of poverty is through economic growth and improved educational opportunities. In the shorter run, however, efforts aimed at improving the functioning of this housing sector must achieve some combination of higher rent-paying abilities and lower costs of operating and upgrading the existing stock of rental housing. The goals should be to prevent the housing stock currently occupied by low-income households from passing into an uninhabitable state of disrepair and to upgrade as much of it as possible through better maintenance and rehabilitation.

If this could be done, modest as it sounds, it would be a massive accomplishment. Failure to deal with this problem, and to achieve a measure of success, could lead to a social crisis in the city. In the 1960s UDC was created to build new housing for the poor. Perhaps the time is right for a contemporary version of UDC whose mission would be to stabilize and upgrade existing low income housing. Armed with ample legal authority and working closely with the City and the private sector, it would aggregate and focus available resources and programs on this objective. Among the latter would be tax subsidies (abatements, exemptions, credits), shelter allowances, low-interest mortgage loans (or outright grants), rent regulation, and code enforcement.

What, if anything, should the State do to stimulate the production of housing for middle-income households? Arguably, the State has an interest in fostering such development within New York City. The growth areas of the city's economy (and thus of the state's as well) are likely to suffer to the extent that the people involved in them find it difficult to obtain satisfactory living arrangements within New York City. New York City's loss of middle-income households might not be offset by gains elsewhere in New York State, but by an increased demand for housing in New Jersey. The further danger is that this would also encourage high-income jobs to relocate across state borders.

In New York City, private housing costs are kept high by the scarcity of developable sites, by the zoning-imposed constraints on development in marketable areas, by investors' fear of rent regulation, and by an archaic building code. High rise development also involves exposure to cost-increasing shakedowns and kickbacks. If ways can be found around those obstacles, then more housing priced within the budgets of middle-income families could be built in New York City.

Property-tax-reduction schemes—such as J-51 and 421—and below-market interest rate mortgage loans only partially offset the negative elements confronting would-be private investors in the city's multi-family residential property market. These programs have worked best in prime Manhattan locations, but the availability of J-51 and 421 has been legislated out of existence in such areas. Recent federal tax reform will curtail the availability of tax-exempt funds to finance below-market interest rate loans. It remains to be seen whether development will now intensify in the outer (or locationally less choice) boroughs. If it does not, then the ability of the city's economy to continue its recent rate of expansion could be checked.

Housing prices in the suburban counties of the New York region have risen rapidly in the last few years. The strengthened demand for housing within this area is a function of the expansion in the economy of the New

York region. However, most of the suburban ring is already developed, albeit at relatively low densities. Redevelopment to higher densities is sharply and effectively resisted by the communities involved. This leaves development to take place on the peripheries of the region. This seems to be the path of least political resistance, and one which will produce the lowest priced housing without government subsidies. But such regional spread will generate a still greater degree of job dispersion within the greater New York area. A strong possibility in this context is that development—residential, commercial, and industrial—within the region will concentrate even more than it has recently toward New Jersey.

NOTES

1. U.S. Bureau of the Census, *Abstract of the Twelfth Census of the United States, 1900* (Washington, DC: U.S. Government Printing Office, 1904), tables 68 and 90.
2. James Ford, *Slums and Housing: With a Special Reference to New York City* (Cambridge: Harvard University Press, 1936), Pt. 1.
3. Roy Lubove, *The Progressives and the Slums: Tenement House Reform in New York City, 1890–1917* (Pittsburgh: University of Pittsburgh Press, 1962).
4. Leo Grebler, *Housing Market Behavior in a Declining Area: Long Term Changes in Inventory and Utilization of Housing on New York's Lower East Side* (New York: Columbia University Press, 1952), pp. 58–61.
5. Peter Derrick, "Catalyst for Development: Rapid Transit in New York," *New York Affairs* 9, no. 4 (Fall 1986):29–59.
6. *Columbia Law School News,* "Residential Rent Control in New York City," May 8, 1967, pp. 30–32.
7. Herbert S. Swan, *The Housing Market in New York City: A Study Made for the Institute of Public Administration* (New York: Reinhold Publishing Corporation, 1944), pp. 39–41.
8. Swan, *Housing Market,* pp. 68–71.
9. Albert Pleydell, *How Tax Exemption Broke the Housing Deadlock in New York City* (New York: Citizens Housing Planning Council, May 1960).
10. Swan, *Housing Market,* pp. 40–42.
11. Roger Starr, *Housing and the Money Market* (New York: Basic Books, 1975), chap. 11.
12. New York State Division of Housing and Community Renewal, *Statistical Summary of Programs* (New York: NYSDHCR, March 31, 1985), pp. 57–64.
13. Bernard Richland, "Constitutional City Home Rule in New York," *Columbia Law Review* 54 (1954):329.
14. New York City Planning Commission, *New Dwelling Units Completed 1921–1972 in New York City,* December 1973.
15. Grebler, *Housing Market Behavior,* pp. 174–175.
16. John C. Weicher, *Federal Policies and Programs* (Washington, DC: American Enterprise Institute, 1980), chap. 3.

17. New York City Planning Commission, *New Dwelling Units.*
18. New York State Temporary State Housing Rent Commission, *Survey of Residential Rents and Rental Conditions in the State of New York,* November 1, 1950.
19. Michael A. Stegman, "The Model: Rental Control in New York City," in Paul L. Niebanck, ed., *The Rent Control Debate* (Durham: University of North Carolina Press, 1985).
20. *New York Times,* February 15, 1962, sec. 1, p. 1.
21. *New York Times,* October 1, 1961, sec. 1, p. 1.
22. *New York Times,* October 16, 1961, sec. 1, p. 1.
23. *New York Times,* February 15, 1962, sec. 1, p. 1.
24. New York City Planning Commission, *New Dwelling Units.*
25. Frank S. Kristof, "Housing: Economic Facets of New York City's Problems," in Lyle C. Fitch and Annmarie H. Walsh, eds., *Agenda for a City: Issues Confronting New York* (New York: Sage Publications, 1970), pp. 332–333.
26. New York City Housing Development Administration, *The Maximum Base Rents Formula: A Cost Index Approach to Controlled Rents,* no date.
27. *New York Times,* June 3, 1971, sec. 1, p. 1.
28. *New York Times,* May 17, 1974, sec. 1, p. 1.
29. Senate Research Service, *Issues in Focus: The Emergency Tenant Protection Act of 1983* (Albany: New York State Senate, February 1984), no. 84–48.
30. Office of the Governor, *Housing Programs of New York State,* no date.
31. *New York Times,* October 14, 1984, sec. 7, p. 1; July 29, 1984; January 11, 1987.
32. David Dreyfuss and Joan Hendrickson, *A Guide to Government Activities in New York City's Housing Markets,* Memorandum RM-5673-NYC (Santa Monica: Rand Corporation, November 1968), pp. 33–41.
33. Frank S. Kristof, *The Origins of the Mitchell-Lama Program,* unpublished manuscript.
34. Robert H. Connery and Gerald Benjamin, *Rockefeller of New York: Executive Power in the Statehouse* (Ithaca: Cornell University Press, 1979), pp. 258–266.
35. John M. Clapp, "The Formation of Housing Policy in New York," *Policy Sciences* 7 (1976):81.
36. Louis Loewenstein, *The New York State Urban Development Corporation: Private Benefits and Public Costs,* Council of State Governments, 1978 (mimeo).
37. Kristof, "Housing," pp. 333–337.
38. Starr, "Housing," p. 154.
39. Cynthia Curran, *Administration of Subsidized Housing in New York State Co-op City: A Case Study,* unpublished doctoral dissertation, New York University, 1978.
40. Unpublished data from New York State Housing Finance Agency.
41. *Mitchell Lama Debt Service Report as of June 30, 1986,* unpublished memorandum from Assistant Commissioner Ruth Lerner to Commissioner Paul Crotty, New York City Department of Housing Preservation and Development.

42. Annmarie H. Walsh, *The Public's Business: The Politics and Practices of Government Corporations*, A Twentieth Century Fund Study (Cambridge, MA: MIT Press, 1978).
43. New York State, Moreland Act Commission on the Urban Development Corporation and Other State Financing Agencies, *Restoring Credit and Confidence: A Reform Program for New York State and Its Public Authorities*, March 31, 1976.
44. New York State Division of Housing and Community Renewal, *Annual Report to be Legislature on Mitchell-Lama Housing Companies in New York State*, various issues.
45. New York City Housing Authority, Research and Policy Development, *Tenant Data: Characteristics of Tenants*, various issues.
46. Gilbert Y. Steiner, *The State of Welfare* (Washington, DC: Brookings Institution, 1971), chap. 4.
47. Dreyfuss and Hendrickson, *Guide to Government Activities*, pp. 14–32.
48. New York City Housing Authority, *Fifty Years of Public Housing*, no date, p. 26.
49. New York City Human Resources Administration, Office of Policy and Program Development, *Quarterly Rent Report*, various issues.
50. Unpublished data from New York City Office of Policy and Program Development, Human Resources Administration.
51. New York City Human Resources Administration, *Quarterly Rent Report*.

16

CRIMINAL JUSTICE

❧

Ester Fuchs

I N NEW YORK and other states, criminal justice is administered
through a complex network of intergovernmental relations. Within
this system the special circumstances of the state's largest city affect
statewide policy. The magnitude of New York City's crime problem, its plethora of active interest groups, and its idiosyncratic political
structure that has five county jurisdictions incorporated in one city make
the administration of criminal justice in New York City particularly
complex and create a need for special adjustments in State policy. This
essay examines how City-State relationships have affected the delivery of
criminal justice services in New York City and how the special needs of
New York City affect State criminal justice policy.

The first section considers how New York City's criminal justice needs
differ from those of other large cities in the state. It compares New York
City with the counties that include three of the state's largest cities and
with all other counties combined. The indicators examined include the
magnitude of the crime problem, the cost of criminal justice services, and
the sources of revenue for these services. The second section analyzes the
legal relationships, including the division of fiscal responsibility between
the City and the State for each criminal justice function. This analysis
reveals how intergovernmental relations affect the delivery of services
and obstruct the development of systemwide policies. The final section
illustrates how State-City relations affect the delivery of criminal justice

services in New York City through a case study of recent problems related to jail overcrowding.

IS NEW YORK CITY DIFFERENT?

In New York City both the nature of the crime problem and the public sector's response to it are different from the rest of the state. The amount of crime, the cost of providing criminal justice services, and the method of funding these services have unique characteristics in New York City.

Amount of Crime and Volume of Services

In 1984, New York City's population was 40 percent of the statewide total; however, 61 percent of all violent crimes reported in New York State occurred in New York City (see Table 16.1). The rate of violent crimes per 100,000 population was 8,397, or more than 50 percent above the statewide average. Among the four other large counties examined, Monroe County, which includes the City of Rochester, had the highest rate, but it still fell well below New York City. Equally important, 56 percent of all felony arrests in New York State occurred in New York City. The next highest county, Monroe, accounted for only 5 percent of the state's felony arrests. These figures suggest that the burden on police is greater in New York City than any other jurisdiction in the state.

The same can be said of New York City's prosecutors and public defenders, who process felony arrests. Over 61 percent of all felony indictments in New York State are handled by the offices of New York City's five district attorneys. Similarly, 76 percent of all felony convictions in New York State occur in New York City. All other jurisdictions in the state handle only a small percentage of the number of felony cases processed and convicted by New York City's criminal justice system.

Once felons have been convicted they receive some form of punishment. The pattern of punishment in New York City differs from that of the rest of the state—relatively more convicts are sent to prison and relatively fewer are placed on probation.

At the end of December 1984 there were 97,441 probationers under supervision in New York State. Of this total, 7,125 were in Family Courts and 90,316 in Criminal Courts. The number of probationers in New York City is over ten times higher than in any other jurisdiction in the state and represents 43 percent of the statewide total (see Table 16.2).

About 58 percent of all occupied jail cells in the state are in New York City (see Table 16.3). New York City has over ten times as many jail

TABLE 16.1
Crime in New York State, 1984

	Erie County	Monroe County	Onondaga County	Westchester County	New York City	New York State
Index Crimes						
Total	44,563	38,300	20,672	33,141	601,634	985,908
Rate	4,422	5,353	4,448	3,804	8,397	5,560
Percentage of State	4.5%	3.9%	2.1%	3.4%	61.0%	100.0%
Felony Arrests						
Total	7,409	7,669	3,939	5,648	95,541	171,420
Rate	735	1,072	848	648	1,333	967
Percentage of State	4.3%	4.5%	2.3%	3.3%	55.7%	100.0%
Felony Indictments						
Total	1,319	1,199	1,196	1,556	28,999	47,470
Rate	131	168	257	179	405	268
Percentage of State	2.8%	2.5%	2.5%	3.2%	61.1%	100.0%
Felony Convictions						
Total	1,094	1,027	932	1,471	28,888	38,268
Rate	109	142	201	169	319	216
Percentage of State	2.8%	2.6%	2.4%	3.8%	75.5%	100.0%

SOURCE: New York State Division of Criminal Justice Services, *New York State County Criminal Justice Profiles: 1984*, September 1, 1985.

NOTE: Rate is per 100,000 population based on 1980 census.

TABLE 16.2

Probation in New York State, 1985

	Number of Probationers	Percentage of State Total	Average Caseload per Officer
Erie	3,726	3.9%	120.2
Monroe	3,882	4.0	110.0
Onondaga	2,211	2.3	74.2
Westchester	5,082	5.3	115.5
New York City	41,682	43.3	203.3
New York State	96,278	100.0	119.0

SOURCE: Unpublished data from New York State Division of Probation and Correctional Alternatives.

inmates as Westchester County (the locality with the second largest inmate population).

Any convict sentenced to incarceration for more than a year serves that time in a State prison. Unlike jails, prisons are operated and funded by the State. New York City's criminal population places a great burden on State facilities. In 1984, 70 percent of the 33,314 inmates in State prisons were sent from New York City (see Table 16.3). New York City's convicted felons are more likely to be sentenced to prison than those from any other region in the state.[1]

Like prison, parole is a State function. New York City residents accounted for nearly 67 percent of the 19,302 persons under the supervision of the New York State Division of Parole in 1985. In per capita terms, the parole population in New York City is over twice as great as in other jurisdictions in the state. The State accommodates this demand by assigning more parole officers to New York City, so that the ratio of parolees to parole officer is similar throughout the State.[2]

The foregoing data indicate that the crime problem in New York City is greater than in other areas and places a disproportionate burden on the criminal justice system at each stage of the process. New York City can be distinguished from the rest of the state in the magnitude of its crime problem and the resulting stress that the City's system must endure.

Criminal Justice Expenditures

New York City's unusually large crime problem requires unusually large local public expenditures for criminal justice agencies. In 1984, the City of New York spent $228.75 per capita for its criminal justice

TABLE 16.3
Persons in Jail, in Prison, and on Parole in New York State, 1984

	Erie County	Monroe County	Onondaga County	Westchester County	New York City	New York State
Jail						
Total	537	488	424	752	9,852	17,000
Rate	53.3	68.2	91.2	86.3	137.5	95.9
Percentage of State	3.1%	2.9%	2.5%	4.4%	57.9%	100.0%
Prison						
Total	992	917	648	1,160	23,337	33,314
Rate	91.5	128.2	139.4	133.2	325.7	187.9
Percentage of State	2.8%	2.8%	1.9%	3.5%	70.1%	100.0%
Parole						
Total	625	681	415	665	12,949	19,302
Rate	62.0	95.2	89.3	76.3	180.7	108.8
Percentage of State	3.2%	3.5%	2.1%	3.4%	67.1%	100.0%

SOURCE: State of New York Division of Criminal Justice Services, *New York State County Criminal Justice Profiles: 1984*, September 1, 1985.

NOTE: Rate is per 100,000 population based on 1980 census.

services (see Table 16.4). This was almost twice as much as the average upstate county and over 50 percent greater than Westchester, its closest competitor. But as a result of fiscal austerity, between 1980 and 1984 the rate of growth in the City's criminal justice budget was less than the average upstate county and the lowest among the sample counties.

The differences between New York City and the rest of the state are more revealing when the expenditures are disaggregated by function. For police services,[3] New York City spent $170.96 per capita, over twice as much as the average upstate jurisdiction and over 50 percent greater than its closest competitor, Westchester (see Table 16.4). Between 1980 and 1984, however, the rate of growth in spending for police services was lower in New York City than in the average upstate county.

New York City's expenditures for its district attorneys was $10.91 per capita, also the highest in our sample and twice as much as the average upstate county. The rate of increase in spending between 1980 and 1984 was slightly higher than the upstate average. The per capita cost of public defenders was also twice as much in New York City as the average upstate county and greater than any other county in our sample. However, New York City increased its spending on public defenders by nearly 68 percent during this period, greater than the average increase for upstate counties and greater than any other county in the sample.

Courts are the only part of the criminal justice system for which New York City spends less per capita than other jurisdictions. In 1984 New York City spent only $0.05 per capita on court operations and it experienced a 98 percent decline in these expenditures between 1980 and 1984. This dramatic decline was the result of a State takeover of court costs beginning in 1977. All New York City court costs, except for maintenance and construction, are now paid by the State. Town and Village courts have remained the fiscal responsibility of local governments. As a result, New York City experienced the greatest benefit from this statewide program.[4]

For criminal punishment, the expenditure data show a mixed pattern. In 1984, New York City spent $3.86 per capita on probation, the lowest amount of the jurisdictions examined and only half as much as the average upstate jurisdiction. Probation has been a political casualty in New York City. Mayor Edward Koch has hesitated to increase City spending on probation because he believes that it should be completely funded by the State. Also, the public generally considers probation to be a "soft" penalty for criminal behavior. Mayor Koch has prided himself as being "tough on crime," and as a consequence probation has lost out to jails as a policy priority. New York City spends much more than any other jurisdiction on correctional services. In 1984, New York City spent $38.15 per capita on correctional services, more than twice as much as

TABLE 16.4
Local Criminal Justice Expenditures, 1984

	New York City	Erie County	Monroe County	Onondaga County	Westchester County	Upstate	Statewide
Total							
Per Capita	$228.75	$97.99	$112.85	$106.52	$163.94	$119.72	$163.65
Percentage Change 1980–1984	42.19%	48.85%	49.00%	71.36%	65.71%	51.03%	45.92%
Police and Sheriff							
Per Capita	$170.95	$70.59	$74.32	$61.96	$114.14	$86.86	$120.73
Percentage Change 1980–1984	37.48%	55.24%	45.75%	63.09%	58.88%	45.25%	40.80%
Prosecution							
Per Capita	$10.91	$5.56	$5.04	$6.16	$7.66	$5.14	$7.47
Percentage Change 1980–1984	72.62%	67.47%	30.23%	161.02%	76.09%	66.34%	69.77%
Defense							
Per Capita	$4.81	$2.11	$2.89	$3.11	$3.71	$2.38	$3.36
Percentage Change 1980–1984	67.59%	46.53%	35.05%	61.14%	26.89%	46.91%	58.49%
Courts							
Per Capita	$0.05	$2.40	$7.17	$1.56	$3.92	$2.85	$1.72
Percentage Change 1980–1984	−97.96%	10.09%	22.35%	−5.52%	7.40%	13.54%	−30.92%
Probation							
Per Capita	$3.86	$3.94	$6.85	$8.27	$5.30	$6.12	$5.21
Percentage Change 1980–1984	33.56%	32.66%	44.82%	71.93%	46.41%	60.21%	51.45%
Correction							
Per Capita	$38.15	$13.39	$16.57	$25.47	$29.21	$16.37	$25.14
Percentage Change 1980–1984	73.64%	28.50%	91.78%	90.78%	133.49%	91.91%	80.34%

SOURCE: New York State Division of Criminal Justice Services, *New York State Expenditures, 1980–1984* (November 1986), Table 14.
NOTE: Per Capita data computed with 1980 census data.

the average upstate jurisdiction. However, all counties in the sample, except Onondaga, show considerable increases in their spending on corrections between 1980 and 1984.

State Aid for Criminal Justice

In sum, New York City spends more per capita on criminal justice than any other jurisdiction in the state. Given this heavy burden, it is reasonable to ask whether State aid plays a major role in helping to make this financial burden more equitable.

In 1984 State aid to all localities for criminal justice totaled $85.6 million, or just 3 percent of total local expenditures. However, 3.5 percent of New York City's criminal justice budget was funded by State revenue (see Table 16.5). This percentage is similar to that for other jurisdictions with large cities, but higher than the average State contribution to all counties. The limited State aid is concentrated in the functions of probation and prosecution. In 1985 New York City's prosecutors received $20,457,000 in State aid, 22 percent of their total expenditures, and the City's Department of Probation received $15,454,000 in State aid, 51 percent of its budget.[5]

As a proportion of all State aid to local criminal justice budgets, New York City is receiving its fair share or more. Of the total State aid to localities for criminal justice services, 65.6 percent is spent in New York City.

The State also plays a major role by paying directly for all prison costs and 95 percent of all court costs. While these direct expenditures are not

TABLE 16.5

State Contribution to Local Criminal Justice Expenditures, 1984
(in thousands)

	Local Expenditures	State Aid	State Aid as a Percentage of Local Expenditures	Percentage of Total State Aid
New York City	$1,617,476	$56,161	3.5%	65.6%
Erie County	99,505	4,756	4.7	5.6
Monroe County	79,248	2,826	3.6	3.3
Onondaga County	49,355	1,714	3.5	2.0
Westchester County	142,071	4,988	3.5	5.8
Upstate	1,225,394	29,444	2.4	34.4
Statewide	2,872,870	85,605	3.0	100.0

SOURCES: New York State Division of Criminal Justice Services, *New York State Criminal Justice Expenditures, 1980–1984*, Table 14; *County Criminal Justice Profiles: 1984.*

included in the aid figures, they are State spending from which New York City benefits significantly. Fully 70 percent of the inmates in State prisons are from New York City, and 53 percent of State expenditures on trial courts go to New York City.

These data show that the cost per capita of providing criminal justice services is greater in New York City than in other jurisdictions. This provides the City with a claim for more State aid than other jurisdictions, and it does in fact receive a "fair" share of the funds that the State allocates for those purposes.

INSTITUTIONAL ROLES IN THE CRIMINAL JUSTICE SYSTEM

The intricate maze of institutional relationships that constitutes the criminal justice system involves numerous independent agencies with little or no legal responsibility to cooperate with each other. The officials of these multiple agencies do not always share common objectives, and decentralized legal arrangements give individual participants an unusual power to block policy change. Accountability also is blurred because there is no single authority responsible for the entire system. But each important actor has a strong stake in the existing arrangement, and there is little incentive to enact needed reforms.

This section describes the institutional roles of the numerous criminal justice system agencies. This information provides a basis for understanding the difficulties in creating rational systemwide policy.

The Chief Executive

In theory, systemwide policy direction and coordination in government is provided by the elected chief executive. For criminal justice services this presumption is complicated by involvement of State and local agencies, each with its own elected chief executive. Moreover, both the governor and the mayor face legal and other restrictions on their power to control State and mayoral agencies. The ways in which these two chief executives are constrained warrants more complete discussion.

The Governor. The scope of the governor's authority is limited in several ways. Not only are there separate local agencies under mayoral control, but independently elected State and local officials also operate in this arena. Specifically there is a separately elected statewide attorney general and separately elected local district attorneys and sheriffs, including five district attorneys in New York City.

Moreover, within the State executive branch there are multiple agencies involved in providing criminal justices services. Because the State constitution limits the number of units having department status, the number of departments involved is relatively small. In addition to the Law Department (under the attorney general) the governor supervises the Corrections Department and an umbrella unit known as the Executive Department. Most of the criminal justice agencies under the governor's direct control are found in the Executive Department. These include the Division of Criminal Justice Services, Division of State Police, Commission of Correction, Division of Parole, Division of Probation and Correctional Alternatives, Crime Victims Compensation Board, and Division for Youth.

The need for coordination among these units led to the creation of the Division of Criminal Justice Services (DCJS) in the Executive Department in 1972. The DCJS merged three agencies: New York State's Identification and Intelligence System, the Division of Criminal Justice in the Office of Planning Services, and the Division for Local Police in the Office for Local Government.

In 1983 Governor Cuomo created the position of Director of Criminal Justice. The director is a member of the governor's senior staff; he is not confirmed by the Senate and did not at first preside over any agency. The Director of Criminal Justice centralized the budget process for State criminal justice agencies by screening all appropriation proposals before submission to the legislature and by clearing all criminal justice legislation before it is sponsored by the governor.

In 1986 the offices of the Director of Criminal Justice and the Commissioner of DCJS were effectively merged with the appointment of one person to both positions. This has allowed the director to further centralize State criminal justice policy, combining the formal authority of a commissioner with the informal authority of the governor's chief criminal justice policy adviser.

The DCJS's program responsibilities also have expanded greatly since 1972, when it was primarily a conduit for distributing federal Law Enforcement Assistance Administration (LEAA) funds and a repository for State fingerprint records. The division is now the official planning agency for the State's criminal justice system. It conducts research, monitors program effectiveness, and acts as a clearinghouse in disseminating information to local and State criminal justice agencies. DCJS is responsible for the Criminal Justice Information System Improvement Project established in 1983 to strengthen State and local information systems. It is still the State's central repository for fingerprint identification records and wanted and missing person information. DCJS prepares statewide juvenile delinquency prevention and justice assistance plans, disperses federal funds on behalf of the Crime Control Planning Board, and provides training to municipal police and peace officers. DCJS programs provide financial aid to selected localities to enhance police and prosecutorial activities which target certain offenders for specialized processing. New York City has been a major recipient of this aid, and many of the programs initiated by DCJS were direct responses to particular New York City problems.[6]

The Mayor. New York City's chief executive has limited authority in the criminal justice arena. He is directly responsible for the municipal Police Department, the Department of Correction, the New York City Board of Correction, the Department of Juvenile Justice, the Law Department, the Department of Investigation, and the Office of the Coordinator of Criminal Justice. The five New York City district attorneys are elected independently of the mayor, while the Legal Aid Society and Victim Services Agency have contractual relations with the City. There are also separate police departments run by the Metropolitan Transportation Authority and the New York City Housing Authority, both not under direct mayoral control. All State criminal justice services provided in New York City are also completely independent from mayoral authority.

The mayor is responsible for formulating the criminal justice budget for all agencies which receive revenue from the City. This includes all City departments, the five district attorneys, contractual agencies, and the specialty police departments. The budget must be approved by the Board of Estimate and the City Council. This fiscal control of agencies that are not legally responsible to the mayor gives him important leverage in informal policy negotiations.

The mayor seeks to affect statewide criminal justice policy through informal meetings with the governor and a staff of City lobbyists. The mayor does not depend on the governor to represent New York City's interests in Albany, but instead proposes an annual criminal justice legislative agenda. This lobbying effort has been a critical means for ensuring representation of the mayor's interests in statewide criminal justice policy, though it is not always successful.

Just as the State has attempted to provide more coordination for criminal justice services through its DCJS, so has the City through its Office of the Coordinator of Criminal Justice (CCJ). As an arm of the mayor's Office, the coordinator's legal authority is limited to those agencies that the City controls.

The Office of the CCJ was mandated by the New York City Charter in 1975. It reviews the budget requests of all agencies for programs related to criminal justice and recommends to the mayor budget priorities among such programs. In addition, it oversees the implementation of three major criminal justice management information systems and, since 1978, oversees the mayor's Arson Strike Force.

The Criminal Justice Agency (CJA) is a contract agency funded through the CCJ's budget. It is responsible for prearraignment investigations to recommend whether or not a defendant should be released on his own recognizance or be detained. The CJA is also responsible for notifying released defendants of pending court appearances.

In addition to the CCJ, several oversight agencies and commissions have authority to investigate criminal activity and political corruption. They usually make recommendations for indictments to the district attorneys or attorney general. For example, New York City's Department of Investigation is responsible for investigating corruption, bribe-taking, and criminal activity among municipal workers. The political corruption scandal that has been unfolding in New York City since the beginning of 1986 has brought serious criticism of this department for failing to discover the corruption earlier. It is the process of being reorganized and revitalized, with critics proposing that it be removed from the mayor's direct control.

Police Services

In New York City, as in other localities across the state, police services are performed primarily by a local agency. But New York City has six police departments, not one. The three major units are the New York City Police Department, the New York City Transit Authority, and the New York City Housing Authority. In addition, the Port Authority, the New York City Marine and Aviation Agency, and the Staten Island Rapid Transit Operating Authority provide police services in the city. The mayor appoints the police commissioner and thus has control over the City Police Department, but he shares authority over the other agencies' police forces with these authorities' boards.

Policing began as a municipal function in colonial days, when constables, watchmen, marshals, and sheriffs patrolled the growing city. New York City's first bona fide police corps, under aldermanic control, was established under authority of the State Municipal Police Act in 1844. This early police force was appointed by local politicians, was undisciplined, and was unable to control street gangs and urban riots. In 1853, in the wake of the Astor Place riots, the State established a commission, which included the mayor, to control police operations in New York City. In 1857 the State legislature reasserted its authority over municipal police and established a Metropolitan Police District consisting of New York City, the City of Brooklyn, and Westchester and

Richmond counties. In 1870 the Metropolitan Police District was disbanded by the legislature and a municipal Police Department was reinstituted. Tammany Hall quickly gained control of the City's Police Department. Corruption became widespread, and in 1894 the State intervened, again. In 1899, two years after consolidation and as a consequence of the corruption scandal, the State legislature put the New York City Police Department under the mayor's control, with the police chief removable by the mayor or the governor. New York City's current charter still allows the governor to remove the police commissioner.[7]

Generally, the New York City Police Department operates within a framework established by State law. The powers of police officers are granted under the State's Criminal Procedure Law. The State determines minimum training standards for police officers and mandates binding arbitration with police unions. The ability of police unions, especially in New York City, to lobby the legislature for salary increases and other benefits also undermines mayoral control over police budgets.

There have been many periods in which the State has reasserted control over the police force, commonly by appointing State commissions to investigate corruption. Examples include the Lexow Commission in 1894 and the Knapp Commission in 1972. The most recent conflict between the mayor and the governor erupted over the issue of merging the Transit Authority and the New York City Police Departments. In 1985 the mayor's Criminal Justice Coordinator recommended consolidation of these two units.[8] Nine previous reports on consolidation had been issued since 1950, most of which favored merger. However, consolidation must be approved by the MTA Board and in the spring of 1986, when it appeared that the proposal would be approved, the governor opposed it. The proposal was then postponed at the last 1986 MTA board meeting. The governor controls the majority of appointments to the MTA board, so it is expected that the proposal for merger will ultimately be defeated.

Outside the city, municipal law enforcement operations are supplemented by sheriff's departments and several specialized police agencies such as the New York State Police, the Niagara Frontier Region Park Police, the New York City Reservoir Police, the State University Campus Police, and the Conrail Police. Their efforts are concentrated in counties where there is little or no municipal police coverage. In other jurisdictions the State Police act as supplemental forces and provide technical assistance to localities through laboratories for crime analysis and through the Bureau of Criminal Investigation. State police also patrol the State's major highways. New York City is not a beneficiary of most of these State police services. The governor has, however, increased the number of

State police investigators assigned to the New York City Drug Enforcement Task Force.

Public Defenders

As a result of a 1972 Supreme Court decision, states became responsible for providing counsel to indigent persons in all criminal cases, including misdemeanors.[9] Like many states, New York has complied with these Court requirements by mandating that localities provide defense counsel to all indigent defendants. Outside New York City it is a county responsibility. New York City provides legal counsel to indigents through a contract with the Legal Aid Society, court-appointed private lawyers (so-called 18-B lawyers), and pro bono lawyers.

The Legal Aid Society's contract with the City has been in effect since 1966. According to the society, its lawyers are assigned to 70 percent of the City's criminal complaints and indictments. In 1985 the caseload of an average staff attorney was 68 defendants, and when adjusted for arraignments was the equivalent of 86.5 cases.[10]

New York State also provides for public defenders who pursue both public and private legal careers (18-B lawyers). Those lawyers are used when the Legal Aid Society has a conflict of interest or a defendant objects to their representation. The court appoints 18-B lawyers on a rotating basis from the public defense pool and the City reimburses them for their services. In New York City the Legal Aid Society has been the primary supplier of attorneys for indigent criminal defendants, but 18-B lawyers have been increasing their share of representation. The funding level and attorney caseload of Legal Aid lawyers have been constant sources of contention between the City and the society. Recently, 18-B lawyers have simply become a less expensive alternative for providing representation to indigents.

Pro bono lawyers are private attorneys who volunteer their services; they account for an extremely small proportion of the lawyers who represent indigent criminal defendants. New York City is one of the few jurisdictions in the state that provides this mixed system of public defense.

Although responsibility to support defense programs is a county mandate, the State supplements county efforts with several defense-related programs. The Target Crime Initiative Program provides funding to enhance staffing levels for those counties and New York City which are participating in special prosecution programs for serious and repeat offenders. The Indigent Parolees Program reimburses counties and the City of New York for legal assistance to indigent parolees and inmates in correctional facilities and at parole revocation hearings.

Prosecution

The attorney general is a statewide official elected to a four-year term. He heads the State's Law Department. The attorney general is independent from the governor and is responsible for prosecuting and defending all proceedings for and against the State. The extent of this independence is part of a long-standing historical dispute that has left the attorney general with, at best, an ambiguous role in the criminal justice system.[11] The recent Liman Commission Report did not even include the attorney general in its evaluation of State criminal justice related agencies.[12]

The State prosecutorial model, unlike its federal counterpart, does not make the attorney general the State's chief prosecutor. Instead, local district attorneys have discretion to establish priorities for the prosecution of criminal activity in their districts. District attorneys became autonomous as a result of provisions in the 1821 State Constitution and are now elected independently in counties or, in the case of New York City, by borough. New York City is unique in that it has five independent prosecutors. No citywide official has legal authority to coordinate the prosecutorial function across all five boroughs or to regulate district attorney relationships with such City agencies as police and corrections. Yet the City must fund the district attorneys' operations from its local revenues.

The attorney general can, separately or together with the governor, appoint special prosecutors and may be directed by the governor to supersede a district attorney. The attorney general has used this authority to take an active role in combating organized crime and political corruption. This has given New York City, unlike other local State jurisdictions, a more direct link to the attorney general. For example, in 1972 Attorney General Lefkowitz appointed a special prosecutor to investigate corruption in New York City's criminal justice system. An Office for the Investigation of the New York City Criminal Justice System remains an active part of the Law Department.

The State supplements the budgets of the district attorneys in New York City and other counties through programs like The Target Crime Initiative Program, designed to enhance the district attorneys' ability to investigate and prosecute serious violent and repeat offenders. New York State also assists the prosecutors of New York City through its Special Narcotics Courts Program, funded by the federal government. A special assistant district attorney is appointed by the five New York City district attorneys and has citywide jurisdiction for the prosecution of narcotics law violators. The special narcotics prosecutor prosecutes the majority of the persons charged with drug offenses in Manhattan. Finally, The New York State Organized Crime Task Force is an independent State prosecutorial agency appointed by the governor and the attorney general. It is headquartered in White Plains and has three other offices, but its primary focus has been organized crime in New York City.

Courts

The general function of the judiciary is to provide for the just resolution of criminal and civil disputes. In the criminal justice system, courts determine the guilt or innocence of people accused of a crime. The New York State Constitution establishes a unified court system, defines the methods for selecting judges, and sets out the organization and jurisdiction of the courts.

Selection of Judges. New York State has a mixed system of elected and appointed judges. The ambivalence of this system is rooted in the problem of keeping political considerations out of the judicial selection process. The State constitution mandates that judges of the Supreme Court, County Court, Surrogate's Court, Family Court (except in New York City), District Court, and Town Court be elected by popular vote. The governor appoints justices of the Appellate Division from sitting Supreme Court Justices, and with the confirmation of the Senate appoints judges for the Court of Claims and for vacancies on the Supreme, County, Surrogate's, and Family courts outside New York City. The mayor appoints Criminal Court and Family Court judges in New York City and can make interim appointments for vacancies in the New York City Civil Court.

Historically, judicial appointments and nominations were part of the patronage system used to reward loyal party members. In 1977, a constitutional amendment established a merit selection system for gubernatorial appointments to the Court of Appeals. A Commission on Judicial Nomination consisting of 12 members was created. The responsibility for appointments to this body was divided among the governor, the chief judge of the Court of Appeals, and the leadership in the Assembly and the Senate. No more than six committee members could be from the same party, nor could they all be lawyers or hold office in any political party. In 1975, by executive order, Governor Carey created a series of judicial nominating committees to evaluate qualifications for applicants for other appointive judgeships. Following this tradition, Governor Cuomo created a State Judicial Screening Committee and four separate judicial department screening committees. The political independence of these committees is weak, however, because the governor retained control over the appointment of committee members.

There have been voluntary screening committees for mayoral appointments in New York City since Mayor Wagner established the Mayor's Committee on the Judiciary in 1962. These committees have had varying degrees of success in ensuring merit selection of judges. Mayor Koch has taken the advisory process seriously, by using a diverse selection committee and by choosing from among only three nominees submitted to him by the committee.

Without a constitutional amendment, merit selection committees, whether at the state or city level, remain voluntary and as such are weak defenses against political patronage. At the same time, party leaders continue to play a major role in determining nominations for elective judgeships.[13]

Court Administration. All courts in New York City except the federal courts are part of the State's unified court system established in 1962. The state is divided into 4 Judicial Departments and subdivided into 11 Judicial Districts (JDs). The First Department comprises the Bronx and Manhattan. The remainder of New York City, along with all of Long Island and the counties of Westchester, Rockland, Orange, Putnam, and Dutchess make up the Second Department. The Third and Fourth Departments are upstate.[14] The JDs in New York City are the First, serving New York County; the Second, serving Kings County and Richmond County; the Eleventh, serving Queens County; and the Twelfth, serving Bronx County.

All courts in New York City function under the administrative supervision of the chief judge of the Court of Appeals, who is also the chief judge of the State. The chief judge appoints a chief administrator for the courts. The chief judge also establishes statewide administrative standards and policies after consultation with the Administrative Board and promulgates them after approval by the Court of Appeals. The Administrative Board is composed of the chief judge of the Court of Appeals and the four presiding justices of the Appellate Division.

The chief administrator supervises the day-to-day operations of the trial courts and directs the Office of Court Administration. His tasks include preparing budgets, designating administrative judges for the trial courts, transferring judges to balance work loads, hiring nonjudicial personnel, and making recommendations to the legislature. The State bears the full cost of court administration, but the City pays for maintenance, construction, and security of court facilities in New York City.

The New York State Commission on Judicial Conduct was created in 1975 to review complaints of judicial misconduct brought by citizens, without compromising the principle of judicial independence. The commission consists of 11 members: four appointed by the governor, three by the chief judge, and one each by the speaker of the Assembly, the majority leader of the Senate, and minority leaders in each house. At least two of the commission's members must be nonlawyers and four must be judges. They serve four-year staggered terms.

Courts' Jurisdiction and Function. Reforming the State court system has been a particularly difficult and politicized task, since it requires amending the State constitution. The partisan nature of the judicial appointment process and the patronage associated with court functions has encouraged legislative support of the status quo. In 1955 there were approximately 1,500 separate and autonomous courts in New York State. The current uniform court system, which took effect in 1962, was brought about by political compromises which allowed New York City to create its own courts to deal with the City's unique criminal justice problems. At the same time, local trial courts were allowed to remain in the control of local political officials.

Trial Courts. The courts in New York are organized into two groups—courts of original jurisdiction, or trial courts, and appellate courts, which hear appeals from trial courts. The Supreme Court of the State of New York is the State's principal trial court. It hears civil matters involving substantial amounts of money; divorce, separation, and annulment proceedings; and equity suits such as mortgage foreclosures and injunctions. In New York City it also handles major criminal matters. Justices of the Supreme Court are selected in partisan elections by the voters of their Judicial District for 14-year terms or until age 70. The Legislature can increase the number of Supreme Court Justices.

The Criminal Court of the City of New York handles arraignments for all crimes and conducts trials for crimes other than felonies (misdemeanors, offenses, and violations). State law provides for 107 City Criminal Court judges who are appointed by the mayor to ten-year terms. County Courts exist outside New York City and are authorized to decide criminal and limited civil cases.

The Civil Court of the City of New York handles civil cases involving amounts up to $10,000. It includes a Small Claims Part and a Housing Part. It is composed of 120 judges elected by the voters in each of the five boroughs for ten-year terms.

Surrogate's Court settles the affairs of decedents (wills, estates). Surrogates are elected by voters of the county to 14-year terms. In New York City, Manhattan has two Surrogate judges and the other boroughs each have one.

The Family Court has jurisdiction over matters involving children and families. It hears cases which involve juvenile delinquency, neglect and child abuse, support, and paternity. In New York City, 42 judges are appointed by the mayor to ten-year terms. Separate Family Court units operate in each borough. Outside New York City, Family Court judges are elected by the voters of each county.

The Court of Claims decides claims against the State. Seventeen judges are appointed by the governor with the consent of the Senate to nine year terms. The constitution requires that there be at least six Court of Claims judges, but the legislature can increase their number. In 1982, 15 Court of Claims judges were added by the Legislature as acting Supreme Court judges. In a special session of the legislature at the end of 1986, 23 more Court of Claims judges were approved primarily to ease the burden on New York City Criminal Court. Partisan political considerations have encouraged the use of Court of Claims judges to relieve the pressure on other parts of the judicial system. The Republican controlled Senate has agreed to these new judicial appointments in exchange for some influence in the selection process.

Local courts outside New York City fall into four categories: District (only in Nassau and Suffolk counties), City, Town, and Village. These local courts are vestiges of the old English Justice of the Peace system, designed to provide convenient justice to a sparsely populated agricultural society. Only the District Courts have judges who must be lawyers and serve full time. Justices in other local courts are either appointed by the local governmental authority or elected. The legislature has the authority to discontinue a City Court or Village Court outside New York City, but may only discontinue a Town Court with the approval of the town's voters. These local courts have been criticized for being inefficient, unprofessional, and a source of local patronage. Currently, these courts hear minor civil and criminal offenses, from traffic violations to misdemeanors. Some hold preliminary hearings for those charged with more serious crimes and decide on bail.

Appellate Courts. Each of the State's four Judicial Departments has an intermediary appeals court known as an Appellate Division of the Supreme Court. They decide appeals from trial courts within their department and conduct proceedings to admit, suspend, or disbar lawyers. Designations to the Appellate Division are made by the governor from among Supreme Court justices, for five-year terms. The governor also designates one justice in each department to serve as presiding justice. There are 24 Appellate justices authorized by law. Additional justices may be designated by the governor if the Appellate justices certify that they are needed. Currently there are 48 Appellate justices, with 14 serving in the First Department and 15 in the Second.[15]

The Court of Appeals, the State's highest court, decides appeals from the Appellate Divisions. Cases involving the death penalty or constitutional questions may come to it directly from the trial courts. The Court of Appeals consists of a chief judge and six associate judges. Judges are appointed by the governor with the consent of the State Senate, under a constitutionally mandated merit selection plan. Terms are 14 years or until the judge reaches age 70.

New York's court system has been described as the most fragmented in the country.[16] Proposals for reform have been numerous, but the most significant in terms of intergovernmental relations is the court consolidation bill and a proposal to increase the number of Appellate Divisions from four to as many as seven. The measure passed both houses of the legislature in 1986, but failed to gain the necessary passage in a second legislative session. Its purpose was to merge the State's principal trial courts (Supreme Court, Family Court, Court of Claims, Surrogate's Court, and County Court) into a single court. Consolidation is expected to improve the efficiency of court management, decrease delays, and save money. While the amendment was supported by most government groups, it was also criticized for not going far enough. The League of Women Voters advocated including New York City Civil and Criminal courts in the merger of the five other major trial courts. They also support a statewide District Court to replace the hundreds of City, Town, and Village courts outside New York City.[17]

Probation and Correctional Alternatives

Probation, defined as contingent release under court supervision, is a function shared by both the State and the City. In other jurisdictions it is a State and county function. The New York State Probation Commission advises and consults with the state director of probation to formulate statewide probation policies. Members of the commission are appointed by the governor. The State Division of Probation and Correctional Alternatives regulates and supervises the administration of probation throughout the State. Direct services are provided by 58 local probation departments.

The State enacted its first probation law in 1901. It permitted Criminal Court judges to appoint "a person or persons to perform the duties of probation officer" on a volunteer basis. Originally intended for a few cities, including New York City, its effectiveness led to statewide legislation in 1903. In 1907 the State Probation Commission was established to run the newly created State Division of Probation within the Department of Correction. In 1928 the office of Director of Probation was formed and the commission assumed an advisory role. In 1955 the State began to partially reimburse local probation departments for their services. In 1970, the division was transferred from the Department of Correctional Services to the Executive Department with the State director of probation reporting directly to the governor. In 1985 the Alternatives to Incarceration program was transferred from DCJS and combined with the Division of Probation to form the Division of Probation and Correctional Alternatives. This merger reflects a more comprehensive approach to community corrections.

The New York City Department of Probation was established as an independent agency in 1974, as part of a statewide effort to remove probation services from local court jurisdiction. The change was fiscal as well as administrative. Since 1974 the State has reimbursed up to 46.5 percent of the City's probation cost.[18] Special programs like the Intensive Supervision Program (ISP) and the Felony Target Crime Initiative Program (TCI) are fully reimbursed by the State.

New York City's Department of Probation conducts presentence investigations, supervises convicted offenders who have been sentenced to a term of probation, and runs the Alternatives to Incarceration programs. The department also provides intake, investigation, and supervision services for the Family Court.

Supervision by the Department of Probation became a source of controversy during New York City's recent period of jail overcrowding. By placing offenders in the community, probation relieves stress on overcrowded jail facilities. It is also less costly than imprisonment. However, in New York City, the current average caseload of 200 probationers per officer makes effective supervision impossible.

The Alternatives to Incarceration program, enacted in 1984, is expressly designed to relieve jail overcrowding. It made State funds available to counties based on their population size and submission of a service plan. The program requires that the mayor or county executive appoint an advisory board which includes other "principal decision-makers" in the criminal justice system. This board designs the Alternatives to Incarceration service plan. The plan is then submitted for approval to the State's Division of Criminal Justice Services. New York City has participated in this program since its inception.

Correction

Correction is another shared function. Adult correctional services in New York involve State facilities operated by the Department of Correctional Services and local facilities operated by county governments or, in New York City, by the New York City Department of Correction. Both the State and the City have oversight agencies for correctional services: the New York State Commission of Correction and the New York City Board of Correction. Correctional services for juveniles also are shared by the City and the State. The Division for Youth is the State agency and the Department of Juvenile Justice is New York City's agency.

The State Commission of Correction (SCOC) dates from 1929, but was reorganized in its present form in 1975. It is within the Executive Department and is composed of three members appointed by the governor, with the advice and consent of the Senate, for five-year terms. All the State's correctional facilities operate under the oversight of the SCOC. The City Board of Correction evaluates the performance of the Department of Correction, establishes and ensures compliance with minimum standards of confinement in all City correctional facilities, reviews inmate and employee grievances, and makes recommendations in planning correctional policy to the mayor and City Council.

The State prison system is administered by the State Department of Correctional Services (DOCS). The department is responsible for all persons convicted of felonies and sentenced to a term of imprisonment that exceeds one year. DOCS maintains inmates in facilities ranging from minimum to maximum security settings. As of January 1987, the State was operating 50 facilities and housing approximately 38,600 inmates at an annual average cost of $26,500 per inmate.[19]

Local governments operate three types of facilities—lock-ups, jails, and penitentiaries. After arrests, individuals are confined to one of over 200 lock-ups operated by towns, villages, or cities. Upon arraignment, defendants may be placed in a local jail, which is usually a county-run facility. Local jails hold both sentenced and unsentenced individuals. Four counties (Monroe, Erie, Westchester, and Onondaga) operate penitentiaries for sentenced inmates.

The New York City Department of Correction (NYC-DOC) is a mayoral agency responsible for operating a citywide corrections system. NYC-DOC prisons house defendants awaiting arraignment, defendants who have been arraigned but not released on bail or their own recognizance, convicts serving sentences for less than one year, and convicted felons awaiting transfer to State facilities. The NYC-DOC operates four institutions for sentenced male prisoners, nine detention institutions, and prison wards in four hospitals.

The State Division for Youth is charged with the care, treatment, and rehabilitation of trouble-prone youth, including those classified as juvenile offenders, juvenile delinquents, and persons-in-need-of-supervision. The division also administers financial assistance to community agencies which provide educational and support services designed to prevent or reduce the incidence of delinquent behavior. The State operates residential programs ranging from controlled, secure settings to family settings.

The New York City Charter was amended in 1979 to establish the Department of Juvenile Justice. It is responsible for the establishment and operation of secure and nonsecure detention facilities for children held at the direction of the Family Court or Criminal Court.

Parole

Parole is a State responsibility, administered through the State Division of Parole. Since its creation as an Executive Department in 1930, the task of the Division of Parole has increased dramatically. At the end of 1930, fewer than 5,000 released offenders were under community parole supervision; in 1986 the number of supervised parolees was 25,755.[20]

The Board of Parole within the Division of Parole is composed of 15 members appointed by the governor with the consent of the Senate. The chairman of the Board of Parole is the head of the division. The board oversees the release of eligible inmates prior to serving their maximum term of incarceration. The board reviews all applicants for early release, decides whether an inmate merits parole, and sets the conditions for the release. The board authorizes warrants for release violators, revokes the release of violators, certifies jail and parole time, and advises the governor on pardon and commutation decisions.

The most important recent innovation in parole services is the Intensive Supervision Program, which began in 1986 as a joint initiative of the Division of Parole and the Division of Budget. Intensive Supervision places all parolees who are within 15 months of release on caseloads structured to average 38 parolees statewide. After 15 months the parolee is moved to the Regular Supervision caseload, which average 97 parolees per officer. Studies have demonstrated that parolees represent the greatest risk to the community during their first 15 months of release, and this program was designed to concentrate Division resources to the best possible effect.

Victim Services

Victims have only recently been included in discussions of the criminal justice system. New York State's 1984 Fair Treatment Standard Act guaranteed victims greater protection as well as emergency social and medical services and increased compensation for injury and loss. The State Crime Victims Compensation Board implements State victim assistance programs. It is composed of five members appointed by the governor with consent of the Senate. The board provides financial compensation to victims of violent crime and their families. The State and localities fund victim assistance through social service, medical, and mental health agencies as well.

New York City established its own Victim Services Agency (VSA) in 1978. It is a contract agency funded primarily by the mayor's Criminal Justice Coordinating Office; it also receives funds from the State and federal governments, foundations, corporations, and individuals.

The VSA offers victim service programs in nine neighborhood offices, Criminal and Family courts, children's centers, and mediation centers. It operates a crime victims hotline and assists victims in obtaining benefits from the State Crime Victim Compensation Board. The agency also works with police, judges, district attorneys, social service agencies, schools, community organizations, and neighborhood businesses in developing crime prevention programs and assisting victims.

EFFECTS OF DIVIDED RESPONSIBILITY: A CASE STUDY OF JAIL OVERCROWDING

The preceding description of institutional roles in New York City and New York State's criminal justice system reveals a system that is highly decentralized. The way in which this divided responsibility leads to dysfunctions is illustrated by examining the decision process for a specific criminal justice policy. The problem of jail overcrowding indicates fundamental weaknesses in the City's criminal justice system that, in part, stem from the division of responsibility between the City and the State governments.

The Crisis

New York City's problem of jail overcrowding reached a crisis point on November 1, 1983, when Judge Morris Lasker of the Federal District Court in Manhattan ordered the mayor to reduce the population held in NYC-DOC facilities to below 10,300. The release was carried out by the mayor in stages and ended on November 15 after 613 inmates were freed on parole.

Initially Mayor Koch responded that overcrowding would be eliminated if judges in the State Supreme Court acted more efficiently. How was the judiciary contributing to the jail problem? The city's jail population includes people awaiting trial, people awaiting sentencing, and those already sentenced. Once prisoners convicted of a felony are sentenced to more than a year they are moved to State prison facilities to serve their time. Koch maintained that there were over 500 prisoners convicted of felonies three weeks before the court order was issued, but still awaiting sentencing.[21] These prisoners should have already been in State facilities, not overcrowding City jails, according to the mayor. The mayor has no legal authority over the judiciary and could only request that the judges expedite their sentencing decisions. At a news conference Koch suggested that courts open on Saturday and that judges be required to work longer hours. He remarked: "I'd like to see some of these judges work eight hours."[22]

The judges swiftly responded to the mayor's charges. Betty Ellerin, the State deputy administrative judge, was spokesperson for her colleagues. She argued that judges were already sentencing prisoners as quickly as possible and that it was the mayor's responsibility to remedy the overcrowding problem. To the judges, more jail space was the obvious solution.[23] She also argued that one of the critical causes of sentencing delays was the inefficiency of the City's Probation Department. It was frequently late in providing sentencing reports, which are necessary before a judge can set a sentence. The reports frequently were completed two to three weeks after conviction, and sometimes it took as much as two months. The Department of Correction was also cited by the judges as contributing to sentencing delays by failing to deliver prisoners to court hearings on time. This forced judges to postpone sentencing of those inmates. These City agencies are under mayoral supervision, making the mayor vulnerable to the judges' public charges of responsibility for overcrowding.

The judges also agreed that sentencing delays were caused when prisoners requested posttrial hearings, when defense lawyers were unable to make court dates, and when psychiatric examinations were needed.[24] These were all courtroom procedures which could be used legitimately or simply as a tactic by defense lawyers to cause sentencing delays.

Judge Ellerin was also intent on not accepting responsibility for the remedy, knowing that the only short-term solution to the crisis would be prisoner release, a solution unacceptable to the public. Instead she was critical of the mayor, saying, "The mayor, instead of fulfilling his responsibility to provide more jail facilities, is seeking to divert attention to the judges."[25]

Other interest groups became involved in the public debate. Thomas Reppetto, chairman of the Citizens' Crime Commission (a watchdog group financed by city businesses), said that freeing prisoners "would be another disaster for the City's criminal justice system."[26] Robert Gangi, executive director of the Correctional Association of New York (a citizen's group), said that the "decision is being made in a crisis atmosphere and is alarming the public."[27]

Causes of the Crisis

New York City is not alone in confronting the problem of jail overcrowding. In 1981 Westchester County formed a task force because its county jail, designed to accommodate 263 prisoners, was often accommodating 400,[28] and Nassau County is under a court order to reduce its jail population.

Overcrowding in jails and prisons is a national problem. Between 1980 and 1985 there was a 52 percent increase in the population of state prisons. New York State experienced a 60 percent increase in its sentenced prison population during the same period. In 1985 State prisons were at 110 percent capacity, housing 35,244 prisoners. At the start of 1985 six states and the District of Columbia were operating their entire prison systems under a court order or consent decree concerning overcrowding, and in 25 other states at least one major prison was under court order or a consent decree. During 1985, on the average, state and federal prison systems were reported as operating at 110 percent of capacity. Fully 19 states reported early release of inmates because of prison overcrowding.[29]

In New York City jail overcrowding has been a long-standing problem. In 1980 there were 7,000 inmates in City facilities; by November 1983 this number had increased to 10,400. In October 1986 the City jail population reached an all-time high of 14,262.[30]

The problem cannot be defined simply in terms of trends. Jail overcrowding and the related issue of jail conditions has been part of an ongoing battle between the City and the Legal Aid Society for over 15 years. Judge Lasker's orders stemmed from a suit filed by the society in 1970 protesting overcrowding among pretrial detainees.[31] Judge Lasker ruled that the City had to improve the conditions in the Manhattan House of Detention (the Tombs) or close the facility, and the Federal Circuit Court of Appeals affirmed his findings in 1974. As a result the City closed the Tombs and did not reopen the facility until renovation was completed in October 1983.

The Legal Aid Society's Prisoner's Rights Project brought another suit in 1976 on behalf of Rikers Island House of Detention for Men (HDM) inmates, also charging the City with constitutional violations as a result of inhumane conditions. The case, *Benjamin* v. *Malcom*, was inherited by Mayor Koch when he took office in 1978. He attempted to resolve the problems through negotiated settlement.

Although the City should have been working on long-term solutions to the increasing jail population, it was and is a problem complicated by State criminal justice policy and State failure to anticipate its own problem of overcrowded prisons. In 1980 the City moved to join the

State as defendants in the *Benjamin* v. *Malcom* case over the status of the "state ready population" in City jails. "State readies" are inmates sentenced to prison terms of more than a year and who should serve their time in State prisons. The City claimed that by leaving state readies in City jails, the State contributed to jail overcrowding.

While the City and the State struggled over responsibility for the state readies, the Legal Aid Society continued pressing its demands for a cap of 1,000 inmates at HDM. In 1980 Judge Lasker prohibited the City from placing more than 1,200 inmates in HDM. The order was temporarily lifted during the 1982 Legal Aid lawyers strike, allowing the City's jail population to rise to 10,600. The limit was reimposed at the end of October 1983 when Judge Lasker ordered 341 beds removed from detention centers on Rikers Island. This ruling effectively imposed a 10,250 ceiling on the City's jail population and eventually led to the court ordered release.[32]

The complicated role of the State in the City's jail overcrowding crisis can be seen most clearly in the court decisions. In 1981 Judge Lasker ruled that the State must remove state ready prisoners within 48 hours of sentencing. Initially the State unsuccessfully sought to have the order lifted on the grounds of excessive burden to its facilities. In February 1986 Lasker vacated his own order after the State successfully argued that the Supreme Court had limited a federal judge's power to act against State officials where the basis for his action was State law.[33] This victory on jurisdictional grounds was short-lived. In March Lasker granted the City a preliminary injunction, put the 48-hour order back into effect, and was upheld by the Second Circuit. In August the City and the State reached an agreement that the State would take state readies in 48 hours, but would no longer hold parole violators. In September 900 inmates were moved out of City facilities.

The case is still not resolved. On December 24, 1986, the State filed a petition for certiorari, seeking review by the Supreme Court. The divergence of State and City interests in this problem are obvious. However, by attempting to resolve this dispute through litigation, both the City and the State have made the courts the critical force in formulating correctional policy.

There are other systemic causes of jail and prison overcrowding that have an intergovernmental dimension. Some State officials attribute the problem of jail and prison overcrowding to the tougher sentencing and parole laws passed by the legislature. In the 1970s the State legislature established sentencing guidelines imposing determinate and mandatory jail sentences for certain offenders. More accused felons awaiting trial contributed to the increase in the City's jail population. The average time for pretrial detention rose from 26 days in 1977 to nearly 44 days in November 1983.[34]

Apparently few legislators considered how these measures would affect the City's jail population and the State's prison population. The seemingly predictable outcome that more prisoners require more jail space suggests that long-term planning and appropriations to expand capacity were required. Edward Hershey, spokesman for the Correction Department, stated the problem clearly, "To an extent the Legislature told us to keep more people in our jails without giving us the resources to do it."[35]

Judges reinforced the trend to send greater numbers of people to jail by setting higher bail rates and releasing fewer accused on their own recognizance. Beginning in 1980 the Criminal Justice Agency found that pleas, dismissals, and "Release-on-Recognizance" had been declining, while arraigning judges were more likely to set a money bail condition for release. The trend seems to have stabilized, but judges are now more likely to set higher bail rates, which also has contributed to the increase in the City jail population.[36]

Gerald Lynch, president of John Jay College of Criminal Justice and chairman of the City's Committee on Jail Overcrowding, argues that the public also was responsible for the jail overcrowding. He observed that the public wants to see more criminals serve time in jails, but it does not want to pay for more jails.[37] New York State voters turned down a prison construction bond issue in 1981 which would have provided $500 million for jail and prison expansion.[38]

Solutions

While the immediate problem of prison overcrowding was resolved in 1983 by releasing inmates, the long-term problem still needs to be resolved. The inmate revolt, job action by guards, and guard brutality that occurred at Rikers Island in October 1986 are a direct result of the overcrowded conditions that have remained a problem in the City's jails.

The 1983 crisis forced public officials to begin addressing the need for a long-term solution. The publicity made it necessary for participants to begin serious bargaining in an atmosphere of public disapproval and fear.

Building more jails and prisons has been the primary long-term solution proposed by the mayor and the governor. In the aftermath of the prisoner release Koch submitted a new jail construction plan to the City Board of Estimate. The budget exceeded $250 million and was more than double that of an earlier plan.[39] In 1983 the City passed a four-year program to add 4,000 inmate spaces to its 10,609-bed capacity. Since 1984 jail capacity has increased by about 3,000 beds.[40] In November 1986 the City approved refurbishing two Staten Island ferries for housing sentenced prisoners on Rikers Island. The City expects to have a 15,900-bed capacity by 1994.

Prison construction also is the cornerstone of Cuomo's criminal justice policy. The 1985 legislative session authorized the State Urban Development Corporation to issue $133 million in bonds to pay for the construction and renovation of prisons. Cuomo currently has a $630 million, 8,600-cell prison expansion program. The projected date for completion for those new prisons is 1988. The State would then have capacity for 40,800 inmates.

The question of cost has been an important part of the ongoing debate around prison and jail construction. According to the Correctional Association, the "real cost" of keeping an inmate in New York City jails in 1983 was $40,000. The City's figure was $26,900. The higher figure includes pension and fringe benefits for employees, debt charges on capital improvements, and jail services provided by other City agencies. It cost about $50,000 for New York State to build one cell in a minimum security prison, $75,000 for medium security, and $100,000 for maximum security.[41]

The New York City Bar Association and the New York Correctional Association advocate early release legislation and have criticized Cuomo's prison construction approach to relieving the prison overcrowding problem. The Citizens Crime Commission and the Correctional Association have for years been proposing more closely supervised probation, community service, and restitution as substitutes for jail terms. They also argue that expanded drug and alcohol treatment efforts, vocational education programs, and counseling services in prisons are necessary so that inmates are more likely to reintegrate successfully into the community upon release.

At the request of Chief Judge Wachtler, the governor and legislature approved the creation of 23 new judgeships. Twenty of these will be assigned to New York City Criminal Court to relieve what the chief judge has termed a "crisis" of backlogs.[42]

Other proposed solutions to the jail overcrowding problem include court reform and a faster and fairer bail processing which would reduce the number of pretrial detainees, an increase in the number of judges, a reduction in time served through alternative sentencing programs, and the reorganization of the City's Probation Department so that some nonviolent prisoners could be released early. The State has supported an expanded alternative sentencing program with important increases in its budgetary allocation. However, probation remains caught between the City and State budgets. New York City has been advocating State takeover of the entire cost of probation and has been reluctant to increase local funding.

Lessons from the Crisis

The jail overcrowding crisis has not been effectively resolved. There were 14,262 inmates in City jails in October 1986, an all-time high. It is clear from the inmate disturbances at Rikers that the short-term solutions have not worked. Even with increased jail space, the City will not be able to cope with anticipated future increases in crime and arrest rates.

The policy that emerged from the jail overcrowding crisis illustrates how one part of the criminal justice system can make a policy decision to achieve a specific objective, without taking into account the potential negative impact on other parts of the system. As a result, the courts have emerged as the key institution, defining City-State relations for corrections policy. The judicial battle over the state readies is not only an example of the failure of the City and the State to cooperate, but an abdication of policymaking authority. The courts are not merely acting as referee, but are compelling action and directing State and City policy.

The State legislature's passage of mandatory sentencing laws without increasing judicial resources and prison space is another example of actions taken without sufficient regard for likely consequences to other parties. Jail overcrowding cannot be separated from police arrest policy, increased demands on prosecutors and defense attorneys, increased caseloads for judges, or mandated prison sentences.

It is not surprising that this type of policy process precipitates crises. There is no coordination and no one is capable of implementing long-term policy proposals. In effect, the courts made criminal justice policy by forcing different participants to meet standards for jail conditions. In retrospect the crisis seemed necessary to begin a discussion of long-term solutions.

Can we plan for the future? In New York City the crackdown on crack created another jail overcrowding crisis in October 1986. Beginning in May 1986 local police began a much heralded policy to increase narcotic felony arrests. Felony arrests were up 13 percent for the first five months of 1986 and the Special Narcotics Prosecutor's office reported a 71 percent increase in felony narcotics indictments over 1985.[43] The result of this policy was jail overcrowding and an inmate revolt. Crisis follows crisis with the system seemingly out of control. It may be time to adopt the recommendations of the numerous studies which have argued for centralizing the criminal justice system.

NOTES

1. According to the New York State Division of Criminal Justice Services, Bureau of Statistical Services, in 1985 47 percent of convicted felons in

New York City were sentenced to prison, 26.3 percent to jail, and 25.2 percent to probation. In the rest of the State 32.3 percent of convicted felons were sentenced to prison, 35.2 percent to jail, and 29.7 percent to probation.

2. According to the New York State Division of Parole, Office of Policy Analysis and Information, in 1985 the ratio of parolees to case-carrying parole officers in New York City was 57, while the State average was 68. These numbers do not reflect the newly implemented Differential Supervision program.

3. This number reflects the total spent on both police and sheriff services. In counties outside New York City police services are provided by both the city police and the county sheriff.

4. According to the Budget Office of the Office of Court Administration, New York State Unified Court System, in 1986 New York State spent $277,361,397 on trial court operations.

5. Unpublished data provided by New York City Office of Management and Budget.

6. New York State, Division of Criminal Justice Services, *County Criminal Justice Profiles, 1984,* September 1, 1985, pp. 293–294.

7. New York State Legislative Commission on State-Local Relations, *New York's Police Service: Perspective on the Issue,* November 1985, pp. 18–27.

8. Kenneth Conboy, *Report to the Mayor: Consolidation of Police Services in New York City,* July 1985.

9. Supreme Court decisions which have mandated states to provide counsel for indigent persons include *Powell* v. *Alabama* 287 U.S. 45 (1932), *Gideon* v. *Wainwright* 372 U.S. 335 (1963), and *Argresinger* v. *Hamlin* 407 U.S. 25 (1972).

10. Legal Aid Society of New York, *Annual Report,* 1985. These figures are critically reviewed in Chester Mirsky and Michael McConville, "Lawyers for the Poor in New York City: The Interdependence and Parallel Growth of Assigned Counsel in Institutionalized Defender Systems," *Review of Law and Social Change* 15, no. 3 (forthcoming, 1988).

11. See Gerald Benjamin, "The Governor and the Attorney General in New York," paper presented at the annual meeting of the American Political Science Association, 1986.

12. See Executive Advisory Commission on the Administration of Justice, *Recommendations to the Governor Regarding the Administration of the Criminal Justice System* (the Liman Commission Report), November 22, 1982.

13. For discussion of the judicial selection process, see League of Women Voters, *The Judicial Maze: The System in New York State* (New York: League of Women Voters of New York State, 1985).

14. There are efforts to create a new Judicial Department exclusively for Long Island. By separating from New York City, suburban counties have increased opportunities for controlling judicial patronage.

15. League of Women Voters, *The Judicial Maze,* p. 13.

16. Fund for Modern Courts, *Justice in New York: A Citizen's Guide to the Courts* (New York: Fund for Modern Courts, 1981), p. 6.

17. League of Women Voters, *The Judicial Maze,* pp. 42–43.

18. Reimbursable costs do not include personnel services.

19. Data from New York State, Department of Correctional Services, Office of Public Information. The Department estimates the costs to be $20,000 per offender, while the Correctional Association of New York provides the $26,500 estimate.
20. New York State Division of Parole, Policy Analysis and Information.
21. *New York Times*, October 28, 1983.
22. *New York Times*, November 4, 1983.
23. *New York Times*, October 28, 1983.
24. *New York Times*, October 29, 1983.
25. *New York Times*, October 29, 1983.
26. *New York Times*, November 1, 1983
27. *New York Times*, November 2, 1983.
28. *New York Times*, October 11, 1981.
29. U.S. Department of Justice, Bureau of Justice Statistics, *Prisoners in 1985* (Washington, DC: Bureau of Justice Statistics, 1986).
30. *New York Times*, October 15, 1986.
31. *Rhem* v. *Malcom* 507 F.2 333 (2d Cir. 1974).
32. For an in depth discussion of the events which led to the 1983 inmate release, see New York State Temporary Commission of Investigation, *The New York City Prisoner Release*, June, 1985.
33. *Pennhurst State School and Hospital* v. *Halderman* U.S. 104 SC 900 (1984).
34. *New York Times*, November 5, 1983.
35. *New York Times*, November 5, 1983.
36. New York City Criminal Justice Agency, *Semi-Annual Report*, 1979, 1980, and 1984.
37. See *Report of the Committee on Jail Overcrowding*, prepared for the New York City Department of Correction, 1983.
38. The bond was successful in New York City. See James B. Jacob, "The Politics of Prison Expansion," *Review of Law and Social Change* 12, no. 1 (1983–1984), pp. 209–241, for a more complete discussion of the electorate's role in prison expansion.
39. New York State Temporary Commission of Investigation, *The New York City Prisoner Release*, June, 1985.
40. New York City Office of Operations, *Mayor's Management Report*, January 30, 1986, pp. 25–37.
41. *New York Times*, September 30, 1984.
42. *New York Times*, December 12, 1986.
43. *New York Times*, November 24, 1986.

17

THE FUTURE OF STATE-CITY RELATIONS

e~ꙩ

Gerald Benjamin
and
Charles Brecher

N EITHER states nor cities make much sense as contemporary governmental units; their boundaries are anachronisms. A strong commitment to the sounder principles of the federal constitution as well as over 200 years of emotional ties to "home" states and cities have dissuaded Americans from undertaking the fundamental revisions necessary to change the building blocks of the national union. But during this period economic and social relations have changed in ways that limit the effectiveness of the inherited political structure.

Most Americans now live their lives within the boundaries of metropolitan areas: They commute to work from suburbs to central business districts; they purchase goods and services advertised through media that respect no political boundaries and they maintain social contacts with friends and organizational members drawn from across a metropolis. Even political campaigns for national and statewide offices are organized around metropolitan media markets. A constitution designed anew logically would form a union of metropolitan areas and delegate local governmental functions to political units whose boundaries more closely coincide with economic and social reality.

More than historical commitments to "home" states and cities prevents the emergence of such a system of metropolitan governance. As many failed efforts to form metropolitan governments demonstrate, contemporary political forces also create obstacles to reform.[1] Large cities tend to be Democratic, their suburbs Republican; neither party is willing to sacrifice its stronghold for the sake of structural reform. Race also keeps the metropolis divided. Blacks—confined for years to the central city by housing discrimination and low incomes—fought hard to establish a power base there; they are reluctant to sacrifice their political toeholds for the promise of a more rational order. At the same time whites, who relocated in the suburbs in part to benefit from exclusionary zoning practices and governmental fragmentation, are unwilling to yield their favored status for the promise of a more just system.

For these reasons, fundamental redesign of the federal system is unlikely. Thus, realistic discussion of intergovernmental affairs should assume that states and cities will remain the basic units for governing urban America and that state-city relations will remain an important arena for political conflict and change. In the past, these assumptions have led social scientists and political activists to seek solutions to urban problems in the framework of state-city relations. A review of developments in the two New Yorks in light of these "old answers" as well as the options emerging more recently provides a basis for some more general conclusions.

THE OLD ANSWERS

Three different methods were proposed in earlier times to reconcile the conflicting needs of large cities and their states. For different reasons, each now is either not practical or not desirable.

The earliest cry of urban reformers was "home rule." It was a call for legally dominant state legislatures to grant localities more political autonomy, particularly in taxing authority. Urban leaders felt they could identify and finance the policies best suited to their problems—provided that the rurally dominated legislatures got out of their way.

When proponents pressed strongly for home rule in the wake of the industrial revolution, the strategy probably made sense. Cities were centers of wealth and had disproportionately large tax bases. If given the authority, they could finance the richer package of public services their residents sought. But in this era, real home rule was politically impractical. Malapportioned legislatures were in the hands of rural interests who both feared the consequences of permitting rapidly growing cities to follow their own course and saw the opportunity to tax urban wealth for their own purposes.

The political realities were altered by the federal Supreme Court in the 1960s, but by then the economic logic of home rule had changed.

Legislative reapportionment required by the one-person-one-vote principle strengthened the representation of urban interests, but the enormous
postwar migration of people, and then jobs, to the suburbs and the influx
of poorer blacks and Hispanics to cities changed the economic realities.

Cities have become centers of poverty, and their tax bases are no
longer sufficient to finance autonomously the services their residents
require. The data assembled by James Musselwhite for this volume make
the point clearly: The average big city now has a per capita income below
that of the rest of its state and a per capita property value only about four
fifths of that in the rest of the state. This lower tax base must finance
services to city populations that include proportionally 50 percent more
poor people than the rest of the state, and whose infrastructure includes
one third more aged housing.

If the now more sympathetic state legislatures were to grant home
rule, they would be granting a license for self-destructive behavior.
Financing urban service needs with local resources alone would require
tax rates so high that big cities would not be viable economically. Home
rule no longer is a sensible answer.

Recognition of local resource constraints led to the view that the
federal treasury should finance big-city service needs. The concept of the
"national city" was popularized by New York City Mayor John V.
Lindsay, who urged direct federal financing of the cities' welfare and
social services.[2] When the National Advisory Commission on Civil
Disorders, on which Lindsay served, issued its 1968 report in the wake of
waves of urban riots, its members stressed that major new federal efforts
would be required to maintain the social fabric of urban America.[3]

Federal aid to cities grew rapidly until the late 1970s, but ultimately
the national response was a dissappointment to urban political leaders. In
this context, the New York City fiscal crisis can be viewed as a lost bet;
local leaders—including Lindsay and his successor Abraham Beame—
counted on new federal aid to sustain sharply escalating local expenditures, but neither the "new" Richard Nixon elected in 1972 nor the
subsequent Democratic administration of Jimmy Carter delivered aid of
the magnitude anticipated. Major policy initiatives like federal welfare
reform and national health insurance never materialized. Then the
widespread conservatism underlying the election and re-election of
Ronald Reagan in the 1980s made a federal solution to urban problems
seem far-fetched.

A third approach to reform of urban governance has been proposed
and experimented with at various times in this century. While more
incremental in nature than dramatic home rule and national city
strategies, "regional authorities" have been proposed to rationalize
metropolitan services. Perhaps the foremost example of this approach is

the Port Authority of New York and New Jersey, a bistate agency established in 1921 to operate selected transportation services in the greater New York region. Another example is the Metropolitan Transportation Authority, which was created in 1968 to operate mass transit services in the region. The defining qualities of these organizations are their regional scope, spanning boundaries of numerous local governments, and their specific rather than "general purpose" functions. In addition, their financial base typically is not dependent on levying taxes; either they are "self-financing" in the sense that they undertake projects paid for through user charges, or they depend on subsidies from state and/or local general governments.

These regional authorities have a record of considerable accomplishment. The Port Authority, for example, has a reputation for quality management and has developed bridges, airports, and economic development projects throughout the region. Moreover, there may be additional functions for which the regional authority approach could prove effective—for example, water supply and treatment facilities and waste disposal.

However, there are serious limits to the use of regional authorities that derive from their basic nature. The authorities rely heavily on user charges for financing, and there are few services besides transportation for which it is practical to rely on user charges for a dominant financing role. Many of the services provided by state or local general governments require substantial tax supported subsidies, and devising regional authorities will not address these needs. Moreover, the authorities typically are not subject to direct electoral accountability. If taxes are to be used to support public services, citizens are likely to require the political accountability associated with general purpose governments.

THE CONTEMPORARY CHOICES

The current situation of declining federal aid and increasing urban needs makes large cities dependent on the rest of the state for help in serving urban residents. To obtain this assistance, cities must rely on the executive and legislative branches of state general purpose governments. In responding to these needs, state officials choose among different assistance strategies.

The case for states providing this assistance derives from two broad purposes of state governments. First, they establish and enforce minimum standards for local services. States rarely mandate absolute uniform service levels across localities, but they are responsible for ensuring that all citizens enjoy some minimum standard of service. Second, states seek to equalize the resources available to localities for meeting these common standards. The area in which this goal is most explicit is elementary and secondary education, where states have enacted "equalizing" aid programs. Recognizing the wide variation in available tax base across school districts, state legislatures have distributed aid to the districts in accord with formulas that make common tax rates applied to differing tax bases yield the same minimum level of per pupil resources. Restated, the states' goal is to equalize the local tax burdens necessary to finance the minimum standards it establishes.

In practice, equalization is constrained by political realities. For services such as education, it is difficult—if not impossible—to prevent local supplementation of state-established minimums. Also, equalization programs generally provide some benefits to even the wealthiest areas, thereby limiting redistribution. Consequently, the extent of equalization achieved is usually less than initially sought, but this does not negate the importance of the basic state policy objective.

The same two goals are shared by the federal government, but for a narrower range of services. The federal government has established minimum standards for certain types of highway transportation, income benefits for the aged and disabled, food stamps, and other specific activities. Similarly, its financing of some of these activities assures equal resources either by fully financing the programs or by distributing aid funds in accord with formulas that take into account relative state income. In functional areas where states and the federal government share objectives, state assistance efforts inevitably are linked to federal actions.

Given these policy objectives, leaders of statewide governments can choose among three different strategies. The strategies are defined in terms of the role state institutions play in financing and delivering services. Each strategy has advantages and drawbacks, but the net benefits of one make it a favored option in light of the experiences recounted in this volume.

Full State Assumption

States can opt to assume full responsibility for both financing and delivering a service. This ensures that the dual objectives of minimum standards and equal resources are met, but poses significant problems. Full state assumption severely limits the possibilities that varying service packages can be tailored to local needs. For most state and local services, political decentralization promotes both effectiveness and efficiency. States have not been exceptionally responsive or efficient in delivering the services for which they have taken full responsibility.

Consider the operations of the New York State Department of Motor Vehicles, particularly its difficulties in adjusting statewide operations to the distinctive needs of New York City. Most residents dread the department's notoriously long lines, and the difficulties in administering driving tests and other regulations among New York City's heterogeneous population have proved formidable to a state bureaucracy. Similarly, the New York State Employment Service has been criticized for failing to provide meaningful assistance to middle-class job seekers and as being inadequate in providing the full range of services needed by disadvantaged residents concentrated in New York City.

Moreover, uniform state delivery of services does not permit local variation above the state-established minimum standard without the creation of separate, and generally uncoordinated, local agencies. For example, the City of New York has established its own employment agencies in several of its poorer neighborhoods in order to supplement the efforts of the State Employment Service, but these efforts are sometimes criticized as duplicating the State's programs. If diversity, responsiveness, and local supplementation of state standards are valued, then full state assumption poses serious drawbacks.

In New York, State officials generally have recognized these difficulties and have avoided assuming service delivery responsibilities. In the social services, where many other states have greater responsibilities, Irene Lurie and Mary Jo Bane document that the New York State Department of Social Services has followed the strategy of supervising local operations. While this is partly related to the distinctive combination of greater local financial responsibility and strong networks of voluntary agencies that characterize New York social services, it also reflects the State's desire to avoid a large-scale operational presence in New York City's unique environment. Similarly, the transfer of City University senior colleges to State auspices did not fold the New York City institutions into the pre-existing State university system, but maintained a separate governing body including local representation to operate the city-based institutions.

Another deterrent to full State assumptions is the practical difficulties State agencies face in locating and staffing New York City operations. State salary scales are predicated largely on living costs in Albany, where rents and prices are significantly lower; the State also has difficulty constructing facilities within the city because of costs that exceed norms elsewhere and unique characteristics of the local building trades.

For the future, it is likely that the conditions making full state assumption unattractive will become even more pronounced. That is, New York City—and other large central cities—are increasingly different from, rather than increasingly similar to, the rest of their states. The essays by Matthew Drennan and by Katherine Trent and Richard Alba highlight the growing disparities between the city and the rest of the state. New York City is becoming poorer, more a concentration of the minority population, more a concentration of female-headed households, and in many other ways a different environment for service delivery than the rest of the state. Thus, expanded statewide service delivery would confront greater diversity than in the past.

More "Marble Cake" Federalism

Among the many metaphors observers have used to describe intergovernmental relations, "marble cake" federalism best captures the mixture of roles each level plays in the delivery of many services.[4] The marble cake metaphor was an intentional contrast to the "layer cake" metaphor, which implied orderly and hierarchical relationships among the federal, state, and local levels. Rather than each government having a clearly defined role, the financial and operational responsibilities are spread among the three levels, with each providing some part of the total package of services. For example, in mental health the states operate hospitals, the federal government funds voluntary community mental health centers, and local governments also provide outpatient services with state financial assistance. Similarly, in criminal justice there are federal as well as state prosecutors, courts, and prisons; and the localities have separate police forces and detention facilities.

As states pursue their objectives for urban service delivery, they could choose to expand activities within the general marble cake pattern. That is, they could select parts of the delivery network for a given service to fund and operate while leaving localities responsible for other parts. This option typically involves creating a State agency to handle some subset of functions which represent added resources devoted to that purpose. Such patterns are evident in Emanuel Tobier and Barbara Gordon Espejo's history of housing programs. In the 1960s the State sought to expand its activities with the creation of the Urban Development Corporation, a new unit created to supplement existing local and State efforts.

The experience of the two New Yorks strongly suggests that marble cake federalism is an inefficient mode of service delivery. The most troublesome areas of State-City relations examined in this volume are those where both governments are engaged in direct service delivery— mental health, criminal justice, housing, and certain social services. In these cases the existence of both State and City agencies permits, even encourages, the shifting of service loads based on fiscal and bureaucratic criteria rather than client needs as well as the shifting of blame for poor performance. This option also makes it difficult for the State to enforce minimum standards within the parts of the system for which it is not directly responsible. Governors and legislators may be tempted to create and nurture programs that they can identify as "their" part of the action, but these efforts often are not the most effective way to use new resources to improve service delivery.

State Funding of Local Operations

Concentration of state resources on urban problems can be achieved by selected expansion of state funding for services delivered by units of local government. These funds can be supplied with virtually no restrictions in the form of general revenue sharing programs or can be directed to priority services through categorical aid programs. Because of the limited accountability inherent in general revenue sharing, state officials, and particularly those in New York State, have favored categorical aid. Consequently, expanded state funding of local government is likely to be in the form of aid programs for specific services.

This policy is generally favored by local officials because it provides them with more funds to carry out their current missions. It also permits the form of decentralized service delivery that appears essential to effective performance within diverse areas of a state.

But greater state funding of other political units raises problems for state officials: They take the political heat of levying taxes to raise funds for local services, but they receive little credit when the local expenditures are made. Beyond this political issue, simply funding local operations does not guarantee fulfillment of the state's objectives. Localities could receive more aid without meeting minimum standards. Added state aid could simply raise the unit costs of services without enhancing benefits to consumers.

In order for this strategy to be effective it must be accompanied by two types of measures. First, states cannot simply write blank checks to localities. State officials need to be able to limit their fiscal commitments. This is done most effectively by relating aid levels to the cost of meeting efficiently minimum service standards. Second, states need mechanisms for enforcing the minimum service standards.

Neither of these measures is easy to design. Many current state aid programs are not rooted in explicit decisions on what is a minimum acceptable standard and how much it should cost to provide that standard. The clearest exception in New York State is the public assistance program. Almost by definition, assistance standards are minimal norms, and the costs are determined by cash benefit levels and allowable rent levels established by State agencies. Similarly, the Medicaid program establishes uniform benefit packages for the indigent, and State agencies determine the unit costs (or provider payment levels) for these services. Perhaps because they are areas in which State objectives are apparently obtainable within a framework of State aid to localities, these programs lead the list of appropriate areas for greater proportional State funding (a policy already adopted by most other states).

Outside the welfare and Medicaid programs, it is harder for states to determine minimum standards and reasonable costs. A complicating factor is that most services are labor intensive, but states have little control over the staffing patterns and pay levels of local government employees—especially those in large cities with independent collective bargaining arrangements. Raymond Horton and David Lewin's essay indicates the difficulties New York State has in shaping the parameters of its own labor costs; regulating those of its localities is an even greater challenge. Yet effective use of new resources by states seems to require their ability to set limits on the outcomes of local collective bargaining. As Kenneth Thorpe's essay reveals, under the Medicaid program the State already has become indirectly involved in collective bargaining between the local service providers (hospitals) and their employees. Efforts by state political leaders to obtain greater returns on state aid for education seem destined to confront the same issue in the schools. There may be a considerable time lag, but greater state fiscal aid seems to require greater state involvement in local collective bargaining.

Enforcing minimum standards is another difficult corequisite of effective expansion of State funding of local operations. The complexities of the process are insightfully described in Irene Lurie and Mary Jo Bane's analysis of State efforts to bolster the child welfare system. Despite the clear legal ability of State agencies to regulate and monitor City agencies, the political realities require bargaining over standards and procedures. In arenas such as social services, where a substantial majority of the service activity is concentrated in one large city, the local unit has a practical capacity to defy and even make demands upon its "regulator." Also complicating the State's regulatory role is the pattern of relying on private nonprofit organizations in several service areas such as child welfare, health, and higher education. These agencies and their board members often exercise considerable political clout in resisting State rules. There is no simple way for State officials to sidestep these realities; tension over enforcement issues is likely to accompany greater State funding of local operations.

THE OUTLOOK

In light of the foregoing analysis, it is possible to discern two general directions of future policy. First, the states are likely to be financing a greater share of combined state and local expenditures. Second, states will rely primarily on existing general purpose local governments to deliver expanded services, but along with this increased financing the states will impose stricter oversight of local activities. A corollary of the second proposition is that state-local conflicts over the enforcement of state-determined standards will intensify.

Movement in these directions implies that direct state operations will not grow along with state financing. In fact, state activities in direct service provision could shrink even while its fiscal role expands. This seems a sensible and feasible approach to rationalizing the organization and improving the effectiveness of some of the service areas characterized as "trouble spots" in State-City relations in New York. The future of mental health, housing, and even criminal justice policy may involve the State shifting some of its direct operations to local governments along with the resources that now underwrite these activities. In exchange, the localities will be more directly accountable for providing services that are of acceptable standards. This solution is implicit in the reforms Blum and Blank discuss for mental health.

Careful consideration of the experience in mental health and other trouble spots in State-City relations identified in the case studies points to the constraints on policy initiatives aimed at following what appears to be a sensible course. Relatively small and narrowly focused interest groups could thwart reforms much as the organized employees of State mental hospitals helped prevent the shifting of resources from inpatient care at State-operated hospitals to community-based care at local government facilities. Similarly, Ester Fuchs's analysis of the fragmented criminal justice system highlights the ways in which narrow, but vocal, constituencies prevent broad reforms.

The critical ingredient for progress toward a more rational pattern of state-city relations appears to be a politically healthy state legislature. The governor, as a highly visible official who is elected statewide, is typically less vulnerable to interest group pressures than are the more numerous, and often more anonymous, legislators. It is reassuring that American state legislatures generally are improving, but troubling to recall how low the standards from which they are progressing were. In New York, the State legislature was embarrassed by revelations of corruption in 1987, but this may lead to favorable responses eliminating some of the more distasteful and inefficient practices of the legislative leaders. Reforms in the financing of campaigns for State office, while less imminent, could enhance further the stature and performance of the State legislature.

For the long-run, however, the most important requirement for a stronger state role in urban affairs is sustained, popular commitment to greater equity. Increasingly, relations between state institutions and big-city governments are matters of economic redistribution and racial justice. Residents of the rest of the state will be asked to help meet the needs of poorer people concentrated in cities. If voters believe this is in their interest—whether for selfish or noble reasons—then politicians will act accordingly; if voters question these goals, politicians need to lead the public.

NOTES

1. See John C. Bollen and Henry S. Schmandt, *The Metropolis—Its People, Politics and Economic Life* (New York: Harper & Row, 1975).
2. John V. Lindsay, *The City* (New York: Norton, 1970), chap. 10.
3. *Report of the National Advisory Commission on Civil Disorders* (New York: Bantam Books, 1968).
4. Morton Grodzins, "Centralization and Decentralization in the American Federal System," in Robert Goldwin, ed., *A Nation of States* (Chicago: Public Affairs Conference Center, 1964).

NOTES

Name Index

Boldface numbers refer to figures and tables.

A

Abrams, Robert, 173
Abramson, Alan J., 47*n*
ACIR. *See* Advisory Commission on Intergovernmental Relations
Addabo, Joseph, 209*n*
Ad Hoc Committee on Deductibility of State and Local Taxes, 205
Adler, Alan, 419*n*
Administrative Board, 495
Advisory Commission on Intergovernmental Relations (ACIR), 4, 5, 6–8, 22*n*, 23*n*, 208*n*, 209*n*, 242*n*
Alba, Richard D., 10–11, 93, 104*n*, 105*n*, 308, 350*n*, 517
Allen, Robert S., 3
Almquist, Calvin, B., 150*n*
Altheide, David, 47*n*
American Federation of State, County and Municipal Employees (AFSCME), 361
American Federation of Teachers, 206
American Hospital Association, 359, 380*n*
American Medical Association, 381*n*
Americans for Conservative Action, 190, **191**
Americans for Democratic Action, 190, **191**
Anderson, Warren, 110, 124, 126, 143, 144, 174
Appellate Division, 495, 497, 498

Archdiocese of New York, 427
Arnold, David D., 23*n*
Arson Strike Force, 490
Arthur Kill Prison, 252
Assembly, 12, 124, 125, 127, 129–146, 152, 163, 172, 175, 324, 369
Assembly Ways and Means Committee, 121
Association for Retarded Children (ARC), 387, 396
Attorney General, 142
Auletta, Ken, 113, 119, 148*n*, 149*n*

B

Bailey, Robert W., 123, 149*n*
Bane, Mary Jo, 19, 516, 519
Barron, James, 209*n*
Battery Park City Authority, 120, 215
Batutis, Michael, Jr., 104*n*, 105*n*
Bayview Prison, 252
Beame, Abraham D., 113, 297, 513
Beame administration, 176
Bellamy, Carol, 139
Benjamin, Gerald, 11, 12, 17, 148*n*, 149*n*, 158, 163, 177*n*, 208*n*, 305*n*, 323, 324, 416*n*, 417*n*, 419*n*, 444*n*, 477*n*, 509*n*
Bergen, Francis, 118
Berger, Renee A., 46*n*
Berke, Joel S., 351*n*
Berne, Robert, 16–17, 350*n*
Bernstein, Blanche, 198, 199, 209*n*, 443*n*

Subject Index

Boldface numbers refer to figures and tables.

A

academic medical centers, 17, 62, 358, 360, 372, 375–377, 379
achievement: scores, 335, 336, 338–348; tests, 335–337, 340, 348, 352n
Acquired Immune Deficiency Syndrome (AIDS), 357, 359
A Decade of Triumph and a Future of Hope: Services to Developmentally Disabled Persons in New York State (NYS OMRDD), 400
Adirondack counties, 72
Adler v. *Deegan*, 117, 149n
administration, 423, 425; court, 495–496; of criminal justice, 479
admissions, 391
Adoption Assistance and Child Welfare Act (1980), 429
adoption services, 433–434
adoptive homes, 428, 431
AFDC. *See* Aid to Families with Dependent Children
affluence, 10, 61, 69, 73, 78
after-care, 391, 403–404
age, 93, **96–97**; structures, 81, 97, 99, 103
agencies, 19–21, 119–120, 147, 215, 244, 275–276, 408–410; Catholic, 428, 432; City, 398, 409–411, 503, 517, 519; contractual, 489; independent, 246, 487; line, 298, 299; local, 487,

516; multiple, 487, 488; municipal, 243, 298; private, 427, 428; with representation in Washington, 189; State, 216, 265, 385, 398, 411, 431, 487, 516, 517, 519. *See also* specific agencies
agency; performance, 431–432; staffing, 276
aging, 81, 95–100
"aging out youths," 410
aid, 11, 14, 114, 120, 278; general purpose, 214; local, 396–397; for mental health, 396–397; operating, 324, 325; programs, 196, 238, 240, 515, 518. *See also* education aid, federal aid, State aid
Aid to Families with Dependent Children (AFDC), **181, 183,** 196–200, 423, 428; financing by localities of, 238; payments, 44, 429
Aid to the Disabled Program, 390
airports, 185
Alabama, 390
Alaska, 238
Albany, 3, 7, 113–120, 162, 313, 425, 516; City in, 123–126, 143; delegation, 146; Democratic dominance in, 161; housing in, 446, 457; mayoral visit to, 11; power in, 107–109, 147
Albany-Schenectady-Troy, 72–75
alcoholism, 388
allowances, 371–372, 470

mortgage arrears, 462–463, 465
mortgages, 451, 458, 460–463, 465;
    low-cost, 459, 474, 475
Mount Vernon, 219
MPU. *See* Metropolitan Placement
    Unit
Multiple Dwelling Law (1929), 449–
    451
multiple dwellings, 450, 451, 468,
    471–473
municipal hospitals, 18, 355, 361,
    364, 378; mental care in, 398,
    401–402, 408–410

N

NAACP Legal Defense Fund, 139
narcotics, 22, 403, 493–494, 508
Nashville-Davidson, 312
Nassau county, 125, 144, 172, 215,
    219, 313, 332–334, 497; housing,
    446, 457; jails, 504
Nassau-Suffolk, 71–72, 73, 74
"national city," 513
National Housing Act (1934), 451
national origin quotas, 88
natural increase, 83–84, 93
navy, 192–193
Nebraska, 38
needs, 31, 46, 322, 479; fiscal, 126;
    human and physical, 33–36;
    public 367; urban, 514. *See also*
    capital, infrastructure, mental
    health
needy, 361, 422. *See also* poor
negotiation, 440–441
New Deal, 36, 155, 158, 160, 458,
    466
New Frontier, 214
New Jersey, 84, 121, 331, 476, 514
New Mexico, 238
New Orleans, 27, 36, 56, 311. *See*
    also big cities, central cities
New York City: debt structure of,
    225–228; difference of, 217–219;
    experiences with productivity,
    297–299; government, 39, 41, 45,
    111, 123, 431; influence,
    128–132; legal capture of, 115–
    116; losses for, 462; political
    influence of, 163, 276; power of,

441; relative decline of, 65–72;
    representation in the Assembly,
    130–131, 163; size of, 30–31,
    218–219; State financial
    involvement in, 249–263;
    Washington office, 188–189. *See*
    also specific issues
New York City Charter, 501
New York delegation, 189–192, 194
New York Journal American, 229
New York Legislative Manual, 130,
    132, 134, 136, 153, 155–157,
    159, 160, 165, 167–172, 178*n*
New York Prospective Hospital
    Reimbursement Methodology
    (NYPHRM), 370, 372–375, 378–
    379
New York State: control, 425;
    dominance, 114–123, 147;
    influence, 435, 436; involvement,
    7, 119, 274; power of, 123, 147,
    367, 423, 435, 439; regulation,
    378; role of, 108, 123. *See also*
    specific issues
New York State Constitutional
    Convention (1938), 467
New York State Developmental
    Center Census, 387
New York State Laws: Chapter 76,
    365, 367; Chapter 520, 369;
    Chapter 620, 397, 408, 414;
    Chapter 957, 363–364. *See also*
    specific laws
New York Times, 110, 112, 123,
    128, 148*n*, 149*n*, 150*n*, 173, 177*n*,
    178*n*, 322, 352*n*, 418*n*, 419*n*,
    477*n*, 510*n*
Niagara Falls, 172
nodal areas, 65, 74
nominations, 494
nonblacks, 67
nonparty enrollments, 156
nonprofit: agencies, 255;
    organizations, 519. *See also*
    charitable organizations
nonresidential facilities, 254
nonretrogression rule, 143
nonwhites, 92, 93, 104
Norfolk, 193
North, 85
North America, 91

productivity *(continued)*
272, 297–299; State experiences
with, 299–300; in workforce, 283
Productivity and Management
Initiatives, 298
Productivity Council, 297, 298, 306*n*
professional staff, 325, **329**, 352*n*
"Professors' Commission," 135
Program Assessment System (PAS),
432
projections, 239–240, 520–521; for
elections, 176–177; for federal aid,
182; for mentally disabled, 412–
416; for population growth, 83,
239; for unemployment, 78. *See
also* forecasts
property: city-state ratio assessment,
32
property tax, 13, 205–207, 212–
213, **226**, 317, 352*n*; assessments,
47*n*; exemptions from, 450, 459–
462, 467, 471; local, 450, 472; as
source of revenues, 219, **222**
property-tax-reduction schemes, 475.
See also subsidy programs
property value, 31–32, **49**, 317, 321,
352*n*, 513; per pupil, 317, **320**,
321, 323; real, 218, 219
proportional representation (PR), 164
prosecution, **485**, 486, 493–494
prosecutors, 480, 486, 493, 508,
517; for narcotics, 494
Protestant agencies, 427, 432
psychiatric: centers, 402, **405**, 406;
services, 408
psychotropic drugs, 18, 390, 391
public assistance, 421–426, 442,
470–471; benefit, 424–426;
eligibility, 424, 425; programs, 20,
182, 184, 200, 421, 422, 446
public authorities, 119–221, 123,
464
public defenders, 480, 484, 492
Public Employees' Fair Employment
Law, 285
public finance, 13, 370; history of,
211–228
Public Housing Law (1939), 466
Puerto Rican Caucus, 139, 144, 145
Puerto Ricans, 10, 85–87, 92–95,
136, 453; in legislature, 139, **140–
141**, 142, 145

punishment, 480, 484
pupils, 17, 337–347, 351*n*;
handicapped, 309, 315, 323, 325,
336, 337, 352*n*; with limited
English, 309, 315, 336, 337; ratios
for, 327, **330**, 335, 348
purchasing power, 278
Pure Waters Bond Act (1965), 246
Putnam County, 72, 83, 215, 495

Q

quality, 283; of care, 433; control,
425
Queens, 145, 212, 258, 388, 451;
County, 495
*The Question of State Government
Capability*, 7

R

race, 67, 81, 92–95, 104, 512
rate: appeals, 372–373; setting, 355,
365–366, 378
rates: interest, 461; Medicaid, 364,
369; Medicare, 370
ratification, 179
ratings, 190, **191**
real earnings: growth of, 75–77. *See
also* income
reapportionment, 11, 128–139,
142–144, 146, 207; legislative, 3,
12, 513; plan, 129, 134–135, 175;
politics, 108
recession of 1970, 64
reconstruction, 5–6
recovery, 56–57, 60, 63
recreation, 283, **284, 292**
redistricting, 12, 145
reelection, 174, 176
referendums, 459, 460
reforms, 88, 429–430, 432–433,
435, 512, 513; implementation of,
436–437
regulatory policies, 180, 185–187,
369
rehabilitation. *See* upgrading
rehospitalization, 402–403
reimbursement, 18, 368–378, 391,
397–398, 423; for foster care,
433; Medicaid, 405; for preventive